The
BARGAIN
Buyer's
Guide

The BARGAIN Buyer's Guide

THE CONSUMER'S BIBLE TO **BIG SAVINGS** ONLINE & BY MAIL

Elizabeth Cline

The Print Project

THE BARGAIN BUYER'S GUIDE. Copyright © 2005 by Lowell Miller. All rights reserved. Printed in the United States of America. No part of this book may be used or reproduced in any manner whatsoever without written permission, except in the case of brief quotations embodied in critical articles and reviews. For information, please write to: The Print Project, P.O. Box 703, Bearsville, NY 12409

Interior Book Design by Stratford Publishing Services

Distributed to the book trade by: Independent Publishers Group, 814 North Franklin Street, Chicago, IL 60610, (312) 337–0747

This book may be purchased for educational, business, or sales promotional use. For information, please write to: The Print Project, P.O. Box 703, Bearsville, NY 12409

FIRST EDITION

ISBN 0-9651750-6-5

Contents

Supplies and equipment for livestock, horses, dogs, cats, small mammals, reptiles, birds, and fish; prescription and over-the-counter health products; pet doors; humane animal traps; equestrian clothing and gear; live baby poultry

Hats, wallets, sunglasses, and pins for men and women; scarves and handbags for women

Diapering and baby supplies; clothing, shoes, and accessories for infants and children

Office, Business, and Professional 441

COMPUTER HARDWARE AND SOFTWARE 441
PC and Macintosh computers and peripherals; software of all kinds;
computer games; computer supplies and accessories; refurbished computers
and computer equipment

OFFICE FURNISHINGS 455
Desks, ergonomic chairs, safes, shelving, workstations, computer furniture;
furnishings for home offices, reception rooms, storerooms, hospitals,
churches, schools, and day-care facilities

OFFICE SUPPLIES AND MACHINES 461
General office supplies; faxes, copiers, shredders, and other office machines;
telephone headsets; shipping materials

PRINTING AND STATIONERY 479
Stationery, invitations, letterhead, logo design, check printing, business
cards, bills of lading, invoices, postcards and other custom printing services

UNIFORMS AND PROMOTIONAL PRODUCTS 487
Uniforms, workwear, and footwear for the medical, food-service, and other
industries; imprintable clothing and miscellaneous goods for promotional
purposes and corporate gifts

Special Needs 495

Adaptive clothing, tools, gadgets, and home and office aids for children and
adults with special physical or medical needs, including products for people
with postoperative conditions, limited mobility, the elderly, left-handed,
allergy-sensitive, ample-sized, and hearing and visually impaired

Sports and Outdoor Recreation 513

CAMPING, HUNTING, AND SURVIVAL 513
Clothing and gear for camping, hiking, rugged outdoor activities, hunting,
and survival; military surplus goods

TEAM AND INDIVIDUAL SPORTS 519
Clothing, footwear, and equipment for all kinds of indoor and outdoor
sports and athletic activities

Introduction

Welcome to the 27th edition of *The Bargain Buyer's Guide,* formerly known as *Wholesale by Mail & Online.* The title was changed to include companies that may not offer wholesale prices, but certainly offer discounts that translate to big savings when it comes to everyday and not-so-everyday items. After each edition is published, I spend the next year comparing prices of items from companies in this book to prices of the exact same items available at the better-known stores at your local mall—the stores that most people would assume offer the best price. If I can buy the same item from one of the online or mail-order vendors I've selected for the comparison, have it delivered, and still save at least 20%—they qualify to be in the book. More often, the savings are between 30% and 40%, and in many cases you'll save 50% or more. In addition to companies that offer the same name-brand items for less, I've included companies that save you money by manufacturing their own products. Cheapass Games, a board company in Seattle, invents and produces cheap and clever games like "Devil Bunny Needs a Ham" for 50% less than you'd generally pay for a board game. If you're willing to buy three pounds of coffee at once, Catskill Mountain Coffee roasts organic, cooperatively-grown coffee beans and sells them for 46% less than I've seen anywhere else. I have listed over 500 large and small reputable businesses that will save you money.

I love finding products online or through mail-order for less than I would have paid if I drove 20 minutes to the mall. For instance, in the furniture category, I priced a brand-name couch at three different dealers in my area for about the same price. When I called Quality Furniture Market in the "Home: Furnishings" chapter, the very same couch was $1,008 less than the local prices I was quoted—delivered! In another price check, I found a famous brand-name vacuum cleaner for $70.99 less (including delivery) than if I had purchased it from a well-known retailer of home appliances at the local mall. In the market for some new flatware or china? Go ahead and buy it at a department store and pay 50% more than if you purchased it from one of the vendors in the "Home: Tableware" chapter. I priced a miniDV camcorder for $149.97 less at B&H Photo-Video in New York than if I had purchased the exact same product at a national home electronics chain store. If you can buy the exact same product for less, have it delivered to your doorstep, from a reputable dealer, why wouldn't you?

The most common question I'm asked is, "How can these companies afford to sell at below-retail prices? What's the catch?" I know, it seems too good to be true. But it isn't. While brick-and-mortar retail stores mark up items double or triple to cover their overhead and to make a profit, the companies in this book have found ways to turn a profit without passing on the extra costs to you.

Some are willing to sell products at a discount if you purchase in bulk—say, three pounds of coffee at a time or 100 tulip bulbs. Other companies sell products to you cheaper because they are the manufacturer. By buying directly from the mill or factory that produces the goods, you bypass the middleman, thus shaving off a couple of layers of price markup. Still others are able to sell to you at below-retail prices because they have cornered a market. This means they purchase in such high volume (thus lowering their per-item cost) that they can take a smaller profit on each individual piece and still make out just fine.

I've also found companies that offer terrific bargains by connecting buyers with manufacturers, with the consumer doing most of the legwork. These are basically brokers who deal in soft goods such as sheets and towels or appliances or furniture. You, the consumer, go to your local store or to the manufacturer's website and pick out the item, recording its make and model number. When you call the broker and ask for a price quote on that item, the broker can afford to give you a tremendous markdown and have the goods drop-shipped directly from the manufacturer to your home. You will also find factory refurbished goods in this book—merchandise that sells for half or more than half off the original sticker price because it was sent back by a customer who decided she didn't want it. When goods have to be reinspected and repackaged, the price plummets. Or perhaps you'll be buying last year's model from some of these companies. Do you really care that your "new" blender was made last year if you can pay a third less for it?

I could go on, but suffice it to say that the vendors I've included in this and other editions don't have to be "tricksters" to bring you great deals. Quite the opposite, in fact. One of the reasons loyal readers have loved this book over the years is that the companies are hand-picked and offer personalized, old-fashioned service in addition to great prices. They stand behind their products and value their customers.

I hope you have a great shopping experience and I know you'll save a lot of money while you're at it.

How to Use This Book

The aim of *The Bargain Buyer's Guide* is to help consumers find great deals on products when buying by mail, phone, fax, or computer. The term *bargain* refers to discounts of 20% or more on list or comparable retail on many or all of a firm's products or services, which is how they qualify to be in this book. Many of the companies here sell at even deeper discounts, up to 90% off of retail. If you're interested in buying in quantity, some of the firms here will negotiate with individuals or small businesses to sell to you on a wholesale basis, often involving a minimum order, and sometimes, but not always, requiring you to have a resale number. Those firms are denoted with a star in the icon line in their listings. For details, see "The Wholesale Star," page xxi.

There are other icons that will help you get the most from the information, so before sending for a catalog or placing an order, please read the key to the symbols in "How to Read the Listings," page xix. For more detailed information on mail-order and internet shopping, see "A Guide to Buying by Mail, Phone, and Internet," beginning on page 611.

Following is a guide to several of this book's features that will help you make the best use of the material.

TABLE OF CONTENTS

I have sympathy for retailers who must find the right aisle and shelf in their store for oddball items. If you were searching for table pads, for instance, would you automatically think to look in the household furnishings department? Think of this book as a print version of a mall. Each chapter comprises a group of companies that make up a wing of the mall selling similar or related goods. Sometimes within a wing (chapter) where there are companies selling very general goods in that product category, there will also be three or more companies that specialize in one particular aspect of that category. When this occurs, I've divided the chapter into themed subchapters (e.g., "Ceramics," "Jewelry Making," and "Textile Arts" in the "Crafts and Hobbies" chapter).

The Table of Contents is designed to help you narrow your product search—or at least to land you into the correct wing of the mall—with brief descriptions of the type of goods found in each chapter or subchapter. These should serve as cues to guide you to the right section, where the Find It Fast list of individual companies, at the beginning of chapters and subchapters, will assist further.

FIND IT FAST

Okay, so you've gotten to the right chapter. To continue the "shopping mall" metaphor, you're now standing in the wing that has store after store of desired goods. But if you're in the "Animals and Pets" chapter looking for tropical fish supplies, you don't need to read every single company listing. Go first to Find It Fast, located immediately after the introduction to that chapter or subchapter. This at-a-glance guide tells you which companies sell the item you're looking for, and outlines different types of products offered by the firms in that section.

COMPANY LISTINGS

At the top of each company listing under the firm's name is an information slug that includes physical and online addresses, contact phone and fax numbers, and other information, such as what they sell; forms of payment they accept; whether they issue a print catalog; and how much it costs, if anything. For a line-by-line rundown and decoding of the symbols and abbreviations used in these information slugs, see "How to Read the Listings," page xix.

Regarding the listings, I have the benefit of seeing the catalogs firsthand or talking to the owners in person. There's a lot of information one can glean from a catalog—ranging from the management's sense of humor to the company's general sense of design and organization. Sometimes owners have stayed on the phone for half an hour regaling me with their business philosophy and vision. As much as possible, I've tried to capture the company character (or characters!) in the listings, as well as to accurately portray their inventory. Obviously, one cannot list everything that a telephone-book-sized catalog of tools sells. So if a company description seems a bit general but leaves you intrigued, go ahead and write or call the firm with your questions, log on to their website, or request a print catalog, if they have one.

A CAVEAT

The Bargain Buyer's Guide is compiled as a resource for consumers to help them find good values available by mail and on the internet. Even if prices or a specific product are mentioned in a listing, *never order directly* from a company based on the listing in this book without first contacting the company. *Don't request extra discounts or wholesale prices, unless the listing states they are available. Attempting to bargain with these firms makes the vendors quite unhappy.* All of the information in this book is based on research and fact-checking as of press time, and is subject to change.

How to Read the Listings

THE BASICS ABOUT THE COMPANY

Each entry begins by presenting the following basic information about the company:

CONTACT INFORMATION: The company's name, mailing address, and phone numbers, including toll-free (800, 888, and 877), fax, and TDD (telecommunications device for the deaf) lines.

FORM OF INFORMATION: This first line tells you right away what form of information you can expect from a company. If the firm issues print material, it might be in the form of a catalog, brochure, flyer, leaflet, price list, or individual manufacturer's brochures. The price of the print material, if any, is included, along with "refundable" or "deductible" if you can redeem the cost by placing an order. In some cases, a company will send you printed information for free as long as you send them a SASE: a long (business-size), self-addressed envelope with a first-class stamp (unless more postage is requested). The text then might read "free with SASE." If the catalog is online only, the information line will read "online catalog only; no print catalog." Many companies have both print and online catalogs. But with the cost of paper and postage going up, some firms are having to charge for their printed material, while the online catalog is still free. As more and more people are shopping over the internet, it makes environmental and economic sense to forgo paper catalogs whenever possible. See "The Online Catalog Symbol," page xxii, for further explanation.

PAY: Methods of payment accepted for orders (catalog fees should be paid by check or money order unless the listing states otherwise):

> **CHECK:** personal check
> **MO:** bank or postal money order
> **MC:** MasterCard credit card
> **V:** VISA credit card
> **AE:** American Express/Optima credit cards
> **DSC:** Discover/NOVUS credit cards
> **CB:** Carte Blanche credit card
> **DC:** Diners Club credit card
> **JCB:** JCB credit card
> **BRAVO:** BRAVO credit card

SELLS: The general type of goods and services sold by the company.

STORE: If there's a physical location—storefront, warehouse, farm, outlet, or factory—the address and hours of operation or visitation are listed. If the line reads "no walk-in location; mail-order only" or "online only," this business doesn't sell to customers in person; when there is no brick-and-mortar store, I try to list the office phone hours.

EMAIL: Email addresses are included if the company doesn't currently have a website. If there's a website, the email address is usually not listed. To email the company, log on to the website and email directly from the site. Every website has a hot button that, when clicked, makes an email form pop up. Usually this hot button will be found by clicking on "Contact Us" or "Email Us."

ONLINE: URL address on the internet; for simplicity's sake and space considerations, I begin all addresses with *www* (www.onlineaddress.com), omitting the *http://* prefix.

WHAT THE SYMBOLS MEAN

THE MAPLE LEAF

This symbol means the firm will ship goods to Canada. Canadian shoppers should ask the vendor about current import restrictions and tariffs before placing an order, and request shipping charges or an estimate before finalizing the order. *Please note:* U.S.

firms generally request payment for goods *and* catalogs in U.S. funds, and may stipulate that payment be drawn on a U.S. bank or paid via postal money order.

⚑ THE FLAG

A small flag in the symbol line means the firm will ship goods to APO and FPO (U.S. military) addresses. For more information, see "Shipments Abroad," page 630.

⊕ THE GLOBE

A small globe on the symbol line means the firm has stated that it will ship goods worldwide. Readers having goods delivered abroad should read the listing before sending for a catalog; check with local authorities to make sure products can be imported, what restrictions may apply, and what tariffs may be charged. For more information, see "Shipments Abroad," page 630.

¡Sí! SPANISH SPOKEN HERE

This icon means the firm has Spanish-speaking sales representatives on staff. Before calling such a company, read the listing and the "Special Factors" notes, since the person's availability may be limited to certain hours or days.

☎ THE TDD SYMBOL

This symbol indicates that the firm can communicate with a TDD (telecommunications device for the deaf). In most cases, the firm uses a separate phone line for the equipment; sometimes it's combined with a fax line. This special number will always be listed when you see the TDD symbol. However, know that all companies have the ability to speak with the hearing impaired, with or without a special TDD line, through a service provided by the phone company.

★ THE WHOLESALE STAR

Such firms will sell at wholesale rates to *qualified individuals or other firms*. To sell to you at genuine wholesale, most firms require proof that you're running a company—a business card, letterhead, resale number, or all three—and may impose different minimum orders and sell under terms different from those that apply to retail purchases. Please note that, unless specified, all information in the listings applies to consumer transactions only, not resellers. For more information, see "Buying at Wholesale," page 616.

THE ONLINE CATALOG SYMBOL

The mouse symbol indicates that this company has a website *that features secure online ordering*. Note that some companies still have websites that function primarily as print ads. In other words, these are websites that tell about the firm's products, but do not enable customers to interactively shop and purchase. Some companies will allow you to browse their online inventory, but do not have online ordering available. In these cases, I have indicated that they have an online catalog under "Form of Information," but I only include the mouse symbol if you can order online securely.

In some cases, the online catalog represents the company's entire inventory. In other cases, it may be a special online catalog that features just that firm's best-selling items or maybe just specials or close-outs. They may offer website-only specials to encourage you to buy online (thus saving themselves a bundle; print catalogs cost money, whereas electronic catalogs are much, much cheaper).

Just because a company's website features electronic ordering doesn't mean you have to use it. Usually firms offer still-wary customers another option: downloading a form and faxing or mailing it in, calling in your order, or e-mailing it. For more about the tricks and traps of online shopping, see "Ordering Online," page 615.

A GUIDE TO BUYING BY MAIL, PHONE, AND INTERNET

This primer on mail-order, phone, and computer shopping, which begins on page 611, will answer other questions you have on everything from sending for catalogs to interpreting warranties. If a problem arises with a mail-order transaction, look here for help in resolving it.

Animals and Pets

Supplies and equipment for livestock, horses, dogs, cats, small mammals, reptiles, birds, and fish; prescription and over-the-counter health products; pet doors; humane animal traps; equestrian clothing and gear; live baby poultry

I live in a house with three dogs, four cats, and a rat. Two of the dogs have to be kept separated or a fight will ensue (in which only the German Shepard will emerge); the cats like to find new and interesting places to throw up in the house; and the rat seems to eat a massive amount of food for a little rodent. Still, all of my pets are as rewarding to own as they are a pain in the neck. And the rewards don't stop with a lick on the cheek. Being around pets has been shown to help people with depression and various illnesses—and has even been linked with lower mortality rates in the elderly.

Is a baby alligator an appropriate pet for a toddler? Will a pot-bellied pig be a good companion in a small city apartment? Will a rabbit gnaw the legs off your antique furniture? Are you likely to outlive your koi carp? These are all valid and important questions. If you're thinking about getting a pet, you might want to first check out the American Veterinary Medical Association's website (www.avma.org), which has wonderful articles about buying a pet, dealing with pet loss, things to know about animal health, animal safety (how to safeguard your pet from poison, how to travel with your pet, safety tips for kids), and how to select a veterinarian, among others. Maybe you'll reconsider the whole idea once you find out about the pitfalls!

A great way to find a pet is through Petfinder.com, an online, searchable database of over 100,000 animals that need homes from over 5,000 animal shelters and adoption organizations across the U.S. and Canada. Organizations maintain their own home pages and available pet database. Launched in 1996, Petfinder was the first site of its kind and is today the largest single force introducing homeless pets to new families. From the comfort of their personal computers, pet lovers can search for a pet that best matches their needs. They can then reference a shelter's web page and discover what services it offers. Petfinder also includes classified ads, discussion forums and a library of animal welfare articles.

Almost all of the companies in this chapter carry books, videos, and CD-ROMs so you can become an expert on just about any kind of animal and pursue any number of related subjects (training, breeding, and grooming, for example). Several of the firms listed in this chapter are owned by or retain veterinarians who will answer your questions on products and their use, but usually won't give specific medical advice. Whether you're seeking discount food for your alpaca or a miniature entertainment center for your favorite hamster, you'll find nearly everything for the winged, scaly, furry, fuzzy, stinky, prickly, or slimy loved one in your life—for a lot less in some cases than you'll pay locally.

Find It Fast

BIRD SUPPLIES
Jeffers, KV Vet Supply, Omaha Vaccine, That Fish Place/That Pet Place, Tomahawk Live Trap, UPCO

DOG AND CAT SUPPLIES
Drs. Foster & Smith, Jeffers, KV Vet Supply, That Fish Place/That Pet Place, UPCO, Valley Vet Supply

EQUESTRIAN CLOTHING, FOOTWEAR, AND GEAR
State Line Tack, Valley Vet Supply

FISH SUPPLIES
Jeffers, Omaha Vaccine, That Fish Place/That Pet Place

HORSE SUPPLIES
Jeffers, KV Vet Supply, Omaha Vaccine, State Line Tack, UPCO, Valley Vet Supply

LIVE BABY POULTRY
Murray McMurray Hatchery

LIVESTOCK/POULTRY SUPPLIES
Jeffers, KV Vet Supply, Murray McMurray Hatchery, Omaha Vaccine, Valley Vet Supply

PET DOORS
Patio Pacific

REPTILE AND SMALL ANIMAL SUPPLIES
Jeffers, KV Vet Supply, That Fish Place/That Pet Place, UPCO

TRAPS (HUMANE)
Tomahawk Live Trap

VET, KENNEL, AND GROOMER NEEDS
Drs. Foster & Smith, KV Vet Supply, Omaha Vaccine, UPCO, Valley Vet Supply

Drs. Foster & Smith

P.O. Box 100
Rhinelander, WI 54501–0100
800–381–7179
FAX: 800–776–8872

FORM OF INFORMATION: free print catalog; online catalog

PAY: check, MO, MC, V, AE, DSC

SELLS: pet, pond, and wild bird supplies

STORE: no walk-in location; mail-order only; 24-hour phones

ONLINE: www.drsfostersmith.com

Doctors Race Foster and Marty Smith, both practicing veterinarians, personally select every product in their catalog to assure high standards for quality and value. Their six different catalogs ("Dogs," "Cats," "Birds," "Fish," "Pond," and "Reptile and Small Mammals") include aquarium supplies, bird products, reptile treats, ferret food, pond kits, bat houses, pet furniture, treats, toys, vitamins, products for skin and hair, vaccines, cat trees, carriers and crates, grooming tools, leashes, training aids, and much more. Helpful sidebars dot the pages on subjects ranging from caring for your older dog to clipping your pet's nails to cat tree criteria. You'll also find an excellent selection of reference books on such subjects as breeds, guides to traveling with your pet, health manuals, and other useful reading sources. Although many of the products in the catalog are Drs. Foster & Smith brand, a spot check of several major brands carried at other discount pet stores showed this company's prices to be the same as or lower than its competitors'. If good prices and the handpicked selection of products aren't enough to win you over, on Tuesdays and Thursdays you can speak to a staff vet on general pet issues and health care. The special vet hotline number is in the current issue of the catalog.

WEBSITE: This company has a beautifully designed online catalog that's easy to use, well organized, and enjoyable to read. In addition to the full inventory, you'll also find on sale and clearance items; and a link to PetEducation.com, the doctors' sister site where you can find and read articles on pet behavior, health, and other topics. The website is set up so you can securely place your order online.

SPECIAL FACTORS: Satisfaction is guaranteed; returns accepted.

Jeffers

P.O. Box 100
Dothan, AL 36302–0100
800–533-3377
FAX: 334–793-5179

FORM OF INFORMATION: free print catalog; online catalog
PAY: check, MO, MC, V, AE, DSC
SELLS: pet care supplies
STORE: 353 W. Inez Rd., Dothan, AL; 7:00 am–7:00 pm daily
ONLINE: www.jefferspet.com

If you're seeking products for your furry, scaly, or feathery little bundles of joy, Jeffers "Pet Catalog" may be your new favorite source. Jeffers specializes in products for the health and care of your pet, at prices that are hard to beat.

The jam-packed 88-page color catalog has photos and descriptions of hundreds of products for the care of cats, dogs, ferrets, birds, fish, exotic pets, and other animals. From alcohol preps (for administering shots) to Zoom Groom (for combing out loose hair), you'll find it all at Jeffers. Jeffers has a livestock and an equine catalog as well, which you can request along with or instead of the "Pet Catalog."

WEBSITE: If you prefer shopping online, the website has a lot of nice features, including secure electronic ordering, an archive of articles on many pet-related topics, a frequently updated bargain bin section full of terrific deals, browsing capability by product type, and a search engine that helps you find specific merchandise by item number.

SPECIAL FACTORS: Money back if not completely satisfied; customs restrictions may apply to certain medicines shipped outside the U.S.; quantity discounts available.

KV Vet Supply Co., Inc.

3190 North Rd.
David City, NE 68632
800–423–8211
402–367–6047
FAX: 800–269–0093

FORM OF INFORMATION: free print catalog; online catalog

PAY: check, MO, MC, V, AE, DSC

SELLS: vet and pet supplies and equipment

STORE: 3190 N Road, David City, NE; Monday to Friday 8:00 am–5:00 pm, Saturday 9:00 am–12:00 pm

ONLINE: www.kvvet.com

KV Vet Supply is a family-owned and -operated business founded in 1979 to bring the very best products to owners of large or small animals. Drs. Metzner and Porter, both veterinarians, sample and review thousands of new products each year and then hand-select them for the catalog. The prices here are excellent—discounted by as much as 45% off retail. Shipping is free on a vast array of items, as well.

Their catalogs—"Livestock," "Equine," "Pet," and "KV Health Links" include products for almost any animal one could imagine—from house pets to horses to livestock. Each is well organized—offering color images of the products, encyclopedic choices, and detailed descriptions.

WEBSITE: If web shopping is your thing, KV Vet's online catalog won't disappoint. The company has taken the same care with the electronic presentation of all their goods, and you can order online after you've browsed the hundreds of products presented here.

SPECIAL FACTORS: Certain shipping restrictions and requirements may apply to vaccines and other large items; authorized returns accepted within 30 days; satisfaction guaranteed.

Murray McMurray Hatchery

P.O. Box 458
Webster City, IA 50595
800-456-3280
515-832-3280
FAX: 515-832-2213

FORM OF INFORMATION: free print catalog; online catalog

PAY: check, MO, MC, V, DSC

SELLS: live baby poultry and poultry-raising supplies

STORE: no walk-in location; mail-order only; phone hours Monday to Friday 8:00 am–6:00 pm CST

ONLINE: www.mcmurrayhatchery.com

I have a friend who grew up in a small, Central Illinois town where almost everyone had a long, sweeping backyard with a vegetable garden and giant elm trees shading their front yard. "Fluff" was a duckling her sister won at a fair. The girls raised Fluff in their backyard. She grew to be a giant duck who didn't mind being dressed up in old T-shirts and pushed around the block in the doll stroller, which had a hole cut out in the canopy where she stuck out her long neck and watched the world bump by. "I don't know why she put up with us, but my sister and I loved her," said my friend. "Even our basset hound loved her—they slept side by side in our barn, where he defended her at night against raccoons and cats." The mother even loved her because she laid giant eggs that made the best brownies this side of the Mississippi. Needless to say, when I found a source for mail-order chicks, ducklings, goslings, and other poultry, I began to fantasize about raising my own ducks up here in the Catskill Mountains.

Murray McMurray Hatchery is a family-owned business that has been around more than eight decades. You can order a free print catalog, or better yet, log on to the website to read about all the wonderful baby poultry this company raises and will ship to you. Murray McMurray has all types of amazing live birds and the equipment you need to raise them. You'll find bantams, Cochin bantams, heavy breeds, white egg layers, rainbow egg layers, rare and unusual breeds, meat birds (sorry, Fluff), feather-footed breeds, crested breeds, ducklings, goslings, peafowl, pheasants, partridge/quail, guineas, turkeys, and all of the necessary supplies: incubators, brooders, batteries, breeding pens, waterers, feeders, building plans, how-to books and videos, and much more. This consumer-friendly online catalog has colorful pictures, detailed descriptions, and a wide range of choices to suit your needs and lifestyle. Do you want pets? Eggs? Meat and eggs both? Do you want to start a small business selling free-range chickens or game birds?

The folks at Murray McMurray Hatchery are in the information business as much as they're in the hatchery business. The FAQ section has fascinating facts about how the "Easter Egg chicken" got its name (by laying pastel blue/green eggs), how long chickens live (10 to 15 years), how many eggs they lay, and so on. There are also interesting "Did You Know" tidbits peppered throughout the website and a section on chick care. I really like this company's friendly approach, well designed online catalog, and devotion to customer service. You're welcome to call or email the company with questions. Raising live animals is a big commitment, but for little money you can get started and reap the benefits for years to come. There are minimums on all types of poultry, with discounts when you buy larger quantities. But if you're one of the many people who wants to raise only a few chicks of any one variety, Murray McMurray is always glad to make up special orders, as long as the total comes to the minimum number required for each type of poultry they sell.

SPECIAL FACTORS: Free shipping on nonpoultry merchandise within the continental U.S.; shipping extra on all poultry shipments; non-U.S. customers should check with the company first to see if their country's regulations permit live-chick shipments; baby poultry is seasonal and not available at all times of the year (see website or print catalog for months of availability).

Omaha Vaccine Company, Inc.

11143 Mockingbird Dr.
Omaha, NE 68137–2332
800–367–4444
FAX: 800–242–9447

FORM OF INFORMATION: free print catalog; online catalog

PAY: check, MO, MC, V, AE, DSC

SELLS: dog, cat, bird, reptile, small animal, horse, and livestock supplies

STORE: several locations in NE, SD, MO, and MN; call for addresses and hours

ONLINE: www.omahavaccine.com

For over 30 years, Omaha Vaccine has been providing veterinarians and pet owners with great service, competitive prices, and a broad selection of products for household pets, as well as for horses and livestock. As you'll see in the catalog, this is a company that values its customers; contests, customer mail, the Pet Birthday Club, various reward programs—all are designed to win and keep your loyalty.

The "Best Care" pet catalog presents 130 well designed pages of prescription and over-the-counter drugs and medical treatments, pet beds and clothing, food, kennels, doors, leashes, odor- and tick-control products, grooming tools, toys, cages, training aids, chewies, and many other items for the most common pets, including birds, reptiles, and fish. The "First Place Equine/Professional Producer" catalog focuses on gear, supplies, and equipment related to raising livestock and horses. Both catalogs have a comprehensive selection of health-care products.

WEBSITE: As one would expect, Omaha Vaccine's web catalog is also excellent and geared toward making the customer comfortable with browsing and ordering online. The interactive table of contents will guide you to the products you seek. Merchandise is pictured and described in detail, making the print versions of the catalog practically unnecessary.

SPECIAL FACTORS: Some medical items may require an authorized prescription from your veterinarian; a $20 charge is added for hazardous materials being shipped by ground delivery; call for other special fees and requirements for shipments outside the U.S.; satisfaction guaranteed; authorized returns accepted within 30 days.

Patio Pacific, Inc.

America's Finest Pet Doors
874 Via Esteban #D
San Luis Obispo, CA
93401–7168
800–826–2871
FAX: 805–781–9734

FORM OF INFORMATION: free print catalog; online catalog

PAY: check, MO, MC, V, AE, DSC

SELLS: pet doors

STORE: same address, Monday to Friday 8:00 am–5:00 pm, Saturday 9:00 am–3:00 pm

ONLINE: www.petdoors.com

Patio Pacific, Inc., also known as America's Finest Pet Doors, solves a problem every pet owner has contemplated: How can I remain in bed eating bon-bons, my feet toasty warm, while Fido braves the blizzard outside so he can "do his business"? Easy, according to Patio Pacific. Buy a pet door. Here you'll find the largest selection in the world, the lowest prices (guaranteed), 24-hour shipment, and free installer referral service.

There are a number of models to choose from: sliding glass pet doors in semi-permanent or temporary installations, some designed for extra security, others for quick installation, still others dual-paned for extra warmth; pet doors for doors and walls; electronic pet doors; pet doors for screens and even windows. The helpful staff is on the other end of a toll-free call to help you with questions you might have about measuring your pet.

WEBSITE: Before placing your order, first check the website for Hot Buy items. Sometimes you can get an even better discount on items that have been returned or lightly damaged in shipping. The website has text and images to help you visualize what this company sells, and you may place and track your order online.

SPECIAL FACTORS: Complete satisfaction guaranteed.

State Line Tack

P.O. Box 910
Brockport, NY 14420–0910
888–839–9640
FAX: 716–637–5198
TDD: 800–468–8776

FORM OF INFORMATION: free print catalog; online catalog

PAY: check, MO, MC, V, AE, DSC

SELLS: equestrian clothing and supplies

STORE: 60 locations nationwide; check website or call for addresses and hours

ONLINE: www.statelinetack.com

State Line Tack bills itself as the world's largest tack shop. If you're a member of the horsey set, you'll love browsing through their "English" or "Western" catalogs. Each catalog features color photographs, detailed descriptions, and State Line's prices next to suggested retail prices so you can readily calculate your savings. Items are discounted anywhere from 15% to 40% off.

The attire sections have proper riding breeches, jodhpurs, chaps, tights, jackets, coats, shirts, and boots for men, women, and children of every shape and size, designed particularly for those who want to dress for competitions . There's plenty of less formal footwear and outdoorsy clothing here as well, including some great hats and caps, rain gear, gloves, and protective riding gear, such as helmets and vests. Lest we forget what riding is all about, State Line Tack has a large selection of wearable items for the horses, too, from horse blankets and mane tamers to traveling boots and even horse pajamas. The gear, equipment, and supplies just keep going: medical and therapeutic aids; shipping and trailering equipment and accessories; grooming tools; portable sheds; feeding equipment; barn and stable supplies; fly and pest control items; nutritional, hygiene, and medical products; bridles; saddlery; horse-themed jewelry and gift items; books; videos; and much more. By the way, State Line Tack has clothing and gear for people of *all* sizes, as well as for people with disabilities.

WEBSITE: The website features online ordering, color pictures, detailed descriptions, and a format that's easy to follow. Browse in the English, Western, or Cowboy sections, and within those categories you can look in the following departments: Rider's Clothing, Horse Clothing, Barn and Stable, Horse Health, Books, Gifts, and Tack.

SPECIAL FACTORS: Complete satisfaction guaranteed; returns accepted for refund, exchange, or credit.

That Fish Place/That Pet Place

237 Centerville Rd.
Lancaster, PA 17603
888–842–8738
717–299–5691
FAX: 717–295–7210

FORM OF INFORMATION: free print catalog; online catalog

PAY: check, MO, MC, V, AE, DSC

SELLS: supplies for aquariums, reptiles, birds, dogs, cats, small animals, and ponds

STORE: same address; Monday to Saturday 9:00 am-9:00 pm, Sunday 10:00 am–6:00 pm

ONLINE: www.thatfishplace.com or www.that-petplace.com

That Fish Place/That Pet Place claims to be the world's largest discount aquarium and pet care supplier. Savings here are up to 60% off regular retail prices. Their three full color, quarterly product catalogs (one aimed at aquarists, one at pond owners, and the other targeted specifically to the needs of dog, cat, bird, reptile, and small animal owners) feature unrivalled product selections, and articles by their resident marine biologists and pet experts. "The Pet Street Journal" will keep you informed, entertained, and up-to-date on special events throughout the pet industry. There's something for every pet—including tropical fish, goldfish, dogs, cats, birds, and reptiles. Among the dozens of name-brand manufacturers represented in TFP/TPP's fish, pond and pet supply catalogs, you're bound to find everything you need to keep your fish and pets healthy and their environment beautiful (including live plants). Check out the aquatic section for good deals on books, plants, fountains, and other supplies for lily ponds, koi ponds, and even patio or balcony ponds for urban dwellers (cool gift idea!).

WEBSITE: Both websites are user-friendly with enhanced product search capabilities and a weekly live online chat with one of their six on-staff marine biologists.

SPECIAL FACTORS: Authorized, unused returns accepted (a 15% restocking fee may be charged).

Tomahawk Live Trap Co.

P.O. Box 323
Tomahawk, WI 54487
800–272–8727
715–453–3550
FAX: 715–453–4326

FORM OF INFORMATION: free print catalog; online catalog

PAY: check, MO, MC, V, DSC

SELLS: humane animal traps and animal handling equipment

STORE: Tomahawk, WI; Monday to Friday 8:00 am–5:00 pm

ONLINE: www.livetrap.com

Q: What's this company doing in the "animal supplies" chapter? A: These are *humane* traps. Tomahawk's box traps are used all over the world by state and federal conservation departments, dog wardens, universities, and others who want to trap animals without harming them. (Capture that garden-munching varmint and then drop it off at your feuding cousin's place down the road!) The prices here are about 30% under retail, and discounts are even greater if you can order 6 or more of the same trap.

Established in 1925, Tomahawk manufactures over 100 different traps and cages for just about any animal of any size: fish, turtle, beaver, grackle, pigeon, raccoon, opossum, skunk, muskrat, cat, dog, rat, mouse, squirrel, chipmunk, armadillo, badger, and many more. Rigid box traps with rear-transfer doors, collapsible traps that fold to 1 inch in height, double-door traps that capture the animal entering from either direction, thumb traps, fish traps, and others are available here. Since trapping requires bait and sometimes special handling equipment such as snake hooks, animal-handling gloves, and pole syringes, Tomahawk carries these items, too.

WEBSITE: You can check out the entire inventory and also order online at Tomahawk's website. This well designed electronic catalog is one I'd recommend over the print version. Why? Because in addition to having the same great inventory pictured and described, you can get on the emailing list and check out current sales and specials.

SPECIAL FACTORS: Quantity discounts available; returns must be authorized and may be subject to a 15% restocking fee.

UPCO

P.O. Box 969, Dept. WBM
St. Joseph, MO 64502–0969
800–254–8726
FAX: 816–233–9696

FORM OF INFORMATION: free print catalog; online catalog

PAY: check, MO, MC, V, AE, DSC

SELLS: supplies for dogs, cats, horses, birds, and small animals

STORE: 3705 Pear St., St. Joseph, MO; Monday to Friday 7:30 am–6:00 pm, Saturday 7:30 am–5:00 pm

ONLINE: www.upco.com

For almost 50 years, veterinarians, groomers and breeders have turned to family-owned UPCO (United Pharmacal Company) for animal supplies and equipment. There are many reasons to buy from UPCO's 194-page color catalog, including quantity discounts, same-day shipping, and special discounts for licensed wildlife rehabilitators. In business for over 48 years, UPCO has managed to carve out a niche for itself in this highly competitive arena by offering wholesale pricing on many items and good selection and service to boot. You'll find health and grooming products, toys, training items, and practical pet supplies for nearly every type of animal except fish: dogs, cats, reptiles, horses, birds, and small animals such as rabbits, hamsters, and ferrets. Notable are the hundreds of books on dog care, training, and breeding in "The UPCO Library."

WEBSITE: UPCO has a searchable website with thousands of products. Since many of the products are neither pictured nor described in detail at the website, at this writing, it makes more sense to shop the old-fashioned way—by thumbing through the print catalog. Once you've perused the goods, you can place your order online, or by phone, fax, or mail.

SPECIAL FACTORS: Quantity discounts available; returns accepted within 30 days; No minimum order. Free shipping within the 48 states on orders over $70.00.

Valley Vet Supply

1118 Pony Express Hwy.
Marysville, KS 66508
800–419–9524
FAX: 800–446–5597

FORM OF INFORMATION: free print catalog; online catalog

PAY: check, MO, MC, V, AE, DSC

SELLS: vet and pet supplies for dogs, cats, and horses

STORE: same address; Monday to Saturday 8:00 am–8:00 pm, Sunday 12:30 noon–5:00 pm

ONLINE: www.valleyvet.com

What distinguishes one pet supply catalog from another? Well, in the case of Valley Vet, it's free shipping on most items, excellent prices (discounts up to 30% aren't unusual here), online ordering, internet specials, and three separate catalogs, each with a different focus. Valley Vet's "Pet Catalog" offers 84 pages of supplies mainly for dogs and cats, including homeopathic remedies, pet vacuums, dog- and cat-themed door-mats and other gift items, and of course the standard leashes, collars, food, cages, pet clothing, toys, grooming tools, and the like. The "Equine Catalog" boasts the best selection of horse blankets and sheets anywhere, and also features an extensive selection of riders' boots and clothing as well as some equine-themed toys, games, and gifts. Here you'll find everything you might need to outfit and care for Mr. Ed. Finally, there's the "Farm and Ranch Catalog," geared toward livestock and their owners. This vet-owned company will do its best to make you a loyal customer.

WEBSITE: Valley Vet's well designed online catalog presents a full line of in-stock products for each of its three branches—pet, equine, or farm and ranch. Click into one of these areas at the website and you'll be able to quickly and easily find any product you seek. Colored images, thorough product descriptions, web-only specials, and secure online ordering make this an attractive alternative to the print catalog.

SPECIAL FACTORS: Satisfaction guaranteed; authorized returns accepted within 30 days.

Apparel, Shoes, and Accessories

Hats, wallets, sunglasses, and pins for men and women;
scarves and handbags for women

When I first moved to upstate New York a friend of a friend wanted to take me and some other people to visit an ashram she belonged to and meet her guru, who happened to be a woman. The place was in a beautiful setting in the hills and there were hundreds of people attending, many of whom had traveled all the way from New York City to receive dharshan from this woman. Translation: she zaps you with her cool vibes and you benefit in some way. A large auditorium was packed with men and women who were directed to their seats on the floor (the better to assume a full lotus position) by women who seemed to be higher up in the ashram's social hierarchy. The women ushers all wore slightly different versions of a peculiar yet curiously stylish outfit. They all wore brightly colored saris (a long cloth worn by Indian women that is wrapped around the body), topped off by a well-tailored Armani-type blazer in a very loud color such as lime green, fuschia, or orange. On top of all that they were all wearing trendy, cosmopolitan, uptown New York type necklaces, bracelets, earrings, and belts. It was an unusual combination of complete opposites of ancient and modern, ethnic and urban that worked perfectly together. After a long day of meditation, lectures, proselytizing, prostrating, and peacock feathers bopped on the bent heads of worshipping devotees, the friend of a friend asked what I thought (hoping for a sign of conversion). All I could think to sincerely say was, "I just love how the women in charge of seating have accessorized!" She stared at me in obvious disgust and then ignored me for the rest of the day. Oh well. The stores listed in this section will allow you to accent all your outfits with the perfect belt, handbag, and jewelry and still have money left over to hand over to the guru of choice.

In addition to the items offered in the "Accessories" section of this chapter, you'll find clothing for women, men, and children in the appropriately named "Clothing for Women, Men, and Children" section on page 29. Be sure to check out the more specialized "Babies and Children" and "Men's Business Attire" subchapters that follow on pages 23 and 65, respectively. Likewise, if you're specifically shopping for men's or women's shoes or boots, see "Shoes," page 71. Underneath it all, you still need hosiery and underthings. You'll find incredible deals in the subchapter called "Intimate Apparel," page 51. And, for the final touch, see the "Jewelry" section on page 57. Some of the stores listed in the clothing section carry shoes for men, women, and children as well

Those searching for work uniforms (chef's whites, hospital scrubs, janitorial jumpsuits) or everyday clothing, such as polo shirts and caps on which to imprint your company slogan, should see the "Uniforms and Promotional Products" section of the "Office, Business, and Professional" chapter.

Many other companies in this book offer clothing and footwear. For example, you'll find outdoor and athletic clothing of all kinds in the "Sports and Outdoor Recreation" chapter; foul-weather gear in "Auto, Marine, and Aviation"; clothing adapted to persons with special physical needs in the "Special Needs" chapter; and safety and protective clothing in "Office, Business, and Professional." There's assorted clothing in the "General Merchandise" chapter, and of course many companies sell themed T-shirts.

Find It Fast

ATTACHÉ AND PORTFOLIO CASES
AnyKnockOff.com

BELTS
AnyKnockOff.com, Freda LA

BRIDAL ATTIRE
Manny's Millinery Supply Center

FRAGRANCES
AnyKnockOff.com, Freda LA

GLOVES
Manny's Millinery Supply Center

HANDBAGS
AnyKnockOff.com, Freda LA

HATS
Baltic Rim, Manny's Millinery Supply Center

JEWELRY
AnyKnockOff.com, Freda LA

MILLINERY SUPPLIES
Manny's Millinery Supply Center

RUSSIAN HATS
Baltic Rim

RUSSIAN PINS
Baltic Rim

SCARVES
AnyKnockOff.com

SUNGLASSES
AnyKnockOff.com

WALLETS
AnyKnockOff.com, Freda LA

AnyKnockOff.com

**860 S. Los Angeles St.,
Ste 1033**

Los Angeles, CA 90014

877–856–5199

FAX: 213–488–0746

FORM OF INFORMATION: online catalog only; no print catalog

PAY: check, MO, MC, V, AE, DC

SELLS: trendy designer knock-off wallets, belts, attaché and portfolio cases for men and women; trendy designer knock-off handbags, jewelry, scarves, and sunglasses for women

STORE: same address (warehouse); phone hours Monday to Friday 9:00 am–6:00 pm PST

ONLINE: www.anyknockoff.com

I had a wealthy boyfriend once who had very specific tastes which included couture clothing. He used to buy me handbags from an Italian designer which ranged from $800 to $1200. They were quite beautiful. Since then I have lived a little in the "real world," had a child, and live quite a different life than I did then and I just can't imagine spending that kind of money on a purse. And now you don't *have* to. If you are attached to what's "in" and currently "hot" in the fashion world, you can have it at a perfectly reasonable price at AnyKnockOff.com. The people behind AnyKnockOff.com are a team of experienced and passionate professionals who believe that trends in fashion are too expensive and transitory to warrant paying an excessive amount of money for them. They created AnyKnockOff.com to allow you to ride the trends, whatever your budget.

What are knock-offs? Well, at AnyKnockOff.com they are "copies" of handbags, jewelry, belts, wallets, sunglasses, fragrances, and scarves, by such designers as Chanel, Fendi, Gucci, Kate Spade, Persol, Paloma Picasso, Prada, JP Tod's, Versace, Coach, Louis Vuitton, Cartier, Blaknik, Volponi, Ferragamo, Tiffany, Calvin Klein, and more. For example, a Prada handbag that would cost $600 for the real "McCoy" will only set you back $40 here. One of the ways they are able to offer their knock-offs for less is by using animal-friendly man-made materials instead of leather for some products. They do carry some leather and suede handbags in addition to many canvas and nylon. AnyKnockOff.com is in no way affiliated with, representing, associated, or sponsored by these designers, nor are their products exact copies. They are quality products inspired by today's fashion trends at great prices. This company is customer certified by BizRate and has an overall rating of 8.9.

SPECIAL FACTORS: Returns or exchanges accepted within 30 days of purchase.

Baltic Rim

1223 Wilshire Blvd., #817
Santa Monica, CA 90403
800–399–0734
FAX: 310–392–3977

FORM OF INFORMATION: online catalog only; no print catalog

PAY: check, MO, MC, V

SELLS: traditional Russian hats and pins for men and women

STORE: no walk-in location; online only

ONLINE: www.balticrim.com

Headquartered in Santa Monica, California, Baltic Rim has been the sole importer of hats from the former Soviet Union since 1991. The Baltic Rim ushanka is the original, manufactured in the factories that once supplied high ranking politburo officials and the Soviet military. Even today the paperwork still bears the trademark bureaucratic hand stamp of the now historic communist regime. Worn by the Russian navy, the fun and animal-safe version of the traditional ushanka is their most popular hat which comes in black, navy blue, forest green, and burgundy for only $25. In addition to hats, Baltic Rim offers a variety of authentic Soviet military dress pins, designer retro-style pins, and a selection of officially licensed college pins representing universities from the rockies to the east coast. Custom pins are available by special order. The pins average around $5 and look excellent on the hats.

SPECIAL FACTORS: Shipping and handling fees are $5.95 for one hat with $2 for each additional hat.

Freda LA

Pursies Galore
9903 Santa Monica Blvd., #349
Beverly Hills, CA 90212
888-987-5678
310-858-7104
FAX: 310-858-8493

FORM OF INFORMATION: online catalog only; no print catalog

PAY: check, MO, MC, V, AE, DC

SELLS: eclectic fashion handbags, gifts, belts, jewelry, and home accents

STORE: same address; Sunday and Saturday 7:00 am–7:00 pm

ONLINE: www.FredaLA.com

If you're one of those shoppers who is always on the lookout for unique merchandise full of life and flair, then you'll love Freda LA's cool, kitschy, new-wave selection of handbags, accessories, gifts, and home accents. Owner Freda Kunin, a Beverly Hills native, has a trendy online fashion boutique that features the wildest handbag selection I've ever seen. Click on the section called Pursies Galore to view dozens of well-made, reasonably priced handbags and carrying cases of all kinds. In addition to the wide selection of handbags you'll find other fashion accessories such as: precious and semi-precious jewelry, belts, fabulous furry business card cases, cell phone cases, mirrored lipstick cases, and wallets; neon fuzzy eyeglass holders, agenda books, and keychains. From tartan plaids and peacock feathers to faux leopard and holograms, the materials and designs here are anything but traditional. One of my favorites: a carrying case made in the style of an 8 mm film can. Freda's philosophy is: Don't buy a handbag after the fact. Buy it first, then build your whole outfit around it! I barely do justice to these handbags, makeup bags, and other totes by describing them. You'll just have to take a look for yourself.

Freda also carries a dizzying array of home accents, such as the classic vintage rooster sets grandma had in her 1950s kitchen, Mexican ceramics, vibrant screen-painted lamp shades, beautiful Victorian era accents, rare antique estate furnishings, and more. For around the home, Freda suggests that you "make all of your decadent dreams come true in the one room of the house where you can truly find tranquillity—your opulent bath." In the bath section, look for unique curios, towel holders, and toiletry items such as the "Unavailable" perfume, which comes with an informational booklet on how to make yourself into an "unavailable" single (because then, of course, everyone will want you!). I also loved the hilariously naughty "Total Bitch" brand soap with accompanying wash towels. Everything at the website can be ordered online. There is much, much more here, so take some time to explore this refreshing website, and be sure to join the FredaLA.com Newsletter Mailing List for updates, specials, and breaking news. Freda LA is a member of the Better Business Bureau, The Beverly Hills Chamber of Commerce, and has received the Yahoo! Top Service Award, which honors e-tailers that receive 95% or higher customer-approval ratings.

SPECIAL FACTORS: Free standard shipping within the continental U.S. on orders over $100.

Manny's Millinery Supply Center

26 W. 38th St.
New York, NY 10018
212–840–2235/2236
FAX: 212–944–0178

FORM OF INFORMATION: $6 print catalog
PAY: check, MO, MC, V, AE
SELLS: hats, millinery supplies, gloves, bridal trimmings
STORE: same address; Monday to Friday 9:30 am–5:30 pm, Saturday 10:00 am–4:30 pm

You're going to fall in love with Manny's Millinery Supply Center when you get the catalog. It will make you want to buy and make hats, throw a hat-making party, and change your whole image. Some catalogs merely show products; this one inspires. Owner Howard Manny, a real character, will get you smiling with his introductory text.

Manny's has two catalogs. (Your $6 with catalog request will get you both.) The "Basic Supply Catalog" offers millinery items such as straw, felt, hat pins, beading, feathers, tapes, sizing, veiling, ribbons, and other professional millinery supplies and equipment, including horsehair braid, hat stretchers, display heads and racks, hatboxes and travel cases, and cleaning products. The 90-page "Hat Catalog" is fabulous and features 600-plus photographed hats—with and without trim. The styles are many, in materials including pari sisal, chenille, velour, felt (both fur felt and wool felt), twisted toyo, and others. Scores of "frames," or fabric-covered hat forms, are offered. The satin frames are suitable for bridal outfits, and the buckram frames provide a base for limitless flights of fancy.

In addition, Manny's hat catalog offers a variety of jeweled, feather, and beaded hat pins; flowered hat pins of every conceivable type; trimmings in a dazzling variety, including cording, wired ribbon, wired mesh, lace, and pleated stretch velvet in many designs, colors, and textures; beaded, sequin, and rhinestone trimmings; wooden hat blocks and basic crowns; oversize hat forms; and hat trees. Savings vary from item to item, but average 33% below regular retail. By the way, if you're into hatmaking or other crafts projects, check out Manny's five "Surprise Grab Bags" (Rounding Assortment, Feather Surprise, Millinery Madness Surprise, Flower Surprise, Triple Flower Surprise). These are 19" × 19" plastic bags crammed full of one-of-a-kinds, remnants, flawed, seconds, or shopworn items, and worth "5 to 10 times the face value of what's in them." They vary in price and are described in detail in the catalog. You can buy them individually, or get 3 for $35. Manny's also sells 6 excellent books on hatmaking.

Please note: If you're buying hats only, the minimum order is three; if you buy one or two hats, you must also buy $15 in assorted items (frames, trims, etc.); if you're buying assorted items only, the minimum order is $25. There is no minimum book order.

SPECIAL FACTORS: Price quotes by phone; minimum order on certain items (see text).

Babies and Children

Diapering and baby supplies; clothing, shoes, and accessories
for infants and children

Although most of the companies in the "Clothing for Women, Men, and Children" section carry clothing and footwear for children, I've included this chapter for companies that focus exclusively on apparel for infants, babies, and children and diapering supplies.

It is easy, especially for new parents, to spend a fortune on tiny matching outfits, little cardigan sweaters, miniature high-top sneakers, down-filled sleeping bags, and on and on for your little bundle of joy. When the little tyke gets a bit older and is in school, though, you'll be appalled at how expensive clothing is. It doesn't take long to learn that buying $50 shoes he'll wear for half a year is fruitless. Thank goodness for some of the companies in this chapter. You can save up to 60% on everything from diapering supplies to velvet-and-lace dresses for your little tykes.

There are numerous firms in other chapters that carry various and sundry child-related goods—from children's crafts projects and games and toys, to tiny protective beekeeping suits and kids' vitamins. It would be impossible to list them all here, so be sure and browse the relevant chapter if there's something specific you seek.

Find It Fast

BABY-CARE PRODUCTS
Baby Bunz, Bareware, Natural E Baby

BABY SLINGS AND CARRIERS
Baby Bunz, Bareware, Natural E Baby

BABY TOYS
Baby Bunz, Bareware, Natural E Baby

CLOTH DIAPERS AND COVERS
Baby Bunz, Bareware, Natural E Baby

INFANTS' CLOTHING
Baby Bunz, Bareware, Basic Brilliance, Natural E Baby, Rubens & Marble

TODDLERS' AND CHILDREN'S CLOTHING
Bareware, Basic Brilliance

Baby Bunz & Co.

P.O. Box 113
Lynden, WA 98264
800–676–4559
FAX: 360–354–1203

FORM OF INFORMATION: free catalog; online catalog

PAY: check, MO, MC, V

SELLS: natural fiber cloth diapering supplies, layette items, toys, books, and accessories for infants and toddlers

STORE: no walk-in location; mail-order only

ONLINE: www.babybunz.com

It all started in 1982 when Carynia, founder of Baby Bunz, was looking for a diaper cover for her newborn son and wanted to make them available to other parents like her. Nearly two decades later, Baby Bunz is a grown-up company that specializes in a variety of natural diapering and other products for babies at below-retail prices. This is not a bargain-basement company. The items in the catalog are high-quality, higher-end products. But informed consumers who shop around for such all-natural items will find the prices at Baby Bunz consistently lower than other retail sources. This company offers Nikky diaper covers in a range of styles—some with waterproof liners, others all-cotton, still others lambswool or breathable poly. The lovely 20-page catalog features detailed descriptions, photographs, and even diagrams for cloth-diaper folding (different for boys and girls). A careful selection of infant items in all-natural, chemical-free, organic cotton—baby buntings, baby caps, blankets, footies, etc.—as well as baby basics, from baby's first books and toys to classic coveralls, are here. There is a new budget line of cloth diapers and covers, including Bummis, that make cloth diapering even more economical. Moms: If you're looking for discounted Weleda products, such as their heavenly calendula cream, Baby Bunz has them, too.

WEBSITE: This is a very nicely designed site. It's aesthetically beautiful and very well organized. The site makes it easy and inviting to shop here. There's no need to get a print catalog if you have internet access. Online ordering is available here.

SPECIAL FACTORS: No wholesale orders please; satisfaction guaranteed; returns of products in original condition accepted within 30 days for refund, credit, or exchange.

Bareware

307 C 14th St.
Courtenay BC V9N 6PS
Canada
877-9-DIAPER
FAX: 250-334-8365

FORM OF INFORMATION: free print catalog; online catalog

PAY: check, MO, MC, V, AE

SELLS: diapering, nursing, and maternity supplies and accessories

STORE: same address; Monday to Friday 9:00 am–5:30 pm PST

ONLINE: www.bareware.net

I really appreciate home-grown companies that specialize in personal service and great value. This one happens to be Canadian, which is great for American shoppers. At the current exchange rate of about 1.50 Canadian dollars to the U.S. dollar, that translates into more than 30% savings on everything you buy here. Incredibly low shipping fees are icing on the cake. So, what kinds of things will mothers find at Bareware? Cloth diapers; diaper covers; diaper accessories (diaper wipes, changing accessories, tote bags, diaper liners); swim and bath items (hooded towels, cradle cap brush); skin care products (massage oil, unpetroleum jelly); adorable Robeez shoes for beginning walkers; maternity items (prenatal heartbeat listening system, maternity underwear, maternity supporters); nursing accessories; breastpumps; and all-natural menstrual products (*very* hard to find), to name a few. There's a free print catalog, too, but the online catalog is so wonderful that you needn't bother with the paper version if you have internet access. With easy-to-understand links to the various product departments, crisp color pictures, and descriptive text, Bareware's website gets our stamp of approval. All prices are listed in both Canadian and American dollars. You can order online, by phone, or you can print out an order form and fax or mail it in. I liked the gently used diapers and clearance page—amazing deals on 100% cotton diapers, which make the absolute best household cloths for dusting, polishing, wiping up disasters, and just about anything else that requires softness and absorbency. You'll also find parenting links here. All products come with the manufacturer's warranty, plus Bareware's own satisfaction guarantee. A mother of toddlers, the owner is extremely accessible should you have questions or problems with your order.

SPECIAL FACTORS: 30-day money-back guarantee; wholesale inquiries welcome.

Basic Brilliance

P.O. Box 1719
Port Townsend, WA 98368
800–409–3835
360–385–3835
FAX: 360–385–4041

FORM OF INFORMATION: online catalog only; no print catalog

PAY: check, MO, MC, V

SELLS: 100% cotton clothing for kids and babies

STORE: no walk-in location; online only

ONLINE: www.basicbrilliance.com

Do you dislike children's clothing that is printed with the designer's logo or cutesy designs? Little dancing frogs and embroidered soccer balls may be cute on other people's kids. But for your kid, is solid-color, 100% cotton what you seek? Well okay, maybe stripes now and then. If this describes your taste, you'll love Basic Brilliance. Log on to the website and feast your eyes on garment-dyed, American-made basics for kids in more than a dozen solid colors, including pastels, rich rainbow colors, and tasteful earth tones and blends. The prices here are fantastic—easily 25% to 50% less than you'd find at a brick-and-mortar store or the famous Swedish baby clothes cataloger. If you're looking for well-made, all-cotton, everyday clothing, with an emphasis on comfort and basic styling, you'll find baby caps and berets, infant snapsuits, long johns sets, leggings, French terry pants, empire dresses, T-shirts, sweatshirts, cardigans, and ballet dresses, among other items. Look for the garment-care page on the website that gives laundering and stain-removal advice. Moms: The children's cotton long johns sets are the least expensive I've seen. I really love this company, and you will, too. The website features online, secure electronic ordering.

SPECIAL FACTORS: Satisfaction guaranteed; returns accepted within 30 days for credit or exchange.

Natural E Baby

78 Freeman Ln.
Manorville, NY 11949
631–874–2334

FORM OF INFORMATION: online catalog only; no print catalog

PAY: check, MO, MC, V, AE, DSC

SELLS: cloth diapers, diaper covers, slings, natural baby care, organic baby clothing, bedding, mattresses, and toys

STORE: no walk-in location; online only

ONLINE: www.naturalebaby.com

Natural E Baby was founded out of a concern for the health of babies and our planet. Cloth diapers are an excellent and superior alternative to disposable diapers. For one, they're cheaper. According to *Consumer Reports,* the average cost to diaper a baby in disposables through potty-training is $1,500 to $2,100. Most diaper services will run about $1,600 in that same time. The costs associated with purchasing your own diapers and laundering them at home, including the cost of detergent, energy, water, etc., for this period will start at about $600. Plus, babies who wear cloth diapers typically have less instances of rash outbreaks, and cloth diapers do not contribute to the landfill. Did you know that disposable diapers are the third most common item found in our landfills? And they take 500 years to decompose.

In addition to a good selection of cloth diapers and diaper covers, you'll find some other great products here for your baby such as slings, organic layettes, undershirts, tops, pants, caps, toys, crib sheets, and comforters. Natural E Baby also has a low price guarantee. If you find a product they carry elsewhere for less, they'll meet or beat the price (cost of shipping is considered). Natural E Baby offers reasonable shipping rates for $5.50 to $6.95 with free shipping within the continental U.S. for any order over $150.

SPECIAL FACTORS: Returns accepted within 30 days of purchase for unused, unwashed items with tags and packaging intact for refund minus a 10% restocking fee; shipping charges will only be refunded if the product was defective and the customer does not want a replacement; contact Natural E Baby before returning defective merchandise—in some instances they will advise you to return the product directly to the manufacturer for repair.

Rubens & Marble, Inc.

P.O. Box 14900–A
Chicago, IL 60614–0900
773–348–6200

FORM OF INFORMATION: brochure, free with SASE
PAY: check or MO
SELLS: infants' clothing
STORE: no walk-in location; mail-order only

Chances are, the first clothes you or your baby wore were made by Rubens & Marble, Inc. That's because Rubens has been supplying hospitals with infant garments since 1890. You can purchase these same items at very low prices directly from their "Baby Wear Factory" flyer. The double-sided flyer shows baby shirt seconds (with small knitting flaws) in snap-side, tie-side, and slipover, in short or mitten-cuff sleeve, at less than a dollar apiece. There are also first-quality gowns and kimonos, all-cotton baby shirts, sheets for crib, bassinet, and porta-cribs, stretch diapers by the dozen, training panties, and terry bibs. Shirt sizes range from preemie and newborn up to 36 months (29–32 pounds).

SPECIAL FACTORS: You must include a SASE to receive the price list; all seconds clearly indicated; minimum order: one package (number of items varies depending on item).

Clothing for Women, Men, and Children

Dress and casual attire for women, men, and children;
outerwear, work, and sports clothing; designer apparel;
progressive and radical T-shirts; new and vintage wedding
gowns; vintage clothing; dance wear; swimwear

I recall a famous ex-wife boo-hooing because the alimony payments from her multi-millionaire husband would prohibit her from maintaining the lifestyle to which she had grown accustomed. Among her *monthly* expenses: $4,000 for clothing and shoes. Gulp! I've never spent that much on clothing in a year.

If you're reading this book, darling, take heart. The companies in this section sell all kinds of clothing for exercising at the gym, knocking about town, tending your garden, dressing up for that important date, accessorizing with flair, and even for getting married in—assuming you have the stomach for it the second time around—all at tremendous discounts, some as much as 75% off!

Find It Fast

BRIDAL ATTIRE
Carla's Vintage Wedding Gowns, Discount Bridal Service

CHILDREN'S CLOTHING
Classic Closeouts, DesignerOutlet, Gohn Bros, REI-OUTLET.com, Sierra Trading Post, The Ultimate Outlet

CHILDREN'S SHOES
Classic Closeouts, DesignerOutlet, Gohn Bros, REI-OUTLET.com, Sierra Trading Post, The Ultimate Outlet

DANCE AND EXERCISE CLOTHING
Dance Distributors, Sierra Trading Post, World Wide Aquatics

FAUX FURS
Fabulous-Furs

HATS
Bluefly, B Coole Designs, Classic Closeouts, DesignerOutlet, Fabulous-Furs, Gohn Bros, REI-OUTLET.com, Sierra Trading Post

MEN'S CLOTHING

Bluefly, Classic Closeouts, DesignerOutlet, Gohn Bros., KingPoodle.com/ RustyZipper.com, The Nth Degree, REI-OUTLET.com, Sierra Trading Post, Sportswear Clearinghouse, The Ultimate Outlet

MEN'S SHOES

Bluefly, Classic Closeouts, DesignerOutlet, Gohn Bros., KingPoodle.com/ RustyZipper.com, REI-OUTLET.com, Sierra Trading Post, The Ultimate Outlet

OUTERWEAR AND FOUL-WEATHER GEAR

Bluefly, Classic Closeouts, DesignerOutlet, Fabulous-Furs, Gohn Bros., REI-OUTLET.com, Sierra Trading Post, The Ultimate Outlet

POLITICALLY THEMED T-SHIRTS

The Nth Degree

SWIMWEAR

Bluefly, Classic Closeouts, DesignerOutlet, Chadwick's of Boston, The Ultimate Outlet, Sierra Trading Post, World Wide Aquatics

VINTAGE CLOTHING

Carla's Vintage Wedding Gowns, KingPoodle.com/RustyZipper.com

WOMEN'S CLOTHING

B. Coole Designs, Bedford Fair Lifestyles, Bluefly, Chadwick's of Boston, Classic Closeouts, DesignerOutlet, KingPoodle.com/RustyZipper.com, REI-OUTLET.com, Sierra Trading Post, The Ultimate Outlet

WOMEN'S SHOES

Bluefly, Chadwick's of Boston, Classic Closeouts, DesignerOutlet, Gohn Bros., KingPoodle.com/RustyZipper.com, REI-OUTLET.com, Sierra Trading Post, The Ultimate Outlet

WORKMAN'S CLOTHING

Gohn Bros., REI-OUTLET.com, Sierra Trading Post

B. Coole Designs

2631 Piner Road
Santa Rosa, CA 95401
800–992–8924

FORM OF INFORMATION: free print catalog; online catalog

PAY: check, MO, MC, V

SELLS: handmade cotton women's clothing; renaissance fair costumes; cotton hats, scarves, and head wraps; handmade and custom kids cotton clothing; diapering supplies

STORE: no walk-in location; mail-order only

ONLINE: www.bcoole.com

It's amazing what you can learn by chatting with strangers. For example, did you know that plus-sized women make up a significant percentage of people who follow the renaissance fair circuit? I didn't even know there *was* a renaissance fair circuit! Well, Barbara Coole, owner of B. Coole Designs, set me straight. Apparently, the romantic clothing fashionable during the time of jousting and wandering bards is well-suited to the ample-bosomed fair lady of today. B. Coole Designs offers handmade cloaks, drawstring blouses, lace-up bodices, skirts in any size you want, romantic low-cut neckline princess dresses, and custom-costumes with as many details and flourishes as your heart desires.

In addition to custom period clothing and costumes, B. Coole carries inexpensive women's clothing (rayon skirts and tops, gauze skirts, jumpers, blouses, twill jackets, vests, skirts); very-hard-to-find and reasonably priced kids cotton clothing (pocket pants, pocket dresses, shorts, tanks, socks, hats); baby clothing, layettes, and plain cotton diapers; blankets; cotton menstrual pads ("just like Granny used to use"); and hats, turbans, scarves, and head cloths suitable for women suffering from hair loss, especially due to chemotherapy and alopecia. Says Barbara: "These plain cotton scarves and wraps do not irritate the sensitive scalp and make women feel lovely at a time when they are recovering and feeling particularly unpretty." The theme here is basic design, comfortable fit, cotton or natural fibers, and low, low prices. What a great find this company is. The 4-page print catalog is less interesting and informative than the online catalog, in my opinion.

WEBSITE: Read the text scattered throughout the website and you'll understand why I love this little home-run business. You may not find a lot of fancy bells and whistles online, but you will be able to easily see what is offered here, read detailed descriptions, and then email or call the owner if you have further questions. There are lots of goodies online too numerous to name here, such as unbleached baby T-shirts, or a huge oversized T-shirt that will even be too big for grandpa. According to the owner, B. Coole Designs has some weak points: no tissue paper wrapping, no fancy stationery, recycled boxes for mailers, and slow work. Hey, she sounds like my kind of gal! If you like well-made clothing and cotton items, and crave a real-life connection with the manufacturer, look no further. I enthusiastically endorse this company. Note: the website does not have secure online ordering. To order, call in your order, or email your credit card information in two parts.

SPECIAL FACTORS: Returns accepted, and refunds given "with no hard feelings."

Bedford Fair Lifestyles

421 Landmark Dr.
Wilmington, NC 28410
800-964-1000, Dept. WBM
FAX: 910-798-2000
TDD: 800-945-1118

FORM OF INFORMATION: free print catalog
PAY: check, MO, MC, V, AE, DSC, Bedford Fair credit card
SELLS: career and casual women's apparel
STORE: no walk-in location; mail-order only

"Unbeatable values!" exclaims text on the inside cover of the Bedford Fair Lifestyles catalog. This source for swingy, inexpensive clothing for women will make you happy with its well-balanced selection of colorful suits, skirts, dresses, and shirt/trouser combos for work and weekends, as well as shoes, sweaters, drawstring pants, and jackets. If you think bargain clothing has to be made out of polyester, you'll be thrilled to discover Bedford Fair Lifestyles. Some of the best deals here are the basics—plain acrylic knit turtlenecks, washable silk blouses, cotton sweaters, A-line skirts, cotton twill trousers, or rayon jumpers that make up the foundation of a fall or winter wardrobe, yet cost about 25% less than what you might pay in stores. Past catalogs have featured pastel party dresses, silk blazers, and crocheted sweaters. Sizes range from petite (starting at size 4) up to misses size 20, and women's 18 to 28; a handy measuring table is included in the catalog to help insure proper fit. Look for the sales catalogs, where items are marked down as much as 50%. I'm sold on this catalog.

SPECIAL FACTORS: Satisfaction guaranteed; returns accepted for exchange, refund, or credit; deferred payment available.

Bluefly

42 West 39th street, 9th Fl. New York, NY 10018	**FORM OF INFORMATION:** online catalog only, no print catalog
877-258-3359	**PAY:** MO, MC, V, AE, DSC, DC, JCB
FAX: 212-354-3400	**SELLS:** designer clothing for men and women, and houseware items
	STORE: no walk-in location; mail-order only
	ONLINE: www.bluefly.com

Did you ever want to indulge yourself with a pair of designer jeans, only to pause as you find that they'll cost you an arm and a leg? Why not indulge you rself with a much friendlier price range by shopping at Bluefly? The brands they offer are the same as those found in many of the finer department stores and can be purchased with all your limbs intact. The top designers are represented here, including Armani, Gucci, Michael Kors, Prada, Fendi, Donna Karan, Calvin Klein, Polo Ralph Lauren, and Versace (just to name a few). A relatively new web business, started in 1998 by the enterprising Ken Seiff, Bluefly was designed to "combine the brands and customer service of an upscale department store with the discounts of an off-price retailer and the convenience of a catalog." It appears to have succeeded, with a huge list of designer clothes available, 25% to 75% discounts, and an easy to use online catalog. Overall, a very convenient way of getting relatively cheap designer clothing. Bluefly also sells gifts, furniture, and other household items such as bedding, dinnerware, and table settings. If you're anything like me, the mall can be the most intimidating and depressing way to shop. Why not avoid the hubbub and noise as well as the prices?

SPECIAL FACTORS: 90-day money-back guarantee; customizable "mycatalog" web feature.

Carla's Vintage Wedding Gowns

FORM OF INFORMATION: online catalog only, no print catalog

PAY: check, MO, MC

SELLS: vintage wedding gowns, cocktail attire for men and women, and costume jewelry

STORE: no walk-in location; mail-order only

EMAIL: Gowns4you@aol.com

ONLINE: hometown.aol.com/gowns4you/index.html

Carla Michaels loves vintage clothing, and so do I. I have a friend who got married in a gorgeous circa 1906 lace gown. It didn't belong to her grandmother; she actually bought it in an antique store in SoHo. Click onto Carla's Vintage Wedding Gowns and you'll be treated to full-color photographs of a variety of gowns from every era and for every dress size. Carla says that many of the vintage gowns she seeks out are perfect for women who aren't necessarily built like Twiggy. In other words, real women.

The website allows you to view not only vintage wedding gowns (for princesses *and* divas), but also swank vintage tuxes for him, cocktail dresses for her, and even faux baubles to accessorize your hip vintage look. Carla photographs and describes the gowns, including the condition they're in and whether they'll require special cleaning, mending, or care. She also provides precise bust, waist, and hip measurements for each dress. The wedding dresses are really inexpensive, most well under $500, at this writing. The other vintage clothing is priced a lot lower than I've seen in New York vintage shops. The website is updated regularly, and Carla keeps a supply of photographs if you need to see more goods that aren't on the website before making your decision. (Send your request by email.) If there's a type of dress you're looking for, email Carla's Vintage Wedding Gowns and they'll do their best to find it for you at a reasonable cost. To place an order simply send Carla an email with the gown number and description. You will be sent an e-mail to confirm availability and the gown will be held for seven days only. Once payment is received, a receipt by e-mail will be sent. This small company wants you to be a satisfied customer, so if you have special requests or problems with your purchase, Carla urges you to get in touch with her right away.

SPECIAL FACTORS: Dresses will be reserved for 7 days, then shipped once your check has cleared; returns accepted for store credit only with 20% restocking fee on wedding items, less shipping. The returned merchandise must be returned in the same condition as sent, mailed back to them priorty mail insured, and they must receive notice of return 2 days after delivery. After that time, it is considered a final sale.

Chadwick's of Boston, Ltd.

35 United Drive
West Bridgewater, MA 02379
800–544–3795
FAX: 800–448–5767
TDD: 800–978–8798

FORM OF INFORMATION: free print catalog; online catalog

PAY: check, MO, MC, V, AE, DSC

SELLS: women's clothing, shoes, and accessories

STORE: Points West Plaza, 21 Torey St, Brockton, MA and Westside Plaza, 9 Northwest Blvd., Nashua, NH; check website for hours

ONLINE: www.chadwicks.com

Chadwick's of Boston, "the original off-price catalog," is full of tremendous deals for women. You'll save 20% to 50% here on stylish sweaters, khakis, skirts, jumpers, jeans, trousers, dresses, business suits, blazers, and coats, in fabrics such as silk, cotton, suede, wool, cashmere, velvet, and rayon. There's also a nice selection of footwear: coordinated-colored pumps, flats, boots, clogs, and more. You won't find a lot of loud prints or outrageous styles in the color catalog. Chadwick's clothes are appealing, to me at least, because they're classic and understated. You'll find items such as cotton cardigans, mix-and-match silk separates, knock-around rayon dresses, and tea-length A-line skirts—many of them in solid colors, and all very inexpensive. You could build a seasonal wardrobe here for very little money by mixing and matching separates.

Note to plus-size readers: Chadwick's of Boston has clothes to fit women of every size. If you're 14W to 26W, ask for the "Jessica London" catalog.

WEBSITE: The website is very extensive. It's easy to shop here by department. I like that you can view a swatch window of alternate colors for any item, plus they have a section to the left of your selection with great coordinate suggestions to complete an outfit.

SPECIAL FACTORS: Satisfaction guaranteed; returns accepted for exchange or refund; deferred billing available.

Classic Closeouts

2 University Plaza
Hackensack, NY 07601

FORM OF INFORMATION: online catalog only; no print catalog
PAY: MC, V, AE, DSC
SELLS: women's, men's, and children's clothing, shoes, and jewelry, electronics, kitchen, home decor, toys, etc.
STORE: no walk-in location; mail-order only
ONLINE: www.classiccloseouts.com

Classic Closeouts explains on their website how they are able to offer such big savings on their merchandise. Their accountants scrutinize each and every dime they spend, all the way down to the coffee filters they use in the office coffee pot. It seems to have paid off because they do have some incredible savings—up to 85% off retail. In the clothes deparment you'll find over 100 brand-names which include Calvin Klein, DKNY, Tommy Hilfiger, J. Crew, Timberland, Anne Klein, Gap, and much, much more. Shop by brand, by price, or by category. There are good deals on all kinds of products including gloves, hats, outerwear, pants, shorts, shirts, shoes, sweaters, vests, swimwear, tanks, t-shirts, ties, watches, handbags, socks and hosiery, sunglasses, electronics, home decor, kitchen, office, school supplies, seasonal outdoors, and toys. They also have plus-size clothing for women. Classic Closeouts is so sure they have the best prices they offer a price guarantee. If you can find any item advertised cheaper, they'll pay the difference. I have purchased some dirt cheap clothing and shoes from this vendor that are high in quality and I am delighted to include them in this book.

SPECIAL FACTORS: Authorized returns accepted for exchange or refund 30 days from the date of purchase in original unworn and/or unused condition with original Proof of Purchase. Shipping is free to APO and FPO boxes.

Dance Distributors

50 S. Cameron St.
Harrisburg, PA 17101
800–333–2623
FAX: 717–234–1465

FORM OF INFORMATION: free print catalog
PAY: check, MO, MC, V, AE, DSC
SELLS: dancewear and accessories for women, children, and men
STORE: no walk-in location; mail-order only
ONLINE: www.dancedistributors.com

Here's a catalog that will appeal to anyone looking for an excellent selection of dance shoes, body wear, and accessories for women, children, and men at prices that are 25% or more off list. (Regular retail prices are listed alongside Dance Distributors' prices so you can see the savings.) The 92-page color catalog features photographs and descriptions of shoes (ballet, pointe, dance sneakers, gymnastic, jazz, tap, and more); a wide variety of dance bodywear from the top-name manufacturers; and dance-related accessories such as dance bags, foot-comfort products, and videos that teach everything from basic pointe to advanced jazz routines—great for the amateur dancer, young choreographer, or dance teacher.

WEBSITE: This full service, easy to use website offers merchandise in the following categories: shoes, tights, leotards, unitards, undergarments, dresses and skirts, tops and bottoms, warm ups, children's, men's, worship dance, and gifts and accessories. They also have a special section for sales and online ordering is available.

SPECIAL FACTORS: 24-hour ordering line; returns accepted—except special orders; sale items; lotions or balms; thongs or panties; CDs, DVDs, VHSs, or cassette tapes that have been opened—within 30 days of receipt, with a $3.95 reshipment charge for exchanges.

DesignerOutlet

242 W. 36th St., 12th Fl.
New York, NY 10018
800-923-9915
212-971-9550
FAX: 212-971-9553

FORM OF INFORMATION: online catalog only, no print catalog

PAY: MO, MC, V, AE, DSC

SELLS: designers' overstocks on women's, men's, and children's clothing, footwear, jewelry, and accessories

STORE: no walk-in location; online only

ONLINE: www.designeroutlet.com

Once you discover this site you'll never want to shop anywhere else. If you're a boutique shopper, you've now died and gone to heaven, because DesignerOutlet has ingeniously come up with a way to buy top designer overstocks and sell them to you at greatly reduced prices. This internet-only store, started by a 15-year fashion industry veteran, can avoid incurring high overhead costs of real estate, catalog printing, and personnel, so the savings are real—to the tune of 35% to 75% off retail. Quantities are limited, so if you see something you love, you'd better buy it right away before it disappears into the ether. All items are top quality and guaranteed, and all merchandise is current season.

The site is really easy to use. Just select Men's, Women's, Plus Size, Toddler's and Infant's, or Girl's or Boy's, and further refine your search by designer. Up will pop the current selection—an evening gown, a sweater, a tie, a shirt, a handbag, a watch, pajamas, jewelry, etc. It's kind of like shopping at a rich person's yard sale. Keep in mind that a designer gown here might be marked down 55%, but it's still not going to be cheap. An informed consumer will find this a great place to shop. If you're looking for a specific designer, email your request and the staff will act as your personal shopper and try to find it for you.

SPECIAL FACTORS: Order by phone, internet, or fax; company will gladly exchange or credit any purchase that doesn't satisfy you completely; returns must be made within 30 days (details on website).

Discount Bridal Service, Inc.

1583 Sulphur Springs Rd
Ste 108
Baltimore, MD 21227
800–874–8794
FAX: 410–595–0140

FORM OF INFORMATION: free referral (see text); website

PAY: varies (see text)

SELLS: women's bridal attire

STORE: no walk-in location; online only; phone hours Monday to Friday 10:00 am–5:00 pm EST

ONLINE: www.discountbridalservice.com

What's the first thing your girlfriend from college asks you when you call to invite her to your wedding (well, maybe the second thing)? "What are you wearing?" And indeed, choosing the right dress is one of the hardest decisions, partly because this is your big day and you want to look flawless, and partly because it will likely end up being one of your biggest expenses. Discount Bridal Service can help out. Recommended by dozens of consumer publications and organizations, this is a network of international dealers who live and work in your community. Your part is to thumb through the national bridal magazines until you find one or more dresses you like. Your local Discount Bridal Service (DBS) dealers can help you verify the style, material, fabric colors, and size for you and your bridesmaids. Once you've made your decision, they'll order the dress on your behalf and have it shipped directly to you. Ordering through DBS can save you from 20% to 40%, which translates into hundreds of dollars. DBS can recommend local seamstresses if you need alterations. Since delivery can take from 6 to 30 weeks, start early!

WEBSITE: If you have access to the internet, I recommend checking out the website, which has a Frequently Asked Questions (FAQ) section that explains this company in detail and how it all works. You can email DBS at the website if you have questions, and there's also a Buyer's Guide section that helps naïve consumers avoid bridal scam artists.

SPECIAL FACTORS: Consult with your DBS rep for terms of sales policy; satisfaction guaranteed.

Fabulous-Furs

601 Madison Ave.
Covington, KY 41011–2403
800–848–4650
859–982–0022
FAX: 859–291–9687

FORM OF INFORMATION: free print catalog; online catalog

PAY: check, MO, MC, V, DSC

SELLS: faux fur coats, hats, and accessories

SHOWROOM: same address; Monday to Friday 10:00 am–4:30 pm; call for Saturday appts.

ONLINE: www.fabulousfurs.com

Unlike their grandmothers, modern women want the luxurious look and feel of fur, but they're in conflict. Why? Because they're animal lovers. And besides, that level of outrageous materialism is out of sync with their other values. Enter Fabulous-Furs. Founded by Donna Salyers, this company sells faux furs combining the beauty, warmth, and luxury of animal fur with exquisite design details and fabrics. These furs are so real that Ms. Salyers has designed a pin to help identify you as an animal lover—just in case you need to fend off outraged animal rights people.

The 44-page color catalog features long coats, jackets, stoles, and vests made to look like sable, chinchilla, crystal fox, white mink, coyote, lynx, Mongolian lamb, Asian raccoon, beaver, leopard, and other furry friends. Although some are most appropriate for formal occasions such as attending the opera, there are plenty of darling examples of more casual coats and jackets appropriate for skiing, shopping, and even cheering on your son at the soccer game. You'll also find fun accessories such as muffs, hats, throws, decorative pillows, and even a few surprises such as faux-leopard thong sandals (Cool!), a faux-fur 18" doll costume, and a throw rug for your dog. Some of these coats aren't cheap, but even the most expensive one is more than $39,000 less than its $40,000 counterpart, a savings of almost 99%! On the other hand, there are quite a few coats here that are really affordable—cheaper, in fact, than my own full-length wool coat cost me, and vastly more elegant. Craftspeople will be happy to learn that Fabulous-Fur is available by the yard and also in scrap boxes—great for sewing toys, collars, or doll clothes.

If you're in the Cincinnati vicinity, stop by the showroom, which offers 20% to 40% off showroom models.

WEBSITE: The online catalog is where you can get more information about this wonderful, future-sighted company and read about the famous people who own these coats. Closeouts, up-to-the-minute sales, and specials are also features of the website, where you can place your order electronically.

SPECIAL FACTORS: Satisfaction guaranteed (see catalog for returns policy).

Gohn Bros. Mfg. Co.

P.O. Box 111
105 S. Main
Middlebury, IN 46540–0111
800–595–0031
219–825–2400

FORM OF INFORMATION: $1 print catalog
PAY: check or MO
SELLS: Amish and plain clothing, hats, and footwear for men, women, and children; general merchandise; and Amish specialties
STORE: same address; Monday to Saturday 8:00 am–5:30 pm

If there's such a thing as a mail-order company that will melt your cold, cold heart, this is it. Gohn Bros. has been offering Amish and plain clothing to everyone for just about 100 years. I really enjoy Gohn's 12-page print catalog. It's like stepping into another world, a world where straw hats "for the summer heat," ear muffs, drop-front work pants, men's garters, suspender web by the yard, ladies' black shawls, and children's bloomers are everyday items. Everything sold by Gohn Bros. is reasonably priced; many are items you just can't find anymore. You'll find thermal and regular underwear, work and dress clothing, hosiery, and outerwear for men, women, and children. The women's intimates section has a number of items for nursing mothers. There's also an extensive section for infants. The footwear ranges from men's leather work boots and dress shoes to women's high-top shoes to children's canvas sneakers. What you'll also love at Gohn are the hard to find items such as white crocheted doilies, buggy blankets, flour-sack towels, and wooden spool holders. The sewing notions and yard goods are a find unto themselves, featuring cheesecloth, 60"-wide denim, and even bandanna fabric. I cannot recommend this company highly enough. If it's plain, well-made clothing you seek, there's not a better source.

SPECIAL FACTORS: Satisfaction guaranteed; C.O.D. orders accepted.

KingPoodle.com/RustyZipper.com

503–233–2259

FORM OF INFORMATION: online catalog only, no print catalog

PAY: MC, V, AE

SELLS: men's and women's vintage clothing, shoes, purses, jewelry, and hats

STORE: no walk-in location; mail-order only

ONLINE: www.kingpoodle.com and www.rustyzipper.com

Launched in March 1996, RustyZipper.com was the web's first vintage clothing store. In the past nearly six years, the husband and wife team behind this company have outgrown their spare closet and now have a warehouse full of thousands of one-of-a-kind vintage clothing items from the 1940's through the 1970's. Jen and Rob Chadwick are the team behind RustyZipper.com and KingPoodle.com. Rob is a long time vintage freak and several years ago had a retail vintage clothing store in the San Francisco bay area. Both Jen and Rob have day jobs and have found the web to be a fantastic way to spread their enthusiasm for vintage clothing across the globe. They are now based in Portland, Oregon.

RustyZipper.com features items that are generally flawless and very reasonably priced. KingPoodle.com features many slightly flawed items and some items in perfect condition—all "absurdly cheap." You won't find anything at KingPoodle.com for more than $10. Both websites are nicely designed and organized with detailed pictures and descriptions that include fabric type, size, measurements, and condition of each item. At RustyZipper.com you'll find shoes, jewelry, purses, hats, and ties in addition to a wide selection of men's and women's clothing. KingPoodle.com sells men's and women's clothing. At both sites, you can browse by era, category, size, or price. If you purchase items from both stores during a visit, they can package them together into one order to save on shipping.

SPECIAL FACTORS: If you're not happy with your purchase, returns are encouraged within 15 days for refund. No checks or money orders.

The Nth Degree

21325 Bradner Rd.
Luckey, OH 43443
800–241–8468
419–837–5982
FAX: 419–837–2513

FORM OF INFORMATION: free print catalog; online catalog

PAY: check, MO, MC, V

SELLS: disability culture T-shirts and sweatshirts

WAREHOUSE: no walk-in location; mail-order only

ONLINE: www.thenthdegree.com

The very hip, exciting online catalog from Nth Degree may change your mind about a few things. This company offers T-shirts and sweatshirts with funny, irreverent, profound, inspiring, and in-your-face messages geared toward both the differently abled and the rest of us who could use some enlightenment about disability culture and the political movements that are springing up around it. For many people living with disabilities, there is often a sense of looking in from the outside, as our culture has adopted an "us versus them" attitude toward the disabled. The Nth Degree is here to break down such barriers by spreading awareness and understanding through their catalog of disability culture T-shirts and sweatshirts. Dan Wilkins, creator of The Nth Degree, sees his T-shirts as a means to create dialogue and make people think about their preconceived notions regarding persons with disabilities.

At the website, you can view themes in one of 7 different categories: advocacy, diversity, empowerment, humorous, inclusion, professional, peace, and community. Some contain quotes by notable figures such as Neitzsche, Ghandi, John F. Kennedy, Victor Hugo, and Martin Luther King, Jr. Others take jabs at politicians, bigots, and the rest of us who are mostly clueless, with messages such as "Not Dead Yet" (in response to Dr. Kevorkian's push to euthanize the terminally ill); "Psychosclerosis (Hardening of the Attitude)," and "Bureaucratically Impaired." There are also humorous messages, such as the cartoon of God and a dog looking at each other, the dog saying, "God?" and God saying, "Dog?" The slogan reads: "A moment of mutual dyslexia." Another favorite: "Your attitude just might be my biggest barrier." Besides great messages, these shirts have professional-quality graphics and are printed with high-tech, no-fade silk-screen ink. T-shirts are heavy-duty 100% preshrunk cotton and the sweatshirts are a 50-50 blend or higher. The website is also a fantastic forum for the latest news and information on disability culture. There are writings, stories, and poetry; cool links to other resources; and a calendar of national disability-rights events. Says founder Dan Wilkins, "The Nth Degree is about turning light bulbs on. We are about helping folks recognize that there is no such thing as 'Us and Them,' just one big 'Us.' We're about increasing awareness and understanding; as much about the celebration of our individuality and our differences, as the search for common ground: the search for shared truths, interests, histories, goals, fears." This business offers secure online ordering.

SPECIAL FACTORS: The Nth Degree will gladly accept returns for defective merchandise only; for a Spanish speaking representative, please email your inquiries to wheelchairboy@glasscity.net.

REI-OUTLET.com

P.O. Box 1938
Sumner, WA 98352-0001
800-426-4840
Fax 253-891-2523
TDD 800-223-1988

FORM OF INFORMATION: online catalog only; no print catalog

PAY: check, MO, MC, V, AE, DSC, JCB

SELLS: outdoor clothing, footwear, and equipment for men, women, and children

STORE: no walk-in location; mail-order only

ONLINE: www.rei-outlet.com

REI-OUTLET.com represents an exciting new phase in Recreational Equipment Inc.'s history—making active outdoor sports affordable and accessible for a whole new generation of outdoor enthusiasts. Since 1938, REI has grown into a well-known international supplier of all manner of outdoor clothing, footwear, and gear. It is one of the internet's largest outdoor stores, providing for a large range of activities including camping, climbing, cycling, cross-training, spelunking, paddling, fishing, snorkeling, or just "hanging out." You'll find a great deal of clothing and footwear for men, women, and children appropriate for these activities. Whether you need a waterproof, windproof, or just a plain old cold-proof suit, REI will have it. They also have plenty of top-quality casual clothing as well—including shirts, T-shirts, sweaters, pants, jackets, dresses, shorts, skirts, long underwear, sleepwear, footwear, slippers, gloves, and hats at 20% to 70% off retail. How do they do it? They keep prices down by offering manufacturer overstocks, product closeouts, cosmetic seconds (no effect on performance, of course), and special buys. You won't find these bargains at REI stores or the REI online store, only here, at REI-OUTLET.com. If you see something you like, grab it before it's gone—items are in extremely limited quantities.

WEBSITE: This website is very convenient and user-friendly, offering the shopper easy to understand instructions on ordering online. There's a special feature called the Bargain Sleuth, which essentially does the work of finding items for you. All you have to do is enter in a broad category and give an email address. You will be emailed as soon as the item you requested is available—so you don't have to waste your time searching and price shopping—the sleuth does it for you. They make it even easier to shop here by adding a feature called Size Finder. Plug in the category and size of the item you seek, and a list will come up which you can sort by brand, price, percentage off, or newest to site. I love when companies let you search by the percentage off retail!

SPECIAL FACTORS: Satisfaction guaranteed; returns accepted for exchange, refund, or credit.

Sierra Trading Post

5025 Campstool Rd., Dept. WBM 04
Cheyenne, WY 82007–1898
800–713–4534
307–775–8000
FAX: 800–378–8946

FORM OF INFORMATION: free print catalog; online catalog

PAY: check, MO, MC, V, AE, DSC

SELLS: casual and outdoor clothing, footwear, equipment, and home furnishings

OUTLET: same address and 1402 8th St., Cody, WY; Monday to Saturday 9:00 am–6:00 pm, Sunday 12:00 noon–6:00 pm; also 2000 Harvard Way, Reno, NV; Monday to Saturday 9:00 am–6:00 pm, Sunday 11:00 am–5:00 pm

ONLINE: www.sierratradingpost.com

Since 1986, Sierra Trading Post has been buying the best clothing, footwear, and outerwear from name-brand manufacturers at low overstock, closeout, and irregular prices so catalog shoppers can enjoy 35% to 70% savings off retail prices. Understandably, quantities on all products are limited, so Sierra encourages phone orders, since orders are filled on a first-come, first-served basis. Greatest savings come under the Super Clearance category, which is a boxed item appearing at the bottom of some pages in the print catalog. Past clearance items have included heavy-weight wool sweaters, first-quality chambray shirts, and Gore-Tex suits, for example, all discounted by half or more. Sierra's inventory regularly includes terry cloth robes, cotton boxer shorts, combed cotton underwear, socks in various fibers, Polar-Tek outerwear, Tekware henleys, down parkas, down comforters, dress wool slacks, hiking boots, cashmere scarves, adult and kids' snowshoes, ski goggles, winter sports boots, Gore-Tex pants and bibs, sunglasses, pup tents, climbing ropes, backpacks, and so on. In other words, you'll find everything you might need to feel great and look fabulous while you hike, ski, boat, fish, or just flirt on the slopes with the nearest snowbuck or bunny. The offerings change frequently, so begin receiving your seasonal catalogs and start saving.

WEBSITE: Log on to the website, which has an extensive inventory, for more super fantastic deals. Here you'll be able to browse by category, see color images of the products, and order online. The online catalog has Bargain Barn items, as well as web-only specials.

SPECIAL FACTORS: Satisfaction guaranteed; insured, prepaid returns accepted for exchange or refund.

Sportswear Clearinghouse

P.O. Box 317746–WBM
Cincinnati, OH 45231–7746
513–522–3511

FORM OF INFORMATION: free brochure with SASE

PAY: check, MO, MC, V, DSC

SELLS: printed sportswear overruns

STORE: no walk-in location; mail-order only

This is the place for printed sportswear—and I don't mean floral and checkered. Sportswear Clearinghouse sells such items as T-shirts (short and long sleeve), caps, casual sports shirts, sweatshirts, athletic shorts, jackets, visors, and nightshirts. The logos may be advertising slogans, company logos, or other miscellaneous subjects. You save up to 70% off store prices on grab bag selections of your size. Okay, so you'll be a walking billboard, but you'll save big on clothing you can wear to the beach, on the golf course, when exercising, to school, and around the house. Where does this merchandise come from, you ask? When clothing items are imprinted with logos, there are bound to be mistakes—colors, wrong sizes, print overruns, or canceled orders, for instance. You'll find lots of great first quality stuff in the 4-page tabloid-style catalog, but everything's in limited quantities, so act quickly. Blank (nonimprinted) items, such as athletic socks, sweatshirts and baseball caps in various designs and colors, are also available here at good prices. Caps from major league sports teams and many colleges are available at good prices. Sizes run from youth XS (2–4) to adult 3X. If your order exceeds $30, you get to choose from a list of free gifts.

SPECIAL FACTORS: Satisfaction guaranteed; unused returns accepted within 30 days for refund, credit, or exchange.

The Ultimate Outlet

A Spiegel Company
P.O. Box 9209
Hampton, VA 23670–0209
800–345–4500
FAX: 800–422–6697
TDD: 800–322–1231

FORM OF INFORMATION: $3 print catalog; online catalog

PAY: check, MO, MC, V, AE, DSC, Spiegel charge card

SELLS: clothing for men, women, and children, and department store goods

STORE: Spiegel Ultimate Outlet Stores in CO, FL, GA, IL, IN, MI, MN, MO, NV, OH, PA, TX, and VA; call 800–645–7467 for addresses and hours

ONLINE: www.ultimate-outlet.com

This company, readers, is a real find. If you're a fan of Spiegel, as American as a BLT on white with mayo, you'll love The Ultimate Outlet, the clearance division of Spiegel. The 91-page color catalog offers 30% to 70% off on a nice selection of goods for your home (decor items such as clocks, candleholders, mirrors, rugs, furniture, window treatment and picture frames), gift items (decorative boxes, writing instruments), soft goods (accent pillows, throws), storage organizers and kitchen utensils, jewelry, handbags, footwear, and wonderful clothing for all ages and both sexes. I am continually surprised at the quality and low prices at The Ultimate Outlet. It's like shopping at the nicest department store you can imagine, with prices that resemble those at the dime store. And Ultimate has one of the best returns policies I've seen anywhere—see the website for details.

WEBSITE: The full inventory is available at the website . Log on for some great deals on women's and men's apparel, bed and bath items, even children's toys. Selection will vary depending on the time of year and what's being cleared out for the next season, but savings here are fantastic—up to 60% on many items. Just click on a category (e.g., Women's Dresses) and you're transferred to a page of photographs accompanied by a brief description and the percentage off (usually 40 to 60%) Want to see that dress in more detail? Just click on the image to zoom in. This consumer-friendly online store features secure electronic ordering.

SPECIAL FACTORS: Satisfaction guaranteed; returns accepted for refund or credit.

World Wide Aquatics

6015 Benjamin Rd., Ste. 312
Tampa, FL 33634–5179
800–543–4459
813–884–0010
FAX: 813–886–9880

FORM OF INFORMATION: free print catalog, $2 outside U.S.; online catalog

PAY: check, MO, MC, V, AE, DSC

SELLS: men's and women's swimwear and accessories

STORE: no walk-in location; mail-order only

ONLINE: www.worldwideaquatics.com

Ladies, what if I told you that you could buy a swimsuit *through the mail* and be a happy customer? The swimsuits from World Wide Aquatics are a great deal and are well designed so women look good in them. No need to suffer the humiliation of department-store swimsuit shopping ever again. Liberate yourself!

Since 1972, World Wide Aquatics has been the mail-order source for competitive swimmers, triathletes, water aerobicizers and water exercisers, fitness swimmers, water polo players, lifeguards, and all other water enthusiasts. The catalog presents products by Speedo, Tyr, Dolfin, Nike, Ocean, Hind, and Aquajogger brands at supercompetitive prices. Here you'll find swimsuits, trunks, shorts, cover-ups, pool equipment, swim caps, goggles, fins, kickboards, triathlon gear, and fitness gear for men and women. Women's sizes run to 24, with a post-mastectomy line available; men's to 40-inch waist. Children's suits are also available. Helpful measurement guides in the catalog steer you to an exact fit. For multiple orders on suits, as for a swim team, greater discounts are offered, so call or consult the catalog for details.

WEBSITE: The website features a full online catalog with electronic ordering, a free e-newsletter, a Water Sports Library, Clearance Corner, and more. Check it out.

SPECIAL FACTORS: Satisfaction guaranteed; except for books and videos, new, unused items with hangtags and labels attached are accepted for return within 30 days of receipt (in original packaging) for exchange, refund, or credit.

Intimate Apparel

Undergarments and hosiery for women, men, and children

Some women are not destined to wear hose. When you have a special event to go to and have to look like a million dollars, do you buy fancy, $16 hosiery, figuring it will last longer than the cheap brands? By the end of the affair, you're likely to have an unsightly run spoiling your look. In fact, recent consumer studies have shown that cheap hose will last you as long as, and possibly longer than, the pricy ones you buy. Fortunately, the companies in this section sell high-quality hosiery of every kind—including socks for men and tights for children—at bargain prices. Problem solved.

As for bras, panties, and other unmentionables, you'll find them here, too. I know many of you out there hold on to your old friends with the holes, tattered lace, and yellowed armpits (you know who you are). Go ahead and treat yourself to some brand-new intimate apparel that's affordable for a change.

Find It Fast

CHILDREN'S SOCKS
Chock Catalog

CHILDREN'S UNDERWEAR
Chock Catalog

NURSING AND POST-MASTECTOMY BRAS
Lady Grace Intimate Apparel, One Hanes Place

PLUS-SIZE UNDERTHINGS FOR WOMEN
Chock Catalog, Lady Grace Intimate Apparel, The Smart Saver

SLEEPWEAR—MEN'S
Chock Catalog

SLEEPWEAR—WOMEN'S
Lady Grace Intimate Apparel

SOCKS AND HOSIERY—MEN'S, WOMEN'S, AND CHILDREN'S
Asiatic Industries, Chock Catalog, One Hanes Place

WOMEN'S LINGERIE
Chock Catalog, Lady Grace Intimate Apparel, One Hanes Place, The Smart Saver

WOMEN'S SWIMWEAR
One Hanes Place

Asiatic Industries

P.O. Box 31
Little Falls, NJ 07424–0031
973–882–8861
FAX: 973–882–8878

FORM OF INFORMATION: $2 print catalog, refundable, $4 outside U.S.; online catalog

PAY: check, MO, MC, V, AE, DSC, DC

SELLS: hosiery for men, women, and children

STORE: no walk-in location; mail-order only

ONLINE: www.sensationshosiery.com

I have sympathy for those of you who actually have to leave your house to go to work. If you have to wear a dress, skirt, or suit to work each day, ladies, why not buy your panty hose by the dozen? Along comes Asiatic Industries, which prides itself on fast delivery and good prices and service. This company, nearly four decades old, distributes quality, affordable hosiery for the entire family. Here you *must* buy by the dozen, and the offerings include knee-highs, ankle-highs, footies, thigh-highs, panty hose, ladies' and girls' socks, men's and boys' socks, opaque panty hose, and girls' and ladies' tights. The 8-page black-and-white catalog features one- or two-line descriptions that include size parameters for each item, but no pictures. If you're not fussy about brand names, you'll save a lot of money here. For example, sheer panty hose are less than a dollar a pair.

WEBSITE: The no-frills online catalog is bare bones and lists inventory in table form with brief descriptions, a lot like the print version. There's no online ordering, although you can download and print out an order form and fax or call in your order.

SPECIAL FACTORS: Minimum order: 12 items of one style and color.

Chock Catalog, Inc.

74 Orchard St.
New York, NY 10002–4594
212–473–1929
800–222–0020
FAX: 212–473–6273

FORM OF INFORMATION: online catalog only, no print catalog

PAY: check, MO, MC, V, AE, DSC, JCB

SELLS: men's , women's, and children's hosiery and underwear, and men's sleepwear

STORE: same address; Sunday to Thursday 9:30 am–5:30 pm, Friday 9:00 am–1:00 pm

ONLINE: www.chockcatalog.com

Guys: Here's a little secret. Although women say they like sexy lingerie, what women actually buy and wear most of the time are practical cotton panties. And there's no better source for this and other underwear and hosiery than Chock Catalog, in business since 1921 bringing top-brand merchandise directly to consumers at prices discounted about 25%.

Log on to Chock Catalog's website and you'll find underthings for men, women, and children; socks and hosiery; and a small selection of toiletries and gifts. The women's items include briefs, slips and camisoles, bras, socks, hosiery, and warmwear. For men there are boxers, briefs, undershirts, long underwear, bathrobes, socks, pajamas and more. Chock also carries boys' and girls' socks and underwear. The manufacturers include Calvin Klein, Hanes, Carters, Bali, Vanity Fair, and others. There's a small section of nonapparel goods that includes Montgomery Schoolhouse wooden toys, Caswell-Massey soaps and lotions, well-priced mineral-salt-crystal deodorant stones, slippers, umbrellas, and handkerchiefs. Chock promises the "lowest prices on the web," so how can you go wrong by ordering your underthings here?

SPECIAL FACTORS: Satisfaction guaranteed; unopened returns with manufacturer's packaging intact accepted within 30 days.

Lady Grace Intimate Apparel

P.O. Box 128, Dept. 74
Malden, MA 02148
800–922–0504
781–322–1721
FAX: 781–321–8476

FORM OF INFORMATION: free print catalog, $2 outside U.S.; online catalog

PAY: check, MO, MC, V, DSC

SELLS: women's intimate apparel and sleepwear

STORE: 13 stores in MA, ME, and NH; call for addresses and hours

ONLINE: www.ladygrace.com

Lady Grace has been "serving the needs of America's women" since 1937, offering a wide range of women's intimate apparel in all sizes, including hard-to-find sizes. The everyday prices are good, but Lady Grace has semi-annual sales where you can find items discounted up to 25%: bras (underwire, soft-cup, full-figure support, minimizers, nursing, post-mastectomy, strapless, low-back, back-support, etc.), underpants, long underwear, nightgowns, slips, swimsuits, girdles, and more. Bra sizes run up to 56, cup sizes up to J. The 32-page color catalog includes photographs, descriptions, and measuring guides. If you prefer, Lady Grace's "intimate apparel buying staff" can assist you by phone.

WEBSITE: On the website you can view virtually all of the styles offered in the print catalog and order online.

SPECIAL FACTORS: Satisfaction guaranteed; authorized returns accepted within 30 days for exchange, refund, or credit.

One Hanes Place Catalog

P.O. Box 748
Rural Hall, NC 27098
800–671–1674
FAX: 800–545–5613
TDD: 800–816–4833

FORM OF INFORMATION: free print catalog; online catalog

PAY: check, MO, MC, V, AE, DSC

SELLS: first-quality and "slightly imperfect" women's hosiery and underwear; women's underwear, loungewear, sleepwear, and casual clothing; men's underwear, socks, workout wear and tees

STORE: no walk-in location; mail-order only

ONLINE: www.onehanesplace.com

Bras and other intimates, cotton leggings, pantyhose, panties, socks, indoor slippers, exercise outfits, even casual wear such as cotton sweater/stirrup pants combos can all be bought at a discount through the One Hanes Place outlet catalog and website. Bras by Bali, Playtex, Hanes Her Way, Hanesport, Just My Size, Wonderbra, Champion, and Jogbra are here in a variety of styles discounted as much as 50%. The hosiery selection comprises the many Hanes lines (of which L'eggs is one) for up to 50% off if you can buy in quantity—a dozen pair of the same style. Besides undergarments and hosiery, the One Hanes Place catalog and website offer some nice casual wear, such as cardigan sweaters and jersey skirts at very good prices.

WEBSITE: I like the website as much as the print catalog. It features online specials, secure online ordering, and customer-friendly features such as order tracking. You can click on any one of several categories—bras, panties and shapers, legwear, clothing, plus sizes, men's and kids', and closeouts and extras—to see pictures of and read text about what's currently being offered.

SPECIAL FACTORS: "Slightly imperfect" merchandise is clearly indicated; returns are accepted; TDD service is accepted Monday to Friday 8:00 am–12:00 midnight EST.

The Smart Saver

P.O. Box 105
Wasco, IL 60183
800-554-4453

FORM OF INFORMATION: free print catalog

PAY: check, MO, MC, V

SELLS: bras, girdles, shapers, and panties

STORE: no walk-in location; mail-order only; phone hours Monday to Friday 8:00 am–3:00 pm CST

If The Smart Saver carries the intimate apparel you love best, you're in luck. This company has first-quality, fine intimates at 35% off (no seconds, no irregulars). Their catalog calls these "styles for the forgotten lady." These aren't the racy numbers worn by Janet Jackson and Madonna. The bras you'll find pictured in Smart Saver's 20-page black-and-white catalog are the classics by Playtex, Exquisite Form, Bestform, Glamorise, Vanity Fair, Venus, Goddess, and Lollipop, among others. You'll find girdles, bras, and panties in real women's sizes, ranging from S to 9XL. There are girdles and shapers for bottoms, thighs, midriffs, and full leg; bras for women who need extra support and room; good, old-fashioned 100% cotton waist-high briefs; and more. There are also bras for nursing mothers and for women who've had mastectomies. You'll see the suggested retail price alongside Smart Saver's, a feature I always appreciate. The owner, who's had the business for 20 years, says her customers are "very loyal."

SPECIAL FACTORS: 100% satisfaction guaranteed; will ship to all 50 states, Canada, and locations with postal zip codes (e.g., Guam, U.S. Virgin Islands, etc.).

Jewelry

Diamonds, investment-grade jewels, wedding rings, fine watches, and jewelry

I had a boyfriend who bought me a beautiful 30" strand of cultured pearls for my birthday many, many years ago. I was so touched. I had never received jewelry like that before. Later, I found out that he had gone to pick out the pearls for me with another women who he made-out with in the parking lot with my recently purchased pearls sitting nearby. I think if he had been able to buy them online, perhaps he might have been able to remain faithful. Of course, then he would have been buying them from the privacy of his home. Never mind.

Does buying jewelry online make you nervous? It shouldn't. Online jewelry sales are growing quite fast, with more than $1 billion in U.S. sales in 2002 and $1.3 billion expected for 2003 (according to Jupiter Research). Even with their high prices, diamonds are one of the easiest jewels to buy online because their quality is precisely defined by technical specifications (the "four Cs": color, cut, clarity, and carat weight). Many sites have detailed buying guides to help make your choices clearer. And always make sure the company you buy from offers a money-back guarantee so that you can return anything you don't like. The jewelry sites I've included in this section are all quite reputable, have been in business for many years, and will save you money.

Find It Fast

DIAMOND JEWELRY
Diamonds by Rennie Ellen, Simply Diamonds, Szul

INVESTMENT-GRADE STONES
House of Onyx

GEMSTONE JEWELRY
House of Onyx, Szul

STERLING SILVER JEWELRY
House of Onyx

WATCHES FOR MEN AND WOMEN
World of Watches

WEDDING AND ENGAGEMENT RINGS
Diamonds by Rennie Ellen, Simply Diamonds, Szul, Wedding Ring Hotline

Diamonds by Rennie Ellen

15 W. 47th St., Rm. 503
New York, NY 10036
212–869–5525
FAX: 212–869–5526

FORM OF INFORMATION $3 print catalog; online catalog
PAY: check, MO, teller's check, bank draft
SELLS: diamond jewelry
FACTORY: visits by appointment only
ONLINE: www.rennieellen.com

Rennie Ellen, a gem-cutter since 1966, not only designs rings, pendants, and earrings with white or colorless diamonds of all shapes, sizes, and qualities, but also offers them at savings up to 75% on prices charged elsewhere for similar jewelry. She specializes in engagement and wedding rings, and she opens her factory to customers on an appointment-only basis. This way she can give her clients, many of them soon-to-be-newlyweds, the personalized attention they deserve. The proprietress, who's a real gem herself, peppers her conversations with *honey* and *darling,* and likes doing business the old-fashioned way—through one-on-one contact with people who inevitably become loyal customers. A one-time professional dancer, Rennie Ellen started working in the diamond center between shows. She started as a diamond cutter and eventually opened up her own company. Now she has several cutters working for her and is one of the very few women manufacturers in the industry. Gals, this company is a real find.

WEBSITE: If you have internet access, I highly recommend the website, where you will get to view Rennie Ellen's line of engagement and wedding rings, earrings, brooches, and necklaces. If you go for understated elegance, you'll love these pieces, in which the beauty of the diamond doesn't get lost in overly busy designs. Once you see the jewelry and read some of the helpful information at the site, give Rennie a call.

SPECIAL FACTORS: Price quotes by phone or letter; each purchase receives a detailed bill of sale; returns accepted within 7 working days for a full refund; minimum charge on shipping (registered mail), handling, and insurance is $25; for an additional charge, orders can be shipped overnight via Federal Express.

House of Onyx, Inc.

120 N. Main St.
Greenville, KY 42345–1504
800–844–3100
270–338–2363
FAX: 270–338–9605

FORM OF INFORMATION: free print catalog; online catalog

PAY: check, MO, MC, V, DSC

SELLS: investment-grade stones, jewelry, and gifts

STORE: same address; Monday to Friday 9:00 am–4:00 pm

ONLINE: www.houseofonyx.com

When you log on to the House of Onyx website or browse the print catalog, be prepared to change your attitude about investing, the government, the diamond industry, and much more. Begun in 1967 as the first quality importer of Mexican onyx, House of Onyx has expanded to include high-grade investment-quality gemstones, imported gifts, jewelry, cloisonné vases, and more, while maintaining their stock of Aztec onyx boxes, statuettes, bookends, and candlesticks—all at 50% to 60% less than you would find elsewhere. The owners, Fred and Shirley Rowe, stand behind their products 100%, and happily give advice on investing in gems, politics, and the economy! Fred is recognized worldwide as an expert on gemstones and their values, and he and his wife have traveled the world gathering information about them. Their goal is to save you a lot of money on your "hard assets," as they call investment-grade gems, and they can do it because they move a lot of merchandise.

The House of Onyx has a complete GIA-equipped laboratory with 3 full-time GIA graduate gemologists on staff for positive identification of all gemstones. Couple this with their absolute commitment to client satisfaction and their "buy-back" policy that insures your investment, and you could not find a more worry-free place to purchase gemstones. The catalog also includes carved soapstone, rose quartz, tiger's eye, semi-precious bead necklaces, freshwater and cultured pearls, diamond and gemstone rings, gold and jeweled watches, earrings, and pendants, all ranging from inexpensive to rare and unusual pieces. Gems are offered, from actinolite to zoisite, minerals from aragonite to smoky quartz crystal, and the fossils offered range from ammonites to trilobites, and include dinosaur eggs and teeth! You'll also find deeply discounted gem videos and encyclopedias, which are useful for the budding enthusiast and collector alike.

International readers, please note: The House of Onyx is not able to ship catalogs or any merchandise to addresses outside the U.S., but they invite you to visit them and if you fly to the Nashville airport and make an appointment with them, they'll "send a car to pick you up."

WEBSITE: The website shows clear full-color photographs of the gems, diamonds, fossils, jewelry, and cloisonné sold here. There are also clearance items and eye-popping specials. But best of all, the website is packed with lively text about why you'll save money here, how to protect your investment, how to maintain privacy (from Uncle Sam) about your assets, how to have a diamond set into a ring, and much more. This is a clear instance where I'd definitely recommend looking at the website before you even request a print catalog. You may find it's not necessary to do so.

SPECIAL FACTORS: Satisfaction guaranteed; returns accepted within 5 days of receipt; minimum order: $25.

Simply Diamonds

P.O. Box 682, Dept. A
Ardsley, NY 10502–0682
800–552–2728
914–693–2370
FAX: 914–693–2446

FORM OF INFORMATION: inquire; online catalog
PAY: check, MO, MC, V, AE
SELLS: diamond jewelry
STORE: no walk-in location; mail-order only
ONLINE: www.simplydiamonds.com
EMAIL: l.g@worldnet.att.net

If there's one thing I've learned through researching and writing this book, it's that dispensing with some of the niceties of typical mail-order shopping can save us a lot of money. Why? Because certain companies offer products at amazing discounts by cutting down on or eliminating their overhead. In many cases, that means no fancy website, no slick catalog or brochure, not even a storefront or retail shop. When you find such a company, you're in luck. Simply Diamonds is just such a place, only better: less like a mail-order company and more like having an uncle in the diamond biz who's your personal broker. This husband-and-wife team will walk you through the extremely scary and perilous process of buying a diamond. They've been doing it for decades and know every facet of New York City's diamond district, including all the tricks and traps. To best use the services of Simply Diamonds, they encourage you to do some shopping first. Get an idea of the type, size, and price range you want. When you're serious about buying a diamond, call or email Simply Diamonds. They take pride in personally talking to you, answering all your questions, giving advice, but above all finding exactly the diamond you seek at a price that's well below retail. Simply Diamonds mounts your gem in a very basic setting; once it's yours, you can pick out a setting at a jeweler's. This is a great source for people who don't know much about diamonds and would make easy targets for unscrupulous dealers. GIA and EGL certificates are available.

WEBSITE: The Simply Diamonds website is direct, to the point, and easy to use. The "Wholesale Diamond Supplier to the Jewelry Industry" brings to your screen beautifully detailed pictures of loose stones, rings, bracelets, earrings, pendants, and pins. This website contains useful and informative definitions on diamond shape, weight, clarity, and inclusions that will leave even the average layman speaking like a true gemologist. There is no online ordering at this time.

SPECIAL FACTORS: Satisfaction guaranteed on every purchase; returns accepted within 5 days of receipt for exchange, refund, or credit; payment must be approved before any diamond is sent.

Szul

12 East 46th St.
3rd Floor East
New York, NY 10017
212–689–7770
800–332–4382
FAX: 212–689–7771

FORM OF INFORMATION: online catalog only; no print catalog

PAY: check, MO, MC, V, AE

SELLS: diamond rings, wedding bands, and accessories for men; diamond, gemstone, and bridal jewelry for women

STORE: no walk-in location; mail-order only; phone hours Monday to Friday 9:00 am– 7:00 pm EST

ONLINE: www.szul.com

Did you know that the name "carat" is derived from the carob seed? These seeds are remarkably consistent in weight and size and, as a result, they were the favored scale balances in ancient markets. By the way, carat weight should not be confused with "karat," the term used to describe gold's fineness or purity. I found out that little factoid in the Jewelry Guide section at Szul's. Szul, an exclusively internet-based company, is one of the first online jewelers to offer a wide selection of diamond, gemstone, and pearl jewelry. Located at the heart of Manhattan's diamond district, Szul sources and manufactures diamond and gemstone jewelry from specialized markets around the world, making it possible to offer their customers fine jewelry at exceptional prices. Prices at Szul are substantially lower than traditional or online jewelers, but they guarantee that product quality is never sacrificed in the bargain. In a price comparison of H-1 color and SI clarity, round, 14 kt yellow gold, diamond stud earrings, in a range of carat weights, I found Szul to be 38% less than a well-known department store and 54% less than a popular jewelry chain store at the local mall. They also have a Clearance section with savings up to an additional 40% off the existing prices. In addition to the Jewelry Guide, mentioned above, you'll find a wealth of information and web links about precious metals, gemstones, and diamonds at the Culture Mine page.

SPECIAL FACTORS: Authorized returns within 30 days of purchase; packages must be returned via insured USPS priority mail service .

Wedding Ring Hotline

172 Rt. 9 North
Englishtown, NJ 07726
800-985-7464
732-972-7777
FAX: 732-972-0720

FORM OF INFORMATION: free brochure; online catalog

PAY: check, MO, MC, V, AE, DSC

SELLS: wedding bands, diamonds, and engagement rings

STORE: same address (by appointment); phone hours Monday to Friday 10:00 am–9:00 pm, Saturday 9:00 am–4:00 pm EST

ONLINE: www.weddingringhotline.com

A division of Bride & Groom's West, Inc., Wedding Ring Hotline makes it possible for you to buy wedding bands, diamonds, and engagement rings factory-direct at savings from 20% to 50%. Manufacturer of its own line of classic-style rings, Wedding Ring Hotline offers wedding band selections in 14 or 18k yellow, white, or pink gold, as well as platinum, with a choice of round plain or flat plain edges, and round, flat, or double milgrain edges (*milgrain* is the technical term for the tiny beading lining the rims). Wedding Ring Hotline also has engagement rings; you specify the cut, carat weight, color, and clarity, and a staff person will quote you prices on GIA lab-certified diamonds currently available. The color brochures show examples of the firm's own designs, and their website features some of the designer lines carried here, including German maker Christian Bauer, Artcarved, Goldman, Gottleib & Sons, Aydin Designs, Britaannia Bridal, Stuller, and many others. Ordering is done by phone, and you are invited to call for price quotes on name-brand rings and information on custom-made jewelry. Engraving is available, and if your order is over $200, there's no engraving charge.

WEBSITE: I recommend the online site, over the printed material, where you'll find stunning photographs of the rings and charts detailing ring features, sizes, and prices. There is no secure online ordering; because there are so many factors when choosing a ring, the folks at Wedding Ring Hotline recommend you call in your order. The website also has monthly specials offering additional discounts, and a lowest price guarantee on traditional bands.

SPECIAL FACTORS: 100% money-back guarantee on most items within 30 days; price quotes by phone and letter.

World of Watches

14001 NW 4th St.
Sunrise, FL 33325
800–222–0077
954-453-2821
FAX: 954–453–2821

FORM OF INFORMATION: online catalog only; no print catalog

PAY: check, MO, MC, V, AE, DC

SELLS: men's and women's watches

STORE: no walk-in location; online only; phone hours Monday to Friday 9:00 am–10:00 pm, Saturday to Sunday 10:30 am–6:00 pm EST

ONLINE: www.worldofwatches.com

When I was in my twenties I had a wealthy boyfriend who took a spill one day taking a curve too fast on his motorcycle. I had to take him to the emergency room—nothing too serious, just a gaping hole in his knee. He was sitting on the examination table and before a doctor came to examine him, he grabbed his sleeve and pulled it over his very expensive watch. He explained to me in a whisper that *"They'll charge me more if they see what an expensive watch I'm wearing!"* I think emergency rooms have had to put a stop to charging for medical services according to watch prices since World of Watches came along, because now you can buy expensive watches at 25% to 60% off of the manufacturer's suggested retail price. World of Watches has been selling fine watches exclusively on the internet since 1997. Because of their discounted pricing, they are not "authorized dealers" as defined by the manufacturer. All of their watches are genuine and authentic. Excepting the pre-owned Rolexes, all watches are new. World of Watches buys their watches through authorized dealers and distributors and other established lines of distribution within the watch industry. In order to provide you with the best savings on the internet, their vendors must protect their sources of supply. For this reason, the serial number has been removed from certain of these new genuine brand-name watches. Under such circumstances, they will match, if not double, the original manufacturer's warranty coverage period and their professional watch technicians service these watches in-house. Name-brands here include Bulova, Bvlgari, Cartier, Piaget, Movado, Omega, Seiko, pre-owned Rolexes, and Swiss Army.

SPECIAL FACTORS: Returns accepted with some restrictions within 30 days of purchase (excludes pre-owned Rolex watches); free ground shipping on all orders of $150 or over within the continental U.S. only.

Men's Business Attire

Traditional shirts, ties, and suits; classic casuals and accessories

Although there are quite a few companies in the "Clothing for Women, Men, and Children" section of this chapter that sell men's apparel of all kinds, including suits and sports coats, I decided to separate out some firms dedicated exclusively to outfitting America's businessman for less. Why? Because high-quality men's business clothing at bargain prices isn't all that easy to come by, and I figure you guys deserve a section of your own. You work hard for your money, after all. You'll find great deals on everything from imported Italian silk ties to custom-sewn Egyptian cotton shirts.

Find It Fast

AUTHENTIC HAWAIIAN SHIRTS
AspencreekSport.com

BIG AND TALL SIZES
Big & Tall Guys, HUGESTORE

MEN'S CASUAL AND DRESS APPAREL
AspencreekSport.com, Big & Tall Guys, eSuits, HUGESTORE

MEN'S FOOTWEAR
AspencreekSport.com, Big & Tall Guys

SHIRTS
AspencreekSport.com, Big & Tall Guys, HUGESTORE, Quinn's Shirt Shop

SUITS
AspencreekSport.com, eSuits, HUGESTORE

TIES
AspencreekSport.com, eSuits, HUGESTORE

TUXEDOS
eSuits

AspencreekSport.com

12765 Via Terceto
San Diego, CA 92130
800–208–9246 pin #2713
858–481–3788
FAX: 858–909–0912

FORM OF INFORMATION: online catalog only; no print catalog

PAY: check, MO, MC, V, AE, DSC

SELLS: men's business attire, Hawaiian shirts, men's shoes

STORE: no walk-in location; mail-order only; phone hours, 7 days a week, 9:00 am–4:00 pm

ONLINE: www.aspencreeksport.com

Men should complain. Business apparel is way too expensive. Fortunately, I discovered AspencreekSport.com on the web. Compared with other retailers of men's clothing, AspencreekSport.com is a bargain. Choose from the finest quality career menswear from some famous designers that they cannot mention. Their suits are made in America by the same manufacturer of many well-known brands, (e-mail them and they'll tell you who they mean).

Among the offerings here are suits, blazers, sportcoats, dress shirts, and trousers—for both business and social occasions. To give you an idea of the pricing, a 100% wool tropical-weight blazer here was about $149; comparable blazers elsewhere were $50 to $100 more. Dress shirts were easily 25% less than one could find elsewhere. The selection of business attire is good, and sizes range from 36 short to 52 long. Another section of the website is devoted to Italian-made suits at about 25% less than suggested retail. All of these are available as three-piece ensembles (with vest), if desired. The prices on these handsome suits are unbeatable, especially if you shop around and see what others are charging. AspencreekSport.com also has an excellent selection of Allen-Edmonds shoes, outerwear, sweatshirts, T-shirts, sweaters, as well as casuals by Sansabelt, Tommy Hilfiger, and Hugo Boss. If you love Hawaiian shirts, this store carries both 100% cotton and 100% rayon classic bird, flower, and themed Hawaiian shirts priced about 25% less than normal retail. They also carry 100% cotton shirts and silk ties from Burberry of London at excellent prices.

The website offers secure online ordering. For best results on questions, orders or comments, please e-mail the folks at AspencreekSport.com. Calling is less efficient.

SPECIAL FACTORS: AspencreekSport.com has a flat-rate shipping fee of $5, at this writing, to any place in the continental U.S. or Canada; returns accepted within 30 days for full refund; returned shoes will be charged a $15 restocking fee.

Big & Tall Guys

101 N. Franklin St.
Titusville, PA 16354
800–479–0164
FAX: 814–827–2464

FORM OF INFORMATION: online catalog only; no print catalog

PAY: check, MO, MC, V, AE, DSC

SELLS: work and casual clothing for big and tall men

STORE: same address; Monday to Friday 9:00 am–6:00 pm, Saturday 9:00 am–5:00 pm

ONLINE: www.bigandtallguys.com

Are you having trouble finding the right kind of clothing because you're a guy who doesn't have an off-the-rack kind of body? I found a great source for affordable pants, shirts, workwear, sportcoats, sweaters, vests, belts, shoes, sleepwear, underwear, and more, available in special cuts and sizes that you won't normally find in retail department stores. Big & Tall Guys started in 1920 with the owner selling shirts and shoes out of an authentic covered wagon. This growing business, headquartered in northwestern Pennsylvania, has managed to stay in the hands of only 2 families over the past 80 years. The objective for present-day owners, brother and sister, Kathy and Scott Linnon, is to make sure that a big or tall man can buy a pair of casual pants for under $50 or a suit for under $200. They carry major brands like Carhart, Wranglers, Lees, Dickies, and Levi's in sizes 2X–7X for big men and L–5XL for tall men. This business offers free alterations, and the website has details on how to take proper measurements for great-fitting clothes. You won't be taking a cut in quality when buying from Big & Tall Guys. The clothing here is durable and stylish. Sign up for the Big & Tall Guys newsletter for coupons, discounts, and promotional info on new products. The Linnons promise you small-town personal service and prices that are hard to beat. Visit the retail store if you happen to be in their neck of the woods.

SPECIAL FACTORS: 30-day money-back guarantee; orders paid by check require a 2-week clearance period before order is processed.

eSuits

2788 Orchard Lake Rd.
Farmington Hills, MI 48334
888–879–7848
FAX: 248–865–9265

FORM OF INFORMATION: online catalog only; no print catalog

PAY: check, MO, MC, V, AE

SELLS: men's suits, blazers, slacks, top-coats, leathers, and tuxedos

STORE: same address; Monday to Saturday 9:30 am– 6:00 pm EST

ONLINE: www.esuit.com

Baron's Wholesale Clothes, a Detroit area wholesaler of fine men's clothing since 1933, launched their internet division, eSuits, in 1995 and they want you to overcome the fear of paying too little. Their inventory of over 10,000 garments include suits, trousers, blazers, slacks, topcoats, trench coats, and leathers. Among the designers represented here you'll find Calvin Klein, DKNY, Oleg Cassini, Jones New York, Kenneth Cole, Haspel, Hugo Boss, Joseph Abboud and Hickey Freeman. Gabardine trousers are carefully tailored by a small family-operated Italian factory. Average savings here start at about 40% off regular retail.

In addition to some incredible savings on top-quality men's wear, you'll find plenty of information on fashion trends, how to judge a suit, caring for wool, and a dictionary of terms. If you prefer the personal touch, you can ask Mr. Baron, himself, to hand select the right suit or sport coat for you. Even greater discounts apply when you order two or more of any item. And to complete your new outfit, eSuits has a Tie-of-the-Month club. Subscriptions for 3, 6, or 12 months are available at $60, $90, and $120 and each month they'll send you a pure silk tie guaranteed to match your new suit

A click on the Tuxedo button will take you to a sister site, eTuxedo.com, where you'll find a wide selection of tuxedos at about 50% off retail. To help clear any confusion you might have with all the choices, they make it easy by comparing the different kinds of tuxes with cars. Their $169 tuxedo is comparable to a Honda Accord 4-cylinder (most popular car in America); the Bill Blass tuxedo is comparable to a 6-cylinder Accord with all the bells and whistles; the Superior tuxedo is comparable to a Lexus or Cadillac; and, the Imperial tuxedo is comparable to a Jaguar.

SPECIAL FACTORS: Payment by American Express preferred for international orders; full refund for any unworn, unaltered merchandise returned within 30 days of purchase.

HUGESTORE.com

800–259–7283
317–321–9999
FAX: 317–321–9988

FORM OF INFORMATION: online catalog only, no print catalog
PAY: check, MO, MC, V
SELLS: men's casual and business apparel
STORE: no walk-in location; online only
ONLINE: www.hugestore.com

Carl Levinson, president of HUGESTORE, began his internet-only store after the longtime family clothier business closed. He launched the company in 1994 with the idea of creating a business that would sell high-quality business and casual attire for men at the lowest prices. Without advertising, print catalogs, and a huge staff, he's been able to do it successfully. This company has received press awards ranging from such notables as the *Wall Street Journal* and *Los Angeles Times* to *MacUser* and Yahoo.

You'll save about 40% on shirts (casual, dress, golf, and T-shirts), pants (dress, casual, and jeans), sports coats, suits, ties, and boxers. This virtual warehouse is basically self-serve. Click onto the shirts, for example, and check off your size, color, fit, and brand, then hit the search button. Your choices will come up with a swatch of the color and price. Click on the swatch to see an image of the item. If you like what you see, put it into your shopping cart. It's as simple as that. If you can get a group at your office to order a total of 12 items of any mix, you'll get an additional $2 knocked off each item. For larger quantities there are greater discounts you'll want to check out here.

SPECIAL FACTORS: 100% satisfaction guaranteed; all items returned for any reason will be refunded.

Quinn's Shirt Shop

Rte. 12, P.O. Box 383
N. Grosvenordale, CT 06255
508–943–7183

FORM OF INFORMATION: $2 price list with SASE, refundable
PAY: check or MO
SELLS: Arrow shirts
STORE: 245 W. Main St., Dudley, MA; Monday to Saturday 10:00 am–5:00 pm

It's lovely to chat with the owner of this company, who's been in the business for decades and knows all about trends in menswear. He says that business attire is getting more casual; fewer men are wearing button-down shirts to the office. Fortunately, if you still work in a place that has classic standards of dress, you'll love Quinn's Shirt Shop—ideal for all you guys who love Arrow shirts and know exactly what you want. According to the owner, this company deals "strictly with Arrow Irregulars in top grade (best of the irregular line) with savings from 40% to 50%." If you know the line (Dover, Brigade, Bradstreet, Kent Collection, etc.), specify the size, SS (short sleeve) or LS (long sleeve), the sleeve length if long sleeve, and color preference. Collars come in regular or button down. Big and tall sizes are available here, too. There's no print catalog, and all orders are C.O.D. The price list is $2 with a SASE, and is refundable with your first purchase. Or you may call for a price quote.

SPECIAL FACTORS: Minimum 4 shirts per order; only C.O.D. accepted; returns accepted for exchange.

Shoes

Men's and women's casual and dress shoes and boots; work boots; and sandals

Nothing can ruin an outfit more than the wrong pair of shoes. It's amazing how the slightest variance in thickness of heel or squareness of toe can compliment or ruin an outfit. A very dear friend once called me over to his death bed, to whisper in my ear, that he thought a chunkier heel would be better with the suit I was wearing. I nodded to him that I understood and would fulfill his request. There are no small matters when it comes to shoes. The key outfits in your wardrobe often require their own pair of shoes. That can get very expensive. But not if you buy your shoes from the companies I've listed in this chapter.

These firms offer everything from doctor-designed women's comfort shoes to lace-up poleclimber boots for men. You'll find a wide selection of shoes in hard-to-find sizes and widths—all at discount prices that will knock your socks off. With savings as high as 50%, it would be hard to find a better way to buy footwear. There's still the problem of fit, however, unless you're ordering more of the same model you've worn before. Here are some tips that might improve your odds of success:

- If you can find the shoes you're buying at a local store, try on a pair before ordering them by mail. Afternoon is the best time, when your feet have swollen slightly.
- Carefully unwrap the shoes or boots and save the packaging. Also, walk around in your new shoes on carpet to avoid scuffing them.
- Try out your new shoes for at least 30 minutes. If they fit, think about ordering a second pair while they're still in stock.
- If the shoes don't fit, return them in the original packaging, according to the firm's instructions.

Even though the companies in this section specialize in footwear, there are many others in the book that have shoes and boots in their inventory. Many of the stores in the "Clothing for Women, Men, and Children" section carry footwear for men, women, and children. Be sure to check the Index for companies selling shoes in other parts of this book.

Find It Fast

ATHLETIC SHOES FOR MEN AND WOMEN
E-Shoe Sale, Shoes on the Web, Zappos.com

CHILDREN'S SHOES
Zappos.com

EXTRA-WIDE, EXTRA-NARROW SHOES FOR MEN
Altman's, Zappos.com

EXTRA-WIDE, EXTRA-NARROW SHOES FOR WOMEN
Zappos.com

GOLF SHOES FOR MEN AND WOMEN
Sha Sha Fine Shoes

MEN'S DRESS AND CASUAL SHOES AND BOOTS
Altman's, E-Shoe Sale, Sha Sha Fine Shoes, Shoes on the Web, Shoespot, Zappos.com

MEN'S AND WOMEN'S SANDALS
Dave's Discount Rope Sandals, E-Shoe Sale, Key West Sandals, Shoes on the Web, Shoespot, Zappos.com

MEN'S WORK BOOTS
Altman's

MEN'S AND WOMEN'S WORK BOOTS
E-Shoe Sale, Shoes on the Web, Zappos.com

OUTDOOR SHOES FOR MEN AND WOMEN
E-Shoe Sale, Shoes on the Web, Zappos.com

ROPE SANDALS
Dave's Discount Rope Sandals

WOMEN'S DRESS AND CASUAL SHOES AND BOOTS
E-Shoe Sale, Sha Sha Fine Shoes, Shoes on the Web, Shoespot, Zappos.com

Altman's

120 W. Monroe St.
Chicago, IL 60603
312–332–0667
FAX: 312–332–1923

FORM OF INFORMATION: free manufacturer's brochures

PAY: check, MO, MC, V, AE, DSC, DC

SELLS: men's shoes and boots

STORE: same address, Monday to Friday 8:30 am–6:00 pm, Saturday 8:30 am–4:30 pm

Since 1932, Altman's Shoes and Boots for Men has provided men of all sizes and walks of life with the largest selection of sizes—5 to 20 in widths ranging from AAAA to EEEE—and one of the most complete selections of men's footwear available. I really enjoyed chatting with the people at Altman's, who were friendly, sincere, and helpful. Discounts range from $15 to $65 a pair, and the top-name brands they sell include Bacco Bucci, Bass, Birkenstock, Bostonian, Carolina, Clark, Dan Post, Dansko, Ecco, Frye, Havana Joe, Justin, Merrell, Mezlan, Naot, New Balance, Rockport, Sebago, Timberland, Tony Lama, and many others. If you like real, old-fashioned service and high-quality shoes, you'll love Altman's.

SPECIAL FACTORS: Special orders are welcome; phone hours the same as store hours; satisfaction guaranteed.

Dave's Discount Rope Sandals

3513 Northcliff Dr.
Fallbrook, CA 92028
866-414-0187
760-731-0186

FORM OF INFORMATION: online catalog only; no print catalog
PAY: check or MO, MC, V
SELLS: rope sandals for men and women
STORE: no walk-in location; mail-order only
ONLINE: www.davesdiscount.com

Just like other great tales, the story of Dave's Discount Rope Sandals began out west almost ten years ago when Dave Cook, newly retired, rediscovered the comfort and appeal of classic rope sandals while exploring Mexico in an RV. After researching and tracking down a low-key manufacturer of these unique-looking sandals, Dave purchased 1,000 pairs and started up Dave's Discount Rope Sandals. So much for retirement! "When I wear them, people go absolutely crazy and ask, 'Where can I get a pair of those?' They're like the Harley Davidson of footwear—one person shows them off and then another has to have them and it goes on like that!" says Dave, who refers to the rope sandal phenomenon as having a "cultlike appeal." Well, this is one cult you won't need deprogramming from, because these rope sandals are sturdy, affordable, and look way cool. They can be worn on rocky beaches and right into the ocean. Constructed from polypropylene rope, the sandals are washable and dryable, and come in size 5 through 13 (or, in inches, 7 3/4" through 11 1/2"), in standard natural, denim, black, and assorted other colors. And best of all—Ready for this?—they're less than $20 at this writing. The per-sandal price goes way down, to $11.99 per pair, if you can buy a dozen pairs (tell your friends). Dave also offers "special purchase" prices on certain color rope sandals—dark blue, red, green, and yellow—at the price of $19.99 per pair, and the cost plunges further if they are bought in conjunction with the aforementioned standard-color rope sandals. I love small companies that do business the old-fashioned way. When you're ready to order, print out the order form at the website, and then mail it to Dave with a check or money order. You can also call or email Dave if you have questions. As for Dave's return policy, "I want to make you happy" is his motto.

SPECIAL FACTORS: To qualify for wholesale prices, minimum order is 12 pairs; see website for details on ordering and shipping procedures.

E-Shoe Sale

P.O. Box 1576
60 Enterprise Ave N
Seacaucus, NJ 07094
877–474–6372
FAX: 201–348–1927

FORM OF INFORMATION: online catalog only; no print catalog
PAY: check, MO, MC, V, AE, DSC
SELLS: men's and women's shoes
STORE: no walk-in location; mail-order only; phone hours 7:30 am–3:30 pm EST
ONLINE: www.eshoesale.com

This is a very straightforward site. In business since 1977, E-Shoe Sale has a wide selection of men's, women's, and children's shoes at savings that average 20% to 40% off retail. Shop by style—sandals, casual, dress, designer, platform, pumps, classic, etc.—or by brand—Birkenstock, DKNY, Havana Joe, Rocket Dog, Chinese Laundry, Dr. Martens, Kenneth Cole, Skechers, and many, many more. I narrowed down a search to sandals, size 8, black, and was shown 120 items. Plus, they were having a special, at this writing, of an additional 25% off their already low prices if you bought two pairs of sandals.

All shipping is free within the continental U.S. and the return policy allows a full year to change your mind for a full refund (shoes must be unworn and in the original box.) E-Shoe Sale has a division called Gary's Off-Price Shoes, with over 530 styles at 50% off. Sizes are limited, but there were quite a few pairs I liked at really good prices.

SPECIAL FACTORS: Returns of unworn shoes in original box 1 year from purchase; shipping and handling free within continental U.S..

Key West Sandals

3119 SW 42nd Ave.
Palm City, FL 34900
772–287–6393
FAX: 772–286–9620

FORM OF INFORMATION: online catalog only; no print catalog
PAY: check, MO, MC, V, AE, DSC
SELLS: men's and women's sandals
STORE: no walk-in location; mail-order only
ONLINE: www.keywestsandal.com

Key West Sandals has been making handmade leather sandals for over 70 years. Dr. Walline, an archeologist who studied Egyptian lifestyles, discovered that the Egyptians wore sandals for all of their activities from work to home wear. Further research revealed that properly made sandals were a great asset to the foot. (Hmmm, if only I had some grant money, I could further that research.) In 1932, Dr. Walline created the Key West Sandal company. Today, they are one of the last remaining leather footwear manufacturers in the United States. They offer quality, custom-fit sandals made by people, not machines. Their basic sandals start at $20 and come in a variety of styles and colors. For an extra $9 any sandal can be custom-fit. You can also send them your own design or an old favorite pair and they will build you a pair of sandals starting at $59! For around $40 you can order sandals made from fish or snake skin. Alligator products are a bit more expensive—but they're harder to catch. This is a very friendly website. Check out the factory photos and the discount page. Nike workers and citizens of Thailand and Germany get a 10% discount. Don't know why. At these prices, I think we all really do need some new sandals.

SPECIAL FACTORS: Authorized returns made in written form within 14 days of receiving order; unless an error on their part a restocking fee will apply; merchandise must be received in proper packaging and in good condition; unless due to error on their part, it is customer responsibility for shipping on all returns.

Sha Sha Fine Shoes

2187 Newcastle Ave. #201
Cardiff by the Sea, CA 92007
877–3–sha–sha
760–436–5373
FAX: 760–436–5385

FORM OF INFORMATION: online catalog only; no print catalog
PAY: MC, V, DSC
SELLS: shoes, T-shirts, and hats for men and women
STORE: call to find a store near you
ONLINE: www.sha-sha.com

Do alternative rock bands play golf when they're not playing nightclubs? Well, if they do, this is where they buy their shoes. "Put some flame in your game." You can shake up the country club with a pair of golf flame shoes with removable spikes for only $32.50, at this writing. And if golf isn't your game, choose from urban sneakers, core casuals, or creepers (a thick-ridged style of outsole). These shoes are very hip and very affordable. Closeouts on limited sizes start at $25. At this writing, there were a pair of 10-eye lace-up boots with contrast stitching and rubber lug outsoles for $30 and Mary Jane style leather uppers with white star inlays and rubber lug outsoles for $30. The shipping and handling is a little pricey at a $9.50 flat rate for the continental U.S. and I can't recommend this store to those of you living in Alaska and Hawaii or outside the U.S. since shipping is very expensive at $30 to $36. But for the rest of us, if you are looking for the unusual and hip in your footwear—there are some very good deals to be found here.

SPECIAL FACTORS: Returns made within 30 days of purchase will be given an exchange or full refund, minus any shipping and handling charges; there will be a $10.00 restocking fee for all items returned for a credit only; all sales to Canada are final.

Shoes on the Web

411 Vine St.
Philadelphia, PA 19106
800–323–2062
FAX: 215–925–4030

FORM OF INFORMATION: online catalog only; no print catalog

PAY: MC, V, AE, DSC

SELLS: men's and women's shoes

STORE: no walk-in location; mail-order only; phone hours Monday to Friday 9:00 am–5:30 pm EST

ONLINE: www.shoesontheweb.com

I just bought my boyfriend some really cool Clarks black nubuck leather shoes at Shoes on the Web. Well, I bought them for him, but I used his credit card. But he won't mind when he finds out that I saved $70 on shoes that retail for $130 and the shipping is free. I mean *he* saved the money. Shoes on the Web has been an internet retailer since 1998 offering brand-name footwear at everyday low prices at up to 50% off retail. Brands offered here include Adidas, Clarks, Earth, Dr. Martens, Guess, Bass, Hush Puppies, New Balance, Reebok, and more. At this writing, the shoes definitely seemed to lean towards the casual side as opposed to the dress side in terms of choices; but, there were some nice selections at very good prices. When prices are marked below retail they list the sale price along with the retail price and the amount you saved.

SPECIAL FACTORS: Returns accepted within 30 days for refund, credit, or exchange; shipping is free on all U.S. orders.

Shoespot

1202 North B St. West
Tampa, FL 33606
888–950–7768
FAX: 509–267–8824

FORM OF INFORMATION: online catalog only; no print catalog

PAY: MO, MC, V, AE, DSC

SELLS: men's and women's shoes, boots, sandals, and accessories

STORE: no walk-in location; mail-order only

ONLINE: www.shoespot.com

Shoespot is a trendy shoe store that caters to a younger, hip crowd. But this old gal found plenty of shoes that she not only liked, but were available at good prices in the Clearance Section. That's where you'll find the discounts at this store. I'm very picky about my footwear. Nothing ruins an outfit more than the wrong pair of shoes. I have spent hours and hours walking around malls going from shoe store to shoe store looking for "the right shoe." Mostly I come home empty-handed. It is so much easier and efficient for me to shop for shoes online and it's even easier to find bargains on the brands I like. I have a special affinity towards Dr. Martens. Shoespot had a number of cool styles of Dr. Martens in their Clearance Section at 49% off list. Other brands in this department include Rocket Dog, Caterpiller, Steve Madden, Chinese Laundry, Skechers, Diesel, Simple, and Kenneth Cole at 40% to 70% off retail prices. I found 86 items in my size. I've been at other other sites that had a larger selection of shoes in their "on sale" sections, but I liked the styles more at Shoespot.

SPECIAL FACTORS: Returns within 30 days of receipt; shoes must be returned unworn and in the original, undamaged packaging; do not ship the shoes back with the original shoebox exposed or wrapped in paper; all shoes must be packaged in a protective box as they were shipped to you.

Zappos.com

1000 Van Ness #213
San Francisco, CA 94109
888–492–7767

FORM OF INFORMATION: online catalog only; no print catalog

PAY: check, MO, MC, V, AE, DSC

SELLS: women's, men's, and children's dress, casual, and athletic shoes

STORE: no walk-in location; mail-order only

ONLINE: www.zappos.com

Zappos.com, derived from the Spanish word for shoes, hasn't been included in this book because they are the most popular shoe store on the web, or because shoppers can choose from a selection of over 100 brands and more than 30 million pairs of dress, casual, and athletic shoes for men, women, and kids. Zappos is not a discount shoe store, per se—however, I've included this great store because if you click your little mouse over the On Sale tab on the homepage, then select your shoe size, many (in my case, 209) pairs of shoes at 30% to 50% off retail will appear.

Most conventional shoe stores are limited by the size of their storage space and shoppers are forced to pick between a much smaller variety of styles and brands. When you finally find a shoe that suits your fancy there is no guarantee that your size will be in stock. Because Zappos.com has such a huge inventory to choose from at their regular prices, it naturally follows that they have a larger selection of On Sale shoes to choose from as well. Brands here include Bass, Birkenstock, Donald J Pliner, Dr. Martens, Skechers, Kenneth Cole, and Ecco—to name a few. Children's discounted shoes are not included in the On Sale section for some reason. Bargains for your little ones can be found by browsing through the regular Kid's Shoes section on the homepage. At this writing, there was a good selection of children's Dr. Martens shoes, sandals, and boots at 46% off list. Shipping, at press time, was free.

SPECIAL FACTORS: Satisfaction guaranteed. Returns or exchanges of unworn shoes for up to 60 days from the purchase date; shoes must be in the condition you received them and in the original box; return shipping is free; see website for details. If you find a shoe for a lower price on another website, Zappos.com will refund you 110% of the difference between the lower price and their price (valid for 10 days after you make your purchase.) See website for details.

Art, Antiques, and Collectibles

Fine art; limited editions; antiques; Americana and militaria collectibles; folk art; comics; popular culture memorabilia; cultural, political, and decorative flags and banners

This is one fun chapter to research and explore. The companies here prove you don't have to be rich to decorate your home with rare or unusual items. I once dated a fresh-out-of-college filmmaker who lived in a run-down top-floor loft in Manhattan's downtown seaport district. Every square inch of his loft was covered with oddities: a 1950s U.S. Army recruitment poster, cracked and yellowed circus flyers, a row of Aunt Jemima syrup bottles, Mr. Peanut banks, cartoon-character salt and pepper shakers— it was fabulous! He would have loved shopping from these companies.

The firms listed here offer an eclectic selection of the rare and unusual, from World War II pinup calendars to fruit crate labels, framed old-master reproductions on canvas to candlestick telephones, patriotic flags to popular comics. Some of these products have excellent resale value; others don't. But because you're buying directly from the dealer, these items are less expensive than if you found them in an antique shop, a traditional art gallery, or a collector's studio.

If you like the feel of a Sunday-morning country auction, your heart racing as you bid $5 on a dusty box full of junk from somebody's attic, you'll love Hake's Americana & Collectibles in this chapter, and eBay in the "General Merchandise" chapter. Both companies require that you bid for their merchandise; both carry an eclectic assortment of collectibles, some valuable, some not. (eBay sells a lot of new merchandise as well, which is why they're not in this chapter.)

If you acquire old maps, photographs, advertisements, or other items that need protection from air and moisture, be sure to check out University Products (in the "Office, Business, and Professional" chapter), an excellent source for display binders, albums, boxes, and restoration materials for artworks, books, manuscripts, photographs, textiles, posters, and postcards.

All of the merchants in this chapter are in their field because they love it. Since most of what they sell are one-of-a-kind items, don't be afraid to ask questions if you're seriously interested in one of their pieces, but are unsure of its value or just want more information about it.

Find It Fast

ADVANCE COMIC BOOK SUBSCRIPTIONS
G-Mart Comics

FINE ART PRINTS ON CANVAS
The Masters' Collection

FLAGS AND BANNERS
American Flag and Gift

FOLK ART
Folkart Market

GRAPHIC NOVELS
G-Mart Comics

HANDMADE DOLLS
Folkart Market

HANDMADE CRAFT FOLK ART
Folkart Market

LABELS
Miscellaneous Man, Original Paper Collectibles

MILITARIA
American Flag and Gift, John W. Poling: Military Collectibles

ONLINE AUCTION
Hake's Americana & Collectibles

PHONES
Phoneco

POLITICAL MEMORABILIA
John W. Poling: Military Collectibles

POP CULTURE COLLECTIBLES
G-Mart Comics, Hake's Americana & Collectibles,
John W. Poling: Military Collectibles

RARE/VINTAGE/POP CULTURE POSTERS
Hake's Americana & Collectibles, Miscellaneous Man

TIN AD REPRODUCTIONS
Desperate Enterprises

American Flag and Gift

930 East Grand Ave.
Arroyo Grande, CA
93420–6108
800–448–3524 (orders only)
805–473–0395
FAX: 805–473–0126

FORM OF INFORMATION: $2 and $5.50 print catalogs, refundable (see text); online catalog

PAY: check, MO, MC, V, AE, DSC

SELLS: historical, patriotic, decorative, and custom-designed flags and banners and accessories

STORE: no walk-in location; mail-order only

ONLINE: www.anyflag.com

What is more American than a giant flag unfurled on the front porch waving gently on a steamy, hot summer day? Green grassy lawns, rows of tidy white houses, and children squealing as they jump through the lawn sprinklers complete the picture. I remember well the gigantic 48-star flag "a real antique" that my father frequently hung on our Victorian front porch on special occasions or whenever he was in a patriotic mood. Well, here's a place to buy those big flags at discount prices. I spent a good deal of time comparing prices of flags and banners at a number of companies. Hands down, this company not only offers the widest selection of high-quality flags, but also the lowest prices. American Flag and Gift claims to be "American's largest and most complete flag shop." If you like to shop by print catalog, there are two. The first has 40 pages and features American flags (indoors and outdoors), state, country, historical, military, holiday, advertising, and custom flags, as well as flagpoles. It is $2, and the cost is refundable when you place your first order. The second has 178 pages and is a comprehensive flag catalog that carries every type of flag one could imagine, as well as banners and flag poles. "If it exists in America, it's probably in this catalog." The cost is $5.50 and is refundable with your first order.

WEBSITE: But why pay for a print catalog when you can browse the fabulous inventory online? The website is easy to use, well-organized, and categorized into sections including American Flags, Historical Flags, State Flags, Military Flags, Patriotic Decor, Flag Poles, International Flags, Holiday Flags, Sports Flags, Flag Products, and Custom Flags. These come in outdoor, indoor, and hand-held. The company provides historical background on every state, country, or American history flag. Flag histories are researched from an extensive library and through membership to various flag research organizations such as the Flag Research Institute and NAVA (North American Vexillological Association).

These flags are well made, with lockstitch seams, quadruple-stitched and back-stitched flyends to ensure maximum longevity, and heavy-duty heading and grommets. Details are embroidered or appliquéd. Unlike many flag and banner stores, American Flag and Gift has several fabrics to choose from: cotton, nylon, polyester, or WindMaster, a long-lasting outdoor material. You can also buy outdoor display sets, designed for ease of use in displaying the flag on your home or business. The flag and banner themes and designs are virtually unlimited—for every reason and every season. Imagine a flag for each holiday, or for special occasions such as a new baby, a birthday, or graduation. If you can imagine it, American Flag and Gift either has it or can make it. They will even screenprint or appliqué your company's logo, trademark, or any other design onto a flag or banner of any size. When you are at the website, be sure to check out the section on flag etiquette.

SPECIAL FACTORS: 30-day money-back guarantee.

Desperate Enterprises

728 E. Smith Rd., #E-8
Medina, OH 44256
800-732-4859
FAX: 888-484-6744

FORM OF INFORMATION: free print catalog; online catalog

PAY: check, MO, MC, V, AE, DSC

SELLS: tin ad reproductions, thermometers, nostalgic light-switch plates, refrigerator magnets, etc.

STORE: same address; Monday to Friday 9:00 am–5:00 pm

ONLINE: www.desperate.com

Talk about a fun catalog to browse . . . Back in 1987, Desperate Enterprises owner Bob Secrist, a nut for advertising collectibles, saw prices for these items going sky-high, and saw diminishing supplies of originals falling into the hands of a very few wealthy collectors. He decided to reproduce some of the most popular images onto tin and make them available at modest prices, thereby sharing his passion with ordinary folks like us. The rest is history.

The 70-page color print catalog presents hundreds of nostalgic images from movies, television, sports, and popular culture adorning tin signs, daily magnetic reminders, light-switch plates, refrigerator magnets, and thermometers. Some of the themes, which include 77 different licensed images, are Marilyn Monroe, Lionel trains, baseball heroes, John Deere, Betty Boop, and famous beverage brands. The back pages feature nostalgic originals. This is a great source for gifts or inexpensive home decor. The prices are a fraction of what the original items would cost—if you could even find them—and Desperate Enterprises offers significant discounts when you order in modest quantity.

WEBSITE: Be sure to visit the website, which features online ordering, color graphics, product updates, and a free electronic newsletter announcing new products and special promotions, plus a 5% discount of website orders.

SPECIAL FACTORS: Satisfaction guaranteed; C.O.D. orders accepted; quantity discounts.

Folkart Market

39W538 Washburn Dr.
Geneva, IL 60134
630–232–8186

FORM OF INFORMATION: online catalog only; no print catalog

PAY: check, MO, MC, V

SELLS: folk art

STORE: no walk-in location; mail-order only; Monday to Friday 9:00 am–5:00 pm

ONLINE: www.folkartmarket.com

Folkart Market offers unique and affordable folk art. These are handmade items created by regional artisans. Now you can decorate your house to your heart's content. Categories on this site include Wreaths, Angels, Boxes and Frames, Game Boards, Candles and Lights, Pillow and Pottery, Primitive Pals, Hang it Up, and Table Toppers. My favorite category is Primitive Pals which features handmade Raggedy Ann-type dolls—but not the kind of Raggedy Annes you're used to. These gals have a lot of personality. They range from 14" to 21" tall and are quite affordable at $13 to $25. The only trouble you'll have is deciding which doll you like best. In addition to rag dolls, you'll find other handmade folk art items such as primitive wooden candle boxes with folk art cut outs, picture frames, berry wreaths, lamps, candles and candle holders, hand embroidered pillows, chessboards, a pumpkin head doll, and signs and samplers. Folkart Market makes shopping for gifts much easier. There's a wide selection of out-of-the ordinary handmade home decor items that range in price from $4.50 to $58.50.

SPECIAL FACTORS: Delivery time is 2 to 3 weeks.

G-Mart Comics

44 East Main St., Ste.101
Champaign, IL 61820–3636
TEL/FAX: 217–356–7733

FORM OF INFORMATION: online catalog only; no print catalog

PAY: check, MO, MC, V, DSC

SELLS: new and back-issue comics, trading cards, and other pop-culture merchandise

STORE: same address; Monday to Friday 12:00 noon–7:00 pm, Saturday and Sunday 12:00 noon–5:00 pm; phone ordering hours Monday to Friday 9:00 am–5:00 pm CST

ONLINE: www.g-mart.com

A long time ago, you could walk into your local drug store with a single dollar and get yourself a handful of great comic books such as *The Amazing Spider Man, The Incredible Hulk, X Men, Daredevil,* and *Howard the Duck.* With the exception of Doctor Doom and his time-travel platform, no one can bring back the good ol' days of 20-cent comics. But G-Mart Comics offers the next best thing. Here you can save 35% on brand-new titles by publishers including Marvel, DC, Image, and Dark Horse. Comic books by smaller publishers are typically marked down about 30%. To take advantage of these great discounts, you will need to place advance orders for your comic books. (An advance order means you contact G-Mart Comics and purchase the new titles two months before they are actually published. Details about payment deadlines for advance orders are laid out at the website.) Since advance orders reduce the risk of overstock merchandise for G-Mart, they reward their customers by offering huge discounts. For slightly damaged, but still readable comics, take off an additional 10%. Though there is no minimum purchase required, it's probably thriftier to place larger orders, since shipping costs have to be taken into consideration. (As comic book junkies tend to travel in packs, it shouldn't be hard to find a friend or two to go in on an order with you.) At the website, you can set up a convenient subscription account, review upcoming issues, and update your orders monthly. You can also view up-to-the-minute inventory listings of new and back-issue comics so there's never any guessing about what issues may or may not be sold out. G-Mart also sells graphic novels, magazines, books, trading cards, toys, games, videos, T-shirts, and other pop culture merchandise.

SPECIAL FACTORS: Call or email G-Mart for comic-related items that you're looking for but may not find online; orders of $85 or more are shipped free of charge; see website for returns and advance payment policies.

Hake's Americana & Collectibles

P.O. Box 1444
York, PA 17405
717–848–1333
FAX: 717–852–0344

FORM OF INFORMATION: print catalog, (see text); online catalog

PAY: check, MO, MC, V, DSC

SELLS: pop culture/nostalgia collectibles via auction and fixed price by phone, fax, mail, or internet

STORE: no walk-in location; mail-order only; phone hours Monday to Friday 10:00 am– 5:00 pm EST

ONLINE: www.hakes.com

Ted Hake is known as the collectible industry's "founding father." Since 1967, he's been running a wildly popular worldwide mail-and-phone auction of pop culture and nostalgia collectibles—from action figures to watches and everything in between. The 168-page catalog comes out five times a year, and you can order a sample catalog for free, or subscribe to a year's worth for $30 (U.S. and Canada) or $45 (if you live overseas).

This is really fun stuff. Hake's offers original, one-of-a-kind collectibles that are *affordable*—as little as $5 and as much as $4,000. Each item is photographed in black and white in the catalog, (color on the website) and described in minute detail. Each item has an opening bid and is sold at that amount or to the highest bidder. All bidding is done by phone, fax, mail, or online. The catalog and website have complete terms of the auction, including the closing time and date, rules and suggested procedures, as well as a bidding sheet—all clearly and carefully spelled out and explained.

Hake's Americana & Collectibles is known and revered by collectors around the world. You'll have lots of fun imagining having your very own Mickey Mouse egg cups, silent movie posters, Li'l Abner and Daisy Mae juice glasses, tin toys, '50s lunch boxes, and more. If the big online auction houses overwhelm you, try Hake's. This company has been around longer than all the rest.

WEBSITE: Auction registration and bidding may be done online. The website has links to related sites, a wonderful biography of Ted Hake (described as "Santa Claus and the Wizard of Oz combined"), details on Hake's price guide books, and thousands of items priced for immediate sale (not for bidding). Why shop the ordinary way when you can get caught up in a global online/mail/phone/fax frenzy and land yourself a deal on some great stuff to jazz up your house or office?

SPECIAL FACTORS: Layaway plans are available on purchases of $75 or more; see catalog or website for terms-of-sale details and auction schedules; auction is conducted online, by phone, by mail, and by fax.

The Masters' Collection

P.O. Box 508
40 Scitico Rd.
Somersville, CT 06072
Dept. 329
800–222–6827
860–749–2281
FAX: 800–437–3329
or 860–763–2028

FORM OF INFORMATION: free print catalog; online catalog

PAY: check, MO, V, MC, AE, DSC

SELLS: fine art oil reproductions on canvas

GALLERY SHOWROOM: same address; Monday to Friday 8:00 am–5:00 pm, Saturday 9:00 am–1:00 pm (except July and August)

ONLINE: www.masterscollection.com

If you're a lover of the best-known European and American painters, and always fantasized about having a Monet in your bedroom, you're in luck. The Masters' Collection is an ingenious company that for 30 years has specialized in museum-quality replicas of masterpieces at affordable prices. Most people spend more on their television set than they will to own one of these beauties. The artworks here are on *canvas*, not paper. To capture the integrity of the original oil paintings, the artisans use a unique process whereby the color image is transferred onto artist-quality canvas, after which surface brush strokes are added by hand to simulate the look and feel of the original oil painting. Then the whole work is sealed for preservation and hand-stretched on wooden stretchers. When you hold a sample piece cut from a finished work in your hands and examine it closely, it really does have the look and weight of an original oil.

The 56-page color catalog from The Masters' Collection offers just a sampling of the hundreds of paintings you can acquire. All paintings come framed in a museum-quality frame and linen liner carefully selected to complement your painting's style, period, and subject matter. (Opting to change the frame or liner costs a bit extra in most cases.) In addition, each comes with a brass name plate identifying the artist and title of the work, if you desire it. And finally, your painting arrives ready to hang—with the proper-size wall hanger included. Most major painters are represented here, from American masters such as Remington and Benson to Europe's best, such as da Vinci, Vermeer, and Renoir.

WEBSITE: Log on to The Masters' Collection website, where you can search for all kinds of paintings (nauticals, hunting and sporting, western, religious, groups and figures, primitives, portraits, landscapes and seascapes, florals and still lifes, impressionists), by artist, or even by price. The website offers secure electronic ordering, special web sales, and a 60-day money-back guarantee. I'll add my voice to the cacophony of raves from happy Masters' Collection art owners, which you can read for yourself at the website. This company will make you feel like a millionaire no matter how modest your budget.

SPECIAL FACTORS: 30-day money-back guarantee. Search eBay for user ID: MASTERSCOLLECTION.

Miscellaneous Man

P.O. Box 1776–WBM
New Freedom, PA
17349–0191
800–647–0069
FAX: 717–235–2853

FORM OF INFORMATION: $7 print catalog
PAY: check, MO, MC, V
SELLS: rare and vintage posters and labels
STORE: no walk-in location; mail-order only; phone hours Monday to Friday 10:00 am–6:00 pm EST

Miscellaneous Man, established in 1970, sells *original* vintage posters on theatrical, movie, military, sports, labor, travel, and advertising themes, *original* pinups and pinup calendars, and handbills, graphics, and product labels. The selection at Miscellaneous Man is far better than that of New York City dealers—at prices ranging from 30% to 70% less. George Theofiles, the "man" in Miscellaneous Man, maintains a 2,000-item catalog of ephemera including collections of cigar box labels and luggage stickers. The catalog indicates item size and condition beside a small black-and-white photo of each item; for a more detailed view, larger photos are available ($2 each). Sale catalogs with reductions beyond the usual 30% are sent to regular customers.

While some posters are sold already mounted on linen or conservation paper, referrals are made to firms that specialize in poster mounting, which aids in preservation without reducing value. Miscellaneous Man also buys vintage posters and ephemera.

SPECIAL FACTORS: Layaway available; returns accepted within 3 days of receipt; minimum order on credit cards: $25.

Original Paper Collectibles

700–W Clipper Gap Rd.
Auburn, CA 95603

FORM OF INFORMATION: free brochure and sample label, with long SASE
PAY: check or MO
SELLS: original, vintage product labels
STORE: no walk-in location; mail-order only

Some are charming, some amusing, others hip—I'm talking about American fruit and vegetable crate labels. Original Paper Collectibles has been in business since 1970, when founder William Wauters noticed that American commercial art was one of the hottest collectibles at antique shops. Mr. Wauters sells his labels for roughly half what you'd pay from an antique dealer. All labels are original American commercial art that, for a variety of reasons, have never been used.

The current stock described in the price list and flyer includes labels originally intended for brooms, soda pop cans and bottles, canned fruits and vegetables, and produce crates. The collections offer the best per-label prices: 150 different fruit crate labels for $29, for example. Imagine walking into a sunny kitchen decorated with framed antique labels or labeled cans perched on the windowsill. Original Paper Collectibles is a great source for fun and inexpensive decorating ideas.

Please note: Payments for orders should be made to William Wauters, not Original Paper Collectibles. Request for brochures must include a SASE.

SPECIAL FACTORS: Satisfaction guaranteed; quantity discounts available; wholesalers should inquire about terms; inquire by mail, not phone.

John W. Poling: Military & Political Collectibles

P.O. Box 333
Dept. WBM
Pendleton, IN 46064
765-778-2714
FAX: 765-646-9229

FORM OF INFORMATION: three print catalogs, $2 each (see text)
PAY: check or MO
SELLS: military and political collectibles and used books
STORE: no walk-in location; mail-order only
EMAIL: polingjw@aol.com

John W. Poling's three catalogs—"Military Collectibles," "Political Collectibles," and "Miscellaneous Catalog"—may turn you into a collector once you see how reasonably priced his merchandise is. The first two catalogs are $2 each, and the "Miscellaneous Catalog" is sent along for free with either or both. The catalogs consist of pages of typewritten descriptions and black-and-white photocopies.

What are political collectibles? Mostly campaign buttons from local and national elections, but also gems such as Mikhail Gorbachev's Official Soviet Government Portrait, an old issue of *National Geographic* with an article by Richard Nixon, a "Senator Sam" T-shirt made during the 1972 Senate hearings, and campaign bumper stickers. There's also a selection of political books at rock-bottom prices. Militaria is Poling's forte—clothing, helmets, insignias and emblems, patches, field equipment, and printed material galore, including used and rare books and manuals, maps, magazines, and newspapers. In the "Miscellaneous Catalog" bargain hunters will find key chains, banners, posters, coffee mugs, shot glasses, and other items commemorating such events as the World's Fair of 1962 and the Seoul Olympics, and such celebrities as the "typical Boy Scout" and Elvis. Description after description of antique postcards, Vietnamese Communist Government Ration Coupons, 1950s motel soaps, and other such gems will keep you entertained for hours and brimming with good gift ideas.

SPECIAL FACTORS: Satisfaction guaranteed; returns accepted within 10 days for exchange or refund.

Auto, Marine, and Aviation

Tires, parts, and accessories for cars, vans, trucks, motorcycles, tractors, ATVs, snowmobiles, riding mowers, etc.; supplies and equipment for marine and air craft; auto brokerage services; motor racing equipment and parts

There are certain goods you don't normally associate with mail-order—auto parts among them. I used to think that way, but no more. I purchased four new snow tires by mail as well as a needed part for my old Honda through two of the companies in this chapter. In both cases, I had the satisfaction of knowing I saved myself some money, and enjoyed the thrill of coming home from work one day to find my purchases waiting on my doorstep. Don't think you have to visit a testosterone-fueled auto parts store to get what you need, or that you have to depend on your mechanic's sources. (One mechanic's "best" local source—a junk parts supplier—was going to charge 25% more for the part!) The companies in this chapter thrive in the mail-order business because they can get it to you for less—in some cases up to 70% less. Even with shipping costs factored in, you'll save. The firms listed here sell all kinds of used and new parts and supplies—including wheels and tires—for cars, vans, trucks, motorcycles, snowmobiles, and ATVs. You'll even find parts for other types of vehicles such as Go-Karts, minibikes, and riding mowers.

The internet is a wealth of information when it comes to automobiles. You can get price quotes on new and used cars, read reviews, check out model specifications, compare cars by two different makers side by side, discover dealers' "real" sticker prices, get general automobile information, learn how to haggle intelligently, check out related links, access bulletin boards, join chat groups, get safety and recall information, and much more.

The internet also offers consumers a whole new way to approach car buying. If you're looking to buy a new car and are willing to do a lot of the initial legwork, American Automobile Brokers, listed in this chapter, rewards your efforts by quoting you a price that's less than the one you got locally.

Perhaps the best known reference for used car pricing is the *Kelley Blue Book Used Car Guide*. The latest consumer edition is less than $10. Or check your local library, which will probably have the book or can get it for you. This company also has a fantastic website (www.kbb.com) where you can find out the value of your used car and motorcycle *for free*.

If you're into boating, you know all too well about insurance, dock fees, and the expense of upkeep and new equipment. But did you know you could save 30% routinely on the cost of maintenance products, gear, and electronics by buying from the marine suppliers listed here? Their vast inventories include every type of coating, tool, electronics, hardware, and instrument you need to keep your vessel shipshape. There's also plenty here for landlubbers, including foul-weather clothing and nifty gadgets for the outdoorsman.

Private pilots will also save on some of the parts, supplies, and electronics from the aviation discounters in this chapter. Like the marine suppliers, these firms also sell goods of interest to those on terra firma, at savings of up to 50%.

Find It Fast

AUTO RACING SAFETY EQUIPMENT
Racer Wholesale

AVIATION
Aircraft Spruce & Specialty

BOATING SUPPLIES AND EQUIPMENT
Defender Industries

CAR PARTS AND ACCESSORIES
The Benz Bin, Car Racks Direct, Cherry Auto Parts, Clark's Corvair Parts, Honda Parts Wholesale, Parts411.com, Trollhattan Auto Parts

MOTORCYCLE PARTS
Parts411.com

MOTOR RACING PARTS
Racer Parts Wholesale

NEW VEHICLES
American Automobile Brokers

SEAT COVERS FOR CARS, TRUCKS, AND SUVS
Webcovers

SNOWMOBILE AND ATV PARTS
Manufacturer's Supply, Parts411.com

TIRES AND WHEELS
Discount Tire Direct, Parts411.com, The Tire Rack

Aircraft Spruce & Specialty Co.

225 Airport Circle

Corona, CA 92880

877–4–SPRUCE

909–372–9555

FAX: 909–372–0555 (West Coast)

or 770–229–2329 (East Coast)

FORM OF INFORMATION: free print catalog within U.S.; $15 international; online catalog

PAY: check, MO, MC, V, AE, DSC

SELLS: aircraft parts, pilot supplies, and building materials

STORE: West, same address; East, 900 S. Pine Hill Road, Griffin, GA; call for hours

ONLINE: www.aircraftspruce.com

Since 1965, Aircraft Spruce & Specialty has been selling aircraft parts and supplies to aviation enthusiasts worldwide. If you know what you're looking for, call for a price quote. Otherwise, they'll send you a phone-book-sized resource with 600-plus pages listing everything under the sun. You'll find an exhaustive inventory of composite materials, aircraft kits, wood products, metals/plastics, airframe parts, landing gear, engine parts and accessories, covering supplies, instruments, electronics, tools, avionics, books, maps and charts, and other pilot supplies at prices that meet or beat other major aircraft supply discounters. There's even nifty stuff here for the nonflyer, such as pedal plane kits for kids, wall thermometers, folding hand trucks, and aviator sunglasses. If you are building a vehicle, there are materials here for you. AS&S also supplies race car teams and builders of boats, bicycles, and motorcycles.

WEBSITE: The online catalog isn't as encyclopedic as the print version, at this writing, but does offer all of the major pilot equipment and tools, as well as online ordering capability.

SPECIAL FACTORS: Satisfaction guaranteed; international representatives for Africa, Japan, Europe, Brazil, Australia, Italy, and Chile.

American Auto Brokers, Inc.

24001 Southfield Rd., Ste. 110
Southfield, MI 48075
248–569–5900
FAX: 248–569–2022

FORM OF INFORMATION: price quotes
PAY: check or MO (see text)
SELLS: new vehicles
STORE: same address; Monday to Friday
10:00 am–6:00 pm

Smart buyers have saved money on new vehicles since 1971 by purchasing through American Auto Brokers, Inc. A licensed dealer/broker, AAB can arrange the sale or lease of new domestic and foreign cars, trucks, and vans at discounted prices. Customers—individuals or corporate fleet accounts—typically know their vehicle choice. Get a quote from your local dealer, then contact AAB to buy or lease for less. Call or write with complete details of the vehicle, including make, model, and options desired. AAB will quote their discounted price which includes: dealer prep, full factory warranty, and all current rebates/incentives. The price is valid by placing your order with AAB, who provides all the purchase arrangements which include factory delivery (for most vehicles) to a new car dealership in your area. You will find their personalized service a convenient and efficient way to buy your new vehicle. This business has thrived for over thirty-two years by *word of mouth* from satisfied customers.

SPECIAL FACTORS: The first quote is free, extra quotes are $5 each. Price quotes by mail, phone, or fax. If request is by mail, please include SASE; checks and money orders are accepted for deposit only—balance payable by certified check, cashier's check, or wire transfer.

The Benz Bin

888–628–3247
609–890–8829
FAX: 609–890–9209

FORM OF INFORMATION: online catalog only, no print catalog

PAY: check (see text), MC, V, AE, DSC

SELLS: Mercedes Benz and other imported auto parts

STORE: no walk-in location; online only; phone hours Monday to Friday 9:00 am–6:00 pm, Saturday 9:00 am–3:00 pm EST

ONLINE: www.thebenzbin.com

The Benz Bin specializes in Mercedes Benz parts and accessories; but, you can get parts for other imports as well, including: Acura, Audi, BMW, Honda, Jaquar, Mazda, Porshe, Rolls Royce, Saab, Subaru, Toyota, Volvo, and Volkswagen. The website is straightforward and easy to use. Select the year, make, and model of your car and then click on the category and part that you are looking for. Parts can also be searched for by part number. Savings here run between 20% to 50%. The retail list price and Benz Bin's price are side by side so you can readily see your savings. Ground shipping is free on orders over $50. If you find what you're looking for you can order it online. If you can't find an item you need give Benz Bin a call because they can get any part you're looking for. Need technical advise? Give them a call—technical advice is given freely, with a smile.

SPECIAL FACTORS: One year unlimited manufacturer's warranty on new and remanufactured Mercedes parts; free ground shipping on orders over $50; satisfaction guaranteed.

Car Racks Direct

80 Danbury Rd.
Wilton, CT 06897
800–722–5734
FAX: 203–761–0812

FORM OF INFORMATION: free print catalog; online catalog

PAY: check, MO, MC, V, AE

SELLS: vehicle racks and vehicle-rack parts and accessories

STORE: same address; Monday to Friday 10:00 am–6:00 pm

ONLINE: www.outdoorsports.com

How can you turn your old VW Rabbit into a sporty funmobile? Easy: Get a car rack, take up hang gliding, and head for the mountains. For 8 years, Car Racks Direct, the mail-order division of Outdoor Sports Center in Wilton, Connecticut, has been selling racks, parts, and accessories for carrying skis, canoes, kayaks, bikes, sailboards, snowboards, luggage, lumber, and other items on motorized vehicles, at great discount prices. You'll find products by such recognized manufacturers as Thule, Yakima, Pack-a-Sport, and Rhode Gear. If you find a lower published everyday price on any product, Car Racks Direct will match it. Car Racks Direct carries multisport systems—racks capable of carrying a variety of items by adding specific attachments to the basic load carrier; single-sport racks—racks designed to carry specific equipment, usually on an occasional basis (bike racks, ski racks, racks for snowboards, canoes, and other large sporting gear); and accessories—locks, pads, load-securing straps, bike covers, boat covers, snowboard and ski bags and cases, bicycle work stands, and ski storage racks. Car Racks Direct has over 500 fit kits in stock to accommodate "any VW Bug, Hummer, or land yacht."

WEBSITE: The online catalog presents a clear explanation of the products available, the retail and discounted prices, and information on how to order. Ordering is available online.

SPECIAL FACTORS: Price quotes by phone, email, or letter; authorized returns accepted; have vehicle make and model ready when ordering. Free UPS ground shipping on all orders.

Cherry Auto Parts

5650 N. Detroit Ave.
Toledo, OH 43612
419–476–7222
800–537–8677
FAX: 419–470–6388

FORM OF INFORMATION: price quotes; online catalog

PAY: check, MO, V, MC, DSC

SELLS: new, used, and reconditioned parts for all kinds of cars, trucks, and SUVs

STORE: same address; Monday to Friday 8:30 am–5:00 pm; also 25425 John R Rd., Madison Heights, MI (Detroit area); Monday to Friday 8:30 am–5:00 pm

ONLINE: www.cherry-auto.com

Cherry Auto Parts Inc., a premiere national automotive parts recycler, has been in business for over 50 years under the same family ownership. They have been serving the needs of auto repair professionals, insurance companies, and the motoring public for over 50 years. Here you'll find hundreds of late model, low mileage, fully warranted and tested recycled engines, transmissions and all other car, sport utility vehicle, and light truck components. Save 30% to 80% compared to new and even more on many "dealer only" items.

The Cherry Auto website has two separate sections: New Parts Catalog and Quality Used Parts. The New Parts section offers over 40,000 new line oem parts (that means premier name-brand original equipment parts that the factory uses, like Bosch, Ate, and Girling) through the country's largest independent import car part importer. Every one of these parts is offered at substantial discounts and can be ordered online. The Quality Used Parts section includes hundreds of late model engines, transmissions, and any other recycled auto part you might be in need of. The website has search and pricing information for both catalogs that makes it simple to look up and check out exactly what you need.

SPECIAL FACTORS: All parts come with a 30-day warranty, extended warranties are available.

Clark's Corvair Parts, Inc.

Rt. 2, 400 Mohawk Trail
Shelburne Falls, MA 01370
413-625-9776
FAX: 888-625-8498
413-625-8498

FORM OF INFORMATION: $6 print catalog, $8 in Canada, elsewhere inquire; online catalog

PAY: check, MO, MC, V, AE, DSC

SELLS: Corvair parts

STORE: no walk-in location; mail-order only; phone hours Monday to Friday 8:30 am– 5:00 pm EST

ONLINE: www.corvair.com

The world's largest Corvair parts supplier, Clark's Corvair Parts, Inc., has been in business for more than a quarter of a century. If you own one of these classic cars, you should know that Clark's can save you up to 40% on mechanical parts, upholstery items, trim, and more for your Corvair. When you order a print catalog, you'll receive about 3 pounds of material: the more than 400-page main catalog, a 250-page specialty catalog ("New Old Stock, Performance, and Used Parts"), and the current 40-page price list. They also have a "1963-1965 Riviera Upholstery Set" catalog with most parts (except for interior items) 10% to 20% less than suggested list. Clark's stocks nearly every part for Corvairs in a number of categories including engine, directional, shifter, transmission, instruments, sheet metal, clutch, harnesses, power top, differential, locks and ignitions, door latches, suspension, turbos, nuts and bolts, steering, generator/alternator, exhaust, brakes, VW conversion, and tools, some from the original suppliers and others specially made for them. Clark's also has a good selection of manuals, and reference books, as well as upholstery sets produced just like the originals, door panels, padded dashes, carpets, top boots for your convertible, cardboard kick panels and package areas, trim and emblems, weather strips, armrests, sun visors, and more.

WEBSITE: The online catalog is basically the print catalog accessible through various searches. Prices are not listed on the catalog pages. Once you've determined the part you want by browsing the catalog pages, click on the part number and a page will come up with the part and description and the option to add it to your shopping cart.

SPECIAL FACTORS: Returns accepted; minimum order: $10.

Defender Industries, Inc.

42 Great Neck Rd.
Waterford, CT 06385
800–628–8225
FAX: 800–654–1616

FORM OF INFORMATION: free print catalog; online catalog

PAY: check, MO, MC, V, AE, DSC

SELLS: marine supplies, gear, equipment, and clothing

WAREHOUSE: same address; Monday to Friday 10:00 am–5:00 pm, Saturday 9:00 am–3:00 pm

ONLINE: www.defender.com

    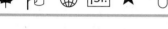

Defender Industries, marine outfitter since 1938, claims to have the largest selection in boating and "the lowest prices all year long." Sit back with the phone-book–sized catalog from Defender and you'll find that many of the hundreds of products offered here are priced 35% or more below retail.

What will you find here? The question more properly should be "What won't you find here?" Defender offers just about anything related to boats and the boating lifestyle: fabrics, knives, paint products, railings, cover accessories, shoes and boots, fishing equipment, pumps, marine stoves and dishes, hammocks, antennae, safety equipment, inflatables, outboard engines, pool floats and toys, fuel products, navigation instruments, radar systems, books and videos, winches, electrical products, binoculars—and that's just skimming the surface. From anchors to Zodiac life rafts, there's a lot here for those who own or live on a boat, and plenty for those who don't. By the way, if you need sunbrellas, boat or sail covers, netting, awnings, pool covers, or the like, Defender has a canvas shop where they've made custom and standard sizes of sewn products in canvas, Naugahyde, Dacron, nylon, and other synthetic fabrics for 60 years. Send a template and sketch for their low price quote.

WEBSITE: Be sure to check out the clearance site, Defender-Outlet.com, which offers great values on overstocks, discontinued, scratch and dent, and one-of-a-kind products.

SPECIAL FACTORS: Minimum order: $25; returns accepted within 20 days for refund or exchange.

Discount Tire Direct

7333 E. Helm Dr.
Scottsdale, AZ 85024
800-589-6789
FAX: 480-483-9230

FORM OF INFORMATION: online catalog only; no print catalog

PAY: check, MO, MC, V, AE, DSC

SELLS: tires, wheels, and suspension

STORE: call for location nearest you; phone hours Monday to Friday 8:00 am–9:00 pm, Saturday 9:00 am–4:00 pm

ONLINE: www.tires.com

Discount Tire Direct is the mail-order division of Discount Tire Co., which has been in business for nearly 40 years selling wheels and all-season, high-performance, snow, and light-truck tires by name-brand manufacturers. Last winter I decided to see how buying tires from home would compare with getting them from my local tire discounter. Surprise! With Discount Tire's new free shipping policy, I saved over $100 on 4 tires for my Honda Civic. Getting product and price information at the website is an easy proposition; search available products by the make and model of your car or truck, or by tire size. The information online guides you through the process. Definitely check out the featured special promotions and closeouts that offer tremendous additional savings. You can place your order electronically at the site, but you can still order by phone or by mail, if you prefer. Whatever method you choose, a sales rep at Discount Tire Direct will check over your order to make sure the tire you want is suitable for your vehicle before your order is processed.

SPECIAL FACTORS: Satisfaction guaranteed; free shipping; returns accepted within 30 days for exchange, refund, or credit.

Honda Parts Wholesale

888–53HONDA

FORM OF INFORMATION: online catalog only, no print catalog

PAY: MC, V, AE, DSC

SELLS: new parts for Hondas

STORE: no walk-in location; online only; phone hours Monday to Friday 9:00 am–5:00 pm EST

ONLINE: www.hondacarparts.com

You don't have to be a grease monkey to buy discount auto parts. Even if you've never done anything more complicated than check the oil, this company makes it simple to get the best prices when you need a new part. Let's face it: Unless you're related to your mechanic, chances are he or she are obtaining car parts from their usual source, which isn't always in *your* best interest. Honda Parts Wholesale sells and ships genuine Honda parts at discount prices to the public. When you call the toll-free number, you'll get a helpful sales rep on the other end who can quote you prices on every Honda part. Or check out the website to find listings of accessories and parts for Honda Accords, Civics, CR-Vs, Odysseys, Passports, or Preludes, as well as current specials. List prices and your cost are side by side so you can calculate the savings—around 25% in most cases. Illustrations of parts can be seen by clicking on the view button. If you don't find what you're looking for, call for a price quote. If you do find what you're looking for, you can order it online.

SPECIAL FACTORS: Parts shipped within the continental U.S. only; minimum order is $20; minimum shipping is $6.

Manufacturer's Supply

P.O. Box 167
Dorchester, WI 54425
800–826–8563
FAX: 800–294–4144

FORM OF INFORMATION: free print catalog; online catalog

PAY: check, MO, MC, V, DSC

SELLS: replacement parts for snowmobiles, chain saws, ATVs, small engines, minibikes, lawnmowers, and Go-Karts

STORE: no walk-in location; mail-order only

ONLINE: www.mfgsupply.com

For 36 years Manufacturer's Supply has been a leading supplier of parts for all-terrain vehicles, chainsaw/harvester/logging equipment, Go-Karts and minibikes, lawnmowers, snowblowers, snowmobiles, trailers, harvesters, and all other kinds of small engines, at savings up to 50% off retail prices. The seemingly endless inventory has pretty much everything you need to get any motorized vehicle or power implement humming again. The beauty of shopping Manufacturer's Supply is that within the 200-plus pages of the catalog, at the website, and via phone, fax, and email, you have access to parts and accessories by major manufacturers for every imaginable make and model. You'll save big by shopping here rather than your local auto parts store.

WEBSITE: The website has more parts available than the print catalog, features online ordering, has product specifications and information in every category, and offers web-only specials. It also has a cool garage feature where you tell it what ATV, snowmobile, or Harley Davidson motorcycle you own and it lists parts and accessories for your specific machine features. Definitely check it out.

SPECIAL FACTORS: Authorized returns (except special orders and electronic components) accepted within 30 days (15% restocking fee may apply); shipping $5.99, within contiguous U.S., except on freight shipments or special orders.

Parts411.com

C&A International dba Parts411
466 W. Arrow Hwy, Suite F
San Dimas, CA 91773
877–484–4860
909–599–4860
FAX: 909–599–6898

FORM OF INFORMATION: online catalog only; no print catalog

PAY: check, MO, MC, V, AE, DSC

SELLS: motorcycle, ATV, and snowmobile parts and related apparel and gear

STORE: same address; Monday to Friday 8:00 am–5:00 pm

ONLINE: www.parts411.com

I'll make a wild assumption that you motorcycle enthusiasts don't demand frills and froufrou in a website. What you're looking for instead is a no-nonsense source for inexpensive bike parts and accessories. Parts411 is your place. This company purchases in large volume so it can pass the savings along to its online customers. Savings here average 20% off list. There are parts for motorcycles, ATVs, automotive air filters, and intake systems. The roster of goods here is encyclopedic: starting with air filters; apparel (gloves, shoes, gear bags, jackets, chaps); ATV parts, including tires and wheels; bike covers; body parts (mirrors, foot pegs, fairing stays, etc.); books and manuals; brakes; chains and sprockets; chemicals; clutch parts; communications equipment—and that's only the first three letters of the alphabet! There's nothing fancy here, just straightforward web shopping. Click on a product category to see everything currently available in that department, with the suggested retail price and Parts411's discounted price side by side. There aren't a lot of product descriptions here. A typical Parts411 customer is an educated consumer who already knows the product description and is looking to save money by buying it here. However, if you have any questions about the merchandise or don't see a part you want, you can reach customer service by phone or by email and they'll happily help you. Speaking of happy, check out the customer testimonials. Even with shipping factored in, they still saved a significant amount on items they bought through Parts411 on what they might have spent by purchasing locally.

SPECIAL FACTORS: Authorized returns accepted within 10 days of receipt (see website for returns policy details); helmets are not returnable; $25 minimum order except for Helmet Quick Release and Tire Flys.

Racer Parts Wholesale

411 Dorman
Indianapolis, IN 46202
800–397–7815
317–639–0725
FAX: 317–639–0722

FORM OF INFORMATION: free print catalog; online catalog

PAY: check, MO, MC, V, AE, DSC

SELLS: motor racing parts and equipment

STORE: no walk-in location; mail-order only; phone hours Monday to Friday 9:00 am– 6:00 pm EST

ONLINE: www.racerpartswholesale.com

Motor racing is one of the hottest spectator sports in the country right now. Not only are more people watching this sport, but more daredevils are becoming participants. If you're one of these, you need a source for bargain-priced racing parts and equipment. Look no further than Racer Parts Wholesale. The 34-page print catalog begins with a warning in bright red capital letters: "Motor racing is extremely dangerous. Injury and death will occur." And it goes on to say that the products sold will protect you from neither injury nor death. Oh well, at least if you go out, you'll go out in style, and you'll save money in the process. Racer Parts Wholesale guarantees that their prices are the lowest. You'll find equipment and parts in the following categories: Ducting, Steering, Scales, Tools, Lubricants, Tire Treatments, Rivets, Cooling, Oil Parts, Filters, Hoses, Fittings, Gauges, Electrical, Mufflers, Brake Pads, and others, including Books.

WEBSITE: Racer Parts Wholesale has a high-functioning website. It's orderly, fast, logical, comprehensive, and consumer-friendly. If you have internet access, the online version of the catalog is as good as or better than the print catalog. Secure online ordering is available here.

SPECIAL FACTORS: Returns accepted except on special and custom orders; a 15% restocking fee applies; lowest price guarantee (see catalog or website for details).

Racer Wholesale

1050 Cambridge Sq., Ste. A
Alpharetta, GA 30004
800–397–7811
770–998–7777
FAX: 678–832–1100

FORM OF INFORMATION: free print catalog; online catalog
PAY: check, MO, MC, V, DSC
SELLS: auto racing safety equipment
STORE: same address; Monday to Friday 9:00 am–6:00 pm
ONLINE: www.racerwholesale.com

Auto racing is one of the fastest growing spectator sports in America. Racer Wholesale, in business since 1985, is known among amateur and professional auto racers for impressive discounts—up to 70% off list prices—on auto equipment, safety equipment, and accessories by name-brand manufacturers. Racers can browse the 50-page catalog for professional driving suits, gloves, boots, helmets, fire extinguishers and fire systems, harness systems, junior racing gear, roll-bar padding, towing accessories, window nets, canopy kits, and more at "guaranteed lowest prices."

WEBSITE: The website appears to have as much or maybe more inventory than the print catalog. Here you'll find the products pictured and described in detail. In addition, the website features current closeouts and offers secure online ordering.

SPECIAL FACTORS: Except for special orders, authorized (and unused) returns accepted within 45 days for exchange, refund, or credit (restocking fee applied).

The Tire Rack

7101 Vorden Pkwy
South Bend, IN 46628
888–541–1777 ext. 360
574–287–2345
FAX: 574–236–7707

FORM OF INFORMATION: free newsletter; online catalog

PAY: check, MO, MC, V, AE, DSC

SELLS: tires, wheels, and packages

STORE: same address; Monday to Friday 8:00 am–8:00 pm, Saturday 9:00 am– 4:00 pm

ONLINE: www.tirerack.com

Tires by mail? Sure! I've done it, and so can you. Never schlep over to the discount automotive joint again. Your tires will likely be less expensive—including shipping— by ordering them through the mail than the ones you can get locally. And they will probably arrive in 3 days to boot! But don't believe me. Check out Tire Rack's website, which is easy to use and will give you all the information you crave—photographs, descriptions, ratings, reviews, tips, and more. You're welcome, too, to call the helpful people at The Tire Rack, who have made serving mail-order customers their main focus since 1982, which makes them America's oldest mail-order tire company. Customer service phone hours are on the website. With access to the single largest supply of O.E. (original equipment) tires available in North America, you'll find most popular brands here, including BFGoodrich, Bridgestone, Continental, Dunlop, Firestone, Goodyear, Hoosier, Michelin, Pirelli, Sumitomo, Yokohama, and others. Besides tires, this firm also sells wheels, packages (tires and wheels together, "expertly balanced"), and accessories. Wheel brands include AMG, ASA, BBS, Borbet, Breyton, EVO, Ford Racing, Mille Miglia, Kosei, Moda, O.Z., and others. Tire Rack's own staff tests and rates all new tire models and can offer informed advice on the best tire for your style of driving and your climate.

SPECIAL FACTORS: Satisfaction guaranteed; returns of unused merchandise are accepted within 30 days for exchange, refund, or credit.

Trollhattan Auto Parts, Inc.

813 Eastern Blvd., Ste. 102
Baltimore, MD 21221
800–328–7655
410–682–2827
FAX: 410–682–4739

FORM OF INFORMATION: online catalog only; no print catalog

PAY: check, MO, MC, V, AE, DSC

SELLS: new parts for Saabs, Volvos, Audis, BMWs, Mercedes, and VWs

STORE: no walk-in location; online only; phone hours Monday to Friday 8:00 am–6:00 pm EST

ONLINE: www.cybertroll.com

Everybody and his uncle drives a Saab in Woodstock, New York, where I live. Saabs handle great in wintry conditions, and besides, they're super cool. However, they're pretty darned expensive to service. Cruising along the information superhighway the other day, I came upon Trollhattan, which will make all Saab and Volvo owners happy. Why? Because this company is devoted to selling Saab and Volvo parts at 20% to 50% off dealer list. The website tells you what Trollhattan does sell (lighting, brake, suspension, tune-up, transmission, fuel-injection, air-conditioning, heating, cooling, electrical, drive train, and clutch components) and doesn't sell (body parts, high-performance accessories, trim parts, interior parts, audio equipment, parts for cars older than 1975). They offer 24-hour shipping; orders delivered to home, office, or shop; a few different ordering options (by phone, fax, online, or mail); and free technical support via phone or e-mail. The folks at Trollhattan are friendly and knowledgeable. Give 'em a call next time a deer hoof knocks out your Saab or Volvo headlight.

SPECIAL FACTORS: Personal checks must clear before your order is shipped; 12-month or 12,000-mile warranty on all parts.

Webcovers

2680 Blake St.

Denver, CO 80205

800-503-2727

303-297-9727

FAX: 303-294-0333

FORM OF INFORMATION: online catalog only; no print catalog

PAY: MO, MC, V, AE, DSC

SELLS: seat covers, floor mats, covers, bras, and accessories for cars and trucks

STORE: no walk-in location; online only; phone hours Monday to Friday 8:00 am–6:00 pm EST

ONLINE: www.webcovers.com

Webcovers has been in business for ten years through mail-order and catalogue, as well as entering into the internet industry in 1997. Their specialties include auto bras, car and truck covers, seat covers, dash covers and other auto accessories.

If you have children and/or dogs you already know that seat covers are a must for the family car. Webcovers offers a wide selection of fabrics, fashions, and colors in their seat covers. I found a pair of charcoal grey tweed universal-fit covers for only $21.95. Their blue velour seat covers were quite a bit cheaper, at $29.32 a pair, than a number of stores I compared them to. And, I priced a four-piece custom floor mat set for my Honda civic at $53.65. A universal rear car seat cover was available at a very reasonable price of $32.28. At these prices, it's time to chuck those old, smelly blankets you're currently using to protect your car seats.

Webcovers also has a clearance section which links to their page on eBay where you can purchase items at up to 60% off retail.

SPECIAL FACTORS: Authorized returns within 30 days of purchase; all returns are subject to a 15% restocking fee.

Books, Audiobooks, and Periodicals

New and used fiction, nonfiction, reference, fine art, how-to, and children's books; books on tape; magazine subscription discounters; college textbooks; technical and computer manuals

If there's one thing you should learn from this book, it's that paying full price for books and magazines is absolutely unnecessary. Every company in this chapter offers deals on books of every kind—from elegant coffee-table art books and thick college textbooks to best-sellers and children's books. You'll find brand-new books as well as collectible antiques; you can shop online or through old-fashioned booksellers who deal strictly through the mail and are willing to answer your questions personally and offer recommendations. There isn't a book in existence you won't be able to find here for substantially less than you'd spend at your local bookstore—up to 90% less.

You won't find every subject category of book listed in the Find It Fast section below. Unless the bookseller specializes in one particular genre of books (cookbooks, say, or fine art), you should assume that the general booksellers in this chapter will have books on your topic of choice.

If you find yourself commuting or traveling a lot, have vision problems, or just love to keep your hands free while improving your mind, you'll enjoy the audiobook offerings, some of which you can rent instead of buy.

Finally, shave dollars off every magazine subscription you're now carrying with the subscription-services firms. If you have a business that subscribes to several magazines, your savings will be substantial.

Please note: Many of the firms in *The Bargain Buyer's Guide* carry books, booklets, guides, and newsletters on subjects relevant to their businesses. If your interest is cooking, see the "Food and Beverages" chapter for companies that stock cookbooks; for books on health-related subjects, check out the listings in the "Health, Beauty, and Fitness" chapter; for how-to and do-it-yourself books, try some of the firms in the "Home: Building, Renovation, and Upkeep" section, or the "Tools, Hardware, and

Shop Machines" chapter, and so on. By the way, Amazon.com is no longer listed in this chapter because it has expanded and diversified its inventory so much that I can no longer call it a "book" store (although, it has some great deals on books). You'll find it in the "General Merchandise" chapter.

Find It Fast

AUDIOBOOKS
AllBooks4Less.com, Blackstone Audiobooks, Barnes & Noble by Mail

CHILDREN'S ACTIVITY BOOKS
Dover Publications

CHILDREN'S LITERATURE
AllBooks4Less, Barnes & Noble Books by Mail, Daedalus Books, Edward R. Hamilton Bookseller

COMPUTER AND TECHNICAL MANUALS
Bookpool, Half Price Computer Books

CONSUMER PUBLICATIONS
Federal Citizen Information Center

COOKBOOKS
Barnes & Noble Books by Mail, Daedalus Books, Edward R. Hamilton Bookseller, Jessica's Biscuit Cookbooks

DO-IT-YOURSELF BOOKS
Woodworkers' Discount Books

FINE ARTS/CRAFTS BOOKS
Dover Publications, The Potters Shop, The Scholar's Bookshelf, Strand Book Store

HARDCOVER BOOKS
AllBooks4Less.com, Barnes & Noble Books by Mail, Edward R. Hamilton Bookseller, Tartan Book Sales, TextbookX.com

MAGAZINE SUBSCRIPTIONS
Barnes & Noble Books by Mail, Below Wholesale Magazines, Delta Publishing Group/Magazine Warehouse

OLD, RARE, USED BOOKS
Strand, Tartan Book Sales, TextbookX.com

PUBLISHERS OVERSTOCK/CLEARANCE/REMAINDERED
AllBooks4Less.com, Barnes & Noble Books by Mail, Daedalus Books, Edward R. Hamilton Bookseller, Tartan Book Sales

TEXTBOOKS
Bookpool, TextbookX.com

UNIVERSITY PRESS/SCHOLARLY PUBLICATIONS
Barnes & Noble Books by Mail, Daedalus Books, The Scholar's Bookshelf, TextbookX.com

AllBooks4Less.com

340 Welland Ave.
St. Catharines, Ontario
L2R 7L9
Canada
888–402–7323
FAX: 905–680–7218

FORM OF INFORMATION: online catalog only; no print catalog
PAY: MC, V, AE
SELLS: audiobooks, and closeout and remaindered books
STORE: same address; Monday to Friday 8:30 am–5:00 pm est
ONLINE: www.allbooks4less.com

AllBooks4Less.com is the online division of The Book Depot, a brick-and-mortar retail outlet. The Book Depot is one of the largest "closeout/remainder" bookstores in North America with shipping facilities in both the United States and Canada. They are a family-run business, established over 10 years ago. When regular bookstores need room for new product, they send their "overstocks" back to the publisher. The publisher marks each book on its end with a little dot or line. AllBooks4Less.com purchases these "remainder" books and offers them to you at bargain prices. The average savings is over 50% off the list price. Because AllBooks4Less.com features closeouts exclusively, you may not find today's best-sellers, but you will find books on your favorite subjects and by your favorite authors. Book categories include Science, Children's, Cooking, History, General Fiction and many more. These books have been in and out of shipping cases a number of times. Many are in pristine condition, while others have suffered damage. AllBooks4Less.com has strict quality control standards and they will not send you a book that has structural damage. However, they may send you a book that has minor cosmetic damage. These books are discounted a further 20%. If you are not happy with the condition of your purchase, you can return it for a full refund.

The books in the Daily Specials section on the home page are hand-selected, quality titles which are discounted up to 90% off the publisher's price. Featured books revert back to their default price at midnight eastern standard time the same day. So, now there's no excuse for putting off a great read by James Joyces, John Steinbeck, John Irving, or Robertson Davies.

SPECIAL FACTORS: Satisfaction guaranteed; returns for full refund, within 15 days of receipt; exchange or refund may not include shipping and handling charges; orders taken by phone for a $2.00 handling charge.

Barnes & Noble Books by Mail

One Pond Rd.
Rockleigh, NJ 07647
800–THE–BOOK
FAX: 201–767–9169

FORM OF INFORMATION: free print catalog; online catalog

PAY: check, MO, MC, V, AE, DC, JCB

SELLS: books, cassettes, videos, gifts, etc.

STORE: call main number for nearest location

ONLINE: www.bn.com

For more than 120 years Barnes & Noble has been presenting readers with the best in new and unusual titles featuring the latest hardcover releases, hard-to-find paperbacks, publishers' overstocks, remainders, and books from small publishers and university presses at savings up to 88%. Every issue of the print catalog offers hundreds of books in a spectrum of subject categories including History, Mystery, The Arts, Science, Literature, Film, Medicine, Biographies, Satire, Juvenilia, Current Fiction, Linguistics, Religion, Reference, Crafts, Self-Help, and Photography.

WEBSITE: Barnes & Noble has a fabulous website as well, where browsers can find discounted books, magazines, music, DVDs and videos. (Subscribing to your favorite magazine through Barnes & Noble will yield savings up to 85%.) Click onto the Half-Price Books section of the bookstore to view overstocks, special values, and Barnes & Noble's own editions. There's where you'll save up to 88%. The Great Deals section features Fiction Under $5, 5,000 Books Under $10, Children's Bargains and Books Published by Barnes & Noble to help you stock up your library without busting your budget. Online ordering is available at the website.

SPECIAL FACTORS: Satisfaction guaranteed; returns accepted; library and school discounts available.

Below Wholesale Magazines

774 Mays Blvd #10
Suite 487, Dept. WBM
Incline Village, NV 89451
800–800–0062
FAX: 530–546–3165

FORM OF INFORMATION: free brochure
PAY: check, MO, MC, V, AE, DSC
SELLS: magazine subscriptions
STORE: no walk-in location; mail-order only; phone hours 24 hours a day
EMAIL: magazines@got.net

With access to over 2,500 titles, Below Wholesale Magazines offers "The deepest discounts in America. Period." This translates into savings up to 90% off newsstand prices. If you find a lower price, they'll not only match it, they'll give you an additional 10% discount. With this kind of deal, it seems crazy to subscribe to magazines the normal, old-fashioned way, doesn't it? Below Wholesale has a 4-page brochure they'll send you for free. If you don't see what you're looking for, call; chances are Below Wholesale Magazines can get it for you. Businesses and self-employed professionals such as doctors, dentists, and lawyers are offered even deeper discounts here and should inquire about the terms. At press time, a website was in the works.

SPECIAL FACTORS: Satisfaction guaranteed; gift service available; allow 6 to 12 weeks for first issue to arrive; special 3- and 4-year rates available (inquire). They sell at wholesale to qualified firms.

Blackstone Audiobooks

P.O. Box 969
Ashland, OR 97520
800–729–2665
541–482–9239
FAX: 541–482–9294

FORM OF INFORMATION: free print catalog; online catalog

PAY: check, MO, V, MC, AE, DSC

SELLS AND RENTS: unabridged recordings of quality books

STORE: no walk-in location; mail-order only

ONLINE: www.blackstoneaudio.com

Many of my artist friends like to listen to audiobooks while they're working. My sister, who travels regularly for her work, loves to listen to audiobooks while driving or flying. They all love Blackstone Audiobooks with their guaranteed lowest prices on full-length (unabridged) high-quality audiobooks. The 274-page catalog shows hundreds and hundreds of titles. Blackstone's catalog is organized alphabetically by category, including 20th-Century Fiction, Poetry, Children's (great for those long car trips or troubled sleepers), Science Fiction and Fantasy, Baseball, Business, Religion, Speeches, Plays, Civil War, Biography, and many others. The cassettes are for purchase or for rent—usually for 30 to 45 days, depending on the book length. They have nearly 300 titles available on CD at this writing. The rentals average around $8 to $10 for children's, or $10 to $15 for adults', which comes to about 60 cents per day. Owner Craig Black says his audiobooks are about 15% to 20% lower than comparable recordings, and he also offers used audiobooks for 50% off. There are quantity discounts for individuals on purchases and rentals (rent 3 books, get an additional 10% off, for example), monthly specials, and discounts for libraries and wholesalers (inquire). See the catalog for details on shipping and returning rentals.

WEBSITE: Blackstone's user-friendly website features online buying or renting, whichever you prefer, and an easy-to-access table of contents. You can also buy gift certificates here and view up-to-the-minute sale items.

SPECIAL FACTORS: Different shipping rates apply outside the contiguous 48 states.

Bookpool LLC

P.O. Box 387
Vineyard Haven, MA 02568

FORM OF INFORMATION: online catalog only; no print catalog

PAY: check, MO, MC, V, AE, DC, DSC, JCB, CB

SELLS: technical books

STORE: no walk-in location; mail-order only; email customer service hours Monday to Friday 9:00 am–5:00 pm

ONLINE: www.bookpool.com

If the terms "parallel computing, fault tolerance, operating platforms, neural networks, and distributed objects" all mean something to you, then I've got a great resource you'll want to know about. Bookpool LLC is an internet-only bookstore that caters to people who are comfortable navigating the world of information technology. This virtual store offers an impressive selection of the best technical books on the net, at prices that beat several of the top book discounters I checked. Discounts of 30% and more are not uncommon here.

At the website the reader can search for books by keyword, browse by category, or view the best-selling technical books by publisher. You won't find gushy romances or potboiler detective novellas here. Instead, you'll find real heart-thumping page-turners in subject categories that include: Business and Culture; Certification; Computer Applications; Databases; Desktop Applications; Distributed Computing; Enterprise Computing; Graphics and Multimedia; Hardware; Networking/Communications; Operating Platforms; Programming; Programming Languages; and WWW and Internet. If there is a book you want but can't find, Bookpool will get it for you. This and other customer service inquiries are done exclusively via email. (Someone will respond to your email within one business day.) The website provides a physical address for those paying by check, as well as a fax number for people who prefer to fax their credit card number. Otherwise, this is a click-and-shop operation, which should be no problem whatsoever for the type of people who desire these books.

SPECIAL FACTORS: Satisfaction guaranteed; books may be returned in original condition (no software seals broken) within 30 days of receipt of your shipment, after requesting a return authorization code from bookpool@bookpool.com.

Daedalus Books

P.O. Box 6000
Columbia, MD 21045–6000
800–395–2665
FAX: 800–866–5578

FORM OF INFORMATION: free print catalog; online catalog

PAY: check, MO, MC, V, AE, DSC

SELLS: book overstocks and remainders, music CDs, and cassettes

STORE: 9645 Gerwig Ln., Columbia, MD; Monday to Sunday 10:00 am–7:00 pm

ONLINE: www.daedalusbooks.com

There's a lot of competition out there between book sellers, so a company has got to be good to make it these days. Daedalus has been around for over two decades selling new and remaindered books up to 90% off the original publishers' prices. Why buy books hot off the press? If you can defer your gratification and buy them a year or so later once they've been "remaindered," you'll be able to buy the best books around at unbelievable savings. Daedalus has volumes of fiction, poetry, and literature; books for children; books on travel, food and health, gardening, crafts, the arts, history, religion, politics, science; and more. Daedalus mails out over twelve print catalogs a year, but for various reasons (quantity, timing, etc.) many of the titles they offer never appear in a print catalog. However, they do appear on their website, which has new titles almost everyday. Because most of the remaindered books that they sell are in limited quantities it is important that you order what you want, which you can do online, as soon as you see it

WEBSITE: The website, which features convenient online ordering, has more to see of what Daedalus currently has in stock. Audiophiles will love the selection of music CDs: classical, jazz, blues, and more, offered at greatly discounted prices in the music section.

SPECIAL FACTORS: Institutional accounts available; returns accepted within 30 days.

Delta Publishing Group/Magazine Warehouse

1243 48th St.
Brooklyn, NY 11219
800–SEND–LIST
718–972–0900
FAX: 718–972–4695

FORM OF INFORMATION: free print catalog
PAY: check, MO, MC, V, AE, DSC
SELLS: magazine subscriptions
STORE: no walk-in location; mail-order only

 ★

How can Delta Publishing Group, a.k.a. Magazine Warehouse, sell you the same magazines for much lower prices than the publishers and clearinghouses? Delta's brochure explains: (1) Their warehouse is stocked with over 850 titles; (2) they don't spend money on glitzy ads, spokespersons, or gimmicks (read: sweepstakes); (3) they save money by requiring prepayment to avoid good customers' subsidizing "deadbeats"; and (4) they cut down on paperwork and staff because 90% of their customers order several magazines for several years, and therefore only get one infrequent renewal notice. Now that you know why it's cheaper, know also that Delta will save you up to 80% on just about any magazine subscription. If you're getting magazines for your office waiting room, Delta will keep track of all your subscription renewals for free. Membership in Delta's 800–SAVE–SAVE Club also gives you discounts on how-to videos, self-help books, CD-ROM software, travel, phone calls, and more.

Please note that some titles require a "trade" address as well as a business name, letterhead, and/or business card. Magazines will be mailed to that address only.

SPECIAL FACTORS: Call 800–SEND–LIST or write for a price list; lowest price guaranteed.

Dover Publications, Inc.

31 East 2nd St., Dept. MC
Mineola, NY 11501–3582
516–294–7000
FAX: 516–742–6953

FORM OF INFORMATION: free print catalog; online catalog

PAY: check, MO, V

SELLS: Dover publications

STORE: same address; Monday to Friday 8:00 am–4:00 pm; also 180 Varick St., 9th Floor, New York, NY; Monday to Friday 9:00 am–4:30 pm

ONLINE: www.doverpublications.com

Dover Publications has more than 20 catalogs to choose from, including "Art–Fine Art," "Art Instruction," "Chess," "Children's Books," "Cookbooks," "Crafts and Hobbies," "Fiction," "Music," "Photography," "Science and Math," and "Social Sciences." The real bargains here are in the "Children's Classics" and "Shakespeare"—books average about $1! Perhaps even more exciting than these books are the other items. For example, if you're in charge of your organization's newsletter, Dover has copyright-free books of illustrations on every topic, copyright-free photographs, clip art in books, electronic clip art, copyright-free graphics specially designed for your copier, instant art stickers, and more. There's a great selection of books on design, ornamentation, calligraphy, every kind of craft and fine art, sheet music; language books; and even wrapping paper. There are gift cards; postcard books; educational posters; stickers and seals; and toy, game, and activity books for children, including an entire selection of those old-fashioned delights: paper doll books. This is a great source for parents.

WEBSITE: Dover is online with a fully operational website describing every Dover book in print—over 7,000 titles in all. This is the way to go if you have online access. All of their other great products—gift gift cards, stickers, wrapping paper—are available here, as well, in an organized, easy to use format.

SPECIAL FACTORS: Satisfaction guaranteed; returns accepted within 30 days for refund; no telephone orders.

Federal Citizen Information Center

Pueblo, CO 81009
888–878–3256
FAX: 719–948–9724

FORM OF INFORMATION: free print catalog; online catalog
PAY: check, MO, MC, V, DSC
SELLS: consumer publications
STORE: no walk-in location; mail-order only
ONLINE: www.pueblo.gsa.gov

Established in 1970, the government's Federal Citizen Information Center "helps federal agencies promote and distribute useful consumer information." Its 16-page "Consumer Information Catalog" is full of booklets and manuals on subjects including cars, children, employment, federal programs, food and nutrition, health, housing, money, small business, and travel. Most of the booklets are a dollar or under, and many are free! For example, the "Consumer Action Handbook" lists contact names and numbers of trade associations, consumer advocacy organizations, and government agencies where you can seek help with consumer complaints and problems. Or there's "A Guide to Disability Rights Laws" that describes your rights regarding housing, public accommodations, telecommunications, education, and more. Both free! For a mere dollar you can obtain "How You Can Buy Used Federal Personal Property," which tells about used equipment and industrial items sold by the government. If your ex is a deadbeat dad, there's a booklet describing whom you can contact to get that back child support. From pruning your trees to saving energy costs, help is here and it's quite inexpensive.

Spanish-speaking consumers: A Spanish-language catalog is available.

WEBSITE: Log onto the website to see the full selection, as well as the full text of most of these booklets; view the text of other consumer publications; get the scoop on current consumer news; find links to other helpful websites; and order the Center's booklets online. This is a great online resource.

SPECIAL FACTORS: A $2 handling fee is charged on all orders.

Half Price Computer Books

Box 115
1125 Fir Ave.
Blaine, Washington 98230
888-663-0063
FAX: 604-945-7229

FORM OF INFORMATION: online catalog
PAY: check, MO, MC, V, AE, DSC
SELLS: new computer books
STORE: no walk-in location; mail-order only
ONLINE: www.halfpricecomputerbooks.com

You have the computer, the software, and the motivation. Now all you need is to know how to use it all. Half Price Computer Books sells new computer books from the original manufacturers for up to 50% off. Their inventory includes over 10,000 different titles, ranging from beginners' guides to obscure programming languages. They cover all sorts of computer programs and problems, answering questions on graphics software, games, internet design, multimedia, networking, operating systems, computer languages, databases, and more. HPCB goes out of their way to buy up books from discontinued businesses enabling their customers to get books that are no longer available elsewhere, as well as save plenty of money. These discontinued book sales offer discounts up to 70%. They also have a Bargain Bin, which lives up to its name with books at 50% to 75% off list prices. Even ultra-new releases are somehow sold at low prices, amounting to a 20% discount. Customer satisfaction is apparent from clicking on the link to BizRate.com which gives percentages of satisfied customers versus unsatisfied customers within a time frame of about three months. HPCB rates at about 98% customer satisfaction. With their exceptional variety and modest prices, it is unlikely you will need to search any further for computer books.

WEBSITE: This site is full of one-time deals, blow-outs, discontinued book sales, and other limited time discounts. It also includes a list of best-sellers and recent arrivals.

SPECIAL FACTORS: Full refund within 30 days of receipt (with unopened CDs); "20% off books" can be exchanged, but not refunded.

Edward R. Hamilton Bookseller

Falls Village, CT 06031–5000

FORM OF INFORMATION: free print catalog; online catalog

PAY: check, MO, MC, V (see text)

SELLS: new, closeout, and remaindered books

STORE: no walk-in location; mail-order only

ONLINE: www.edwardrhamilton.com

This wonderful bookseller has been featured in this book for a long time. New, hardbound books are mostly what you'll find in Edward R. Hamilton's monthly print catalog, which lists thousands of high-quality books selling for up to 80% off the original price. Categories include Biography, Crime, Sports, U.S. and World History, Politics, Native American Culture, Religion, Travel, Archaeology, The Occult, Gardening, Hobbies, Animals, Cooking, Fashion, Collecting, Art and Crafts, Fine Art, Photography, Music, Children's Books, Current Fiction, Classic Literature, Science Fiction, Self-Help, Psychology, Reference, and much more. You will enjoy the thoughtful but brief text that describes each title. To offer the lowest possible prices all orders must be prepaid. They do no billing and do not accept credit cards. The postage and handling charge is only $3.50 per order. If any book is sold out your money will be refunded by bank check.

WEBSITE: This site is an extension of their mail-order catalog. Newly arrived titles, because of their limited quantities, are not listed on the site until it is determined that they can meet the demand for them. Many titles included on the website are no longer listed in the catalog. To order from this site you will need to fill out the order form online and print it out (or print it out first and fill in) and then send it with a check or money order to the address listed above. If you wish to shop on the web using a credit card, you may click on the link for HamiltonBook.com on the home page. This is a separate business that obtains its inventory from Edward R. Hamilton Bookseller and accepts payment by credit card. HamiltonBook.com charges postage and handling of $3.50 per order plus an additional 95¢ per book.

SPECIAL FACTORS: Satisfaction guaranteed or your money refunded; shipment is normally within 48 hours; some titles may be temporarily out of stock, in which case a second shipment will be made, normally in 14 days, no later than 60 days.

Jessica's Biscuit Cookbooks

P.O. Box 301
Newtonville, MA 02460
800–878–4264
617–965–0530
FAX: 617–244–3376

FORM OF INFORMATION: free print catalog; online catalog

PAY: check, MO, MC, V, AE, DSC

SELLS: cookbooks, and food and wine reference

STORE: no walk-in location; mail-order only

ONLINE: www.ecookbooks.com

Here's a great idea: a whole mail-order operation devoted to nothing but cookbooks offered to you at 20% to 75% below original price. Jessica's Biscuit Cookbooks has something for everyone: books on ethnic, regional, and international cooking; classic cookbooks from well-known chefs and celebrities; books on desserts, baking, vegetarian cuisine, wine and beer, cake decorating, children's cookery, and many others. The 48-page print catalog is fun to read and lists special offers on brand new cookbooks, food commentary books and even features recipes. Jessica's also sells food-related posters.

WEBSITE: If you have online access head straight for the Jessica's Biscuit website. Not only are hundreds of cookbooks to be found here, easily searchable by author, title, or description, but there are scores of articles you can read on subjects such as Hawaiian regional cuisine or summer drinks. All articles include recipes and excerpts from various cookbooks. This is a great hands-on way to sample what's cooking in the book world. The website also features closeouts and online ordering.

SPECIAL FACTORS: Satisfaction guaranteed; returns accepted.

The Potters Shop

31 Thorpe Rd.
Needham Heights, MA 02194
781–449–7687
FAX: 781–449–9098

FORM OF INFORMATION: free print catalog

PAY: check, MO, MC, V, DSC

SELLS: books and videotapes on ceramics and pottery, ceramics tools

STORE: same address; Monday to Thursday 11:00 am–5:30 pm, Friday 9:00 am–12:00 noon

EMAIL: pottersshop@aol.com

Established in 1977, The Potters Shop issues a poster-size catalog that lists hundreds of pottery-related books discounted between 15% and 70%. This is a great source for anyone interested in the subject. Categories include Technical Books (clay, glaze, kilns, firing), Throwing, Hand Building/Sculpture, Tiles/Mosaic, Decoration/Casting/Mold Making, Porcelain, Health/Business/Marketing, Potters' Philosophy, World Pottery, Children's Books, and much more. Dolan tools are also sold here at a 10% discount.

SPECIAL FACTORS: Defective products will be exchanged; other returns accepted for credit; purchase orders accepted from schools and institutions.

The Scholar's Bookshelf

110 Melrich Rd.
Cranbury, NJ 08512
609–395–6933
FAX: 609–395–0755

FORM OF INFORMATION: free print catalog; online catalog

PAY: check, MO, MC, V, Eurocard, Access Card

SELLS: scholarly and university press books

STORE: no walk-in location; mail-order only

ONLINE: www.scholarsbookshelf.com

Here's a bookseller that specializes in university press and scholarly imprint remainders on a wide range of subjects for the serious reader, researcher, teacher, and student. The Scholar's Bookshelf, in business since 1974, sweetens your scholarly pursuits with discounts that average 30% below the publisher's price, although savings can run up to 75%. You'll also find wonderful videos here at a discount.

The general sale catalog has concise descriptions of volumes on philosophy, religion, history, travel, literature, cinema, music, science, reference, and more. Throughout the year, The Scholar's Bookshelf produces themed catalogs as well, including "Literature," "Fine Arts Books," "Military History," and "History." The videos offered are the kind of documentaries that would make wonderful teaching or presentation aids on subjects such as World War II and African-American history.

WEBSITE: If you prefer to shop online, The Scholar's Bookshelf website features the full inventory and online ordering. Titles are arranged by broad subject for easy browsing, or you can search for a specific title by author, subject, or title.

SPECIAL FACTORS: Returns accepted within 30 days for exchange, refund, or credit; minimum order: $10.

Strand Book Store

828 Broadway
New York, NY 10003–4805
212–473–1452
800–366–3664
FAX: 212–473–2591

FORM OF INFORMATION: free print catalog; online catalog
PAY: check, MO, MC, V, AE, DSC, DC, JCB
SELLS: new, old, rare, and used books
STORE: same address; Monday to Saturday 9:30 am–10:30 pm, Sunday 11:00 am–10:30 pm; see website for addresses and hours for Strand Book Annex and Hacker/Strand Art Books in New York, NY.
WEBSITE: www.strandbooks.com

"Eight miles of books!" Strand Book Store, New York City's legendary bookstore, offers thousands of new titles at 50% off the cover price as well as a wide variety of "front list" books ordered directly from the publisher and obtainable at 20% or more off cover price. Some are remainders, others "fine second-hand," still others hard-to-find or out of print. Americana, art, children's books, cookbooks, fiction, film and drama, history, literature, medical, music, natural history, religion, science, sports, and travel are among the subject categories. This 76-year-old family business also features the largest rare book collection in New York city, containing first and signed editions of many collectibles in every field. The 80-page catalog is nicely organized with succinct, well-written descriptions of every title. Parents: This is a great source for affordable hardcover children's classics.

WEBSITE: Strand is online with their entire stock. This site is easy to navigate. Books are categorized by subject matter and clearly listed as new, used, or rare. If you prefer to shop offline you can download the print catalog by subject matter or in its entirety (it's big). Online ordering is available.

SPECIAL FACTORS: 100% satisfaction guaranteed; appraisals are available; used books also bought.

Tartan Book Sales

500 Arch St., Dept. 5N
Williamsport, PA 17705
800–233–8467, ext. 6789
FAX: 800–999–6799

FORM OF INFORMATION: online catalog
PAY: check, MC, V
SELLS: used hardcover books
STORE: no walk-in location; online only; phone hours Monday to Friday 7:00 am–5:00 pm
ONLINE: www.tartanbooks.com

Tartan Books are bestsellers, book club selections and other award winning titles that have had limited circulation in libraries. You'll find today's most popular authors in fiction, non-fiction, mystery and science fiction at discounts up to 75% off the publisher's price. Tartan hardcovers are circulated with patented book covers from Brodart Co. which ensure they are protected and in the best condition possible. All Tartan titles are carefully inspected, reconditioned and conservatively graded in "very good" condition. With a warehouse of constantly changing stock they cater to individuals and the largest booksellers. To view the current inventory you must download the catalog from their website and then phone, fax, or mail in your order. There is also the option of viewing inventory at the Tartan Z-Shop at Amazon by clicking the link from the home page. I found the Z-Shop a more convenient way to browse the current selections. If you're like me, you usually don't buy hardcover books because they're just too pricey. But here you can buy a $23 book for only $1.50. Now that's a bargain! Terms for books purchased for resale or use by an institution are explained at the website.

SPECIAL FACTORS: Quantity discounts available; institutional and retail accounts available.

TextbookX.com

Akademos, Inc.
25 Van Zant St. Ste 1A-2
Norwalk, CT 06855
800–887–6459
FAX: 203–866–0199

FORM OF INFORMATION: online catalog only; no print catalog

PAY: MC, V, AE, DSC

SELLS: new and used college textbooks

STORE: no walk-in location; online only; customer service hours Monday to Friday 9:00 am–6:00 pm EST

ONLINE: www.textbookx.com

One of the most shocking things about going to college, apart from the *most* shocking fact that you're suddenly free to do anything you want while your parents are halfway across the country, is the cost of textbooks. I was a real hayseed when I went to college. Just clueless. When I purchased my first Russian history textbook I nearly fainted when the check-out gal told me it was $60. I decided it would be worth the money since it could also serve as an end table next to my futon on the floor. Well, now smart, hip college kids who surf the internet (and read this book) will discover a way to avoid the campus bookstore. TextbookX.com is just what it sounds like: a source for deeply discounted college textbooks. Direct ties with major academic publishers allow this company to purchase books at the lowest possible prices and then mark them up just enough to cover their operating costs. It's an all-around great deal for students seeking new and used textbooks and nonacademic books. The site is easy to use and understand—search for books by title, keyword in title, author's last name, or ISBN number or browse by category and sub-category. You can order your books right online, and there's a customer service number if you should have questions or problems. The founder of TextbookX.com, himself a former college professor, is committed to quality higher education, which of course means being able to afford the necessary academic materials.

SPECIAL FACTORS: Books in original condition returnable within 30 days of confirmation of order for refund less a 10% restocking fee; no international orders.

Woodworkers' Discount Books

4460 Tierra Rojo Drive
Colorado Springs, CO 80926
800–378–4060
719–579–8330
FAX: 719–579–8287

FORM OF INFORMATION: free price list; online catalog

PAY: check, MO, MC, V, AE, DSC

SELLS: woodworking books, videos, and plans

STORE: no walk-in location; mail-order only; phone hours Monday to Friday 8:00 am–5:00 pm MST

ONLINE: www.discount-books.com

I would love to be able to design and make my own furniture—if only I had the time. When you have the time, perhaps you'll log onto Woodworkers' Discount Books online catalog and get yourself a book that shows how to do fine woodworking. The website is straightforward with detailed descriptions of titles and images of the cover art. You'll find every kind of book and manual for beginners and experts alike on subjects ranging from furniture making, clock making, and boxes, to design philosophy, power tools, and fine home building. Book prices are discounted an average of about 20% and shipping is very reasonable. Check out current specials and the very latest editions—online ordering is available. This is a nice company with real people on the other end of the phone ready to chat with you and give you the help you need.

SPECIAL FACTORS: Satisfaction guaranteed.

Cameras, Photographic Equipment/Services, and Optics

Cameras, darkroom equipment, photo supplies, film- and slide-processing services, binoculars, telescopes, and other optical instrumets

The companies in this chapter sell cameras, lenses, filters, tripods, lighting equipment, screens, splicers, batteries, and everything else for the amateur or professional shutterbug, including basic darkroom supplies (chemical, paper, film, etc.), darkroom equipment and furnishings, digital imaging supplies, and other high-tech equipment. Some of the firms here also provide services such as very low cost film and slide processing. And you can't talk lenses without including other optics such as microscopes, spotting scopes, telescopes, and binoculars. If you're looking for just about anything related to cameras and optics, you're in luck—you can save up to 48% by buying from these companies.

If video is your thing, you'll find most of the companies that sell video cameras, camcorders, videotape, VCRs, and other video-related goods in the "Music, Audio, and Video" chapter.

THE GRAY MARKET AND OTHER CONCERNS

Years ago, the camera and electronics industries came up against some problems caused by the gray market—a market that legally circumvents authorized channels of distribution to sell goods at prices lower than those intended by the manufacturer (the trademark owner); these gray-market goods were originally produced to be sold in other countries. Less expensive than their "authorized" counterparts, gray-market goods have one major disadvantage: They definitely don't come with a warranty that's honored in the U.S. They may also be of lesser quality and contain substances not approved for use in the U.S.

I spoke to one of the oldest firms in this chapter to find out why the term *gray market* has such negative connotations. In short, she explained, companies that sell gray-market goods are unethical *unless they inform customers about what they're buying*. In other words, a gray-market product isn't necessarily bad in and of itself as long as the customer understands the gamble: Buy cheap and take your chances, because there's no manufacturer's warranty. She told me you should be very suspicious of a name-brand camera, for example, that's sold for a hundred dollars less in one place than in another. Find out why, she urged. A vendor who doesn't advertise the product's real origins up front isn't worthy of your business.

If you see such an item sold at an unbelievably low price, just make sure the vendor is an authorized distributor and that the product has a valid warranty honored by the service centers of the U.S. manufacturer. Some merchants offer gray-market products with a store warranty equal to the original manufacturer's, which may end up being a good deal as long as you're happy with the quality of the product. Don't forget: Buying by credit card is always a good way to get certain protections under the Fair Credit Billing Act.

While gray-market activity has abated somewhat, another form has become prevalent—"diversions" of products from the authorized path, say by a wholesaler or mass merchant. In this case, the product was intended for the U.S. market, but not for the store in which it's sold. This isn't always bad; the consumer benefits, for example, when major department stores buy in enormous quantities to get the lowest possible price, and then resell the surplus "out the back door" to other stores and discounters. The problem is that the manufacturer might not assume any liability for the product's poor performance if that product wasn't sold to you by an authorized dealer. If you're the conscientious type, take the time to contact the manufacturer about the model you've chosen and find out what's normally included with the item—case, lens, cap, strap, coupons, etc.—and especially if there's a manual that's supposed to come with it explaining proper use and care. Most manufacturers have toll-free numbers and websites.

Find It Fast

BINOCULARS, TELESCOPES, MICROSCOPES
B&H Photo-Video–Pro Audio, Camera World, Mardiron Optics

CAMERAS AND PHOTOGRAPHY/DARKROOM EQUIPMENT
B&H Photo-Video–Pro Audio, Buydig.com, Camera World, Porter's Camera Store

DIGITAL IMAGING EQUIPMENT
B&H Photo-Video–Pro Audio, Buydig.com, Camera World, Porter's Camera Store

FILM AND SLIDE PROCESSING
Owl Photo

B&H Photo-Video–Pro Audio

420 Ninth Ave.
New York, NY 10001
800–606–6969
212–444–6615
FAX: 800–947–7008
or 212–239–7770

FORM OF INFORMATION: free print catalogs (see below); online catalog

PAY: check, MO, MC, V, AE, DSC

SELLS: equipment and supplies for photography and digital imaging, video, and pro-audio

STORE: same address; Monday to Thursday 9:00 am–7:15 pm, Friday 9:00 am–1:00 pm, Sunday 10:00 am–5:00 pm, closed Saturday

ONLINE: www.bhphotovideo.com

If you're a photographer living in the New York metropolitan area, you already know about B&H. This company has been "the professional's source" for more than 3 decades. Some of the best deals on photo, video, audio, and imaging equipment can be found here. Add to that good service and one of the largest inventories on the face of the globe and you'll know why I love this company so much.

B&H caters to the mail-order crowd with an experienced sales force ready to help you negotiate the incredible spectrum of products: photography equipment, including large-format options for both studio and field operations; every imaginable accessory, from tripods and lights to umbrellas and stands; darkroom equipment and supplies; video equipment suited for professionals as well as home hobbyists; computer equipment, such as scanners, nonlinear editing apparatus, and hardware and software; and pro audio equipment, such as high-end microphones, earphones, and mixing devices. B&H has a free catalog which includes more than 10,000 of their most popular products. They also offer a "Digital Photography SourceBook," a "Prosumer Video SourceBook," a "Professional Lighting SourceBook," and a "Professional Audio SourceBook."

WEBSITE: B&H's online catalog is a great way to shop here, as well. Click on one of the product categories—Photo, Film, Digital Photo, Consumer or Professional Video, Computer Video, Lighting, A/V Presentation, Pro Audio, Binoculars, Scopes or Used Equipment—and you'll see a good selection of items currently available, complete with photographs and detailed product specs. Check out the specials, books, and helpful links to sites of interest to photographers, videographers, and audiophiles while you're there.

SPECIAL FACTORS: Gray-market goods are not sold without the consumer's knowledge, and these come with a B&H warranty; satisfaction guaranteed; authorized returns accepted within 7 days of receipt (14 days for photographic equipment) for refund, credit, or exchange.

Buydig.com

Worldwide Direct
203 Route 22 East
Dunellen, NJ 08812
800–617–4686 x1
732–752–4466
FAX: 732–424–5136

FORM OF INFORMATION: free print catalog; online catalog

PAY: check, MO, MC, V, AE, DSC

SELLS: photography, digital imaging, and video equipment; office equipment; computers; and home electronics

STORE: no walk-in location: mail-order only; phone hours Monday to Thursday 10:00 am-7:00 pm, Friday 9:30 am–2:00 pm EST

ONLINE: www.buydig.com

Buydig.com is committed to providing you with the best selection and lowest price on everything digital. They specialize in digital cameras, printers, scanners, and digital video camcorders for home or professional use, as well as DVD players and DV editing decks. Shop by category: Photography, Camcorders, Audio/Video, Office Equipment, Computers, or Electronics or by brand: Canon, Casio, Fuji, Hewlett Packard, Kodak, Minolta, Nikon, Olympus, Panasonic, Toshiba, and more. In a price comparison between other popular online electronics stores, I found an Epson scanner for $67 less at Buydig.com and a Panasonic plasma TV for $527 less at Buydig.com. There are some very good deals here.

Note: If you're ordering a plasma TV, DVD player, scanner, fax machine, printer, receiver, or home theater, do your research and make sure this is the model and make you want. These items are not returnable after the box is opened unless there is a defect, in which case returns can be made to the manufacturer for replacement. This is one of the ways Buydig.com is able to save overhead and save you money. Over 50,000 customers have rated Buydig.com with an "outstanding" overall rating since 2000.

SPECIAL FACTORS: Authorized returns within 10 days of receipt; 10% restocking fee

Camera World

P.O. Box 19705
Irvine, CA 92623
800–226–3721
FAX: 877–552–2244

FORM OF INFORMATION: online catalog only
PAY: check, MO, MC, V, AE, DSC
SELLS: photography, digital imaging, and video equipment; home electronics
STORE: no walk-in location; mail-order only; phone hours Monday to Friday 9:00 am– 9:00 pm, Saturday 9:00 am–3:00 pm PST
ONLINE: www.cameraworld.com

Wow! When you find a company like this one, it's worth an exclamation. Rarely does one find an online merchant offering such a vast inventory of products at bargain prices coupled with user-friendly, unintimidating, easy-to-understand online shopping. As you can tell, I really like Camera World's website, and if you're in the market for video, photography, or digital imaging equipment, you're going to love it, too. This isn't a fly-by-night e-company with no retailing experience. Camera World began as a husband-and-wife operation in the late 1970s, and since that time has grown into the second largest retailer of photo and video gear in the U.S. and Canada. Prices here are excellent—routinely 20% or more below retail, with specials and clearance items dipping as low as 60% off list price. In fact, you'll notice that some items don't even have prices posted; you have to email the company for a prompt price quote because some manufacturers don't want prices this low to be advertised. But you'll save money here in other ways, too, because there's no tax, and shipping in the continental U.S. is free with any order over $100 (excludes auction, clearance, oversized and heavier items).

Camera World's departments include: Photography (cameras, lenses, flashes, bags, tripods, filters, film); Video (camcorders, editing equipment, VCRs, pro monitors, projectors); Digital (cameras, scanners, printers, camcorders, and accessories); and Electronics (CD players, DVD players, mini disc players, receivers, speakers, televisions, and tape decks). Although the inventory is broad and deep, you won't have trouble navigating around the site. Camera World is an authorized dealer for everything they sell, which means you'll find no gray-market or foreign-market goods. The customer-service people here are attentive and knowledgeable, as proven by the customer testimonials, which you can read on the site. There's also a free e-newsletter you can subscribe to and photo/video related articles.

SPECIAL FACTORS: Authorized returns in original condition accepted within 14 days of receipt (see website for detailed policies); business, school, and government accounts welcome (details at website).

Mardiron Optics

The Binocular Place
4 Spartan Circle, Dept. WBM
Stoneham, MA 02180–3230
781–938–8339

FORM OF INFORMATION: catalogs, brochures, and price lists

PAY: check or MO

SELLS: binoculars, telescopes, night-vision scopes, rangefinders, opera glasses, microscopes, rifle scopes

STORE: no walk-in location; mail-order only

 ★

I love companies with attitudes like this one. Mardiron sells high-quality products at a discount—up to 48% off—in the belief that "a customer well served is often a source of future referrals." Look no further if you're in the market for binoculars, spotting scopes, astronomical telescopes, nightvision scopes/binoculars, laser rangefinders, microscopes, opera glasses, or pistol and rifle scopes from a great range of manufacturers. Call or write to request information about manufacturers' product brochures and catalogs, price lists, and/or specific product comparisons and price quotes. Mardiron carries all models that are in current production, and sells everything at prices that are far below retail. If you can't find what you need, they'll have it shipped to you directly from the manufacturer. Recently discontinued or superseded models are further discounted; ask for this special list (which may also include models that are current, but overstocked).

Top name brands here include: Bushnell, Nikon, Swift, Steiner, Leica, Pentax, Canon, Minolta, Fujinon, Bausch & Lomb, Newcon, and many others.

At this time Mardiron does business the old-fashioned way: by phone or mail.

SPECIAL FACTORS: Price quotes by phone; shipping free within the continental U.S.

Owl Photo Corp.

701 E. Main St.
Weatherford, OK 73096
580–772–3353
FAX: 580–772–5804

FORM OF INFORMATION: free mailers and price list

PAY: check, MO, MC, V

SELLS: photo finishing and video transfer services

STORE: same address; Monday to Friday 7:30 am–5:00 pm, Saturday 9:00 am–1:00 pm

I adore straightforward, unpretentious businesses that offer impeccable service, give personal attention, and have a no-fuss attitude. By that I mean no flashy website, no glossy print catalog—just unbeatable prices and good service. Owl Photo Corp. is a real find. Talk about great deals! It would be hard to find any place—mail order, internet, or local one-hour joint—with prices lower than Owl's for color and black-and-white film processing. The prices here were 35% lower than every other discount photo developer I checked! Just give Owl a call with your name and address, and they'll send you free mailers and their current price list. Reprints and film are available here as well. Owl uses high-quality Kodak paper and chemicals. Give the friendly staff a call if you need a price quote on other photo-finishing services or video transfers. I think you'll find that doing business the old-fashioned way—by phone and mail—will pay off.

SPECIAL FACTORS: Satisfaction guaranteed; free shipping.

Porter's Camera Store, Inc.

P.O. Box 628
Cedar Falls, IA 50613
800–553–2001
319–268–0104
FAX: 800–221–5329

FORM OF INFORMATION: free print catalog within U.S., $3 for Canada, $10 international; online catalog

PAY: check, MO, MC, V, AE, DSC

SELLS: photographic, darkroom, video, and digital imaging equipment and supplies

STORE: 323 W. Viking Rd., Cedar Falls, IA; Monday to Saturday 9:30 am–5:30 pm

ONLINE: www.porters.com

Porter's Camera Store has been selling photographic and darkroom equipment since 1914. They carry more than 4,000 photo, video, and digital photography products—including many hard-to-find and unusual goods—at prices which run about 20% to 40% off list. Items in both the catalog and website are fully described and illustrated. Professionals and serious hobbyists will find the major manufacturers (over 200) and supplies represented here, but there's photography-related stuff here for everyone else, too, from kids' craft projects to gifts for grandma. Product categories include: Cameras, Digital Cameras, Lenses, Flash, Film Tripods, Camera Filters, Studio Lighting and Backgrounds, Darkroom Equipment and Supplies, Binocular and Telescopes, and Video Accessories.

WEBSITE: Porter's entire inventory is online at a site that has been redesigned and is easy to navigate. For deeper discounts check out the clearance, used equipment, and rebate and promo pages. I found the Q & A section very helpful. Online ordering is available.

SPECIAL FACTORS: Authorized returns are accepted; institutional accounts are available.

Crafts and Hobbies

All-category Craft Supplies

Craft and hobby materials, supplies, tools, and equipment for general crafts including shell craft, tole, basketry and caning, clock making, doll making, leather crafting, glass crafting, floral and potpourri, embossing, and woodworking

The firms in this general section of the "Crafts and Hobbies" chapter can provide the materials for nearly any artsy diversion—miniatures, stenciling, basketry, embossing, caning, clock making, leather crafting, stained glass, tole, decoy painting, floral and potpourri, doll making, music boxes, lamp making, candle making, woodworking, paper making, and much more.

The companies listed in this section are either general crafts suppliers with a very broad selection spanning many disciplines or are firms specializing in one item or type of goods—feathers, stained glass supplies, leather, basketry and caning, etc. For help in locating a particular item, see Find It Fast, below.

If you're looking for ceramics, pottery, or sculpture supplies, you'll find some here. But for companies that *specialize* in these goods, see the section in this chapter called "Ceramics," page 161. If creating wearables such as earrings and necklaces is your thing, check out the "Jewelry Making" section, page 167. And if you're looking for materials and equipment for the arts of spinning, weaving, knitting, sewing, quilting, soft sculpture, or other fabric and fiber art or craft, you'll find many such companies in "Textile Arts," page 171.

Soap-making supplies can be found in the "Personal Care and Beauty" section on page 295. And there are many craft-project supplies in the "Toys, Games, and Party Supplies" chapter, page 555. Depending on where you draw the line between art and craft, you're likely to find useful and related goods in the "Fine Art Supplies" chapter, page 191, as well.

Find It Fast

CANING, BASKETRY, GOURD CRAFT
The Caning Shop, Frank's Cane and Rush Supply

CLOCK-MAKING SUPPLIES
National Artcraft, Turncraft Clocks

CRAFT KITS
The Artists Club, The Caning Shop, Frank's Cane and Rush Supply, Gramma's Graphics, Vanguard Crafts, Warner-Crivellaro Stained Glass Supplies

DOLL- AND BEAR-MAKING SUPPLIES
Craft Catalog, National Artcraft

FEATHERS
Gettinger Feather

FLORAL AND POTPOURRI
Craft Catalog, Tom Thumb Workshops

GENERAL CRAFTS SUPPLIES
Craft Catalog, National Artcraft, Sunshine Discount Crafts, Vanguard Crafts

GLASS CRAFTS
Craft Catalog, Glass Crafters, Warner-Crivellaro Stained Glass Supplies

LEATHER CRAFTS
Leather Unlimited Corp.

RUBBER STAMP SUPPLIES
Sunshine Discount Crafts, Think Ink

SHELLS AND SHELL CRAFT
Benjane Arts

"SUN-PRINTING" SUPPLIES
Gramma's Graphics

THERMOGRAPHY AND EMBOSSING
Think Ink

TOLE AND DECORATIVE PAINTING
The Artists Club, Craft Catalog

The Artists Club

P.O. Box 8930
Vancouver, WA 98668–8930
800–845–6507
FAX: 360–260–8877

FORM OF INFORMATION: free print catalog; online catalog
PAY: check, MO, MC, V, AE, DSC
SELLS: tole and decorative painting supplies
STORE: Vancouver, WA; call for directions
ONLINE: www.artistsclub.com

Tole is the name of the game here. For those of you who are unfamiliar with the term, *tole* is the American folk craft of hand-painting things. If there's something you want to decorate, The Artists Club no doubt carries it. Discounts run up to 40% on items in the 88-page catalog and the sales flyers published 10 times a year. Unpainted items include wooden holiday decorations, picture and mirror frames, napkin holders, tic-tac-toe boards, end tables, bulletin boards, boxes, plant stands, jewelry boxes, children's step stools, and much more. This is *the* source for books on tole projects and techniques, which make up about half of The Artists Club business. There are also project kits and, of course, tole supplies, such as tiny brushes, paints, and stencils.

WEBSITE: Here's a nice website. It lets you search for tools and supplies, books and videos, and projects and surfaces galore. Perhaps this store should be called "Everything Unpainted"—including wood, glass, paper, canvas, and tin surfaces. Clicking through the website inspired me to think about gifts I could personalize. The friendly website also features internet-only bargains, articles, helpful hints, and secure online ordering.

SPECIAL FACTORS: Satisfaction guaranteed; returns accepted within 30 days for exchange, refund, or credit.

Benjane Arts

P.O. Box 298
West Hempstead, NY 11552
516–483–1330

FORM OF INFORMATION: $5 print catalog
PAY: check, MO, MC, V, AE
SELLS: seashells and shell craft jewelry and gift items
STORE: 111 Hempstead Turnpike, West Hempstead, NY; every day but Tuesday 10:00 am–6:00 pm

The beautiful color catalog from Benjane Arts does not get updated. Why, you ask? Don't feel bad. I asked too. It's because the inventory hasn't changed for several thousand millennia. Proprietress Lynn Rubinowitz sells seashells and shell craft in her seashore store and has been doing so for over thirty years.

Collectors, craftspeople, science teachers, children, day-care workers, and artists will love this catalog. Pictured in the catalog are examples of dozens of shells ranging from exotic pink striated conch shells and speckled multicolored bivalves to delicate sand dollars and tiny seahorses. In addition to the wonderful assortment of shells, Benjane sells treasures made from them: jewelry (earrings, shark's teeth pendants, chokers, lockets, keyrings) and gift items (paperweights, shell-decorated boxes, lamps, mirrors, napkin rings). Those in the shell business will find display items such as tripod stands, easel holders, and Lucite pronged stands. For only $1 at this writing and a self-addressed, stamped envelope, you can purchase detailed, illustrated instructions for various shell craft projects (to make shell mosaics, seascapes, and coral wreaths, for example). Benjane also carries an impressive selection of shellcraft books and supplies.

The wonderful thing about shell craft is that it requires no fancy tools or equipment. Shells are not expensive, either, in part because they are manufactured by slimy sluglike animals who don't even charge for their labor! Ms. Rubinowitz takes pride in the fact that you can purchase just one shell if you so desire. There is no minimum order. It is worthwhile, however, to stock up, since the shipping may end up costing you more than the shells themselves! Many items are discounted if you buy them in quantity, and there are a number of prepackaged shell assortments. Not everything mentioned on the accompanying price sheets is pictured. And there are frequently new and unusual items that are rare or in limited stock. If you have questions, call Benjane and they will be happy to help you find what you want. At this writing there is no website in existence, nor one planned. This is a good, old-fashioned business that deals directly with customers in person or through snail mail.

SPECIAL FACTORS: Special discounts given to museums, aquariums, and educational groups; all shipments made UPS unless otherwise requested; all jewelry and gift items are fully guaranteed; qualified wholesale buyers with I.D. may inquire for terms.

The Caning Shop

926 Gilman St.
Berkeley, CA 94710–1494
800–544–3373
510–527–5010
FAX: 510–527–7718

FORM OF INFORMATION: free print catalog, online catalog

PAY: check, MO, MC, V, DSC

SELLS: seat-reweaving, gourd-crafting, and basketry supplies

STORE: same address; Tuesday to Friday 10:00 am–6:00 pm, Saturday 10:00 am–2:00 pm

ONLINE: www.caning.com

To explore the catalog from The Caning Shop is to become immersed in a world of natural materials and quiet industry. Founded by caning expert and author Jim Widess in 1969, The Caning Shop repairs woven furniture, holds crafts workshops, and sells tools, supplies, and instructional materials for furniture repair, basketry, gourd crafts, and egg decorating. Prewoven cane webbing (in traditional and modern patterns), rawhide (especially for chair seats), genuine Danish seat cord (for Danish chairs of the 1950s), and rubber webbing (for modern Danish chairs and sofas) are some of the repair materials detailed in the catalog, along with reed splint, fiber rush, and Hong Kong grass, which can all be used on chair seats and in basketry. Pressed fiber (imitation leather) seats, easily cut and suitable for staining, are available in square, round, and quilted patterns. Professionals can pick up caning tools—awl, caning chisel, hooked spline chisel, hand clamp, utility knife, caning nippers, spline cutters, and sliver gripper; weaving tools—small, regular, heavy-duty and extra-long, with straight and bent tips; and electric tools—a miniature jig saw and a high-speed drill. Also available here are Danish nails, upholstery tacks, and "official" caning pegs (to replace those golf tees!) as well as bone and stone fetish assortments, long leaf pine needles, and kits for making baskets and keepsake pouches. About half of the 40-page catalog is devoted to instructional books on many craft topics including gourd crafting, papermaking, book binding, handmade musical instruments, and Native American designs.

WEBSITE: I liked the website, which at press time did not offer secure online ordering, but did present the full range of products, complete with excellent descriptions and photographs. Gourd crafts, basketry, furniture caning—you name it, all the supplies and books you want are here. You can download an order form off the website, fill it out, and fax or mail it in.

SPECIAL FACTORS: Satisfaction guaranteed; returns accepted for a full refund.

Craft Catalog

P.O. Box 1069
Reynoldsburg, OH 43068
800-777-1442
740-964-6210
FAX: 800-955-5915

FORM OF INFORMATION: $4 print catalog within U.S., $8 in Canada, $10 all other countries; online catalog

PAY: check, MO, MC, V, DSC

SELLS: general craft supplies

STORE: 2087-K Rt. 256; Monday to Friday 10:00 am–9:00 pm, Saturday 10:00 am–6:00 pm, Sunday 12:00 noon–5:00 pm

ONLINE: www.craftcatalog.com

Here's a catalog that will get you thinking about all the projects you wish you had time for. This would be a great resource for camp counselors, people who work with the elderly, and others looking for a one-stop craft supply source. The 96-page catalog is filled with supplies and equipment for virtually every kind of crafts discipline: woodworking, miniatures, clocks, dolls, sewing, tole, fabric painting and dyeing, wood antiquing, glass crafts, papier-mâché, box making and decorating, ornament making, stenciling, needlework, quilting, candle making, floral design, decoupage, jewelry making, potpourri, lamp making, rub-on art, lettering, folk toys, and more. And there are scores of books peppered throughout on everything from window design to foil finishing. The catalog is well indexed and organized, and the prices here are excellent, about 20% to 50% less than normal retail. You'll find coupons for certain items that bring greater savings.

WEBSITE: The website offers secure online ordering. The online version of the catalog presents a good selection of inventory, as well as new additions, current specials, and a bookrack. Every Friday they add featured specials.

SPECIAL FACTORS: Free shipping on orders of $85 or more in the continental U.S.; no C.O.D. orders accepted; quantity discounts available; free catalog with first purchase.

Frank's Cane and Rush Supply

7252 Heil Ave.
Huntington Beach, CA 92647
714-847-0707
FAX: 714-843-5645

FORM OF INFORMATION: free print catalog; online catalog

PAY: check, MO, MC, V, AE, DSC

SELLS: seat-reweaving supplies, furniture, kits, books, natural fiber matting, grasses, tropical fencing, etc.

STORE: same address; Monday to Friday 8:00 am–4:00 pm

ONLINE: www.franksupply.com

For 25 years, Frank's Cane and Rush Supply has been supplying craftspeople and shop owners with the materials and tools for chair caning, seat weaving, wicker repair, hat making, basketry, and other fiber arts. The catalog is practically a handbook on how to repair furniture and select the right materials for different jobs, with several pages devoted to instructional and reference books, posters, and topical instruction sheets you can order for a tiny sum. Frank's recommends ordering a materials sample for any product you're not sure of—for example, reed spline, oak and ash splints, Shaker tape, flat, round, and oval reeds, and colored rush—and suggests *sending in* samples to match weaves or widths. Frank's sells cane webbing, strand and binding cane, fiber and wire-fiber rush, fiber wicker, and Oriental seagrass in twisted or braided coils, matting, and carpet. While some items, such as tissue flex and welt cord (braided or twin), require a minimum yardage (10 yards), for most products you receive discounts when ordering in quantity or large sizes. The catalog depicts wood hoops and handles, wire handles, rattan rings, broom corn, wheat straw, fleece twine (for hamper repairs), sisal, jute roving, sugar plum and raw coconut fiber, and an assortment of raffia. The section on rattan poles, bamboo poles, and bamboo splits and cuts provides detailed information about sizing, condition, and uses, and offers discounts on bales of 10, 25, and 100 poles. Seat weaving kits are a simple low-cost way to learn flat-fiber seating, hand caning, and rush weaving, and pages of furniture kits (rockers and ladder-back chairs), standard tools, wood parts, and hardware provide a complete shopping opportunity.

WEBSITE: The website gives the same information and tips as the printed catalog, and orders can be placed by email.

SPECIAL FACTORS: Minimum order $10 on credit cards; authorized returns accepted (no exchanges on bamboo).

Gettinger Feather Corp.

16 W. 36th St.
New York, NY 10018
212–695–9470
FAX: 212–695–9471

FORM OF INFORMATION: free price list, samples, and website
PAY: bank check or MO
SELLS: feathers
STORE: same address (8th floor); Monday to Thursday 8:30 am–5:30 pm, Friday 8:30 am–3:00 pm
ONLINE: www.gettingerfeather.com
EMAIL: gettfeath@aol.com

Founded in New York City in 1915, Gettinger Feather Corp. is one of the leading suppliers of feathers for carnivals, theatrical companies, fashion designers, Indian crafts, and general craftspeople. This a fine source of turkey, guinea hen, pheasant, peacock, rooster, marabou, and goose feathers as well as feather boas, feather pads, and ostrich plumes. First-quality ostrich plumes, 20" to 21", run $190 per pound, but second quality, 22" to 28", in assorted colors, go for $125 per pound. An "A" quality marabou boa is $2 per yard; "B" quality, $1. Turkey feathers, packaged in 1-, 5-, and 10-pound units, start at $29 for 1 pound and drop to $16.50 for 10 pounds. Solid-color quills range from $35 per pound to $19.75 for 10 pounds. Goose feathers, in loose-soft, strung-soft, loose-stiff, and strung-stiff biots range from $69 to $72 per-pound. Coque tail feathers, either white or bronze, strung or loose, cost a pretty penny, in 1- or 5-pound units, but they are so impressive! For something more affordable and fun, the 4-page price list shows a marabou fan of 12" feathers that's under $10 at this writing. If you're seeking a good source for bedding feathers to replenish your comforter or pillow, this is the place.

WEBSITE: The website has color images of all the feathers Gettinger's offers, but you will still need to call or get a price list as prices are not included here, nor is online ordering.

SPECIAL FACTORS: Accounts welcome; minimum order: $25.

Glass Crafters

398 Interstate Ct.
Sarasota, FL 34240
800−422−4552
941−379−8333
FAX: 941−379−8827

FORM OF INFORMATION: free print catalog; online catalog

PAY: check, MO, V, MC, AE, DSC

SELLS: stained-glass and other glass-craft supplies

SHOWROOM: same address; Monday to Saturday 9:00 am−5:00 pm

ONLINE: www.glasscrafters.com

Whether you're new at stained glass or a professional craftsperson, Glass Crafters is a godsend. In business since 1975, Glass Crafters offers a wide selection of instructional videotapes, pattern books, projects, tools, supplies, and, of course, stained glass. Their 74-page catalog lists a unit price for most items and a discount price, which usually nets a 15% savings or more, even if you buy in small quantity. On many of the items, you can "mix and match" and still get the quantity discount. Bimonthly 8-page sales flyers offer specials that will save 30% to 50% on selected items (these flyers can be viewed on the company's website). But even the routine prices are better than most everyone else's—some as much as 50% better—a fact verified by a local glass artist who constantly bargain hunts for the best suppliers.

The catalog features all kinds of glass-crafting equipment and accessories: glass cutters, diamond glass grinders, specialty cutters, soldering tools, copper foil and tools, lead and brass came, glass mosaics, and more. There are sections devoted to lamp making, bead making, clock making, and box and frame making, with all the tools, parts, and hardware you'll need. You'll find cast figures, etching stencils, paints, markers, jewels, and a wide selection of patterns and pattern books for projects ranging from mosaics to quick-and-easy lamps to distinctive vases.

WEBSITE: I like this online catalog, which lets you browse for products by category and then click on the item of interest to view an image and read well-written descriptive text. The site also features web-only specials, a section for those just getting started that offers videos, books, and kits for beginners, and secure online ordering.

SPECIAL FACTORS: Satisfaction guaranteed. Returns within 14 days of receipt, not including glass, lead came, or videotapes, unless defective; minimum order is $20.

Gramma's Graphics, Inc.

49 Starview Place
Lancaster, VA 22503
800–262–1546
804–462–0884
FAX: 804–462–0882

FORM OF INFORMATION: $1 brochure if sent with LSASE; $3 outside U.S.; website

PAY: check or MO

SELLS: blueprint cloth-imaging materials

STORE: no walk-in location; mail-order only

ONLINE: www.bubblink.com/donnelly and www.grandloving.com

The "Gramma" of Gramma's Graphics is Sue Johnson, co-author of *Grandloving: Making Memories with Your Grandchildren,* which features over 200 innovative and inexpensive activity ideas to do with grandchildren or to send in the mail. An expert on fun craft projects, Johnson built an entire business around Sun Print kits, which "blueprint" an image on prepared fabric, creating a photographic representation in shades of blue that can be toned to brown, charcoal, tan, amethyst, or green. You must use 100% cotton or other natural fiber, since the imaging solution will bead up and roll off synthetics, sizing, or resins. Gramma's Graphics sells all the Sun Prints ingredients—from the imaging solution to the fabric—as well as instructions for creating the prints, assembling a pillow, and making an heirloom quilt. The 6-page brochure suggests a number of subjects for projects—family portraits, wedding invitations, certificates and degrees, treasured photographs—and other applications including clothes, banners, wall hangings, doll faces, place mats, tote bags, and more. This quick-and-easy printing process can be done right in your own backyard and results in permanent prints. With a Sun Prints kit you can make unique, unforgettable, *inexpensive* gifts.

Wholesale buyers: Minimum order for wholesale prices is 24 kits.

WEBSITE: Check out the color photographs of some finished products made with Sun Prints, such as a vest, a wedding pillow, and a keepsake quilt, and read other information about these interesting and unique prints. To purchase a Sun Print kit you will need to send them a check or money order as there is no online ordering—see website for details.

SPECIAL FACTORS: Satisfaction guaranteed; quantity discounts available.

Leather Unlimited Corp.

7155 Cty. Hwy. B, Dept. WBM
Belgium, WI 53004-9911
920-994-9464 cust. service
800-993-2889 credit card orders
FAX: 920-994-4099

FORM OF INFORMATION: $3 catalog, refundable; online catalog

PAY: check, MO, MC, V, DSC

SELLS: leather-crafting supplies and equipment and finished products

STORE: walk-in location; customer service hours Monday to Friday 7:00 am–4:00 pm

ONLINE: www.leatherunltd.com

In business since 1970, Leather Unlimited issues an 84-page catalog with photos and line drawings depicting everything from finished leather products to raccoon skins. Leather crafters will find hardware, tools, and kits; every conceivable kind of skin (caribou, rattlesnake, impala, curly sheep, rabbit, coyote, and more); leather for garments, upholstery, and belts, including dyed leather; and plenty of books and videos. Interested in Native American craft? You'll find feathers; drum parts; beads; porcupine quills; warrior headdresses; horsehair; tomahawks; replica animal talons, claws, and teeth; looms; silver buttons and conchos; and other items for making modern-day Indian-style clothing, ritual objects, jewelry, and weapons. Cowboys, Hell's Angels, and Vermont soccer moms will all find something they need among the finished items sold here: cycle gear and clothing; Western chaps and saddlebags; ladies' handbags, wallets, and cigarette cases; hats; mittens; slippers; briefcases and computer bags; bicycle seat covers; luggage tags; earrings; and more. Everything in the catalog is 30% to 50% off retail, and there is no minimum order. Extra discounts are given for quantity purchases, detailed in the catalog.

WEBSITE: The website features the print catalog pages which you can scroll through page by page, browse by category, or search by item. Click on the product descriptions along the images and you will get a larger image, for some items, and the option to order securely online if you so desire.

SPECIAL FACTORS: Authorized returns are accepted within 30 days of receipt; no minimum order; 100% satisfaction guaranteed.

National Artcraft Co.

7996 Darrow Rd.
Twinsburg, OH 44087
888-937-2723
330-963-6011
FAX: 800-292-4916 or
330-963-6711

FORM OF INFORMATION: various print catalogs (see below for prices and details); online catalog

PAY: check, MO, MC, V, DSC

SELLS: musical movements; lighting and electrical parts; doll-making, ceramics/sculpture, glass candle, snow globe, fountain pump, and clock-making supplies; and general craft supplies

STORE: no walk-in location; mail-order only; phone hours Monday to Friday 8:30 am–6:00 pm EST

ONLINE: www.nationalartcraft.com

National Artcraft is a wonderful find if you love to make lamps, clocks, music boxes, dolls, fountains, ceramic and pottery items, and just about anything else. You can buy many items in small quantities at a good price, but the prices are really great—up to 50% less—when you buy in larger quantity. Price breaks vary for each item, and unit prices are listed under each quantity so you can calculate the discounts. National Artcraft sells "wholesale direct"—they ship directly from their warehouse—but anyone can buy here as long as they meet the $40 minimum.

If, to be a happy shopper, you prefer print catalogs (as opposed to browsing and buying online), you can choose from a number of catalogs: the main catalog ($3) contains their line of craft, ceramic, and gift accessories and supplies. For doll makers, two catalogs are available: a supply catalog ($3) and a Byron doll mold catalog ($10).

The tabloid-size main catalog is currently 56 pages and growing. It contains an eclectic selection that includes all types of craft accessories: beveled glass mirrors, ballpoint desk pens, lotion pumps, oil lamp and candle accessories, decorative egg stands, fountain pumps, brushes, ceramic tools and supplies, clock movements, musical movements, and lamp-making supplies. The "Doll-making Supplies" catalog features 48 pages of eyes, hair, teeth, parasols, doll bodies, and all the tools and supplies for making dolls of every kind. The Byron mold catalog contains plaster molds and bodies for an enormous range of antique porcelain dolls. All print catalogs can be ordered online.

WEBSITE: National's website has all of their products shown in color. New items are being added daily. You can choose the items you want, place them in a shopping basket, fill out the shipping and payment information, and then order directly online. The system will price your order and calculate your discount based on quantity ordered or combinations of certain items. When you check out, a nice feature compares the "each" price with the discounted price you earned by buying in quantity or combination.

SPECIAL FACTORS: Satisfaction guaranteed; returns made within 45 days will be fully refunded if company error or manufacturer defect; quantity discounts available; main catalog to Canada and Mexico—add $1; to South America, Central America, and overseas—add $3. Byron doll mold catalog—add $3 and $8 respectively; shipping within 48 hours (2 working days) for domestic orders, foreign orders allow 5 working days.

Sunshine Discount Crafts

P.O. Box 301, Dept. WBM
Largo, FL 33779–0301
800–729–2878
727–538–2878
FAX: 727–531–2739

FORM OF INFORMATION: $5 print catalog, refundable; $10 international; online catalog

PAY: check, MO, MC, V, AE, DSC

SELLS: general crafts and hobby supplies; soap and candlemaking supplies

STORE: no walk-in location; mail-order only

ONLINE: www.sunshinecrafts.com

Leafing through Sunshine Craft's 160-page, closely printed catalog gives you the feeling of being in a giant warehouse, where one might find buckets of plastic animal eyes, barrels of colorful beads, aisles of paints, and cases of polymer clays and mosaic tiles. In fact, this catalog boasts over 14,000 products for the craftsperson and hobbyist, and you won't be disappointed by the prices—25% to 35% below regular list, with better prices on some items when you order in even small quantities. There are supplies here for doll makers, clock makers, jewelry crafters, home decorators, glass artists, woodworkers, tole fanatics, miniatures fanatics, and more. They have added soapmaking and candlemaking supplies to their vast inventory this year. There's also plenty here for the kids—beading, glitter, feathers, barrettes, baskets, dream catchers, rub-on transfers, and on and on. Whether you're making a stuffed animal, creating Easter ornaments, or decorating your own bridal headpiece, you'll find what you need here.

WEBSITE: The website has all 14,000-plus items available and secure online ordering. Check out the Sale Items for internet-only specials. All orders come with a free catalog.

SPECIAL FACTORS: See catalog for returns policy; orders under $20 require an additional $2.50; quantity discounts available on some items; wholesale buyers should inquire for terms.

Think Ink

322 NE 162nd St.
Shoreline, WA 98155
800–778–1935
425–778–1935
FAX: 206–366–2771

FORM OF INFORMATION: $2 print catalog, refundable; online catalog

PAY: check, MO, MC, V, AE, DSC

SELLS: thermography/embossing powders, GOCCO printers and supplies

STORE: same address; call for an appointment

ONLINE: www.thinkink.net

If you're part of the rubber-stamp-art craze, you're going to be very happy to find out about Think Ink. This company, says the enthusiastic owner, has perhaps the largest selection of embossing (also called thermography) powders anywhere—222 colors and counting—at prices that are about 50% to 60% less than you'll find anywhere else. When most of us think of rubber stamps, we think "Return to Sender!" or "Second Notice!" in red block letters. But today's rubber stampers are creating beautiful, masterful art. This is an unbeatable source.

In addition to stocking embossing powders, Think Ink sells GOCCO printers, supplies, and creative accessories for printing your own colorful flyers, bulletins, cards, tote bags, T-shirts, and nearly anything else made of paper, card stock, fabric, leather, or wood. More than 7 million GOCCO printers have been purchased in Japan and elsewhere for home use since their introduction a generation ago. (In Japan, serious artists use large-format GOCCO printers to produce limited-edition, fine-art prints, an art form known as Shin Kohanga.) Think Ink sells 3 models of Print GOC-COs, the B6 model (with a 4" × 5³/4" image area) and two Print Arts, one for paper (6.9" x 9.3" image area) the other for cloth (5.7" x 9.3" image area). These printers work by creating a master of your design that can be inked like a silkscreen and printed. Until you have a good look at the catalog and website, you may not be exactly sure what these printers are capable of. Once you do, you'll be tempted to buy *The New GOCCO Guide,* a 245-page guide penned by no other than Think Ink's owner, Claire Russell, that offers project ideas, steers you through tricks and traps, and generally aids you in getting the most out of this marvelous home printer.

WEBSITE: The website, which offers online ordering, is a good place to find out more about these extremely cool presses and the bargain embossing powders. By the way, if you find yourself at an online tattoo site, you made the same mistake I did and typed *.com* rather than *.net.*

SPECIAL FACTORS: Wholesale orders accepted; inquire for terms.

Tom Thumb Workshops

59 Market St.
Onancock, VA 23417
800-526-6502
757-787-9596
FAX: 757-787-3136

FORM OF INFORMATION: free price list; online catalog

PAY: check, MO, MC, V, AE, DSC

SELLS: crafting supplies for potpourri, soap making, candle making, pressed flowers, etc.

STORE: same address; Monday to Friday 9:30 am–5:00 pm, Saturday 9:30 am–1:30pm EST

ONLINE: www.tomthumbworkshops.com

With items from a Tom Thumb Workshops catalog, you could make your own personal massage oil or create beautiful pressed-flower art. You could make your own soaps or seashell art. Or you could order herbs and dried flowers, fabric sachets, and potpourri boxes and then make heartfelt Christmas gifts throughout the year—at prices 20% to 45% below those charged elsewhere. Tom Thumb carries booklets and crafting designs, patterns and illustrated how-tos, and full-sized texts to help take the mystery out of potpourri crafts, card crafting, wreath making, herbal soap making, blending of essential oils, and many more activities that are good for the soul and have practical application. There are a lot of little goodies here you won't find elsewhere, such as simmering spices, little decorator boxes and bottles, incense, and refresher oils for potpourris. An additional saving of 25%, except for items from the "bulk oil list," applies on orders of $100 and higher.

WEBSITE: Do check out the nice website that includes beautiful color images of many items. If you're looking for a particular dried flower, for example, and don't know what it looks like, the online catalog is a better option than the printed price list that has no product photographs. Online ordering is available.

SPECIAL FACTORS: Satisfaction guaranteed; authorized returns accepted within 21 days.

Turncraft Clocks, Inc.

P.O. Box 70
Mound, MN 55364–0070
800–544–1711
FAX: 952–471–8579

FORM OF INFORMATION: free print catalog; online catalog

PAY: check, MO, MC, V, DSC

SELLS: clock plans and movements, general woodworking plans

STORE: 4310 Shoreline Dr., Spring Park, MN; Tuesday to Friday 10:00 am–4:00 pm, Saturday 10:00 am–2:00 pm

ONLINE: www.meiselwoodhobby.com

With nearly 30 years of experience, Turncraft Clocks continues to offer woodworkers and clock makers plans for cabinets (curio, jewelry, gun), humidors, coffee tables, desk sets, lamps and floor, wall, mantle, and patio clocks. They also stock the parts (but not the wood, in most cases): a full selection of movements—regular mini-quartz, pendulum, dual chime, six-melody chime—decorative tubes, clock hands, clock dials, numbers, hardware, and decals. Clearly written descriptions in the 32-page catalog help with selecting correct sizes and appropriate styles. Lamp parts packages (basic, universal, and three-way), drill bits, glue, stains, and router bits are also available.

WEBSITE: The design of this website is simple and clean. Turncraft shares this site with Meisel Hardware Specialties and Wood to Paint. In the online catalog you'll find over 170 different wood clocks and a good selection of clock movements, dials and hardware. They offer web specials and online ordering.

SPECIAL FACTORS: Satisfaction guaranteed; school accounts with purchase order.

Vanguard Crafts

P.O. Box 340170
Brooklyn, NY 11234
800–66–CRAFT
718–377–5188
FAX: 888–692–0056

FORM OF INFORMATION: free print catalog, online catalog

PAY: check, MO, MC, V, DSC

SELLS: crafts kits and materials

STORE: 1081 E. 48th St., Brooklyn, NY; Monday to Saturday 10:00 am–5:00 pm

ONLINE: www.vanguardcrafts.com

If you manage a classroom, an after-school program, a day-care center, or a household of children, the catalog from Vanguard Crafts can help you plan instructive, interesting, even "cool" projects—not only for the kids! Since 1959, Vanguard has made crafts kits and projects affordable while updating the inventory to keep apace with current fads. One year it may be friendship pins and hemp 'n bead bracelets; the next it may be granulated candles and no-bake suncatchers. The colorful 79-page catalog introduces kits for fantasy masks complete with decorating materials, mini-totes, preassembled wooden boxes ready for finishing and decoration, papier-mâché dance rattles, creative collage boxes, Wonderfoam mosaic tiles, plastic jewels, button picture frames, pom-pom pals, coil baskets, and many more fun, unique, and interesting projects. Vanguard has kits and supplies for tissue art, printmaking, tie dyeing, weaving, basket making, sponge painting, scratch art, modeling, calendar making, crocheting, beading, and almost every art or craft you can think of, including leather and woodworking, calligraphy, and stenciling. Brushes, artists' supplies, and tools are also available—for example, brush packs ideal for classrooms, art papers, paints, craft scissors, knife sets and snips, and jewelry pliers.

WEBSITE: The website is well organized and easy to use with colorful pictures, clear descriptions and you can order online.

SPECIAL FACTORS: Minimum order $25; institutional accounts from accredited organizations are welcome, and bids and quotations are invited.

Warner-Crivellaro Stained Glass Supplies, Inc.

1855 Weaversville Rd.
Allentown, PA 18109
800–523–4242
FAX: 800–523–5012

FORM OF INFORMATION: $4 print catalog, $10 outside U.S.; online catalog

PAY: check, MO, MC, V, AE, DSC

SELLS: stained-glass tools and supplies

STORE: same address; Monday to Wednesday and Friday to Saturday 9:00 am–5:00 pm, Thursday 9:00 am–8:00 pm EST

ONLINE: www.warner-criv.com

Allentown, Pennsylvania, is home to Warner-Crivellaro's 40,000-square-foot warehouse and showrooms of glass, bevels, filigree, wooden boxes, flowers, lamp prisms, and more for the stained-glass enthusiast. The 236-page catalog and the comprehensive website bring the quality and service of Warner-Crivellaro into your home. Shoppers can order boxed sample sets of glass (2" × 3") marked with a manufacturer's color number and representing everything available from a particular manufacturer. "Bargain Boxes" are an economical way to stock up on first-quality glass (10 sheets, 8" × 10" or 12" × 12") at great prices. Bevels—plain, engraved, in holiday and seasonal themes—drop in price when ordered in mix-and-match quantities; nuggets, nugget foilers, marbles, jewels, and night-light filigrees receive quantity price breaks, too. If you're looking for a grinder, a soldering iron, a tubing cutter, or an electric engraver to fashion your own tables, windows, and lamps, all are here in name-brand models. Warner-Crivellaro is so determined to win you over that they offer a lowest price guarantee, as well as excellent customer service and policies.

WEBSITE: I recommend logging on to the website, where you'll be able to shop online for the same merchandise available in the print version, as well as hundreds of other items you'll find only online. At the website, Technical Tips offers lessons on working with lampshades, copper foil, soldering, leading, and glass cutting. Online sales run limited-time discounts of 10% to 30% off Warner's usual prices, and web specials offer additional reductions. Over 159 free patterns which include night-lights, quilt squares, and Pennsylvania Dutch designs are available online, too.

SPECIAL FACTORS: Phone orders available 24 hours a day; call about matching glass and making special orders; authorized returns accepted; minimum order $25.

Ceramics

Materials and equipment for pottery, sculpture, and other ceramic crafts

Most people think of mugs, pots, and bowls when they think of ceramics. But people who love to work with clay also make lamps, clocks, jewelry, mirrors, tile, ornaments, sculptures, candlesticks, porcelain boxes—the list is as endless as the craftsperson's imagination. For all of the little parts, tools, and accessories you need to create these items, look to the companies below, but don't forget that many of the general craft companies in the previous section, starting on page 141 carry them, too. You'll find ceramics supplies, tools, and even heavy equipment, such as kilns, carried by the companies in this chapter. Because they want your mail-order business, most companies will give you incentives to buy kilns and other heavy goods by offering free or very inexpensive shipping.

Find It Fast

BOOKS ON CERAMIC ART AND TECHNIQUE
Aftosa, Axner Pottery Supply, Bailey Ceramic Supply, Clay-King.com

CLAYS, SLIPS, AND GLAZES
Axner Pottery Supply, Bailey Ceramic Supply

CRAFT PROJECT SUPPLIES
Aftosa, Axner Pottery Supply, Lou Davis Wholesale

INSTRUCTIONAL VIDEOS
Axner Pottery Supply, Bailey Ceramic Supply, Clay-King.com

LARGE EQUIPMENT (WHEELS, KILNS)
Axner Pottery Supply, Bailey Ceramic Supply, Clay-King.com, Lou Davis Wholesale

POTTER'S SAFETY GEAR
Axner Pottery Supply, Clay-King.com

POTTERY DISPLAY ITEMS
Aftosa

POTTERY SUPPLIES, TOOLS, AND ACCESSORIES
Bailey Ceramic Supply, Clay-King.com

UNPAINTED BISQUEWARE
Aftosa

Aftosa

1034 Ohio Ave.
Richmond, CA 94804
800–231–0397
510–233–0334
FAX: 510–233–3569

FORM OF INFORMATION: free print catalog; online catalog

PAY: check, MO, MC, V, AE, DSC

SELLS: pottery accessories, craft supplies and bisqueware

STORE: no walk-in location; mail-order only; phone hours Monday to Friday 8:00 am–5:00 pm PST

ONLINE: www.aftosa.com

For over 20 years Aftosa has been a leader in providing accessories for the potter and ceramic artist. Their mission is to search the world for accessories that help you "finish" your designs. There are supplies here for all your ceramic projects. Dispenser pumps; pin frogs for flower arranging (you create the container/base); wire, cane, and rattan handles for ceramic baskets, teapots, and other vessels; metal stands for candle holders; bottle spigots and stoppers; cotton and fiberglass wick, as well as oil burners and glass chimneys; wooden accessories such as honey sticks and salad servers; mirrors; clocks and jewelry parts; display stands; cork (composition, bark-top, and natural); metal and glass shades; wooden trivet boxes; and, of course, potter's tools and supplies can all be found here at prices that are 35% to 50% less than retail. Aftosa also carries white bisqueware kits ready to be glazed and fired. All items, including bisqueware, are shipped freight free in the contiguous United States. Expedited shipping is available at the customer's cost. The handling and packaging charge for orders under $100 is $6 and $3 for orders over $100.

WEBSITE: Aftosa's complete catalog is online with specials and new product updates. Product images are in color as well as some black-and-white illustrations. In addition to the ceramic accessories, the website offers bisque, display items, books, closeouts (20% to 50% off), information on contract manufacturing, an online gallery, and a resource page. You can order online.

SPECIAL FACTORS: Orders to Hawaii, Alaska, Canada, and other international orders are charged the actual freight cost; returns are subject to a 15% restocking fee; shipping free in continental U.S.

Axner Pottery Supply

P.O. Box 621484
Oviedo, FL 32762–1484
800–843–7057
407–365–2600
FAX: 407–365–5573

FORM OF INFORMATION: free print catalog; online catalog

PAY: check, MO, MC, V

SELLS: pottery supplies, books, and videos

WAREHOUSE/SHOWROOM: 804-A Eyrie Dr., Oviedo, FL; Monday to Friday 9:00 am–5:00 pm, Thursday 9:00 am–7:00 pm, Saturday 9:00 am–2:00 pm

ONLINE: www.axner.com

A professional potter recommended Axner Pottery Supply as a good source with reasonable prices. Axner's goods average about 20% less than what you'd find in a ceramic supply shop—if you're lucky enough to live near one. The 192-page catalog has a lot of explanatory text alongside the photographs of products, which makes it a good resource. Quantity price breaks are included for many items, and suggested retail prices versus Axner's prices are also listed on some, but not all, products. Here you'll find equipment, tools, and supplies for making tile, jewelry, pots and dishes, lamps, clocks, and more. You'll find the big equipment here—kilns, wheels, and mixers, for example—as well as clay and glazes of all types. (There's an 8-page color insert for the glazes.) Axner claims to have the largest supply of pottery supplies and equipment "in the known universe," so just about any tool, finishing supply, or other pottery-related item you seek will be here. Be sure to leaf through the pottery/ceramics books and videos section, for which Axner is renowned.

WEBSITE: What about Gerstley Borate? Go to the website to find out. While you're there, you'll find Axner's complete inventory: books, videos, equipment, clay and materials, glazes, tools, and supplies—plus monthly specials and closeouts—laid out in a comprehensive, easy to use format with clear color product images. You can order right off the website.

SPECIAL FACTORS: Satisfaction guaranteed; 30-day return policy; wholesale orders accepted.

Bailey Ceramic Supply

P.O. Box 1577
Kingston, NY 12402
800–431–6067
845–339–3721
FAX: 845–339–5530

FORM OF INFORMATION: free print catalog; online catalog

PAY: check, MO, MC, V

SELLS: professional ceramic supplies and equipment

SHOWROOM: 62 Ten Broeck Ave., Kingston, NY; by appointment, Monday to Friday 9:00 am–12:00 noon, 12:30–4:30 pm; phone hours Monday to Friday 9:00 am–5:00 pm EST

ONLINE: www.baileypottery.com

Jim Bailey and his wife, Anne Shattuck Bailey, are dedicated ceramists. Since 1984, Bailey has been supplying professional potters with great products that are up to 25% less than retail when you buy in quantity, and major name-brand pottery equipment at "the lowest prices in the USA." Bailey also manufactures many of its own products, such as extruders, slab rollers, potters wheels, and kilns, and sells them at factory-direct prices. The 184-page color catalog offers chemicals, clays, and glazes; small tools and accessories; hand-building equipment; wheels and wheel accessories; mixing equipment; kilns; safety, production, storage, and spray equipment; packing materials; display and accessory items; lamp and jewelry accessories; an extensive video and book library; and much more.

WEBSITE: Bailey's entire inventory is available online. This is the place to get the most updated information and prices as the print catalog is produced every two years. Online ordering is available. However, for large items, such as gas kilns, it is best to call Bailey and speak with one of their advisor staff so that you can be assured of selecting the best engineered system for your specific application.

SPECIAL FACTORS: Satisfaction guaranteed on every order; five professional potters on staff to answer questions; most orders shipped within 48 hours.

Clay-King.com

108 Garner Rd.
Spartanburg, SC 29303
864–585–6014
888–838–3625
FAX: 864–582–3936

FORM OF INFORMATION: online catalog only, no print catalog

PAY: check, MO, MC, V, AE, DSC

SELLS: professional ceramic supplies and equipment

STORE: no walk-in location; mail-order only

ONLINE: www.clay-king.com

My sister, a professional sculptor, bought an L & L kiln last year from a good local discount ceramic supplier. If she had bought the same kiln from this company, she would have saved $300 (including shipping). Clay-King.com is a great online source for basic and specialized pottery supplies, tools and accessories of all kinds. They carry known brands such as Olympic, Paragon, Creative Industries, North Star, Scott Creek, Doo Woo, Sherrill Mudtools, Kemper, and more at discount prices. In addition to kilns, you'll find potters wheels, slab rollers, extruders, ware carts, wedging boards, pottery tools, air brushes, and books and tapes. This site is nicely designed and provides plenty of information about choosing, buying, installing, and firing your kiln. Click on links to manufacturers' websites to learn more about their warranties and guarantees for different kilns and wheels.

The staff at Clay-King.com are experienced and knowledgeable with over 35 years combined experience. They are dedicated to giving you full customer support—both before and after the sale.

SPECIAL FACTORS: Satisfaction guaranteed; return any undamaged products, new or used, for any reason within 14 days; return any unopened and unused items within 3 months; no restocking fees; full refund of purchase price, less shipping; always inspect your shipment before signing for it.

Lou Davis Wholesale

N3211 County Rd. H
P.O. Box 21
Lake Geneva, WI 53147
800–748–7991
262–248–2000
FAX: 262–248–6977

FORM OF INFORMATION: $2 print catalog
PAY: check, MO, MC, V, AE, DSC
SELLS: hobby ceramic and craft supplies
STORE: no walk-in location; mail-order only; phone hours Monday to Friday 8:00 am–8:00 pm, Saturday 8:00 am–4:00 pm CST
ONLINE: www.loudavis.com

If you've seen one crafts supply catalog, you've seen 'em all, right? Well, no, not exactly. For instance, I found that Lou Davis Wholesale, in business for over 40 years, stood out from the pack. This is a straightforward company presenting real savings to ceramists by offering a lowest-price guarantee, quantity discounts, and a good selection of basic supplies for hobby ceramics, lamp making, music boxes, clocks, dolls, and many items for crafting. The 40-page newsprint tabloid-style catalog has hundreds of products drawn or photographed, with descriptions and different price breakdowns—the more you order, the more you save. If you're serious about saving, you can even phone and ask for higher quantity discounts.

WEBSITE: At the website a sampling of products, which include brushes, clocks, doll items, electrical/lampmaking, fountain pumps, and paints and finishes, are presented in the context of projects. This site is a good resource for project ideas, articles, and tips—but you will need a print catalog to see all of the products Lou Davis offers. There is no online ordering available. There is an online order form that you can download and print out and then call in your order with your order form all filled out in your hot little hand. This makes it easier for the kind folks at Lou Davis to process your order. Or, you can mail or fax the order form.

SPECIAL FACTORS: Complete satisfaction guaranteed; returns accepted within 90 days.

Jewelry Making

Beads, stones, gems, findings, and supplies for making fine and craft jewelry

There are some mail-order catalogs that make you dream. I've really enjoyed reading and learning about cultured pearls, Czechoslovakian beadery, Native American silver-smithing, investment-grade stones, and many other eclectic and fascinating subjects you'll find in this section's company literature. If you've ever considered making your own earrings, rings, pendants, bracelets, pins, and necklaces, or wanted to turn an ordinary item such as a pill box, barrette, or money clip into something valuable and precious, the firms below will provide you with many-faceted avenues to do so, from inexpensive materials, tools, and accessories to rare and precious metals and cut gems. Have fun!

Find It Fast

BEADS
Fire Mountain Gems, Hong Kong Lapidaries

GEMSTONES
Eloxite, Fire Mountain Gems, Hong Kong Lapidaries

JEWELRY-CRAFT "BLANKS" (NONJEWELED ITEMS)
Eloxite

JEWELRY FINDINGS
Eloxite, Fire Mountain Gems

PEARLS
Fire Mountain Gems, Hong Kong Lapidaries

THREAD AND SILK
Eloxite, Fire Mountain Gems, Hong Kong Lapidaries

Eloxite Corporation

P.O. Box 729, Dept. 8
Wheatland, WY 82201
307–322–3050
FAX: 307–322–3055

FORM OF INFORMATION: free print catalog; online catalog
PAY: check, MO, MC, V, DSC
SELLS: rock hound, jewelry craft, and beadmaking supplies
STORE: 806 Tenth St., Wheatland, WY; Monday to Friday 8:30 am–4:00 pm, Saturday 8:30 am–2:30 pm
ONLINE: www.eloxite.net

Since 1955, Eloxite has been selling jewelry craft supplies, and supplies and equipment for those who collect agates, gems, and minerals for cutting, polishing, or engraving to create their own jewelry and rock crafts. Prices here are up to 75% below those charged by other crafts sources for findings and jewelry components. Jewelry findings with a western flair are featured in the 100-page catalog: bola ties and slide medallions, belt buckles and inserts, and coin jewelry are prominent offerings. Also shown are pendants, rings, earrings, lockets, tie tacks, jewelry boxes, money clips, barrettes, pins, and more, made to be set with cabochons or cut stones, as well as jump rings, chains, pill boxes, screw eyes, and ear wires. The stones themselves are solid-cut cubic zirconia and synthetic gemstones and oval cabochons of abalone, agate, black onyx, garnet, opal, obsidian, jasper, and malachite. There's also a full range of beads and beading supplies, tools and equipment, including tumblers, soldering tools, grinding wheels, and more.

Sandwiched between the pages of jewelry components are quartz clock movements and blanks for clock faces, clock hands, and ballpoint pens and letter openers for desk sets. Discounts are available on most items, and specials are usually offered with orders of specified amounts.

WEBSITE: At the website, there aren't any fancy bells and whistles, only quick links to the items you seek. Products are photographed, in most cases, and accompanied by detailed descriptions. Click on a category and you'll be zipped to the next section, where your choice is narrowed, until you've found precisely the diamond blade, rock hammer, or freshwater pearls you need. Online ordering is available.

Fire Mountain Gems

One Fire Mountain Way
Grants Pass, OR 97526–2373
800–423–2319
FAX: 800–292–3473

FORM OF INFORMATION: free print catalog; online catalog

PAY: check, MO, MC, V, AE, DSC

SELLS: beads, jewels, gems, and supplies for jewelry making

STORE: no walk-in location; mail-order only

ONLINE: www.firemountaingems.com

You know you've found a gem of a company when you read their mail-order catalog and want to meet the owners. They share their philosophy about working cooperatively with village people in 14 developing countries to obtain interesting products ethically and constructively. Fire Mountain Gems has been around for 25 years and publishes a 580-plus page color catalog that's a jewelry-maker's dream come true. I'm not talking plastic beads here. This is a serious source for serious artisans. Price breaks are listed for each item; buying a single item in small quantity can net you a savings of 40%. Czech glass beads; Austrian crystal beads; seed beads; shell strands; porcupine quills; porcelain beads; pewter pendants; freshwater cultured pearls of every size, color, and description; gem beads; gold, silver, and other metal beads; cloisonné beads and pendants; faceted gems; cabochons; findings; tools; supplies such as beading twine, hemp cord, and suede thong—the list goes on and on. Suffice it to say that if you want to make jewelry, Fire Mountain Gems will have what you're looking for at prices you can live with.

WEBSITE: The website has the full inventory available—26,000-plus products. At the outlet store, you'll find many items at low closeout prices—up to 75% off. Don't forget to check out the weekly specials. Online ordering is available and there is no sales tax.

SPECIAL FACTORS: Any unaltered item can be returned for refund, credit, or exchange; see catalog for details.

Hong Kong Lapidaries, Inc.

2801 University Dr.
Coral Springs, FL 33065
954–755–8777
FAX: 954–755–8780

FORM OF INFORMATION: $5 print catalog request by fax, email, or mail; online catalog
PAY: check, MO, MC, V
SELLS: jewelry supplies, beads, cabochons, pearls, and loose stones
STORE: no walk-in location; mail-order only
ONLINE: www.hklap.com
EMAIL: menash1@aol.com

Hong Kong Lapidaries, established in 1979, sells a wide range of precious and semi-precious stones in a variety of forms. The 80-page catalog lists items of interest to hobbyists as well, and the prices run as much as 70% below comparable retail. Thousands of cabochons; beads; loose-faceted and cut stones (heart shapes and charms, flowers and leaves, rings, donuts, and more); mosaic stones; strung chips of pearl, garnet, amethyst, onyx, abalone, and other kinds of semiprecious stones are offered through the catalog, which comes with a separate 12-page color brochure that shows representative pieces. Egyptian clay scarabs, coral, cameos, cubic zirconia, yellow jade, cloisonné jewelry and objets d'art, and 14k gold-filled and sterling silver beads are available. Hobbyists should note the necklace thread—100% silk or nylon—in a score of colors and sizes, as well as stringing needles. Prices per piece are lower when you order in quantity. If you're serious about jewelry making, you'll appreciate this catalog, which is packed with good value, but not overly concerned with flashy illustrations or jazzy presentation. Most of the items are listed in chart form for the educated consumer.

WEBSITE: The website lets you view the print catalog on your screen, page by page, in black and white. Orders should be faxed as there is no secure online ordering. There's also a section of dazzling color images of stones, gems, and beads that add appeal to the lackluster pages in the online catalog.

SPECIAL FACTORS: Satisfaction is guaranteed; price quotes by fax; quantity discounts available; returns accepted within 12 days; minimum order: $50.

Textile Arts

Material and equipment for sewing, spinning, knitting, weaving, quilting, needlework, dyeing, and other textile arts and crafts

Once upon a time—and not so long ago, either—sewing, quilting, and knitting were common activities in most homes. Today, making your own clothes, curtains, table-cloths, blankets, and other home accessories is a great way to save money, assuming you have the time. The companies in this chapter can help you find all the right tools and materials for your projects. You'll find everything from raw fleece for spinning and large looms for rug weaving to professional dress forms for designing your own gowns and undyed silk for batiking. There's also lots here for the everyday knitter or mender just looking for some bargain supplies. Every kind of textile artist will find plenty here to love, at huge savings.

Other chapters in this book sell textile-related supplies and equipment, particularly "Fine Art Supplies" and two sections of the "Home" chapter: "Appliances and TVs" and "Wall and Window Treatments, Decorator Fabrics."

Find It Fast

BATTING, PILLOW INSERTS, FIBERFILL
Buffalo Batt & Felt, Connecting Threads, Monterey Incorporated

BEADING SUPPLIES
Newark Dressmaker Supply

CUSTOM-MADE ZIPPERS
The Button Shop, A. Feibusch

DOLL-MAKING SUPPLIES
Newark Dressmaker Supply, Taylor's Cutaways and Stuff

DRAPERY HARDWARE
Atlanta Thread & Supply

DRESS FORMS
Atlanta Thread & Supply, Solo Slide Fasteners

FABRIC
Connecting Threads, Fashion Fabrics Club, Taylor's Cutaways and Stuff, Thai Silks, Utex Trading Enterprises

FABRIC DYES
Dharma Trading

FAKE FUR
Monterey Incorporated, Taylor's Cutaways and Stuff

LOOMS
Great Northern Weaving, Webs

PERSONAL SEWING MACHINES
Solo Slide Fasteners

PROFESSIONAL SEWING, PRESSING, AND DRY CLEANING MACHINES
Atlanta Thread & Supply, Solo Slide Fasteners

QUILTING PATTERNS AND SUPPLIES
Connecting Threads, Taylor's Cutaways and Stuff

RUG-MAKING SUPPLIES
Great Northern Weaving

SEWING MACHINE PARTS
Atlantic Thread & Supply, The Button Shop, Newark Dressmaking Supply, Solo Slide Fasteners

SEWING NOTIONS AND TOOLS
Atlanta Thread & Supply, The Button Shop, A. Feibusch, Newark Dressmaker Supply, Solo Slide Fasteners

UNDYED FABRIC AND CLOTHING BLANKS FOR DYEING
Dharma Trading, Thai Silks

UPHOLSTERY SUPPLIES
Atlantic Thread & Supply, The Button Shop, Newark Dressmaking Supply, Solo Slide Fasteners

YARNS AND RAW FIBER FOR SPINNING
Mangham Manor Fiber Farm, Smiley's Yarns, Bonnie Triola Yarns, Webs

Atlanta Thread & Supply

695 Red Oak Rd.
Stockbridge, GA 30281
800–847–1001
770–389–9115
FAX: 800–298–0403

FORM OF INFORMATION: free print catalog; online catalog

PAY: check, MO, MC, V, AE, DSC

SELLS: sewing tools, notions, and pressing equipment

STORE: no walk-in location; mail-order only; phone hours Monday to Friday, 8:30 am–5:30 pm EST

ONLINE: www.atlantathread.com

Atlanta Thread & Supply, a division of National Thread & Supply Corp., has been in the business of providing professionals with sewing equipment and supplies since 1948. Extremely competitive pricing—30% to 40% less than retail, in many cases—and a high level of customer service make this a worthy company to know about, particularly if you can buy items in quantity, where deeper discounts apply.

The 64-page catalog presents photographs or line drawings with no-nonsense product descriptions. Tailors, upholsterers, dressmakers, and those who do serious sewing at home will appreciate the wide selection of threads (all-purpose, embroidery, serging, buttonhole, etc.), dress and tailoring forms, sewing supplies, linings, buttons, scissors, cleaning items, drapery-making supplies and hardware, crinolines, tapes, irons and pressing tables, professional and at-home sewing machines and machine parts, and more. I liked the Uniquely New dress form and pant/skirt forms; when you lose or gain weight, adjust the form's cover and it will compress or expand to your new size! Don't be looking for cutesy arts and craft items in this catalog. This is a serious supplier of top-name products for professional-caliber sewing.

WEBSITE: The website is straightforward and easy to use. Clicking on a product yields a color photograph, product description, and suggested retail price next to Atlanta Thread's price, which is significantly lower. You can order right on the website, but be aware that the online catalog does not carry as many items as the print catalog.

SPECIAL FACTORS: Satisfaction guaranteed; returns accepted for refund or exchange; quantity discounts apply; C.O.D.s accepted; same day shipping on orders received before 2:00 pm EST.

Buffalo Batt & Felt Corp.

3307 Walden Ave.
Depew, NY 14043
716–683–4100
FAX: 716–683–8928

FORM OF INFORMATION: $1 brochure and samples, refundable; online catalog

PAY: check, MO, MC, V

SELLS: fiberfill, quilt batts, pillow inserts, decorative "snow"

STORE: no walk-in location; mail-order only

ONLINE: www.superfluff.com

Haven't you always wondered what made cloth dolls and hand-crafted pillows so springy, washable, *and* affordable? Buffalo Batt & Felt Corp. probably has the answer, with its Super Fluff bouncy polyester stuffing; Ultra Fluff, a premium fiberfill; Soft Heart Quallofil pillow inserts; and "thermabonded" quilt batt. With an array of desirable properties (high loft, nonallergenic, flame-retardant, machine washable, easy to sew), Buffalo Batt's fiberfill, quilt batts, and pillow inserts are available in convenient small sizes as well as bulk, at substantial savings on normal retail prices. Buffalo Batt & Felt also sells Buffalo Snow products—Christmas tree skirts, loose flakes (for window or display decorating), snow blankets, and other items. The sample-laden catalog gives details about thicknesses, sizes of rolls and inserts, and the differences among products. Since there's a two-case minimum, you'd do well to team up with a friend.

WEBSITE: The website has lots of information, as well as excellent photographs and descriptions of the products and a FAQ section that textile artists especially will appreciate. Online is also where you'll find out about industrial products (minimum order 1,000 pounds) with bedding, furniture, and even acoustical applications. Prices are not listed at the website, nor is online ordering. Go ahead and give them a call and they'll be happy to give you prices and assist you.

The Button Shop

P.O. Box 272
Des Plaines, IL 60016–0272
TEL: 847–795–9964
FAX: 847-795-9968

FORM OF INFORMATION: free print catalog
PAY: check, MO, MC, V
SELLS: buttons and sewing supplies
STORE: no walk-in location; mail-order only
EMAIL: ButtonShop@aol.com

The Button Shop calls itself "America's source for discount sewing supplies for over 100 years." Among the items offered in the 18-page black-and-white catalog are zippers (cut to any size and color-matched to your fabric if you send in a 2" fabric swatch); a good selection of top-name scissors; odds and ends, such as vest buckles and suspender clips; Signature thread; thread for serger machines; interfacings; tapes; binders; elastics; quilting supplies; shoulder pads; pins and needles; hooks and eyes; sewing machine parts; miscellaneous sewing gadgets; and of course, buttons. There are buttons for children's wear and craft projects, plain white buttons, make-your-own covered buttons, buttons of glass or wood, military-style buttons, colored buttons, gold-rimmed buttons, pea-coat buttons, fancy ladies' buttons—you name it. In spite of the fact that the catalog lacks detailed descriptions or colors, I like this company's old-fashioned approach to mail-order that relies more on its customers' knowledge than on glitsy layouts. The Button Shop's prices are about 30% to 40% below what you'd find in retail stores.

SPECIAL FACTORS: Minimum order $5, or $10 if paying with credit card; returns accepted within 30 days.

Connecting Threads

P.O. Box 8940
Vancouver, WA 98668–8940
800–574–6454
FAX: 360–260–8877

FORM OF INFORMATION: free print catalog; online catalog

PAY: check, MO, MC, V, AE, DSC, JCB

SELLS: fabrics, quilting patterns, materials, and supplies

STORE: 13118 NE 4th St., Vancouver, WA; Monday to Friday 10:00 am–6:00 pm, Saturday 10:00 am–5:00 pm

ONLINE: www.connectingthreads.com

Newfound respect at auctions these days for traditional early-American quilts has spawned a resurgence in the art of quilting. Connecting Threads is an invaluable source for "the busy quilter" with its 64-page color catalog of fabrics, patterns, instructional books on quilting and other textile arts, and a full inventory of quilter's handy tools and basic supplies: quilting stencils, frames and batting, cotton thread, slash cutters, slice rulers, bias tape, flexible-angle lamps, thread, basting guns, cutting mats, pencil remover solution, and much more. Prices here are about 20% below retail.

WEBSITE: If you are a quilter, you will want to bookmark Connecting Thread's website. This firm now carries thousands of fabrics and hundreds of fabric samplers. The website is definitely the better way to shop over the print catalog, particularly to mix and match patterns and colors together. First you pick your fabrics out—search by individual fabrics, designer collection, manufacturer, subject, color, or scale. When your search results come up, you can look at an enlarged picture of the fabric by clicking on the sample. And then—here's the really cool part—you can send up to 32 fabrics to the Design Table to see how they work together. Then you can view them four ways: "close up," "arms length," "from across the room," and in gray scale (to see the contrast). There are all sorts of weekly web-only bargains available, and, of course, online ordering.

SPECIAL FACTORS: Satisfaction guaranteed; returns accepted for credit, refund, or exchange within 30 days.

Dharma Trading Co.

P.O. Box 150916
San Rafael, CA 94915–0916
800–542–5227
415–456–7657
FAX: 415–456–8747

FORM OF INFORMATION: free print catalog; online catalog

PAY: check, MO, MC, V, DSC

SELLS: textile craft supplies and clothing "blanks"

STORE: 1604 Fourth St., San Rafael, CA; Monday to Saturday 10:00 am–6:00 pm

ONLINE: www.dharmatrading.com

It's a pleasure to pass along information about firms like Dharma Trading Co. This consumer-friendly company sells undyed fabric, garments, hats, and accessories for women, men, and children of all sizes, and the dyes, fabric paints, batik supplies, markers, and tools to color and decorate them. Dharma's policies are as plain as their goods: Prices are discounted from list about 20%, and the per-unit prices drop even more if you can order in a small quantity. Quantity discounts apply to the total amount ordered, not the type or style, which means you can mix and match and still get the best prices. The wearables in the 133-page catalog include silk items, including baseball caps, sun visors, hair bows, neckties, T-shirts, ponchos, tank tops, skirts, over vests, boxers, chemises, and camisoles; cotton, jersey, and hemp items, including infant rompers, toddler T-suits, short-and long-sleeved shirts, underpants, baby wraps, bubble suits, kids' caps, shorts, shirts, dresses, tights, all types of outer- and underclothing for men and women; and other fabric "blanks," including gloves, tablecloths, laundry bags, placemats, tote bags, aprons, bandannas, tea towels, sarongs, headbands, silk fans, silk-covered earring blanks, pillow covers, muslin dolls, and much more. There are books on every aspect of the textile arts, and, of course, the supplies you'll need to turn these textiles into one-of-a-kind masterpieces. The catalog is full of useful information such as safety tips, how-to articles, and techniques involving shrinkage and fabric types.

WEBSITE: The website is well designed, informative, and offers online ordering. This is a real find for textile craftspeople, moms or schools looking for great keepsake craft ideas, or creative types in search of a thoughtful gift that's inexpensive and unique.

SPECIAL FACTORS: Satisfaction guaranteed; returns accepted within 30 days with some conditions (see catalog for details). Will ship to Japan, Singapore, and the West Indies.

Fashion Fabrics Club

10490 Baur Blvd.
St. Louis, MO 63132
800–468–0602
FAX: 314–993–5802

FORM OF INFORMATION: free swatch portfolio and membership information packet; online catalog

PAY: check, MO, MC, V

SELLS: dress fabric

STORE: no walk-in location; mail-order only; phone hours Monday to Friday 9:00 am–4:00 pm CST

ONLINE: www.fashionfabricsclub.com

Are you envious of women who can afford designer clothes? Did it ever occur to you that a beautifully dressed woman in a stunning designer suit might have sewn her own outfit with fabric selections from Fashion Fabrics Club? It's altogether possible, since this company carries the very fabrics used by such notable designers as Evan Picone, Jones NY, Polo, and Liz Claiborne and sells them to you at savings of 50% or more. You don't have to be a member of this fabric club to buy. However, for a fee of $4.95 (which at the time of this writing included a $5 gift certificate), you'll receive a monthly portfolio of the latest fabric consisting of 15 to 35 swatches. The samples are $1^1/_2$" × 2" in size and are often coordinated with interesting solids, prints, and textures. The kits consist of an ever-changing variety of fabrics—cottons, silks, polyester, linen, wool, microfiber, Tencel, and more. Members also receive clearance-sale information, members-only rebate coupons, which you can use to save even more money when you purchase, frequent-buyer benefits, and access to a professional thread-matching service from a selection of 262 colors by Gutermann Thread. There's never an obligation to buy, and all uncut fabrics will be accepted for return anytime.

WEBSITE: The website is a convenient way to find out more about this fabric club, view current fabrics, order a free introductory sample packet, join the club, or just order fabric online. There are also attractive internet specials where savings of 75% are not unusual.

SPECIAL FACTORS: Satisfaction guaranteed; returns accepted; club membership available only in the U.S. and possessions.

A. Feibusch

27 Allen St.
New York, NY 10002
888–947–7872
212–226–3964
FAX: 212–226–5844

FORM OF INFORMATION: price quotes; brochure; online catalog

PAY: MO, MC, V, AE

SELLS: zippers, thread, notions, and garment supplies

STORE: same address; Monday to Friday 9:30 am–5:00 pm, Sunday 10:00 am–5:00 pm

ONLINE: www.zipperstop.com

Write a company to buy a zipper? Not so silly once you realize that this company, A. Feibusch, regularly handles mail and telephone orders and has been doing so since 1941. They are a fully authorized YKK zipper distributor and have the best selection and inventory of anyone else on the internet. (But there is no secure online ordering.) From tiny doll zippers to heavy-duty zippers for luggage, A. Feibusch either stocks your zipper or can have it custom-made. A. Feibusch also carries all kinds of sewing notions—"everything but buttons"—and sells them for about 50% less than you'll find elsewhere. This is an especially good source for just about any color of all-cotton and polyester thread. Since there is no print catalog, you will need to know the product number of the zipper. These are listed at the website alongside all the scanned color swatches available for each type of zipper. Call, email, or mail it in with your order. If you don't know, mail a fabric swatch and A. Feibusch will match it for you. The salespeople here speak many languages, including Spanish, French, Chinese, and German.

SPECIAL FACTORS: Price quotes by email or mail.

Great Northern Weaving

451 East D Ave.
Kalamazoo, MI 49009
800-370-7235 orders
269–341–9752
FAX: 269–341–9525

FORM OF INFORMATION: print catalog and samples, $2.50; online catalog

PAY: check, MO, MC, V

SELLS: rug-making supplies and tools

STORE: 451 E. D Ave., Kalamazoo, MI; Monday to Friday 9:00 am–4:00 pm, closed on Wednesdays

ONLINE: www.greatnorthernweaving.com

Ask rug weavers for a great source and they're likely to cite Great Northern Weaving. That's because Great Northern offers high-quality supplies and equipment for rug weaving, and crocheting at prices that are below everyone else's. The 14-page catalog features rug warps (cotton/poly, 100% cotton, spun nylon, and multifiber); rug wefts (rag coils, loose rags, wool rags, cotton rag filler, poly rug filler, rug roping, fuzzy loopers, colored loopers, and white loopers); weaving yarns; weaving equipment such as shuttles, warping board, rag cutters, and spool racks; loom parts and looms, new and used; crochet supplies and yarns; and weaving and pattern books. You'll even find a little pot holder loom to recreate those pot holders you made as a Brownie Scout. Best of all, these are nice Midwesterners who are happy to answer your questions and help you get started.

WEBSITE: The website is well designed with helpful and detailed descriptions and color pictures of all the products—plus there is online ordering.

SPECIAL FACTORS: Add $6 on C.O.D. orders.

Mangham Manor Fiber Farm

901 Hammocks Gap Rd.
Charlottesville, VA 22911
434–973–2222
FAX: 434–973–2228

FORM OF INFORMATION: $3 brochure and price list; website

PAY: check, MO, MC, V, AE

SELLS: raw fleece from sheep and Angora goats, yarn, dyed mohair locks, wool and mohair socks, shawls, blankets, hats, etc.

FARM STORE: farm visits by appointment; phone hours Monday to Friday 10:00 am–4:00 pm EST

ONLINE: www.woolmohair.com

The Manghams of Mangham Manor Fiber Farm, in the foothills of the Blue Ridge Mountains, have been raising naturally colored sheep and Angora goats for 20 years. This is a great place to know about if you're a spinner, knitter, or weaver, because you'll get the finest quality raw wool and mohair here for 50% less than what you'd pay in a retail shop. In fact, it's likely that the Manghams are your supplier's supplier.

If you were to chat with Michelle, half of the Mangham husband-wife team, it would remind you that shepherds see themselves as loving caretakers of a large family—in this case 250 breeding head with *triple* that number in the spring! The Manghams are careful to practice "green" farming techniques to insure that the soil and animals remain healthy for the next generation of Manghams and beyond. Many of their "girls" have names and have been with them for many years. (Spinners from all over the globe have favorite animals they know by name whose fleece they reserve each year!) The fleece comes in various shades of gray, black, white, red, and brown. The Manghams sell washed and dyed mohair; raw mohair; raw wool; 50% wool/50% mohair carded, batted, and in roving form; white or black mohair socks (the softest and warmest socks ever!); and white, gray, or chocolate brown mohair blankets. Other products include gorgeous dyed mohair locks (great for yarn, doll wigs, tassels, felted hats, etc.), mill-spun yarn (dyed mohair and soft gray wool—perfect for tweeds), long tail hairs from the horses that work on the farm, and "how to" felt ball packages. Samples are available by request.

WEBSITE: The website has very charming and humorous descriptions of products, with prices—there are no images and online ordering is not available.

SPECIAL FACTORS: C.O.D. orders accepted.

Monterey Incorporated

1725 E. Delavan Dr.
Janesville, WI 53545
800-432-9959
608-754-2866
FAX: 608-754-3750

FORM OF INFORMATION: free price list; free print catalog; $5 sample packet

PAY: check, MO, MC, V, AE

SELLS: fake-fur fabric, stuffing, throw blankets, and wool mattress pads

STORE: same address; Monday to Friday 8:00 am–4:30 pm; Saturday 8:00 am–12:00 noon

For over 30 years, Monterey Incorporated has been able to sell fake fur fabric at discount prices—up to 50% off—because it manufactures the popular deep-pile fur fabrics it sells. It supplies toy, apparel, craft, costume, and pet markets as well as the over-the-counter market. Here you'll find the country's largest selection of knitted deep-pile fabrics in first-quality, closeout, overrun, discontinued, and substandard items.

Available fabrics are 58"–60"wide consisting of a variety of colors in plush, short pile, shag novelty, and shearling. You can also order such "fun" luxury furs as seal, fox, teddy bear, giraffe, dalmation, and jaguar by the cut yard, by the roll (15 to 20 yards per roll), and, for remnants, by the pound ($4.50 per pound or $4 per pound over 35 pounds). A carton of fake-fur remnants would keep an elementary school art teacher happy for a year. A sample set is available for $5 in the States, $10 to addresses in Canada. Inexpensive stuffing (from 85 cents per pound) for crafts projects is also available. Do you love furs but love nature's critters more? Then get a fake fur coat from Monterey. Wow! Wait till you see the luscious full-length hooded cheetah coat for only $160! And finally, Monterey sells 100% Merino wool sleepers (mattress pads). This company is a great find.

SPECIAL FACTORS: Minimum yardage: 1 yard; minimum order: $25.

Newark Dressmaker Supply, Inc.

P.O. Box 20730, WMR
Lehigh, PA 18002–0730
800–736–6783
610–837–7500
FAX: 610–837–9115

FORM OF INFORMATION: free print catalog; website
PAY: check, MO, MC, V, DSC
SELLS: sewing, craft, bridal, and quilting supplies
STORE: no walk-in location; mail-order only; phone hours Monday to Friday 8:00 am–4:30 pm EST
ONLINE: www.newarkdress.com

If you think Newark Dressmaker Supply, Inc., only serves home sewers, get ready to cheer, because the 68-page color catalog also has some unusual products for year-round and theme-based craft making. Not surprisingly, two-thirds of the catalog is devoted to sewing needs: thread, specialty zippers, machine accessories, and tools such as rotary cutters and scissors. There's no shortage of interfacing and interlining, home-decor items (tassels, fringe, Shir-rite tape, plastic rings), upholstery tools, and clothing and utility fabrics (gingham check, waterproof flannel, broadcloth, mosquito netting, Jiffy-grip, duck). For home sewing of bridal outfits, you'll find several pages of heir-loom, cluny, and eyelet lace; ribbon; sequins and pearls; wired flower garlands; and $^7/_{16}$" metal boning. There are even some handy household items such as fix-it kits for securing everything from loose wallpaper to slippery rugs.

Crafters and workshop students will appreciate the pages of supplies and how-to books for paper crafting, toy and doll making (animal fabrics, eyes and noses, 18" doll patterns and clothes), beading, rhinestones, spangles, jewelry findings, and the odd decoration. So many unexpected items pop up throughout the catalog—patriotic rib-bons, glue guns, miniatures for florals and doll houses—that it's worth a look.

Wholesale customers: Request wholesale order form with catalog; $125 minimum; no other specials or bonuses apply to wholesale orders.

WEBSITE: At the website you can shop by category, find out about the company, request a catalog, and order online.

SPECIAL FACTORS: Satisfaction guaranteed.

Smiley's Yarns

92–06 Jamaica Ave., Dept. W
Woodhaven, NY 11421
718–847–2185 (mail order)
718–849–9873 (store)

FORM OF INFORMATION: online catalog, no print catalog

PAY: check, MO, MC, V

SELLS: yarn for hand knitting and crocheting

STORE: same address; Monday, Tuesday, Thursday, Friday, and Saturday 10:00 am–5:30 pm

ONLINE: www.smileysyarns.com

Since 1935, Smiley's Yarns has been the ultimate yarn source for the serious knitter and crocheter. Purchase premium-quality yarns starting at the incredibly low price of just $1 a ball. Among the manufacturers represented are Paton's, Bernat, Lion Brand, Phentex, and Reynolds, at up to 75% off retail. More than 100,000 balls of yarn are on sale at prices guaranteed to be the lowest in America.

WEBSITE: Click on to Smiley's user-friendly website to see color images of the various yarns, complete with detailed descriptions—fiber, country of origin, weight, laundering instructions, yardage, ideal needle and hook size, and even how much you'd have to order to make a long-sleeved sweater. The One Dollar Sale section has unbelievable deals any frugal textile artist won't want to pass up. And of course, you can order online.

SPECIAL FACTORS: Returns accepted within 30 days of receipt; minimum order of $25; flat rate shipping charge is $8.95 per order.

Solo Slide Fasteners, Inc.

8 Spring Brook Rd., Dept. WB
P.O. Box 378
Foxboro, MA 02035
800–343–9670
FAX: 800–547–4775

FORM OF INFORMATION: free print catalog; online catalog

PAY: check, MO, MC, V, AE, DSC

SELLS: dressmaking and dry-cleaning equipment, sewing and alteration supplies

STORE: no walk-in location; mail-order only

ONLINE: www.e-sewing.com

This family-run business has been supplying cleaners, tailors, dressmakers, bridal shops, hospitals, hotels, and schools with sewing and alteration supplies, large and small, for nearly half a century. And they've kept up with the times by offering online ordering at their website of some popular items. To take advantage of Solo's excellent wholesale (50% off retail) prices, the minimum order is $25; many items are further discounted if you can order them in quantity. The 100-page catalog has everything from Ace staplers (used by dry cleaners) to zippers, and everything in between—large (e.g., pressing machines) and small (e.g., suspender buttons). Even if you're not a professional, there are many items for home use, such as lint brushes and thread organizers.

Please note: Solo Slide has a Korean-speaking sales rep.

WEBSITE: As mentioned, the online catalog features electronic ordering. Click on one of the product categories, which includes threads, buttons, scissors, sewing machines, books, notions, and dress forms, to see hundreds of items listed and described, although not always clearly pictured. If you need more information about a product or can't find the one you seek, feel free to call a friendly customer service rep.

SPECIAL FACTORS: Authorized returns accepted (except custom-ordered or cut goods); minimum order: $25; free shipping on orders over $100; C.O.D. orders accepted.

Taylor's Cutaways and Stuff

2802 E. Washington St., Dept. WBM
Urbana, IL 61802–4660
FAX: 217–367–1976

FORM OF INFORMATION: $1 print catalog; $2 outside U.S.; online catalog
PAY: check, MO, MC, V
SELLS: cutaways and patterns
STORE: no walk-in location; mail-order only
ONLINE: www.taylorscutaway.com

Taylor's Cutaways and Stuff has been serving crafters by mail since 1977. It has based its business on the fabric that's left when garment pieces are cut away—to the benefit of doll and toy makers, quilters, and sachet-lovers. Instead of saving up your own scraps, you can order from an assortment of packs: calico, Christmas, solid, doll clothes, and mini-calico, each filled with different prints, some generously sized at 9" × 44". Remnants of satin, velvet, polyester, silk, cottons, and craft fur come in ½- to 2-pound bundles, in sizes suitable for quilts, toy animals, and baby clothes. Taylor's simplifies toy and doll making with precut items such as hearts, stockings, and teddy bears; teddy patterns and kits; and soft toy patterns, all full-size and complete with instructions. The 32-page catalog abounds with surprise bargains and items you won't find in your local store: fashion doll clothing patterns (for Barbie-sized dolls), instructions for making an apple head doll, patterns for high-button-leather doll shoes, recipes for making your own pet food, beef jerky, instructions on subjects such as drying flowers in the microwave oven, satin rosebuds, elastic assortment (woven edges, picot, and grosgrain), crochet patterns, precut stencil books, iron-on transfers, bags of buttons, animal (or doll) joints, animal noses, and eyes for toys.

WEBSITE: If your interests are eclectic enough to include both folk doll making and web surfing, log on to the website, which presents listings, but not images, of the full inventory and an order form you can download and fax or mail in. The website also lists the latest specials and bargain packages available.

SPECIAL FACTORS: Quantity discounts available.

Thai Silks

252 State St.
Los Altos, CA 94022
650–948–8611
800–722–7455
FAX: 650–948–3426

FORM OF INFORMATION: free print catalog; online catalog

PAY: check, MO, MC, V, AE

SELLS: silk and other all-natural fabrics, silk scarves, silk clothing, etc.

STORE: same address; Monday to Saturday 9:00 am–5:30 pm

ONLINE: www.thaisilks.com

With direct access to foreign loomers, Thai Silks brings artists, clothing makers, interior decorators, and upholsterers savings of 30% to 50% on regular retail prices for silks, velvets, satins, and accessories. An assorted sample set at $40 plus $3 for shipping is not a bad idea when you consider the wide choices and low prices (or choose a specialty sample: bridal, $12; artists', $5; brocades, $6; prints, $13.50; velvets, $12; closeout, $3). For $20, you can enroll in the silk fabric club and receive quarterly mailings of Thai Silks' newest colors, prints, and fabrications and a sample of the current closeout.

The easy to read fold-out catalog lists, but does not picture, a dozen or more variations in each of these categories: habotai or China silk, used for flower making; silk crepe of every description; silk charmeuse; fancy and regular silk chiffons; Jacquard Georgette; silk/rayon chiffons; velvet (8% silk/82% rayon); stretch silks (silk with a small percentage of Lycra); silk noil; organza; Shantung silk; silk Doupioni; natural satins; tapestry brocades; matelasse; silk prints; hand-painted silks; beautiful iridescent taffeta silks; assorted white silks and Pongees used for painting and batiking; and much more. Thai Silks also carries such interesting fibers as fine pima cotton batik, cut linen, and silk/wool suiting. In addition, you'll find scarves, shawls, and capes here: white silk, hand-hemmed scarves for artists; Devoré satin scarves; burn-out-pattern velvet/rayon scarves; novelty Jacquard chiffon scarves; dyed silk scarves; and white silk shawls and capes. Men's silk neckties, sarongs, T-shirts, tank tops, habotai pants, pincushions, and sewing kits round out the catalog.

WEBSITE: The website offers over 1400 silk fabrics from China, Korea, Thailand, and India. All of the fabrics have a color image of a swatch which can be enlarged for a closer look at the weave and pattern. Most of the finished goods also have color images which you can click on to enlarge. Online ordering is available.

SPECIAL FACTORS: Wholesale pricing applies when yardage and price minimums are met (inquire); discounts (1 yard minimum) for artists, dressmakers, and boutiques; minimum order: ½ yard.

Bonnie Triola Yarns

343 E. Gore Rd.
Erie, PA 16509–3723
814–825–7821
FAX: 814–824–5418

FORM OF INFORMATION: $10 print catalog for U.S residents; $12 print catalog for Canadian residents; samples (see text); online catalog

PAY: check, MO, MC, V

SELLS: yarns

STORE: no walk-in location; mail-order only; phone hours Monday to Friday 7:30 am–3:00 pm EST

ONLINE: home.earthlink.net/~bonnietriola/

For those of you who love to use knitting machines, looms, and even embroidery machines, you should know about Bonnie Triola. She tests and works with all of her yarns and will happily answer any of your questions regarding their use. For $10, you receive a year's worth of mailings with yarn samples, price lists with special closeout sales, and newsletters full of helpful hints, resources, seminar notices, and new product reports and reviews. On top of Bonnie's already discounted prices, many of her yarns are eligible for quantity discounts where you can save up to 25% additionally. She also has a wholesale catalog (no minimums) for qualified buyers, with deep discounts on everything. She carries her own lines of natural and synthetic fibers, overruns from New York designers, and yarns by Tamm and Sunray. (Samples and color cards on these latter two are not included with the $10 catalog; inquire for prices.) Her metallic yarns are popular with people who use embroidery machines, but almost any textile artist or craftsperson will find great choices and buys here. Most of Bonnie's yarns are sold as full cones only, and many of the markdowns are close to 75% less than retail.

WEBSITE: The website presents current specials, yarn selections including designer closeouts, and books and accessories. There are color photographs of all yarn selections—but no online ordering. The website is worth a look as it gives you a good idea about Bonnie Triola's fabulous discounts and her careful product selection.

SPECIAL FACTORS: C.O.D. orders accepted; net-30 billing for qualified wholesalers (request the wholesale price list).

UTEX Trading Enterprises

826 Pine Ave.
Niagara Falls, NY 14301
TEL/FAX: 716–282–8211

FORM OF INFORMATION: free price list with SASE
PAY: check, MO, MC, V
SELLS: imported silk fabric
STORE: same address; by appointment only
EMAIL: utextrade@aol.com

If you're a decorator, seamstress, tailor, or textile artist, you'll want to know about UTEX, America's largest silk source. Since 1980, this company has been importing silk fabric directly from mills around the world and passing the savings on to the public by selling fabric as well as silk sewing thread, silk knitting/weaving yarns, silk neckties, and silk scarves directly through the mail. UTEX issues a no-nonsense price sheet with the discount schedule, fabric selection table to help you locate the right fabric for your needs (wedding gowns, evening wear, casual clothing, suits, interior decoration, etc.), and fabric weights, widths, and swatch numbers. Once you select the sample(s) and send in a deposit (to cover the cost of the samples), you have 20 days to make a decision to purchase or return, after which you get a partial refund. This is a great source for people knowledgeable about silk, since the flyer descriptions are minimal. The more you order, the more you'll save, as quantity discounts apply to both scarf and fabric orders.

SPECIAL FACTORS: Sample deposits refundable, less handling charges; C.O.D. orders accepted.

Webs

P.O. Box 147, Dept. WBM
Northampton, MA
01061–0147

800–FOR–WEBS

413–584–2225

FAX: 413–584–1603

FORM OF INFORMATION: $2 print catalog; online catalog

PAY: check, MO, MC, V, AE, DSC

SELLS: yarns, and spinning and weaving equipment and books

STORE: Service Center Rd., Northampton, MA; Monday to Saturday 10:00 am–5:30 pm

ONLINE: www.yarn.com

Webs, in business since 1974, keeps the world of fibercrafts spinning with yarns discounted up to 80% off suggested retail prices and equipment for weavers, spinners, and knitters at all levels of development. The already-low yarn prices receive additional discounts of 20% and 25% on purchases of $60–$119 and $120 or more, respectively, and looms and spinning wheels are shipped freight-free.

The catalog has photographs and descriptions of looms; knitting supplies; spinning wheels and supplies; weaving tools; and yarns. Because Webs manufactures many of its own yarn lines, the firm offers them at terrific savings. Samples are available for $2. Individual color cards can be ordered for $5; the complete loose-leaf binder color book, with generous samples, is $39.50. Webs also is a major mail-order source of mill ends and closeout yarns. Some items are subject to a 1-pound minimum purchase; others are available only in 1-pound cones, but these details are evident in each product description. Webs is oriented toward providing the right equipment and yarns, so indicate your specialty in your correspondence, and look forward to some getting-to-know-you questions when you shop for equipment.

WEBSITE: The website is extensive, very easy to navigate and you can order online.

SPECIAL FACTORS: Shipping not charged on looms (except for children's looms), spinning wheels, or drum carders; quantity discounts available; authorized returns accepted within 30 days, with possible 15% restocking fee; minimum order: $20 on credit card orders.

Fine Art Supplies

Art supplies and equipment for drawing, painting, etching, lithography, and other fine arts; graphic arts supplies; studio furniture

If you're an artist living in New York City, you're lucky to have access to large, well-stocked art-supply stores that sell art materials of all kinds at reasonable prices. If it weren't for mail-order, the rest of us would be stuck with tiny retail stores that might as well be selling liquid gold in those tubes of oil paint. Art supplies are one area in which you can get *excellent* deals by mail. Mail-order art-supply discounters routinely offer savings of 20%; some of the vendors in this chapter can save you as much as 70%. The firms listed here sell supplies and materials for fine arts and some crafts: pigments, inks, drawing material, paper, brushes, canvas, mats and frames, stretchers, studio furniture, vehicles and solvents, silk-screening supplies, carving tools, and much more.

The Art Materials Labeling Act of 1988 together with the Consumer Products Safety Commission have created standards for the art materials industry and banned hazardous materials from being used in elementary schools. Although many art materials have been reformulated to conform to the legal standards, toxic ingredients are still an unavoidable problem. Most artists are aware of the risks, but for more information about art materials in general, as well as toxicity issues, pick up a copy of *The Artists' Handbook of Materials and Techniques,* by Mayer and Sheehan. Another book, Michael McCann's *Health Hazards Manual for Artists,* has become something of a classic and is a must for every artist's studio library. The fully revised edition has the most current information on safety, labeling, and new chemicals. It outlines the dangers for artists in such fields as painting, photography, ceramics, sculpture, printmaking, woodworking, textiles, and many others, and has a special section on health hazards for children working with art materials. Both of these titles are available from many of the bookstores listed in this book.

If you're a commercial artist, you'll be glad to know some of the firms in this chapter sell graphic design–related software and computer goods, but you'll do well to consult the computer section of the "Office, Business, and Professional" chapter as well. Some of the firms in the "Crafts and Hobbies" chapter carry supplies for fine artists and graphic artists, too.

Find It Fast

ANIMAL AND HUMAN-FORM MANNEQUINS
Pearl Paint, Daniel Smith

ART AND GRAPHIC DESIGN BOOKS/VIDEOS
Cheap Joe's Art Stuff, Jerry's Artarama, Daniel Smith, Utrecht

CHILDREN'S ART SUPPLIES
Jerry's Artarama, Ott's Discount Art Supply, Pearl Paint, Daniel Smith

COMPUTER GRAPHICS SUPPLIES
Utrecht

FRAMING SUPPLIES
American Frame, Graphik Dimensions, Jerry's Artarama, Pearl Paint, Daniel Smith, Utrecht

GENERAL ART SUPPLIES, TOOLS, AND EQUIPMENT
Cheap Joe's Art Stuff, Jerry's Artarama, Ott's Discount Art Supply, Pearl Paint, Utrecht

PROJECTORS AND LIGHTBOXES
Cheap Joe's Art Stuff, Jerry's Artarama, Ott's Discount Art Supply, Pearl Paint, Utrecht

READY-MADE FRAMES
American Frame, Cheap Joe's Art Stuff, Jerry's Artarama

SCULPTURE MATERIALS
Jerry's Artarama, Ott's Discount Art Supply, Utrecht

SPECIALTY PAPERS
Daniel Smith

STUDIO FURNITURE
Cheap Joe's Art Stuff, Jerry's Artarama, Pearl Paint, Daniel Smith, Utrecht

American Frame Corporation

400 Tomahawk Dr.
Maumee, OH 43537–1695
888–628–3833
FAX: 800–893–3898

FORM OF INFORMATION: free print catalog; online catalog

PAY: check, MO, MC, V, AE, DSC

SELLS: custom-cut wood and metal frames, mat board, framing tools, and supplies

STORE: 477 W. Dussel Dr. (Suffolk Square), Maumee, OH; Monday to Friday 10:00 am–6:00 pm

ONLINE: www.americanframe.com

Confess: Do you have friends' valuable artwork tacked on your wall with push pins? Once you've had a gander at American Frame Corporation's 46-page color catalog of frames, mats, and framing hardware, you might start thinking of changing your ways. You need this catalog, especially if you've looked at frame prices recently. You can save up to 70% off retail prices on all types of frames and mats, and the excellent website, with the complete inventory, offers another way to view the selection and place an order.

American Frame's catalog boasts that it's "more than just a catalog. It's a handbook." The print and online catalog are full of tips to help a novice through the tricks and traps of framing, such as how to choose the right frame and mat color for the artwork, how to determine the mat's border size, and other nifty snippets. The catalog offers over 275 metal and wood frames in a variety of styles and gorgeous colors, and over 170 Bainbridge matboards. Color photographs, precise cross-section line drawings, and clearly written descriptions guide the reader through the world of framing. You'll also find the framing hardware and accessories you'll need. All frames and mats are cut to your specification, and if the detailed instructions on how to measure them aren't clear enough, there's a friendly support staff on hand to answer your questions.

WEBSITE: The website is a joy. It takes you through a very clear and concise process of choosing frames, mats, Plexi-glass, mounting boards, and linen liners for your artwork. Along the way, if you want to know more about Plexi-glass, for example, one click and up comes more information. Well done. Web shoppers can also take advantage of web-only specials and ready-mades at great prices as well as tips and hints and framing ideas.

SPECIAL FACTORS: Measure twice, cut once is the rule; a restocking fee applies to all returns, and custom-cut mats cannot be returned.

Cheap Joe's Art Stuff

374 Industrial Park Dr.
Boone, NC 28607
800–227–2788
828–262–0793
FAX: 800–257–0874
or 828–262–0795

FORM OF INFORMATION: free print catalog; online catalog

PAY: check, MO, MC, V, DSC

SELLS: fine artist supplies and equipment, studio furniture, art books, videos, etc.

WAREHOUSE: same address; Monday to Friday 10:00 am–6:00 pm; phone hours Monday to Thursday 9:00 am–9:00 pm, Friday and Saturday 9:00 am–5:00 pm EST

ONLINE: www.cheapjoes.com

You'll get a good feeling when you shop for art supplies at Cheap Joe's. The Joe behind Cheap Joe's has established a program called Brushes for Vincent, inspired by Van Gogh's brother, Theo, who kept the impoverished Vincent stocked with art supplies. This program donates art supplies to Native American schools, cancer hospitals, and other groups that can't afford to buy them. But you'll be even more pleased with the selection and prices at Cheap Joe's. The catalog is 144 colorful pages of papers, canvas, all kinds of media, and brushes by well-known manufacturers as well as Cheap Joe's own line. A 30% discount is typical throughout the catalog, with 60% possible on quantity purchases of select items. Cheap Joe's also sells easels, shrink-wrap systems, projection equipment, print racks, and studio furniture. Since equipment and materials work best if you know how to use them, Joe plants tips throughout the catalog and carries books and videotapes on painting and art history. Cheap Joe, whose artistic medium is watercolor, invites questions and suggestions regarding materials and equipment.

WEBSITE: The website is a lovely place to visit. In addition to secure online ordering and the full inventory of supplies and equipment, you can check-out upcoming workshops, subscribe to an instructional magazine for watercolorists, send a musical postcard of a painting by Joe, or peruse some high country photographic images. And if that's not enough, you can go to art-related links, get art questions answered, or have free sales flyers and news emailed to you. Shopping online here makes you feel as if you are part of a community.

SPECIAL FACTORS: Satisfaction guaranteed; returns within 30 days; shipping and handling is free on orders of $250 or more.

Graphik Dimensions Ltd.

2103 Brentwood St.
High Point, NC 27263
800–221–0262
336–887–3700
FAX: 336–887–3773

FORM OF INFORMATION: free print catalog; online catalog

PAY: check, MO, MC, V, AE, DSC

SELLS: sectional ready-made and custom-made frames and accessories

STORE: same address; Monday to Friday 9:00 am–6:00 pm, Saturday 9:00 am–2:00 pm

ONLINE: www.pictureframes.com

For 40 years, the husband-and-wife team of Joan and Stephen Feinsod has been stocking a huge inventory of quality framing materials and selling them to artists and photographers at discount prices. Graphik Dimension's 60-page color catalog has a frame to suit every kind of artwork and every kind of surrounding, from castle to rustic cabin, in styles that are austere or minimal, youthful or cheery. There are standard-depth frames for use with glass as well as "canvas" depth for paintings on stretchers. Whether you seek a gilded, ornate frame for an heirloom painting or a glossy, gulf-blue frame for that whimsical print to hang in your bathroom, you'll find it here. Graphik Dimensions offers framing kits in your choice of wood frames or metal frames including the acrylic, backing board, retainer clips, hanging hardware, and wire—no tools necessary.

WEBSITE: The full inventory can be viewed online. Web specials are added every two weeks with savings up to 50% off their regular low pricing. Online ordering is available.

SPECIAL FACTORS: Satisfaction guaranteed; quantity discounts available; authorized returns accepted.

Jerry's Artarama, Inc.

5325 Departure Dr.
Raleigh, NC 27616
800–827–8478
919–878–6782
FAX: 919–873–9565

FORM OF INFORMATION: $6 print catalog; online catalog

PAY: check, MO, MC, V, AE, DSC

SELLS: fine art materials, picture frames and mats

STORE: stores in West Orange, NJ; West Hartford, CT; Bellerose, NY; Raleigh, NC; Deerfield Beach and West Palm Beach, FL; Knoxville, TN; and Fort Collins, CO (call for hours and addresses); phone hours Monday to Friday 9:00 am–8:00 pm, Saturday 11:00 am–5:00 pm EST

ONLINE: www.jerrysartarama.com

In business since 1968, Jerry's Artarama promises you'll "always save up to 75% off manufacturer's list prices" on commercial and fine arts materials and furniture, and there's a lowest-price guarantee to boot. The 350-page full color print catalog details name-brand easels, canvas, paints, pastels, brushes (individual and in sets), palette knives, gold finishes, drawing and sketch media, film and frame hardware, portfolios, files, and heavy-duty studio equipment. Prices drop on quantity purchases of such items as brushes, palette cups, Gessobord, unprimed linen, and stretcher bars. Some minimum-order requirements apply.

A quick glance and you'll find big savings—oil paints at 45% off list, brushes at 48% off, inks at 40% off, canvas at 50% off, furniture priced 60% below list, frames at 50% off—and I could go on. Products by TV artists Bob Ross and Susan Scheewe, instructional videos, and classic books *(Drawing on the Right Side of the Brain, The Artists' Handbook)* are discounted, too. For everything from Academy watercolors to Zippy art totes, Jerry's Artarama is the place. Jerry calls his catalog "the encyclopedia of artist materials," and that's not too far off.

WEBSITE: The website has all of Jerry's products online plus some good buys at the closeout section and secure online ordering.

SPECIAL FACTORS: Satisfaction guaranteed; color charts and product specifications available on request; quantity discounts available; minimum order: $20.

Ott's Discount Art Supply

102 Hungate Dr., Dept. WBM
Greenville, NC 27858–8045
800–356–3289
FAX: 252–756–2397

FORM OF INFORMATION: online catalog only, no print catalog
PAY: check, MO, MC, V
SELLS: art, graphics, and craft supplies
STORE: no walk-in location; mail-order only; phone hours Monday to Friday 9:00 am– 5:00 pm EST
ONLINE: www.otts.com

Since 1972, Ott's Discount Art Supply has catered to the supply needs of artists and arts programs with savings up to 75% off manufacturers' list prices. Ott's carries standard artist's supplies—sketch books and parchment, charcoal, and pastel papers; drawing inks; synthetic or natural bristled brushes—by Liquitex, Grumbacher, Winsor & Newton, Strathmore Berol, Weber, and others; oil and watercolor paints; and studio equipment such as projectors, magnifiers, easels, lamps, and light boxes. Among the other items found here are mat cutters, swing-arm desk lamps, artist portfolios, Japanese rice paper and origami kits, clay guns, how-to books, bags of balsa wood for carving, and jeweler tools. Many of the products shown at this website are not pictured and do not have very detailed descriptions. This is a good discount source for supplies that you are already familiar with or have researched. Secure online ordering is available.

SPECIAL FACTORS: Satisfaction guaranteed; returns accepted within 30 days; institutional orders accepted; see catalog for additional fees or shipping charges on heavy or flammable items.

Pearl Paint Co., Inc.

308 Canal St., Dept. WBM
New York, NY 10013–2572
800–221–6845
212–431–7932
FAX: 212–274–2290

FORM OF INFORMATION: $2.50 print catalog; online catalog

PAY: check, MO, MC, V, AE, DSC

SELLS: fine art, craft, and graphics supplies, studio furniture, etc.

STORE: same address, also 22 other locations in CA, FL, GA, IL, MA, MD, NJ, NY, TX, and VA; call for locations

ONLINE: www.pearlpaint.com

Pearl Paint Co., Inc., knows that although New York City teems with artists, not all artists live in New York. That's why in addition to 22 store locations (listed in the print and online catalogs), Pearl Paint makes its many craft, fine arts, and graphic arts products available through the mail. Strolling through Pearl is a young artist's quintessential New York experience, and Pearl has managed to transfer that hip, well-organized, service-intensive atmosphere to the catalog. You'll find great values here, with discounts that go as high as 50% on some items. Pearl Paint also stocks studio furniture and, yes, house paint. In business for over 60 years, Pearl Paint is the place for tools, canvas, manuals, handmade drawing and writing books, poster paper, foam core, frames and framing supplies, pens, stretchers—you name it! If you need an item that's not listed in the catalog or on the website, call, fax, write, or email for information.

WEBSITE: The website is not as extensive as the print catalog at this writing, but it does feature online ordering and a good spectrum of best-selling products at prices that are lower than if you purchased them at one of their stores.

SPECIAL FACTORS: Quantity discounts available; all orders (except FireArts catalog) under $50 will incur an extra $6.95 handling fee; all flat-wrapped paper will incur an additional $2.50 packing charge.

Daniel Smith

P.O. Box 84268
Seattle, WA 98124–5568
800–426–6740
206–223–9599
FAX: 800–238–4065

FORM OF INFORMATION: free print catalog, with rebate; online catalog
PAY: check, MO, MC, V, AE, DSC
SELLS: fine art supplies and equipment
STORE: 3 stores in WA, call for locations and hours; phone hours Monday to Friday 6:00 am–6:00 pm PST
ONLINE: www.danielsmith.com

After thumbing through dozens of discount mail-order catalogs with blow-out, blast-off deals and enough exclamation points in the text to give you a headache, it's always a great relief to settle back each year and open up the most recent catalog from Daniel Smith. The 200-page reference catalog is an example of informed design, respect for an artist's intelligence, well-written and informative text, fabulous selection, and wonderful prices. Although it doesn't look like a discount catalog, it is; prices here are well below list in most cases, and there are many items you just won't find anywhere else. Daniel Smith manufactures their own paints (oils, acrylics, and watercolors), etching and lithographic inks, painter's canvas and linen, and other products. Serious artists consider these products some of the best in the biz. You'll also find an extensive selection of paints of every kind by top-name manufacturers, as well as brushes and other painting tools, drawing and printing supplies, an incredible variety of paper and canvases, framing supplies, studio furniture, books, and much more. If you're a paper freak, check out the single-sheet papers from all over the world—German etching paper, Italian intaglio paper, Japanese woodblock print paper, French marble paper, Nepalese block printing paper, and others too exotic and gorgeous to believe.

WEBSITE: The website is every bit as lovely as the print catalog. Here you can view the full range of products complete with excellent color images and thoughtful product write-ups, download the print catalog for free, get artist's material tips, browse through technical leaflets, contribute to or just peek at the artist bulletin board, look up societies and organizations, read art events news, and view artist profiles. You can also order online. Bravo to this classy company!

SPECIAL FACTORS: Satisfaction guaranteed; authorized returns accepted for exchange, refund, or credit; minimum order on paper: 10 sheets.

Utrecht

6 Corporate Dr.
Cranbury, NJ 08512-3616
800–223–9132
609–409–8001
FAX: 800–382–1979

FORM OF INFORMATION: free print catalog; online catalog

PAY: check, MO, MC, V, AE, DSC

SELLS: general art supplies

STORE: locations in AZ, CA, CO, CT, DC, FL, GA, IL, MA, MI, MD, MN, MO, NM, NY, OH, OR, PA, RI, TX, UT, WI AND WA; call for addresses; phone hours Monday to Friday 8:00 am–9:00 pm, Saturday 9:00 am–5:00 pm EST

ONLINE: www.utrecht.com

It's so rewarding to have looked through and rejected a great many art-supply mail-order catalogs and found one that truly deserves to be in this book. Utrecht is something of an institution for New York City artists as a great source for discount artist's paints. (Utrecht manufactures their own paints and sells them directly to the customer, saving you a bundle.) But the paints by top-brand manufacturers such as Winsor & Newton, Rembrandt, and Liquitex are also discounted 40% and more. On many items, savings run as high as 66% off. Brushes, canvas, drawing implements and supplies, paper, framing supplies, printmaking tools and inks, portfolio/presentation cases—these and other fine-art needs can be found in Utrecht's 63-page color print catalog as well as on their website.

WEBSITE: The online catalog is well organized, and easy to use—although not all of the products have images. You'll find clearance sales with deeply discounted goods, free freight on orders over $150, web-only specials, and online ordering.

SPECIAL FACTORS: Institutional accounts available; quantity discounts available.

Flowers

Fresh-cut flowers, arrangements, bouquets, and potted plants

According to recent behavioral research conducted at Rutgers, The State University of New Jersey, nature provides us with a simple way to improve emotional health—flowers. The presence of flowers triggers happy emotions, heightens feelings of life satisfaction and affects social behavior in a positive manner far beyond what is normally believed. I can believe that. When I drive by a field speckled with orange, purple, and yellow wildflowers it certainly does trigger some happy emotions. However, the last time I purchased a bouquet of red roses at my local florist, my heightened feelings started to sink as I pulled three 20 dollar bills out of my pocket.

A dozen long-stemmed roses, while quite beautiful, can be pretty expensive for something that is going to be dead in about a week. It's more practical to give a potted plant, or a toaster—but they just aren't as romantic. We all know when you walk in with a potted plant as a gift, you are trying to save a few bucks. I have found some companies here that are going to make your future Valentine's Days and anniversaries a little less embarrassing. Prices from online and brick-and-mortar florists can range quite a bit for a dozen long-stemmed red roses (no vase). A popular online florist was selling them, at this writing, for $68.98 delivered. All the firms I've listed here will sell you a dozen long-stemmed, red, grower-direct roses (no vase) for $36.98 to $44.90 delivered (at this writing). Goodbye potted plant! I don't mean to knock potted plants by any means—they have a place. For instance, a dozen red roses from an elementary student to a teacher is bad. Potted plant is good. A dozen red roses to a married co-worker is bad. Potted plant is good. A potted plant to a Green Party member is always better than cut flowers. I'm sure you'll make the proper choice and if you use the companies here you'll pay up to 42% less for fresh-cut, grower-direct flowers and plants.

Find It Fast

FRESH-CUT FLOWER ARRANGEMENTS AND BOUQUETS

Grower Flowers, KaBloom, Proflowers

FRESH-CUT SNAPDRAGON BOUQUETS

Evergreen Farms

LONG-STEMMED ROSES

Grower Flowers, KaBloom, Proflowers

ORGANIC FLOWERS

Proflowers

POTTED PLANTS

Evergreen Farms, Grower Flowers, KaBloom, Proflowers

SEASONAL FLOWERS

KaBloom, Proflowers

TULIPS

Proflowers

Evergreen Farms Inc.

11769 Nubbin Dr.
Coker, AL 35452
205–333–1234
FAX: 205–333–1236

FORM OF INFORMATION: website only; no print catalog
PAY: check, MO, MC, V, AE, DSC
SELLS: fresh-cut snapdragon bouquets
STORE: mail-order only; phone hours Monday to Friday 8:00 am–5:00 pm CST
ONLINE: www.evergreenfarms.com

★

What could be more luxurious than having fresh flowers delivered to your door (or to the door of your surprised mother, employee, or girlfriend)? Bouquets from Evergreen Farms last so long that you will able to keep receiving gratitude long after most recipients would have thrown out the dead blooms. Evergreen Farms is a find, and here's why. When you buy flowers from a florist, not only are the flowers 7 to 10 days old by the time you buy them, but the florist is acting as middleman, thus adding to the price tag of the flowers. Evergreen Farms, the largest grower of greenhouse-cut fresh flowers in the deep South, harvests their snapdragons daily, and ships them out within 36 hours of harvest. These will be the freshest, longest-lasting flowers you've ever gotten. And because they're coming straight from the grower, they'll also be the cheapest.

Evergreen offers fresh-cut snapdragons (their specialty), a refreshing change of pace from the usual roses. They can drop-ship your order to that special someone and enclose a card with a note from you. Each order contains over 35 stems of snapdragons giving you well over 100 blooms. All orders are shipped the day they receive them by UPS Next Day Air Service. At this writing, a bouquet was $49.97 with free shipping. When I looked at smaller bouquets from a few FTD florists—with many fewer blooms, lots of filler green, and froufrou stuff you don't need or want—I found their prices a lot higher than Evergreen's. You can order online, by phone, or by fax, whichever is most convenient for you. The website, in addition to offering online ordering, has an interesting section on do's and don'ts for handling and preserving your fresh-cut flowers.

SPECIAL FACTORS: Orders received after 12 noon CST on Friday will be shipped on Monday for Tuesday delivery; wholesalers should inquire for terms.

Grower Flowers

P.O. Box 44800
Detroit, MI 48244
888–321–ROSE

FORM OF INFORMATION: online catalog only; no print catalog

PAY: MC, V, AE, DSC

SELLS: long-stemmed roses, lilies, iris, and chrysantemum bouquets, and potted plants

STORE: no walk-in location; mail-order only

ONLINE: www.growerflowers.com

One of my biggest problems with giving an arrangement of fresh-cut flowers is that I usually don't like the way they're arranged or the choice of fillers and I don't like when they come in containers in baskets with that big soggy green "brick-thing" and little fru-fru plastic things stuck in it. I prefer a simple, classic arrangement which consists of mostly flowers. I really like the simplicity and beauty of the fresh flower bouquets at Grower Flowers. Grower Flowers offers some of the freshest flowers on the internet through their greenhouse facilities in Watsonville, CA and Ontario, Canada. As a result of providing extra lighting and additional carbon dioxide to their roses and increasing the growth rates, they are able to cut their roses twice a day, 365 days of the year, ensuring a constant supply of the freshest possible product. At the point of cutting, it is only 24 more hours until they are at the recipient's door. When you purchase your roses direct from the grower, you are getting roses that will open beautifully and last longer.

In addition to long-stemmed roses in a wide variety of colors, you'll find lilies, iris, chrysanthemums, and some quite lovely potted plants. Prices for bouquets generally range from $29.95 to $39.95 plus $9.95 for overnight shipping (Tuesday through Friday). All orders are securely packaged in attractive, insulated gift boxes to ensure that only the freshest possible product arrives at its destination. Your gift selection will not arrive arranged in a vase even if a vase is purchased. Since the flowers are cut fresh and sent from the grower, there are no Sunday or Monday deliveries. Orders are only delivered Tuesday through Saturday (delivery is $14.95).

SPECIAL FACTORS: Orders with U.S. destinations received before 3:00 pm EST and orders with Canadian destinations received before 12:00 pm EST can be shipped and delivered the next available day or on selected delivery date

KaBloom

200 Wildwood Ave.
Woburn, MA 01801-2031
800–KaBloom
800–522–5666

FORM OF INFORMATION: online catalog only; no print catalog

PAY: MC, V, AE, DSC

SELLS: fresh-cut flowers, long-stemmed roses , seasonal flowers, fresh flower bouquets, wreaths, and potted plants

STORE: Over 70 stores nationwide, see website for retail store locator; phone hours Monday to Saturday 8:00 am–11:00 pm, Sunday 9:00 am–6:00 pm EST

ONLINE: www.kabloom.com

KaBloom opened its doors in December 1998, with three avenues to purchase flowers: through the internet, by telephone, and at retail locations in greater metropolitan Boston. Consumer acceptance of KaBloom was immediate. Their combination of quality flowers, attractive prices, and easily accessible locations, with knowledgeable and friendly service is a winner. They now have over 70 retail locations nationwide. At KaBloom you'll find exciting varieties of the freshest, highest quality flowers at some of the best prices. Because they purchase in volume, they are able to negotiate the best prices. By buying direct from growers all over the world, they can pass the savings on to you. Even on holidays, you'll find that their prices remain consistent. At this writing, KaBloom was offering all of their online visitors the opportunity to become a KaBloom preferred customer, which means you will be notified of incredible additional savings that regular visitors to the site might never see. These savings often amount to 20%, 40%, and sometimes even over 50% off their already low online prices.

SPECIAL FACTORS: Weekday overnight delivery by FedEx and UPS for most flowers from Tuesday to Friday, at a cost of $9.95 (some items may be more); "Saturday Priority Overnight" for most flowers, at a cost of $19.95 (some items may be more); order by 1:00 pm EST for next day delivery; satisfaction guaranteed, if you not satisfied with the freshness of your purchase, call KaBloom and they will gladly replace it at no charge, valid for 21 days from the date of delivery.

Proflowers

5005 Wateridge Vista Dr.
Suite 200
San Diego, CA 92121
888–373–7437

FORM OF INFORMATION: online catalog only; no print catalog

PAY: check, MO, MC, V, AE, DSC, DC, JCB

SELLS: fresh-cut roses, tulips, mixed bouquets, seasonal flowers, organic flowers, and potted plants

STORE: no walk-in location; mail-order only

ONLINE: www.proflowers.com

Proflowers, which launched in August 1998, only ships fresh flowers that come direct-from-the-grower, thus ensuring that the flowers you buy were cut only 24 to 48 hours before you or your recipient receives them. And because their flowers never wait around in warehouses, trucks or retail florist's coolers, they're able to guarantee that their flowers will last at least seven days. Proflowers offers a wide selection of high-quality, unique, freshly-cut flowers that include over 85 bouquets and plants to choose from that are not easily found in local markets. Offerings include roses in fourteen different colors (including an assortment of bi-colored roses), tulips, irises, lilies, Birds of Paradise and a variety of mixed bouquets. In a price comparison with the FTD site, I found Proflowers to be about 30% to 35% less for their flower selections. They also offer gift baskets, gourmet desserts, and chocolates; but, I did not find them to be any less expensive than leading competitors for these items.

According to an independent survey conducted by BizRate, Proflowers is the top ranked fresh flower site for product selection, price, customer support, website design, ease of ordering and on-time delivery for two straight years. And Forrester Research, one of the nations top market analyst firms, has ranked Proflowers number one in the Flower category of their PowerRankings for two consecutive periods in 2000.

SPECIAL FACTORS: All flowers are guaranteed to last at least 7 days or your money back; if for any reason you are not satisfied with the freshness of your flowers, they will gladly replace the bouquet or refund your money.

Food and Beverages

All-category Foods and Drinks

Ethnic and gourmet foods; cheese-making supplies; steaks, chops, and smoked meat; organic citrus and tropical fruit; fresh-baked cookies and brownies; coffee and tea; beer- and wine-making supplies; caviar and truffles; Amish-style pickled vegetables and fruit preserves

Food items sold through catalogs and the internet generated nationwide sales of $6.3 billion in 2001, according to the Direct Marketing Association, a New York-based trade group. Those sales totaled $5.8 billion in 2000. Direct-marketing sales for food and other items have been increasing around 10% annually for the past several years. People enjoy the convenience of shopping at home whenever they want; exotic or ethnic ingredients may not be available for some people locally; and food items are particularly popular as corporate gifts or just as gifts in general to friends and family. Of the top 100 catalog marketers compiled by *Catalog Age* magazine, there are three that primarily sell food items: "Harry and David," a gourmet food catalog; "Swiss Colony," known for its cheese, chocolate and other items; and "Omaha Steaks," a catalog that sells meats and fish. These companies sell food items for gift giving in baskets and decorative boxes. Many of the stores I've listed in this chapter will save you 20% to 70%

off food gift baskets and boxes compared to the three companies listed above. I have also included stores that will save you money on specific items that you purchase for yourself and your family. You need to compare the prices with prices at your local market and then factor in the shipping. And be sure to compare organic products to organic products—they generally are more expensive (but worth it in my opinion). When I do a price comparison, I compare not only to prices in stores that sell the same product in my area, but also to other online/mail-order companies. The stores that I have listed are all the best bargains as far as gift packages go and some offer specific food products (like coffee or oranges) that are not only better quality, but still save me money (even with the shipping costs) than if I were to buy locally. But you may have access to a local farmer's market where you get very good deals on fresh, high-quality produce or other food items. You need to compare for yourself with what is available to you locally. And don't forget to factor in the shipping.

I have not found a national source for online grocery shopping that will save you money over shopping "in person." Although online grocery shopping is certainly more convenient, you will generally pay the same as if you went to the supermarket. Unless, of course you figure in the time saved by shopping online. Or, if you happen to live in midtown Manhattan or the lower east side of New York city. FreshDirect is a new online grocer who offers consumers 10% to 35% off supermarket prices and has a low delivery price of $3.95. It may be a matter of time until we all find online grocers like FreshDirect delivering in *our* neighborhoods. Datamonitor, a premium business information company specializing in industry analysis, announced that the U.S. online grocery sector will reach a market value of $26.8 billion by 2005. And, according to the report, *Online Grocery in the US, 2001,* the market for online grocery shopping is growing strongly, with total consumer expenditure increasing at a compound annual growth rate of 108.6% from $80 million in 1996 to $1.5 billion in 2000. Perhaps in a future edition of *The Bargain Buyer's Guide* I will be able to include some online grocery vendors who can save you money on something you need everyday. For now, the companies listed herein are specialty food stores that sell one type of item or items and/or food gift baskets and have been selected over hundreds for their quality, good service, and best bargains.

If you're seeking out companies that primarily sell herbs, spices, condiments, extracts, and other flavorings, see the section that follows entitled "Spices, Condiments, and Flavorings," page 225.

CAVIAR
Caviar and Imported Gourmet Foods Warehouse

CHEESE
Amana Meat Shop & Smokehouse, Gibbsville Cheese Company, New England Cheesemaking Supply

COFFEE AND TEA
Catskill Mountain Coffee, Northwestern Coffee Mills

COOKBOOKS
E.C. Kraus, Sultan's Delight

COOKIES AND BROWNIES
Bellows House Bakery

DRIED NUTS AND FRUIT
Sultan's Delight

FRESH ORGANIC CITRUS AND EXOTIC FRUIT
Starr Organic Produce

GIFT BASKETS AND BOXES
Amana Meat Shop & Smokehouse, Bellows House Bakery, Gibbsville Cheese Company, E.C. Kraus, Jake & Amos, New England Cheesemaking Supply, Northwestern Coffee Mills, Starr Organic Produce, Sultan's Delight

GOURMET FOODS
Caviar and Imported Gourmet Foods Warehouse, Sultan's Delight, The Truffle Market

HERBS AND SPICES
Sultan's Delight

JARS OF PICKLED VEGETABLES AND FRUIT PRESERVES
Jake & Amos

MEAT AND FISH
Amana Meat Shop & Smokehouse, Gibbsville Cheese Company, Caviar and Imported Gourmet Foods Warehouse

TRUFFLES
Caviar and Imported Gourmet Foods Warehouse, The Truffle Market

WINE- AND BEER-MAKING SUPPLIES
E.C. Kraus

Amana Meat Shop & Smokehouse

P.O. Box 158
Amana, IA 52203
800-373-6328
FAX: 800-373-3710

FORM OF INFORMATION: free print catalog; online catalog

PAY: check, MO, MC, V, AE, DSC

SELLS: smoked meats, steaks, chops, and food gift boxes

SMOKEHOUSE: Amana Colonies, Amana, IA; open daily; phone order hours Monday to Friday 8:00 am–5:00 pm CST

ONLINE: www.amanameatshop.com

This is a great source for mail-order meats and cheeses and gift boxes, with prices up to 25% less than the better-known food-by-mail companies. I was ecstatic to find this company. But first, a little history: In the 1850s a group of German immigrants settled in east-central Iowa, calling their new home Amana after a passage in the Song of Solomon meaning "to remain faithful." In the seven villages they established, known as the Amana Colonies, they lived communally, embracing a pure and simple way of life. In those days each village had a meat shop and smokehouse for curing ham, bacon, and sausage. Today thousands of visitors to the colonies and now readers of this book can buy delicious meats made using the same centuries-old recipes.

Flipping through the print catalog is a mouth-watering experience. Here you'll find hams in a bountiful variety, including smoked bone-in and boneless, honey smoked and spiral sliced; smoked turkey; several types of German sausage; bacon; pork chops; steaks (rib-eye, filet mignon, New York strips); beef jerky, and more. In addition to meats, there are wonderful gift boxes with assortments of cheeses, condiments, and meats. Prices here include shipping if you're within the continental U.S.; this is the best deal around on mail-order meats.

WEBSITE: At the website you'll not only get to see all the delicious selections Amana Meat Shop & Smokehouse has to offer—in full color with descriptive text—but you can also take advantage of amazing web specials and then order online.

SPECIAL FACTORS: Complete satisfaction guaranteed; shipping included in price within the continental U.S.; shipping extra on products shipped to Alaska, Hawaii, Puerto Rico, and Canada; corporate customers please inquire for pricing.

Bellows House Bakery

P.O. Box 818
Walpole, NH 03608
800–358–6302
603–445–1974
FAX: 603–445–1973

FORM OF INFORMATION: free print catalog; online catalog
PAY: check, MO, MC, V, AE
SELLS: cookies, brownies, shortbread, blondies, scones, and whoopie pies
STORE: no walk-in location; mail-order only; phone hours 7:00 am–6:00 pm EST
EMAIL: bhbakery@sover.net
ONLINE: www.bellowshouse.com

Looking for a company that sells delectable desserts that make great gifts at reasonable prices through the mail? Readers will be thrilled to learn about this company, Bellows House Bakery. When Lou and Lois, the proprietors of Bellows House Bed and Breakfast, decided to make their guests feel special by leaving a plate of home-baked goodies on the nightstand each evening, they didn't guess what this would lead to. Guests begged to take the cookies home with them or to order as gifts for friends and business associates. That's how it started, and today this company, with the same love and care baked into their cookies, wins national awards, gets written up in major news media, and has loyal customers all across the country. In 2001 and 2002, *New Hampshire Magazine* voted Bellows House Bakery the best cookies, brownies, and whoopie pies in the state.

All cookies are handmade and baked from scratch using only real butter, fresh whole eggs, high-quality chocolate, premium sugars, and unbleached flour. And no preservatives are used, not that these goodies could possibly remain uneaten for long! The selection here is fantastic, and the prices unbeatable. With quantity price breaks to bring the prices down ever further, it's especially penny-wise if you can do all your shopping for friends, family, and clients in one order. Offerings include traditional cookies—frosted chocolate nut, chocolate peanut butter, molasses, chocolate chip, almond butter, oatmeal raisin, and mint chocolate chip; shortbread cookies—almond, orange walnut, lemon, butter, chocolate chip, caramel nut, chocolate orange chocolate chip, chocolate cherry chocolate chip, chocolate peanut butter chip, apple pie, maple, raspberry chocolate chip; and heavenly brownies—fudge, raisinut, macaroon, mint chocolate chip, peanut butter chip, chocolate chip, chocolate cherry, and caramel pecan (my favorite). The bakery offers a variety of buying options—individually wrapped, in various small packages, in decorative gift assortments and gift tins, and in bulk packages. A great deal for the money, incidentally, are the sinfully rich brownies, which you can order in sheets. I found the price and quality here almost too good to be true, and you will, too.

Corporate clients: Bellows House Bakery does a lot of business with corporate clients. Inquiries welcome.

WEBSITE: Bellows has all of their delicious gift boxes and tins pictured with descriptions at their website. A price list can be viewed and downloaded here. Ordering is done by fax (order forms can be printed from the website), phone, or email.

SPECIAL FACTORS: 100% satisfaction guaranteed.

Catskill Mountain Coffee

906 Rt. 28
Kingston, NY 12401
845–334–8455
888–SAY–JAVA

FORM OF INFORMATION: free brochure; online catalog

PAY: check, MO, MC, V, AE, DSC

SELLS: organic, cooperatively grown coffee

STORE: same address; hours Monday to Friday 7:30 am–5:00 pm, Saturday and Sundays 10:00 am–4:00 pm

WEBSITE: www.catskillmtcoffee.com or www.buyorganiccoffee.com

Catskill Mountain Coffee sells some of the best beans in the world. And what's more, all of the coffee is certified organic *and* kosher. And on top of all that, the prices here are about 30% less than what you'd pay in a store (50% less than if you bought organic beans from a very popular national chain coffee store).

The coffee is roasted, flavored, and blended in small batches to ensure high quality and freshness. CMC is certified organic by the Northeast Organic Farming Association, Certified Organic, LCC. The Vaad Hakashrut of the Capital District, Albany, New York provides the supervision for their kosher certification. Owners, Emma Missouri and Katherine Keefe are committed to the principles of organic farming, which helps to replenish and rebuild our world's topsoil while protecting human and animal life. Many of their coffees are also certified Fair Trade. In other words, you can feel good about buying this coffee.

The full-color brochure lists the available beans—from Colombia, Ethiopia, Papua New Guinea, Guatemala, Peru, and so on; the blends, imaginatively named and described (for example, Dancin' On the Ceiling, Wired!, and Sophisticated Lady); and flavors, including Go Nuts!, Hazelnut, and Mud Pie (Chocolate, Pecan, and Vanilla). There are also a variety of Swiss-water processed decafs. Emma, Katherine, and the staff custom-roast the beans to one of five choices—Viennese, Full City, French, Espresso, or Turkish, all described in the brochure. This is without a doubt the least expensive organic and kosher coffee anywhere; the current wholesale prices at this writing were $6/pound for beans and blends, and $7/pound for decafs. The only catch is that you have to order 3 pounds of one type to get these prices. No problem! CMC also sells samplers so you can try all their delicious coffees.

WEBSITE: The website is informative very easy to navigate and has secure online ordering.

SPECIAL FACTORS: Minimum order: 3 pounds of one type.

Caviar and Imported Gourmet Foods Warehouse

888–889–1949

404–843–2047

FAX: 404–843–4465

FORM OF INFORMATION: online catalog only; no print catalog

PAY: MC, V, AE, DSC

SELLS: caviar, mushrooms, truffles, foie gras, smoked salmon, and other imported gourmet foods and gifts

STORE: no walk-in location; mail-order only; phone hours Monday to Friday 8:00 am– 5:00 pm EST

ONLINE: www.freshcaviar.com

★

I used to be fairly ignorant when it came to caviar. But a visit to the Caviar and Imported Gourmet Foods Warehouse (CIGFW) website was illuminating. There I learned how long caviar lasts (caviar's total shelf life is 2 to 3 weeks, which means it's important that you buy caviar from a reputable store that orders it fresh and sells in large volumes), why it's sold in colored tins or jars (color determines the type: Beluga is packed in blue; Osetra in yellow; Sevruga in red), and how it's processed (the *ikrjanschik,* or Russian caviar maker, has to apprentice 15 years before he's allowed to process caviar on his own, a delicate procedure involving running the large sac, or roe, over a fine mesh screen until the tiny eggs separate out). There's lots to learn here, but the most important thing for readers to know is that this is America's largest importer of fine gourmet foods, which results in prices that range from 20% to 60% below those of its competitors. If you're addicted to this expensive stuff, get ready to indulge yourself.

CIGFW sells caviar in many different styles, grades, and sizes; smoked salmon and other preserved gourmet fish (kippers, trout, and mackerel); mushrooms (morels, chanterelles, porcini, shiitake, oyster, and more); exotic imports (Spanish squid ink, saffron, and French prunes in Armagnac); foie gras of many types; truffles aplenty; and gift items including mother-of-pearl caviar sets. CIGFW even has an in-house executive chef who can help you plan a meal or recipe using any of these exotic products. Perishable items are shipped Federal Express overnight at $25 (you should consume your caviar within 2 to 3 days); nonperishable items are shipped UPS ground. Believe it or not, even with shipping factored in, CIGFW is still far ahead of the pack in terms of price. So don't shop for luxury foods anywhere else until you've checked out this website.

SPECIAL FACTORS: Wholesale inquiries welcome.

Gibbsville Cheese Company, Inc.

W2663 CTY OO
Sheboygan Falls, WI
53085–2971
920–564–3242
FAX: 920–564–6129

FORM OF INFORMATION: free price list; web-site

PAY: check or MO, MC, V

SELLS: Wisconsin cheese and summer sausage

STORE: same address (5 miles south of Sheboygan Falls on Hwy. 32); Monday to Saturday 8:00 am–5:00 pm

ONLINE: www.gibbsvillecheese.com

I have a portly friend who claims there's a part of the human brain that requires the "snap" of cheddar once a day to function properly. Gibbsville Cheese Company is the place where all cheese addicts can satisfy their needs at standout prices. For example, at this writing a pound of mild cheddar is $3.18/pound if you purchase it in 5-pound bulk packaging. My local supermarket charges $4.99/pound for mild cheddar at this writing. Gibbsville offers several types of Wisconsin summer sausage (regular, beef, or garlic) and beef sticks, too, in addition to well-priced gift boxes to suit every budget and taste. Their gift boxes—which include an assortment of cheeses, cheese spreads, and summer sausage—are 40% to 50% less than some of the better-known meat and cheese mail-order companies.

In business since 1933, Gibbsville produces the most popular kinds of cheese, including cheddar (mild, medium, aged, supersharp white, tomato basil, and car-away), Monterey jack (including garlic, dill, vegetable, and pepper versions), two-tone cheese, colby, colby with salami, and reduced-fat colby. Among the cheeses they sell, but do not produce, are: Swiss, Muenster, Parmesan, Romano, Gouda, Mozzarella, brick string, blue, and provolone. If you're into flavored cold-packed cheese spreads, you'll find them here ranging from sharp cheddar, Swiss almond, hot pepper, and bacon-flavored cheeses to port wine, garlic-and-herb, and horseradish cheese spreads. Dieters will appreciate the lower-fat varieties, clearly marked in the catalog.

Please note: Gibbsville doesn't ship during the summer months—from approximately May to September—as UPS doesn't have refrigeration.

WEBSITE: The website is very nice and easy to use—you can browse all of their products here, download a catalog, and order online.

SPECIAL FACTORS: UPS will not deliver to post office boxes; price quotes by letter with SASE.

Jake & Amos

P.O. Box 7595
Lancaster, PA 17602
866-JA-PICKLE
866-527-4255

FORM OF INFORMATION: online catalog only; no print catalog

PAY: check or MO, MC, V, DSC

SELLS: all natural Amish-style pickled foods, condiments, jams, jellies, fruit preserves, fruit spread, and other jarred fruit products

STORE: Rt 340, Bird In Hand, PA; see website for hours

ONLINE: www.jakeandamos.com

Jake & Amos, a family-owned company which began in 1993, sells all natural Amish style canned vegetable and fruit products in clear glass quart jars. Their ever-growing line of products currently include over 60 different choices of pickled vegetables, salads, relishes, spreads, fruit butters, sauces, mustards, and salad dressings.

Jake & Amos believe that canning is an art. They know that the way a product is canned can affect the quality of its flavor. In addition to using only the finest ingredients, what makes their products so delicious is that they employ different canning processes for each product, they select the process that will best maintain the goodness and full flavor of all the ingredients.

This is an original and quaint, not to mention inexpensive, source for gift giving. An assortment pack of six 16 oz. jars of preserves at Jake & Amos is $27, with shipping included. If you purchased four 10 oz. jars of preserves from a very well-known food mail-order company (H & D), it would cost you $28.90. That means, with shipping figured in, at H & D you're paying 72¢ an ounce and at Jake & Amos you're paying 28¢ an ounce. That's 61% less! All orders must be in multiples of 6 jars of any combination and shipping is free.

SPECIAL FACTORS: Shipping is free of charge within continental U.S.; AK, HI, U.S. territories, and Canada require a $2.00 per jar shipping charge; 100% money-back guarantee.

E.C. Kraus

P.O. Box 7850–WC
Independence, MO 64054
816–254–7448
FAX: 816–254–7051

FORM OF INFORMATION: free print catalog; online catalog

PAY: check, MO, MC, V, DSC

SELLS: home wine- and beer-making supplies

STORE: 733 S. Northern Blvd., Independence, MO; Monday to Friday 8:00 am–5:30 pm, Saturday 9:00 am–1:00 pm

ONLINE: www.eckraus.com

Save up to half the cost of wine, beer, and liqueurs. How? Make them yourself! One of the gals in my college dorm used to whip up batches of "Kahlua" made from vodka, instant coffee, and artificial sweetener. Yuck! Fortunately, our palates get more sophisticated with age, and E.C. Kraus is just the place to get started anew with a home wine-making hobby. For over 30 years, they've made it simple by selling kits through their "Home Wine and Beer Making Equipment and Supplies" catalog that include everything you need to make 4 gallons of beer, or 5 gallons of wine, including ingredients and instruction books. This is a one-time investment, after which you need only buy the ingredients and a few other supplies, sold here as well. Yeast (for beer and wine), fruit acids, wine clarifiers, purifiers and preservatives, grape concentrates, fermenting vats, malted barley grains, kits for specific beers and soft drinks, liqueur extracts, measuring tools and gauges, and a great selection of books, manuals, and videos are a few of the items E.C. Kraus sells. By the way, a note in the catalog mentions that it's legal for a one-person household to make 100 gallons of beer or wine a year, as long as it's consumed and not sold. If there's more than one adult, the limit is 200 gallons. Hmm. That comes out to almost 4 gallons a week per couple. No problem!

WEBSITE: Not only does the E.C. Kraus website have all of their products online, you'll find plenty of articles and recipes to get you started or keep you going. Online ordering is available now as well.

SPECIAL FACTORS: Please check your local ordinances regarding home production of alcoholic beverages; shipment to APO/FPO addresses "at buyer's risk"; C.O.D. (UPS) orders accepted; shipping is free in the continental U.S. on orders over $25.

New England Cheesemaking Supply Co.

292 Main St., Dept. WBM
Ashfield, MA 01330
413–628–3808
FAX: 413–628–4061

FORM OF INFORMATION: $1 print catalog; online catalog

PAY: check, MO, MC, V

SELLS: cheese-making supplies and equipment

STORE: same address; Monday to Friday 8:00 am–4:00 pm (call for appointment)

ONLINE: www.cheesemaking.com

Making cheese at home is easier than you might think. It's also economical. The only problem is, according to Ricki, owner of New England Cheesemaking Supply, once you've tasted your own freshly made cheese, the store-bought variety will never quite live up to your expectations again. The 20-page newsprint catalog will help you feel confident about starting your cheesemaking endeavor with some wonderful products for beginners (Mozzarella and Ricotta Kit), books, equipment such as cheese presses, molds, and pasteurizers, supplies such as cheesecloth and cultures (starters), and much more. What kinds of cheese can one make at home? Cheddar, Gouda, Monterey jack, cottage cheese, buttermilk cheese, ricotta, mozzarella, mascarpone, gourmet soft cheeses, crème fraîche, chèvre—you name it, and you'll find everything necessary to do so right here.

WEBSITE: If you can, skip the print catalog (save a tree, save a dollar) and go right to the adorable website, where you can order online, get recipe ideas, and link to related sites.

SPECIAL FACTORS: A 10% restocking fee applies to all returned items.

New Global Marketing

P.O. Box 652
Stone Ridge, NY 12484
845–658–7610
FAX: 845–658–7618

FORM OF INFORMATION: online catalog; print catalog
PAY: MO, MC, V, AE, DSC
SELLS: cigars, humidors, and smoking accessories
STORE: no walk-in location; mail-order only, phone hours Monday to Friday 9:00 am–5:00 pm EST
ONLINE: www.bestcigarprices.com

New Global Cigars and their premier website BestCigarPrices.com purchase only the major brand cigars including many of the smaller boutique lines that have come out over the last few years, then resells them with only a small mark-up. This company also seeks out brands that aren't top sellers, but are of good quality and at a price they consider a great deal for you. Fabulous prices resulting in high-volume sales means that the cigars you buy here are really fresh. The website, frequently updated to reflect the latest price fluctuations, lists hundreds of cigars alphabetically along with their near-wholesale price tag. There are no fancy photographs or descriptions, so this is a great place to shop if you already know cigars. However, if you're looking for some friendly guidance, the nice people at New Global assured me they're happy to field phone calls and answer questions. ("It happens all the time," says the owner.) You can order online, by phone, or download an order form, fill it out by hand, and fax it in. If you don't have internet access, a print catalog is available by request.

SPECIAL FACTORS: New York State residents must pay the appropriate tobacco and sales taxes; a $5 surcharge is waived if you order 2 or more items or if your order totals $100 or more.

Northwestern Coffee Mills

30950 Nevers Rd.
Washburn, WI 54891
800–243–5283
715–747–5555
FAX: 715–747–5405

FORM OF INFORMATION: free print catalog, $2 outside U.S.; online catalog

PAY: check, MO, MC, V, AE, DSC

SELLS: coffee, tea, herbs, spices, coffee filters, coffee flavors, and syrups

STORE: 30950 Nevers Rd., Washburn, WI; Monday to Saturday 10:00 am–4:00 pm

ONLINE: www.nwcoffeemills.com

Northwestern Coffee Mills has had long experience in their specialty coffee and tea business that began 125 years ago as Robertson's, the first coffee roaster in Wisconsin. They have moved their landmark Milwaukee roasting mill and vintage 1914 roasting equipment to northern Wisconsin where they continue their long established tradition of superb coffees, teas, and spices. To keep apace with today's coffee and tea drinkers, not to mention the competition, Northwestern offers a selection that's broad and deep, good prices that become even better when you order in quantity, flat-rate shipping, and excellent service. Using gas-fired, slow-roasting ovens creates especially delicious coffee. Whole bean or ground to order, the coffees here include blends, estate straights (Brazil Serra Negra, Guatamala Antigua, Mexican Custapec Altura, Ethiopia Harrar, to name a few), natural decaffeinated (CO_2 or Swiss water–processed) blends and straights, and dark roasts as well as some organic coffees. Teas include black-tea single estates and blends, Oolong and green teas, flavored and herb teas, decaf, and organic, all loose. Interesting gift packs and samplers are available here, as well as coffee flavors and syrups and an assortment of coffee filters. The expanded spice offerings include many varieties of chili peppers and dried mushrooms. If you're an unabashed caffeine fiend, join the Coffee-of-the-Month club and have incredible coffee delivered right to your door for less. Now if only someone could make it for you each morning!

WEBSITE: This no-nonsense website in coffee-colored type describes their roasting process, explains how tea leaves are typed and graded, and gives hints on how to brew a good cup of coffee or tea. You'll find their full selection of coffee, tea, spices, coffee flavors, and brewing equipment here. The kind owner at Northwestern told me they expect to be taking secure online orders soon so do check in as they may be taking them now as you read this.

SPECIAL FACTORS: Satisfaction guaranteed; quantity discounts available.

Starr Organic Produce, Inc.

P.O. Box 551745
Ft. Lauderdale, FL 33355
888–262–1242
FAX: 954–723–0779

FORM OF INFORMATION: online catalog only
PAY: check, MO, MC, V
SELLS: organically grown fresh-picked tropical fruit
STORE: no walk-in location; mail-order only; phone hours Monday to Friday 12:00 noon–6:00 pm EST
ONLINE: www.starrorganic.com

All right readers, we're going to have a little lesson in comparing apples to oranges now. It has come to my attention that some of you (you know who you are) call this wonderful company and order produce and then after the shipping is added on, you complain that you can buy oranges locally for cheaper. First of all, I hope you are making a proper comparison. It would be so embarrassing if you were comparing some dried up, bland, waxed, gassed, dyed, genetically modified, irradiated and pesticide treated orange-colored round sphere called an orange at your local supermarket with one of these hand-picked, hand-selected, naturally ripened, unbelievably fresh, juicy, vibrant, sweet yet tangy, untreated, organic, at the peak of ripeness oranges. At this writing, I have purchased twelve organic Valencia oranges from my local health food store, twelve organic Valencia oranges from a very popular online organic store, and twelve organic Valencia oranges from Starr. Please don't make me explain the pros of organic produce over non-organic—that's another book. The price per pound for the oranges at my local health food store were .99¢. These were less expensive than Starr at

$1.55 per pound, but the oranges from my local store were so dry and tasteless that I couldn't/wouldn't eat them. The oranges from the online organic store were quite delicious, but more expensive than Starr at $2.69 a pound. Since shipping was similar from both places, Starr was the clear winner here with delicious oranges at 47% less than the online organic grocer. But, you might live in an area where delicious, and hopefully organic, citrus is readily available at good prices. Check your prices first, locally, before you call Starr.

If you'll indulge me for a little more, I would like to give another price comparison which I think you'll be very happy with. I receive numerous gifts throughout the year of food gift baskets and boxes—most often purchased from a very popular mail-order food gift company. (Hint: their name starts with an H and ends with a D). A Royal Citrus Combo Box weighing in at 7-pounds 6-ounces of non-organic, albeit very delicious, oranges and grapefruits from this company costs, at this writing, $4.06 a pound. A 10-pound citrus mix of organic oranges and grapefruits from Starr will cost you $1.90 a pound. That's a 53% savings. Shipping costs are similar for both companies. I prefer receiving organic fruit and am happier knowing my gift-giver saved money in the process.

For over 25 years Starr Organic Produce has been in the business of delivering fresh-picked *certified organic* tropical fruits to folks across the U.S.. It's hard to fathom that one could get avocados, Florida papayas, oranges (juice, navel, temple, Valencia), honey tangerines, Mineola tangelos, red/pink grapefruit, mangoes, and limes delivered to your home at these prices. The very personable co-owner of this company told us that while other growers in Florida allow gassing of their fruit, Starr Organic is committed to bringing only the most impeccably grown fruit to their customers, which means hand-picked, hand-selected fruit that has been naturally ripened and has never been waxed, gassed, treated with poison pesticides, or irradiated. The website presents a list of tropical fruits and the months in which they're generally available. Boxes range from 8 to 40 pounds. Sign up for the Monthly Organic Plan and receive a monthly 10- or 20-pound box of different in-season fruit throughout the whole year.

SPECIAL FACTORS: Starr Organic cannot ship to Hawaii, Alaska, or California; certified health-food stores and co-ops are welcome to inquire about wholesale terms; satisfaction guaranteed.

Sultan's Delight

P.O. Box 090302
Fort Hamilton Station
Brooklyn, NY 11209
800-852-5046
718-745-2121
FAX: 718-745-2563

FORM OF INFORMATION: free print catalog with SASE; online catalog

PAY: check, MO, MC, V, AE, DSC

SELLS: Middle Eastern and Mediterranean foods and gifts

STORE: no walk-in location; mail-order only

ONLINE: www.sultansdelight.com

Sultan's Delight, a division of Nuts About Nuts, Inc., is frequently cited in magazines and cookbooks as a source of Middle Eastern and Mediterranean foods and ingredients. The prices here are good and, in some cases, tremendous—at least 30% below what they'd be in gourmet specialty shops. Whether you familiarize yourself with these products over the internet or by requesting a print catalog (include a SASE), Sultan's Delight provides a very smart and convenient way to stock your kitchen with ready-to-serve Middle Eastern specialties, grains and beans, spices, dried or candied fruit, preserves and syrups, bread and pastry dough, Turkish coffee and tea, tahini, flower water, olives, specialty oils, pistacios and other nuts. Sultan's Delight also carries Italian items (such as olive oil and black olive sauce), henna, and even Turkish coffee cups. If you're into cooking, this is a company you'll want to get to know. The nice handful of cookbooks here offer introductions to cooking with spices, and primers on Lebanese, Moroccan, Armenian, and Greek cuisine. For the kitchen there are also items such as falafel molds, Arab head dress cloth (great for tablecloths), and frankincense.

WEBSITE: If you're an experienced cook or know just what you want, the website is a fast and easy way to shop here. You won't find elaborate descriptions or fancy pictures for most of the goods here. Items are listed in table form, and you can place your order electronically right on the site.

SPECIAL FACTORS: Minimum order: $20; inquire about shipping options other than UPS.

The Truffle Market

P.O. Box 4234
Gettysburg, PA 17325
800–822–4003
718–745–2121
FAX: 717–337–3936

FORM OF INFORMATION: online catalog only, no print catalog

PAY: check, MO, MC, V

SELLS: Italian truffles and mushroom products

STORE: no walk-in location; mail-order only

ONLINE: www.trufflemarket.com

After paying the bill for a white truffle in December, you may not believe that companies in the truffle industry offer sales. Well, you're wrong! The Truffle Market offers many delicious products at reduced prices. Their permanent Products on Sale page on their website hosts items that the Truffle Market is either considering to stock or discontinuing. This page offers a great opportunity to try new products and save money on the ones you already love. You'll want to check out the very informative and interesting fact section about truffles. You'll find everything you need to know about truffles here, including descriptions of types of truffles, handling of truffles, and hunting and cultivating them. Did you know that the only evidence that supports the myth that truffles are an aphrodisiac is that the odor of the truffle contains alpha-androstenol—a chemical found on the breath of pigs? This chemical is suspected to be a pheromone which attracts female pigs and would explain why sows have a natural talent for finding truffles. However, it is more likely attributed to another chemical also present in the fungus, dimethyl sulfide.

In addition to white truffles, black summer truffles, and bianchetto truffles, The Truffle Market carries white truffle oil, truffle butter, truffle carpaccio, truffle and porcini cream, olive cream, truffle flour, dried mushrooms, black truffle juice, black truffle peelings, truffle and porcini pasta, truffle puree, truffle sauce, fondue truffle cheese, truffle slicers, Spanish saffron, truffle vinegar, and their exclusive, truffle cheese.

SPECIAL FACTORS: Minimum order: $25; shipping and handling in continental U.S. is $5 per order.

Spices, Condiments, and Flavorings

Bulk herbs and spices; spice blends for instant dishes; international condiments; flavoring oils and extracts

The companies in this section carry all the little items that jazz up our palates, whether it's exotic and unusual oils for flavoring, Cajun spices, Indian chutneys, or Vermont maple cream. These are some of the best items to buy mail-order, since they're often sold in bulk, which can mean up to 95% savings! Just be sure that you store your herbs and spices in airtight bottles or jars, away from heat and light.

Find It Fast

CONDIMENTS
The CMC Company, Palmer's Maple Products, Wildtree Herbs, Wood's Cider Mill

ETHNIC SEASONINGS, SAUCES, CONDIMENTS
The CMC Company, Wildtree Herbs

FLAVORINGS, ESSENTIAL OILS, EXTRACTS
Atlantic Spice, Bickford Flavors, Rafal Spice, Wildtree Herbs

GIFT BOXES
Palmer Maple Products, Wildtree Herbs, Wood's Cider Mill

HERBS AND SPICES
Atlantic Spice, Rafal Spice, Wildtree Herbs

MEDICINAL HERBS AND BOTANICALS
Atlantic Spice

POTPOURRI INGREDIENTS
Atlantic Spice, Rafal Spice

TEA AND COFFEE
Rafal Spice

Atlantic Spice Co.

P.O. Box 205
North Truro, MA 02652
800–316–7965
508–487–6100
FAX: 508–487–2550

FORM OF INFORMATION: free catalog with potpourri recipes; online catalog

PAY: check, MO, MC, V, DSC

SELLS: culinary herbs and spices, teas, potpourri ingredients, dehydrated vegetables, nuts, seeds, botanicals, and essential oils

OUTLET: Junction of Route 6 and 6A, North Truro, MA; Monday to Friday 9:00 am–5:00 pm, Saturday 10:00 am–2:00 pm

ONLINE: www.atlanticspice.com

Atlantic Spice Co. will add spice to your life whether you're cooking up gourmet meals; healing with herbs, botanicals, and essences; or creating scented wreaths and potpourri. All ingredients are free from irradiation. Most of the items are sold in bulk and wrapped in 1-pound packages made of biodegradable plastic. Cooks will find spice blends (apple pie, curry powder, pickling spice, etc.); culinary herbs and spices; extracts and flavors; bulk teas; baking items; dehydrated vegetables; and shelled nuts and seeds at savings of 50% and more. There's lots here for the New Ager, such as St. John's Wort, Valerian root powder, golden seal root powder, and ginseng powder, not to mention those essential oils used by aromatherapists. Craftspeople will appreciate the fragrance oils, potpourri ingredients, and fabulous, detailed recipes for potpourri, sachets, pomander balls, and simmering fragrances.

Rounding out the double-sided, maplike catalog are related supplies and equipment—muslin sachet bags, potpourri jars, self-seal tea bags, spice jars, gel caps and capsule fillers, plastic gallon jars, and the like. The listings are flagged to note items that shouldn't be used in food or drink. Atlantic's low prices drop 10% on orders of 5 pounds of the same item (based on the 1-pound rate), 15% off on 25 pounds, and orders over $200 get an additional 10% off, orders over $500 get 15% off.

WEBSITE: Atlantic Spice's website is straightforward and easy to use—the full inventory is online and you can order electronically.

SPECIAL FACTORS: Satisfaction guaranteed; quantity discounts available; minimum order: $30; add $6 to C.O.D. orders.

Bickford Flavors

19007 St. Clair Ave.
Cleveland, OH 44117
800–283–8322
TEL: 216–531–6006
FAX: 216-531-2006

FORM OF INFORMATION: free price list; online catalog
PAY: check, MO, MC, V
SELLS: flavorings
STORE: same address; Monday to Friday 9:00 am–5:00 pm EST
ONLINE: www.bickfordflavors.com

If you or someone you know objects to foods that have alcohol as an ingredient, you've just found an unusual and excellent source for nonalcoholic flavorings. Established in 1914, Bickford Flavors makes and sells their own concentrated flavorings from naturally derived oils. You won't find any added alcohol, sugar or salt here; you will find a dizzying selection of flavors in their flyer—over 100 at last count—as well as food colorings and odd ingredients, such as vanilla powder and carob syrup. Get a load of some of these flavorings (in soy or propylene base): cola, banana, banana strawberry, cheesecake, cranberry, rootbeer, watermelon, butter rum, wild cherry, caramel, cinnamon, chocolate almond, maple, peach, raspberry, strawberry, Irish cream, malted milk, vanilla butternut, peanut butter, kahlua, creamcheese, cream de menthe, grand mariner, hazelnut, praline, pistschio, garlic, and of course pure vanilla. Most flavors Bickford carries are in an oil extract and are certified Kosher. Imagine the unusual candies, cakes, chocolate, ice cream, lollipops, and flavored waters you could make! All flavors are sold in a variety of sizes ranging from 1-ounce to 1-gallon. The selection here is unparalleled and prices are good. If you can buy in larger sizes (8 ounces and up), the prices go down even further.

WEBSITE: The website has a searchable database of all of their flavorings, a price list, along with a little bit of history about their company. Online ordering is available.

SPECIAL FACTORS: Flavorings are free of alcohol and sugar; wholesalers should inquire about terms.

The CMC Company

P.O. Drawer 322
Avalon, NJ 08202
800-CMC-2780
FAX: 609-861-3065

FORM OF INFORMATION: Refundable $5 print catalog; online catalog

PAY: check, MO, MC, V, AE, DSC

SELLS: gourmet seasonings and ethnic specialties

STORE: no walk-in location; mail-order only

ONLINE: www.thecmccompany.com

If English is your second language and you're living in Snowfall, Idaho, you may have a problem. Namely, where are you going to find that crucial Pakistani, Malaysian, Mexican, or Thai ingredient to make your family's favorite dish? Don't worry, because The CMC Company specializes in hard-to-find ingredients and food specialties for both gourmet and gourmand, and they're less expensive here—by 10% to 50%—than in most gourmet shops.

Some of the items CMC carries include dried, powdered, and canned chiles for Mexican cuisine, Mexican hot sauce, hot chile peanuts, tomatillos, Mexican dried shrimp, and more. If ingredients from Thailand, Malaysia, Singapore, or Indonesia are what you seek, check out the sambals, sauces, spices, curry pastes, and rice at CMC. You'll also find ingredients for the following cuisines: Chinese, Indian, Pakistani, Japanese, Creole, Cajun, Jamaican, French, Greek, and Middle Eastern. The 38-page catalog from CMC offers the very best ethnic cookbooks from around the world, and special implements needed in preparing such cuisine such as a tortilla press, a food smoker bag, and more. "It is our hope," says the catalog text, "that we can help you prepare authentic ethnic dishes without resorting to unsuitable substitutions or unfortunate omissions."

Wholesale customers, please note: Discounts are given to resellers and food-service professionals.

WEBSITE: The website is really great and offers some specials you won't get from the catalog. Ingredients are categorized by country or region (Japan, India/Pakistan, China/Hong Kong, etc.), with brief descriptions included. The website features online ordering.

SPECIAL FACTORS: Updates to the catalog can be found at the website.

Palmer's Maple Products

72 Maple Ln.
Waitsfield, VT 05673–9710
TEL/FAX: 802–496–3696

FORM OF INFORMATION: brochure and price list, free with long SASE

PAY: check, MO, MC, V

SELLS: maple syrup, cream, candy, and jelly

STORE: Mehuron's Market and Bisbee's Hardware, Waitsfield, VT

Maple sap harvesting is an art that's been passed down from generation to generation. How does one know when it's time to head out into the woods and begin the arduous process of tapping the trees? The Palmers of Waitsfield, Vermont, claim "a certain scent is in the air." Delbert Palmer, the fourth generation to be involved in producing this all-American nectar, along with his wife, Sharlia, their two children, Shawn and Susan, and even their grandchildren (that's 6 generations!), run a world-renowned maple farm complete with a new sugar house that's wheelchair accessible. The brochure details the process of sugaring, relates the history of the Palmers' operation, includes happy-customer testimonials as well as recipes, and presents the wonderful products they make on their farm. You can buy grade A maple syrup (light amber, medium amber, dark amber) in various sizes and formats, including a log cabin and a gift jug; maple cream in 2, 4, 8, and 16 ounces; maple jelly; a variety box of maple candy; and even honey. Prices here are excellent, especially when you buy in larger quantities. If you have a kid who eats oatmeal, waffles, and pancakes, you'll go through that ½ gallon in no time! Talking with the Palmers was a lovely experience, and their company literature reflects their old-fashioned integrity and family values. Visitors are welcome to drop by.

SPECIAL FACTORS: Be sure to include a long SASE when you request a price list and brochure.

Rafal Spice Company

2521 Russell St.
Detroit, MI 48207
800–228–4276
313–259–6373
FAX: 313–259–6220

FORM OF INFORMATION: free print catalog; online catalog
PAY: check, MO, MC, V, AE, DSC
SELLS: spices, herbs, coffee, tea, flavorings, cookbooks, etc.
STORE: same address; Monday to Saturday 7:00 am–4:00 pm
ONLINE: www.rafalspicecompany.com

Rafal is a good source for a wide variety of flavoring items: spices and herbs, food specialties from anchovy paste to Wright's Liquid Smoke, extracts (pure, imitation, and alcohol-free), and coffee flavorings, among others. On select items you can save as much as 30%, and even more when you buy in bulk. If ethnic cooking is your thing, be it Cajun or Chinese, you'll find a wide range of unusual ingredients here, such as Creole seasonings; French beignet mix; fiery condiments with saucy names like Dis Stuff Really Hot Mon!, Endorphin Rush, and Ass Kickin' Sauce; cellophane noodles; Swiss spaetzle dumplings; Thai satay (spicy peanut) sauce; and much more. Rafal also sells coffee beans by the pound, teas, cookbooks, spice jars, essential oils, and potpourri ingredients.

WEBSITE: The website is pretty straightforward. You'll find all of Rafal's products here. There are no product descriptions or images, however you can order online.

SPECIAL FACTORS: Satisfaction guaranteed; allow 3 weeks for delivery.

Wildtree Herbs, Inc.

11 Knight St.
Warwick, RI 02886
800–672–4050
401–732–1856
FAX: 401–732–1968

FORM OF INFORMATION: free brochure; web-site

PAY: check, MO, MC, V, AE

SELLS: herbs, spices, soup mixes, and culinary blends

STORE: same address; Monday to Friday 9:00 am–6:00 pm EST

ONLINE: www.wildtreeherbs.com

How wonderful to have discovered this family-owned business. Wildtree Herbs, in business since 1995, was founded on the notion that busy people deserve to have meals that are inexpensive, fast, and convenient—without having to resort to eating in fast-food restaurants or microwaving a frozen brick of stuff called food.

Instead, what you will find in the brochure are culinary spice and herb blends that turn cooking interesting food into a no-brainer. Every packet comes with recipes and instructions. Examples: Scampi Blend, for an impressive meal in minutes; Fajita Seasoning Blend, the perfect marinade for chicken and steak fajitas; Sun-dried Tomato Pesto; Hearty Spaghetti Sauce Blend, which transforms a can of crushed tomatoes into a quick and delicious fat-free sauce; and Blasted Bloody Mary Blend, the perfect cocktail concoction but also a secret ingredient for salsa. My favorite—Carol's Cranberry Horseradish Blend: just mash it into some softened cream cheese and spread it on crackers. Yum! The herbs and spices here have no additives, no fillers, and are not irradiated. Because Wildtree Herbs does all the blending themselves, you get higher quality, fresher products—there is no wait between the manufacturer, distributor, and your shelf. Most items are available in a small and a larger size, and the prices here are very reasonable. Wildtree also has soup mixes, dressings and marinades, infused grapeseed oils, bread dipping oils, single herbs and spices, small kitchen accessories, fudge sauces, and even treats for dogs and cats.

I liked the themed gift sets (for instance, garlic lovers, pasta assortments, quick and easy meals) that they will wrap according to any holiday, year-round.

WEBSITE: You can download the brochure at the website. At press time the shopping page was under construction and may be up and running by the time you read this. In the meantime, you will need to call and order by phone.

Wood's Cider Mill

1482 Weathersfield Center Rd.
Springfield, VT 05156
802–263–5547
FAX: 802–263–9674

FORM OF INFORMATION: free brochure with SASE; online catalog

PAY: check, MO, MC, V

SELLS: apple cider jelly and syrups

FARM: call for appointment; phone hours Monday to Friday 9:00 am–5:00 pm EST

ONLINE: www.woodscidermill.com

Willis and Tina are the Woods behind Wood's Cider Mill. Their small southern Vermont farm, on which they keep cows, sheep, chickens, and a vegetable garden, has been in the family since 1798. Luckily for us, the Woods produce 4 items they sell by mail. The first 2 are cider jelly and boiled cider. They grind and press apples on the original 1882 screw press to make sweet cider, then evaporate it in a wood-fired stainless-steel evaporator to make boiled cider. Boiled cider is concentrated to about 7 to 1, and cider jelly about 9 to 1. Use boiled cider with hot water for a delicious drink, in cooking, or as a topping for pancakes, yogurt, or ice cream. Cider jelly is great with peanut butter on sandwiches, on bagels, or along with stews and meats. (The Woods will send you a recipe sheet if you request one with a SASE.) You'll also find maple syrup here, for which Vermont is famous, and the Woods' own cinnamon cider syrup—half maple syrup, half boiled cider with a stick of cinnamon in each bottle. Yum! Some say it tastes like apple pie in a bottle. The prices here are excellent, especially if you order larger-format bottles and jars.

WEBSITE: You can find out about apple pressing and tree tapping at their website, plus they have a short description of each of the four products along with a few recipes. There was no online ordering at press time and there were no prices listed for the four products.

SPECIAL FACTORS: Satisfaction guaranteed; quantity discounts available.

Garden, Farm, and Lawn

Seeds, bulbs, and live plants; supplies, tools, and equipment
for vegetable and flower gardening, small-scale farms and
nurseries, beekeeping, and land- and waterscaping

While most of the country waits every year to see if Punxsutawney Phil will see his shadow, avid gardeners are already well into their plans for spring and beyond. Why? Because as soon as the first seed catalog arrives at year's beginning, they have big decisions to make. Soon they'll be enjoying the bounty of fresh vegetables that grace every meal and giant bouquets of roses, gladiolas, zinnias, and snapdragons that decorate every room. If you've never experienced gardening, I highly recommend it. Ask anyone who grows vegetables, tends flowers, or just putters around the yard taking pride in weedless borders: Working the land is a proven cure for malaise.

Print and online catalogs provide one of the best ways to extensively plan your garden. Not only can the companies in this chapter bring you a fantastic selection of bulbs, plants, flowers, herbs, seedlings, as well as tools and equipment, but they can do so at considerable savings compared to your local farm and garden centers.

If you're a beginner, don't fret. Most of these firms have catalogs or websites jam-packed with tips and information. Many also sell great reference books as well. And all are staffed with people who want to answer your questions and offer advice. Gardening isn't hard as long as you buy plants, bulbs, and seeds appropriate to your climate, conditions, and soil. Ohio Earth Foods, listed in this chapter, will test your soil for $18, which is less than half the price of the best-known home gardener kits. Want to start a new hobby? Why not take up beekeeping? Brushy Mountain Bee Farm listed in this section can help you get started.

If you're ready to quit that corporate job and begin a whole new life, then move out of the city and start a Christmas tree farm. Flickinger's Nurseries sells evergreen seedlings at wholesale prices. Or you can order tree seedlings and transplants to plant around your new country home from Carino Nurseries.

From tractors to garden tools to lawn furniture, there are plenty of companies located elsewhere in this book that sell goods related to farming, landscaping, and gardening.

Find It Fast

BEEKEEPING SUPPLIES
Brushy Mountain Bee Farm

BULBS
Dutch Gardens, Mellinger's, Miller Nurseries, Pinetree Garden Seeds, Van Dyck's, Van Engelen

FLOWER, VEGETABLE, HERB SEEDS
D.V. Burrell Seed Growers, Butterbrooke Farm Seed Co-op, Fedco Seeds, Johnny's Selected Seeds, Mellinger's, Miller Nurseries, Pinetree Garden Seeds, Rohrer's Seeds, Twilley Seeds

GARDEN AND LAWN DECOR AND FURNITURE
Turner Greenhouses

GARDENING BOOKS
D.V. Burrell Seed Growers, Butterbrooke Farm Seed Co-op, Fedco Seeds, Johnny's Selected Seeds, Mellinger's, Pinetree Garden Seeds, Turner Greenhouses

GREENHOUSES
Bob's Superstrong Greenhouse Plastic, D.V. Burrell Seed Growers, Mellinger's, Turner Greenhouses

LIVE PLANTS
Carino Nurseries, Fedco Seeds, Flickinger's Nurseries, George's Plant Farm, Mellinger's, Miller Nurseries, Nor'East Miniature Roses, Pinetree Garden Seeds, Prentiss Court Ground Covers

POND LINERS AND POND EQUIPMENT
Bob's Superstrong Greenhouse Plastic

TOOLS AND SUPPLIES
D.V. Burrell Seed Growers, EON Industries, Fedco Seeds, Johnny's Selected Seeds, Mellinger's, Ohio Earth Food, Pinetree Garden Seeds, Rohrer's Seeds

TREES
Carino Nurseries, Flickinger's Nurseries, Miller Nurseries

Bob's Superstrong Greenhouse Plastic

Box 42–WM, Neche, ND 58265

Box 1450–WM, Altona, MB R0G OBO Canada

204–327–5540

FAX: 204–327–5527

FORM OF INFORMATION: brochure, $1 or 2 first-class stamps

PAY: check or MO

SELLS: greenhouse plastic and fastening systems, and pond liners

SHOWROOMS: Neche, ND, and Altona, Manitoba, Canada (by appointment); phone hours Monday to Friday 6:00 am–8:00 pm CST (The best time to get Bob, himself, is 6:00 am–9:00 am.)

Bob and Margaret Davis started their business in 1980 when they decided to combine his gardening experience with her business-management skills to market their UV-stabilized superstrong woven poly, the only greenhouse plastic they found that was strong enough to resist the violent winds, hail, and temperature changes on their Manitoba prairie farm. Their 32-page newsprint catalog is a joy to thumb through; the Davises show us the many uses for this miracle stuff and wax poetic on their missions to aid troubled teens through promoting greenhouse projects in the U.S. and Canada, to encourage solar heating and wind power, and to help ordinary folk get the most out of their gardens in every season.

The woven poly comes in 7-, 10.5-, 13- and 20-mil thicknesses, in clear (also called translucent) or opaque. The catalog text describes the different properties and possible uses for each. There are two anchoring systems to choose from: the Cinchstrap, a plastic lath to nail down the poly, and Polyfastener, a two-part plastic channel-and-insert strip. Prices for the woven poly run from 17 cents to 27 cents per square foot. Custom-made barn curtains, tarps, plastic mulching, terrariums, and greenhouse kits are also offered here. Besides the detailed measurement and price charts and descriptions, there are testimonials from happy customers who have used Bob's Superstrong Poly for everything from sails and water-tank liners to boat sheds and skywalks.

Note to Canadian readers: Please write to Canadian address for literature.

SPECIAL FACTORS: C.O.D. orders accepted.

Brushy Mountain Bee Farm

610 Bethany Church Rd.
Moravian Falls, NC 28654
800-233-7929
336-921-3640
FAX: 336-921-2681

FORM OF INFORMATION: free print catalog; online catalog

PAY: check, MO, V, MC, DSC

SELLS: supplies for beekeeping and candle, soap, mead, and books on vinegar making

STORE: same address; Monday to Friday 8:30 am–5:00 pm

ONLINE: www.beeequipment.com

You'll like this company, whether you're a seasoned beekeeper or merely interested in the subject. The 88-page catalog makes for a great read. For example, did you know that queen-marking colors are internationally standardized so that any queen's age anywhere in the world can be easily determined? (I didn't even know queens were marked.) The catalog is jam-packed with articles, calendars, suggested references, product descriptions, personal anecdotes, checklists, and advice. Best of all, prices here are about 20% to 30% below retail. The owners, who've been in business since 1978, have a friendly attitude toward their customers. You'll find beekeeping supplies and equipment aplenty, from complete hives to all necessary components, tools, and accessories; protective clothing for adults and children; mite treatments; queens and package bees; bee food; queen-marking kits; honey-producing presses, extractors, and other equipment; honey jars, bears, and bottles in every size and style; honey products; mead-making books and equipment; candle molds and supplies; soap-making supplies; recipes for furniture and tin polish; children's bee-related books, and games; and books and videos on many subjects, from instructional videos to a natural cosmetics primer. There's so much more, but you'll want to discover all the goodies in this catalog yourself.

WEBSITE: The website has a broad array of products, and features online ordering. Most of the items listed have the same black-and-white illustrations as the catalog; however, the descriptions aren't as detailed here as in the print version. This is a good way to order if you already know what you want and like the convenience of ordering from home.

SPECIAL FACTORS: Wholesale orders available to qualified buyers (inquire); satisfaction guaranteed; unused merchandise must be returned within 30 days (see catalog for details).

D.V. Burrell Seed Growers Co.

P.O. Box 150–WBM
Rocky Ford, CO 81067
719–254–3318
FAX: 719–254–3319

FORM OF INFORMATION: free print catalog
PAY: check, MO, MC, V, DSC
SELLS: flower, herb, gourd, and vegetable seeds, and growing supplies
STORE: 405 North Main, Rocky Ford, CO; Monday to Friday 8:00 am–5:00 pm
EMAIL: burrellseeds@rmi.net

If you have dreams of turning your home garden into an income-producing roadside stand, Burrell is a great source to know about. This company, which has been serving commercial growers and florists since 1900, sells vegetable, fruit, and flower seeds in large quantities (100 pounds), tiny quantities (individual packets), and everything in between. There are price breaks at 1, 5, 25, 50, and 100 pounds. Naturally, if you can go in with a friend and buy more, your prices will be lower and you'll save on shipping costs as well. The 105-page catalog pictures and describes everything you would want to grow, from artichokes to watermelons. You get the feeling everything in Burrell's catalog has been carefully and thoughtfully selected for its hardiness and reliability. And in fact, the catalog's introductory text says it all: "No seedsman can hope to survive the critical judgment of the trade unless his product consistently delivers satisfaction." The back of the catalog features some useful items: a hand-held broadcast spreader, a push-type cultivator, soil-heating cables, reference books, and more.

Customers outside the U.S., please note: Catalogs cost $5 (in U.S. funds), and orders must be paid in U.S. funds.

SPECIAL FACTORS: Shipping included on certain items; quantity discounts available; institutional accounts available.

Butterbrooke Farm Seed Co-op

78 Barry Rd.
Oxford, CT 06478–1529
203–888–2000

FORM OF INFORMATION: free price list with long SASE

PAY: check or MO

SELLS: chemically untreated herb, vegetable, and flower seeds

STORE: no walk-in location; mail-order only

"We're not sure why everyone's rushing around so much." So says Tom Butterworth, owner of Butterbrooke Farm. This company still does business the old-fashioned way: They don't accept plastic, and there's no website—just good values by mail. Butterbrooke Farm, where helping you become "seed self-reliant" is their goal, is a membership organization of organic farmers, home gardeners, and seed savers. While you don't have to become a co-op member to buy from Butterbrooke, the membership fee is low ($15/year at this writing) and with it you receive a lot of benefits: 33% discount on all seeds, a quarterly newsletter, access to unlimited free advice, and the opportunity to buy heirloom seeds, among others. The price list, free when you send in a long SASE, has many varieties of seeds available in small packets (enough for one or two 20-foot rows) and larger packets (for planting four to six 20-foot rows), both at extremely reasonable prices. All seeds, which are fresh and chosen specifically for short growing seasons, have been derived from raised beds using biodynamic growing methods and no machine-powered equipment or chemicals. Buying nonhybrid seeds such as Butterbrooke's means you can harvest your own seeds to use next year. Be sure to check out Butterbrooke's inexpensive booklets (most of them only $1.75) on everything from mulching to making compost.

SPECIAL FACTORS: All orders shipped first class within 24 hours of receipt.

Carino Nurseries

P.O. Box 538, Dept. BBG
Indiana, PA 15701
800–223–7075
724–463–3350
FAX: 724–463–3050

FORM OF INFORMATION: free print catalog; online catalog

PAY: check, MO, MC, V, DSC

SELLS: tree and shrub seedlings and transplants; fresh-cut Christmas trees and wreaths, deer repellent products

STORE: no walk-in location; mail-order only; phone hours Monday to Friday 9:00 am–4:00 pm EST

ONLINE: www.carinonurseries.com

★

Located in Indiana County, Pennsylvania, "the Christmas tree capital of the world," Carino Nurseries has been around since 1946 and is now run by the third generation of Carinos. Here you can get evergreen and deciduous seedlings and transplants direct from the grower *at wholesale prices.* To get an idea of what this nursery has to offer, check out the website. There you'll see the many varieties of trees, in transplant and seedling form, you can buy here: all kinds of spruce, fir, pine, hemlock, chestnut, walnut, butternut, dogwoods, locusts, olive, ash, oak, and birch, among others. Carino's trees are suitable for Christmas trees, ornamentals, windbreaks, noise barriers, landscaping, timber, wetlands restoration, wildlife food, and cover. The specials are great deals and come with the added benefit of free shipping. The print catalog includes details about the variety, age, and approximate height of the plants, and other relevant information regarding shipping, planting zones, pruning, and selecting the right tree.

WEBSITE: The website offers about the same information as the print catalog, except here, availability is updated weekly. The website features secure online ordering.

SPECIAL FACTORS: Shipments made by UPS; some minimum orders apply; shipping takes place October 1 to November 15 and March 20 to May 15 only.

Dutch Gardens

144 Intervale Road
Burlington, VT 05401
800–944-2250
FAX: 800-551-6712

FORM OF INFORMATION: free print catalog; online catalog

PAY: check, MC, V, AE, DSC

SELLS: Dutch bulbs, perennials, speciality plants, and roses

STORE: no walk-in location; mail-order only

ONLINE: www.dutchgardens.com

If you've seen one bulb catalog you've seen 'em all, right? Not exactly. Both the Fall and Spring catalogs, and the Perennial and Rose catalogs from Dutch Gardens are stunners that stand out from the pack. These catalogs feature page after page of gorgeous photographs of hundreds of varieties of flower bulbs, perennials, specialty plants and roses, most shipped grower-direct from Holland at prices that are 20% and more below retail. Everything is guaranteed to grow, and there are quantity price breaks that help you save more money when you buy in larger quantities.

What's lovely about these catalogs, besides the presentation, is the amazing selection. In the "Fall Planting" catalog alone there are 33 pages devoted to daffodils and 39 pages devoted to unusual specialty bulbs, with detailed and interesting text about the history of these flowers, the types of conditions each is best suited for, height, blossom size, and more. And the grower profiles are especially interesting. The "Spring Planting" catalog features over 70 new introductions, including daylilies, dahlias, gladioli, allium, and hostas. The catalogs are also a treasure trove of information ranging from fertilizing your bulbs to forcing bulbs indoors. If you want to design a garden, rather than just plant one, look to Dutch Gardens for top size, top quality, and top value.

WEBSITE: I give the online version of the catalog high marks. This website is easy to navigate, features lots of helpful information about planting zones, flower characteristics, and soil and climate requirements, and offers online ordering. Look at the photographs on a cloudy, chilly day and you'll be ready to order and plant some bulbs for spring.

SPECIAL FACTORS: All bulbs and plants are guaranteed to bloom within the first year after planting; Check catalogs or website for fall and spring planting deadlines.

EON Industries, Inc.

P.O. Box 11, Dept. WBM
107 W. Maple St.
Liberty Center, OH
43532–0011
419–533–4961

FORM OF INFORMATION: free brochure; online catalog

PAY: check, MO, MC, V

SELLS: metal garden markers

STORE: no walk-in location; mail-order only; phone hours Monday to Saturday 8:00 am– 8:00 pm EST

ONLINE: www.eonindustries.com

Since 1936, the family behind EON Industries has focused on the production of one thing: metal plant markers. This focus allows them to give their personal attention to each detail of the process, which results in a superior product—at half the price of those shown in upscale garden catalogs! These simple yet elegant markers come in a number of styles and lengths—Rose Markers and Nursery Markers for larger, easy-to-read labels, and the smaller Swinging Label marker and Staff marker for the more understated areas in your garden. And for your tiniest and most inconspicuous marker needs, try Mini-Nursery and Mini-Swinger markers. EON also sells a variety of marking pens and pencils, and has advice on the most weather-proof methods for labeling the markers.

WEBSITE: You can view all of EON's products online. At this time there is no online ordering available, but you can download and print the order form, and then mail it to EON at the P.O. box listed above. Make sure you use a current order form to insure that the prices are not outdated.

SPECIAL FACTORS: Markers are sold in multiples of 25 and 100 only.

Fedco Seeds, Inc.

P.O. Box 520-WBM
Waterville, ME 04903
207–873–7333
FAX: 207–872–8317

FORM OF INFORMATION: $2 print catalog (see text); online catalog

PAY: check, MO, MC, V

SELLS: seeds, trees, seed-starting and cultivation tools, potatoes, bulbs, and supplies

STORE: no walk-in location; mail-order only

ONLINE: www.fedcoseeds.com

 ★

In 1978, the Fedco garden seed cooperative was formed, working with the now-defunct Maine Federation of Cooperatives and the still-thriving Maine Organic Farmers and Gardeners Association. Now, nearly a quarter of a century later, Fedco is going strong, providing high-quality seeds at the lowest possible prices (20% to 70% less than you'll pay elsewhere).

This isn't your ordinary seed catalog. Fedco doesn't have an individual owner or beneficiary: "Profit is not our primary goal." Consumers own 60% of the cooperative, and workers 40%. About half of Fedco's customers are individuals, and the other half are cooperatives. If you order in a group with co-workers, friends, or neighbors, you can minimize your costs. (The order form for individuals or groups is the same.) Fedco will individually package each order in a group order and then ship to one address. There is a strict schedule by which you must place your order for volume discounts. Once you've filled out the form, you can either mail or fax it (no phone orders). Fax orders incur a $2 charge, however.

One of three catalogs—"Bulbs," "Trees," and "Seeds, Tubers and Organic Growers Supply"—will come to you at the appropriate time of year with an ordering deadline. Each of these catalogs is a labor of love and intelligence, full of standard and interesting varieties, some heirloom, with valuable descriptions, historical sidelights, instructions for growing, plenty of witty and wise philosophy, and good, sound advice. There are books, mostly of the "politically green" variety, about medicinal herbs, organic gardening, earth-friendly insect management, coloring and comic books, and more; T-shirts; and tools, supplies, and accessories, particularly for the organic gardener.

WEBSITE: The website has five categories to choose from: Seeds, Moosetubers, Organic Growers Supply, Trees, and Bulbs. At each division you can find out the ordering schedule and current availability. There are also planting guides and charts, resources, links, and events. You can download an order form for each print catalog and mail or fax it in (again, faxing incurs a $2 charge).

SPECIAL FACTORS: Satisfaction is guaranteed; minimum $5 for check or money orders; minimum $25 for credit card orders; free shipping on seed orders; quantity discounts are available.

Flickinger's Nurseries

P.O. Box 245
Sagamore, PA 16250
800-368-7381

FORM OF INFORMATION: free print catalog
PAY: check, MO, MC, V
SELLS: evergreen and deciduous tree seedlings
NURSERY: Rt. 85, Sagamore, PA; call for hours

For three generations, Flickinger's has supplied landscapers, nurseries, and Christmas tree farms with quality seedlings and transplants at wholesale prices. Their color catalog features over 18 species of pine, fir, and spruce trees suitable for Christmas tree, ornamental, and reforestation uses, and includes hemlock, arborvitae, paper and European birch, white and red dogwood, European larch trees, and even some ground covers, such as myrtle. These top-quality seedlings have excellent root systems, thick stems, and good color, and will be freshly dug for your order. Seedlings and transplants are sold per 100 and per 1,000, but their low prices hold for quantities as low as 50 (their smallest order amount). These people move a lot of trees, which is what makes their thrifty prices possible. If you're looking to start your own tree-farm business, the people at Flickinger's can give you advice regarding pricing, invoicing, and advertising to help you get off the ground. The catalog also presents helpful suggestions regarding pruning, planting, and general care of your trees.

SPECIAL FACTORS: Orders under $30 include $5 handling fee; pick-up-order customers must notify nursery 3 days in advance.

George's Plant Farm

1410 Public Wells Rd., Dept. WBM

Martin, TN 38237

TEL/FAX: 731–587–9477

FORM OF INFORMATION: free flyer; online catalog

PAY: check, MO

SELLS: sweet potato plants and home-grown sweet potatoes

STORE: no walk-in location; mail-order only; January through April: phone hours Monday to Friday 2:00 pm–10:00 pm, Saturday 7:00 am–10:00 pm CST; May through June: 7:00 am–10:00 pm CST, 7 days a week

ONLINE: www.c-us.com/tatorman

The Dellingers of George's Plant Farm have been growing sweet potato plants and selling them at grower-direct prices to people all across the U.S. since 1985. George's Plant Farm is a small-time operation that values its customers and guarantees all plants will have strong stems, healthy roots, and can withstand cross-country shipping. What makes these sweet potatoes even sweeter is that prices here are well below everyone else's, there are quantity price breaks offering even greater savings, and there's free shipping. The current flyer has several varieties to choose from, each described in detail as to best features: color, yield, flavor, cooking characteristics, etc. Growing instructions and recipes come with your sweet potato plants, as well as "George's guarantee."

WEBSITE: The website offers seven varieties of sweet potato plants to choose from. Each plant has a description and picture. And you can let George's grow your sweet potatoes for you, by contract. Email them at tatorman@ecsis.net, or call for details. Deadline for contract is June 1. There is no online ordering available at this time; but you can print out an order form and fax, mail, or call in your order.

SPECIAL FACTORS: No plants shipped to California or outside the continental U.S.; no C.O.D.s please.

Johnny's Selected Seeds, Inc.

955 Benton Ave.
Winslow, ME 04901
207-861-3900
FAX: 800-437-4290

FORM OF INFORMATION: free print catalog; online catalog

PAY: check, MO, MC, V, AE, DSC

SELLS: seeds, roots, tubers, seed cultivation supplies

STORE: no walk-in location; mail-order only

ONLINE: www.johnnyseeds.com

Johnny's Selected Seeds, Inc., established in 1973, is a firm that cultivates both customer satisfaction and an inventory of exemplary-quality flower, vegetable, and herb seeds, equipment, tools, and supplies at good prices. Johnny's encourages the use of the "organic" method and is a certified organic farm. Customers appreciate the easy to use catalog and outstanding rate of seed germination. Seeds—flower, vegetable, legume, grass, and herb—are sold in fractions of an ounce as well as by the pound (1, 5, 15, 50, and, for corn, 100). To make sure you benefit from the fruits of your labors—and to help keep them coming—Johnny's also carries food mills and dehydrators, flower-drying materials, seed-station supplies, weather instruments, pest control products, and all kinds of books.

WEBSITE: If you prefer to shop online, you can visit Johnny's website. There you can search for items by category or by description and then order online. You can also pick up gardening tips, find links to related sites, or check out the internet specials.

SPECIAL FACTORS: Satisfaction guaranteed; no shipping charges (continental U.S. only) on orders over $150; quantity and volume discounts given; returns accepted for exchange, refund, or credit.

Mellinger's

P.O. Box 157
2310 W. South Range Rd.,
Dept. WBM
North Lima, OH 44452–0157
330–549–9861
FAX: 330–549–3716

FORM OF INFORMATION: free print catalog; online catalog

PAY: check, MO, MC, V, DSC

SELLS: seeds, bulbs, live plants, and home and garden supplies

STORE: same address; Monday to Saturday 8:30 am–5:00 pm (June 16 to March 31); 8:00 am–6:00 pm (April 1 to June 15)

ONLINE: www.mellingers.com

For 76 years, the Mellinger family has been committed to going the extra mile for their customers. Their business has been built on offering the very best products at the best possible prices, backed with knowledgeable salespeople who take the time to help their customers. This company sells everything you need for successful ornamental and vegetable gardening—terra cotta pots, arbors and trellises, greenhouse accessories and greenhouses, pest control products, bird feeders, plant fertilizer, and more. Many types of vegetable, flower, fruit, and grass seeds are sold here. You'll find all your old favorites here, as well as some rare and unusual tropical plant seeds. Mellinger's also sells a collection of gardening books and useful kitchen gadgets.

WEBSITE: Mellinger's website was created with as much regard for their customers as the lovely print catalog. Not only is the full inventory presented online with online ordering capability, but browsers can check out fantastic web-only specials and clearance items where the savings are quite significant.

SPECIAL FACTORS: Plants are warrantied for 13 months (see catalog for terms); authorized returns accepted (a 10% restocking fee may be charged).

Miller Nurseries

5060 W. Lake Rd., Dept. WBM
Canandaigua, NY 14424
800–836–9630
FAX: 585–396–2154

FORM OF INFORMATION: free print catalog; website

PAY: check, MO, MC, V, AE, DSC

SELLS: plants, shrubs, trees, and nursery stock

GARDEN CENTER: same address; Monday to Friday 8:00 am–4:30 pm, daily from March 13 to June 14

ONLINE: www.millernurseries.com

There's nothing more beautiful than an arbor trailing with grapevines and heavy with bunches of frosty purple fruit; or aisles of ruby-red raspberries, ready for the picking. There's just something satisfying about being surrounded by the bounty and sweetness of nature. For over a century, the Miller family has provided access to nature's riches in the form of 65 varieties of crisp, hardy "Olde-Tyme" apples, strawberries, raspberries, blackberries, blueberries, pears, cherries, nut trees, grapevines, and much more, at savings of 50% off typical nursery prices. Miller Nurseries is a major supplier of trees, shrubs, and vines for the backyard fruit and nut grower. They even provide possible garden layouts, suggesting that edibles can be a beautiful, productive, and cost-effective part of any landscape. Miller Nurseries also offers shade trees, ornamental grasses, and decorative flowers, and rounds out the catalog with mulches, wheelbarrows, and other gardening supplies and equipment. This family-owned, family-operated nursery is dedicated to their customers, and each purchase is backed with Miller's "Canandaigua Quality" guarantee.

WEBSITE: At this writing, the website was mostly informational and did not list Miller's products or feature online ordering.

SPECIAL FACTORS: Some stock is shipped only in spring.

Nor'East Miniature Roses, Inc.

P.O. Box 440
Arroyo Grande, CA 93421
805–481–2234 ext. 65
800-426-6485
FAX: 805–481–7374

FORM OF INFORMATION: free print catalog; online catalog

PAY: check, MO, MC, V

SELLS: miniature roses

STORE: 58 Hammond St., Rowley, MA; Monday to Friday 8:00 am–4:00 pm

ONLINE: www.noreast-miniroses.com

One never tires of the beauty of a rose. Nor'East Miniature Roses, Inc., one of the largest miniature rose nurseries in the U.S., makes miniature roses available at prices significantly below those of other dealers. What are miniature roses? Quite simply, they are naturally dwarf roses, hardy perennials that grow on their own roots. They come in every color imaginable—apricot, luscious reds, mauve, yellows, white, pinks, oranges—and are perfect for perennial borders, in mass plantings, in containers, as climbers, or anywhere where a splash of color is needed in the garden. The pricing is simple: All minis are $6.45 and collections are priced as marked . In addition, quantity discounts apply, so the more you order, the less you spend per plant (10% off for 10 or more plants, 15% off for 20 or more plants. Great service is a hallmark of Nor'East, whether you're buying through the catalog or off the website.

The approximately 16-page color catalog details the specifics of many kinds of miniature bush roses (micro-minis, climbers, and tree roses). To help you plan a suitable garden for your climate and landscape, the catalog describes plant height at maturity, blooming pattern and coloring (roses come in solid colors and blends), best conditions for growth, and scent. Nor'East helps novices enjoy the rewards of growing roses by offering easy-to-cultivate choices. If Nor'East selects the roses for you, or if you order in quantity, additional savings will apply.

WEBSITE: The well designed website has gorgeous color images of all rose offerings, with descriptions, cultivating suggestions, and online ordering. A nice feature of the online catalog lets you search for your ideal rose by color or by category (hanging minis, fragrant minis, tree roses, etc.).

SPECIAL FACTORS: Plants that don't perform are accepted for replacement within 90 days.

Ohio Earth Food

5488 Swamp St., NE
Hartville, OH 44632
330–877–9356
FAX: 330–877–4237

FORM OF INFORMATION: free print catalog; online catalog

PAY: check, MO, MC V, DSC

SELLS: natural fertilizers and natural pest controls

STORE: same address; Monday, Tuesday, Thursday, Friday 8:00 am–5:00 pm; additional days and hours between March 25 and June 1

ONLINE: www.ohioearthfood.com

Ohio Earth Food has been serving gardeners and farmers since 1972 with natural fertilizers and pest control products. The 24-page catalog offers dozens of products certifiable for organic crop production by NOP Standards at the time of this printing. If you have a summer roadside vegetable stand, participate in farmers' markets, have a large garden, or even own a full-scale farm, Ohio Earth Food has great prices when you buy in bulk. (Growers' price breaks include ton lots.) You'll find natural fertilizers such as Re-Vita Compost Plus, Jersey greensand, cottonseed meal, liquefied seaweed, fish products, rock phosphate, and others; insect and disease controllers such as diatomaceous earth (made of ground fossil shell), rotenone and milky spore powder—great for Japanese beetles; herbicides for killing weeds and grass; natural products for livestock; growing supplies such as potting soil, compost makers, soil test kits, and powdermill dust applicators; and a small selection of books about bio-friendly growing. Detailed contents and descriptions accompany each product listing, as well as quantity price breaks. Send in a soil sample, and for $18, Ohio Earth Food will analyze it for the base exchange capacity of your soil; organic matter content; levels of nitrogen, potassium, phosphorous, calcium, magnesium, and sulfur; and the amount of lime needed, if any. This is a nice company to know about.

Wholesalers, please note: Ask for the grower price list with your catalog.

WEBSITE: The website is great—easy to use. You can search by category or by product index, but there is no online ordering at this time.

SPECIAL FACTORS: Shipments over 500 pounds are generally shipped by commercial truck; see catalog for all shipping rates and requirements.

Pinetree Garden Seeds

P.O. Box 300
New Gloucester, ME 04260
207–926–3400
FAX: 888–52–SEEDS

FORM OF INFORMATION: free print catalog, $1.50 outside U.S.; online catalog

PAY: check, MO, MC, V, AE, DSC

SELLS: seeds, bulbs, plants, garden equipment, and books

STORE: no walk-in location; mail-order only

ONLINE: www.superseeds.com

Remember those beautiful old-fashioned cornucopias, luscious-looking and brimming over with fruits of the harvest? That's what you'll find in this 164-page closely printed color catalog, a cornucopia of over 800 varieties of vegetable and flower seeds, bulbs, plants, tools, and a distinguished selection of gardening books—all at old-fashioned prices. In many cases, their prices are a third less than that of competitors. Established in 1979 to serve home gardeners with the best products at the best prices, Pinetree Garden Seeds has grown into a larger company that has kept its original philosophy. They believe their typical customer is a sophisticated gardener who wants to try many of the things he or she has heard or read about, hence their line of "vegetables from around the world." This amazing selection includes traditional vegetables from France (haricots vert, cornichon cucumbers, dandelion greens), the Orient (snow peas, daikon, Thai peppers), Italy (artichokes, eggplant, fennel) and, Latin America (black beans, cilantro, many chiles). Where else could you find this variety at the best prices around, and all backed with an ironclad guarantee? You'll want to place this fat little catalog on your shelf to refer to again and again throughout the year. Don't overlook the nongarden products in the back of the book.

WEBSITE: If you're computer savvy, be sure to check out Pinetree's full catalog online. It's wonderfully organized and easy to use. Although most items are not pictured, this won't be an impediment to the experienced gardener. Detailed descriptions accompany each product, and you can order right at the site.

SPECIAL FACTORS: Satisfaction guaranteed; returns accepted for exchange, refund, or credit.

Prentiss Court Ground Covers

P.O. Box 96
Saluda, NC 28773
864–271–1577
FAX: 815–642–9105

FORM OF INFORMATION: $1 brochure; online catalog
PAY: check, MO, MC, V
SELLS: live ground-cover plants
STORE: no walk-in location; mail-order only; phone hours 9:00 am–6:00 pm EST
ONLINE: www.GroundCoversUSA.com

Want to spend less time mowing the lawn? Would you like a visually interesting, easy-care carpet to cover "difficult" areas around your home? Or are you just looking for wide sweeping beds of color, lush borders, and sunny expanses of daylilies? Well, look no further than Prentiss Court Ground Covers for all of this at very reasonable prices. In business since 1978, Prentiss Court currently offers over 50 varieties of ground cover, at savings of up to 50% below nursery prices. The types of plants offered range from the shade-loving hosta (4 varieties) to the sun-loving daylily (8 varieties), and include jasmine, Japanese honeysuckle, liriope, and traditional and Algerian ivy, as well as ornamental grasses, Virginia creeper, bronze-improved ajuga, dianthus, and cotoneaster, among others. Cost at this writing ranges from 56 cents for honeysuckle or euonymus to $1.56 for the Stella a De Oro daylily. Wow! No nursery mark-ups here. Available in pots or bare root, plants are "pampered" by the skilled horticulturists at Prentiss Court, packed carefully, and shipped quickly. Some minimums apply, so check the website or brochure carefully.

WEBSITE: The website features just about everything one needs, including detailed descriptions of the various plants, information on how often they bloom and where they grow best (shade versus full sun, for instance), beautiful color images, prices, and company information. You can even click on the sound icons to hear the correct pronunciation of botanical names like *dianthus gratianopolitanus*. The only thing you can't do here is order electronically. You still need to order by telephone, at this writing.

SPECIAL FACTORS: Minimum order varies with bare-root or potted orders.

Rohrer's Seeds

P.O. Box 250
Smoketown, PA 17576
717–299–2571
FAX: 800–468–4944

FORM OF INFORMATION: free print catalog; website

PAY: check, MO, MC, V, DSC

SELLS: flower and vegetable seeds, gardening supplies, lawn seed, forage, crop seed, etc.

STORE: 2472 Old Philadelphia Pike, Smoketown, PA; call for hours

ONLINE: www.rohrerseeds.com

For flowers and vegetables with an historic twist, simply flip through the pages of Rohrer's 63-page seed catalog. Our great-grandmothers grew many of the heirloom seeds listed here, and probably paid a similarly low price. For larger agricultural interests, Rohrer's supplies pasture mixtures, grasses and crop seed, and both organic/natural and conventional herbicides and fungicides. Most of the catalog, however, is devoted to the home gardener, and highlights the local, organically grown historical heirloom variety seeds of the Landis Valley Museum, grown by Pennsylvania settlers from the mid 18th century. These include the sweet Amish Moon and Stars watermelon, extra-white German Gilfeather turnips, and green Jenny Lind cantaloupes. Savings increase when you order in quantity, even if it's a small quantity. Rohrer's guarantees that every seed, old-fashioned or modern, must satisfy you, or you will get your money back.

WEBSITE: Rohrer's has information about their products at their website and you can view the pages of their print catalog online. A printable order form is available as there is no online ordering.

SPECIAL FACTORS: Orders of 15 or more seed packets are shipped free; returns accepted for exchange, refund, or credit.

Turner Greenhouses

Hwy 117
P.O. Box 1260, Dept. 131
South Goldsboro, NC 27533
800–672–4770
FAX: 919–736–4550

FORM OF INFORMATION: free print catalog; online catalog
PAY: check, MO, MC, V, DSC
SELLS: greenhouses and accessories
STORE: primarily mail-order; visitors are welcome, call for directions
ONLINE: www.turnergreenhouses.com

Imagine plucking baby greens for dinner from your own steamy indoor garden beds in the middle of a blizzard. Did you think greenhouses were only found at wealthy estates or commercial growing operations? After receiving Turner's catalog, with prices over 35% less than their competitors, the day is not far off when you could be the proud owner of a Turner greenhouse—"the affordable greenhouse that grows with you!" The three expandable types of greenhouses Turner sells are backed by three generations of expertise in the manufacture, care, and set-up of greenhouses. They believe that your purchase is too important not to make a thorough investigation, so they encourage potential customers to look at their competitors' catalogs and compare price and service. Turner provides a complete set of assembly plans and a list of Turner Greenhouse owners in your area for you to talk to. And best of all, they don't forget you after the sale. They promise a lifelong relationship of service, and will take time to answer any questions you may have for as long as you own your greenhouse. The catalog includes useful greenhouse accessories, such as circulators, benches, misters, thermometers, and cooling units, as well as handy items like propagation mats and the gardener's phone pack that allows you to bring your phone wherever you go!

WEBSITE: Make sure to check out the website. Once you do, you'll understand why 12% of this company's business every year is from repeat customers. In addition to the clear presentation of products with pictures and descriptions and online ordering, you'll find enthusiastic customer testimonials, gardening and greenhouse tips, Turner Greenhouses' clear statement of policies and guarantees, "The Dirt" monthly newsletter, links to gardeners' sites, and much more. I heartily endorse this company.

SPECIAL FACTORS: Satisfaction guaranteed; authorized returns in original condition accepted within 30 days for refund or credit less freight costs.

Twilley Seeds

121 Gary Rd.	**FORM OF INFORMATION:** free print catalog
Hodges, SC 29653	**PAY:** check, MO, MC, V
800-622-7333	**SELLS:** seeds and small-grower supplies
FAX: 864-227-5108	**STORE:** no walk-in location; mail-order only

If you're a truck farmer, u-pick, or bedding plant grower, Twilley is the place to buy your seeds in bulk. Claiming they sell "the best seeds your money can buy," Twilley puts their money where it counts—back in your pocket. Prices for small quantities are comparable to most seed catalogs, but if you buy in quantity—from 1 to 500 pounds of seed—the price quickly drops from 40% to 50% off the original. Twilley's carries everyone's favorite garden vegetable seeds, and both annual and perennial flower seeds. Symbols in the catalog will alert the discerning grower to All-America Selections winners, Twilley's own "Professional Seed Series," and seeds that are particularly well suited to roadside stands or u-pick operations. You'll also find charming and helpful money-making ideas throughout, ranging from how to display and preserve your vegetables in the searing summer heat at your roadside stand to this year's "chic" crops and hot sellers to the gourmet trade.

Organic growers, please note: Twilley supplies untreated seed only upon volume request in advance of season.

SPECIAL FACTORS: Discounts for bulk orders over $100; minimum order: $25 on credit card or C.O.D. orders.

Van Dyck's

P.O. Box 430
Brightwaters, NY
11718-0430
800-248-2852
FAX: 800-639-2452

FORM OF INFORMATION: free print catalog; online catalog
PAY: check, MO, MC, V, AE, DSC
SELLS: flower bulbs and perennials
STORE: no walk-in location; mail-order only
ONLINE: www.vandycks.com

If you're looking for a company that's serious about flowers, Van Dyck's is the place to start. The Van Dyck family has sold bulbs in Holland for generations, and has been doing business in the U.S. since 1990. The family tradition continues today with discounts of at least 40%, excellent service, and their "no quibble" guarantee of satisfaction. The prices and selection here beat everyone else's. Their catalog blooms with pages and pages of full-color photographs of tulip, crocus, iris, hyacinth, lily, narcissus, allium, daffodil, muscari, amaryllis, hosta, and peony flowers. As with most companies, the more you buy, the more you save—so Van Dyck's recommends combining orders with friends and family or with a garden co-op to get the lowest prices possible. If your order exceeds $30, the nice people at Van Dyck's will throw in free tulip bulbs.

WEBSITE: At the website, you can shop online, order a print catalog, subscribe to the free e-newsletter, and read helpful articles on gardening-related topics. It's nicely designed and easy to use.

SPECIAL FACTORS: Bulb bonuses available with quantity orders, quantity discounts available; satisfaction guaranteed.

Van Engelen, Inc.

23 Tulip Dr., Dept. WBM
P.O. Box 638
Bantam, CT 06750
860–567–8734
FAX: 860–567–5323

FORM OF INFORMATION: free print catalog; online catalog

PAY: check, MO, MC, V

SELLS: Dutch flower bulbs

STORE: no walk-in location; mail-order only; phone hours Monday to Friday 8:30 am–7:00 pm, weekends 10:00 am–3:00 pm EST

ONLINE: www.vanengelen.com

Over 800 varieties of exhibition-quality Dutch flower bulbs grace this catalog, which is the only wholesale collection of Dutch bulbs in the U.S. Bulbs are sold in multiples of 50, with special collections of the most popular varieties available in smaller units. If you're looking for a large number of bulbs at a very low price, this is the catalog for you (you can always go in on an order with friends). The types of flower bulbs sold include varieties of tulip, narcissus, crocus, daffodil, anemone, allium, freesia, iris, fritillaria, hyacinth, amaryllis, and lily. The height of the plants and colors of the flowers are described in detail, so you can get the type of plant that would complement your garden perfectly.

WEBSITE: The website is well designed and lets you order online after you have browsed the extensive inventory of flower bulbs. Click on an image of a flower to see more images and detailed descriptions of the varieties available. You can also check out the bulb food section, horticultural tips, and end-of-season specials.

SPECIAL FACTORS: Satisfaction is guaranteed; quantity discounts are available; minimum order: $50.

General Merchandise

Surplus and overstock goods; online auctions; great values on a wide range of products—household and supermarket goods, gadgets, nonelectric appliances, goods imported from China, handcrafted works, vegan products, and department store items

Most of the companies listed in this chapter offer such a wide range of products it might be confusing to put them elsewhere: everything from solar-powered radios and cruelty-free nonleatherware to sports equipment, department store goods imported from China, 1960s home decor, and handcrafted works from artists in developing countries. These are some of the best print and online catalogs to browse, equivalent to a big Sunday-morning 6-family yard sale. Go through the listings carefully since there are some real finds here. You're bound to get lots of gift ideas for holidays, birthdays, and other occasions.

Find It Fast

APPAREL
Bennett Brothers, eBay, NetMarket, Novica, Overstock.com, Pangea Vegan Products, Pearl River

BOOKS
Amazon.com, eBay, Half.com, NetMarket

CAMERA AND PHOTO
Amazon.com, Bennett Brothers, eBay, Overstock.com

COLLECTIBLES
Amazon.com, eBay, Novica, Pearl River

COMPUTERS
Amazon.com, eBay, Half.com, Overstock.com

FOOD AND BEVERAGES
Amazon.com, eBay, NetMarket, Pangea Vegan Products

FOOTWEAR
eBay, Pangea Vegan Products, Novica, Overstock.com, Pearl River,

FURNITURE
Amazon.com, eBay, NetMarket, Pearl River

GIFTS
Amazon.com, American Science & Surplus, eBay, Novica, Overstock.com, Pearl River, Real Goods

HOME DECOR
Amazon.com, eBay, NetMarket, Novica, Overstock.com, Pearl River, Real Goods

HOME ELECTRONICS
Amazon.com, Bennett Brothers, eBay, Half.com, NetMarket, Overstock.com

INDEPENDENT SELLER MERCHANDISE
Amazon.com, eBay, Half.com

JEWELRY AND WATCHES
Bennett Brothers, eBay, Half.com, NetMarket, Novica, Overstock.com, Pearl River

LUGGAGE
Bennett Brothers, Overstock.com

MUSIC CDS
Amazon.com, eBay, Half.com, Overstock.com

MUSICAL INSTRUMENTS
Novica, Pearl River

NONELECTRIC TOOLS AND HOUSEHOLD AIDS
Lehman's Non-Electric Catalog, Real Goods

ONLINE AUCTIONS
Amazon.com, eBay

OVERSTOCKS AND CLOSEOUTS
American Science & Surplus, NetMarket, Overstock.com

PERSONAL CARE ITEMS
Amazon.com, Bennett Brothers, Cook Brothers, eBay, NetMarket, Pangea Vegan Products

SPORTS EQUIPMENT
Amazon.com, eBay, Half.com, NetMarket, Overstock.com

TOOLS, ELECTRONICS, AND GADGETS
Amazon.com, American Science & Surplus, Bennett Brothers, eBay, Half.com, NetMarket, Overstock.com, Real Goods

TOYS AND VIDEOGAMES
Amazon.com, American Science & Surplus, eBay, Half.com, Overstock.com

Amazon.com

P.O. Box 80387
Seattle, WA 98108–0387
800–201–7575 (not for orders)
206–266–2992

FORM OF INFORMATION: online catalog only; no print catalog

PAY: check, MO, MC, V, AE, DSC, DC, JCB

SELLS: books, music CDs, DVDs and videos, electronics, tools, toys, baby items, kitchen and housewares, independent-seller merchandise

STORE: no walk-in location; online only

ONLINE: www.amazon.com

Amazon.com is continually branching out into many different fields in addition to books and music, including cameras, tools, toys, auctions, kitchen and housewares, wireless phones, outdoor living, baby items, and z-shops, which are minisites launched by individuals, but hosted by Amazon.com, where you can find virtually everything, from Japanese trading cards and Amish quilts to salmon chili.

This is still an awesome site for book buying. This virtual bookstore has millions of titles, a wealth of reviews, personal recommendations, author interviews, excerpts, and much more. (Readers: Feel free to submit your own review of this book. I'd love to hear from you!) At Amazon.com, you'll enjoy savings of 20% to 40%. It's hard to beat for selection, price, and service. (It's not unusual to receive books from Amazon.com just 2 days after ordering.) Not only is this a good place to buy books at a discount, but it's a godsend for writers and others who are looking for references and sources on any subject, since you can search by author, title, subject, or keywords.

But don't stop at books. Amazon.com has branched out into other fields with music CDs and videos (listen to musical selections right on your computer before you buy), DVDs, electronics, tools, kitchen items, outdoor living, auctions, and just about anything else under the sun. All at a discount! The toys and games department is awesome. I bought presents online for my son last year only 10 days before Christmas and received them in plenty of time. I can also highly recommend the tools, which are well priced; Tool Crib of the North, featured in this book for many years, is now part of Amazon's Home Improvement section.

The website is designed both for comfort and for speed. Efficient search engines, shopper-friendly featured lists and gift ideas, and an extensive FAQ section with detailed customer service information make this a model for other online vendors to follow. But unlike other web-only shopping sites, you can also call the Amazon.com staff to have a real human being answer your questions.

SPECIAL FACTORS: Satisfaction guaranteed; returns accepted within 15 days for exchange, refund, or credit; no phone orders.

American Science & Surplus

P.O.Box 1030
Skokie, IL 60076
847–647–0011
FAX: 800–934–0722

FORM OF INFORMATION: free print catalog; online catalog

PAY: check, MO, MC, V, DSC

SELLS: industrial, educational, military, and scientific surplus goods

STORE: Milwaukee, WI, and Chicago and Geneva, IL; see website or call for addresses

ONLINE: www.sciplus.com

  ★

"Incredible stuff, unbelievable prices," is their motto, and the 64-page black-and-white catalog from American Science & Surplus doesn't disappoint. This collection of kits, tools, toys, teaching aids, arts and crafts, models, gadget parts, and miscellaneous useful products is a bargain hunter's dream come true, with savings reaching over 75% on some items. Junior inventors, teachers, students, and tag-sale aficionados will find lots to love about this catalog.

Established around 1937, American Science & Surplus issues 12 catalogs per year. Because quantities are finite, the inventory is always changing, and therefore somewhat defies description. However, past catalogs have included such items as science projects both wacky (Rubber Flubber and Goofy Gel) and serious (ecology kits to test pond water, make-your-own geodes), magnets, toys, tools, batteries, electronic parts, computer educational software, arts and crafts kits and supplies, microscopes and telescopes, film mailers, talking doormats, fanny packs, hospital robes, seasonal decorations, and on and on. Line drawings and amusing descriptive text make this indescribable spectrum of surplus goodies the catalog equivalent of strolling through a flea market sponsored by Mensa.

WEBSITE: Since inventory is always changing at American Science & Surplus, the online catalog is a great way to see what's currently in stock. You'll find it as entertaining as the print catalog, and there is secure online ordering.

SPECIAL FACTORS: Minimum order: $10; returns accepted within 30 days; no manufacturer warranties apply.

Bennett Brothers, Inc.

30 East Adams St.
Chicago, IL 60603–5676
800–621–2626
FAX: 312–621–1669

FORM OF INFORMATION: free print catalog; online catalog

PAY: check, MO, MC, V, AE, DSC

SELLS: jewelry, appliances, electronics, luggage, home furnishings, etc.

STORE: same address; Monday to Friday 8:15 am–5:00 pm (see catalog for holiday shopping hours); also 211 Island Rd., Mahwah, NJ; Monday to Friday 8:15 am–5:00 pm

ONLINE: www.bennettbrothers.com

Once a year, Bennett Brothers, in business since 1906, issues their "Blue Book," a 148-page glossy color catalog filled with brand-name products including jewelry, watches, silver, housewares, appliances, electronics, cameras, luggage, toys, sporting goods, furniture, blankets, and more—all at prices well below retail, up to 45% below on some items. The three Bennetts (father and two sons) smile out at you on the inside page, and promise that their honest and equitable business practices will make you a loyal customer.

What's this catalog all about? Gifts, gifts, and more gifts—from luxury items, such as diamond and gold jewelry for people with discretionary income, to sterling silver flatware and Black Forest cuckoo clocks. And then there are more modest and practical items, such as gourmet gadgets, cordless telephones, and even toys. Everything here is name-brand and high quality, and the suggested retail price (provided in most cases by the manufacturer) is listed alongside Bennett's so you can see the savings. Corporate buyers should contact Bennett Brothers for details on the firm's "Choose-Your-Gift" booklets for employee award and incentive programs at price levels from $16 to $1,000.

WEBSITE: Bennett Brothers now has the entire inventory from the "Blue Book" available in an online version that is comprehensive and easy to use. All products are clearly pictured with detailed descriptions, and can be ordered online.

SPECIAL FACTORS: Authorized returns are accepted within 10 days for exchange or credit.

eBay

FORM OF INFORMATION: website only; no print catalog

PAY: seller's discretion (see text)

SELLS: collectibles, gadgets, jewelry, shoes and clothing, electronics, etc.

STORE: no walk-in location; mail-order only

ONLINE: www.ebay.com

This is the largest person-to-person trading area on the internet and functions as an online auction: You bid for goods, and the highest bidder wins—often at significant savings. It is also the longest-running and the most innovative online auction, with hundreds of categories divided into easy to use subcategories, from antiques, collectibles, and computers, to magazines, jewelry, toys, and dolls. The site features literally millions of items for sale and appears to be growing by leaps and bounds daily.

eBay recommends your making phone or email contact with the seller before you begin bidding. People interested in buying from a vendor can look up the vendor's selling history, a collection of actual buyers' reviews of this vendor. If the vendor turns out to be reliable, get started! Friends who have used this site love it. However, if it's possible for a virtual bazaar to be hectic, this one surely is. I find that the sheer magnitude of choices is a tad overwhelming. Nevertheless, it makes for an interesting shopping experience and can end up saving you a bundle. It's best if you have a general idea of how much an item costs before you catch the bidding bug. For example, a pair of women's suede boots starting at $1 looks promising, but not if the winning bid eventually exceeds the boots' suggested retail price!

eBay's site map is a table of contents that links you to pages that will explain the whole bidding or selling process, will give you tips on how to have the best experience, and will offer hints on how to find what you're looking for. Bidding time spans and starting bids vary for each item. Most items are pictured, which is helpful. Credit card payment, shipping requirements and procedures, and warranties and guarantees will vary from seller to seller.

SPECIAL FACTORS: Valid email address is required.

Half.com

FORM OF INFORMATION: website only; no print catalog

PAY: MC, V, AE, DSC

SELLS: books, CDs, movies, video games, computers, consumer electronics, sporting goods and trading cards

STORE: no walk-in location; mail-order only

ONLINE: www.half.com

Half.com, (derived from the rule, since abandoned, that an item should cost no more than half its list price) an eBay company, offers people a fixed-price, online marketplace to buy and sell high quality, new, overstocked, remaindered and used products at discounted prices. Unlike auctions, where the selling price is based on bidding, the seller sets the price for items at Half.com at the time an item is listed. The site's expanding marketplace currently includes books, CDs, movies, video games, computers, consumer electronics, sporting goods and trading cards. Shoppers can easily search for specific items or browse for items that are categorized. Items have product descriptions, reviews, and, often, a photo.

Half.com was founded in July 1999 and is one of the most visited shopping sites on the internet. Through its ever-growing community of sellers, Half.com offers more than 50 million items for sell. Unlike eBay, Half.com bills the buyer and pays the seller, which means there's no danger that a seller will have to grapple with a bounced check. Half.com offers a buy-protection guarantee on all sales. What's more, they require all sellers to ship items within 24 hours of confirming (which has a 48 hour limit).

SPECIAL FACTORS: Sellers set their own shipping costs and methods.

Lehman's Non-Electric Catalog

P. O. Box 321
One Lehman Circle, Dept. WBM
Kidron, OH 44636
888–438–5346
330–857–5757
FAX: 888–780–4975

FORM OF INFORMATION: $3 print catalog, $6 to Canada; $10 to all other countries; online catalog

PAY: check, MO, MC, V, DSC

SELLS: nonelectric appliances and products for self-sufficient living

STORE: same address; Monday to Saturday 8:00 am–5:30 pm, Thursday 8:00 am–8:00 pm

ONLINE: www.lehmans.com

Want to get "off the grid"? Or are you just someone who loves old-fashioned, high-quality products and ingenious gadgets that hark back to simpler days? Then you're going to *love* Lehman's, which began in 1955 as a hardware and appliance store catering to the Amish population in Ohio.

Lehman's has the country's largest display of wood cookstoves and a huge selection of nonelectric appliances, including gas refrigerators and wringer washers, as well as people-powered products. You'll find cooking aids (butter churns, nonelectric yogurt incubators, grain mills for making flour, giant cast-iron kettles on legs, nonelectric toasters); household items (doorbells, oil lamps, wind-up flashlights, composting toilets, water pumps, solar power systems), children's toys and games, farm and garden tools and equipment, snowshoes, a terrific assortment of books, and more. This company is included here not so much for their discount prices (although products that are people-powered do save money on electricity) but for the range of hard-to-find products they carry.

WEBSITE: Lehman's itself is very much "on the grid," as witnessed by their fantastic website, which features online ordering and an easy-to-navigate format.

SPECIAL FACTORS: Free shipping on most orders within the U.S.; satisfaction guaranteed; authorized returns accepted within 30 days; order by phone 24 hours, 7 days/week.

NetMarket

100 Connecticut Ave.
NORWALK, CT 06850-3561
888–MY–MARKET
TDD: 800-462-1768

FORM OF INFORMATION: online catalog only; no print catalog

PAY: MC, V, AE, DSC

SELLS: electronics, home furnishings, personal-care products, office equipment, toys, apparel, groceries, etc.

STORE: no walk-in location; online only; phone hours Monday to Friday 8:00 am–11:00 pm, Saturday 9:00 am–8:00 pm EST

ONLINE: www.netmarket.com

"Save time. Save money. Save your sanity." This sounds like a mantra for the information age, but it's really NetMarket's slogan. NetMarket, "your one-stop superstore," is an online company that connects shoppers directly to manufacturers so you can save from 10% to 50% on everything you buy here, and up to 80% on items found in the special-purchase or closeout bins. When you become a member—$79.99 annual membership fee at this writing—you get the best prices as well as other benefits. But you don't have to be a member to shop at NetMarket.

The inventory here is phenomenal—800,000 items at press time—in the following departments: electronics, home and leisure, sports and fitness, computers and office, babies and toys, fashion, books, and closeouts. But this is just the beginning. Click on a main category such as Home and Leisure to find 15 more subcategories, from appliances and home furnishings to pet-care products and vacuums. We're talking about a megastore here. NetMarket is able to present so much inventory because all products come directly from the manufacturer or distributor.

So, why pay money to shop here when you can shop elsewhere for free? NetMarket claims their members won't find the same merchandise anywhere else at this price. They back up this claim with a 200% low-price guarantee: They'll refund you double the difference in price if you can find the same item you purchased from them anywhere else for less. For example, if you buy a product for $100 from NetMarket and then find the product elsewhere for $90, NetMarket will give you a check for $20. Other benefits of membership include an automatic extended 2-year warranty on all goods purchased with a U.S. manufacturer's warranty, a personal shopper to help you locate just about anything, "ask the expert" (for detailed product questions), a $200 travel voucher on a major airline, and NetMarket cash back, where qualifying purchases earn credits toward future NetMarket buys. You'll recognize the brands—all top-name manufacturers. A consumer-friendly interface lets you find specific products in your category by brand or by price range.

SPECIAL FACTORS: Shipping within the U.S. and Puerto Rico only; preauthorized returns accepted (see website for returns policy).

Novica

11835 W. Olympic Blvd.
Suite 750E
Los Angeles, CA 90064
877–266–8422
310–479–6115
FAX: 310–479–7246

FORM OF INFORMATION: online catalog only; no print catalog

PAY: check, MO, MC, V, AE, DSC

SELLS: art, books, clothing, collectibles, eco-friendly items, furniture, home decor, gifts, jewelry, masks, musical instruments, toys, and games created by artisans from around the world

STORE: no walk-in location; online only; phone hours Monday to Friday 9:00 am–6:00 pm PST

ONLINE: www.novica.com

Novica exists so that artists and artisans can do what they love best—create unique and beautiful work. To be an artist is extremely difficult in developing nations, where men and women who otherwise would be recognized—if not celebrated—for their abilities are making shoelaces on assembly lines or slapping stamps on agricultural crates. Novica, (derived from the Latin root of "novus" which means new) in association with National Geographic, serves as an online arts agent for more than 1,700 artists in countries around the world. At the website you can read about the artists, explore their cultures, view photographs of their work and select from more than 8,500 handcrafted works. Staff of Novica's teams, based in offices around the world, interview each artist, photograph their artwork, post the interviews and photographs online, and handle all packing and shipping on behalf of the artist. International couriers deliver the artwork directly to customers, eliminating numerous middlemen and transferring the savings to creator and customer alike. Artists set their own prices, earning more than they can locally, while customers benefit by paying far less than traditional retail for beautiful works of art. Novica has been so successful that it is today the leading world arts site on the internet. And Novica founders vow to uphold two cardinal rules: The artist must earn more than the going local rate, and the consumer must pay below-market prices. That means anywhere between a 10% and 50% price boost for local artisans and savings up to 75% for consumers—giving buyers a chance to do the right thing while saving money. The types of categories here include animals, art, books, clothing, collectibles, eco-friendly items, furniture, home decor, gifts, jewelry, masks, musical instruments, paintings, rugs, sculptures, toys, games, and vases from Andes, Bali and Java, Brazil, India, Mexico, Thailand, and West Africa.

SPECIAL FACTORS: Authorized returns for a full refund (including shipping charges) within 60 days of purchase; all furniture returns that are not the result of Novica's error are subject to a 10% restocking fee; many large or oversized items, including furniture, are only available to customers in the 48 contiguous U.S. states.

Overstock.com

800–989–0135

FORM OF INFORMATION: online catalog only; no print catalog

PAY: MC, V, AE, DSC

SELLS: apparel, footwear, computer hardware and software, electronics and cameras, hardware and garden, home decor, housewares, jewelry, luggage, sports gear, and toys

STORE: no walk-in location; online only; phone hours Monday to Friday 6:30 am– 11:00 pm, Saturday and Sunday 8:00 am– 4:00 pm PST

ONLINE: www.overstock.com

I'm so glad I found another source for deeply discounted shoes. When I clicked on the footwear department at Overstock.com there were Jill Sanders, Skechers, Dr. Martens, Reebok, Nike, Tommy Bahama, and Gucci shoes all at 40% to 60% off the regular retail rate. How happy am I now?

Overstock.com is about as wonderful as a website can be. The first thing you'll notice is the impressive variety of name-brand products they carry. Besides the above-mentioned footwear, the departments include: Apparel for Men and Women; Computer and Home Office; Electronics and Cameras; Hardware and Garden; Home Decor; Housewares; Jewelry; Luggage and Business; Sports Gear; and Toys. And here's a tiny sampling of some of the brand-names: Bosch, Bulova, Calvin Klein, Fila, Fossil, Head, Hewlett-Packard, Hoover, Krups, Sharp, Ralph Lauren, Sony, and Seiko.

How can they sell these products at such low prices? Name-brand companies are forced to sell their excess inventory for a number of reasons: Their products must be removed from shelves to make room for newer models; overproduced products must be sold; a change in financial circumstances or strategy may result in canceled orders; manufacturers may be downsizing or moving facilities; and/or companies may need to reduce inventories for accounting reasons. One thing to remember about shopping at Overstock.com—inventory comes in limited quantities and is added frequently. So check in often, and if you see something you want, get it—it might not be there tomorrow. All products are described and pictured, and searching is possible by brand or department. You'll find this one of the quickest, easiest, most friendly websites around.

SPECIAL FACTORS: Products returned within 30 days from the date received, in original condition, for money-back guarantee; flat shipping rate of $2.95 on all orders within the continental U.S.

Pangea Vegan Products

2381 Lewis Ave.
Rockville, MD 20851
800–340–1200
FAX: 301–816–8955

FORM OF INFORMATION: free print catalog; online catalog

PAY: check, MO, MC, V

SELLS: vegan goods including food, clothing, cleaning products, and personal care items

STORE: same address; Saturday and Sunday only, 11:00 am–6:00 pm

ONLINE: www.veganstore.com

Don't have a cow, man! With so much current media attention focused on the foods we eat, there's been a growing interest in vegetarianism and "cruelty free "products made with no animal-based derivatives or animal testing. So, what's the difference between vegetarian and vegan? While vegetarian or "veggie" goods often contain eggs, milk, cheese, lactose, or other ingredients that come from animals, vegan products use only nonanimal-based ingredients and materials to create delicious foods and quality items for every need imaginable. Enter Pangea Vegan Products, which first opened its doors in a Bethesda, Maryland, storefront 7 years ago, and has since expanded online to offer a great selection of the very latest and best in vegan products. At the Pangea website, check out the huge collection of fantastic vegan goods in 17 product categories, items such as shoes and boots (nonleather Birkenstocks and Dr. Marten's, for example), belts, men's dress wear, foods (meat and dairy alternatives, sauces and gravies, baked goods and candies), vitamins, animal-free soaps and candles, makeup, products for your cat and dog (vegan doggie bones and shampoo, for example), household cleaners, and much more. I liked Pangea's own line of VeganSweets chocolate and

No Bull clothing, "the best-quality, breathable faux leather products available on the market today," featuring the unisex Harley jacket and Soho zip-up jacket, the stylish Urban Legend shoe, the Savage Hiking boot, and The Liberator combat boot (cool.) This website has an easy to use search engine, FAQ section, and secure online ordering. You may also be interested in the great library of cookbooks, informational books, children's reading, CDs, and videos.

This store is included here not so much for the discounts—but because I think it's a great source for a wide variety of vegan products that generally would not be available under one "roof."

SPECIAL FACTORS: All returns for exchange, refund, or credit must be returned to Pangea in unused condition within 30 days.

Pearl River

393 W. Broadway
New York, NY 10012
800-878-2446

FORM OF INFORMATION: $5 print catalog; online catalog

PAY: check, MO, MC, V, DSC

SELLS: kitchenware, footwear, clothing, home decor, bedding, musical instruments, stationery, dolls, gifts, and novelties imported from China

STORE: 477 Broadway, New York, NY; 7 days a week 10:00 am–7:30 pm

ONLINE: www.pearlriver.com

A quarter of a century ago, a small group of young overseas Chinese men and women decided to start a small retail store in New York City's Chinatown. Back then there was no direct trade between China and the U.S. and they, knowing that China had much to offer America, set off to introduce quality Chinese goods to the country. From this idea came Pearl River, the first Chinese-American department store. Thirty years later Pearl River has evolved into a large company carrying a full line of quality Chinese goods. The 112-page catalog offers products from the practical to the curious and exotic. I found some great prices on organic green tea, sandlewood soap, cotton print kimonos, window blinds, folding screens, slippers, silk comforters, opera masks, classic Chinese note and address books, lanterns, tote bags, herbal products, and much more. There's also a nice selection of infant shoes and clothes. This store is a great find, not only for inexpensive household and apparel basics, but also for very reasonably priced and out-of-the-ordinary gift items.

WEBSITE: The website is well organized and easy to use. Click on the names of items to see a picture and read a brief description. Ordering is available online.

SPECIAL FACTORS: No refunds; exchanges or store credit only within 14 days of receipt.

Real Goods

360 Interlocken Blvd.
Ste. 300
Broomfield, CO 80021
800-508-2342
FAX: 800-508-2342

FORM OF INFORMATION: free print catalog; online catalog

PAY: check, MO, MC, V, AE, DSC

SELLS: products for ecological sustainability

STORE: locations in Hopland and Berkeley, CA; see website for addresses and hours

ONLINE: www.realgoods.com

There are some companies you just feel good about patronizing. Real Goods is one of them. Founded the same year as this book—1978—Real Goods began in owner John Schaeffer's garage as a source of useable products for followers of the "back to the land" movement. Today this company has grown tremendously along with the number of people who realize the value of goods that save money on fuel and electricity, decrease reliance on ecologically unsound companies and their practices, or make us healthier and happier. Many items here are unique or hard to find. And since Real Goods offers a lowest-price guarantee on everything they sell, you'll also save money by shopping here. What type of sensible products does Real Goods sell? How about solar-powered radios and lanterns, recycled computer disks, woven-jute storage bins, recycled glass tableware, air and water purifiers, natural bedding, combination litterbox-composters, bat houses, and kiddie worm farms, to name a few.

WEBSITE: If you're committed to earth-friendly products, it makes more sense to shop online than to use the print version of the catalog. Real Goods makes it worth your while with the inventory online, clear and easy to use browsing, web-only specials, and secure electronic ordering. Product categories include Healthy Lifestyles, Home and Garden, Energy Efficiency, The Library, Gifts and Seasonal, and Kids and Toys. Or click on the Renewable Energy Catalog to view products aimed to get you off the grid: from smaller items such as battery- or propane-powered refrigerators to elaborate systems harnessing wind, solar, or hydro power for your home.

SPECIAL FACTORS: Satisfaction guaranteed; returns accepted (a restocking fee may apply).

Health, Beauty, and Fitness

Eye Care and Eyewear

Contact lenses, prescription eyeglasses, reading glasses, sunglasses, eyeglass frames, and contact lens supplies

I live in a small town where everybody knows everybody else. I used to think when I smiled and nodded hello to people as we passed on the street that they were choosing to ignore me because I'm an opinionated, often overbearing, know-it-all who only listens sporadically, and tends to minimize her faults. But as I've gotten older, I've realized that they just couldn't see me because they weren't wearing their glasses or contact lenses.

If you're a contact lens wearer, you know how much you spend every year on lenses, eye check-ups, cleaning and soaking solution, contact lens insurance, etc. You'll still need to see your doctor once a year, but you can save a great deal of money—up to 75%—by using the companies in this section for replacement lenses and contact lens supplies. You'll also find firms here that specialize in eyeglasses, reading glasses, and sunglasses at a discount. If you don't think buying attractive, well-fitting eyeglass frames by mail is possible, think again. Some of the companies below have made mail-order their sole venue for many years, and that means customers who have been satisfied with both the end result and the price they paid for the services.

Find It Fast

BIFOCALS
ReadingGlasses.com

CONTACT LENSES
1–800 CONTACTS, Contact Lens Replacement Center, Prism Optical

LENS-CARE PRODUCTS
1–800 CONTACTS

PRESCRIPTION EYEGLASSES
Prism Optical

READING GLASSES
ReadingGlasses.com

SUNGLASSES
1–800 CONTACTS, Contact Lens Replacement Center, Prism Optical

1–800 CONTACTS

51 West Center
Orem, UT 84057
800–CONTACTS
FAX: 801–924–9900

FORM OF INFORMATION: online catalog

PAY: check, MO, MC, V, AE, DSC, DC, CB

SELLS: contact lenses

STORE: no walk-in location; mail-order only; phone hours Monday to Thursday 8:00 am–12 midnight, Friday 8:00 am–1:00 pm, Saturday 9:00 am to 11:00 pm, Sunday 10:00 am–6:00 pm

ONLINE: www.1800contacts.com

1–800 CONTACTS was founded in 1995 by two entrepreneurs who sought to address contact lens wearers' basic frustrations. Wearing contacts themselves, they understood that contact lenses could be expensive and inconvenient to replace. With that in mind, they set out to offer low prices, convenient ordering and fast delivery to their customers. Their plan to accomplish this centered on buying contact lenses in large quantities to get the best prices and housing a large contact lens inventory so customers' prescriptions would be in stock and ready to ship. 1–800 CONTACTS sells approximately 150,000 contact lenses a day, which is why they can sell you the same brand-name lenses prescribed by your doctor for much less than you'd pay elsewhere—from about 20% to 50% less. You can call the company with your prescription information, order online, or have the 1–800 CONTACTS staff call your doctor to get the prescription.

1–800 CONTACTS offers contacts by Bausch & Lomb, CibaVision, CooperVision, and Johnson & Johnson. With the largest inventory of contact lenses in the world, they are able to stock most of the parameters that customers order—with very few exceptions. In fact, they have many contact lenses in inventory that are only stocked by two companies (1–800 CONTACTS and the manufacturer themselves). They even stock most colors, torics, bifocals and multifocals.

Most contact lenses aren't custom-made anymore. Daily wear and disposable contact lenses are made by automated equipment in very large quantities on heavily automated production lines. As a medical device, they must be nearly identical every time —no matter where they are sold. This means you will receive the exact same contact lenses from 1–800 CONTACTS as you have been getting from your eye care provider's store—the only difference is the delivery to your door (and the lower price).

The average customer saves about $20 to $50 per year by ordering from 1-800 CONTACTS. If you are already going to a large national optical chain, or a really competitive optical store, you may find that you only save $5 or $10 dollars by ordering from 1-800 CONTACTS.

SPECIAL FACTORS: Satisfaction guaranteed; quantity discounts available; free standard mail shipping to the continental U.S. and Canada.

Contact Lens Replacement Center

P.O. Box 615
Wheatley Heights, NY 11798
800–779–2654
FAX: 516–643–4009

FORM OF INFORMATION: free price list with long SASE; website
PAY: check, MO, MC, V, AE, DSC
SELLS: contact lenses and sunglasses
STORE: no walk-in location; mail-order only
ONLINE: www.clrc.com

Did you almost faint after the last bill you got from your eye doc? Then join the ranks of savvy consumers who visit their eye-care professionals for medical check-ups, but purchase their lenses elsewhere. You'll love the prices in Contact Lens Replacement Center's current brochure. You could have spent 50% less had you ordered through the Center. This company is for experienced lens wearers—people who have a current prescription and wish to save money by ordering the lenses themselves (instead of paying their eye doctors to do it, and suffering the consequent mark-up). The Center offers gas permeable and hard lenses, soft lenses, disposables, and program replacement lenses from the best known manufacturers. You provide a current prescription, the Center's staff can help you from there—they have a licensed optician on staff to answer your questions. There are no membership fees. Should you find lower prices elsewhere, the folks at CLRC want you to let them know. In addition to contact lenses, the Center sells high-fashion top-quality sunglasses. For a current listing of available brands, please call. All sunglasses come with cases and the manufacturer's warranty.

WEBSITE: At press time the website was under construction and only provided contact information and an email link.

Prism Optical, Inc.

10992 NW 7th Ave.
N. Miami, FL 33168
800–637–4104
FAX: 305–754–7352

FORM OF INFORMATION: free print catalog
PAY: check, MO, MC, V, AE, DSC
SELLS: prescription eyeglasses, sunglasses, and contact lenses
STORE: same address; Monday to Friday 8:30 am–5:00 pm
ONLINE: www.prismoptical.com

Prism Optical has been saving customers up to 75% on prescription eyewear for over 40 years. At Prism, you can get precision eyewear ground to your doctor's prescription with "painstakingly precise" workmanship; a full-range of men's, women's, and children's frames in popular sizes, shapes, and colors; just about every kind of lens made—single-vision, bi- and tri-focals, invisible progressive lenses, tinted, plastic, super-lite polycarbonate, etc.; and custom-fit glasses with lenses made to fit *your* eye size, with bridge and temples made to fit *your* face. Prism also carries a complete line of value-priced contact lenses.

So how do you get great-fitting frames by mail? You can either send in your present frames for duplication (Prism's specialists will duplicate temple and bridge size, frame width, and lens size) or use Prism's Precision Frame Fitting Guide that has diagrams against which you can place your current frames to determine these measurements. There are pages of Prism's frames to choose from; Prism can also get you a good deal on designer frames not listed in their catalog if you call or fax them with the manufacturer's name, frame color, and size (information found on the inside of the frame, usually the temple). Service is quick, and all glasses are guaranteed, so what do you have to lose?

WEBSITE: At the website, you can email for a print catalog, but there was no online inventory or electronic ordering at press time.

SPECIAL FACTORS: If not satisfied with glasses within 30-day trial period, they can be returned for full refund.

ReadingGlasses.com

9131 King Arthur Drive
Dallas, Texas 75247
800–238–0904
FAX: 214-688-1046

FORM OF INFORMATION: online catalog only; no print catalog

PAY: check, MO, MC, V, AE, DSC

SELLS: reading glasses

STORE: 10 stores in LA, OK, and TX; call or see website for addresses

ONLINE: www.readingglasses.com and www.readingglassesforcheapskates.com

Recently I was lost on a New York City subway with my 9-year-old son and was astonished to find I couldn't read the subway map because no matter how close or far I moved the map from my eyes, it was a blur. Fortunately, I was able to depend on the kindness of strangers, but realized the time had come for me to get reading glasses. Enter ReadingGlasses.com and ReadingGlassesForCheapskates.com. You've got to love a reading glass company that quotes Fran Lebowitz, Gary Shandling, and Jimmy Durante on eyeglasses. Since opening the world's first Reading Glasses Boutique in 1987, Reading Glasses To Go has been recognized as the leading specialty retailer of upscale reading glasses and accessories, all at great prices. At their website, Reading-Glasses.com, prices are about 25% below retail and at ReadingGlassesforCheap-skates.com you'll find stylish, sturdy, and lightweight reading glasses starting at $14.50 a pair. ReadingGlasses.com has a very cool feature (for IBM compatibles) where you can scan or mail in a photo of your face and then "try on" glasses. Domestic standard shipping is free. I love this company and I bet you will too.

SPECIAL FACTORS: Satisfaction guaranteed; Returns accepted within 30 days for any reason, no fine print, no arguments.

Fitness and Exercise

Home and professional aerobic, resistance, and weight-lifting equipment and machinery; health-monitoring devices

My grandmother, born at the end of the nineteenth century, was absolutely disgusted by joggers. When she would see early-morning joggers in brightly-colored outfits running along her road, past red barns and pigsties, she'd snort. "Why don't they jist pick up a shovel an' hoe?" It's a different world now. She'd be cursing me, too, if she'd lived to see the day when her own flesh and blood would spend hard-earned money for the privilege of running *indoors* on a treadmill three times a week.

If you're into exercise machines, free weights, and other indoor work-outs, this is your chapter. Some of the firms here sell professional-quality machines at factory-direct prices. They won't be cheap, but they'll be less expensive here than elsewhere.

Icon Fitness, the manufacturer of many of the fitness equipment brands you are familiar with, started offering new and refurbished equipment for bid, at eBay, a couple of years ago. I've seen new equipment go for almost 50% off of retail and because you're buying from the manufacturer, you get the same return policies and warranties as if you bought it for twice as much at the name-brand websites. See the details in their listing under Fitness Auction in this chapter.

If you're into jogging, aerobics, swimming, bicycling, surfing, or any other type of rigorous fitness routine, be sure to check out the companies in the "Sports and Outdoor Recreation" chapter.

Find It Fast

FREE WEIGHTS
Fitness Factory Outlet, Smooth Fitness

PRO GYM AND INSTITUTIONAL EQUIPMENT
Fitness Factory Outlet, Smooth Fitness

HEALTH/FITNESS MEASURING DEVICES
Creative Health Products

HEALTH, FITNESS, AND TRAINING VIDEOS
Creative Health Products

TREADMILLS, STATIONARY BICYCLES, ELLIPTICALS, AND HOME GYMS
Fitness Auction, FitnessFactory Outlet, Smooth Fitness

Creative Health Products

5148 Saddle Ridge Rd., Dept.
WBM

Plymouth, MI 48170

800–742–4478

734–996–5900

FAX: 734–996–4650

FORM OF INFORMATION: free print catalog; online catalog

PAY: check, MO, MC, V, AE, DSC

SELLS: fitness testing equipment, health-monitoring products

STORE: no walk-in location; mail-order only

ONLINE: www.chponline.com

Creative Health Products has been selling health/fitness testing and measuring products as well as exercise equipment since 1976, and has some of the best product lines available. Savings run up to 30% on most items, and the company offers a lowest price guarantee, lest you need more incentive to shop here. This is a wonderful source for those involved with physical therapy, cardiac rehabilitation, or just general fitness. The online catalog includes products, in 38 categories, such as exercise bikes, blood-pressure monitors, pulse oximeters, body-fat calipers, moist heating pads, physioballs, scales, stopwatches, flexibility testers, alignment and posture grids, and much more. Creative Health also offers an impressive array of health and fitness books, videos, and training software. Products are all pictured (mostly in black and white) with descriptions and CHP's price next to the retail price. There are also articles and guides on products such as heart-rate monitors and skinfold calipers. Creative Health's knowledgeable staff is ready to answer any questions you have about their products or about how to find the best equipment for your needs. This website features online ordering.

SPECIAL FACTORS: 30-day satisfaction guarantee; returns within 30 days for refund or exchange (except exercise bikes, videos & software); products must be returned in new condition with all original packaging, instructions, manuals, etc.; shipping charges are not refundable.; quantity discounts and institutional accounts available; C.O.D. orders accepted.

Fitness Auction

ICON Health & Fitness
1500 South 1000 West
Logan, UT 84321
800–822–6357

FORM OF INFORMATION: online catalog; no print catalog

PAY: MC, V, AE, DSC

SELLS: fitness equipment available by auction direct from the manufacturer

STORE: pickup locations throughout the U.S.

ONLINE: www.fitnessauction.com

ICON Health & Fitness owns and manufactures some of the most well-known brands in the fitness industry including ProForm, NordicTrack, HealthRider, Image, Weslo, and Weider. Through Fitness Auction, and in conjunction with eBay, ICON offers new and refurbished fitness equipment available for sale by bidding direct from them, the manufacturer. You'll find new and refurbished treadmills, ellipticals, crosstrainers, home gyms, exercise bikes, steppers, and more at much less than you would pay for the exact same models elsewhere.

The new products are shipped directly from ICON with a standard 30-day satisfaction guarantee. When I checked at the Fitness Auction site there were a number of ellipticals and treadmills at winning bids that were up to 45% less than retail prices. For instance, a new ProForm 380X treadmill was sold at a winning bid of $330. When I checked the same model at the ProForm website and also at a popular online sports store, the same treadmill was selling for $600. New equipment also comes with a 90-day warranty with extended warranties available for an extra fee.

Fitness Auction refurbished items are those items that have been used during a 30-day trial period from the manufacturer and returned for minor scratch and dent reasons. These products have been refurbished to top quality and include a 90-day warranty. All sales are final. When I checked refurbished NordicTrack products, the savings on winning bids were as high as 90% off of the price of the same new products offered at the NordicTrack site. The two catches are: refurbished products are pick-up only from regional warehouses and they hold no return policy or trial period. The pick-up sites on products available included Atlanta, GA; Chicago, IL; Los Angeles, CA; Oakland, CA; Detroit, MI; Seattle, WA; Chantilly, VA; and Dallas, TX. And I was told a Boston, MA pick-up site would be available soon. When you pick up the refurbished products, they are fully assembled and unboxed. If you are close to the pick-up areas and you're willing to live with the no return, you could own a NordicTrack CX985 elliptical that retails for

$799 for just $80! All refurbished equipment comes with a standard 90-day warranty. Extended warranties are not available on these items.

SPECIAL FACTORS: Shipping is only available in the 48 contiguous U.S.; shipping is curbside delivery in 10-15 business days; all sales final for refurbished equipment; refurbished equipment is for pick-up only at warehouse location stated in product description.

Fitness Factory Outlet

877–336–7483

FORM OF INFORMATION: online catalog only; no print catalog

PAY: check, MO, MC, V, AE, DSC

SELLS: fitness and exercise equipment

SHOWROOM: same address; Monday, Wednesday, Friday 11:00 am–7:00 pm, Tuesday, Thursday 11:00 am–6:00 pm, Sunday 12:00 noon–4:00 pm

ONLINE: www.fitnessfactoryoutlet.com

Since 1988, Fitness Factory Outlet has been selling aerobic and strength training equipment at discounted prices to schools, gyms, and individuals who want the convenience of working out at home. You'll save about 10% compared to other fitness dealers by shopping here. But remember, a 10% savings here can mean $100 depending on the equipment you are in the market for. At the website you'll find treadmills and cardio equipment, multistation gyms, combination and utility benches, leg machines, various presses, power racks, dumbbells and dumbbell racks, boxing equipment, and Olympic and standard weight plates. There is a category dedicated to commercial equipment. Also listed are cable attachment bars, abdominal straps, chinning bars, inversion boots, Olympic and standard bars and collars, rubber flooring, belts, nutritional products, awesome accessories, and much more. Fitness Factory Outlet takes pride in strong customer service policies, which translates into free tech support, a 31-day money-back satisfaction guarantee, and knowledgeable salespeople who can answer all your questions. If you find any of their products on sale for a lower price, they will gladly sell you the item at the same price. Likewise, if you have purchased an item and see it advertised for less, they will refund the difference to you up to 31 days after your purchase.

SPECIAL FACTORS: Authorized returns (exclusive of shipping and handling charges) are accepted for refund within 31 days if in like-new condition; free freight for orders over $99 within the continental U.S. (See website for products not included in this offer).

Smooth Fitness

112 Gaither Dr.
Mt. Laurel, NJ 08054
888-211-1611
FAX: 215-362-5546

FORM OF INFORMATION: online catalogs only; no print catalogs

PAY: check, MO, MC, V, AE

SELLS: treadmills, home gyms, and, elliptical trainers

STORE: 4 store locations in PA, NJ, and DE, call for addresses and hours.

ONLINE: www.smoothfitness.com

Starting over six years ago, InternetFitness.com began selling quality fitness equipment online through smoothfitness.com. They introduced their Smooth brand of treadmills, home gyms and elliptical trainers. InternetFitness.com has been in the business of providing health and fitness solutions for over 19 years. The company started by selling fitness equipment in brick-and-mortar stores. With the advent of the internet, they realized the potential for offering these same products online. Here you'll find their exclusive Smooth brand of treadmills, home gyms and elliptical trainers. They are the only manufacturer of quality fitness equipment to primarily sell over the internet. By selling factory direct and online, they eliminate the overhead costs of retail sales. That is why they are able to sell comparable equipment well below the price of competitors. You get the convenience of shopping online combined with factory direct savings of 40% to 45%.

All of their Smooth Fitness equipment is made to the highest standards. The Smooth brand is not your "Blue Light Special." For example, the Smooth 9.3 treadmill is built with the industry leading Baldor motor—a powerful treadmill motor known for its durability. These products are designed to exceed normal requirements with equipment that is built to last, which is reflected in the warranties they provide.

You may find when shopping for brand fitness equipment like True, Landice or Precor you are restricted to online purchases of only dealers in your regional area (beware of warranty limitations) and consequently you are required to pay state taxes. The Smooth brand of fitness equipment is available throughout the U.S. and Canada (no warranty limitations). They ship not only through their two manufacturing facilities, but also their warehouses in New Jersey and Nevada.

Customers are assured of satisfaction through a 30 day money-back guarantee. All treadmills and elliptical trainers are backed with a 1-year in-house repair warranty (lifetime parts warranty on home gyms). Should your equipment require service, there is an extensive nationwide network of certified technicians. In addition, customers can call or email inquiries to their service group.

SPECIAL FACTORS: Shipping charges for contiguous U.S. destinations are included in prices and are clearly indicated on your order; inside delivery and/or setup can be requested for an additional charge; satisfaction guaranteed; see website for returns policies.

Medications and Vitamins

Prescription and generic over-the-counter drugs and medications; Chinese herbs and alternative medicines and treatments; vitamin and mineral health supplements

Consider this section of the "Health, Beauty, and Fitness" chapter a print version of a trip to the drug or health-food store. Here you'll find companies selling prescription drugs and other drugstore items by mail, which is not only convenient, but also a great way to save money. Even generic drugs may be cheaper by mail, affording you savings of up to 60% on some commonly prescribed remedies.

Since many people are into alternative treatments such as homeopathy, nutritional therapy, and Chinese herbs, I've included several companies that specialize in these as well. When it comes to vitamins and nutritional supplements, you definitely shouldn't pay full price. The companies here can cut your vitamin expenses by more than half.

I find the whole subject of herbs, vitamins, and alternative health approaches daunting. If you're a parent, you have had to become something of an expert. After all, you can't be running to the doctor every time your kid has a runny nose. Just about every bookstore sells a multitude of books on health-related topics. My advice is to read as much as you can—and then read some more. Naturally, you'll need your physician's cooperation when ordering prescriptions by mail. If you're considering nonprescription remedies, it's always a good idea to consult a professional before you start self-treatments.

Find It Fast

ALTERNATIVE MEDICINES AND REMEDIES
All Star Health, East Earth Trade Winds

HEALTH-RELATED BOOKS
East Earth Trade Winds

PRESCRIPTION AND GENERIC OVER-THE-COUNTER MEDICATIONS
AARP Pharmacy Services, Drugstore.com

SENIORS HEALTH PRODUCTS
AARP Pharmacy Services, Drugstore.com

VITAMINS AND NUTRITIONAL SUPPLEMENTS
AARP Pharmacy Services, All Star Health, Drugstore.com, East Earth Trade Winds, Freeda Vitamins

AARP Pharmacy Services

Department #258390
P.O. Box 40011
Roanoke, VA 24022
800–406–1662
800–260–4452 (Spanish)
FAX: 800–530–5014
TDD: 800–933–4327

FORM OF INFORMATION: free print catalog; online catalog

PAY: check, MO, MC, V, DSC

SELLS: generic drugstore and pharmaceutical items

STORE: no walk-in location; mail-order only; phone hours Monday to Friday 8:00 am–10:00 pm, Saturday 8:30 am–5:00 pm EST

ONLINE: www.aarppharmacy.com

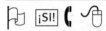

AARP Pharmacy Services has been serving the needs of AARP Members for over 40 years. They offer programs to help you save money on prescription drugs, over-the-counter medications and products for healthy living.

The print catalog specializes in generic products—items that have the same active ingredients as common brands such as Tylenol, PreparationH, and Imodium A-D but are sold for much less, sometimes half—under the AARP Pharmacy label. The catalog offers generic vitamins, nutrition formulas, antacids, face creams, sleep aids, toothpaste, sunglasses—just about anything you'd find in a drugstore. Additionally, the catalog carries products to assist elderly folk with everyday living, featuring items such as elevated toilet seats, heating pads, cholesterol home test kits, humidifiers, and on and on. AARP Pharmacy functions as a full-service pharmacy and can fill any prescription with brand-name or generic medications. Using the latter will net you 20% to 30% savings. See the catalog for details on prescription and other ordering. There's a full-time pharmacist on duty at the main number to answer all of your prescription drug queries.

WEBSITE: There's an online version of the catalog that features easy product searches and online ordering. To get prices on prescription drugs, simply enter the product name in the search box on their Drug Prices page or click on a letter for an alphabetical list.

SPECIAL FACTORS: AARP Pharmacy honors most prescription insurance plans; prescription medications can be labeled in Braille upon request when you order; free shipping for purchases over $50.

All Star Health

3101 W. MacArthur Blvd.
Santa Ana, CA 92704
800-875-0448
714-210-5989
FAX: 714-751-8422

FORM OF INFORMATION: online catalog only; no print catalog

PAY: check, MO, MC, V, AE

SELLS: vitamins, herbs, nutritional supplements, homeopathic medicines

STORE: no walk-in location; mail-order only

ONLINE: www.allstarhealth.com

Remember when most people never thought about the consequences of their eating habits, and referred to health-conscious individuals as "health nuts"? Thank goodness most of us have gotten with the times! Now you can order all of your supplements by going to All Star Health on the web, and save 30% to 60% off retail prices when you do. All Star Health offers a lowest-price guarantee on many of the top names in health, nutrition, and homeopathic supplies, such as Twin Lab, Nature's Way, Schiff, Hyland's, Klamath, Natrol, and many more. This firm carries a full line of vitamins, herbs, minerals, antioxidants, amino acids, essential oils, protein bars, shakes, superfoods, and weight loss/gain products that can all be securely ordered online and shipped to your doorstep. All Star Health takes full advantage of selling their goods over the internet, forgoing the expensive overhead of a brick-and-mortar operation, thus enabling them to drastically reduce the overall cost to their customers. This is a great website. I love the feature that lets you sort the product list you are browsing by percentage of discount or by price or brand. Plus, they calculate the exact amount of how much you've saved off retail in your cart. You'll also find monthly specials and categories for women's and children's supplements. Not all of the 15,000 products carried by All Star Health are found on the site, so contact them for special orders or items that you don't find online.

SPECIAL FACTORS: Flat-rate shipping charge of $4.95, no matter what size the order; see website for details about international shipping; products may be returned within 30 days of purchase; orders paid by check will not be shipped until check has cleared.

East Earth Trade Winds

P.O. Box 463151
Redding, CA 96049–3151
800–258–6878
FAX: 530–223–0944

FORM OF INFORMATION: $1 print catalog; online catalog
PAY: check, MO, MC, V, DSC, AE
SELLS: Chinese medicinal herbs, books
STORE: 144 Hartnell Ave., Redding, CA; Monday to Friday 10:00 am–5:00 pm
ONLINE: www.eastearthtrade.com

Chinese traditional medicine is many centuries older than the Western style practiced by U.S. physicians. With the growing Asian population in the U.S. and increasing awareness of the effectiveness of Chinese herbalism by non-Chinese patients and physicians alike, demand for Chinese medicines has soared. If you live in a big city with a Chinatown, you're in luck—sort of. The shopkeeper at the Chinese herb shop may or may not speak English. The product you're looking for may not be fresh or in stock. Parking may be an expensive nightmare. You might be overcharged and not realize it. You won't have any way of verifying the reputability of the manufacturer—do they sell products derived from endangered species, for example, and are their trade practices sound?

Enter East Earth Trade Winds. This company has been in business since 1985 selling unique Chinese herbal products from reputable Chinese and American manufacturers. All of their products are carefully selected by herbalists, not marketers. East Earth's products are inexpensive—much less than their competitors'. The 24-page print catalog offers herbs used for tonics (health-promoting/maintaining formulas) or for treating minor health complaints (cold, flu, indigestion, insomnia, overweight, hay fever, PMS, eczema, etc.). If you don't know a lot about this revered branch of medicine, you'll find the catalog absolutely fascinating, with detailed descriptions of the products and their ingredients (deer antlers or crushed pearls, for example) and what they're used for. You can also call East Earth with questions; they're used to that. This company also carries incense, tea, essential oils, and a variety of books relating to Chinese herbs, medicine, and culture.

WEBSITE: The website offers secure online ordering and a broad array of products. Descriptive text accompanies each item. Just reading about the formulae and what they're used for will prove stimulating.

SPECIAL FACTORS: No products derived from endangered species are stocked; no C.O.D. orders accepted; wholesale buyers should inquire about minimums and policies; satisfaction guaranteed; returns and claims should be made within 10 days of receipt.

Drugstore.com

13920 SE Eastgate Way Ste. 300

Bellevue, WA 98005

800–378–4786

FORM OF INFORMATION: online catalog only; no print catalog

PAY: check, MO, MC, V, AE, DSC

SELLS: drugstore and pharmaceutical items

STORE: no walk-in location; mail-order only

ONLINE: www.drugstore.com

Drugstore.com, inc. is a leading online drugstore and information site offering a very healthy way to shop for health, beauty, wellness, personal care, and pharmacy products. The web store offers thousands of brand-name personal health care products at competitive prices; a full-service, licensed retail pharmacy; and a wealth of health-related information, buying guides, and other tools designed to help consumers make informed purchasing decisions. Drugstore.com's corporate headquarters are located in Bellevue, Washington and the company's 290,000 square foot distribution center is located in Bridgeport, New Jersey. Since opening for business in February 1999, Drugstore.com boasts more than 1,800,000 customers. They offer approximately three to four times as many health, beauty, and wellness products that are stocked in brick-and-mortar stores, stocking both the most popular and hard-to-find, unique product lines.

The website has many helpful editorial features, including shopping guides, product comparisons, related articles and additional product content. Customers can receive a secured e-mail reminder if it's time for a prescription refill; and through the eMedAlert program, customers can choose to be notified via a privacy-protected email alert if they have purchased a product that's been recalled.

The Drugstore.com pharmacy is fully licensed in all 50 U.S. states and certified by the National Association of Boards of Pharmacy's Verified Internet Pharmacy Practice Sites (VIPPS) program. And, they offer free standard shipping on most prescriptions as well as the option to arrange for pick up at any one of 3,800 Rite-Aid stores nationwide. Drugstore.com customers pay almost 20% less on average for prescription drugs compared to brick-and-mortar pharmacy prices for top-quality generic and brand-name drugs. Customers can access comprehensive, easy-to-understand drug interaction information and the Ask Your Pharmacist feature allows customers to ask Drugstore.com pharmacists questions about over-the-counter and wellness products as well as prescription drugs.

SPECIAL FACTORS: Returns within 30 days of receipt for nonprescription items (see website for details on conditions).

Freeda Vitamins, Inc.

36 E. 41st St.
New York, NY 10017–6203
800–777–3737
212–685–4980
FAX: 212–685–7297
TDD: 800–777–3737

FORM OF INFORMATION: free print catalog; online catalog

PAY: check, MO, MC, V, AE, DSC

SELLS: dietary supplements and prescriptions

STORE: Freeda Pharmacy, same address; Monday to Thursday 8:30 am–6:00 pm, Friday 8:30 am–4:00 pm

ONLINE: www.freedavitamins.com

It's always refreshing to find a family-run business like this one that really cares about its customers. It's obvious that Freeda is just such a place when you read this vitamin company's literature. A leading consumer guide found Freeda to be the most reasonably priced among leading vitamin manufacturers—20% less than everyone else. Freeda Vitamins was founded in 1928 by Abraham Freeda and his daughter, Lillian Zimmerman. The firm is now headed by Dr. Philip Zimmerman and his wife, Sylvia. The fourth generation of Zimmermans are actively involved with the company, which keeps tight control over the quality and service of their products. Today this company has been written up and praised everywhere as one of the only sources for all-natural, kosher vitamins that are 100% yeast- and wheat-free. All Freeda vitamins are dated to guarantee freshness; are free from coal-tar dyes, artificial colors, and flavors; and have vegetarian fillers or binders. So if you're someone who has a hard time tolerating commercial vitamins, despair no more.

The comprehensive print catalog lists vitamins, digestive supplements, nutrients, and nutriceuticals in a wide variety of sizes and strengths. Parents: This is a wonderful source for children's vitamins; all Freeda children's products are found on the Feingold Approved Food List for hyperactive children. Freeda will send your doctor, dentist, chiropractor, podiatrist, or veterinarian their Physicians' Information Packet on request.

WEBSITE: Freeda's has kept up with the times with a straightforward website that's information intensive. Read articles by Dr. Zimmerman on a range of subjects, from "Allergies and Nutrition" to "Getting Enough Calcium." All the products manufactured here are thoroughly described at the website and can be ordered online. I like and trust this company.

SPECIAL FACTORS: Courtesy discounts are given to health-care professionals; C.O.D. orders accepted; $10 minimum charge on credit cards; free shipping on orders $100 and above.

Personal Care and Beauty

Products for skin and hair care; name-brand and natural cosmetics; wigs; handmade soaps; fragrances and perfumes; soap-making and aromatherapy supplies

When my twin sister and I were in high school, our recently divorced mother brought her first post marriage date home. My mother and her date were sitting in the living room having some cocktails and chatting. My sister and I hadn't come out of our room to be introduced yet, when we decided to play a hoax on them. We got out all of mom's red lipsticks and proceeded to paint my sister's face, neck, and arms bright red. My sister stood in the hallway outside of the living room, out of sight, and called out to my mother that she wasn't feeling well. When my mother asked what was wrong, my sister stumbled out into the living room, announced that she thought she had a fever, and pretended to pass out on the floor. The date was alarmed and was forever wary of us after the performance piece, and mom wasn't very happy that we had used up all of her expensive lipstick.

The companies in this section can save you a solid 50% on everything from lipstick to wigs. If you really want to save money and have an interest in making your own soaps, cosmetics, and even natural remedies, Liberty Natural Products, listed in this section, has all the bulk ingredients for aromatherapy, soap making, herbal remedies, and more.

Find It Fast

AROMATHERAPY
Kettle Care, Liberty Natural Products

COSMETICS
Fragrance Wholesale

FRAGRANCES AND PERFUMES
Fragrance International Inc., Fragrance Wholesale, Perfumania.com

SKIN AND HAIR PRODUCTS
Cal Ben Soap Company, Dreamsoap.com, Fragrance Wholesale, Kettle Care, Perfumania.com, The Soap Factory

SOAP-MAKING SUPPLIES
Liberty Natural Products

WIGS
Beauty by Spector

Beauty by Spector, Inc.

**1 Spector Pl.,
Dept. BBG–04**
McKeesport, PA 15134–0502
412–673–3259
FAX: 412–678–3978

FORM OF INFORMATION: print catalog (see text)
PAY: check or MO (see text)
SELLS: wigs, hairpieces, wig accessories
STORE: no walk-in location; mail-order only

Beauty by Spector, Inc., offers the Alan Thomas line of wigs and hairpieces at savings of up to 50% compared with salon prices. The 32-page color catalog features a number of designer styles for women, modeled in gorgeous full-page photographs. The wigs range from neat, softly coifed shorter styles to the magnificent below-shoulder-length drape "Obsession." The styles are contemporary and fashionable—pretty, relaxed, and well shaped. Included in the catalog are wiglets, cascades, and extensions ideal for everyday wear as well as for dressy occasions. There are men's hairpieces here, too, in several styles. Thermal-conductive monofilament and polyurethane are available in the men's pieces for maximum comfort.

The wigs and hairpieces are available in a wide variety of synthetic fibers as well as human hair and are offered in dozens of colors. For color selection, you may purchase a set of actual hair samples, or if you prefer, send a sample of your hair for color matching. You'll also find shampoos, conditioners, hair accessories (turbans and scarves, for example), brushes and combs, and wig stands and mannequins.

Beauty by Spector now offers a new line called Dermafix, designed specifically for women suffering from hair loss due to chemotherapy and alopecia. These wigs use a special material that naturally adheres to the scalp without glue or tape. The styles and colors are adorable and will contribute to a feeling of self-esteem and security.

Beauty by Spector has been in business since 1958 and is extremely knowledgeable in the field. Wig specialists are on duty 24 hours a day to answer your questions.

SPECIAL FACTORS: Specify men's or women's styles when requesting information, as added material and flyers pertaining to your gender will be enclosed with the catalog; call to inquire regarding the price of the catalog; pay by money order and receive an additional discount; quantity discounts are negotiable.

Cal Ben Soap Company

9828 Pearmain St.,
Dept. WBM

Oakland, CA 94603

800–340–7091

510–638–7091

FAX: 510–638–7827

FORM OF INFORMATION: free print catalog; online catalog

PAY: check, MO, MC, V, AE, DSC

SELLS: natural, earth-friendly soaps for bath, hair, laundry, and dishes

STORE: no walk-in location; mail-order only; phone hours Monday to Friday 8:30 am–4:00 pm PST

ONLINE: www.calbenpuresoap.com

"The third planet from the sun deserves clean air, quality water, and 'Pure Soap'," according to the exciting, colorful literature sent by Cal Ben Soap Company. Here's a company that believes in environmentally friendly household soaps at great prices. This company has taken a leadership role since 1947 in providing consumers with soaps for laundry, face and body, hair, and dishes that do the job better than their common commercial counterparts, but that also last a lot longer (they're triple concentrated) and don't harm the environment in any way. Each of the Five Star Soap Products has multiple uses detailed in the accompanying literature. For example, the Seafoam laundry soap can also be used for toilets, greasy driveways, and as an all-purpose household cleaner. The shampoo doubles as a bubble bath, rug shampoo, and delicate-fabrics soap. And on and on.

Since these economical, all-natural products seemed almost too good to be true, I decided to sample some products, including the Gold Star Shampoo Concentrate, the "Pure Soap" bar, the liquid Five Star Dish Glow (great for scrubbing grass-and-dirt-scuffed sneakers with), and the Seafoam Destain automatic dishwashing soap. All were truly wonderful. You will feel excellent about the fact that you aren't contributing to groundwater pollution. The prices here are good, too. Since the soaps are concentrated, savings run up to 85% off normal retail. All products come in a variety of sizes, and gift and sample packs are available as well as yearly collections. In addition to soaps, Cal Ben also sells almond hand/body lotion, glass cleaner, crystal deodorant stones, natural scouring pads, countertop seafoam finger pump dispensers, and other cleaning/hygiene accessories and products. Lathering up with pure soap for kitchen and bathroom hygiene rinses away 95% of harmful bacterial.

WEBSITE: Online you can read all about Cal Ben's products, check out pricing, and order online, or call your order in or download an order form to mail or fax in. Accessing the online catalog is an environmentally friendly way to check out these nice products without acquiring print material that eventually becomes waste.

SPECIAL FACTORS: Satisfaction guaranteed; returns accepted for exchange, refund, or credit. Be sure to mention *The Bargain Buyer's Guide* when ordering.

Dreamsoap.com

2842 Main Street #146
Glastonbury, CT 06033-1036

FORM OF INFORMATION: online catalog only; no print catalog

PAY: check, MO, MC, V, AE, DSC

SELLS: 100% vegetable-based soap, bath foam, shower gel, and lotion

STORE: no walk-in location; mail-order only

ONLINE: www.dreamsoap.com

Featuring French soaps made from shea butter, organic olive oil, and essential oils of Provence, this site offers high-quality soap that one would ordinarily pass up as soon as they confronted the prices. For those of you who might think gentle French soap would be nice but not worth the extra expense, Dreamsoap.com can give you the best of both worlds, with low enough prices to allow you to use it for more than just special occasions. I found the soap prices here easily 50% lower than comparable soaps offered in local shops where I live. This site offers extra gentle soaps, shower gels, foam baths, olive oil soaps, wash creams, and body lotion from the "Rêve de Provence" line made with essential oils from the heart of the French southern region of Provence, in Manosque. It is a very sunny region, and very well-known for the quality of its perfumes and scents such as lavender, vervain, rosemarin, peach of vineyard, and fig tree. These soaps are not tested on animals and contain no added dyes or colors. All in all, this site is perfect for those who take delight in healthy and affordable cleanliness, with soap that is gentle on your face, your pocketbook, and the environment. (Products will arrive packed in all-natural fill made from renewable wood resources.) In addition to Dreamsoap's affordable prices, they also have a "Department of Dents and Dings"

that features the same quality products in slightly damaged packaging at large discounts. I like this company and have ordered from them a number of times for myself and for gifts. Online ordering is available.

SPECIAL FACTORS: Satisfaction guaranteed.

Fragrance International, Inc.

398 E. Rayen Ave.	**FORM OF INFORMATION:** price quotes
Youngstown, OH 44505	**PAY:** check, MO, MC, V, DSC
800–543–3341	**SELLS:** men's and women's fragrances
330–747–3341	**STORE:** same address; Monday to Friday
FAX: 330–747–7200	10:00 am–5:00 pm phone hours Monday to Friday 8:30 am–5:00 pm EST (see text)
	EMAIL: fii@cisnet.com

Fragrance International has been featured in this book for a number of years for their comprehensive selection of fragrances at discount prices—28% to 33% below retail. If you happen to be hooked on an expensive perfume, Fragrance International should be able to save you a lot of money. Their inventory has grown so huge that they no longer publish a print catalog. Instead, this company maintains a massive database updated daily of just about every line of fragrance one could imagine—from brand-new hot items to the hard-to-find old brands and everything in between, including mass-market lines. Give them a call with your fragrance brand, and they'll quote you a price over the phone. If you call after hours, an answering machine is on duty to take your order or message. A helpful representative will get back to you on the next business day.

SPECIAL FACTORS: No minimum order; freight free on orders of $250 or more.

Fragrance Wholesale

P.O. Box 358
Pebble Beach, CA 93953
FAX: 831–648–1678

FORM OF INFORMATION: online catalog only; no print catalog

PAY: MC, V, AE, DSC

SELLS: cosmetics, men's and women's fragrances, and hair and nail accessories

STORE: no walk-in location; mail-order only

ONLINE: www.fragrancewholesale.com

Since 1986, Fragrance Wholesale has been a leading wholesaler/retailer of designer fragrances and cosmetics. Now this company is able to offer merchandise directly to consumers through their website at a discount because they have no brick-and-mortar overhead, they obtain merchandise in extremely large quantities, and they have established relationships with manufacturers. Thanks to the wonders of technology, regular guys and gals today can buy top-name cosmetics at great prices.

Having surfed around for the best cosmetics source on the web, I have to say this one gets very good marks. Not only are the prices better than retail—to the tune of 10% to 30% less, in some cases—but the selection is far better than elsewhere. For example, if you are a fan of Clinique, it's almost impossible to find the pricey but wonderful Dramatically Different moisturizing lotion anywhere but in department stores. Fragrance Wholesale had it at the time of this writing, along with some other popular Clinique products, at about 15% less than our local retailer. What one often finds with wholesalers is off brands, or odd products from mainstream brands, making shopping a frustrating endeavor. Not here. Fragrance Wholesaler sells only top-quality goods, no imitations or products that are old or expired. Occasionally, they obtain special merchandise in which there may be an aesthetic variance from standard. Examples of this are unboxed products or products that may have been originally designed as a demonstrator. Nonstandard products will always be clearly denoted.

Cosmetics brands include such names as Estee Lauder, Lancome, Clinique, Arden, and Dermablend. You'll also find hair accessories (a wide assortment of twists, banana clips, and jaw clips), nail polish, gift sets, and collectable miniatures (fragrances) for men and women—cute tiny bottles of fragrances that were originally produced for promotional purposes but are now hot collectibles. The Clearance section had awesome deals on a variety of cosmetics by such names as Almay, L'Oreal, Revlon, and

Ultima II. Interestingly, Fragrance Wholesale was not always the cheapest place to find fragrances when I shopped around. However, the Specials section did have a few stupendous deals on selected designer fragrances. This site gets enthusiastic endorsements from customers, whose main rave seems to be great prices and extremely fast service.

If you want to find out such information as why Fragrance Wholesale does not publish a phone number, or why they are able to sell to you at such good prices, see the informative Frequently Asked Questions section of the website. Please note that this company responds to all emails promptly.

SPECIAL FACTORS: 100% satisfaction guaranteed. Returns accepted up to 30 days from date of purchase; minimum order: $25; shipping free on orders over $100; no products shipped to APO/FPO addresses; see website for information on shipments to Canada and overseas.

Kettle Care

**6590 Farm to Market Rd.,
Dept. WBM
Whitefish, MT 59937
TEL/FAX: 406–862–9851**

FORM OF INFORMATION: free print catalog, $2 outside U.S.; online catalog
PAY: check, MO, MC, V, AE, DSC
SELLS: natural skin-care and bath products
STORE: same address; 7 days a week 10:00 am–6:00 pm; call for appointment
ONLINE: www.kettlecare.com

What a lovely woman owns this company, and what lovely products she makes. Breezing through Kettle Care's print catalog is like strolling through a Montana field of wildflowers. Since 1984, Lynn Wallingford has grown the very herbs and wildflowers in her garden that go into Kettle Care products. I don't include this company just because I happen to love high-quality, handmade, ecologically sound, all-natural, beautifully packaged personal-care products. Compare Kettle Care's products with other high-end companies such as Weleda, Camocare, and Aubrey, and you'll see that on selected items Kettle Care's prices are as much as 50% less. Ms. Wallingford says she hand-blends and personally fusses over each jar and bottle; testimonials from happy customers throughout the catalog confirm that the packaging is beautiful and the products out of the ordinary. Among the products here are moisture creams and lotions, sprays, bath powders, cleansers and soaps, hair products, mineral baths, massage oils, balms and salves (for lips, babies, sore muscles, feet, sunscreen, the delicate eye area, varicose veins, and chapped and callused workers' hands), aromatherapy products, and essential and fragrance oils. I liked the "pocket perfumes"—in ¼-ounce screw-top jars so you can apply fragrance wherever you please, in the amount you please. I also liked the handmade Workers Soap, with pumice and clove oil for your tough guy who also wants to smell nice. This is a company that inspires loyalty in its customers.

WEBSITE: Check out the great website, where you can order online from the full spectrum of products. When well-designed online catalogs like this are created with the consumer's needs in mind, there's really no reason to use the print version at all.

SPECIAL FACTORS: 25-cent refund for returned bottles and jars to recycle; satisfaction guaranteed.

Liberty Natural Products

8120 SE Stark
Portland, OR 97215
800–289–8427
503–256–1227
FAX: 503–256–1182

FORM OF INFORMATION: free print catalog; online catalog

PAY: MC, V, AE, DSC, DC

SELLS: botanical ingredients and related accessories

STORE: no walk-in location; mail-order only; phone hours Monday to Thursday 7:30 am–10:00 pm, Friday 7:30 am–4:00 pm, Sunday 4:00 pm–10:00 pm PST

ONLINE: www.libertynatural.com

Did you know that an attar is extracted through the distillation of flowers? Could you define the difference between an essential oil and a tincture? Log on to Liberty Natural Products' website and you'll start to understand the world of knowledge occupied by soap makers, aromatherapists, herbal and holistic practitioners, and massage therapists. Liberty Natural Products is one of the leading sources for bulk botanicals—from vials to drum sizes—at the lowest prices around. To benefit from wholesale prices, the only requirement here is a minimum order of $50.

But that won't be hard, because there's so much here you'll want to buy. Product categories in the online catalog include aromatherapy (eye pillows, distillate waters, diffusers, air fresheners, and accessories); baby care; books; bulk ingredients (from absolutes, attar, balsams, and concretes to distillate waters, herbs, soaps, resins, and tinctures—with a lot in between); massage oils; medicinals (homeopathic, tea tree products, cold care, etc.); New Age music; packaging (amber, clear, and cobalt blue glass bottles, droppers and caps, pipettes, sprayers, jars, and much more); personal care; andvitamins. The bulk ingredients, in particular, are impressive. Click on Absolutes, for example, and you'll find a lengthy list ranging from arnica and beeswax to violet leaves and ylang ylang. There's really great stuff here even for those of us not into soapmaking or the healing arts. You'll love the air fresheners—little 2-ounce spray bottles in a wonderfully eclectic spectrum of fragrances, like orange spice, flower garden, nag champa incense, and cedarwood. Buy a box of these inexpensive little goodies to give as hostess gifts or to keep in a basket in your bathroom.

You will also appreciate the informational section of the website that included a botanical database, a glossary of botanical terms, soapmakers' resources, essential oil safety information, and articles on exotica such as jasmine, shea butter, and grapefruit seed extract. The print catalog is the same as the online catalog, so it makes more sense to shop from the electronic version and save some trees in the process. You can order directly online, and there are customer service people available to answer your questions if you call during business hours.

SPECIAL FACTORS: Some items are not returnable; qualified returns accepted within 60 days of receipt (see details on website).

Perfumania.com

251 International Pkwy.
Sunrise, FL 33325
866–557–2368
954–335–9100
FAX: 954–335–9185

FORM OF INFORMATION: online catalog only; no print catalog

PAY: check, MO, MC, V, AE, DSC

SELLS: fragrances for men, women, and children; bath and body products, watches

STORE: retail stores nationwide, check website for locations; online only

ONLINE: www.perfumania.com

When you're surfing the web for your favorite perfume, you'll notice there's a lot of competition out there. Savings at Perfumania.com average 20% off suggested retail prices on most items, with "red tag" specials marked down by as much as 80%. But loyal readers of this book know that a bargain isn't a bargain without great customer amenities—fabulous selection, sound return policies, reasonable shipping charges, and helpful customer service representatives, among others. I'm happy to report that Perfumania.com gets good marks in all of these categories.

Perfumania.com professes to have the largest assortment of fragrances (for men, women, and even kids), bath and body products, cosmetics, and skin-care treatments anywhere. The website is easy to navigate. Browse by category or search for a product with a brand name. I particularly like Perfumania.com's specials: pages and pages of top-name brands marked down by more than half, and the "5 for 25" promotions where you can choose any 5 items and pay only $25. To win you over even more, Perfumania.com will help you choose the right fragrance based on your gender, the season, and the style desired (classic, work, formal, sport, trendy, romantic, and casual). And I actually thought just one fragrance was good enough for all occasions!

SPECIAL FACTORS: Unopened, authorized returns accepted within 30 days of receipt; returns will incur a 20% restocking fee unless the result of a company error; authorized wholesale customers may inquire for terms.

The Soap Factory

3 Burlington Rd.
Bedford, MA 01730
888-227-8453
781-275-8363

FORM OF INFORMATION: $2 print catalog; online catalog

PAY: check, MO, MC, V

SELLS: handmade castile soaps

STORE: no walk-in location; mail-order only; phone hours weekdays 8:00 am–10:00 pm EST

ONLINE: www.alcasoft.com/soapfact

★

Readers of this book know by now that I love small companies that take pride in what they sell, have old-fashioned relationships with their customers, and deliver real value. The Soap Factory fits the bill. In the 1960s, owner Marietta Ellis researched home soap recipes in order to help field workers teach women in developing countries to make soap for their families. She then began making her own soap and selling it at local craft fairs. Now more than 30 years later The Soap Factory sells to customers from all over the country.

Lots of companies make and sell soap, but few produce castile soap. Using a traditional formula from the 19th century, Marietta's authentic castile is a combination of olive oil and animal fat. Olive oil gives the soap mildness and gentleness, while animal fat, in this case lard, gives soap superior cleaning and lasting qualities. The Soap Factory uses lard in their recipe because, unlike tallow, it causes the soap to lather well in warm rather than very hot water. Also, the fatty acids in lard are very similar to those in human skin—perfect for people with ultrasensitive skin. The result is an unbelievably firm, creamy, mild, long-lasting soap that cannot be produced from plant oils alone. Many modern soaps claim to be true castile but aren't—they don't have the required 40% to 60% olive oil, if any, or they use coconut oil instead, which can cause skin irritation. For those of you who object to using animal products of any kind, The Soap Factory makes a castile soap that's made of olive oil in combination with other vegetable oils. You can buy bars of soap here in boxes of 2 or 4 in a dazzling array of scents and varieties, as well as scent-free. The Soap Factory sells gel soap and liquid soap, too—great for taking camping or hiking. Click through the website to see the array of choices—mint-scented soap with added aloe vera, luxurious Victorian-style rose-scented bars with real milk added, gentle-scrubbing bars made with oatmeal, and bars scented with pine, apple, rosemary, lavender, and patchouli.

There's a helpful glossary that describes such terms as *cold-process, saponification,* and *glycerin,* a page of information about the bad stuff found in commercial soaps, and even a page of glowing customer feedback. The Soap Factory's soaps are about 30% less than comparable products found through other catalogs and your local health food store. The print catalog is merely a print-out of the website and will cost you $2, so I'd recommend browsing and shopping online.

SPECIAL FACTORS: Orders may be placed by phone, mail, or online; wholesale customers welcome (see website for details).

Home

Appliances and TVs

Refrigerators, stoves, microwaves, dishwashers, washers and dryers, small kitchen appliances, vacuum cleaners, sewing machines, televisions, air conditioners, etc.

The companies featured in this section offer primarily white goods (washers, dryers, refrigerators, microwaves, and ranges), brown goods (TVs, air conditioners, etc.), personal-care appliances, sewing machines, vacuum cleaners, and floor machines. For companies that specialize in other "pluggables" such as home entertainment systems and audio and/or video equipment, see the "Music, Audio, and Video" chapter. For office equipment and machines such as computers, telephone headsets, copiers, and printers, see the "Office, Business, and Professional" chapter.

One thing you'll notice about the companies below is that many of them aren't what you'd think of as mail-order companies. That is, they may not have a glossy print catalog that comes in the mail each month; they may not have a print catalog at all. But don't let that discourage you. Some of the companies here offer price quotes, which means *you* do the homework and footwork, and they'll reward you for your efforts. You can save hundreds on appliances by shopping this way—up to 70%.

Here's how price quotes work: Shop around locally for the appliance, or log onto the manufacturer's website and get information that way. When you find a model you like, write down the details (make and model numbers, color, etc.), then call or email the firm. You'll be pleasantly surprised at the price you're quoted, even with shipping costs factored in. This is a great way to shop for vacuum cleaners and sewing machines, too.

When you've got your choice down to one or two models, you can talk to a sales representative and have him or her send you the manufacturer's brochure. Or you can obtain this directly from the manufacturer, most of whom will send brochures on specific models upon request. Manufacturers' addresses are usually found on product packaging, and most have websites as well. The consumer contacts and addresses of hundreds of major corporations are also listed in "Consumer's Resource Handbook," available from the Federal Citizen Information Center on page 123.

Find It Fast

AIR CONDITIONERS
Dial-a-Brand, LVT Price Quote Hotline

MAJOR APPLIANCES
Beach Sales, Cole's Appliance & Furniture, Dial-a-Brand, LVT Price Quote Hotline

SEWING MACHINES AND SERGERS
All Brands.com

SMALL APPLIANCES
All Brands.com

TVS
Cole's Appliance & Furniture, Dial-a-Brand, LVT Price Quote Hotline

VACUUM-CLEANER REPAIRS
ABC Vacuum Cleaner Warehouse

VACUUM CLEANERS, RUG SHAMPOOERS, FLOOR POLISHERS
AAA Vacuums, ABC Vacuum Cleaner Warehouse, LVT Price Quote Hotline, Vacuum Cleaner Discounter

AAA Vacuums

3462 Catclaw Dr.
Abilene, TX 79606
800–533–8227
325–795–0954
FAX: 325–698–0468

FORM OF INFORMATION: price quote; online catalog

PAY: check, MO, MC, V, DSC

SELLS: vacuum cleaners, rug shampooers, floor polishers

STORE: same address; Monday to Friday 9:00 am–6:00 pm

ONLINE: www.aaavacuums.com

Save up to 50% on some of the best names in the cleaning biz at AAA Vacuums, in business since 1975. AAA buys in volume, doesn't publish a print catalog, spends little on PR, and therefore can pass the savings directly on to the customer. Canister, upright, convertible, and mini vacuum models; rug shampooers; and floor buffers are available from Sharp, Panasonic, Hoover, Sanyo, Fantom, Kirby, Filter Queen, and Rainbow. AAA also carries supplies and accessories for all of these brands. Whether you're looking for a home model or a commercial model, it will be well worth your while to call AAA Vacuums for a price quote before you venture out into the crowded and overpriced stores. A sales rep with a Southern lilt and a helpful demeanor can quote you current discount prices and provide other product information as well.

WEBSITE: AAA's website features a handful of their most popular models—but by no means represents their full inventory. The site is fairly minimal with very brief product descriptions, photographs, prices that include delivery fees, and an online order form. If the model you want is here, you're in luck. Otherwise, you'll still need to call or email the store for information on other lines and models.

SPECIAL FACTORS: All merchandise comes with AAA Vacuum's Parts and Service Contract and/or the original manufacturer's warranty; satisfaction guaranteed; returns accepted within 10 days.

ABC Vacuum Cleaner Warehouse

6720 Burnet Rd., WBM
Austin, TX 78757
800–285–8145
512–459–7643
FAX: 512–451–2352

FORM OF INFORMATION: free price list;
online catalog
PAY: check, MO, MC, V, AE, DSC
SELLS: vacuum cleaners
STORE: same address; Monday to Saturday
9:00 am–5:00 pm
ONLINE: www.abcvacuum.com

Once you know about ABC Vacuum Cleaner Warehouse, it seems silly to go out and buy a machine at a department store. For more than two decades, ABC has been purchasing machines from suppliers who are overstocked or going out of business, then selling them to the consumer at greatly discounted prices. You'll find models by Royal, Sharp, Samsung, Filter Queen, Nilfisk, Sanitaire, Oreck, Eureka, Hoover, Kirby, Rainbow, Panasonic, Sanyo, Bissell, Fantom, and others, at amazing prices—some 70% off original list. You won't find prices lower than this, and if you do, tell ABC. They "want to have the lowest prices in America." All machines are new and in the original box, and shipping is free. Most people who buy from ABC have already visited a vacuum cleaner store and know what they want. But if you have questions, call ABC to discuss your needs, and they'll mail you a price list and even product brochures if you request them.

WEBSITE: If you have a computer, you'll go bonkers over ABC's website and will probably opt to shop this way instead of over the phone. Why? Because it basically has all the information a normal shopper would need, including product descriptions and photographs, as well as suggested retail price alongside ABC's so you can see how much you're saving. It's well organized and easy to use, features electronic ordering, and even has a questionnaire you can fill out and email if you're in need of guidance and want ABC to get back to you with a model recommendation based on the information you provided online (type of floors, square footage of house, pets, allergies, upright or canister, etc.).

SPECIAL FACTORS: Satisfaction guaranteed; returns accepted within 30 days for exchange, refund, or credit; all machines come with a warranty.

AllBrands.com

20415 Highland Rd.
Baton Rouge, LA 70817
866–255–2726
FAX: 225–408–7148

FORM OF INFORMATION: online catalog only; no print catalog

PAY: check, MO, MC, V, AE, DSC, JCB

SELLS: sewing machines, sergers, embroidery, industrial, and knitting equipment, and accessories

STORE: same address; Monday to Friday 9:00 am–5:00 pm

ONLINE: www.allbrands.com

All Brands Sewing, Vacuum, & Appliance, established in 1976, offers its online shoppers such a comprehensive inventory of home and industrial sewing machines, vacuums, appliances, important product news, and valuable customer service information that you'll be delighted and eager to deal with a firm that also happens to have the lowest prices available. When it comes to buying sewing machines (portables or industrials), knitting machines, embroidery machines, irons, presses, steam cleaners, and other equipment, super deals are possible. You can assume products are new, unless a different status—refurbished (R) or demonstrator (D)—is indicated. All Brands also sells cabinets, needles, rotary cutters, shears, dress forms, and design software. Some models come with how-to-use videos or workbooks; other informational materials are available (manufacturers' brochures, product comparisons, consumer reports, and details about warranties, accessories, and parts) by snail-mail, if you request them. Your order will either ship from inventory or be drop-shipped from the manufacturer or distributor within the U.S. and Canada. Look to this firm as your buying agent. First, tell them what sewing, quilting, embroidery, and knitting operations you need equipment for. For instance, do you do straight lockstitch, zigzag, satin stitch, appliqué, blind hem, overlock, stretch stitches, buttonhole styles, monograms, embroidery, serging, rolled hem, differential feed, cover hem, steaming, pressing, ironing, or machine knitting? Second, let them know what price range, brands, or features are important to you. (They know which machines have the features you are looking for at the least cost.)

WEBSITE: The website is friendly, informative, and features online ordering. Complete details about shipping options, warranties, and return policies are spelled out here, too.

SPECIAL FACTORS: $25 minimum order; authorized returns accepted within 90 days for exchange only; a 15% restocking fee may apply.

Beach Sales

80 VFW Pkwy.
Revere, MA 02151
781–284–1515
800–562–9020
FAX: 781–284–9823

FORM OF INFORMATION: price quotes by phone, fax, mail, or email

PAY: check, MO, MC, V

SELLS: large and small appliances and entertainment and communications electronics

STORE: same address; Monday to Wednesday and Friday 9:00 am–6:00 pm, Thursday 9:00 am–8:00 pm, Saturday 9:00 am–5:00 pm; expanded hours during holiday season

ONLINE: www.beachsalesinc.com

Since 1947, Beach Sales has provided the Boston area with major discounts on large and small appliances and electronic items. You can take advantage of these same savings by calling, faxing, emailing, or writing to Beach Sales for a price quote on appliances (dishwashers, washing machines, microwaves, dryers, vacuum cleaners, refrigerators, snow blowers), entertainment equipment (VCRs, televisions, car stereos, camcorders, audio and video accessories), and communications items (dictators, fax machines, two-way radios, transcribers, pagers, telephones, and word processors). All you need are the manufacturer's name and the model number of the item. There's no catalog, but Beach Sales sells the products of so many major manufacturers that you'd do well to get a quote first from the friendly staff before going out and buying anything pluggable from a retail store. Even smaller items such as film and audio- and videotape are available at quantity discounts.

A special note to non–New England customers: Beach Sales doesn't want to turn any customers away. However, be aware that the cost of transporting very large appliances (e.g., refrigerators, stoves) to your home may counterbalance any initial savings if you live far from New England. However, you'll still save a lot on smaller items such as electronics or countertop appliances.

WEBSITE: The website will give you an idea of the types of products the company sells, but there's no online ordering and you still need to get the item's make and model on your own before you contact the staff for a price quote.

SPECIAL FACTORS: Returns in their original packaging are accepted for exchange, refund, or credit; large appliances shipped within New England area only.

Cole's Appliance & Furniture Co.

4026 Lincoln Ave.
Chicago, IL 60618
773-525-1797
FAX: 773-525-0728

FORM OF INFORMATION: price quotes; website

PAY: check, MO, MC, V, DSC

SELLS: appliances and home furnishings

STORE: same address; Monday and Thursday 9:30 am–9:00 pm, Tuesday and Friday 9:30 am–5:00 pm, Saturday 9:30 am–5:30 pm (closed Wednesdays and Sundays)

ONLINE: www.colesapplianceandfurniture. homeappliances.com

Cole's was founded in 1957 with the idea that an educated consumer would be the company's best customer. (Savvy readers of this book have been buying their appliances here for many years.) Cole's sells home electronics (TV and video), major appliances, and home furnishings and bedding at discounts of up to 50%. It's a good idea to check out your item locally, write down its make and model, and then call, write, or fax the nice people at Cole's. They'll give you a price quote that will more than likely knock your socks off. If you don't know exactly what you want, the helpful people at Cole's will be happy to give you recommendations, steer you to the right manufacturers, and generally assist you in buying the right appliances for your needs. The following manufacturers are carried by Cole's: Amana, Asko, Brown, Dacor, DCS, Frigidaire, General Electric, Hotpoint, Insinkerator, Jenn-Air, KitchenAid, Magic Chef, Maytag, Panasonic, Premier, Speed Queen, Sub-Zero, Tappan, Thermador, Viking, Whirlpool, Wolf, and Zenith, among others. Deliveries are made by Cole's in the greater Chicago area, and via UPS or common carrier elsewhere.

WEBSITE: The website is basically an electronic version of window shopping for your appliances. Once you log on to Cole's home page, click on the Brands button and a list of featured brand names will come up that will link you to the manufacturer's site. Not all of the manufacturer's sites I checked had prices, so you may need to shop around elsewhere on the internet to get suggested retail prices, then give Cole's a call and they'll be happy to quote you their low price.

SPECIAL FACTORS: Price quotes by phone or letter.

Dial-a-Brand, Inc.

2208 Sunrise Hwy.	**FORM OF INFORMATION:** price quotes
Merrick, NY 11566	**PAY:** check, MO, MC, V, DSC
516–378–9694	**SELLS:** appliances, TVs, and video equipment
800–237–3220	**SHOWROOM:** same address; Monday to Friday 9:00 am–5:30 pm, Saturday 9:00 am–4:00 pm
FAX: 516–867–3447	

 ★

It never occurs to most people that they could buy a major appliance through the mail. But all kinds of people do, and that's one of the reasons Dial-a-Brand is still in business after 3 decades. You'll save from 20% to 40% when you buy your major appliances, TV, or VCR from Dial-a-Brand. They'll give you a price quote right over the phone when you call them with the make and model you seek; you *must* provide the make and model to get a price quote. If you live across the country from Dial-a-Brand, the shipping costs on very large appliances would normally be prohibitive. But Dial-A-Brand has a contract with GE that allows you to have major GE appliances such as refrigerators or dishwashers shipped directly to you. Dial-a-Brand represents most major manufacturers including, at this writing, Amana, Bosch, Dacor, Miele, Frigidaire, Gagganau, GE, Jenn-Air, JVC, Kitchen Aid, Maytag, Panasonic, RCA, Sony, Sub-Zero, Thermador, Toshiba, Viking, and Whirlpool. Shipping is free if you live in the tristate region of New York/New Jersey/Connecticut. Deliveries elsewhere are made via UPS on smaller items.

SPECIAL FACTORS: Returns accepted for exchange if goods are defective or damaged in transit; C.O.D. orders accepted.

LVT Price Quote Hotline, Inc.

Box 444–W03
Commack, NY 11725
888–225–5588
631–234–8884

FORM OF INFORMATION: online catalog only; no print catalog

PAY: cashier's check or bank wire transfer

SELLS: major appliances, televisions, air conditioners

STORE: no walk-in location; mail-order only; phone hours Monday to Saturday 9:00 am–7:00 pm EST

ONLINE: members.aol.com/appliances

The internet has turned American shoppers into informed consumers. We now know what we want, and we know who's got it cheapest. Enter LVT Price Quote Hotline. This company had the same idea years before the internet popularized the notion. Their approach was to provide the lowest prices if the consumer did all the work—the work of shopping around for the right make and model before calling LVT. You can still call LVT for a price quote on just about any appliance, television, or air conditioner, and they're likely to beat any price you've found anywhere else by up to 30%.

WEBSITE: Better yet, check out LVT's website and you'll get a good idea of what this company is all about. There you'll have access to LVT Brands Links, a page of website links and 800 numbers of major manufacturers such as Amana, Emerson, Fedders, Friedrich, Frigidaire, GE, Hitachi, KitchenAid, Maytag, Panasonic, RCA, Samsung, Sharp, and Whirlpool. Go directly to the manufacturer to get product information on major appliances (dishwashers, washers and dryers, freezers, and ranges), microwave ovens, televisions, and air conditioners. When you've specked out the make and model you want, call LVT for a price quote. Be sure to specify make, model, and choice of color, if applicable. Not only will you receive a low price quote, but LVT picks up all shipping costs and processes your order within 48 hours. (Very large major appliances are shipped to metropolitan NJ, NY, and CT only.) No wonder this company has been written up and featured in so many consumer magazines.

SPECIAL FACTORS: Shipping, handling, and insurance charges are all included in quotes; manufacturers' rebates honored; all sales are final; all goods have manufacturers' warranties; minimum order: $300.

Vacuum Cleaner Discounter

3421 Bosque
Waco, TX 76710
800–388–1738
FAX: 254–756–3689

FORM OF INFORMATION: online catalog only; no print catalog

PAY: check, MO, MC, V, AE, DSC

SELLS: vacuum cleaners and steamers

STORE: same address; Monday to Saturday 8:30 am–5:30 pm

ONLINE: www.vacuumcleanerdiscounter.com

Which is better, bagged or bagless? I have been pondering that question for some time now. Look for some insights into this topic and more at the FAQ section of Vacuum Cleaner Discounter. Not only have they been selling vacuums for over 20 years, they are one of the largest independent vacuum cleaner discounters in the world. Savings on brands such as Bissel, Eureka, Hoover, Panasonic, Royal, Sanitaire, Sanyo, Sharp, and more are between 30% to 60% off retail. You'll find a wide selection of upright (bag and bagless), lightweight, canister, handheld, steam, and commercial vacuums. Bags, belts, and accessories are also available. All new vacuums carry a least a one year warranty from either the manufacturer or from Vacuum Cleaner Discounter. VCD also carries a more limited, but still discounted, selection on sewing machines, irons, air conditioners, and some small kitchen appliances. Don't forget to check out the Bargain and Clearance sections and if you find something you like, you can order online.

SPECIAL FACTORS: Returns within 15 days; 10% restocking fee; ground shipping within the continental U.S. only.

Bed, Bath, and Table Textiles

Sheets, bedspreads, and other bedding; towels, shower curtains, and bathmats; table linens; bedroom and bathroom accessories

The first time you sleep on 380-thread-count, all-cotton sheets, you will never want to go back to your own bed again. In fact, your bargain sheets will suddenly feel a lot like burlap. Okay, maybe I'm exaggerating just a bit. But I find that the older I get, the more luxury I feel I deserve. The only problem is, fine bedding and thick, oversized spa towels are usually prohibitively expensive. That's why I love the companies in this chapter.

You, too, will love the firms listed here, which can save you 40% and more on soft goods for your bathroom (towels, shower curtains, toilet seat covers, bathmats), bedroom (sheets, comforters, duvet covers, blankets, bed ruffles, mattress pads, pillow shams), and dining room (place mats, tablecloths, table runners, cloth napkins). One firm, J. Schachter, offers deep discounts to those who do the footwork; shop around on your own, then call this firm for a price quote on brand-name bed and bath textiles, and they'll get the goods to you for a lot less. For other firms that sell household textiles, such as upholstery fabric and curtains, see "Wall and Window Treatments, Decorator Fabrics" page 391.

Find It Fast

BEDSPREADS AND BLANKETS
 Designer Linens Outlet, The Domestic Bin, Eldridge Textile, LinenPlace, J. Schachter

CUSTOM-MADE SOFT GOODS
 J. Schachter

DOWN COMFORTER AND PILLOW REFURBISHING
 J. Schachter

SHEETS
 Designer Linens Outlet, The Domestic Bin, LinenPlace, J. Schachter

TABLE LINENS
 Eldridge Textile

TOWELS AND OTHER BATHROOM SOFT GOODS
 Designer Linens Outlet, The Domestic Bin, Eldridge Textile, LinenPlace, J. Schachter

Designer Linens Outlet

c/o American Pacific
3901 Gantz Rd.
Grove City, OH 43123
866-725-3356
FAX: 614-539-7030

FORM OF INFORMATION: online catalog only; no print catalog;

PAY: check, MO, MC, V

SELLS: high quality bedding, bath, and home decor

STORE: no walk-in location; mail-order only; phone hours Monday to Friday 8:00 am– 5:00 pm EST

ONLINE: www.designerlinensoutlet.com

Designer Linens Outlet is a manufacturer-direct bed, bath and home products discount website. Their goal is to offer the finest name brand home products at 50% off retail prices—everyday. All of the product offerings are brand new merchandise that are either overstocks, retailer returned goods, or discontinued items from the manufacturer and are in the original good condition as in retail stores. They are able to make these products available at highly discounted prices because they are coming directly from the original manufacturer of the brand and selling direct to the consumer.

Designer Linens Outlet offers a great selection of high-quality bedding, bath, and home décor from top brands including Nautica, Ralph Lauren, Liz Claiborne, Dockers and Calvin Klein. Their current selection of designer merchandise includes popular styles in categories such as: comforters, duvet covers, quilts, sheets, pillows, shower curtains, window curtains, window hardware, and more. New items are added each week to keep the selection exciting. Because Designer Linens Outlet sells direct from the manufacturer, they are able to offer their great selection at discounts from 35% to 85% off retail.

SPECIAL FACTORS: Satisfaction guaranteed; returns accepted within 30 days for refund or exchange; flat shipping rate of $4.95 within the contiguous 48 states.

The Domestic Bin

369 Fairview Ave.
Westwood, NJ 07675
877-233-2284

FORM OF INFORMATION: online catalog only; no print catalog;

PAY: MC, V, AE, DSC

SELLS: bedding, towels, and drapes

STORE: no walk-in location; mail-order only; phone hours Monday to Friday 9:00 am–5:00 pm EST

ONLINE: www.domesticbin.com

The Domestic Bin is a family owned full line linen store, established in 1977, that offers only top quality name brand linens, bedding and bath items at discount prices. They carry an extensive line of children's bedding by Dan River, and a complete line of sheets, towels, comforters, bed in a bag sets, comforter ensembles, mattress pads, pillows, drapes, valances, towels, kid's furniture, kid's sleeping bags, bath rugs, kid's novelty rugs, shower curtains and bath accessories. Top name brands include Croscill, Dan River, Wamsutta, Springmaid, Scent-Sation, Fieldcrest, Cannon, Simmons, and West Point Stevens. The Domestic Bin also offers a full line of bedding for infants, toddlers, and teens. Their sports bedding includes major league baseball, NFL football, Nascar and NCAA college bedding.

SPECIAL FACTORS: Returns within 30 days for full refund with authorization; opened packages of sheets, pillowcases, wall borders and/or items which have been used or washed cannot be returned.

Eldridge Textile Co.

17 E. 37th St.
New York, NY 10016
212–576–2991
800–635–4399
FAX: 212–576–2994

FORM OF INFORMATION: online catalog only; no print catalog

PAY: check, MO, MC, V, DSC

SELLS: bed, bath, and window textiles

STORE: same address; Monday to Friday 9:00 am–6:00 pm

ONLINE: www.eldridgetextile.com

Since 1940, Eldridge Textile Company has been selling fashions for the home—table linens, cloth napkins, comforters, sheets, curtains, towels, and other bed and bath textiles, such as mattress pads, throw pillows, bed skirts, shower curtains, sleeping pillows, and upholstered headboards—at the guaranteed lowest prices, and well below "white sale" prices. You can save about 20% on goods by major manufacturers such as Croscill, Wamsutta, Laura Ashley, Sheftex, Royal Sateen, Bay Linens, Thomasville, Pillowtex, Fieldcrest, Christine Designs, and United Feather and Down, among others. If you don't see something you're looking for, call. The folks at Eldridge will do their best to accommodate all requests.

WEBSITE: At the website you can view hundreds of products in gorgeous color from one of the dozens of manufacturers listed on the site. You can search for products by color scheme or description, or just click onto one of the categories (Bedroom, Bathroom, Windows, Living Room, Dining Room or Solid Colors) to view the merchandise. You can email the company to inquire about products, to special order a specific pattern from one of the manufacturers they represent, or to request a fabric swatch. Secure online ordering is available, and there's a toll-free number you can call during business hours if you need to speak with a customer service rep.

SPECIAL FACTORS: Free shipping on all orders over $250 (excluding international, Hawaiian, and Alaskan orders); return of unused goods accepted within 30 days for refund or credit.

J. Schachter Corp.

5 Cook St.
Brooklyn, NY 11206
800–468–6233
718-384-2732
FAX: 718-384-7634

FORM OF INFORMATION: price quotes
PAY: check, MO, MC, V
SELLS: down-filled bedding, linens, and custom services
STORE: same address; Monday to Thursday 9:00 am–5:00 pm, Friday 9:00 am–1:00 pm

J. Schachter has been manufacturing high-end down comforters and pillows for the bedding industry and refurbishing old ones since 1919. I'm not talking about $99 mass-produced comforters; the ones manufactured here are lifelong investments. Off the record, the owner told me which stores buy his comforters to resell under their labels. I'm sworn to secrecy, but I can tell you they're the crème de la crème of New York's department stores; the same $1,500 comforter at one of those stores can be bought factory-direct under the J. Schachter label for at least 40% less. Before the advent of the yuppies' throwaway culture, people used to spend a lot on best-quality down comforters and pillows. These "old timers" still return to J. Schachter to have their pillows, sofa cushions, and comforters restuffed while they wait; the cost is far less than buying a new one of the same quality.

The other portion of Schachter's business is being a dealer of sheets, towels, and bedding (yes, this includes inexpensive down comforters manufactured by others) from the major U.S. linen mills, including but not limited to Bellino, Croscill, Fieldcrest, Cannon, Stevens, Wamsutta, Burlington, Palais Royal, Hudson Bay, Thomasville, Nancy Koltes, Faribo, Fino Lino, and many others. Since there's no print catalog, shop around in your local stores. When you see what you want, call, fax, or write to J. Schachter with the brand, size, and color or pattern and they'll be glad to give you a price quote. J. Schachter's price will save you 25% to 40% off retail. This type of shopping takes more time than just looking at a catalog and making one call. On the other hand, if you're making some major purchases for your bed and bath, the extra legwork could end up saving you hundreds of dollars on a large purchase. It's well worth your while to call the nice people at J. Schachter. They've been in the biz for a long time and know how to deliver old-fashioned value in a highly competitive market.

SPECIAL FACTORS: Know the brand and style of goods before you call for a price quote; store closed Saturdays and Sundays.

LinenPlace.com

135 W. 29th St., Suite 602
New York, NY 10001
212–629–0300

FORM OF INFORMATION: online catalog

PAY: MC, V, AE

SELLS: bed and bath textiles and accessories

STORE: no walk-in location; mail-order only; customer service hours Monday to Friday 10:00 am–5:00 pm EST

ONLINE: www.linenplace.com

Refreshing. That's the word I would use to describe this wonderful company, which sells high-quality bed and bath textiles such as sheets, blankets, duvet covers, towels, and shower curtains, in addition to some nice bathroom accessories. The sheets here are of the higher end or luxury variety, mostly 400 thread count. Discounts here run as high as 58% less than comparable bedding. LinenPlace aims to "revolutionize the way people buy home furnishings." Hey, I'm all for that. Who wants to drive to the mall for cotton sheets? How does LinenPlace keep their prices so low? They have a merchandise team with years of experience working with the best manufacturers in the world. Because they buy directly from the manufacturers, they can bring customers the lowest possible price. Most of these products are made exclusively for LinenPlace and are tested by their quality-control team and used by their employees. Prices here are some of the best of the web for high-quality, 400 thread count, sheet sets. On the sheets, for example, savings average 40% off retail. If you have to outfit several beds, that could amount to hundreds of dollars in savings, money you can spend elsewhere. The website is extremely user-friendly. A well-designed feature helps you find exactly what you're looking for. It's a "find by" chart, in which you check the boxes that apply to the product you seek, in the following categories (for sheets): color, type, weave, style, fabric, and thread count. Check any combination and—*Voila!*—you'll be whisked to a page with thumbnail images and descriptions of what's currently being stocked in your specifications. I also loved the Design Guide, which featured a glossary, informative articles, and color guides. If you need assistance, there are customer-service people who can answer your questions by phone during the hours listed above.

SPECIAL FACTORS: Returns can be made for any reason within 30 business days; all orders shipped UPS.

Building, Renovation, and Upkeep

*Materials and supplies for designing, constructing,
improving, maintaining, and cleaning your home*

This section features all kinds of great companies every home owner will want to know about. Whether you're looking to build a new home, spruce up your old one, or just find a way to keep your house clean, you'll find firms here that sell plumbing supplies, old-timey bathroom fixtures, screen doors and shutters, cleaning supplies and gadgets, spiral staircase kits, logs for log-home kits, and more.

If you're focusing on the interior of your house, all the other sections of this "Home" chapter will have what you're looking for: flooring, furniture, appliances, kitchen accessories, lighting, wallpaper, shades, upholstery fabric, and tableware.

Thinking of building a home? The Shelter Institute in Bath, Maine, offers a wide variety of classes for individuals and couples who want to do it themselves. The Institute leads hands-on courses of varying length on just about every aspect of home design and building. For more information on the Institute, visit their website (www.shelterinstitute.com); call them at 207–442–7938; or write to Shelter Institute, 38 Center St., Bath, ME 04530.

Find It Fast

BATHROOM AND KITCHEN HARDWARE AND FIXTURES
Baths from the Past

CLEANING SUPPLIES
The Cleaning Center

DOORS, WINDOWS, GLASS PANELS, AND COMPONENTS
Arctic Glass & Window Outlet, Oregon Wooden Screen Door

FLOOR-PLAN AND 3-D MODEL KITS FOR BUILDING
Design Works

HOUSE SHUTTERS AND SHUTTER SUPPLIES
Shuttercraft

LOGS FOR LOG-HOME CONSTRUCTION
Wholesale Log Homes

SPIRAL STAIRCASE KITS
The Iron Shop

Arctic Glass & Window Outlet

I-94 @ exit 16
Hammond, WI 54015
800–428–9276
715–796–2291
FAX: 715–796–2295

FORM OF INFORMATION: $4 print catalog and brochures, refundable; website

PAY: MO, MC, V, DSC

SELLS: exterior doors, windows, skylights, sunroom glass

STORE: same address; also 1232 W. Clairemont Ave., Eau Claire, WI, and 1481 Marshall Ave., St. Paul, MN; Monday to Friday 8:00 am–6:00 pm, Saturday 9:00 am–3:00 pm

WEBSITE: www.kissourglass.com

Behind every company there's an interesting tale or two. When you receive a catalog from Arctic Glass & Window, you'll also get to read the whole charming story, "How We Got Here." I won't give up all the good parts, but the gist of it is this: When the Bacons moved from Alaska to western Wisconsin, one thing led to another, and they ended up with a truckload of surplus glass. More than 2 decades later, the Bacons' family-owned business has customers in 49 out of the 50 states. "We supply the highest quality product available at the lowest possible price," according to their brochure. They also offer free design advice if you need it, as well as generous returns and warranty policies.

Arctic Glass & Window sells tempered insulated glass panes that can be used in workshops, sun rooms, offices, storefronts—even barns and chicken coops. Besides bringing in more sunlight, which is known to help fight wintertime depression, these glass units contribute passive solar heat. In the Bacons' home, which is heated by a wood stove, their wood consumption went from 15 cords per year down to 3 when they added their sun room. You can buy both seconds and surplus panes here. The surplus panes have no defects; the seconds have minor visual imperfections, such as a fingerprint between the panes or a slight dimple or scratch, imperceptible from 5 feet away. Both units carry the same 10-year seal warranty. In addition to glass, the Outlet also sells Kolbe & Kolbe aluminum-clad doors and Velux roof windows and skylights. The brochures you'll receive have clear instructions and detailed information about storing, transporting, and installing, and the staff is willing to answer any other questions.

WEBSITE: At the website you'll be able to see pictures of some of the beautiful windows, skylights, and entry doors available. They list in-stock thermopanes and have a page of product information, as well as monthly specials. There's a Link Page with links to manufacturers' sites so you can get more information on products. When you decide on what you want, it's best to call or send a fax for a current price list, as there is no online ordering. You also need to call Arctic for an updated inventory of regular windows and doors.

SPECIAL FACTORS: Quantity discounts available; minimum crating charge is $40; returns accepted up to a year after sale for full refund or credit, provided panes have not been installed and are in salable condition. Arctic Glass can only ship Kolbe & Kolbe windows and Velux skylights to the following states: IA, IL, MI, MN, ND, SD, and WI

Baths from the Past, Inc.

83 E. Water St.
Rockland, MA 02371
800–697–3871
781–871–8530
FAX: 781–871–8533

FORM OF INFORMATION: free print catalog; website

PAY: check, MO, MC, V, AE, DSC

SELLS: reproduction bathroom and kitchen hardware and systems

STORE: same address; Monday to Friday 9:00 am–5:00 pm

ONLINE: www.bathsfromthepast.com

Is your bathroom the most ignored room in your house? Thumbing through the 40-page color catalog from Baths from the Past, you'll be struck by how little it would take to jazz up your old claw-foot tub or pedestal porcelain sink.

Baths from the Past makes it affordable to buy authentic-looking brass faucets, porcelain shower heads, telephone-style tub fillers, or old-fashioned shower systems at prices up to 30% below other sources for comparable quality. Whether you're going for Deco Edwardian or Victorian, you'll find a sink, commode, tub, faucet, bath accessories, shower fittings, and other related items to complete or enhance the look you're after. Baths from the Past has been in business since 1981 and offers warranties on all items and finishes (details outlined in catalog).

WEBSITE: The website is not very easy to navigate and the images do not do justice to the beautiful products that Baths from the Past offers. When you click on an image, you'll get a larger picture with the description, price, and shipping estimate. Ordering is not available online so you will need the catalog or to call them.

SPECIAL FACTORS: Satisfaction guaranteed; returns accepted for refund or exchange within 30 days of receipt, but see catalog for details.

The Cleaning Center

311 S. 5th Ave
Pocatello, ID 83201
800-451-2402
FAX: 208-235-5481

FORM OF INFORMATION: free print catalog; online catalog
PAY: check, MO, MC, V, AE, DSC
SELLS: cleaning tools and products
STORE: same address, Pocatello, ID; Monday to Saturday 9:00 am–6:00 pm
ONLINE: www.cleanreport.com

Everyone has a gift. Don Aslett, president of The Cleaning Center, has found his niche as "America's number one cleaning expert" and travels the media circuit donning his famous toilet briefcase and preaching cleanliness. At least, he used to. I was saddened to see in the new catalog that he's "cleaned up" his image; there's no longer a photo of Don and the famous toilet attaché. Author of many best-selling books on every aspect of cleaning, organizing, and decluttering, Mr. Aslett is a motivator, which you'll immediately grasp from the perky catalog text. You'll be treated to delightful prose on the company's history, the full selection of Aslett's books, and an inventory that includes the best in buckets, sponges, cleaning cloths, gloves, dusters, squeegees, vacuums, mops, cleaning-supply organizers, brushes, and of course his famous brand cleaners for everything from toilets and rugs to tiles and wood. All of the cleaning products are highly concentrated and therefore extremely economical if used correctly. The gadgets and items have all been hand-selected by Aslett, who appears to know more about this subject that anyone else. Price checks on similar items show The Cleaning Center to be 20% or more lower than comparable name-brand products.

WEBSITE: Online you'll be able to browse products for cleaning, disinfecting, and deodorizing just about everything. Photographs and vivid descriptions make the website as accessible as the print catalog, and you'll also be able to order online. Looking to start your own business in the "exciting and profitable field of construction cleanup"? You'll find a book on this subject, as well as many others that will help you get control over clutter, improve the quality of your surroundings, and save money.

SPECIAL FACTORS: Satisfaction guaranteed; returns accepted for exchange, refund, or credit.

Design Works, Inc.

11 Hitching Post Rd.
Amherst, MA 01002
413–549–4763

FORM OF INFORMATION: online catalog only; no print catalog

PAY: check, MO, MC, V, AE

SELLS: reusable peel-and-stick furniture and architectural symbols and 3-D model kits for home-building

STORE: no walk-in location; mail-order only

ONLINE: www.homeplanner.com

If you've ever tried to plan a new home, addition, or remodeling project, you know the hardest parts are organizing the floor plans and visualizing your ideas in 3 dimensions. Sure, there's computer software for home design, but when you are obsessing about your new, sunny kitchen nook, the last thing you want to do is master a new computer program. If you're like me, you'll appreciate Design Works, which has come up with a unique (and inexpensive) solution. In business since 1982, owner Dan Reif has developed some ingenious products. With the Home Quick Planner, $24.95 at this writing, you receive 700 precut, reusable, peel-and-stick furniture and architectural symbols, plus a 1/4" floor plan grid, to plan a home up to approximately 2,000 square feet. Go ahead: Knock down walls, move furniture and fixtures, put in too many windows and bathrooms—you can always change your mind later for free. A Deluxe version for $10 more has additional symbols that make the Planner suitable for floor plans up to approximately 5,000 square feet. There are also separate Quick Planners just for kitchen, bathroom, office, or interior design. The kitchen one, for example, gives you every conceivable option—single sinks, double sinks, 33" refrigerators, 36" refrigerators, and so on, so you can really fiddle around with islands, windows, cabinets, and appliances until you're absolutely batty. It's fun.

The 3-D Home Kit—Basic (2,000 square feet), $33.95 or Deluxe (5,000 square feet), $47.95—lets you visualize your dream house, sun room, or new wing in 3 dimensions. You can use the kit's printed posterboard building materials—from brick, stone, siding, roofing, and decking, to windows, doors, skylights, kitchen cabinets, and appliances—to construct a detailed 1/4" scale model of your own design. There are also materials for interior walls, stairs, floor plan, even scale people and pets! Both 3-D Home Kits include a "Hands-on Design and Math" booklet to help you solve some common design problems: for example, how to calculate the minimum size for windows, design the roof and calculate its slope, and determine the amount of paint, paneling, or concrete needed. Whether you're teaching architecture to students or daydreaming about how you'll spend that lottery win, this will be a fun and illuminating project.

WEBSITE: The website is really fun to visit, but also helpful if you're having trouble conceptualizing how these kits are used. There you'll get to see photographs of actual house plans and models assembled, and see other examples of how one might use the kits for interior design, educational projects, and decorating. You can order the kits right on the website.

SPECIAL FACTORS: Shipping and handling is $4.95 for 1 kit, $6.95 for 2 or more kits within U.S.

The Iron Shop

400 Reed Rd.
Broomall, PA 19008
800–523–7427
610–544–7100
FAX: 610–544–7297

FORM OF INFORMATION: free print catalog; online catalog
PAY: check, MO, MC, V, AE, DSC
SELLS: metal, oak, and cast-aluminum spiral stair kits and accessories
STORE: locations in PA, CA, IL, CT, FL, and TX; call for addresses and hours
ONLINE: www.theironshop.com

If you have a house—that could use a brilliant solution to that age-old question of how to get from down here to up there, here is a great company for you. The Iron Shop has been manufacturing metal, oak, and cast aluminum spiral stair kits since 1931 and selling them factory-direct to smart home owners at way less than you'd pay anywhere else. Installing these stairs is remarkably easy, takes 2 people, and can be accomplished in less than 1 or up to 2 full days, depending on the style and accessories you choose.

You'll be inspired by the 36-page color print catalog from The Iron Shop, with gorgeous photographs of assembled stairs in metal, oak, and Victorian-style cast aluminum. Complete features, installation details, and other specs are given for each model. The Iron Shop also has every accessory you need to make your stairs your own: handrails, spindles, center pole caps, balcony landing railings, top landing gates, tread coverings, and so on. Whether you're looking for a pair of grand, sweeping staircases to swirl up either side of your front foyer, homey oak stairs to lead up to your teenage son's converted attic pad, or a high-tech metal version to connect the bedroom with your basement studio below, The Iron Shop has every possible variation you could imagine. A skilled technician can walk you through the ordering process. Every stair comes with a how-to video and detailed installation instructions, but you'll get plenty of tech support from the folks at The Iron Shop whenever you need it. This company has a long history of customer satisfaction.

WEBSITE: This well-designed online catalog speaks volumes about the company's level of competence and concern for quality. If you know what you're doing and have done it before, you can get an exact price quote by filling out the online worksheet with information such as floor-to-floor height and diameter, code requirements, well-opening dimensions, and accessories, and then order your kit online. (It's recommended, however, that beginners and less-experienced do-it-yourselfers talk to a service representative before ordering online.)

Note: There are so many customizing options, this company couldn't list them all on their website, so be sure to inquire if there's a particular option you're seeking but don't find here.

SPECIAL FACTORS: No returns accepted once assembly has begun (see catalog or website for details); satisfaction guaranteed.

Oregon Wooden Screen Door Company

2767 Harris St., Dept. WBM
Eugene, OR 97405
541–485–0279
FAX: 541–484–0353

FORM OF INFORMATION: $3 brochure and price list
PAY: check, MO, MC, V
SELLS: wooden screen and storm doors
STORE: same address; Monday to Friday 8:00 am–5:00 pm

The specialty of Oregon Wooden Screen Door Company is obvious in its name. That dedication to wooden screen doors has created 30 door styles in categories dubbed Ornamental, Classic, Muscular, and Designer's Collection, any of which can be modified with spandrels, brackets, and other hardware. Doors have their own character depending on their design, be it simple or more ornate and complex. The doors sold here are constructed of ¼" thick vertical-grain fir, strengthened and made warp resistant with mortise-and-tenon and dowel joinery. For seasonal changes, screen and storm inserts (both wood framed) are available, primed with wood preservative in a finish of your choosing. The final touch—solid brass hardware—can be ordered from Oregon Wooden Screen Door or from your favorite shop. Prices for doors range from $200 for a kit to several hundred. To custom-order a door or to discuss questions you may have about choosing a design, give the staff a call.

SPECIAL FACTORS: Authorized returns accepted.

Shuttercraft, Inc.

282 Stepstone Hill Rd.
Guilford, CT 06437
203–245–2608
FAX: 203–245–5969

FORM OF INFORMATION: free brochures and price lists; website
PAY: check, MO, MC, V
SELLS: interior and exterior house shutters and hardware
SHOWROOM: call for directions and hours
ONLINE: www.shuttercraft.com

Details, details. What makes your house different from every other one on the block? Details such as authentic exterior wood shutters. You can get them by mail through Shuttercraft at prices well below those charged elsewhere for custom-milled shutters. Shuttercraft offers wood shutters for the exterior and interior of your house. Authentic exterior wood shutters are available in all sizes and traditional styles, including moveable louvers, fixed louvers, raised/flat panels, board and batten, combination louver and panel, arch tops, curve tops, gothic arches, and endless cutout possibilities. Made of western red cedar, these shutters are appropriate for restoring vintage homes, public buildings, or dressing up your new house. They are naturally ventilating and won't cause the wood behind them to rot. Interior wood shutters are available in small louvers, wide plantation louvers, raised panels, and open frame for fabric insert. Woods used include poplar, basswood (for painting), and red oak (for staining). Shutters are delivered nationwide unfinished, primed, or fully painted in your color choice. Sample shutters can be shipped for a $20 refundable deposit. Hardware is also available for all shutter types.

WEBSITE: The website lists the kinds of shutters available, and pictures most of the shutter types. There is a form you can fill out online that makes it easy to find out how much your shutters will cost, but there is no online ordering.

SPECIAL FACTORS: Free shipping/delivery on most orders; painting services available; 50% deposit required when ordering; price quotes by phone, fax, or email.

Wholesale Log Homes

P.O. Box 177
Hillsborough, NC 27278
TEL/FAX: 919–732–9286

FORM OF INFORMATION: online catalog; print brochure

PAY: check or MO

SELLS: logs for log-building construction

STORE: no walk-in location; phone hours Monday to Friday 9:00 am–5:00 pm EST

ONLINE: www.wholesaleloghomes.com

In my neck of the woods, it's not uncommon to find "kit" log homes built by the proud owners themselves. These do-it-yourselfers thought they were saving money by buying all-inclusive packages consisting of detailed house plans, precut, ready-to-assemble wood components, and windows, doors, and roofing. And in fact, compared to hiring an architect and a general contractor to design and then build a home from scratch, they did save some money. But they would have saved a lot more had they known about Wholesale Log Homes, which sells the high-quality milled heartwood logs, timbers, finished boards, log siding, and log accessories for log home construction at wholesale prices. Even with shipping charges added on, you can still shave hundreds and even thousands of dollars off the cost of your log home.

This company *does not* sell floor plans or model kits. You design your home or purchase a house plan. Then the experienced people at Wholesale Log Homes will give you an estimate—free of charge—on the amount of logs and timber materials your plan will require, as well as the cost. In the home-construction business for 3 decades, owner Ron Wolfe explained the advantages to building your log home this way. First is cost: You're not paying for items you could buy locally, such as roofing, windows, and doors. (Not to mention the convenience of having these items delivered *when you need them,* rather than all at once at the beginning of the project.) Nor are you paying for wood that's been premeasured and precut. Second is flexibility: Wholesale Log Homes sells by the linear foot. All necessary cutting to length is done on the building site. Not only does this method guarantee tight-fitting joints and precise cuts, but it also allows maximum control of log placement and appearance. In addition, the linear-foot method of construction allows you to make design changes during construction, giving you far more flexibility than precut packages do.

The finest-grade Eastern White Pine goes into their logs and wood products, which are properly kiln-dried and graded. Logs are delivered in 8′, 10′, 12′, 14′, and 16′

lengths, with your choice of shape, thickness, and double or single tongue-and-groove. All of this is laid out clearly at the website. Clear product descriptions, prices, shipping policies, and even an Image Gallery with beautiful color photographs will convince you that you're dealing with smart, high-quality people at this company. If you're going to build your own log home, this is definitely a company you should check out before paying retail prices on the wood components that come with a kit.

SPECIAL FACTORS: 30% deposit required at time of order; on-time delivery assurance on orders of all sizes; wholesale inquiries welcome; Log Homes Council member.

Flooring

Hardwood flooring; new and antique Oriental rugs; Persian and Persian-design rugs; area rugs; carpeting; vinyl floor coverings; padding; tiles

How is it possible to save money by purchasing a huge item such as carpeting or hardwood flooring by mail? Here's how: Many of the firms in this section are either flooring manufacturers themselves or get their goods directly from the mill. Special relationships with trucking companies allow them to move very large items at low cost to you. You're saving on tax as well as the normal retailer markup, and all of this can translate into savings of 50% on large rugs and wall-to-wall carpeting, normally one of the biggest single expenses in redecorating a room. Whatever your flooring preference—from gorgeous cherry floors to hand-woven Oriental runners—you'll find it here for a lot less.

For information on carpet installation, maintenance, and stain removal call The Carpet and Rug Institute's toll-free information line at 800–882–8846. Their website is exceedingly useful, too (www.carpet-rug.com). Not only are there great articles about the care and maintenance of rugs, how to choose carpet, carpet and the environment, and more, but here you'll find the Spot Removal Computer. This is a real find. Search for a stain in the alphabetized list of hundreds and then click on it. You'll get a succinct but detailed, step-by-step solution to your particular rug or carpet stain. It's a gold mine of free information.

Find It Fast

CARPETING AND AREA RUGS
79th Street Rug Shop, Carpet Universe, Prestige Carpets, S&S Mills, Warehouse Carpets

NEW AND ANTIQUE ORIENTAL RUGS
Jacobsen Oriental Rugs, Wall Rug & Carpets

PERSIAN RUGS AND PERSIAN-DESIGN RUGS
79th Street Rug Shop

VINYL FLOORING
Carpet Universe, Prestige Carpets, Warehouse Carpets

WOOD FLOORING
Prestige Carpets

79th Street Rug Shop

2829 Peachtree Rd.
Atlanta, GA 30305
877–603–8155
404–231–2108
FAX: 404–231–4967

FORM OF INFORMATION: online catalog only; no print catalog

PAY: MC, V, DSC

SELLS: antique Persian rugs, Persian-design rugs, cotton rag rugs, dhurries, hand-hooked rugs, kilims, and Oushaks

STORE: no walk-in location; mail-order only; phone hours Monday to Friday 8:00 am–5:00 pm EST

ONLINE: www.79thstreetrugshop.com

In twenty plus years, 79th Street Rug Shop has cultivated an extensive collection of loyal suppliers of one-of-a-kind antique and semi-antique Persian rugs. They take pride in finding very special pieces at great values. Their suppliers range from Boston to London and they want to offer you two things: bargain prices and wonderful quality. The vast majority of their business is exceptional and decorative Persian rugs. All of their rugs are clean, restored if needed, and ready to go. This is their specialty and they take great pride in it. In addition to Persian rugs, they offer Persian-design rugs, cotton rag rugs, dhurries, hand-hooked rugs, kilims, and Turkish Oushak rugs. You'll find plenty of information about all of the types of rugs they sell, in addition to information about rug making and rug styles at the website.

Often times, the folks at 79th Street Rug Shop have the opportunity to buy a package of, say, sixty rugs of which they sell fifty-eight. Guess what? The last two go on the Specials & Closeouts section. Or, other times, they buy discontinued patterns of needlepoints, etc., and they go on this page as well. Sometimes one of their rugs may have a small "problem"—they will describe it—and you will find it on this page. Their same 30-day return policy applies to these items. This is an excellent opportunity for you to save bunches on hand-loomed treasures.

SPECIAL FACTORS: Satisfaction is guaranteed; returns within 30 days; return freight and insurance must be paid by the customer; it is best to keep the original packaging; shipping and insurance are free via UPS within the 48 states (UPS does not accept P.O. boxes); an adult signature is required upon receipt of order.

Carpet Universe, Inc.

4109 S. Dixie Hwy.
Dalton, GA 30721
800–433–0074
FAX: 706–277–1754

FORM OF INFORMATION: free print catalog (see text), brochures, and samples; online catalog

PAY: check, MO, MC, V, AE, DSC

SELLS: carpeting, rugs, padding, and vinyl flooring

STORE: same address; Monday to Friday 9:00 am–5:00 pm

ONLINE: www.beardenbrothers.com

Family-owned and-operated Carpet Universe, Inc. is in Dalton, Georgia, the "Carpet Capital of the World." This company offers a wide selection of carpets, vinyl, tile, and wood floor coverings, as well as carpet cushion—all from the best-known manufacturers, factory-direct to you. The savings are substantial—up to 70% off retail—and they'll ship door-to-door. The shipping fees are surprisingly inexpensive—averaging 60 cents a square yard, depending on where you live.

Here's how it works. If you find and price a carpet or vinyl locally, call Carpet Universe and they'll get you the same product and price it for you when you call their toll-free number. Just provide them with the manufacturer and style number, as well as the square yards needed. You can also send a sample and they'll try to match it. They can send carpet samples to you or a catalog with beautiful color photographs for $4. The catalog features area rugs—hand-hooked, woven, Oriental, braided, and more. Carpet Universe has thrived in the competitive carpet business by providing top-quality goods and by saving customers a "considerable amount off any retail price, guaranteed!"

WEBSITE: Billing itself as "the largest floorcovering website on the internet," this site lets viewers tour the inventory—from area rugs to gym floors. If you're thinking about flooring, logging on to the website is a great way to get ideas and acquaint yourself with the universe of choices. You cannot order online, but a call to the Dalton store will get the ball moving for clearing up questions and having samples sent.

SPECIAL FACTORS: Payment must be received prior to shipment; satisfaction guaranteed; all floor coverings come with factory warranties; quantity discounts available.

Jacobsen Oriental Rugs

Learbury Center
401 N. Salina St., Dept. WBM
Syracuse, NY 13203
315–422–7832
FAX: 315–422–6909

FORM OF INFORMATION: free print catalog; online catalog

PAY: check, MO, MC, V, DSC

SELLS: new and antique Oriental rugs

STORE: Syracuse, Saratoga Springs and Fair-port, NY; call or see website for addresses and hours

ONLINE: www.jacobsenrugs.com

This employee-owned company has been selling fine Oriental rugs since 1924 at prices kept surprisingly low. The beautiful 26-page catalog shows photographs of dozens of rugs from the more than 8,000-rug collection. Jacobsen buys the rugs directly from the countries where the rugs are woven, then imports them to his Syracuse showroom. Doing business this way eliminates the middleman; coupled with large-volume sales, the net effect saves the consumer money.

You'll find genuine, handwoven rugs of recent vintage from India, Pakistan, Turkey, Afghanistan, Iran, Nepal, and China. Sizes vary depending on the type of rug, but range from 2′ × 3′ to some as large as 12′ × 20′. Both the catalog and website include lots of information about the unique characteristics of different rug-making regions and styles, history of rug weaving, parts of an Oriental rug, information on looms and design, the ins and outs of judging rug quality, and more. Since Jacobsen wants you to be satisfied, you'll fill out a questionnaire, after which a company representative will write you back with details and colored slides of rugs available that seem to fit your needs. Once you've made your selection, you can have the rug sent on approval to see how it fits in its new surroundings.

WEBSITE: The lavish photographs at the friendly website offer a wonderful way to view all of the gorgeous rugs Jacobsen has in stock. Click on the section Rugs on Sale to check out recently acquired beauties further discounted around 20%. There's no online ordering, but you'll get plenty of guidance as to how to proceed by phone or email when you're ready to seriously consider making this kind of investment.

SPECIAL FACTORS: Satisfaction guaranteed; rugs sent on approval require you to first fill out a credit form and/or submit a deposit.

Prestige Carpets, Inc.

P.O. Box 516
Dalton, GA 30722
800–887–6807
706–217–6640
FAX: 706–217–2429

FORM OF INFORMATION: free brochure, website

PAY: check, MO, MC, V, AE, DSC

SELLS: carpeting, vinyl and wood flooring, area rugs, and padding

STORE: no walk-in location; mail-order only; phone hours Monday to Friday 8:00 am–6:00 pm EST

ONLINE: www.prestigecarpet.com

Prestige sells its own line of residential and commercial carpeting that's guaranteed against stains and wear just like the national brands—all at wholesale prices. Carpet samples are available showing the range of colors, fiber content, guarantees, and so on for each style. This firm also offers custom area rugs that can be produced to match wallpaper and furniture. In addition to Prestige's own brand, the company has access to about 95% of all carpet mills and flooring manufacturers to get you great deals on carpet, vinyl, and wood lines at prices up to 60% below those charged at retail outlets and department stores. You can check out the website to see photos of carpet and vinyl flooring samples and their custom designer rugs. There is no online ordering, so your best bet is to contact Prestige by phone, email, fax, or mail, once you've decided on your flooring, to get a price quote. You'll need to provide the manufacturer's name, the style number and name, and square yardage. Padding, adhesives, and tack strips for installation are also available. Prestige doesn't publish a catalog, but you'll find the people there amiable and happy to answer your questions.

SPECIAL FACTORS: A deposit is required when you place your order, and final payment must be made before shipment (common carrier is used); both residential and commercial carpeting needs are served here.

S&S Mills

200 Howell Dr.
Dalton, GA 30721
800–363–9126
FAX: 706–277–3922

FORM OF INFORMATION: sample books; online catalog

PAY: check, MO, MC, V

SELLS: carpet and padding and hardwood flooring

SHOWROOM: 200 Howell Dr., Dalton; Monday to Friday 8:00 am–5:00 pm EST; toll-free phone hours 24 hours/day, 7 days/week

ONLINE: www.ssmills.com

S&S Mills manufactures carpeting and sells and ships it factory-direct to consumers at prices that are a solid 50% less than retail. At the website you'll find a wide variety of high quality carpet products for every room in your home or business in different styles and color combinations. Also at the website you can read about the mill's generous limited wear warranty and shipping policies. Click on Bargain Remnant to see a list of in-stock remnants—"short rolls" of brand-new, unblemished carpeting left over from commercial and home sales. Short rolls are discounted another 25% to 40% off the mill's already discounted prices! If you see something you like, call them or fill out an online form and they will send you free samples and swatches so you can experience the feel of each texture and look at each color under your own lighting. There is never any obligation to purchase or return the samples. S&S Mills is also happy to answer your questions every day of the week. This company is committed to saving you time and money, and to making carpet buying a convenient, hassle-free experience. S&S also carries hardwood flooring. Since color, size, and style change frequently, check here often for real deals.

SPECIAL FACTORS: Satisfaction guaranteed; all carpeting comes with a warranty; free Installers Referral Network available for your area.

Wall Rug & Carpets

3719 Battleground Ave.
Greensboro, NC 27410
800–877–1955
336–545–6899
FAX: 336–545–6524

FORM OF INFORMATION: free brochure
PAY: check, MO, MC, V
SELLS: reproduction Oriental rugs
STORE: same address; Monday to Saturday
10:00 am–6:00 pm

Wall Rug & Carpets is the distributor for Mastercraft Imports, Ltd. and Karastan—two of the finest machine-made area rug lines in the world. These rugs combine the beauty of classic Oriental design with the long-lasting comfort and performance of New Zealand wool. Best of all, these stunning reproductions are priced affordably—about 50% less than the hand-woven versions—so as to be available to regular consumers and not just the world's nobility.

Great care is taken in the manufacture of these rugs to make them as close to the originals as possible. The Karastans, for example, start with 100% worsted New Zealand wool, the traditional fiber of fine Orientals, and each color is individually skein-dyed in the yarn. The modern-day looms are designed to capture the luxury of the hand-woven originals. Once woven, the rugs are "lustre-washed" in much the same way the native weavers of antiquity washed their creations; finally, the damp rug is buffed with the "Sultan's Slipper," bundles of old wool drawn across the surface to impart a rich patina to the finish. The beautiful rugs sold by Wall Rug & Carpets are, above all, practical, unlike their priceless, hand-woven counterparts, with warmth, comfort, dirt resistance, wearability, and affordability at the forefront.

In addition to their Mastercraft and Karastan line, Wall Rug & Carpets also carries rugs by Oriental Weavers Sphinx Division, Obeetee, 828 International Trading Company, M.E.R., Michael Aziz Oriental Rugs Inc., Bashian, and Noo Noo Rue Company.

SPECIAL FACTORS: All rugs are guaranteed; inquire about return policy; call to get price quotes and delivery information.

Warehouse Carpets, Inc.

P.O. Box 3233
Dalton, GA 30719
800–526–2229
706–517–2229
FAX: 706–517–6984

FORM OF INFORMATION: free brochure
PAY: check or MO
SELLS: carpeting, vinyl flooring, and padding
STORE: 5724 Smyrna Church Rd., Chatsworth, GA; Monday to Friday 8:00 am–5:00 pm

Here's another example of a place that rewards consumers who do some of the footwork themselves. Warehouse Carpets has been around for more than 20 years and specializes in serving mail-order customers through direct home delivery. They ship only first-quality carpets from the following manufacturers: Queens Carpet, Mohawk, Galaxy Carpets, Shaw Salemcarpets, Coronet Carpets, Horizon, and Mannington, among others. There's an informational brochure that basically tells you to shop around for the carpet you want, then call Warehouse Carpet's toll-free number, or fax or write them, with the manufacturer's name and the style name to receive a price quote. Savings on carpeting here run up to 50%, so it's worth the trouble.

SPECIAL FACTORS: A 50% deposit is required when order is placed, with the balance due before shipment; all carpet shipped via common carrier.

Furnishings

*Classic, contemporary, reproduction Victorian, Danish,
Adirondack, hand-crafted, high-tech Plexiglas, inflatable,
and wicker furniture for living room, bedroom, dining
room, study, and patio; accessories and decor including
chair cocoons, radiator enclosures, custom-made table pads,
and wooden baskets*

The companies listed here give new meaning to the term *armchair shopper.* You can save as much as 50% on the suggested retail price of furniture of all kinds by sitting back and ordering it directly from North Carolina, the manufacturing center of the furniture industry. Discounters like the ones in this section don't take the staggering markups that make furnishings and home accessories prohibitively expensive in department and furniture stores. So great are the deals in this part of the country that it's not uncommon for people to plan their vacations around furniture shopping. After a week at the North Carolina golf resorts, they hit the showrooms and have a truck-load of new furniture shipped home.

Unless you're planning a trip to the area, your choices as a savvy consumer include: finding furniture you like locally and then calling these firms for price quotes, or consulting with the company sales reps for guidance. Most of the firms listed here can supply brochures and swatches, give decorating advice over the phone, and take orders for furniture and accessories from hundreds of manufacturers. Some have gorgeous and elaborate catalogs, the cost of which is refundable when you purchase; others have interactive websites; still others operate solely by price quote. All will deliver real value.

Speaking of delivering, many offer "in-home delivery service"—your furniture will be uncrated exactly where you want it, and if there are damages, you'll see them right away and can contact the company while the shipper is there to find out what to do. In-home delivery is usually made either by the company's own truck or with a moving service that's accustomed to handling furnishings. Understand that these companies couldn't be in business if they didn't make buying from them worth your while. You'll pay a lot less here—including shipping—than you will at the local strip-mall furniture outlet.

There are also lots of other great finds in this section, such as amazing chair cocoons, beautiful and functional radiator covers, custom-made table pads, high-tech acrylic bathroom accessories, inflatable furniture, hand-made wooden baskets, throw pillows, and rugs.

There are also handsome desks, bookshelves, and other furnishings for the home office. But if you're specifically looking to furnish your office space, consider the companies listed in the "Office Furnishings" section of the "Office, Business, and Professional" chapter. Many of the companies below sell lighting as well. Companies that *specialize* in lighting, however, are grouped in "Lighting," page 371.

Find It Fast

ACRYLIC FURNITURE AND ACCESSORIES
Plexi-Craft Quality Products

CHAIR COCOONS
Masacco New York

CHILDREN'S FURNITURE AND ACCESSORIES
Coppa Woodworking, FurnitureOnline.com, Marion Travis

COUNTRY-STYLE TABLES, CHAIRS, AND ACCESSORIES
Coppa Woodworking, Genada Imports, Marion Travis

HOME AND OFFICE FURNITURE
Carolina Interiors, Ellenburg's Furniture, FurnitureOnline.com,
Priba Furniture Sales & Interiors, Quality Furniture Market, Sobol House

INFLATABLE FURNITURE
Bubble Furniture

MODERN AND CONTEMPORARY
Genada Imports

RADIATOR ENCLOSURES
ARSCO, Monarch Radiator Enclosures

TABLE PADS
Factory Direct Table Pad

UNFINISHED FURNITURE
Marion Travis

VICTORIAN- AND FRENCH-STYLE FURNITURE AND ACCESSORIES
Heirloom Reproductions

WICKER AND RATTAN FURNITURE AND ACCESSORIES
Ellenburg's Furniture

WOODEN BASKETS
West Rindge Baskets

ARSCO Manufacturing Company, Inc.

3564 Blue Rock Rd.
Cincinnati, OH 45247
800-543-7040
513-385-0555
FAX: 513-741-6292

FORM OF INFORMATION: free brochure; online catalog

PAY: MO, MC, V, DSC

SELLS: radiator enclosures and metal cabinetry

STORE: same address; Monday to Friday 8:00 am–4:00 pm

ONLINE: www.arscomfg.com

Does your home or office suffer from naked radiator syndrome? Oh no! Actually, naked radiators are more than just unsightly. Here are some of the benefits of installing a radiator enclosure by ARSCO: enhances your decor; saves fuel by preventing outside wall heat absorption; increases comfort by circulating warm air directly into the room; protects drapes, walls, and ceilings from airborne dust; and protects occupants from burns. ARSCO's prices are a solid 35% below those charged by local sources for the same kinds of enclosures.

If you live within 600 miles of Cincinnati, ARSCO can send someone to measure your conventional steam radiator, fan coil unit, or fin tube (baseboard) heater. Or you can do it yourself with the easy measuring guide provided in the ARSCO literature. Standard sizes run up to 42" high and 96" long. There are 14 very pretty stock colors of baked enamel, and other options include special notches, doors, or cutouts for valve access, a built-in humidifier pan, insulated tops, and adjustable legs for uneven floors. Once you get the enclosure, you can assemble it in about 20 minutes. ("If you can put together a simple 5-piece puzzle, your can assemble our enclosures," says ARSCO's literature.) The brochure and flyers from ARSCO make the whole process clear and easy. This is one of those household details that you can't live without once you see it.

ARSCO also manufactures functional steel cabinetry. Their low-cost steel furniture comes in a wide variety of colors, in finishes of durable baked enamel. These metal cabinets are ideally suited to schools, institutions, industrial settings, libraries, hospitals, churches, and offices. They'd look great in the home, too.

WEBSITE: Even though the website does not offer online ordering, I still recommend it because it's well put together. There you can see color images of ARSCO's radiator covers and metal cabinets, read about the products, and find out more about ARSCO.

SPECIAL FACTORS: Since all enclosures are custom-made, they aren't returnable; ARSCO does, however, guarantee the workmanship and durability of the products.

Bubble Furniture

ONE, Inc.
P. O. Box 1729
Tampa, FL 33601
800–704–9684
813–486–1096
FAX: 813–888–7034

FORM OF INFORMATION: online catalog only; no print catalog
PAY: MC, V, AE, DSC
SELLS: inflatable furniture and accessories
STORE: no walk-in location; mail-order only
ONLINE: www.bubblefurniture.com

Bubble Furniture sells inflatable chairs, sofas, beds, and accessories (flowers, pillows, picture frames, and more) in lots of bright colors and styles at great prices. Furniture products are made of extra thick and durable .40 mm material for high weight tolerances. A twin bed holds 400 pounds! You can get a groovy sofa that holds 500 pounds in orange, purple, lime, red, or "cosmic glow in the dark" for only $44.99 each, at this writing. For even better deals, click onto Specials where I found a four-piece living room set (a sofa, two chairs, and a foot stool) for $96.99. Colors can be mixed and matched for maximum effect. And, in case you were getting worried about the thought of blowing up a household of inflatable furniture, don't—because they sell sturdy inflation pumps in six different styles to make your inflating job easier. Bubble Furniture also sells inflatable duffel bags, sports bags, and backpacks in plenty of cool colors and at bargain prices.

SPECIAL FACTORS: Authorized returns in original retail packaging accepted within 30 days of shipment for exchange or refund.

Carolina Interiors

115 Oak Ave.
Kannapolis, NC 28081
800–438–6111
707–933–2261
FAX: 704–932–0434

FORM OF INFORMATION: free brochure
PAY: check or MO
SELLS: home furnishings and accessories
STORE: same address (1–85, Exit 63); Monday to Saturday 9:00 am–6:00 pm
ONLINE: www.carolinainteriors.com

Imagine strolling through a showroom the size of a city block lavishly furnished with furniture and accessories for dining rooms, living rooms, and bedrooms, complete with wall coverings, floor coverings, rugs, and bedding. That's what you'd find if you could visit Carolina Interiors, 30 miles north of Charlotte. Carolina Interiors' central location (in the heart of America's furniture-manufacturing belt) and high sales volume permit them to offer an outstanding selection from the finest furniture manufacturers at 30% to 60% off suggested retail prices. The brochure and website list some of the best-known names of over 350 manufacturers you can choose from. Chances are that bedroom ensemble, desk, or dining-room set you're in love with can be gotten for less at Carolina, so give them a call when you know what you want. Provide them with the manufacturer's name; they'll give you a price quote and discuss the cost of having the furniture delivered right to your door. Carolina's even has a low price guarantee, ask one of the nice salespersons for details. (Even factoring in shipping costs, you still end up saving a bundle when you furniture shop this way.) The brochure explains Carolina's deposit requirements.

WEBSITE: At the website you can find out about Carolina Interiors, view a list of manufacturers, and submit inquiries for furniture you are looking for.

SPECIAL FACTORS: Price quotes by phone, fax, email, mail; satisfaction guaranteed.

Coppa Woodworking, Inc.

1231 Paraiso Ave.
San Pedro, CA 90731
310–548–5332
FAX: 310–548–6740

FORM OF INFORMATION: $1 print catalog; online catalog

PAY: check, MO, MC, V

SELLS: Adirondack furniture, wood screen doors, dressing screens

STORE: same address; Monday to Friday 8:00 am–5:00 pm

ONLINE: www.coppawoodworking.com

 ★

If you've shopped around for Adirondack chairs lately—those classic American wooden chairs with the fan-shaped backs and broad flat arms on which to rest your summertime gin and tonic—you know they're not cheap. But Adirondack chairs are the specialty at Coppa Woodworking, and you can get them up to 50% less here than from several other places I've checked. The 4-page color flyer shows chairs made in 2 different styles, the classic Fanback and the traditional Westport. You can also find Adirondack loveseats, children's chairs, footrests, coffee tables, spindle baskets, and end tables. All are made of unfinished pine and come unassembled, but assembling them is easy. For $10 more you can have your piece stained with a semi-transparent color. But, as they say on late-night TV, that's not all. Coppa also manufactures really stunning wooden dressing screens into which you can insert fabrics such as Irish lace, cotton floral patterns, and the like. A unique tension bar in these screens allows you to use fabric without doing any sewing. And finally there are Coppa's wood screen doors. From plain Mission-style doors to gingerbreadlike doors with whimsical cut-outs, there are dozens of styles to choose from.

WEBSITE: Go to the website, and you'll see the entire inventory in full color. The only way to fully appreciate the fine craftsmanship and design employed by Coppa Woodworking is to view these pieces. After you've fallen in love with a door, screen, or chair, you'll still have to call, as there's no online ordering.

SPECIAL FACTORS: Satisfaction guaranteed; returns accepted except on custom orders; Alaska and Hawaii require special shipping charges.

Ellenburg's Furniture

I–40 at Stamey Farm Rd.
P.O. Box 5638
Statesville, NC 28687
704–873–2900
FAX: 704–873–6002

FORM OF INFORMATION: $6.50 print catalog, refundable; website

PAY: check, MO, MC, V, DSC

SELLS: home furnishings

STORE: same address; Monday to Friday 9:00 am–5:30 pm, Saturday 9:30 am–5:00 pm

ONLINE: www.ellenburgs.com

Ellenburg's Furniture is a family-owned and -operated business committed to saving you 40% to 60% off the suggested retail cost of fine furniture. They say they'll "go the extra mile" when their larger competitors will not. The $6.50 catalog fee (refundable with purchase) brings you a list of manufacturers Ellenburg's represents, as well as a collection of brochures from some of the best furniture makers. Flipping through these will definitely get you started thinking about the decorating style you favor. Ellenburg's staff is ready to help you in any way they can, whether by discussing your preferences and sending you more information on a certain style or manufacturer, mailing you fabric swatches, or giving you a price quote on a line that's not listed in their catalog.

WEBSITE: The website has been expanded to include a large portion of their inventory, in addition to a Closeout Corner, where you'll save an additional 10% to 40% off their normal discount. You will need to call, fax, or email Ellenburgs's for price quotes and to order.

SPECIAL FACTORS: Price quotes by phone or letter; only damaged and defective goods are accepted for return; call for shipping and deposit details.

Factory Direct Table Pad Co.

1501 W. Market St.
Indianapolis, IN 46222
800–737–4194
FAX: 317–631–2584

FORM OF INFORMATION: prices and samples, $1; online catalog

PAY: check, MO, MC, V, AE, DSC

SELLS: custom-made table pads

STORE: no walk-in location; mail-order only; phone hours Monday to Saturday 8:00 am–8:00 pm CST

ONLINE: www.tablepads.com

Factory Direct Table Pad Co. has been helping us protect our treasured dining tables, servers, coffee tables, desks, piano tops, end tables, and other wood pieces from scratches, heat, stains, spills, burns, dents, and watermarks for over 20 years. All table pads are custom-made to fit any surface. They have a heavy-duty, washable, leatherette top surface, a cushiony cotton bottom, and fold for easy handling and storage—but still have an attractive no-seam surface. The fiberboard core is unaffected by humidity, doesn't bow when stored upright, and is lighter in weight than most other table pads. At Factory Direct Table Pad, you get your choice of over 20 designer wood tones and solid colors, and these pads come with limited guarantees of up to 30 years. Since about half of the cost of a custom-made table pad is the fee paid to the person who measures your table, you'll save a lot by doing it yourself using the free measuring kit or by getting assistance from the highly accurate "phone measuring service." And since this company manufactures and sells the pads factory-direct, you're saving even more money.

WEBSITE: You'll find just about everything you need at the excellent website. It presents the company's products complete with color charts, photographs, and measuring instructions, and includes forms that enable you to email the company for a kit or a price quote, plus you can order online.

SPECIAL FACTORS: Inquire about return policy.

FurnitureOnline.com

735 N. Water St. #440
Milwaukee, WI 53202
800-343-4222
FAX: 800-468-1526

FORM OF INFORMATION: brochures and samples; online catalog

PAY: check, MO, MC, V, AE, DSC

SELLS: home furnishings and accessories

STORE: no walk-in location; mail-order only; phone hours Monday to Friday 6:30 am–9:00 pm, Saturday 8:00 am–9:00 pm, Sunday 11:00 am–9:00 pm CST

ONLINE: www.furnitureonline.com

I often flip through some of the higher end furniture catalogs and imagine the items I would get if I won the lottery or suddenly inherited a large fortune from some long, lost relative. I was delighted to discover FurnitureOnline.com and realize that I don't need a fortune to acquire some nice furniture. I particularly liked their bedroom furniture selections and found one queen size headboard, footboard, and side panel set from the Virginia collection that I compared to a very similar set at the Pottery Barn, and found I liked the one from FurnitureOnline.com every bit as much, plus it was $500 less (with delivery included).

FurnitureOnline.com is a National Business Furniture company. National Business Furniture's customers include 451 of the Fortune 500 companies, 97 of the 100 largest universities, the White House, the Capitol, most military bases and over 400,000 individuals and businesses around the country. Not only does this company have 25 years of experience providing customers with outstanding products and services, they have buying power that means you will always get an excellent value. The website is well organized and easy to use—shop by category or manufacturer. Most of their vendors have finish and fabric samples. Samples available at no charge are available online via their special Color Sample Cart. Shipping is fast and direct from the manufacturer to save you time and money.

SPECIAL FACTORS: Free of charge 9-year guarantee; return policy on most items is considered round trip freight, call customer service for details.

Genada Imports

P.O. Box 204, Dept. W–04
Teaneck, NJ 07666
TEL/FAX: 973–569–9660

FORM OF INFORMATION: $1 print catalog

PAY: check, MO, MC, V

SELLS: Danish, modern, and contemporary furniture

STORE: no walk-in location; mail-order only

Since 1968, Genada has been importing Danish-design furniture from Europe and selling it factory-direct to Americans at significant savings. I really like the 48-page black-and-white catalog with photographs and descriptions on every page. What is it about this style of furniture? It's '50s retro and futuristic chic at the same time: clean, classic lines, beautiful wood, form and function in harmony, comfort without pretense. Here you'll find armless chairs, sofas, and divans; convertible foam furniture (couch or chair into guest bed); sectional corner couches; tables (end, coffee, card, dining room, stackable, snack, etc.), leather office chairs straight out of *The Jetsons;* bookcases, including foldable designs; computer and office furniture; bunk beds and captain's beds; and much more. The unifying element here is design and quality of materials (teak, rosewood, walnut, etc.). If you've a flair for design, or just want some well-made, affordable pieces that will go with anything, Genada Imports is a wonderful source.

SPECIAL FACTORS: Full money-back guarantee; specify upholstery and finish preferences when ordering.

Heirloom Reproductions

1834 W. Fifth St., Dept. WBM
Montgomery, AL 36106–1516
800–288–1513
334–290–3390
FAX: 334–290–2085

FORM OF INFORMATION: $10 print catalog, refundable; online catalog

PAY: check, MO, MC, V

SELLS: Victorian and French reproduction furniture, clocks, lamps, etc.

STORE: same address; Monday to Friday 10:00 am–5:00 pm

ONLINE: www.heirloomreproductions.com

I know an old belle whose house is like a museum of Victoriana. She has ladies' chairs, a red velvet camelback sofa, a chiming clock on the marble mantel, and gorgeous hurricane lamps dripping with crystal baubles and hand-painted with pastel flowers. Heirloom Reproductions can help you achieve that same look in your own home with their collection of New Victorian reproductions shipped to you directly from the factory at savings of 40% to 55%. They represent the top names in the industry: Kimball, Victorian Classics, Carlton McLendon, and Victorian Lighting, to name a few. The color catalog (its $10 cost is refundable with your first purchase) presents chairs (ladies' and gents'), parlor sets, fainting sofas, marble-top tables, dining sets, beds, dressers, armoires, hall trees, clocks, display cabinets, grandfather clocks, hurricane lamps, and much more. Heirloom Reproduction's helpful staff will answer questions you might have regarding your decorating scheme, fabric choices, shipping, and the company's sales policy.

WEBSITE: I like the website because it allows you to view the actual print catalog for free, page by page, and it has some great links to a line of curio collector's cabinets by Howard Miller and Victorian reproduction lamps as well. As of this writing, you cannot order online.

SPECIAL FACTORS: Price quotes by phone, letter, or email; swatches are available on request; orders shipped from factory in insured truck.

Masacco New York

53 Leonard St., Suite 2W
New York, NY 10013
212–925–8667
FAX: 212–925–3575

FORM OF INFORMATION: free brochure and price list; online catalog

PAY: check or MO

SELLS: "chair cocoons"—stretch slipcovers for folding chairs and banquet chairs

STORE: no walk-in location; mail-order only; phone hours Monday to Friday 9:00 am–5:00 pm EST

ONLINE: www.masacco.com

It is difficult to describe the "chair cocoons" dreamed up by Masacco New York. This husband and wife team in Manhattan offers a unique solution to the problem of folding chairs too ugly to use every day, but too necessary to get rid of altogether. Depending on the fabric, these nifty chair cocoons turn an ordinary metal folding chair into an elegant seat for an ultra-formal candlelit dinner, a retro-funky seat for your stylin' urban apartment, or a classy, understated perch for your tropical sunroom. Two years ago, creator Anne Moss thought about the hideous chairs she kept hidden away except when company came. What if these could be made attractive enough to actually use as furniture? The solution was Masacco stretch covers, which have since been voted "Best New Product" by the New York Home and Textiles Show, and have been featured in *Metropolitan Home* and other design magazines.

Think "slipcover" and you are apt to visualize those baggy, wrinkly, ill-fitting covers sold by upscale décor catalogs to "disguise" the homely folding chair. Now, put that image out of your mind altogether. Part of the success of Masacco's ingenious covers is due to the original design itself. Imagine a slipcover that stretches over the top of a metal folding chair and comes to points at each of the four small feet bottoms. By means of a clever pattern that utilizes both the tension of the chair legs and Velcro to "pinch" the seat front to the seat back, the resulting futuristic, star-like shape looks nothing like the folding chair that makes up its underlying structure. The other half of the success equation is the delicious fabrics Anne chooses: shimmering silvery metallics, champagne crushed velvets, glossy maroon velours, "harlequin" black-and-cream. These slipcovers fit any standard folding chair and are fully washable. They are easy to pull on and off and need no ironing. Best of all, they are inexpensive, especially if you pick up folding chairs at yard sales or used furniture shops, enabling you to change your room décor for every season.

Masacco's other line was originally designed for commercial use—hotels, catered events, and conventions—with round-backed banquet chairs. The "wedding collection" features such sumptuous fabrics as gold satins, crushed ivory velours, and gold floral laces; backslips can be added to a basic white cocoon to turn an ordinary banquet chair into a formal chair.

When you request a color brochure, with crisp color photographs that perfectly portray the goods, Masacco New York will send you a price list and order form that lists the available fabrics and colors, as well as wholesale and retail prices. To qualify for wholesale prices, you must have a reseller ID number.

WEBSITE: At the website you can see and read about these chair cocoons, look at all the different fabric samples, and check out all the prices, whereas the print material is less comprehensive. Even though at this writing Masacco was still taking only checks and money orders online, I recommend you check out the website first, before or instead of requesting print material. The owner promised that credit cards would be accepted soon. At this writing, everyone who orders online receives a 15% discount.

SPECIAL FACTORS: Custom designs available on orders of 50 pieces or more; special orders welcome.

Monarch Radiator Enclosures

P.O. Box 326, Dept. WBM
Carlstadt, NJ 07072
201–507–5551
FAX: 201–438–2820

FORM OF INFORMATION: free brochure; online catalog
PAY: check, MO, MC, V
SELLS: all-steel radiator enclosures
STORE: no walk-in location; mail-order only
ONLINE: www.monarchrad.com

What could be more money-saving than turning your ugly radiator into a functional piece of furniture that also happens to save on energy costs? That's the idea behind Monarch's stock and custom radiator covers. Don't let exposed radiators spoil the charm of your home. For little money you can get a steel cover that's easy to assemble and install, comes in several colors, and has an attractive grill front for maximum air circulation. The units are designed for safety; not only will your radiator protect your walls, drapes, and children from burns, but you can now use the insulated top as a surface for plants, books, and knickknacks. Monarch's custom radiator enclosures are even more tempting, with built-in bookshelves, hinged tops, concealed humidifiers, and designer colors and grill styles among some of the features available. The two brochures you'll receive—one for stock, the other for custom models—explain in detail all the features of these nifty products and guide you step-by-step through the task of measuring your radiator for the right cover.

WEBSITE: If you have online access, visit the website, which offers online ordering and features photographs, information, and a price chart for the stock enclosures. I think once you see the beautiful images at the site and read about the advantages of a covered versus an uncovered radiator, you won't be able to resist.

SPECIAL FACTORS: Most enclosures can be shipped by UPS; larger enclosures are shipped via common carrier.

Plexi-Craft Quality Products Corp.

514 W. 24th St., Dept. WBM
New York, NY 10011
800–24–PLEXI
212–924–3244
FAX: 212–924–3508

FORM OF INFORMATION: $2 print catalog; online catalog

PAY: check, MO, MC, V, AE

SELLS: Plexiglas and Lucite home furnishings and accessories

STORE: same address; Monday to Friday 9:30 am–5:00 pm

ONLINE: www.plexi-craft.com

Plexi-Craft Quality Products Corp. manufactures Lucite and Plexiglas furniture and household accessories that are available direct from the factory at about 50% less than what they'd cost at department stores. The 16-page print catalog includes tables (Mandarin, Parson, coffee, console, vanity, TV, etc.), a variety of table bases of unusual shape and design, display cases, futuristic-looking stools and chairs, and lots of practical accessories such as telephone caddies, pedestals (for plants or art), coat racks, wine racks, place mats, and towel bars. These Lucite/Plexiglas pieces are shatterproof and durable, built to last a lifetime, and will add practicality with a minimalist flair to any surroundings. Never, *ever* use window cleaner; Plexi-Craft recommends and sells a special cleaner that will keep your furniture looking new with just an occasional wipe. Tabletops come in a variety of sizes, shapes, and thicknesses, in glass or acrylic; cushion colors are white or beige. Plexi-Craft welcomes custom orders.

WEBSITE: The website is informative and easy to use, with crisp color images and online ordering. Plexi-Craft's full catalog is represented here and can be viewed either by category or by specific keyword search.

SPECIAL FACTORS: Call, fax, or write for custom-order quotes; no returns accepted without prior written permission.

Priba Furniture and Interiors

210 Stagecoach Trail
Greensboro, NC 27409
336–855–9034
FAX: 336–855–1370

FORM OF INFORMATION: free brochure; website

PAY: check, MO, MC, V, DSC

SELLS: furniture, accessories, bedding, rugs, etc.

STORE: 210 Stage Coach Trail, Greensboro, NC; Monday to Friday 9:00 am–5:30 pm, Saturday 9:00 am–5:00 pm

ONLINE: www.pribafurniture.com

Priba Furniture and Interiors wants to make you a customer for life. They are so determined that if you come to visit their Greensboro showroom, Priba will arrange transportation from the airport and will credit 1% of your total order toward lodging (hotel/motel receipt required)! If visiting North Carolina isn't on your agenda, shop around your own neighborhood until you find the furniture, lamps or accessories, fabrics, carpet, wall coverings, or bedding you want. To take advantage of Priba's discounts (which run up to 48% on over 300 lines of furniture and accessories) you'll need the manufacturer's name and style number. For upholstery, get the fabric and grade name or number. Both the print brochure and the website list the manufacturers Priba represents. If you're not quite sure what you want, Priba can help narrow your preferences and then send you photographs or brochures of a particular manufacturer's items. Priba uses van-line service, so your furniture will be uncrated and set up in your home.

WEBSITE: For readers unfamiliar with the concept of North Carolina furniture discounters—why they're able to offer such low prices to folks halfway across the country and how it all works—a quick visit to the website will be well worth your while. There you'll find out more about this pocket of bargain America, and Priba's corner of it in particular. You can also view pictures of selected pieces or styles, but there's no online ordering or inventory to speak of at this writing. However, you can email Priba at the site with queries or to obtain price quotes.

SPECIAL FACTORS: Credit cards accepted for deposit only; a 30% deposit required when you place your order; 150-pound minimum for shipment.

Quality Furniture Market

2034 Hickory Blvd. SW
Lenoir, NC 28645
828–728–2946
FAX: 828–726–0226

FORM OF INFORMATION: free brochure and price quotes; website

PAY: check, MO, MC, V, AE, DSC

SELLS: furnishings, bedding, and accessories

STORE: same address; Monday to Saturday 8:30 am–5:00 pm

ONLINE: www.qualityfurnituremarket.com

Quality Furniture Market, in business since 1955, takes its name seriously: You're invited to check the firm's ratings with Dunn and Bradstreet, the Lyons listing, the Lenoir Chamber of Commerce (800–737–0782, and the Better Business Bureau (800-727-1861) before you buy. The firm's magnificent selection of furnishings for every room and taste is offered at prices that are 20% over cost, compared with the usual 110% to 125% markups. In a random check of comparison shopping, I found a better-known brand-name couch available at Quality Furniture Martket for over $1,000 less (including delivery) than I would have paid for the very same couch at a local dealer! The easiest way to shop here is to link to manufacturers' sites from the Quality Furniture Market's Manufacturers page to view products. Then, find a nearby dealer so you can see the piece in person, note the price, then call Quality Furniture Market and get their price. I think you'll be more than pleased. This company has been recommended as a "great price" store by Oprah Winfrey and *Woman's Day* magazine, among others.

Quality Furniture sells indoor and outdoor furniture, bedding, and home accessories by hundreds of firms. The list of brands is given in the brochure, as well as terms of sale and other conditions. Readers have written to say they were very pleased with Quality's prices and the firm's in-home delivery service. If you're traveling near Lenoir, drop by and get lost in the 40,000 sq. feet of furniture galleries and display rooms.

WEBSITE: Although the website does not present inventory for sale online, I still recommend that you pay the site a visit. The website has information on present and near-future clearance sales and closeouts, as well as a list of hundreds of furniture manufacturers they represent (and this is just a partial list) with links to their sites where you can view products. Additionally, you'll get a good sense of what this company is all about by reading abut their policies and services.

Sobol House

141 Richardson Blvd.
P.O. Box 219
Black Mountain, NC 28711
828–669–8031
FAX: 828–669–7969

FORM OF INFORMATION: free brochure; website

PAY: check, MO

SELLS: home and office furnishings

STORE: same address; Monday to Saturday 9:30 am–5:30 pm

ONLINE: www.sobolhouse.com

Sobol House was a pioneer in the mail-order furniture business. Since 1970 this company has been offering first-quality modern and traditional furniture at savings of 40% to 50% to customers in places as far flung as Saudi Arabia. Like other companies of this sort, Sobol asks that you do some of the work: Visit showrooms in your area; compare brand names, cost, and quality; take notes. When you find the furnishings you like, call Sobol with the manufacturer's name, the model number, and finish or fabric. Sobol will give you a price quote and answer any other questions you might have about the hundreds of manufacturers they represent. The money you'd spend on sales tax will pay a major portion of your freight cost. In-house delivery and setup are available, or you can have the furniture delivered to your sidewalk, which is more economical. "All we ask," says the brochure, "is the chance to give you a competitive bid!" Okay, so give 'em a chance.

WEBSITE: The website provides information about Sobol House and a list of the over 200 manufacturers they carry; but the photo gallery contains only the tiniest fraction of their inventory, and there is no online ordering. They do have a Specials page with clearance items (prices on specials are listed). Call, email, fax, or write Sobol House to get price quotes on all other items.

Price quotes by phone, fax, or letter; Sobol House requires a signed order form or handwritten letter with the appropriate information and a 50% deposit; see website for refund policy.

Marion Travis

P.O. Box 1041	**FORM OF INFORMATION:** $1 print catalog
Statesville, NC 28687	**PAY:** check, MO, MC, V
704–528–4424	**SELLS:** reproduction Early American chairs,
FAX: 704–528–3526	benches, and tables
	STORE: 354 S. Eastway Dr., Troutman, NC; Monday to Thursday 8:00 am–3:30 pm, Friday 8:00 am–12:00 noon

The owner of Marion Travis tells a little story that demonstrates what this company is all about. Years ago he bought property that had a run-down house on it. From the shambles, he salvaged an intriguing old chair. A well-made example of 1800s craftsmanship, the chair inspired him to create a modern-day reproduction, the Lillie Ladderback, one of his best-sellers to this day. When the people at Marion Travis say their Early American reproduction chairs last a lifetime, they mean it. This is furniture that collectors will be collecting a hundred years from now. But you can collect them now and spend 25% to 50% less than you'd pay elsewhere for furniture of this caliber.

The skilled craftsmen of Marion Travis construct the chairs—of ash, oak, maple, and other hardwoods—in such a way that the natural contraction of the wood, only partially seasoned, causes the joints to grow even stronger and tighter with the years. The 12-page black-and-white catalog from Marion Travis shows beautifully made ladderback chairs with hand-woven cord seats, bar stools, tables, rockers, children's chairs and rockers, porch swings, foot stools, and much more. Seats are made with cord, wood slats, and palm cane rush; furniture can be unstained (machine sanded) or finished in natural, walnut, or golden oak. If you're in the vicinity of Troutman and can pick up your furniture unboxed, you'll get an additional 25% off.

Wholesale customers: Request the wholesale catalog and price list from Shaver Woodworks, P.O. Box 946, Troutman, NC 28166. Minimum wholesale order is 12 pieces.

SPECIAL FACTORS: Minimum order is 2 pieces of furniture; authorized returns of defective goods accepted within 30 days.

West Rindge Baskets, Inc.

47 W. Main St.
Rindge, NH 03461
TEL/FAX: 603–899–2231

FORM OF INFORMATION: free brochure
PAY: check or MO
SELLS: handmade, hand-woven wooden baskets
STORE: same address; Monday to Thursday 8:00 am–4:00 pm (all year), Friday and Saturday 10:00 am–4:00 pm (May 30 to Christmas)

I adore this company, and you will, too, once you chat with the down-home folks at West Rindge. West Rindge has been making baskets from local New Hampshire wood since 1925. The baskets here start as rough-cut, slab-edge white birch or oak from local forests, and are hand-made, hand-woven, and individually inspected for flaws. Don't be expecting the $5 made-in-Asia basket you'd buy in a dime store. West Rindge baskets are upscale, impeccably made baskets to keep over a lifetime. The color brochure shows the selection—40 in all—that includes baskets for shopping; pie and cake holders (including a double pie holder); picnic baskets; wastebaskets; baskets designed for apple picking, wine-toting, plants, barbecue utensils, French bread, and many more, including ones with swing handles, stiff handles, and hinged lids. The baskets here sell for less than what you'd pay for items of comparable quality in a gourmet shop or decorator store. Prices are extremely reasonable—averaging around $30. This nice, family-run business is a great find.

Wholesale buyers: West Rindge has a wholesale price list with prices at about 30% less, which you can request if you're a reseller. In New Hampshire, a "reseller" is not required to have a resale number. The only requirement is that you purchase a minimum of $150 on your first wholesale order.

SPECIAL FACTORS: Satisfaction is guaranteed; C.O.D. orders accepted for an additional charge.

Kitchen Equipment

Small kitchen appliances and gadgets; pots and pans; chef's knifes and cooking utensils; restaurant-grade supplies; gourmet cooking and baking accessories

Cookware is one area where quality makes a big difference. I have three fry pans, all the same size, made from three different manufacturers. When I make a batch of pancake batter and pour my batter into each of the three pans, all on the same heat setting, I get three very different results. I can't stress enough the importance of good cookware. But, it is not cheap.

The firms in this chapter sell all the great brands of cookware: All-Clad, Bodum, Bourgeat, Braun, Calphalon, Chicago Metallic, Le Creuset, Cuisinart, Kaiser, KitchenAid, Krups, Omega, Pavoni, Pelouze, Vollrath, and more. (They also sell everything else from measuring spoons and butcher's knives to bread-making machines and cappuccino makers.) I have found that generally most dealers of cookware and cutlery offer the same "on sale" specials on identical products at the same time. What does this mean to you, the consumer? It means that there isn't one particular store I can send you to for the best all-around deals. The most economical way to buy new kitchenware is to check the sources I have listed and look for specials on the kind of cookware or cutlery you're in the market for. You can save 30% to 50% on cutlery and cookware if you wait and watch for special sales. Be careful to compare apples to apples. Many manufacturers carry a number of product lines that vary in quality and price. And don't forget to compare shipping prices and applicable tax.

For large kitchen appliances such as refrigerators, stoves, and ovens, see the section entitled "Appliances and TVs," page 307. As long as you'll be creating culinary masterpieces, you'll want to set an impressive table for your guests. See "Tableware," page 379, for flatware, glassware, and china—this is one area where the everyday savings are big, generally 50% less than department store prices. Check out "Bed, Bath, and Table Textiles" for tablecloths, place mats, and napkins, page 317.

Find It Fast

COOKWARE AND BAKEWARE
A Cook's Wares, Broadway Panhandler, Kitchen Etc., Peerless Restaurant Supplies, Professional Cutlery Direct

A Cook's Wares

211 37th St.

Beaver Falls, PA 15010–2103

800–915–9788

FAX: 800–916–2886

FORM OF INFORMATION: $2 print catalog; online catalog

PAY: check, MO, MC, V, AE

SELLS: gourmet cooking supplies and ingredients

STORE: same address, Monday to Friday 9:00 am–4:00 pm, Saturday 9:00 am–1:00 pm

ONLINE: www.cookswares.com

What if you were to see an interesting recipe that required a bird's nest—a utensil that holds potatoes in the shape of a nest for deep-frying? Unless you live in an area that happens to have a fabulous gourmet kitchen store, you'd be out of luck. Luckily, I've discovered A Cook's Wares, a great source for gourmet cookware, bakeware, gadgets, and ingredients. The deals here can be found on specials and closeout sales.

I like the 64-page, black-and-white, text-heavy catalog illustrated with line drawings. If you're looking to outfit your kitchen with chef's-quality cookware and bakeware—items you'd be proud to hang from the ceiling in full view of your guests—you'll find such brands as All-Clad, Bourgeat, Calphalon, Cuisinart, Demeyere, Kaiser, Le Creuset, Mauviel, and many others. A Cook's Wares also carries top-name cutlery from such notables as Henckels and Wüsthof-Trident, appliances and gadgets from the likes of KitchenAid and Waring, and wondrous, hard-to-find gourmet ingredients and condiments: exotic-flavored and imported vinegars and olive oils, sweet sauces, spices and herbs, syrups, and vanillas, to name a few. This is a great source for gift ideas.

WEBSITE: The company's website lets you view the full inventory and place your order online. I give this site high marks because it also features news, discussions, recipes, product reviews, gift suggestions, and articles of interest to gourmets and gourmands. The reals savings here are from web-only specials and current closeout sales, plus you can choose to join the e-club to receive free e-newsletters and be eligible for member-only special offers.

SPECIAL FACTORS: Complete satisfaction guaranteed; returns accepted within 30 days for exchange or refund; orders shipped only within the U.S. (Hawaii, Alaska, and APO/FPO addresses included).

Broadway Panhandler

477 Broome St.
New York, NY 10013
212–966–3434
FAX: 212–966–9017

FORM OF INFORMATION: price quotes; online catalog

PAY: check, MO, MC, V, AE, DSC

SELLS: cookware, cutlery, kitchenware, bakeware, and tabletop accessories

STORE: same address; Monday to Friday 10:30 am–7:00 pm, Saturday 11:00 am–7:00 pm, Sunday 11:00 am–6:00 pm

ONLINE: www.broadwaypanhandler.com

When it comes to cookware and all its accoutrements, the more products, the better, for there's excitement in a store's kaleidoscopic mix of materials and textures, shapes and culinary promise. Hold that image in mind when you call or write Broadway Panhandler for quotes on appliances and professional equipment (there's no print catalog); manufacturers include All-Clad, Bodum, Bourgeat, Braun, Calphalon, Chicago Metallic, Le Creuset, Cuisinart, Kaiser, KitchenAid, Krups, Omega, Pavoni, Pelouze, and Vollrath. They also carry knives by such notables as Global, Lamson & Goodnow, Sabatier, and Wüsthof-Trident; for the cutlery, price lists and manufacturers' brochures may be available. There is a brick-and-mortar store, and since most roads lead to New York City you'll want to stop in for cookbooks, serving pieces, kitchen linens, baskets, and assorted gadgets. You can expect savings up to 30% on select items, especially on open-stock cutlery and various lines of cookware.

WEBSITE: Broadway Panhandler's homepage features a busy chef chopping his greens in a lovely brick walled kitchen, with links to the following departments: Chef's Corner, Cookware, Bakeware, Tabletop, Knives, Electrics, and Kitchen Tools Plus. At Chef's Corner, read interviews and get some good cooking tips from top New York chefs. At press time, Cookware, Knives, Kitchen Tools Plus, and Electrics had a limited selection available; however, the Bakeware, and Tabletop departments were still under construction. But check in often, because this company, with more than 10,500 products for the professional and home cook, is sure to have more and more inventory available online as the website develops.

SPECIAL FACTORS: Price quotes by phone or letter.

Cutlery Shoppe

357 Steelhead Way
Boise, ID 83704–8362
800–231–1272
208–672–8488
FAX: 208–672–8588

FORM OF INFORMATION: free print catalog; online catalog

PAY: check, MO, MC, V, AE, DSC

SELLS: cutlery, knives, sharpeners, etc.

STORE: no walk-in location; mail-order only; phone hours Monday to Friday 8:00 am–6:00 pm, Saturday 12:00 noon–5:00 pm

ONLINE: www.cutleryshoppe.com

I don't think there's a person reading this who won't find something to love in Cutlery Shoppe's current print or online catalog. This company, which has been in business since 1985, specializes in knives—sport, military, kitchen, self-defense, and survival. Besides high-quality knives, there are lots of tools and neat gadgets here as well. And you'll like the discounts that run as high as 40% on many items.

The well-designed, 64-page color catalog features photographs and descriptive text of items that appeal to a wide range of people, from chefs to survivalists, from old-time whittlers to jungle explorers, from Navy SEALs to handymen. They also have an impressive line of flashlights. (Their Photo Micro Light II is about the size and weight of a quarter and has been approved by NASA.) Cutlery Shoppe sells self-defense items such as pepper spray, as well as Leatherman Tools, Swiss Army knives, knife sharpeners of every type and description, kitchen knives, and more. I really appreciate companies that specialize in one type of product—and do it right.

Please note: Consult your local ordinances regarding the purchase, possession, and use of weaponry and personal-protection devices.

WEBSITE: The website offers online ordering, detailed product descriptions, and nice photographs and design. The Gift Ideas section will no doubt solve some of your most trying birthday-gift dilemmas.

SPECIAL FACTORS: Satisfaction guaranteed; returns accepted within 30 days for exchange, refund, or credit.

Kitchen, Etc.

32 Industrial Dr.,
Dept. WMB–01
Exeter, NH 03833–4557
800–232–4070
603–773–0020
FAX: 603–778–0777

FORM OF INFORMATION: free print catalog; online catalog

PAY: check, MO, MC, V, DSC

SELLS: tableware and kitchenware

STORE: locations in CT, MA, NH, RI and VA; see catalog or website for locations; phone hours Monday to Friday 9:00 am–5:00 pm EST

ONLINE: www.kitchenetc.com

Ask anyone who's bought high-quality pots and pans lately and they'll tell you it's not that easy to find great deals on stuff for your kitchen. But you can save from 20% to 50% from their Hot Buys and Clearance sections when you buy your china, stemware, small appliances, flatware, kitchen gadgets, pots and pans, baking accessories, and other kitchen supplies through Kitchen Etc. This company has been around since 1983 and offers a fat catalog overflowing with great buys, color photographs, and product descriptions to make this a one-stop shopping experience for culinary-related goods. One half of the catalog is devoted to fine and casual tableware, stemware, and flatware from the best names in the biz, including Dansk, Mikasa, Noritake, Pfaltzgraff, Waterford, Wedgwood, and many others. It's a great selection, and discounts are deep. The other half of Kitchen Etc.'s catalog is devoted to everything else one might need for the kitchen, from the exotic (ravioli makers and bread machines) to more basic supplies (turkey roasters and chef's knives). Kitchen Etc. also maintains a bridal registry.

WEBSITE: But wait, as they used to say on the late-night TV commercials, there's more! The website is fantastic, and I highly recommend it. Search for more than 23,000 products with the easy-to-use search engine, or just click on an image (a pot takes you to cookware, a wooden stool to furniture, and so on) to cyberwalk down the aisles of the online store and view merchandise grouped by category. The categories include casual dinnerware, fine dinnerware, casual china, glassware, flatware, cookware, bakeware, serveware, cutlery, textiles, electrics, gadgets, storage, giftware, food, and furniture. And once you've found the merchandise you want, you can order directly online.

SPECIAL FACTORS: Satisfaction guaranteed.

Peerless Restaurant Supplies

1124 S. Grand Blvd.,
Dept. WBM
St. Louis, MO 63104–1090
800–255–3663
314–664–0400
FAX: 314–664–8102

FORM OF INFORMATION: $10 print catalog; online catalog

PAY: check, MO, MC, V

SELLS: commercial cookware and restaurant equipment

STORE: same address and 1001 Fay St., Columbia, MO; Monday to Friday 8:00 am–5:00 pm, Saturday 9:00 am–12:00 noon in November and December only

ONLINE: www.prls.com

If you're setting up a small catering business, sidewalk bar/café, or bakery, Peerless has been a great source for commercial restaurant supplies for over 50 years. But even individuals find lots to like in the mammoth 224-page catalog. For a $10 investment, you'll get the annual Peerless catalog, which is well organized, descriptive, and has a fantastic selection. There are some good deals on select items here.

Here's a tiny sample of the kinds of items you'll find in the catalog: plain, restaurant-grade tableware (including adorable art deco pastels from Fiesta); plastic and glassware for poolside, bar, or table; stainless flatware; tablecloths, table skirts, ice sculpture molds; cutlery; serving trays; chafing dishes; punch bowls; urns; everything for the kitchen, from lettuce slicers to vacuum-packing machines; bus-boy utility carts; open-wire shelving; garbage containers; and large appliances, such as fryers, mixers, and ranges. Get the picture? Peerless also has amazing deals on used equipment; if you register your special need with their used equipment Wish List, Peerless may be able to save you a bundle. (Used equipment comes with a 30-day parts and labor guarantee.)

Those who live in the St. Louis area would be well advised to stop into the 25,000-square-foot showroom and visit the Bargain Room, where everything is drastically reduced. Food-service professionals should note that Peerless also provides 3-D design services for commercial kitchens and interior decorating design services for restaurants and bars, nursing homes, hotels, nightclubs and more. See catalog for details.

WEBSITE: The website features secure online ordering of over 5,000 items, and you can browse alphabetically by merchandise or by manufacturer.

SPECIAL FACTORS: Minimum credit card order is $25; quantity discounts available; authorized returns are accepted within 30 days of receipt (see catalog for return policy).

Professional Cutlery Direct

242 Branford Rd., Dept. WBM
North Branford, CT 06471
800–859–6994
203–871–1000
FAX: 203–871–1010

FORM OF INFORMATION: free print catalog; online catalog

PAY: check, MO, MC, V, AE

SELLS: kitchen cutlery, cookware, cookbooks, etc.

STORE: no walk-in location; mail-order only; phone hours Monday to Friday 8:30 am–8:00 pm, Saturday 9:00 am–5:00 pm, Sunday 12:00 noon–5:00 pm EST

ONLINE: www.cutlery.com

Professional Cutlery Direct specializes in commercial-quality equipment for at-home cooks who take cooking seriously. The 72-page catalog features cutlery of high-carbon stainless steel, as well as hardwood cutting boards, bakeware, cookware and utensils, grills and griddles, chef's attire, knife accessories (such as sharpeners and steels), specialty tools, cookbooks, cookware racks, butcher block carts, and more. Discounts range between 20% and 30% on select items. Don't fret if you're new to the kitchen; the catalog gives enough information to help you choose your cutlery wisely. Professional Cutlery Direct offers a shipping cap of $24.95, at this writing, so that you can purchase heavy pots and pans, cutting boards, and kitchen furniture without the usual punitive shipping charges.

WEBSITE: If you'd rather shop online, the website displays an extensive inventory and includes online ordering capability. I really enjoy shopping online at sites like this one. Web-only specials increase the incentive to do so. The site is easy to understand, has lots of color images, and is well organized.

SPECIAL FACTORS: Price quotes by phone or letter; quantity discounts on some items; returns accepted within 60 days for exchange, refund, or credit.

Lighting

Indoor and outdoor lighting fixtures; reproduction Tiffany
lamps; crystal chandeliers; lamps and lamp shades; candles

If you know people who have a special talent for choosing the right lamps and shades, you probably understand that it is, indeed, a gift. Somehow, their homes always feel inviting, and all details seem to pull together. A warm pool of yellow light next to a big fluffy chair invites you to sink down in its glow with a cup of tea. But for the rest of us, successful lighting is a design challenge. Luckily, some of the firms listed here have on-staff designers who can advise you on how to light your home. You'll also find the basics in interior design textbooks and decorating manuals. And you'll definitely be inspired by the fabulous catalogs and websites.

The companies below sell lighting for the home—lamps, ceiling fixtures, bathroom and kitchen fixtures, patio and walkway lighting, building lanterns, etc.—and related electrical accessories, shades, and replacement parts. Some also sell ceiling fans and attachments. Discounts average about 30% to 40% on name-brand goods, and the firms that manufacture their own fixtures sell at competitive prices as well. Don't forget about old-fashioned lighting. I'm talking about candles. You'll find a great source for candles at bargain prices in this section.

Find It Fast

CANDLES
NJCandle.com

CEILING FANS
Nationwide Lighting, USA Light & Electric

CHANDELIERS
King's Chandelier, Union Lighting

COMMERCIAL LIGHTING AND SUPPLIES
USA Light & Electric

LAMPS, LIGHT FIXTURES, SCONCES
DiscountTiffanyLamps.com, Nationwide Lighting, Union Lighting,
USA Light & Electric

OUTDOOR LANTERNS AND PENDANTS
NJCandle.com, Union Lighting, USA Light & Electric

REPRODUCTION TIFFANY LAMPS
DiscountTiffanyLamps.com

DiscountTiffanyLamps.com

Star Tiffany Studios
70 Broadway
Greenlawn, NY 11740
877–651–7827

FORM OF INFORMATION: online catalog only; no print catalog

PAY: MC, V, AE, DSC

SELLS: reproduction Tiffany lamps and lighting

STORE: same address; Monday to Friday 10:00 am–5:00 pm

ONLINE: www.discounttiffanylamps.com

In 1893, Louis Tiffany opened his glass factory in Queens, NY. More than a century later, his collectible lamps and shades are sold at auction and in antique stores for thousands of dollars. If you're a fan of these beautiful stained-glass lampshades, take heart. Anyone can afford a Tiffany reproduction manufactured and sold by DiscountTiffanyLamps.com. This company carries on the Tiffany tradition by manufacturing stunning lamps and lighting based on the designs of Louis Tiffany, and making them available to glass lovers at affordable prices. In fact, the online store sells all pieces directly to consumers at an average of 50% off retail price. Click on one of the following categories to view full-color pictures and detailed product descriptions: table lamps, floor lamps, copper foil fixtures, wall lamps, beveled glass, lamp bases, odd & end table lamps, and odd & end hanging shades. Feast your eyes on the gorgeous birds, flowers, twisting ivy, insects, and exotic fish-scale and geometric patterns that adorn Tiffany-style pieces. There are some super deals to be had in the odd & end sections. These are one-of-a-kind artist samples that for one reason or another did not get into production. They are in perfect condition and sell for way less than similar pieces. I really like this store's no-nonsense approach to saving you money. If you adore Tiffany but are on a Wal-Mart budget, you'll love this company as much as I do.

SPECIAL FACTORS: 100% satisfaction guaranteed; returns must be made within 10 days of receipt for refund, within 30 days for exchange; no international orders; will ship to Alaska, Hawaii, and Puerto Rico, but call first for shipping rates.

King's Chandelier Co.

Dept. WBM, P.O. Box 667
Eden, NC 27289–0667
336–623–6188
FAX: 336–627–9935

FORM OF INFORMATION: $6 print catalog, $8 outside U.S.; online catalog

PAY: check, MO, MC, V, AE, DSC

SELLS: Czechoslovakian, Italian, and Swarovski trimmed chandeliers

STORE: 729 S. Van Buren Rd. (Hwy. 14), Eden, NC; Monday to Friday 9:30 am– 4:30 pm, Saturday 9:30 am–1:00 pm

ONLINE: www.chandelier.com

It's nice to know that quality has staying power. That goes for businesses like King's Chandelier Company, owned and operated by the same family for over 60 years, as well as their products—elegant crystal chandeliers, sconces, and candelabras that are instant heirlooms. Discount chandeliers, you ask? Compare King's crystal lighting fixtures with others' and you'll see that their prices are close to wholesale. The reason is that King's Chandelier Company is the manufacturer, so you're getting these goods direct from the factory without retailer markups. The full-color catalog shows all 100 designs dripping with cut crystal, glowing with soft light, and shining in silver or brass finishes. The styles range from extravagant and complex designs fit for royalty to more understated old-timey Victorian. King's imports the finest materials, such as Austrian Swarovski crystal, and has artisans who create each piece as it's ordered. The company claims the full beauty of these crystal wonders can't be captured in photographs, so they invite customers to come visit their North Carolina showroom. Barring that, however, you can have a videocassette made with up to 6 designs of your choosing. The VHS is $20, refundable when you place your order.

WEBSITE: To get an idea of how beautiful these lighting masterpieces are, log on to the website. There you'll find all of the chandeliers in full color with prices and information on how to order—there is no online ordering, as yet. You can also find out about the history of this company.

SPECIAL FACTORS: An additional 15% discount is extended to designers, decorators, and contractors; satisfaction guaranteed; returns accepted within 15 days (see catalog for details).

Nationwide Lighting

1073 39th St.
Brooklyn, NY 11219
800–586–1675
FAX: 800–736–4886

FORM OF INFORMATION: price quotes; web-site

PAY: check, MO, MC, V, DSC

SELLS: high-end lamps, chandeliers, and ceiling fans

STORE: open everyday except Wednesday 9:00 am–5:00 pm EST

ONLINE: www.nationwidelighting.com

If you're not accustomed to shopping by price quote, maybe it's time you saw the light. Why? Because companies like Nationwide Lighting will reward you for your footwork by saving you up to 50% off normal retail prices on high-end lamps, chandeliers, and ceiling fans. Here's how it works: If you're in the market for quality brands such as Waterford Crystal, Schonbek, Nulco, Wilshire, Estiluz, Casablanca ceiling fans, or Hubbardton Forge (to name just a few brands this firm represents), shop around for them—either locally or through the manufacturers' links at Nationwide's website—and then contact Nationwide Lighting for a price quote. You can do so by phone, fax, email, or by letter (with an SASE). Since they represent so many high-quality manufacturers, big and small, Nationwide Lighting can offer you a low price that will save you a bundle. Be aware that there is a $250 minimum order. However, buying lighting this way, particularly if you are furnishing a whole house or apartment, makes a lot of sense. You'll need to provide the manufacturer's name and the product style number when you ask for a price quote. Nationwide Lighting will do the rest.

SPECIAL FACTORS: Please note there is no print catalog; price quotes by phone, email, fax, or letter (please enclose a SASE); store closed Wednesdays; minimum order: $250.

NJCandle.com

Remeli Enterprises
567 52nd St.
West New York, NJ 07093
201–558–1800
FAX: 419–831–8748

FORM OF INFORMATION: online catalog; no print catalog
PAY: V, MC, AE, DSC
SELLS: scented and unscented candles
STORE: no walk-in location; mail-order only
ONLINE: www.NJCandle.com

Did you know that refrigerating candles before a party will cause them to burn more slowly and evenly? Do you know how to remove melted wax from a tablecloth, how to make candles light more easily, or how to prevent colored candles from fading? You will, after reading Candle Care Tips at NJCandle.com's website. NJCandle.com is a small company that likes to offer personable service to keep its customers happier. The prices alone will make your face light up, but the selection is also wonderful. If you buy candles regularly, you know they're not cheap. But log on to NJCandle.com's website and you'll be amazed. Prices here average 20% less than elsewhere, and there are additional discounts when you order in bulk.

Don't be expecting cutesy candles adorned with unicorns, sparkles, and clown characters. These are classy solid-color candles made fresh when you order them. You'll find scented and unscented pillars in many sizes, as well as jar candles, votives, and tea-lites. There are about 30 attractive scents to choose from—bayberry, eucalyptus, hazelnut coffee, magnolia, sugar cookie, and vanilla among them—and even more colors. For weddings, corporate events, or other special occasions where you want your candles coordinated to match tablecloth and centerpiece, send NJCandle.com a swatch and they'll custom-dye your candles! All candles use lead-free wicks and are scented and colored all the way through. The website has pictures, descriptions, and online shopping capability. You can tell a lot about a company by their website. While you won't find bells and whistles, fancy graphics, and super-cool sound and animation at NJCandle.com's website, you will find no-frills, you-get-what-you-see good value, and nice product selection. Here's your new candle source!

SPECIAL FACTORS: Satisfaction guaranteed; qualified wholesale customers welcome (see website or call for details).

Union Lighting

2386 Morris Avenue	**FORM OF INFORMATION:** online catalog only; no print catalog
Union, New Jersey 07083	**PAY:** check, MO, MC, V, AE, DSC
800-839-9001	**SELLS:** table and floor lamps, chandeliers, recessed, outdoor, and bathroom lighting; and dimmers, bathroom fans and accessories
FAX: 908-688-7362	**STORE:** same address; Monday and Friday 9:00 am–9:00 pm, Tuesday to Thursday, and Saturday 9:00 am–5:00 pm
	ONLINE: www.unionlighting.com

Union lighting has been providing for the lighting needs of both homeowners and professionals for over 40 years. With a home lighting inventory of over 3,000 discounted fixtures from the world's most prestigious lighting manufacturers, there's little chance Union doesn't have what you want. But you don't need me to tell you that. Just go to their website and pick through their enormous online catalog offering chandeliers, table lamps, floor lamps, wall sconces, flush mounts, recessed lighting, outdoor lighting, bathroom lighting, Nutone fans, Lutron dimmers (fancy light switches), as well as some basic home and bathroom accessories like doorbells, candleholders, and towel racks. Union provides prompt shipping, quality service, and low prices. Now I know that talking about "cheap" chandeliers is probably making some of you look nervously for the fine print that says they are made from recycled glass. Stop looking. This is the real thing. Union's chandeliers are of the finest quality coming from world renowned manufacturers such as Schonbek, Hubbardton Forge, and Nulco. So relax, these fixtures are not cheap imitations, and they really are at discount prices.

WEBSITE: Union's website provides crisp images of most of their inventory, along with brief descriptions and online ordering. Their customer service representatives are very helpful and can answer any questions you might have—they even received a 5-star rating from Yahoo! Shopping.

SPECIAL FACTORS: Returns accepted within 30 days for refund.

USA Light & Electric

P. O. Box 296
Patton, CA 92369
800–854–8794
505–891–8696
FAX: 800–851–7651
or 505–891–3389

FORM OF INFORMATION: free print catalog; online catalog

PAY: check, MO, MC, V, DSC

SELLS: track, recessed, outdoor, and commercial lighting; and lighting supplies and accessories

STORE: no walk-in location; mail-order only; phone hours Monday to Friday 8:00 am–4:30 pm PST

ONLINE: www.usalight.com

USA Light & Electric, which sounds like a utility company, is a wonderful firm geared toward high-quality goods and low prices for homes and businesses. There is a print catalog, if you request it, but the website is definitely the way to go, as the 20% discount is not offered when you order by phone or mail, nor does the print catalog have the most recent or complete inventory.

USA Light & Electric, which has been in business for 26 years and on the internet for 7, has a comprehensive selection of recessed and track lighting, outdoor and landscaping lights and lanterns, and lighting supplies. When you visit the website, you can click on one of several broad product categories: Lighting, Bulbs, Energy Saving, Generators, and Landscape Lighting. One click on Lighting zips you quickly to another section, where you can narrow your search by selecting Track and Display, Recessed, Metal Halide and High-Pressure Sodium, or Work Lights.

Besides the vast and tasteful selection of goods geared toward both homeowners and designers, the website has some other nifty features. For instance, there is an informative section with common lighting terms and definitions, some unusual layout examples, information on track lighting, articles on halogen lamps, and a warning about the aforementioned track lighting kits found at home improvement stores. There is also a free design service. For almost any layout for track, recessed, and outdoor lighting, there are lighting designers ready to help. (Send an email with a short description of your project, your phone and fax numbers, and they will get back to you usually the same day.) If you do not find what you are looking for, email the company and they will try to "point you in the right direction." I love this value-and-service-oriented firm.

SPECIAL FACTORS: Returns require an authorization number and a 20% restocking fee applies; see website for details on warranties, shipping, and returns; checks must clear before goods are shipped.

Tableware

New and estate tableware including fine and everyday china, Japanese tableware, crystal stemware and everyday glasses, silverware and stainless flatware, and hollowware; giftware, ornaments, and fine collectibles

I had a wealthy boyfriend who had very expensive tastes. Among his collection of fine china, he had a set of eight intricately decorated diamond and olive-cut crystal Waterford drinking glasses. Each glass was about $175. In the five years that I was with him, they were never used. When my mother came to visit, and the boyfriend was out, she used one of the glasses to get a drink of water. Unfortunately, she also dropped it and shattered it to pieces. I don't know if you ever saw the movie *Sleeping With the Enemy*, with Julia Roberts; but, life with my boyfriend was kind of like *Lucy Sleeping With the Enemy*. I told my mother that this would be our little secret and I swept up the glass and put its remains in a brown paper bag which I took out to the garbage and buried at the bottom. Later that evening, when the boyfriend had returned, my mother mentioned that she thought she had gotten a splinter in her toe from walking barefoot on the deck (I doubt the boyfriend had splinters in *his* deck). He got a flashlight and some tweezers to help get the splinter out. He pulled out what looked like a grain of sand and said, "This looks like a piece of crystal from one of my Waterford glasses!" My mother and I dropped our jaws in unison. We were speechless. Too bad we didn't know about the companies in this section. We would have offered to replace it if we knew we could have gotten it for half price.

Don't pay full price for fine china, stemware, and flatware—period! Every discounter in this section can save you lots—up to 50%—on active patterns of tableware. And if your wedding china is a pattern that's been discontinued, don't worry. There are firms here that have replacement pieces for your pattern at great prices, too. The same is true for silverware and crystal. Some of the companies below are also great sources of fine giftware for less. Luxuries at a discount? Why not!

Remember that many of the companies in the "Kitchen Equipment" section, page 363, also carry tableware, albeit mostly of the everyday variety. See also "Bed, Bath, and Table Textiles," page 317, for linens, cloth napkins, and table mats to complete your dining table's well-dressed look.

Find It Fast

CHINA AND OTHER DISHWARE
Barrons; Michael C. Fina; Replacements; Rogers & Rosenthal;
Rudi's Pottery, Silver & China; Silverwarehouse

CRYSTAL
Michael C. Fina, Replacements, Rogers & Rosenthal, Silverwarehouse

CUSTOM ENGRAVING
Michael C. Fina

ESTATE STERLING
Beverly Bremer Silver Shop, Replacements, The Silver Queen, Silverwarehouse

FIGURINES AND COLLECTIBLES
Replacements

FLATWARE
Barrons; Beverly Bremer Silver Shop; Michael C. Fina, Gatherings; Replacements;
Rogers & Rosenthal; Rudi's Pottery, Silver & China;
The Silver Queen; Silverwarehouse

GIFTWARE
Barrons , Gatherings

HOME ACCENTS
Barrons; Beverly Bremer Silver Shop; Michael C. Fina, Gatherings; Rogers & Rosenthal; Rudi's Pottery, Silver & China

JAPANESE TABLEWARE
Utsuwa-No-Yakata

SILVERWARE REPAIR SERVICES
Silverwarehouse

Barrons

P.O. Box 994
Novi, MI 48376-0994
800-762-7145
FAX: 800-523-4456

FORM OF INFORMATION: free print catalog; online catalog

PAY: check, MO, MC, V, AE, DSC

SELLS: tableware, giftware, and home accessories

STORE: mail-order only; phone hours Monday to Friday 8:00 am–10:00 pm, Saturday 9:00 am–9:00 pm, Sunday 11:00 am–7:00 pm EST

ONLINE: www.barronsdinnerware.com

Since 1975, Barrons has been selling steeply discounted, name-brand tableware, crystal, giftware, and home accessories for people who like the convenience of shopping at home. The color catalog leads you through sparkling and elegant glass: crystal goblets and pitchers, delicate glass stemware, holiday ornaments of cut glass and sterling, candlesticks and wall sconces, and whimsical figurines; china sets and pieces by all the greats; gift items (such as a silver-plated child's tea set, baby items, and porcelain boxes); and silverware, serving pieces, and hollowware. The prices here are about 35% less on dinnerware than normal list and 50% less for flatware. The manufacturers represented here are the leaders in their fields, including Waterford, Wedgwood, Lenox, Oneida, Spode, Fitz and Floyd, Reed & Barton, Swarovski, Lladró, Johnson Brothers, and Mikasa.

WEBSITE: You may get as carried away at the website as I did, because there are so many great deals in the Outlet Store section and fabulous items in the section called Entertaining. Although not as comprehensive as the print catalog, this site features a nice selection of products, of which many, but not all, are pictured, and is a great source for gift ideas. In addition to collectibles and tableware of every kind, the website offers home decor and holiday items. You can order online at the website.

SPECIAL FACTORS: Satisfaction guaranteed; returns accepted within 30 days for exchange, refund, or credit.

Beverly Bremer Silver Shop

3164 Peachtree Rd. NE, Dept. WBM

Atlanta, GA 30305

800-270-4009

404-261-4009

FAX: 404-261-9708

FORM OF INFORMATION: price quotes; online catalog

PAY: check, MO, MC, V, DSC

SELLS: new and estate sterling flatware, hollowware, gifts, etc.

STORE: same address; Monday to Saturday 10:00 am–5:00 pm

ONLINE: www.beverlybremer.com

Nicknamed the "Silver Belle," Beverly Bremer presides over her glistening eponymous Georgia shop that has more than 1,200 sterling flatware patterns in stock, including American, English, Italian, French, and Danish designs. Her new and nearly new sterling silver flatware is priced up to 75% off regular retail. If you're missing a piece of your pattern, chances are you'll find it here, including active, discontinued, antique, and hard-to-find patterns.

You can request, by phone or mail, an inventory of your silver patterns showing the pieces in stock. If you don't know the name of the pattern, send along a photocopy or sketch (be sure to sketch any identifying marks on the back of the handles). Ms. Bremer says that, unless noted, there are no monograms on the old silver she carries. (She doesn't sell silver on which monograms have been removed, either.) Beverly Bremer also offers a wide selection of new and antique, investment-quality hollowware, new and antique sterling gifts, and a sterling appraisal service. Here's a great place to buy a wedding gift, a romantic gift, or an instant heirloom (antique sterling pieces make good investments), and Beverly Bremer will wrap and ship it according to your specifications.

WEBSITE: The website is a fun place to visit. Here you'll learn about caring for your silver and setting a table properly for different occasions. You can also search for your pattern and see what pieces are available, or you can shop for gifts such as sterling silver Christmas ornaments, baby rattles, or berry servers. The website gives visitors a taste of what Bremer's shop has to offer and lets you order online, but if there's something specific you seek, your best bet is to call or write the firm.

SPECIAL FACTORS: Complete customer satisfaction guaranteed.

Michael C. Fina

545 Fifth Ave.
New York, NY 10017
800–BUY–FINA
718–937–8484
FAX: 718–937–7193

FORM OF INFORMATION: free print catalog; online catalog

PAY: check, MO, MC, V, AE, DSC

SELLS: jewelry, tableware, and giftware

STORE: Fifth Ave. at 45th St.; Monday to Friday 10:00 am–7:00 pm, Thursday 9:30 am–8:00 pm, Saturday 10:00 am–6:00 pm, Sunday 12:00 noon–6:00 pm

ONLINE: www.michaelcfina.com

In business since 1935, Michael C. Fina has been known locally as a great place to buy jewelry at substantial savings—10% to 50% below list. In a recent price comparison check, I found their Gorham "Fairfax" flatware was 30% less than a very well-known department store's "sale" price. Manhattanites, out-of-towners, and mail-order shoppers alike can also choose from an exhaustive roster of name-brand manufacturers of tableware and sterling flatware way too numerous to list here. If there's a particular maker of china, stemware, or flatware you seek, chances are excellent that this company stocks it. The print catalog presents a lovely selection of estate silver, giftware (such as sterling baby picture frames and rattles), dazzling stemware for every type of table setting, pages of exquisite china, stainless and sterling flatware, and much more. Most items show the list price alongside Fina's price; these luxury items are priced well below what you'd pay elsewhere. If you're soon to be wed, Michael C. Fina can maintain your bridal registry, too. The salespeople are fluent in French, Italian, Russian, and Spanish.

WEBSITE: Michael C Fina's website is designed well and is easy to navigate. The images of the merchandise are nice and clear and can be enlarged with a click to get a closer look. If you like what you see, you can add it to your shopping cart and buy it online.

SPECIAL FACTORS: Satisfaction guaranteed; returns accepted within 3 weeks for exchange, refund, or credit (except for engraved and personalized items).

Gatherings

10311 W. Hampden Ave., #A100	**FORM OF INFORMATION:** free print catalog; online catalog
Denver, CO 80227	**PAY:** check, MO, MC, V, AE, DSC
800–468–2769	**SELLS:** Oneida stainless flatware, giftware, home accents
303–215–1111	
FAX: 303–215–1115	**STORE:** no walk-in location; mail-order only
	ONLINE: www.gatheringscatalog.com

Formerly known as Kaiser Crow Gatherings, this new company does what the old one did: sells Oneida stainless flatware at prices more than 50% below suggested list price. The color catalog shows the current patterns of Oneida stainless, Oneida Golden Accents (stainless accented with 25k gold electroplate), and service pieces (butter knives, sugar spoons, gravy ladles, pie servers, etc.) in every pattern. Additionally, Gatherings sells china, giftware, seasonal home accents, collectibles, and kitchen cookware. The best deals are still on the Oneida, however.

WEBSITE: Online you can view clearance items, as well as the full inventory of merchandise. There's secure online ordering at the website.

SPECIAL FACTORS: Satisfaction guaranteed; returns accepted (see catalog or website for details).

Replacements, Ltd.

P. O. Box 26029, Dept. W7
Greensboro, NC 27420
800–737–5223
336–697–3000
FAX: 336–697–3100
TDD: 800–270–3708

FORM OF INFORMATION: price quotes and online catalog only; no print catalog

PAY: check, MC, V, DSC

SELLS: replacement china, crystal, and silver, and collectibles

STORE: Interstate 85/40, exit 132, NC; 7 days a week 9:00 am–8:00 pm EST

ONLINE: www.replacements.com

"We replace the irreplaceable," says the heading at the top of Replacement, Ltd.'s Internet home page. Imagine that your beloved Wedgwood china pattern has been discontinued. You'd be sad if it weren't for the fact that you would be able to replace that broken coffee cup and soup bowl through Replacements, Ltd. Your "new" pieces will be indistinguishable from the originals and cost a fraction of the original price. Replacements carries over 160,000 patterns of china, crystal, and silver (flatware and hollowware) from such manufacturers as Lenox, Royal Doulton, Wedgwood, Noritake, Mikasa, Spode, Oneida, International Silver, Pfaltzgraff, Gorham Silver, Towle Silver, Franciscan, and thousands more. Replacements also carries a large selection of collectibles, including plates, bells, and figurines by makers such as Hummel, Royal Doulton, Lladro, Lenox, Precious Moments, Franklin Mint, Swarovski, and others. The website is very informative and allows you to register your pattern so that Replacements can inform you when sales are happening or special pieces have come in. Online, you can also identify your pattern, read about manufacturers' histories, browse current specials, and more. Since the inventory is large and ever-changing, this company doesn't publish a print catalog. However, they're ready to answer your phone inquiries and will even fax, email, or mail you an inventory listing of your pattern. All orders are placed by phone, as there's no electronic ordering capability at the website.

SPECIAL FACTORS: 30-day, no-questions-asked returns policy; satisfaction guaranteed.

Rogers & Rosenthal, Inc.

2337 Lemoine Ave., Ste. 101
Fort Lee, NJ 07024–0212
201–346–1862
FAX: 201–947–5812

FORM OF INFORMATION: price quotes
PAY: check or MO
SELLS: tableware
STORE: no walk-in location; mail-order only

Rogers and Rosenthal, two recognizable names in the china and silver trades, have been in the business of providing customers with fine table settings at up to 60% below list price since 1930. They don't have a fancy website. They publish no highfalutin catalog. But if you know the pattern of china, flatware (stainless, silver-plate, or sterling), crystal, stemware, hollowware, or pewter you're looking for by just about any top-name manufacturer, write down the maker and style and leave the rest to Rogers & Rosenthal. Please call or write for a price quote (written requests should be accompanied by a SASE); you'll be glad you did.

Canadian readers, please note: Only special orders are shipped to Canada.

SPECIAL FACTORS: Price quotes by phone or letter with SASE; returns accepted for exchange.

Rudi's Pottery, Silver & China

182 Rt. 17 N
Paramus, NJ 07652
800-631-2526
201-265-6096
FAX: 201-265-2086

FORM OF INFORMATION: price quotes; online catalog

PAY: check, MO, MC, V, AE, DSC

SELLS: tableware, cookware, linens, and luggage

STORE: same address and 357 Rt. 9 S., Manalapan, NJ; Monday to Saturday 10:00 am–5:30 pm, Tuesdays and Thursdays 10:00 am–9:00 pm

ONLINE: www.rudispottery.com

Rudi's Pottery, Silver & China has been family-owned and -operated for over 40 years. That means they've been selling the best names in china, crystal and flatware, at savings from 30% to 50% off list prices, for three generations. You can log onto their website and search the 28,000 plus items by department, manufacturer, or keyword. Rudi's tableware brands include Lenox, Dansk, Vera Wang, Noritake, Waterford, Spode, Wedgewood, and more. Although tableware has been Rudi's mainstay since 1968, they carry limited-edition Christmas ornaments and collectibles. They also carry cookware by All-Clad, 800 thread count luxury linens, and luggage by Atlantic, Boyt, Delsey, Pathfinder, and TravelPro.

Even if you don't have internet access, when you find any pattern of stemware, for example, that you fancy, call Rudi's for a price quote. It is likely that they can get it to you for less. The nice people at Rudi's tell us this happens "all the time, every day!" So don't be shy about calling; you may be pleasantly surprised at the quoted price. You can also write Rudi's for a price quote, but please enclose a SASE when you do.

SPECIAL FACTORS: Prices quoted by phone or letter (include SASE); flat shipping rate of $6 for any order under $50.

The Silver Queen Inc.

1350 W. Bay Dr.
Largo, FL 33770
800–262–3134
727–581–6827
FAX: 727–586–0822

FORM OF INFORMATION: free print catalog; online catalog

PAY: check, MO, MC, V, AE, DSC

SELLS: estate silver flatware, new flatware, china, crystal, and gifts

STORE: same address; Monday to Friday 8:30 am–5:30 pm, Saturday 9:00 am–5:00 pm

ONLINE: www.silverqueen.com

Since 1973, The Silver Queen has specialized in estate sterling flatware. With over 6,000 patterns in stock, they have one of the largest inventories of active and discontinued patterns in the U.S. They obtain their flatware from estate collections and jewelry buyouts, and then pass the savings on to you. In the catalog, the estate patterns' prices listed next to the new versions prove that if you're willing to buy "like-new" flatware, rather than brand-new, you'll save 25% or more on perfectly restored estate silverware. If there's a pattern you're interested in, you can also call to get the latest computerized list of prices and availability. The Silver Queen's 60-page color catalog offers new and estate sterling silverware, stainless flatware, silverplated flatware, hollowware, baby gifts, new china and crystal, and Christmas ornaments, many of these priced below normal retail by about 35% to 50%.

WEBSITE: I found the website to be a little too busy and cluttered and hard to navigate. That aside, once you are there you can register online if you're a bride-to-be; take a crystal, china, flatware, or hollowware "tour" to see what's currently in stock; check out baby gifts; view current sale items; sell your silver online; email for a list of your own china pattern pieces in stock; read interesting articles on topics including silver care, household hints, and information on china; and even announce your engagement on the site. They have secure online ordering as well.

SPECIAL FACTORS: Orders can be placed by phone, online, mail, or in person; authorized returns accepted within 10 days of receipt.

Silverwarehouse

4311 NE Vivion Rd.,
3rd Floor

Kansas City, MO 64119–2890

816–454–1990

FAX: 816–454–1605

FORM OF INFORMATION: online catalog only; no print catalog

PAY: check, MO,MC, V, DSC

SELLS: silver, stainless, and silverplate flatware; china, crystal, holloware, etc.

STORE: same address; Monday to Saturday 10:00 am–6:00 pm closed Wednesdays and Sundays

ONLINE: www.silverwarehouse.com

   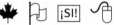

Silverwarehouse, founded in 1970, has the largest selection of silverware worldwide, offers active and discontinued patterns, and is a full-service company for sterling silver flatware, silverplate, stainless, Dirilyte flatware and hollowware, pewter, crystal, and china. The website reminds shoppers that Silverwarehouse also buys, sells, and repairs silverware and hollowware, offering professional knife reblading and garbage-disposal damage repair. Here you can also get free pattern identification and free pattern search to supplement those missing spoons. A bridal registry is maintained, and a no-interest layaway is available. The attractive website allows you to order online or view the inventory—which includes lots of tableware, flatware, china, and stemware in addition to books on silver care, polish, storage chests and cloths. The Silverwarehouse site permits a search/order of china and an identification and match of silverware patterns, both current and discontinued. The same information can be obtained by sending a SASE for a price quote form.

SPECIAL FACTORS: Returns with authorization accepted within 15 days for full refund, less shipping charges, providing flatware is in original sealed bags and has not been opened.

Utsuwa-No-Yakata

Tajimi USA Inc.
Attn: MOD
240 South Main St., Ste. K
South Hackensack, NJ 07606
800–269–5099
FAX: 800–281–2136

FORM OF INFORMATION: free print catalog; online catalog

PAY: check, MO, MC, V, AE

SELLS: Japanese tableware

STORE: stores located in CA, IL, NY, NJ, WA, Canada and London, see website for addresses and hours; phone hours Monday to Friday 10:00 am–6:00 pm EST

ONLINE: www.utsuwa.com

There's a small family-owned Japanese restaurant in the town I live in that I love eating at. I love everything about it. The food, of course, the small soup bowls and ceramic soup spoons, the delicate tea cups, the plates, the little dishes for the soy sauce and wasabi. On more than one occasion, I have ordered sushi there and have had the waitress stop me during my order to tell me that was enough, I was ordering too much.

I was very happy to discover Utsuwa-No-Yakata, North America's largest Japanese tableware chain. They sell beautiful tableware directly from Japan that is great for any type of cuisine. Here you'll find tea sets, sake sets, bento boxes, sushi items, bowls, plates, small dish sets and many more. They also have a wedding gift section where you'll find tea sets, bowl sets, and wedding dolls sets for $18 to $25. Prices are as much as 50% off retail. You can order online securely by adding items to a shopping cart, plus they give you the option of filling out an order form online and submitting—but I only recommend the online shopping cart.

SPECIAL FACTORS: Returns within 14 days; please make sure to pack returned items well so they do not break during transit; if they receive your item broken, or not in a condition to re-sell it, you will be issued a percentage of the refund; no refunds for any of the shipping fees; orders $100 or less the shipping fee is $10; orders over $100.01, the shipping fee is 10% of the subtotal

Wall and Window Treatments, Decorator Fabrics

Wallpaper, wall stencils, curtains, shades, blinds, and window accessories; upholstery, drapery, and other interior-decorating fabric

Companies that specialize in window treatments, such as shades and blinds, also often carry wallpaper. And companies that specialize in wallpaper often carry decorator fabric. Well, it makes sense if you think about it. If you want to pull a room together, what better way than to coordinate your curtains or shades with your wallpaper and upholstery? So here they are together: wall and window treatments and decorator fabric. The firms in this section carry all the fabrics and materials you'll need to create window ruffles, throw pillows, fabric room dividers, and coordinated upholstery. There's also every kind of shade and blind, as well as the hardware you'll need. And if you have the energy for hanging wallpaper or stenciling a border around your room, you'll find these here, too. The companies listed below can save you as much as 80%.

Find It Fast

CURTAINS AND TOPPERS
American Blind and Wallpaper Factory, Homespun 10-Foot-Wide Fabrics and Draperies

DECORATOR FABRICS AND TRIM
Hancock's of Paducah, Homespun 10-Foot-Wide Fabrics & Draperies, Marlene's Decorator Fabrics, Silk Surplus

DECORATOR STENCILS
Stencil House of N.H.

NATURAL FIBER AND GRASS GOODS
American Blind and Wallpaper Factory

WALL COVERINGS AND RELATED SUPPLIES
American Blind and Wallpaper Factory

WINDOW TREATMENTS AND HARDWARE
American Blind and Wallpaper Factory, Homespun 10-Foot-Wide Fabrics & Draperies

American Blind and Wallpaper Factory

909 N. Sheldon Rd.
Plymouth, MI 48170
800-575-8016
FAX: 800-575-2558

FORM OF INFORMATION: $2 print catalog for wallpaper; free print catalog for blinds; online catalog

PAY: check, MO, MC, V, AE, DSC, DC

SELLS: wallpaper, shades, blinds, rugs, home accents, paint, curtains and toppers, lighting fixtures, and custom framed art

SHOWROOM: same address; Monday, Wednesday, and Friday 10:00 am–7:00 pm, Thursday 10:00 am–9:00 pm, Saturday 9:00 am–6:00 pm, Sunday 11:00 am–5:00 pm; also 6615 19½ Mile Rd., Sterling Heights, MI

ONLINE: www.decoratetoday.com

American Blind and Wallpaper Factory claims to have the largest selection of national brand special-order blinds and wallpaper in the U.S. Their inventory includes paints (over 1800 colors), area rugs, lighting fixtures, curtains and toppers, home accents and wall art. You can save from 25% to 85% by buying here.

This company offers products from top national brand manufacturers and has access to wallpaper patterns from over 5,000 special-order wallpaper books. You can browse the wallpaper catalog ($2), which features hundreds of the most popular patterns, or log on to the website (which is much more extensive) to view thousands of patterns. If you need a closer look at a pattern, they'll send you a sample for $5. The free American Blind Sample Kit, which you can request, includes samples of the most popular styles of mini-, micro-, pleated, cellular, vertical, and wood blinds, as well as directions for mounting and measuring. The kit is a great way for you to touch and see the actual materials and colors you'll be dealing with. With either blinds or wallpaper, if you shop your local decorating store and write down the brand, color, and pattern number, a quick call or email to the company will get you an express quote. American Blind and Wallpaper guarantees the lowest prices anywhere, and offers a free lifetime guarantee against product defects.

WEBSITE: This is a nice website. There's lots of consumer-friendly information here about how to shop and measure for blinds, wallpaper, and paint, plus there's a good selection of area rugs, home accents, lighting fixtures, curtains and toppers, and custom-framed art. This is a great way to decorate your home or office. Sit back, relax, and start mixing and matching items you like by sending them to your own online scrapbook. Once you choose wallpaper, blinds, or paint that you like, you can use an easy form that calculates square footage for you based on the dimensions of the area you're decorating. Other items, such as area rugs and lamps, can be sent to your scrapbook (which will keep everything you send to it for 90 days). Scrapbook items are organized in neat rows with a photo and unit price for each product. If you're not sure what you want and need guidance, there's even a "Personal Shopper" service that hooks you up with a rep who will contact you by phone and guide you through the process. You can order electronically at the website using a nice step-by-step procedure that verifies your measurements, color choices, and other specifications each step of the way.

SPECIAL FACTORS: Satisfaction guaranteed; free shipping in the continental U.S.

Hancock's of Paducah

**3841 Hinkleville Rd.,
Dept. WBM–01**

Paducah, KY 42001

800–845–8723

270–443–4410

FAX: 270–442–2164

or 270–442–3152

FORM OF INFORMATION: free print catalog;
online catalog

PAY: check, MO, MC, V, DSC

SELLS: home-decorating fabrics, quilting
fabrics, pillow forms, quilting supplies, etc.

STORE: same address; Monday to Friday
9:30 am–5:30 pm, Saturday 10:00 am–
5:00 pm, closed Sunday

ONLINE: www.hancocks-paducah.com

Down in Paducah, Kentucky, is "America's largest quilting and home-decorating store," Hancock's of Paducah. For over 3 decades, this company has operated a brisk mail-order business serving 2 primary markets—home decorators and quilters—by offering goods priced 50% lower than anywhere else. Some other nice features include a custom-laminating service (great for patio furniture, tablecloths, place mats, rain gear, and more) and an inexpensive sample service.

The full-color, 64-page "Fabrics for the Home" catalog features hundreds of fabrics for bedding ensembles, window treatments, upholstery, and decorative pillows, along with accessory items, such as cords, tassels, fringes, and drapery hardware. The catalog for quilters has thousands of fabrics appropriate for quilting, along with tools, notions, and other supplies that are often hard to find, especially in less-populated areas.

WEBSITE: Both quilters and decorators would be well served to check out Hancock of Paducah's website, where you can view fabric samples, check out specials, and order online. If you order through the website, incidentally, shipping is free.

SPECIAL FACTORS: Free shipping within continental U.S. when you order online; satisfaction guaranteed; see catalog or website for returns policy.

Homespun 10-Foot-Wide Fabrics & Draperies

P.O. Box 4315-WBM
Thousand Oaks, CA 91359
888–543–2998
FAX: 206–338–2576

FORM OF INFORMATION: $2 planning kit and fabric samples; online catalog

PAY: check, MO, MC, V, AE, DSC

SELLS: 10-foot-wide fabrics, custom-made draperies, etc.

STORE: no walk-in location; mail-order only

ONLINE: www.homespunfabrics.com

Homespun 10-Foot-Wide Fabrics & Draperies has a solution to some of the biggest drapery headaches—bulkiness, sun rot, the expense of dry cleaning, and the hassle of pleater hooks among them. Homespun Fabrics sells all-cotton material that's 10′ wide, or about 105" to 109" after shrinkage. The fabric includes homespun, hobnail, barley, and monkscloth weaves, in white and natural. The width makes the fabric perfect for "seamless draperies," and even eliminates some of the finishing work. Homespun Fabrics manufactures all styles of draperies (suitable to the fabric) and can also custom-make "Fan Pleat" draperies. These operate on a track system that's hung from the ceiling or mounted on the wall, with a buckram header tape with nylon tabs that engage the track. The drapery folds are 4" or 5" deep, so the stackback (the area covered by the curtain when it's drawn back) that would be 37" deep with conventional pinch-pleat draperies is only 11" deep with the Fan Pleat system. Made in Homespun Fabrics' heavyweight cottons, this system produces handsome, neutral window coverings that give you maximum glass exposure. They have a crisp, tailored appearance that's ideal for modern decor and office settings, and are machine washable and dryable and guaranteed against sun rot for 7 years. An added bonus: The fabric can be tolerated by people with chemical sensitivities.

Besides draperies, Homespun also works great for slipcovers, wall upholstery, tablecloths, bedcovers and throws, napkins, bedskirts, and more, not to mention the hardware for accessorizing your drapes (fanwood poles and decorative ends of all kinds). The fabrics lend themselves nicely to labor-saving and attractive wall coverings that hide ugly plaster and old wallpaper. In addition to the heavy cottons, Homespun Fabrics offers open-weave casement fabric, wide muslin, wide prewashed canvas in white or natural, and ultra-wide semi-sheers and lace—batiste, voile, and bouclé slub—in lots of colors. Homespun can create the draperies, or you can do it yourself. You'll find helpful books on home decorating and guides to making fan pleat draperies, slipcovers, bedspreads, table linens, and accessories.

WEBSITE: Homespun's website is very informative. Here you will find out about the advantages and uses for wide fabrics, plus learn a thing or two about how to best go about decorating or redecorating your home. Fabric samples and the planning kit can be ordered online.

SPECIAL FACTORS: Returns are accepted within 10 days for exchange, refund, or credit.

Marlene's Decorator Fabrics

301 Beech St., Dept. 7B
Hackensack, NJ 07601
201-843-0844

FORM OF INFORMATION: free flyer with SASE
PAY: check, MO, MC, V, AE
SELLS: decorator fabrics
STORE: mail-order only; phone hours Monday to Friday 9:30 am–6:00 pm EST

The brochure from Marlene's is about as straightforward as one could be. It lists the manufacturer names of first-quality fabrics and trims with which Marlene's deals. If the decorator fabric you seek is on that list, you're in luck, because this company can get it to you at 35% to 50% off retail prices as long as you can meet the minimum yardage requirement (5-yard minimum on some, 15-yard minimum on others). Write or call for a price quote, or send a SASE with a sample if you're not sure of the manufacturer name or pattern number, or to request a brochure. Specify the yardage needed and whether you're interested in upholstery, drapery, or other decorator fabrics.

SPECIAL FACTORS: Minimum orders apply; no returns unless damaged by UPS or manufacturer.

Silk Surplus

1127 2nd Ave
Manhattan, NY 10027
212–753–6511

FORM OF INFORMATION: price quotes

PAY: check, MO, MC, V, AE

SELLS: discontinued decorator fabric and trim

STORE: same address; Monday to Friday 10:00 am–6:00 pm, Saturday 10:00 am–5:30 pm

All good things—even decorator fabrics—come to an end. Luckily, there's Silk Surplus to rescue discontinued Scalamandré and Boris Kroll fabric as well as silks, cottons, velvets, woolens, chintzes, brocades, damasks, and other weaves, at savings up to 75%. Since 1962, Silk Surplus has welcomed walk-in shoppers to its store. Since there's no catalog, mail-order customers must know in advance the exact discontinued Scalamandré or Boris Kroll fabric and color they want. Serious mail-order buyers can query by mail and enclose fabric samples. Design professionals should inquire about additional trade discounts.

SPECIAL FACTORS: Price quotes by phone or letter (with SASE); free sample cuttings; all sales final; minimum order: 3 yards.

Stencil House of N.H., Inc.

P.O. Box 109, Dept. WBM
Hooksett, NH 03106
800–622–9416
603–625–1716

FORM OF INFORMATION: $4.50 print cata-
log, refundable
PAY: check, MO, MC, V
SELLS: decorator stencils
STORE: no walk-in location; mail-order only

Jan Gordon's husband is afraid to turn his back on his wife, president of Stencil House of
N.H. "If I see a plain surface, I want to stencil it," she says. The 20-page color catalog
from Stencil House offers a dazzling array of decorator-quality stencil designs at craft-
store prices. While common craft stencils are one-piece designs, Stencil House's designs
are multilayered to allow for two or more colors. The current catalog has over 250 different designs appropriate for walls, floors, stair risers, fireboards, wooden furniture, fabric,
and more. New designs are added each year. The stencils come precut or "uncut"; you can
save an average of $2 to $3 on each by cutting out the designs yourself. Most of the stencils are under $10, and all are one-of-a-kind items designed by Gordon, although the
starred items in the catalog are modeled after authentic stencil designs found in museums
and old homesteads. There are quaint country motifs, such as a bird with birdhouse and a
laundry line; Shaker-inspired designs; Pennsylvania-Dutch stylized vines, flowerpots,
hearts, birds, and flowers; and themes for children. Stencil House can also custom-design
stencils to go with your wallpaper and fabric. If you send in a fabric sample, they'll help
you match the paint color and give other color and design advice for free.

Stencil House, "your one-stop shop for home-decorating stencils," sells various stencil supplies, including acrylic and oil-based paints (2 different paint charts are offered),
stencil brushes, brush cleaner, floor cloth, and unprinted Mylar sheets (for making your
own stencils). Stencil House has a "frequent stenciler's plan"—when you've ordered 5
stencils (no time limit), you get 1 stencil for free. See catalog for details.

Wholesale customers: Please inquire about wholesale prices and policies

SPECIAL FACTORS: Custom designs and sizes available; no returns on custom orders.

Luggage

Luggage, briefcases, attaché cases, computer bags, and backpacks, etc.

I had a boyfriend once who left me for a much younger woman. The ink from the messages written by her classmates on her high school yearbook hadn't dried yet. Did I mention he was about 26 years her senior? When I found out that he was having an affair with her, I packed all of my clothes, two cooking pots (extra ones he didn't use), one coffee maker (an extra one), and some bedding (extra) and left one night when he was out. I didn't have much in the way of luggage to pack my things except for one black, nylon, soft, zip-up suitcase that he had purchased for me a few years earlier. I had to put most of my clothes in plastic garbage bags. I didn't tell him that I was leaving. I just left to go live with my sister (in the same town). I didn't hear from him until two weeks had passed and I heard a knock on the door. I opened the door and there he was. I was able to squeak out a weak "Hello," as my heart pounded in my chest. He then asked me if his new girlfriend could borrow the black suitcase he had given me because they were going on a trip to Hawaii and she didn't have a suitcase. I walked over to the closet and picked up the empty suitcase and threw it at him and said, "She can have it." I think, to this day, he still doesn't understand why I was so "rude." Perhaps if he had known about some of the companies in this chapter he could have bought his new girlfriend some of her very own brand-new luggage.

The luggage discounters here can deliver big savings on everything from suitcases, attaché cases, and rolling garment bags to smaller items, such as travel kits, fashion handbags, cosmetics cases, and backpacks. I have compared the prices of luggage sold from the companies listed in this chapter to the very same make and model sold in major department stores and have found the stores here to be about 50% less on the average. And, in many cases, the items sold from the vendors listed here are much less at their regular price than a department store's "sale price" of the same luggage. Don't buy your luggage at a department store!

Find It Fast

ATTACHÉ CASES
BaggageForLess.com, eBags, LuggageBase.com, Luggage Online

BACKPACKS
BaggageForLess.com, eBags, LuggageBase.com, Luggage Online

BIKE BAGS
BaggageForLess.com, eBags, LuggageBase.com, Luggage Online

BRIEFCASES
BaggageForLess.com, eBags, LuggageBase.com, Luggage Online

FACTORY AUTHORIZED REPAIRS
BaggageForLess.com

LUGGAGE
BaggageForLess.com, eBags, LuggageBase.com, Luggage Online

HANDBAGS
BaggageForLess.com, eBags, LuggageBase.com, Luggage Online

PORTFOLIOS
Luggage Online

WALLETS
eBags, LuggageBase.com, Luggage Online

BaggageForLess.com

6688 Perimeter Loop
Dublin, OH 43017
877–422–4243
FAX: 614–761–9556

FORM OF INFORMATION: free print catalog; online catalog

PAY: check, MO, MC, V, AE

SELLS: luggage, briefcases, backpacks, and bike bags

STORE: no walk-in location; mail-order only

ONLINE: www.baggageforless.com

BaggageForLess.com has guaranteed low prices on name-brand luggage. If you find a lower advertised price on any product they sell, they'll offer you a lower price and a free travel gift (digital alarm clock, neck rest, or neon padlock, for example). What they really pride themselves in, is—not their low prices—but their "genuine personal service," the kind you get in neighborhood stores where you're a regular customer. And to get you to be *their* regular customer, they offer extras like free monograms (up to 12 letters) embroidered on your luggage. (That will certainly make it much easier to find which black, carry-on, wheeled, suitcase is yours next time you're at the baggage claim area.) They also offer free travel gifts on purchases that total over $150. The travel gifts may include a Fisher space pen, an international adapter, a money belt, a combination padlock, or an alarm clock. Kids can embroider their bags with their name and an image to choose from such as horses, dinosaurs, pandas, ladybugs, motorcycles, fairies, mermaids, skateboarders, and more.

BaggageForLess.com carries all the top-brands including Atlantic, American Tourister, Briggs & Riley, Ricardo, Samsonite, and Swiss Army. Shipping charges are a flat charge of $5 for ground shipping on orders up to $75. And, for a limited time, at this writing, ground shipping is free for orders over $75.

WEBSITE: You won't need the print catalog if you just log on to their website where they have their full inventory and online ordering is available.

SPECIAL FACTORS: Returns accepted; customer is responsible for return shipping charges; if order was part of the free shipping program customer will be credited for the cost of the order less the actual shipping charges; free gifts must be returned with your returned merchandise.

eBags

6060 Greenwood Plaza Blvd.
Greenwood Village, CO 80111
800–820–6126

FORM OF INFORMATION: free print catalog; online catalog

PAY: MC, V, AE, DC

SELLS: luggage, handbags, business cases, backpacks, and wallets

STORE: same address; Monday to Saturday 10:00 am–8:00 pm, Sunday 12:00 noon–6:00 pm

ONLINE: www.ebags.com

With over 180 name-brands and 8,000 products to choose from, eBags is one of the largest online retailers of luggage, business cases, handbags, backpacks, sports and duffel bags, urban bags, and wallets. They carry a complete line of premium and popular brands including Samsonite, JanSport, The North Edge, Eagle Creek, and Liz Claiborne, to name a few.

WEBSITE: In the Urban Gear section on the website you'll find funky, colorful, stylish slings, shoulder packs, waist packs, and messenger bags (those are the bags that strap over one shoulder that every other person in New York city wears). In the Kids and Parents section you can get a stuffed Curious George purse or a stuffed lamb backpack. The luggage inventory is large and when you click on a product, in addition to a color photo and description, on many items there is a consumer product rating for appearance, organization, price/value, and overall rating. They even include customer testimonials. Jump into the Outlet section to find sales and closeouts at 20% to 70% off on brands such as Atlantic, Samsonite, American Tourists, Skyway, and Ricardo.

SPECIAL FACTORS: Satisfaction unconditionally guaranteed; returns of any unused merchandise accepted within 30 days of receipt; your credit card will be credited for the price of the bag and any taxes, excluding shipping costs; eBags will coordinate and pay the return freight charges, but will deduct a restocking fee of $5.00 per item; if the return is due to a manufacturing defect or eBags shipping error, the initial shipping will be credited and the restocking fee will not be charged.

LuggageBase.com

670 S. Frontage Rd.
Nipomo, CA 93444
888-832-1201
FAX: 805-929-8192

FORM OF INFORMATION: online catalog only; no print catalog

PAY: check, MO, MC, V, AE, DSC

SELLS: luggage and travel accessories, business cases

STORE: same address; Monday to Friday 8:00 am–5:00 pm, Saturday 10:00 am–4:00 pm; also San Luis Luggage, 1135 Chorro St., San Luis Obispo, CA

ONLINE: www.luggagebase.com

LuggageBase.com offers first-quality travel and business bags and cases at up to 60% off suggested retail prices. Don't buy cheap luggage at that mega discount store in the mall if you want your luggage to last more than a year. For the same price, you'll be able to buy better quality items at LuggageBase for less. If you have internet access, log onto the website, where you can click on a major brand name and view pictures and descriptions of the full line of offerings. Some prices aren't listed on the website, so you still have to call LuggageBase's toll-free number for a price quote. When I did this, I discovered that LuggageBase's price was 30% less than that of a major department store's "sale" price. There are some truly amazing sale items on the website for those looking to buy an entire set of brand-new luggage from last year's stock, and other incentives such as free shipping on certain lines. There are also some nifty features such as the "durability scale"—a rating from 1 to 10 assigned to each piece sold here to let you know specifics about the materials, structure and design, warranties, and damage and repair records for that line, if known. What's good about this company is that they've been around the block a few times and are endorsed by the Better Business Bureau and other consumer organizations. If you don't have web access, you can still call LuggageBase if you've seen a bag you're considering buying. Provide them with the maker's name and model number so they can quote you a price.

SPECIAL FACTORS: Satisfaction guaranteed; returns accepted within 30 days for exchange, refund, or credit.

Luggage Online

5 Rock Hill Rd., Bldg. #1
Cherry Hill, NJ 08003
888–958–4424
FAX: 877–478–4462

FORM OF INFORMATION: online catalog only; no print catalog

PAY: check, MO, MC, V, AE, DSC

SELLS: luggage, briefcases, backpacks, travel and business accessories

STORE: no walk-in location: mail-order only; phone hours Monday to Friday 9:00 am–9:00 pm, Saturday and Sunday 12:00 noon–6:00 pm EST

ONLINE: www.luggageonline.com

When I was a young gal, just starting out in the printing industry, I was in a business meeting with the higher-ups of a large printing company when the owner of the company stopped the meeting and looked at the paper-stock accordion file I was using as a briefcase and announced to the group that he would like to buy me a briefcase as a welcome gift. Gee, ahhh, thanks. If only I had know about Luggage Online, the internet division of a well-established luggage enterprise founded in 1927, which specializes in high quality brand-name luggage and business accessories for all requirements and budgets. They offer name-brand luggage, briefcases, and portfolios with a low price guarantee. If you see your luggage selling elsewhere for less, contact them within 30 days of your purchase and they'll refund you the amount you paid over the lowest price (internet advertised prices only). Some of the many brands they carry include American Tourister, Atlantic, Briggs & Riley, Ricardo, Samsonite, Victorinox, Tumi, and Wally Bags. They also have a backpack section which includes a wide selection of wheeled backpacks, book bags, messenger bags, and daypacks. In the business and travel accessories category you will find cosmetic cases, toiletry kits, travel wallets, waist packs, leather portfolios, writing pads, and more. Check out the Best Buy section to get an additional 30% to 60% savings off their already low prices.

SPECIAL FACTORS: Authorized returns within 10 days of receipt; 10% restocking fee; free ground shipping on orders over $125.

Music, Audio, and Video

Music, instructional, and entertainment recordings of all types

I used to think that before anyone went out on a date with someone else, they should both be able to agree on three books, three movies, and three albums that they both like. If you can't agree on any, then just walk away. I made an exception to my own rule and dated a man who only liked one music album that I liked. It was "Blonde on Blonde" by Bob Dylan. The relationship eventually failed miserably and I realized that one music album in common just wasn't enough to sustain a relationship. But, I'm pretty sure three albums (and three movies and three books) are.

The companies in this section sell music of all types, in all forms—from old-fashioned vinyl LPs to high-tech DVDs. Music never gets old. If you're willing to buy used CDs, for example, or last year's titles, you can build an enormous music library for yourself for up to 80% less than the cost of buying everything brand-new and hot off the press. You'll also find music, movie, stand-up comedy, and educational videos in every conceivable category, including vintage, alternative, documentary, self-help, and many hard-to-find selections.

For books on cassette, see the "Books, Audiobooks, and Periodicals" chapter. And don't forget that many of the other companies in this book sell videos—on animal training, cooking, exercise, art and craft technique, and much more.

Find It Fast

AUDIOCASSETTES
Berkshire Record Outlet

EDUCATIONAL AND INSTRUCTIONAL VIDEOS
Homespun Tapes, Video Learning Library

LPs
Berkshire Record Outlet, Harvard Square Records,
Record-Rama

MUSIC CDs
Berkshire Record Outlet, Mymusic.com

MUSIC DVDs
Berkshire Record Outlet

MUSIC VIDEOS
Berkshire Record Outlet

RENTABLE HOW-TO VIDEOS
Video Learning Library

USED OR VINTAGE CDs, LPs, AND AUDIOCASSETTES
Berkshire Record Outlet, Harvard Square Records,
Record-Rama Sound Archives

Berkshire Record Outlet

R.R. 1, Rte. 102 Pleasant St.
Lee, MA 01238–9804
413–243–4080
800–992–1200
FAX: 413–243–4340

FORM OF INFORMATION: $2 or $5 print catalog (see text); online catalog

PAY: check, MO, MC, V

SELLS: classical recordings on LPs, CDs, cassettes, music videos, and video discs

STORE: same address; Saturday 10:00 am–5:00 pm

ONLINE: www.berkshirerecordoutlet.com

Berkshire has been selling classical music since 1974, long before online shopping became a reality. Whether you're someone who still has a mint-condition turntable and collector-quality LPs, or own a state-of-the-art CD player, Berkshire has classical recordings in your preferred form, including audiocassettes. While you can pay $2 in cash (make it $5 if you enclose a check instead) to receive a hard copy of Berkshire's big print catalog, viewing the 14,000-plus titles is probably easier and more fun by accessing the up-to-date catalog online, which is free.

WEBSITE: Online there's a powerful catalog-search engine that lets you browse CDs, LPs, audiocassettes, video discs, music videos, DVDs or CD-ROMs by label, composer, title, or even part of a title. Prices start as low as $1.99. Every conceivable classical label is here, from Abbey to Xenophone. Berkshire also has a selection of sound tracks, books about classical music, videotapes, and folk and ethnic music titles.

SPECIAL FACTORS: Minimum order, including shipping: $15.

Harvard Square Records, Inc.

P.O. Box 381925-WH
Cambridge, MA 02238
877–465–7669
617–868–3385
FAX: 617–876–4364

FORM OF INFORMATION: online catalog
PAY: check, MO, MC, V, AE, DSC
SELLS: out-of-print LPs
STORE: no walk-in location; mail-order only
ONLINE: www.LPnow.com

LPNow.com, which is run by Harvard Square Records, Inc., in business since 1985, has 50,000 titles of rare and out-of-print vinyl LPs at their website. Called cut-outs, the record-industry version of remainders, these discontinued records are categorized under Jazz and Easy Listening, Gospel, Children's Music, R&B and Dance, Blues, Rock, Country, World and Traditional, Spoken Word, Sound Effects, Soundtracks, Classical, and others. Prices range from $5 to $20, depending on the title and whether it's an import. The website, where you can order online, has an Audiophile category of higher-priced out-of-print LP titles that are hard to find elsewhere. (Don't you wish you had saved your Rolling Stones "Sticky Fingers" album with the zipper? Now it's worth a fortune!) Stock in all categories moves quickly, so if you see what you want, order promptly, as items cannot be put on hold. If your title is sold out when you order, your credit card will not be charged.

SPECIAL FACTORS: Returns (defective, unplayable goods) accepted within 14 days for replacement or merchandise credit.

Homespun Tapes

Box 340, Dept. WH
Woodstock, NY 12498
800-338-2737
845-246-2550
FAX: 845-246-5282

FORM OF INFORMATION: free print catalog; online catalog

PAY: check, MO, MC, V, DSC

SELLS: music instruction videos, DVDs, CDs, books, and miscellaneous recording and music supplies

STORE: no walk-in location; mail-order only

ONLINE: www.homespuntapes.com

If the best way to learn is by doing, then pick up that banjo, flute, or dulcimer collecting dust in your attic and start playing. Have no fear, because Homespun Tapes, founded in 1967 by Jane and Happy Traum (the latter of the folk/blues duo Happy and Artie Traum), will guide you through the learning or mastering process with their unique instructional music tapes. If you've been wanting to take lessons but have been too busy or broke, these tapes will restore your confidence and save you money at the same time.

Homespun's 72-page print catalog features instructional videotapes, DVDs, and CDs by the very best musicians in their fields. You can learn guitar from Keb' Mo', jazz piano from Donald Fagen of Steely Dan, singing techniques from Maria Muldaur, fingerpicking and flatpicking from Doc Watson, banjo from Pete Seeger, Appalachian dulcimer from Lorraine Lee, and on and on. There are instructional tapes for children and tapes for musicians at all levels of expertise. The tapes are created with close-ups and split-screen imaging techniques, 3-camera systems, good studios, and top camera operators to present the clearest possible angles. There are about 350 titles in the current catalog, spanning accordions to whistling, averaging in price from about $15 to $40. Homespun Tapes also has a small selection of musician supplies, such as study recorders, Keith tuners, and slides and strings, as well as scores of books. But the real bargain here is the time and money you'll save by taking lessons from a pro right in your own home.

WEBSITE: Homespun's website features new releases, important updates, in-depth listings of all the lessons, and online ordering, so check it out. You can custom design your search by artist, instrument, music style, and level. You can also download tabs from selected lessons or listen to a sample of a particular lesson of interest.

SPECIAL FACTORS: Overseas customers can wire money directly into Homespun's bank account or pay by credit card or in U.S. funds; returns accepted, but see catalog for more details; wholesale orders available (call 800–554–0626); most videos available in PAL (European) format.

Mymusic.com

499 Terry Fox Dr., Unit 85
Kanata, Ontario K2T 1H7
Canada
800–465–7905
613–271–9494
FAX: 613–599–8323

FORM OF INFORMATION: online catalog only; no print catalog
PAY: MC, V, AE
SELLS: CDs
STORE: no walk-in location; mail-order only
ONLINE: www.mymusic.com

Mymusic.com has grown out of a company that's been around for ten years with two warehouses, hundreds of thousands of titles and a huge storehouse of music knowledge. There are many sites that sell music, but Mymusic.com wants to cater to your own musical interests in a different and personalized way. In addition to over 270,000 titles in categories such as Rock, R&B, Country, Rap, Jazz, International, and Blues to pick from, you'll find reviews by the knowledgeable music staff and musical bios to give you an idea of the variety of interests that are offered here. Check out the staff's and various musical artists' list of the only five albums they would take with them if they were stuck on a deserted island. You can list your five choices as well. Their top 200 CDs are always just $9.90 and CDs in the Bargain Bin start at $5.99. Song samples are available to listen to online for most CDs and if you're still not sure what CD to get, you can read the quotes and star ratings from reviews by such magazines as *Rolling Stone, Spin, Mojo, Entertainment Weekly,* and more. This is a great site that I highly recommend.

SPECIAL FACTORS: Authorized returns or exchanges within 45 days of receipt.

Record-Rama Sound Archives

1130 Perry Hwy.
Pines Plaza Shopping Center
Pittsburgh, PA 15237–2132
412–367–7330
FAX: 412–367–7388

FORM OF INFORMATION: price quotes; online catalog

PAY: check, MO, MC, V, AE, DSC

SELLS: vintage 45s, LPs, and CDs; phonograph needles and deejay supplies

STORE: same address; Monday to Saturday 10:00 am–6:00 pm

ONLINE: www.recordrama.com

When word reached the Library of Congress that a retired paper goods salesman was claiming to have the country's largest known collection of 45s, a curator was sent over to check it out. Sure enough: Record-Rama Sound Archives holds the record with 1.5 million oldies on 45s, plus a million LPs. Paul C. Mawhinney's collection began with his youthful purchase of Frankie Lane's "Jezebel," and an obsession was born.

Mr. Mawhinney isn't sitting on this national treasure; he has created *MusicMaster: The 45 RPM Singles Directory,* the ultimate reference on 45s produced from 1948 to the present. The *MusicMaster,* organized by artist and title, is now the most-used reference in the New York Public Library, and is a must-have for any library or serious collector. Record-Rama offers the MusicMaster Database and other directories—the CD-5 Singles Directory and the 45 RPM Christmas Singles Directory, both by artist/title. (Call for current directory prices.)

If you check out the website, you'll see that Mr. Mawhinney's CD collection currently numbers over 600,000. If you're looking for a CD or LP title, he probably has it—just call and ask. Better yet, use the Record-Rama World Search online database that allows you to search for an artist and access his or her entire discography on the web, as well as place orders right from your computer. You'll also find maintenance products for LPs and CDs as well as, phonographs, over 10,000 phonograph needles, jukebox title strips, and other supplies for deejays.

SPECIAL FACTORS: Price quotes by phone limited to 2 requests per call.

Video Learning Library

15838 N. 62nd St., Dept. 702	**FORM OF INFORMATION:** $29.95 print catalog (see text); online catalog
Scottsdale, AZ 85254	**PAY:** check, MO, MC, V, AE, DSC
800–383–8811	**SELLS AND RENTS:** how-to, self-help, hobby, and educational videos
480–596–9970	**STORE:** no walk-in location; mail-order only
FAX: 480–596–9973	**ONLINE:** www.videolearning.com

The Video Learning Library is the brainchild of James Spencer, editor and publisher of the massive 768-page reference entitled *Complete Guide to Special Interest Videos.* What a great idea! Suppose, for example, you want to learn ballroom dancing, floral design, Vietnamese cooking, chi gong, or pet grooming; or suppose you want to get some fishing instruction, bowling tips, or hints on giving yourself a home perm. You could either enroll in an expensive course or you could buy or rent a video from Video Learning Library. There are over 12,000 titles in the current edition selected for their usefulness, uniqueness, and availability. The videos are arranged by broad subject categories (for instance, Automotive, Home Improvement, Travel and Adventure, Photography, Games and Magic, and Languages, to name a few) and indexed in the back by specific subject. The individual listings include brief descriptions or reviews and plenty of user-friendly icons denoting closed-captioned for the hearing impaired, star ratings by independent media consultants and reviewers, videos available in PAL (European) format, and titles endorsed by Kids First! for their kid-friendly content. Scanning the catalog or the website evokes an "Oh, wow!" response, as in, "Oh, wow, maybe I should get that feng shui tape and redo my house." This is a wonderful source for teachers looking to enhance a classroom presentation, documentarists looking for subject material, administrators needing training materials, camp counselors or elder-care workers wanting to educate and/or entertain, newly retired people seeking a hobby, or just folks on a never-ending quest for self-improvement.

WEBSITE: The online catalog costs you nothing and allows you to browse the massive inventory by subject. A sister site, Rent-by-Mail (www.rentbymail.com), has a link here in case you'd prefer to rent your special-interest video rather than buy it.

SPECIAL FACTORS: Shipping charges are $5 per order within the U.S.

Home Audio Equipment

Stereo and speaker systems; home entertainment systems; last-year's-model audio/video equipment; refurbished vintage audio equipment

Once, when I was on a dinner date with a fellow that I met from a mutual friend, we went to his house after dinner for a drink. This was the third date we had been on and the first time I had come to his house. We were sitting in the living room, having our drinks, when he got up and said he wanted to put some music on but he only had a stereo system in his bedroom. He walked over to his TV set and turned it on to the weather channel which had Muzak running while the current and forecasted weather conditions were being displayed. That was pretty much the disqualifer. Too bad he didn't know about some of the firms in this chapter. He could have had a stereo system for both the bedroom and the living room.

Whether you're a regular Joe wanting a pair of good speakers for your home or car or a sound nut who can't stand to listen to R&B CDs without a subwoofer, the firms in this section will please you with audio supplies and equipment up to 50% off regular retail. For companies that sell related goods, particularly professional sound equipment for stage, studio, and DJ, as well as electronic instruments and supplies, see "Musical Instruments, Accessories, and Sound Equipment," page 421.

Find It Fast

AUDIO EQUIPMENT
Cambridge SoundWorks

SPEAKER KITS
Cambridge SoundWorks, Gold Sound

SPEAKERS
Audio Concepts, Cambridge SoundWorks, Gold Sound

USED, DEMO, AND CLOSEOUT AUDIO AND VIDEO EQUIPMENT
Gold Sound, Vintage Electronics

VINTAGE AUDIO EQUIPMENT
Vintage Electronics

Audio Concepts, Inc.

901 S. 4th St., Dept. WBM
La Crosse, WI 54601
608–784–4570
FAX: 608–784–6367

FORM OF INFORMATION: online catalog only; no print catalog

PAY: check, MO, MC, V, AE, DSC

SELLS: ACI speakers and speaker accessories

STORE: no walk-in location; phone hours Monday to Friday 9:00 am–5:00 pm CST

ONLINE: www.audioc.com

If you're a speaker aficionado, you're no doubt familiar with the legendary Sapphire and Titan, made by Audio Concepts, Inc. (ACI). What if I told you that you could buy these and other ACI products at up to 50% off the suggested retail price? Well, it's true. This company sells ACI speaker systems, ACI home theatre packages, and audio accessories such as speaker stands, passive high-pass filters, speaker cables, interconnects, and more at tremendous savings. The website provides all the basic information you'll need, including ACI's 100% money-back guarantee if you're not completely satisfied (see website for details). When you log on to the website you can read about and view all the products in their full-color splendor. There's an excellent FAQ section that gives detailed information on various ACI products, an audio glossary, a page of demos and specials, audio-related links, and much more.

SPECIAL FACTORS: Satisfaction guaranteed; authorized returns in new condition sent in the original packaging accepted within 30 days for exchange, refund, or credit.

Cambridge SoundWorks

100 Brickstone Square
Andover, MA 01810
800–945–4434
978–623–4400
FAX: 978–475–7265

FORM OF INFORMATION: free print catalog; online catalog

PAY: check, MO, V, MC, AE, DSC

SELLS: high-performance stereo and home theater products

STORE: 25 stores located in CA, ME, MA, and NH, call or see website for addresses; phone hours Monday to Friday 9:00 am–8:00 pm

ONLINE: www.cambridgesoundworks.com

Cambridge SoundWorks, the pioneering manufacturer and direct marketer of high-performance stereo and home theater products, sells their award-winning speakers direct from the factory, eliminating distribution costs and passing the savings directly to you, the consumer. This same high-value formula allows them to match their high-performance speakers with electronics from brands like Sony, Onkyo, and Marantz and offer incredible deals on great-sounding complete audio systems. Cambridge SoundWorks, founded in 1988 by Emmy Award-winner and Audio Hall of Fame member, Henry Kloss, started as an inventive speaker manufacturer over 14 years ago. A catalog business was formed, which evolved into a chain of retail stores, and became one of the first companies to sell consumer electronics on the internet. This is a company that makes great speakers and sells them at great prices. What you will find here are well-designed, well-made, great-sounding, and great-looking audio and video products at unbeatable prices.

Nervous about buying a stereo or home theater system online? Don't be. Whether you buy stereo or home theater equipment at a retail store or online, ultimately the best place to audition your system is in your own home. All rooms have an acoustic character of their own. A store showroom literally sounds different than any room in your home. The true test of the acoustic quality of a product is when you listen to it in the environment where it's going to "live." Cambridge SoundWorks offers a liberal 45 day No Risk Return Policy. If you buy from them and don't like what you get, return it for a full refund—no questions asked. You can try out your new system in your home, listening to your favorite music and watching your favorite movies. Besides their inexpensive stereos, CSW offers all sorts of audio and video equipment such as cassette decks, DVD players, MP3 minidiscs, powered subwoofers, radios, turntables, satellite TVs, VCRs, digital video recorders, and portable CD players. Their accessories include antennas, headphones, surge protectors, blank tapes and CDs, speaker wire, and remote controls.

WEBSITE: Not one to wrestle with putting together an audio system? Not to worry. This website makes it easy with a number of "Help Me Choose" type features throughout the site. There is even a library of technical terms that helps you figure out exactly what you're getting. This is especially helpful when there are a lot of bells and whistles attached to the stereo you're looking at and you're not sure whether it's worth the extra 50 bucks. Oh yeah, they also have pages and pages devoted to hooking up your stereo or DVD player or whatever, from basic installation to general troubleshooting. If you'd still like to talk to a real person, CSW live experts are available offering customer service before and after the sale.

SPECIAL FACTORS: If you make a purchase from Cambridge SoundWorks, and then find the same product for less within 45 days, at an authorized retailer, prove it and they'll refund the difference, see details at website.

Gold Sound

4285 S. Broadway, Dept. WBM
Englewood, CO 80110
303–789–5310
FAX: 303–762–0527

FORM OF INFORMATION: online catalog only; no print catalog

PAY: check, MO, MC, V, AE, DSC

SELLS: high-end speaker kits; used, demo, and closeout home and professional audio equipment

STORE: same address; Monday to Friday 11:00 am–6:00 pm, Saturday 11:00 am–5:00 pm

ONLINE: www.goldsound.net

If you thought you had to spend thousands to get high-end speakers, think again. Gold Sound has designed and sold quality speaker kits for home and professional use since 1976. Speaker kit advantages include: (1) better sound, deeper bass, greater clarity; (2) lower cost (up to 80% savings!); (3) greater flexibility in size, wood finish, and appearance, plus space-saving units you can build into walls, ceilings, and furniture; (4) easy upgrades for newer technologies (you can dramatically improve your existing 25-year-old speakers); and (5) they're educational and fun! *Stereo Review* has praised Gold Sound speakers as "the high end of the high end"; they've won the International Consumer Electronics Show's Innovation Design Award; and they're used by NASA, Boeing, and scores of institutions and corporations.

In prebuilt speakers, you pay mainly for labor, advertising, overhead, and store markup. Use your time and only pay for what makes sound: the working parts. A Gold Sound kit for $299 has better parts and sound, says owner/designer Ron Gold, than $1,000 of assembled units. All kits use high-quality European- and U.S.-made components. The kits include detailed, easy-to-follow plans. Kits with completely built cabinets need as little as one evening to assemble. The kits are also available without cabinets, for people who prefer to make their own. Home kits for stereo or home theater use include subwoofers, satellites, bookshelves, towers, centers, surrounds, and in-wall models. Pro models are popular for clubs, musicians, deejays, schools, and churches. At the website you'll find descriptive text and glowing reviews of Gold Sound's speaker kits, and other useful information that will help you get started. At this time, however, there was no online ordering. You can phone or email the staff at Gold Sound and they'll help hook you up with the system you seek. If you're in the area, stop by Gold Sound's Denver showroom, where you can hear many assembled kits.

SPECIAL FACTORS: Speaker kits have a 30-day money-back guarantee and a 2-year replacement warranty; quantity discounts are available.

Vintage Electronics

627 Kinnikinnik Dr.
Colorado Springs, CO 80906
Bob@vintage-electronics.net

FORM OF INFORMATION: online catalog; eBay

PAY: paypal

SELLS: refurbished vintage audio equipment and accessories

STORE: no walk-in location; mail-order only

ONLINE: www.vintage-electronics.cc

Have you been itching to find a functional, like-new 8-track player for all of your tapes that survived the 1970s? Vintage Electronics specializes in classic amplifiers, cassette decks, turntables, 8-tracks and other reconditioned vintage audio equipment at discount prices that are truly amazing. And, unlike other dealers who sell vintage stereo equipment, Vintage Electronics offers a full 90-day repair warranty on most of the items they sell. If you are shopping for a new sound system, take a moment to consider the benefits of purchasing vintage stereo equipment. Most quality consumer products made in the 1960s through the 1980s were built to last (I still have my grandmother's fully operating heavy-duty Hamilton Beach blender). Retail audio equipment made available at that time is no exception to the rule. Many items feature sturdy metal and wood frames that are not only cool and sleek in appearance, but also offer added protection, unlike the lightweight frames that are often part of current design standards for retail electronics. Of course, as distinguished music afficionados, the most important detail we all look for when purchasing stereo equipment is superior sound and clarity. Music played on vintage solid state and analog equipment has a great warm, full feeling that just can't be reproduced by much of today's digital technology. The quality of classic electronic equipment has certainly met the test of time and has attracted the keen interest of thousands of dedicated audiofiles from all over the world. Also, out-of-date equipment may have unique features such as dubbing, multi-speaker outlets, filters, and neat LED meters that aren't available on most modern units. I recently ordered an awesome 1977 Sansui RA-500 reverb amp with psychedelic display screen for $25 from Vintage. Talk about a blast from the past. This is the same amp that I used while listening to albums by the Ramones, The Who and Blue Oyster Cult! Vintage Electronics sells fully reconditioned items that are in good to excellent condition by notable manufacturers such as Marantz, Sansui, Tandberg,

Harman/Kardon, Pioneer, Sherwood, Kenwood, Denon, Technics, and Akai. The owner of Vintage, Bob Toepfer, and staff have nearly 30 years experience repairing home electronics—so all of their products are professionally refurbished, aligned, lubed, cleaned, and inspected before being placed in their detailed online showroom. This equipment is high quality and the original retail sticker price may have placed great-sounding audio gear out of your price range back in the day. Take advantage of Vintage Electronic's discount prices and purchase the classic stereo system that you always wanted.

Vintage Electronics also offers repair service for classic audio equipment that you may already own. With a detailed description of the problems, Vintage Electronics will determine an exact service charge before you even ship the unit to their headquarters in Colorado Springs. All repairs come with a 90-day warranty. The website is regularly updated with new products and contains useful links to other sites for vintage equipment, parts, accessories, and out-of-print manuals.

SPECIAL FACTORS: Returns only on approval

Musical Instruments, Accessories, and Sound Equipment

New and used musical instruments and musician supplies; sheet music; professional sound and recording equipment for stage, recording studio, and deejay

Whereas the firms in the previous section carry goods primarily for people who *listen* to music, this section features companies that cater to those who *play* or *produce* music. The firms listed here sell top-quality instruments—everything from school band recorders to grand pianos. Professional musicians rarely pay full price for their instruments, and if you buy from the same sources they use, neither will you. You'll also find electronic equipment and supplies for professional or at-home studio recording, as well as stage electronics, deejay equipment, and even karaoke machines. Get ready to save up to 75% from some of these firms.

Find It Fast

ACCORDIONS AND CONCERTINAS
Accordion-O-Rama

BAND INSTRUMENTS
Giardinelli, Interstate Music Supply, National Educational Music, West Manor Music

BRASS AND WOODWINDS ACCESSORIES
Discount Reed

ELECTRONIC KEYBOARD
American Musical Supply, Interstate Music Supply, Musician's Friend

GENERAL MUSICAL INSTRUMENTS
American Musical Supply, Sam Ash Music, Elderly Instruments, Giardinelli, Interstate Music Supply, National Educational Music, West Manor Music

GUITARS, STRINGED INSTRUMENTS, AND ACCESSORIES
American Musical Supply, Carvin, Interstate Music Supply, Mandolin Brothers,- Metropolitan Music, Musician's Friend, Shar Products, Weinkrantz Musical Supply

MUSICAL CHIMES
American Musical Supply

PERCUSSION INSTRUMENTS
American Musical Supply, Sam Ash Music, Interstate Music Supply

PIANOS AND ORGANS
Altenburg Piano House

SONGBOOKS AND SHEET MUSIC
Accordion-O-Rama, Elderly Instruments, Patti Music Company, Shar Products

STAGE AND STUDIO ELECTRONICS AND EQUIPMENT
American Musical Supply, Sam Ash Music, Carvin, Interstate Music Supply, Musician's Friend

USED INSTRUMENTS
Accordion-O-Rama, Altenburg Piano House, Elderly Instruments, Mandolin Brothers

Accordion-O-Rama

236 N. Stevens Ave.
Dept. WBM

South Amboy, NJ 08879

732-727-7715

FORM OF INFORMATION: $1 print catalog; website

PAY: check, MO, MC, V, DSC

SELLS: accordions, concertinas, amps, accessories, and services

STORE: same address; Tuesday to Friday 10:00 am–5:00 pm, Saturday 11:00 am–3:00 pm (may be open longer; call)

ONLINE: www.accordion-o-rama.com

So you're in the market for an accordion. Once considered the instrument of old world Europeans, the accordion has a rejuvenated, hip, new image in today's rock, folk, and cajun bands. Where do you go to find the widest selection of new and rebuilt instruments, personalized service, and specialists in tuning, repairs, and electronics? Accordion-O-Rama is your place. Accordion-O-Rama is a specialty store for accordions, if you couldn't tell by the name, whose staff will help you select the best one for your taste and budget. The current set of flyers at the time of this writing featured a number of famous-name models marked down from the suggested retail price to the tune of 25% to 40%. There are several ways you can go about finding the right accordion. If you call or write, the staff will ask that you give them detailed information about what you're looking for so they can best respond. The color catalog is $1; the black-and-white catalog is free. Or you can take a video "Demonstration" tour of Accordion-O-Rama for $25, or receive an instructional video on "The Basics of MIDI," also $25 (or get both videotapes for $45). There is the additional option of going to their website and filling out the electronic questionnaire or contact form.

WEBSITE: Ordering is not available on the website because when it comes to getting the right accordion or concertina there are so many variables that it is best to speak with one of the very helpful and knowledgeable people at Accordion-O-Rama before making the final decision. The website is a good place to start as it is very informative and you can start the process of choosing the right accordion for you by filling out the online questionnaire. The website features just a sample of the hundreds of accordions that they have in stock, all with detailed descriptions, clear images, and the discounted prices listed next to the suggested retail.

Altenburg Piano House, Inc.

1150 E. Jersey St.
Elizabeth, NJ 07201
908–351–2000
FAX: 908–527–9210

FORM OF INFORMATION: free brochure; website

PAY: check, MO, MC, V, AE, DSC

SELLS: new and used pianos and organs

STORE: same address; Monday to Friday 8:00 am–6:00 pm, Saturday 9am–5:00 pm, Sunday 12:00 noon–5:00 pm; also Asbury Park and Trenton, NJ

ONLINE: www.altenburgpiano.com

Of all the old, original European piano makers who came to America more than 100 years ago, only one company still remains family owned and operated: Altenburg Piano House. Established by Frederick Altenburg in 1847, this company is still going strong. Altenburg sells pianos and organs in all styles and finishes by "almost all" manufacturers, including various one-of-a-kind pianos and Altenburg's own models, the Otto Altenburg line (recommended by Franz Liszt and other luminaries). Besides the Otto Altenburgs, you'll find pianos by Baldwin, August Forster, Bohemia, Bluthner, Petrof, Wurlitzer, Pleyel, Chickering, Sauter, and others; and organs by Johannus, and Hammond, as well as complete church organ systems.

If you call for literature, you'll receive a 2-page price list on Altenburg's own line of vertical and grand pianos. To find out about other brands, you can visit the website. But the best way to get all the information you seek is to call and talk to the salespeople about what you're looking for in terms of price, finishes, and manufacturer. If you're lucky enough to live near Elizabeth, New Jersey, stop by the art deco showroom where you can stroll around and tickle the ivories of an authentic Altenburg.

WEBSITE: The website is not set up for electronic ordering, for obvious reasons. But online you can read about the history of the company and see some current models available from various manufacturers.

SPECIAL FACTORS: All models come with a full warranty.

American Musical Supply

P. O. Box 152
Spicer, MN 56288
800–458–4076
320–796–2088
FAX: 320–796–2080

FORM OF INFORMATION: free print catalog; online catalog

PAY: check, MO, MC, V, AE, DSC

SELLS: musical instruments and recording equipment

STORE: Victor's House of Music, 762 Rt. 17 N, Paramus, NJ; Monday to Thursday 10:00 am–9:00 pm, Friday 10:00 am–7:00 pm, Saturday 10:00 am–6:00 pm

ONLINE: www.americanmusical.com

I like companies like this one, where service and customer satisfaction are high priorities. American Musical Supply (AMS) is a musician's discount catalog that offers the hottest brands at the lowest guaranteed prices, in addition to some super deals (up to 60% off for some items) by way of closeouts, "dent & scratch" specials, and "nonfactory sealed." They offer a 45-day money-back guarantee, free 1-year extended warranties on many items, extended payment plans, 7-day-a-week phone hours, and more.

Among the hundreds of products at American Musical Supply are microphones and mic accessories, studio and recording equipment, studio furniture, speakers and amps, guitars and basses, guitar accessories, drum sets and percussion accessories, keyboards, MIDI gear, books and videos, and more. Color photographs and well-written text make it easy to navigate through this catalog. AMS is the mail-order division of Victor's House of Music, a third-generation family business.

WEBSITE: The full catalog is online, with a convenient product search capability, secure online ordering, links to many of the manufacturers they carry, internet-only specials, weekly giveaways, rebates, gift certificates, and much more, all presented in a musician-friendly format that suggests they're on the side of the artist.

SPECIAL FACTORS: Lowest price guarantee; products can be returned within 45 days for full refund; 100% customer satisfaction is their goal.

Sam Ash Music Corp.

P.O. Box 9047, Dept. WBM
Hicksville, NY 11802
800–472–6274
FAX: 800–818–9050

FORM OF INFORMATION: free print catalog; online catalog

PAY: check, MO, MC, V, AE, DSC

SELLS: instruments and electronics

STORE: locations in CT, FL, IL, NY, NJ, OH, PA, TN, and CA; call or check website for addresses; customer service hours Monday to Friday 9:00 am–8:00 pm, Saturday 10:00 am–5:00 pm EST

ONLINE: www.samash.com

In 1924, Sam and Rose Ash had to pawn Rose's engagement ring for $400 to make the first down payment on the first Sam Ash Music Store, eventually to become known as "The Musical Instrument Megastore" 75 years later. Today, there are nearly three dozen Sam Ash stores scattered around the U.S. famous for their wide selection of musical instruments at the lowest prices anywhere. In addition to the regular discounts, Sam Ash runs frequent half-off sales and Deals of the Month; will give you money for your trade-in guitars (acoustic and electric), basses, tube amplifiers, drums, brass and woodwind instruments, and electronic equipment; and pledges to beat any price that's lower. The full-color print catalog is filled with the latest products from the best names in the business, from guitars, keyboards, drums, and percussion instruments to recording, live sound, and band and orchestral equipment.

WEBSITE: The website is a fully functioning online musical megastore that, in my opinion, is actually superior to the print catalog. Here you can shop online by clicking on a broad category (Guitars & Amps, Keyboards, Pro Audio, DJ & Lighting, Software, Music and Videos, etc.) and browse the selections. The suggested retail price next to Sam Ash's discounted price showed savings of about 40% or more on most items. Online, you can also check out specials, read classifieds posted by like-minded musicians, check out music-industry news and look at musicians' home pages, and sign up for the free Sam Ash catalogs. You can place your order directly online at the website.

Spanish-speaking consumers, please note: For a Spanish-speaking sales representative, call 800–472–6274 or 212–719–2299 (NY) or 305–628–3510 (FL).

Carvin Corp.

12340 World Trade Dr.
San Diego, CA 92128–3742
800–854–2235
858–487–1600
FAX: 858–487–8160

FORM OF INFORMATION: free print catalog; online catalog

PAY: check, MO, MC, V, AE, DSC

SELLS: Carvin guitars, basses, and accessories

STORE: same address; Monday to Friday 9:30 am–6:00 pm, Saturday 10:00 am–5:30 pm; also Hollywood, Santa Ana, Sherman Oaks, and West Covina, CA, locations; phone order hours Monday through Friday 6:30 am–6:00 pm and Saturday 9:00 am–5:00 pm PST

ONLINE: www.carvin.com

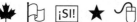

What do James Brown's band, Mariah Carey's guitarist, and YES all have in common? Yes, I *know* they're all musicians! Besides that, though, they all have a soft spot for Carvin guitars and basses. Award-winning Carvin manufactures its own line of instruments and equipment, then offers them to consumers at factory-direct prices from the catalog and website. The 64-page color catalog features photographs, detailed descriptions, specifications, and prices that are up to 65% off list. All Carvins are "Born in the USA."

In addition to guitars and basses of every type and description, Carvin offers such equipment as power amps, mixers and sound systems, loudspeakers, monitors, mics and cables, pickups, amplifiers, racks and stands, and speaker parts. In the current catalog are raves from both customers and professional reviewers, including *Bass Player* magazine and *Pro Audio Revue*. You'll also find a small selection of instructional books and videotapes.

WEBSITE: The website features online ordering and the full inventory of pro sound equipment, guitars, and amps. There's also a great "build your guitar online" virtual custom shop, where you choose the options you want, view your very own guitar before it's even built, and then buy it at factory-direct prices. Cool.

SPECIAL FACTORS: Money-back guarantee if you're not completely satisfied within 10-day trial period; 1-year warranty against manufacturing defects.

Discount Reed Co.

24307 Magic Mountain Pkwy.,
#181
Valencia, CA 91355
800-428-5993
661-294-9437
FAX: 661-294-9762

FORM OF INFORMATION: free price list; online catalog
PAY: check, MO, MC, V, DSC
SELLS: reeds for musical instruments
STORE: no walk-in location; mail-order only
ONLINE: www.discountreed.com

Discount Reed, in business since 1980, specializes in clarinet and saxophone reeds, many of them at savings up to 50% off retail prices. The 8-page catalog chronicles one deeply discounted product after another: from Rico Jazz sax reeds and Mitchell Lurie clarinet reeds to hand-selected clarinet and sax reeds from France. The reeds here come in a variety of canes, strengths, cuts, and even coatings—the Rico Plasticover, used by Tom Scott, has a coating that significantly reduces moisture absorption, allowing the reed to be played longer. The huge in-stock reed inventory includes all the major players, including Olivieri, Daniel's, La Voz, Zonda, Jones, Fibercane, Grand Concert Select, Peter Ponzol, Pete Fountain, Fred Hemke, Van Doren, Rico Select Jazz, and Marca, plus synthetic reeds by Fibracell and Bari. There is also a limited selection of reeds for oboe and bassoon. Accessories include a Pisoni reed knife, Qwik-Time metronome, Hodge silk swabs, Claricord elastic clarinet neckstrap, Kiwi NeckPak, Blue Note sax straps, bore and key oils, and reed cases, guards, trimmers, and much more.

WEBSITE: The website is where you'll find the most up-to-date inventory, as well as specials. After you've viewed the large selection of products and read the detailed descriptions, you can order in one of four ways—by phone, by email, or by downloading the order form and faxing or mailing it in. There's no secure electronic ordering at this writing.

SPECIAL FACTORS: School purchase orders accepted; minimum order: $20 on U.S. credit cards, $30 on international credit card orders.

Elderly Instruments

P.O. Box 14249-WM01
Lansing, MI 48901
888-473-5810
FAX: 517-372-5155

FORM OF INFORMATION: free print catalog; online catalog

PAY: check, MO, MC, V, DSC, JCB

SELLS: new and vintage musical instruments, books, audio- and videotapes, and music CDs

SHOWROOM: 1100 North Washington, Lansing, MI; Monday to Wednesday 11:00 am–7:00 pm, Thursday 11:00 am–9:00 pm, Friday and Saturday 10:00 am–6:00 pm; mail-order phone hours Monday to Saturday 9:00 am–5:00 pm EST

ONLINE: www.elderly.com

Since 1972, Elderly Instruments has been known for its huge selection of new and used guitars, basses, amplifiers, effects, banjos, ukuleles, mandolins, fiddles, dulcimers, harmonicas, accordions, bodhrans, and other instruments at terrific prices. Concertinas, autoharps, folk harps, bowed psalterys, harmonicas, kalimbas, recorders, didgeridoos, flutes and fifes, Andean pipes, pennywhistles, steel drums, bongos, and tambourines are among the many instruments you'll find. There's also a good selection of left-handed instruments here. Elderly supplies all types of accessories such as picks, strings, electronic tuners, capos, slides, cases, instrument parts, software, postcards and posters, building and repair tool parts, books, hard-to-find music CDs, and much more. Book subjects include instrument building and repair, songbooks (country, gospel, folk, Irish, Christmas, bluegrass), self-instruction for every instrument sold (with the possible exception of kazoo!), biography, and recording techniques. For electronics users, Elderly's catalog details specifications for home recording equipment, microphones, wireless systems, amps, overdrive and distortion effects, foot pedals, processors, and much more.

In addition to their regular 200 page catalog which is issued three times a year, Elderly publishes the *Vintage and Used Instrument List* every six weeks. Unless you request otherwise, the general catalog is the one they'll send.

WEBSITE: If you can, check out Elderly's website, where, among other things, you can scan the amazing selection of Elderly's hard-to-find CDs, cassettes, and books; see the current Cheapo Depot specials and closeouts; and order online. The comprehensive site is easy to use and to navigate. If you're in the market for a used instrument, you can fill out and electronically submit the used-instrument-wanted form.

SPECIAL FACTORS: Satisfaction guaranteed (see catalog for policies); unused, authorized returns accepted within 5 days; Elderly appraises, buys, and swaps used instruments.

Giardinelli, Inc.

P. O. Box 4370
Medford, OR 97501
800–249–8361
FAX: 800–652–4534

FORM OF INFORMATION: free print catalog, $7 outside U.S.; online catalog

PAY: check, MO, MC, V, AE, DC, DSC

SELLS: brasses, woodwinds, string, percussion, and accessories

STORE: same address; Monday to Friday 8:30 am–5:00 pm, Saturday 9:00 am–1:00 pm

ONLINE: www.giardinelli.com

When you see the high school band parade and the school orchestra perform, it's likely they're playing instruments from Giardinelli, Inc., a seller of fine brasses and woodwinds since 1947. Over the years, the catalog offerings have been expanded to include violins, violas, cellos, and basses; electronic and portable keyboards; electric guitars and basses; and amplifiers. Giardinelli describes its prices as "thrifty," which is a term of modesty; prices here dip as low as 45% off suggested retail.

The 252-page catalog is easy to use with inventory categorized by instrument (woodwind, brass, concert and marching percussion, orchestral, guitars, and keyboards), accessories (mouthpieces and mutes; reeds, caps, and ligatures; cases, covers and gig bags; metronomes and tuners; stands), and care and maintenance. Forty-five pages are dedicated to publications, notably methods books and music for flute, clarinet, tuba, bassoon, trumpet solos, trombone solos and ensembles, and brass ensembles. Many additional name-brand products available from Giardinelli are not listed in the catalog, so calls are invited.

WEBSITE: Giardinelli's online catalog is logically organized, making it easy to find the right instrument or accessory from the broad inventory. There are also Scratch and Dent specials here, clearance items, links to music resources, and a lot more. This is one instance where I'd recommend you skip over the print catalog and go directly online to shop. You can place your order online.

SPECIAL FACTORS: Satisfaction guaranteed; returns accepted; institutional accounts welcome.

Interstate Music Supply

P.O. Box 510865
New Berlin, WI 53151
877-213-2580
FAX: 800-529-0382

FORM OF INFORMATION: free print catalog; online catalog

PAY: check, MO, MC, V, DSC

SELLS: instruments, electronics, and accessories

OUTLET: Cascio Interstate Music Co., 13819 W. National Ave., New Berlin, WI; Monday to Thursday 10:00 am–8:00 pm, Saturday 10:00 am–5:00 pm; also 6835 West Mequon Rd., Mequon, WI; Monday to Thursday 12:00 am–8:00 pm, Friday 12:00 am–5:00 pm, Saturday 10:00 am–4:00 pm

ONLINE: www.interstatemusic.com

How does one company top another? Interstate Music Supply (IMS) claims to have "the lowest prices on the planet." Unless you're from another galaxy, you won't do any better than to shop here for everything from acoustic basses to zonda reeds. Their three catalogs, "Drums and Percussion", "Guitar/Bass/Keyboard/MIDI", and "Educator/Band/Orchestra" have every kind of musical instrument for band or orchestra, including children's instruments; sound, stage, lighting, and recording equipment; parts and accessories for every type of instrument; storage units; stage furniture and riser setups; and much, much more. This is a major source for schools and other institutions looking to fully equip their departments and musicians. But you don't have to be an institution to enjoy 60% off list prices on these products. Individuals get the same savings. And the catalog features closeouts, blowouts, and other great sale items where savings are even greater.

WEBSITE: The website is a great resource for musicians—it has over 20,000 items available and more being added daily. If you can't find what you're looking for, use the quick search or give them a call. They now have secure online ordering.

SPECIAL FACTORS: Satisfaction guaranteed; returns accepted within 14 days for exchange, refund, or credit; 20% restocking fee; institutional accounts available.

Mandolin Brothers, Ltd.

629 Forest Ave.
Staten Island, NY
10310–2576
718–981–8585, 3226
FAX: 718–816–4416

FORM OF INFORMATION: free print catalog; online catalog

PAY: check, MO, MC, V, AE, DSC

SELLS: new and vintage guitars, banjos, and mandolins and accessories

STORE: same address; Monday to Saturday 10:00 am–6:00 pm

ONLINE: www.mandoweb.com

Mandolin Brothers, Ltd. inspired a lovely Joni Mitchell lyric about going to Staten Island to buy a mandolin, and prompted the *Boston Globe* to call this "one of the best guitar shops in the world." Since 1971, Mandolin Brothers has been the home for vintage, new, and used American fretted instruments at reasonable prices; new products sell at discounts up to 35% off list.

Fine guitars, mandolins, mandolas, banjos, ukuleles, and other stringed instruments are featured in the 76-page catalog along with such new equipment as electronics, guitars, and accessories. In stock are pickups, cables, strings, straps, frets, books, videos, and more. In addition to instrument repairs, Mandolin Brothers offers written appraisals of instruments, maintains a "want list" service for individuals, and has an online and print newsletter, *Vintage News,* offering comprehensive listings of available vintage instruments (subscription to print version of monthly newsletter is $20/year domestic and $25 international). In-stock new as well as vintage instruments can be shipped on a 3-day approval basis.

WEBSITE: The website will give you a good idea of what this company is all about, what they sell, and the great specials they're currently running, but there's no online ordering; you still have to phone, fax, or mail in your order.

SPECIAL FACTORS: Satisfaction guaranteed; returns accepted within 3 days.

Metropolitan Music Co.

P.O. Box 1415
Stowe, VT 05672
802–253–4814
FAX: 802–253–9834

FORM OF INFORMATION: free print catalog; online catalog
PAY: check, MO, MC, V
SELLS: stringed instruments and accessories
STORE: no walk-in location; mail-order only
ONLINE: www.metmusic.com

Since 1920, Metropolitan Music Co. has been a source for stringed instruments and accessories primarily for professional and otherwise experienced musicians. The 36-page print catalog includes violins, violas, cellos, basses, and bows by Ibex, Resonance, and Juzek, among others. In stock are such parts as bridges, pegs, chin rests, and shoulder rests. Wood and tools are also available, as are books on the repair and construction of instruments. Catalog prices are 30% to 50% less than you'd pay retail.

If you need overseas delivery, Metropolitan Music will refer you to worldwide distributors.

WEBSITE: At the website you will find all of their violas, cellos, basses and 4/4 violins. They also have their full line of cases, bows, strings, parts, tonewoods and accessories online. Click on the blue model numbers to see large photographic images of the instruments. If you want to order, you will have to call, fax, email, or write, as there is no online ordering.

SPECIAL FACTORS: Price quotes by phone or letter, with SASE; minimum order: $15.

Musician's Friend

P.O. Box 4370
Medford, OR 97501
800–391–8762
FAX: 541–776–1370

FORM OF INFORMATION: free print catalog; online catalog

PAY: check, MO, MC, V, AE, DSC

SELLS: guitar, bass, and keyboard electronics, stage and studio gear, etc.

STORE: 5 locations in OR, WA, and NV; call main number for addresses

ONLINE: www.musiciansfriend.com

Musician's Friend, in business since 1981, calls its inventory of professional recording equipment and electronics "gear" and dubs itself "the world's largest direct marketer of music." The color catalog offers everything for guitar and bass, including amps and combos, effects processors, pedals, pickups, stands, straps, strings, tubes, tuners, and cases and gig bags; everything for keyboards and MIDI—more amps, more stands, more cases and gig bags, plus software, sequencers, samplers, and synth and sound modules; and everything for stage and studio: acoustic foam, cables, CD players and recorders, cassette decks, compressors, drum machines and drums, microphones, mixers, rack accessories, speakers, and wireless systems. Prices are lowest on the most popular gear, with additional savings available on back-of-the-catalog closeouts.

WEBSITE: The website offers the full inventory, a product search engine, online ordering, good web-only specials, a free online newsletter subscription, articles, and musician-related links. There's also an extensive list of blowout merchandise priced to move quickly, so check it out.

SPECIAL FACTORS: Satisfaction guaranteed; price quotes by phone; authorized returns accepted within 45 days.

National Educational Music Co., Ltd.

1181 Rte. 22, Dept. WBM
Mountainside, NJ 07092
800–526–4593
908–232–6700
FAX: 908–789–3025

FORM OF INFORMATION: free print catalog; website

PAY: check, MO, MC, V, AE

SELLS: instruments and accessories

STORE: no walk-in location; mail-order only; Monday to Friday 8:30 am–5:00 pm

ONLINE: www.nemc.com

National Educational Music Company, NEMC for short, offers an excellent selection of band and orchestra instruments at up to 60% off suggested list price. These are brand-new, first-quality instruments—no damaged goods or manufacturer's seconds. The savings improve if you can buy in quantity, and NEMC makes it attractive for schools and other institutions to do so through a coupon program that enables frequent or large buyers to earn free instruments.

Every type of band and orchestra instrument is available here, from alto horns to xylophones—all well-known, top-quality brands. NEMC sells accessories, too: carriers and cases, drum hardware, reeds, sound systems, and tuners, for example. By the way, NEMC offers one of the best warranty coverages in the industry at no additional cost (except for fretted instruments).

WEBSITE: I recommend the website to find out about NEMC and the services they offer. Schools and dealers will find helpful information at the website about special programs for buying or leasing instruments in quantity.

SPECIAL FACTORS: Eligible returns accepted within 7 days (a restocking fee may be charged).

Patti Music Company

4253 W. Beltline Hwy.
Madison, WI 53711–3814
800–777–2884
FAX: 608–257–5847

FORM OF INFORMATION: free print catalog; online catalog

PAY: check, MO, MC, V, DSC

SELLS: piano and organ sheet music, music books, teaching methods and aids, metronomes, etc.

STORE: same address; Monday to Friday 10:00 am–7:00 pm CST

ONLINE: www.pattimusic.com

People at all ages and stages of life study or teach piano and organ, and for them Patti Music Company sells sheet music, methods books, MIDI diskettes, teaching aids (flash cards, dictionaries, manuscript paper), and instructional videos, always below list price, sometimes at discounts up to 30%. Patti Music offers the complete series of over 60 different piano and organ methods, all the major piano libraries, the complete and current National Federation list, as well as thousands of supplementary sheets, ensemble offerings, seasonal titles, and pedagogical materials. You'll find over 35,000 titles, 17,000 of which are listed in the hefty catalog, all oriented to the keyboard teacher and performer. Foreign publications are available as well. The hefty newsprint catalog (192 pages) also offers popular standards by The Beatles, Billy Joel, and Elton John, and scores from Broadway shows and movies. The piano methods section, running 24 pages, presents annotated entries on all the major instructional methods currently available, detailing levels and grades and availability of instructor's handbooks. Teachers and musicians can choose music from piano collections, libraries, National Federation Junior Festivals selections, piano solos and ensembles, and organ methods and repertoire. There are excellent books for parents who want to help their children develop musically, as well as general-interest titles about composers and performers. Piano furniture is also offered toward the back of the catalog, as are music stands, lamps, and gifts.

WEBSITE: At the website you can browse their online catalog, which has the list price next to their price so you can see what you're saving. Online ordering is available.

SPECIAL FACTORS: Only defective merchandise can be returned; flat rate for shipping and handling $5.95 to $6.95.

Shar Products Company

P.O. Box 1411
Ann Arbor, MI 48106
800–248–7427
734–665–3978
FAX: 800–997–8723

FORM OF INFORMATION: free print catalog; online catalog

PAY: check, MO, MC, V, AE, DSC

SELLS: sheet music, stringed instruments, videos, accessories

STORE: 2465 S. Industrial Hwy., Ann Arbor, MI; Tuesday to Friday 9:00 am–6:00 pm, Saturday 9:00 am–5:00 pm; also Toronto, Ontario (see website or call for location and hours)

ONLINE: www.sharmusic.com

Since 1962, Shar has been "proudly serving the needs of string players" and is still setting the trend for bowed string instruments. This family-owned business has a wide selection, prices up to 35% off retail on many items, and excellent customer service. In the 64-page color print catalog you'll find violin, viola, cello, and bass instruments and outfits; bows, strings, and general accessories, such as rosin and instrument cleaners/polish, chin and shoulder rests, metronomes, tuners, pitchpipes, tuning forks; and more. There's a separate print catalog for sheet music with thousands of titles (string music, chamber music, jazz, Christmas, fiddle, Broadway, etc.) that also carries such items as manuscript paper, educational materials, and really wonderful and innovative music games. In addition to products, Shar offers services for bowed-instrument players: instrument and bow appraisal, restoration services, and a personal consultant program to help you identify the ideal stringed instrument for your specific needs.

WEBSITE: The online version of the catalog features an easy to use search engine for music titles that doubles as an excellent reference for teachers and students. The website, which has online ordering, is arranged by the proficiency level of the musician. In other words, the instrument offerings are grouped by beginning players and instruments, intermediate, advancing, and advanced and professional players, since a cello for a student would be a very different instrument from that needed by a world-class recording artist. If you have internet access, I recommend skipping the print version of the catalog and going right online, since the website features the full inventory of products, as well as current specials and product news.

SPECIAL FACTORS: Satisfaction guaranteed; sheet music not in catalog can be special-ordered.

Weinkrantz Musical Supply Co., Inc.

325 Hayes St.
San Francisco, CA 94102
800-736-8742
415-399-1201
FAX: 415-581-0305

FORM OF INFORMATION: free print catalog; website

PAY: check, MO, MC, V

SELLS: bowed instruments and accessories

STORE: same address; Monday to Friday 9:00 am-5:00 pm

ONLINE: www.weinkrantzmusic.com

Since 1975, Weinkrantz Musical Supply Co., Inc., has been devoted to selling bowed instruments, accessories, and supplies at prices that usually range from 30% to 50% below retail. This company offers strings, violins and violas, basses, and cellos. Instruments are available as part of outfits, or you can purchase bows, cases, rosin, and other equipment separately. Metronomes, tuners, bridges, chin rests, bow hair, and instrument bags and cases are all sold at discount here. Some new items include Mooradian bass bags and Realist acoustic bass pickups. If you're looking for an instrument produced by a limited-run small workshop, call or write; it's likely the folks at Weinkrantz will be able to find it for you.

WEBSITE: At press time, the website was still under construction.

SPECIAL FACTORS: Satisfaction guaranteed.

West Manor Music

831 E. Gunhill Rd.
Bronx, NY 10467
718–655–5400
FAX: 718–655–1115

FORM OF INFORMATION: free print catalog
PAY: check, MO, MC, V, AE
SELLS: musical instruments
STORE: same address; call for hours

 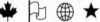

West Manor Music has been supplying schools and institutions with musical instruments since 1956, and it offers a wide range of equipment at average discounts of 45%. The 16-page newsprint catalog lists clarinets, flutes, piccolos, saxophones, oboes, English horns, cornets, trumpets, flugelhorns, trombones, French horns, euphoniums, tubas, violins, violas, cellos, string-basses, electric and acoustic guitars, snare drums, drum sets, cymbals, xylophones, timbales, marimbas, orchestra chimes, congas, tambourines, bongos, and other instruments. Drum stands and heads, strings, reeds, cases, music stands, metronomes, mouthpieces, amplifiers, music books, manuscript pads, cases, and other supplies and accessories are here, too. All of the instruments are new and guaranteed for 1 year. West Manor also offers an "overhaul" service for popular woodwinds and brasses, and it can perform repairs as well.

SPECIAL FACTORS: Quantity discounts are available; minimum order: $25, or $100 with credit cards.

Office, Business, and Professional

Computer Hardware and Software

PC and Macintosh computers and peripherals; software of all kinds; computer games; computer supplies and accessories; refurbished computers and computer equipment

Just because you spend inordinate amounts of time in front of your computer at the office, have a portable you tote home with you on nights when you have to work late, and own still another computer at home that sits in the family room for your kids to play educational games on, doesn't necessarily mean you are techno-savvy, especially when it comes to buying a new computer or upgrading the ones you have. Like many of you, I find the whole competitive world of computer vendors overwhelming. If you compare prices, which I've done quite a bit while researching this section, you'll find that one company can be cheaper by $200 to $300 on one model, but more expensive by the same amount on another product. Thankfully, the advent of the world wide web has brought help to consumers like us in the form of *computer shopping agents*.

What are they? They're sites you can log onto *for free*, type in the product you're looking for, and the shopping agent scans their database to list all the stores that sell that product and the price at which they sell it. There are dozens of good ones, so I recommend trying several so you can get a real cross section. Any good search engine can help you find a list of price-comparison "bots" (technoslang for robots).

The companies in this chapter are all good firms that have managed to survive in the vicious dog-byte-dog world of technology by offering good products at a discount. Because competition is so fierce in this industry, there's absolutely no need for us consumers to pay full price for computer hardware and software. Many of the companies in other chapters, by the way, also sell computer-related goods. For computer workstations and other computer furniture, be sure to check out "Office Furnishings," page 455. And for many computer-related supplies such as printer paper and diskettes, see "Office Supplies and Machines," page 461.

Find It Fast

ACADEMIC SOFTWARE
Academic Superstore

COMPUTER BOOKS AND MANUALS
CDW, Zones

COMPUTER FURNITURE AND ORGANIZERS
Dartek.com

HARDWARE
CDW, Computer Geeks, Dartek.com, Dell Outlet, Epson, RefurbDepot.com, Zones

MACINTOSH-COMPATIBLE PRODUCTS
CDW, Epson, MacWholesale (under Dartek.com), Softwareoutlet.com, Zones

NETWORKING EQUIPMENT
CDW, Dartek.com, Zones

PRINTER SUPPLIES
CDW, Dartek.com, Zones

REFURBISHED COMPUTERS
Dell Outlet, RefurbDepot.com

SOFTWARE
Academic Superstore, CDW, Softwareoutlet.com, Zones

USED SOFTWARE FOR IBM-COMPATIBLES
Recycled Software

Academic Superstore

223 W. Anderson Ln. Suite
A110

Austin, TX 78752

800–817–2347

512–450–1199

FAX: 512–450–0263

FORM OF INFORMATION: free print catalog;
online catalog

PAY: check, MO, MC, V, AE, DSC

SELLS: computer software and some hardware for students, teachers, school administrators, and faculty members (see text)

STORE: no walk-in location; mail-order only

ONLINE: www.academicsuperstore.com

If you are a student, teacher, school administrator, or faculty member, or are purchasing for an accredited school, college, or a hospital directly affiliated with an educational institution, then you probably know that you can get some amazing deals on software programs. However, you may not know about one of the great sources for discounted software for the academic community, Academic Superstore. The software (for both Macintosh and Windows) categories include business, education, graphics, program-ming, music, screenwriting, teaching tools, and even learning languages. In addition to the wide range of educational programs offered here, they have an impressive selection of graphics programs. You'll also find miscellaneous items designed to organize one's money and time. Whether you need computer aids for teaching or advanced organizing software, Academic Superstore can provide for you. They also offer a "Buy Now Shop Later" policy which allows you to buy your software with complete peace of mind. If you purchase an item from Academic Superstore and find the same item for less at another academic reseller within 25 days of your purchase, they will refund the difference. Need-less to say, they're confident you'll be satisfied.

WEBSITE: This website is extensive but fairly simple. There is a list on their homepage with all of the top-selling products and hot deals currently offered. Their products are listed by category (business, education, etc.) and some of the descriptions include helpful hints to the software illiterate.

SPECIAL FACTORS: Returns accepted on unopened software within 30 days; see web-site for details on qualifications for discounts.

CDW

CDW Computer Centers, Inc.
200 North Milwaukee Ave.
Vernon Hills, IL 60061
800–838–4239
847–465–6000
FAX: 847–465–6800

FORM OF INFORMATION: free print catalogs; online catalog

PAY: check, MO, MC, V, AE, DSC

SELLS: PC and Mac computer hardware and software, peripherals, etc.

STORE: showrooms in Chicago and Vernon Hills, IL; call for hours and addresses; phone hours Monday to Friday 7:00 am–9:00 pm, Saturday 9:00 am–5:00 pm CST

ONLINE: www.cdw.com

Computer Discount Warehouse (CDW) is a leading provider of technology solutions for business, government, and education. In business since 1982, this company publishes a comprehensive print catalog, 5 specialty catalogs, and has one of the best computer-related websites around. Top name brands carried by CDW include APC, Apple, Cisco, HP, Microsoft, Sony, Symantec, Toshiba, and ViewSonic. Want to know what keeps CDW winning praise in the consumer media year after year? Customer service by trained professionals (all graduates from CDW University!), custom configurations, toll-free technical support for the life of your product, manufacturer warranties, leasing options, fast delivery, and a broad selection of everything under the sun that's computer-related.

International customers, please note: There's a $25 handling fee charged on all orders shipped outside the U.S.

WEBSITE: If you have internet access, skip the print catalog and go right to the website. Once you're there, you can search in the CDW or Mac Warehouse sections for hardware, software, networking products, and accessories. Searches can also be made by manufacturer, category, or keyword. The site has a CDW Outlet section which offers high quality outlet items at significantly discounted prices. Outlet items are products which have been returned for a variety of reasons, such as: missing user manuals, cosmetic blemishes, incorrect orders, and duplicate orders. All outlet items have been inspected by CDW certified technicians, have a 30-day return period if you are not completely satisfied, and are up to 50% off retail.

SPECIAL FACTORS: Authorized returns within 30 days of invoice date, with some restrictions (see website or catalog).

Computer Geeks Discount Outlet

1890 Ord Way
Oceanside, CA 92056
760–726–7700

FORM OF INFORMATION: online catalog only; no print catalog

PAY: MC, V, AE, DSC

SELLS: computer components and peripherals

STORE: no walk-inlocation; will-call order pick-up only Monday to Friday 9:00 am–4:00 pm PST

ONLINE: www.computergeeks.com

Computer Geeks Discount Outlet sells computer-related excess inventory and manufacturer-closeouts to tech-savvy, "geeky" consumers. If you don't feel like you meet the geeky criteria, I'm sure they will be willing to make an exception. Formerly operating only at the dealer and corporate levels, Computer Geeks is entering its sixth year as an online retailer, and ships over 1,000 individual orders each business day. They purchase overstocked products and slightly obsolete inventories in enormous quantities, allowing them to set their own prices despite a highly competitive market. Along with the great value you will find great variety. Computer Geeks offers all sorts of computer hardware and consumer electronics shipped directly from their own warehouses, including printers, monitors, scanners, sound and video cards, CD-rom drives, cooling fans, CPU's, DVD drives, joysticks, keyboards, modems, memory, radios, speakers, motherboards (pant pant!) network accessories and cards, ethernet adapters, cell phones, cables, digital cameras, MP3 gear, media accessories, microphones, floppy drives, zip drives, and other stuff. Most items are new—some are used or refurbished—all are clearly marked. They also offer a modest amount of software.

The Computer Geeks website is driven by a sophisticated inventory-management database engine that updates website content in real time. What this means is that you will never see an item that has sold out. This, combined with the fact that Computer

Geeks owns and warehouses all of their inventory, insures that all products that are visible on their website are in stock and ready to ship.

SPECIAL FACTORS: All sales are final; authorized returns on non-working items accepted within 30 days of receipt; return of products, other than for exchange or replacement, are subject to a 15% return fee.

Dartek.com

175 Ambassador Dr.,
Dept. WBM
Naperville, IL 60540
888–432–7835
FAX: 800–808–1106

FORM OF INFORMATION: free print catalog;
online catalog
PAY: check, MO, MC, V, AE, DSC
SELLS: PC computers and related supplies
STORE: no walk-in location; mail-order only
ONLINE: www.dartek.com

Dartek.com, for PC users, and its sister company MacWholesale (800–531–4MAC), for Macintosh people, can help you save money on the equipment you need to make the most out of your PC or Mac. This self-proclaimed "ultimate discount computer superstore" has been around since 1978 serving the ever-changing needs of technophiles with a wide range of products, including hardware, software, printers, modems, supplies and accessories, computer furniture, and much more. The print catalog will make you dizzy flipping through page after page of color photographs with detailed product specifications and descriptions along with list-versus-their price on items ranging from accelerator boards to zip drives. This company, in business for more than 20 years, holds its own in the computer market by offering impeccable customer support services, including expert technical advice and client-centered warranty, return, and service policies.

WEBSITE: At the website you can search for product by category, by brand, by description, and even by price. Another advantage of the website is the sheer number of products—over 100,000 at this writing. If you have questions, you can still call for technical support or customer service. The response rate on emails is very quick here, too. Along with web-only promotions, you'll find the latest closeouts and sales. Secure online ordering is offered at the website.

SPECIAL FACTORS: Satisfaction guaranteed; quantity discounts available; authorized returns accepted within 30 days (see catalog or website for policies).

Dell Outlet

One Dell Way
Round Rock, Texas 78682
800-WWW-DELL

FORM OF INFORMATION: online catalog only; no print catalog

PAY: check, MO, MC, V, AE, DSC

SELLS: refurbished computer hardware and peripherals

STORE: no walk-in location; mail-order only for refurbished products

ONLINE: www.dell.com

Although the Dell Outlet offers some decent savings online on their computers and peripherals with mail-in rebates of up to $150 on select items, I've included them in this book because of the savings of up to $300 on refurbished products. What, exactly, is a refurbished computer? I'll tell you. All of Dell's computers come with a 30-day satisfaction guaranteed policy. As a result of this policy, some computers are returned. While only a small fraction of this equipment is returned because of technical issues, (number one reason for returns is "Customer Sales Error"—ordered wrong system, etc.) all systems are put through the production process again. They are taken apart and rebuilt to original factory specifications, then retested to ensure that the customer gets the same quality and award-winning workmanship as a new Dell computer. Even the systems that are returned unopened are refurbished. Although warranties on refurbished systems are not changed, the price is significantly lowered. Refurbished systems will save you up to $300 off list price. Not bad for a name-brand computer company. Oh yeah, and they also have a Hot Deals section on the Refurbished Systems page, offering shoppers easy access to the best prices Dell Outlet has to offer.

To get to the Dell Outlet where you'll find refurbished items, click on either Consumer: Home & Office or Business: Small Business on the homepage of Dell.com and then click again on Refurbished Systems at the top of the next page that comes up. At press time, Dell Outlet was offering free UPS ground shipping on select items within the continental U.S.

SPECIAL FACTORS: Dell refurbished systems come with the same limited warranties as new systems

Epson

P. O. Box 93107
Long Beach, CA 90809-3107
800–873–7766

FORM OF INFORMATION: online catalog only; no print catalog

PAY: check, MC, V, AE, DSC

SELLS: discontinued and refurbished printers, scanners, and digital cameras

STORE: no walk-in location; mail-order only

ONLINE: www.epson.com

Recently a friend of mine mentioned he was going to order an Epson flatbed scanner from a well-known mail-order company. I immediately checked the Clearance Center at the Epson website and found the exact same scanner he was looking for, refurbished, and $50 less than where he was planning to get it. He loves it.

Epson America, Inc. is the U.S. affiliate of Japan-based Seiko Epson Corporation, a global technology company that manufactures printers, computers, liquid crystal displays (LCDs), integrated circuits, electronic and crystal devices, optical products, factory automation systems, and watches. EPSON's history spans over 100 years with a heritage that began in watchmaking and led to the invention of the world's first quartz watch, along with many other technology "firsts." I have been using Epson products for years and I recommend them highly. Imagine my delight to find out that these great products are now available at 50% to 60% off retail as clearance and refurbished items. When you log on the the Epson site, click on the map for the Canada/United States link. This will take you to the North America page. Under the Products index, click on the Clearance Center (are you with me so far?) and you'll find deeply discounted printers, scanners, and digital cameras. Clearance items are new products in original factory condition and packaging that have recently been discontinued by

Epson. Refurbished products are items that have been returned, inspected, and tested to ensure they perform properly. Some may have minor blemishes due to handling. Refurbished printers may or may not contain a media pack or the same software package as new models. Because refurbished and clearance products are discounted to move final quantities, they do not accept returns on these items except if the product arrives defective, in which case your remedy is replacement with the same model or equivalent. Both clearance and refurbished items come complete with a User's Manual and the same Epson limited warranty as if the product was purchased new.

SPECIAL FACTORS: Clearance and refurbished items only accepted for return if product arrives defective, in which case product will be replaced with the same model or equivalent.

Recycled Software, Inc.

7329 Painted Shadows Way
Las Vegas, NV 89149
800-851-2425
702-655-5666
FAX: 702-655-5662

FORM OF INFORMATION: free price list; online catalog

PAY: check, MO, MC, V, AE, DSC

SELLS: used PC-compatible computer software

STORE: no walk-in location; mail-order only; phone hours Monday to Friday 7:00 am–3:00 pm PST

ONLINE: www.recycledsoftware.com

Contrary to popular belief, most software can be resold or transferred to a new owner, as determined by the manufacturer's agreement that's included with the software. Recycled Software took this concept and built a successful mail-order business around it that benefits all of us. The software sold here (IBM-compatible) can be gotten at amazing prices—up to 80% off. So who cares if it was preowned? In the free price list you'll be happy to see the original price listed next to Recycled Software's deeply discounted prices. The categories here include popular titles of all kinds—Antivirus and Backup, Business/Contact Managers, Computer-aided Design, Communication, Databases, Desktop Publishing, Financial and Statistical, Flowcharting Tools, Graphics and Design, Integrated Packages, Online/Web Utilities, Operating Systems, Print Utilities, and much more. Many titles have not been preregistered, which means you'll be able to register them in your own name and get all the accompanying perks: technical support in many cases, warranty services, reduced-rate upgrades, etc. Recycled Software sells only English-version software as sold in the U.S., guaranteed to be free of viruses or defects.

International customers, please note: Recycled Software honors prohibitions on sale of programs outside the U.S. when such restrictions are imposed.

WEBSITE: The current price list of stock on hand can be viewed online or downloaded (zipped) from the website, which is updated weekly, but there's no online ordering. You'll still need to call, fax, or mail in your order.

SPECIAL FACTORS: Satisfaction guaranteed; returns accepted within 30 days for refund, exchange, or credit.

RefurbDepot.com

800–660–4443

FORM OF INFORMATION: online catalog only; no print catalog

PAY: check, MO, MC, V, AE, DSC

SELLS: factory refurbished computers, cameras, office equipment, audio and video equipment, small appliances, and other pluggables

STORE: no walk-in location; mail-order only; phone hours Monday to Thursday 10:00 am– 6:00 pm, Friday 10:00 am–2:00 pm EST

ONLINE: www.refurbdepot.com

Over the years of doing this book, I've become a jaded, suspicious shopper. How can they sell that item for so little? What's the catch? Well, I found a great company called RefurbDepot.com that tells you up front why they are able to sell name-brand pluggables at up to 80% off. Everything at RefurbDepot.com, as the name suggests, is factory refurbished. What does this mean? I got a little education, and it's worth passing along the lesson to readers, as you may never want to buy "new" again once you've learned about refurbished goods. Here are some examples of why a product would be classified as "refurbished": (1) The product was returned to the manufacturer before the 30-day money-back guarantee, and is simply reinspected and repackaged like new; (2) The box or casing was damaged in shipment, and the item is repackaged; (3) The item was returned because of a slight defect, and the defective part is replaced by the manufacturer, tested, and then the item is repackaged like new; (4) The item was returned because of a minor cosmetic blemish on the casing, which is corrected; (5) The item was a demonstration model; or (6) The box was opened. Overstocked items that are brand new are also sometimes called "refurbished." It is impossible to know the history of each item, but whatever the reason it gets labeled refurbished, all you need to know is that it is inspected, serviced, tested, and repackaged to meet the original product specifications. Everything this vendor sells comes with the manufacturer's original warranty, from 90 days to 2 years. Here's the icing on the cake: Refurbished products have a lower defect rate than new products, which are 50% more likely to be defective.

Okay, so now that you know about as much as I do, here's what you'll find at the RefurbDepot.com online store: computers (desktops, digital cameras, monitors, notebooks, printers, scanners); audio (audio systems, car stereo, personal stereos and portable stereos); electronics (cameras microwaves, shavers, telephones); office equipment (copy machines, fax machines, label makers); and video (camcorders, DVD, televisions, VCRs). You can search by specific product or by manufacturer, but I found even more items by clicking on "category" under "power search," where goods such as Palm Pilots, bread makers, and vacuum cleaners also showed up. All major manufacturers are represented here, including Brother, Canon, Casio, Compaq, Epson, GE, Hewlett Packard, IBM, JVC, Lexmark, Minolta, and dozen of others. The website offers secure online ordering, and there is a customer service number you can call if you need to speak with a human being. This is a great find for bargain hounds.

SPECIAL FACTORS: If paying by check, please allow up to 7 business days after receipt for clearance of funds; a $25 fee will be charged on all returned checks; see website for details on return, exchange, and refund policies; all products come with manufacturer's warranty.

Softwareoutlet.com

2431 S. Anne St.
Santa Ana, CA 92704
800–230–7638
714–979–6800
FAX: 714–434–4799

FORM OF INFORMATION: online catalog only; no print catalog

PAY: check, MO, MC, V, AE, DSC, purchase orders

SELLS: PC and Macintosh business, graphics, educational, and game software

STORE: no walk-in location; mail-order, will call available

ONLINE: www.softwareoutlet.com

Softwareoutlet.com president Bill McIvor began selling closeout and surplus software fifteen years ago, when we were all using DOS machines with the big floppy disks. Now he has a booming online store, as well as thousands of happy customers who appreciate his sound, underlying business model: "Buy software in huge lots and blow it out dirt cheap." I found my favorite educational children's software for 40% less, which is fairly typical here. Many goods are discounted even more. To sweeten the whole experience, read the president's letter in the "About Us" section and you'll learn that this is a small company run by real people you can talk to—my favorite kind of business.

I was also pleasantly surprised to discover the comprehensive selection and the no-nonsense design of the website, which enables customers to search either by category or by key word. Categories include Games, Graphics, Kids and Education, Utilities, Family, Business, Macintosh, and Accessories. Bargain hunters: be sure to check out the $5 or Less and the $10 or Less sections. Every week there are also a dozen or so super specials. This is a firm that has a lot of experience with one type of product and really does it well. It's doubtful you'll find such a good selection of software elsewhere at these prices. If you don't believe me, read the customer testimonials. They're about as gushing and effusive as I've ever seen!

SPECIAL FACTORS: 20% restocking fee on all returned items; returns must be made within 30 days (see website for details); quantity discounts available to qualified resellers.

Zones, Inc.

1102 15th St. SW, Ste. 102
Auburn, WA 98001–6509
800–248–9948

FORM OF INFORMATION: free print catalogs; online catalogs

PAY: check, MO, MC, V, AE, DSC

SELLS: PC and Mac hardware and software

STORE: no walk-in location; mail-order only

ONLINE: www.zones.com

Zones was founded in 1986 and has continued to evolve along with the technology industry. They are a single source, direct marketing reseller of multi-vendor IT products and services. Zones offers over 150,000 products from more than 2,000 vendors. This computer superstore comprises the IT Zone, Creative Pro and Mac Zone, and is regularly rated one of the top web-merchant sites. If you prefer print catalogs, you can request a Zones or Mac Zone catalog for free for the same good selection and service.

WEBSITE: Whether you have a PC or a Mac system, one click will take you to the appropriate store, where you can shop by brand, system, hardware, software, networking solutions and storage/media. Some of the non-Mac and -Apple manufacturers represented here include Adobe, Microsoft, Epson, Hewlett-Packard, Intel, IBM, NEC, and Sony.

Zones has been serving the education and government community for over 16 years, offering an extensive selection on technology products and services. Their dedicated account representatives are committed to working with your institution to find the right computing solutions for your budget.

SPECIAL FACTORS: Due to certain manufacturers' return polices, you will be required to contact those manufacturers (including Apple, IBM, Compaq, Hewlett-Packard, Sony and others) directly to repair, replace or return your products. With manufacturer's allowance, a return authorization number may be requested 14 days from the invoice date; all products must be received within 10 days of receipt of a return authorization number.

Office Furnishings

Desks, ergonomic chairs, safes, shelving, workstations, computer furniture; furnishings for home offices, reception rooms, storerooms, hospitals, churches, schools, and day-care facilities

Whether you're looking for an inexpensive, ergonomic desk chair for home or computer workstations for two dozen employees, these companies will have what you need. Many of the firms here carry furnishings for institutional settings—church pews, stacking cafeteria chairs, gymnasium bleachers, chalkboards—while others are more focused on the needs of small businesses. Every company listed here will save you significant amounts of money.

Some of the companies that carry office machines and shipping supplies also sell office furniture, shelving, and other furnishings for your stockroom or office, so be sure to see the listings in "Office Supplies and Machines," page 461.

Find It Fast

CHILD CARE AND SCHOOL FURNITURE, PLAYGROUND AND PARK EQUIPMENT
Alfax Wholesale Furniture, Dallas Midwest, K-Log, National Business Furniture

CHURCH AND RELIGIOUS FURNISHINGS
Alfax Wholesale Furniture, Dallas Midwest

CORPORATE AND MIDSIZE OFFICE FURNISHINGS
National Business Furniture

DESIGN SERVICES
National Business Furniture

HOME OFFICE, BUSINESS, AND COMPUTER FURNITURE
Alfax Wholesale Furniture, K-Log, National Business Furniture, OfficeFurniture.com

LIBRARY, CONFERENCE, AUDIO/VISUAL FURNITURE
Alfax Wholesale Furniture, Dallas Midwest, K-Log, National Business Furniture

MEDICAL OFFICE FURNITURE
Alfax Wholesale Furniture

OTHER INSTITUTIONAL FURNITURE
Alfax Wholesale Furniture, Dallas Midwest

STAGES, RISERS, LOCKERS
Alfax Wholesale Furniture

Alfax Wholesale Furniture

1250 Broadway, Ste. 1600
New York, NY 10001–3701
800–221–5710
212–947–9560
FAX: 800–638–6445

FORM OF INFORMATION: free print catalog; online catalog

PAY: check, MO, MC, V, AE, DSC

SELLS: school, church, and institutional furniture

STORE: no walk-in location; mail-order only; phone hours Monday to Friday 7:30am–9:00 pm, Saturday 10:00 am–3:00 pm EST

ONLINE: www.alfaxfurniture.com

If you're opening a day-care center, refurnishing a school or religious institution, or looking to update your company's offices, Alfax Wholesale Furniture offers "guaranteed quality at wholesale prices" on institutional furniture. The furniture and equipment, such as file cabinets, literature storage systems, lockers, and heavy steel shelving, are designed for heavy use, with many products suitable for the home as well. Prefabricated office and computer cabinetry and stations; nursery and child-care furnishings (mats, play-study stations); stages, risers, and lecterns; cafeteria, banquet, and library furnishings; conference-room seating; mobile medical cabinets and quick-set-up medical couches; and miscellaneous fixtures such as PA systems, trophy cases, hat racks, flag stands, and coat racks can be ordered from the 140-page catalog.

WEBSITE: Alfax has an easy to use website complete with online ordering. I like that they include the list price next to the discounted price, along with the shipping charges.

SPECIAL FACTORS: Satisfaction guaranteed; institutional accounts and leasing available; additional 3% discount if payment made in full upon purchase.

Dallas Midwest

4100 Alpha Rd., Ste. 111
Dallas, TX 75244
800-527-2417
972–866–0101
FAX: 800–301–8314

FORM OF INFORMATION: free print catalog; online catalog

PAY: check, MO, MC, V, AE, DSC

SELLS: church, school, and institutional furniture

STORE: no walk-in location; mail-order only; phone hours Monday to Friday 7:30 am–7:00 pm, Saturday 9:00 am–1:00 pm CST

ONLINE: www.dallasmidwest.com

Dallas Midwest sells school, church, and government agency furniture at discounts of 30% to 60% off list prices, with special savings offered on orders over $1,000. The catalog presents furnishings and fixtures, such as benches and chairs, desks, credenzas, pulpits, cabinets, and shelving. Stacking chairs, folding chairs, and folding and adjustable worktables are available, as are post and rope systems for managing crowds, mobile stages and risers, and directory boards.

The catalog devotes sections to school and day-care equipment for indoor use (classroom desks, chairs, wooden storage units for toys and books, activity tables, cribs, nap mats) and outdoor use (sandboxes, slides, seesaws, playground sets). The section on church furnishings features pulpits, kneelers, credence and communion tables, and stands. School and church furnishings available in unfinished wood are detailed in a separate catalog, available on request.

WEBSITE: The website is comprehensive and user-friendly. Shop by category, department, or style—all products are clearly depicted with list prices beside the Dallas discount price. If you like what you see you can order online.

SPECIAL FACTORS: Price quotes by phone; quantity discounts available; authorized returns accepted for exchange, refund, or credit; institutional accounts available; furniture leasing packages available.

K-Log

P.O. Box 5
Zion, IL 60099
800–872–6611
847–872–6611
FAX: 847–872–3728

FORM OF INFORMATION: free print catalog; online catalog

PAY: check, MO, MC, V, AE

SELLS: office, A/V, and computer furniture and equipment

STORE: no walk-in location; mail-order only

ONLINE: www.k-log.com

Luckily for mail-order shoppers, all discount furniture enterprises are not created equal. K-Log clearly excels in its inventory of training/hospitality, utility, folding, and activity tables, and other conference room furniture that ranges from boat-shaped, slab-base tables and traditional plinth-base tables to modular conference and computer tables. For a less institutional feel, there are solid American red oak and oak-veneer furniture lines, a classic cherry executive series, and, for computer work, a traditional-style oak set, all in a variety of configurations, with most products discounted 50%. K-Log can equip school audio-visual and computer labs with two-student stations, split-top workstations, and computer lab desks with space for both computer and desk work. Electric-lift, adjustable work centers allow for computer work while standing or sitting, and tower workstations accommodate multiple monitors for LAN systems or video editing. The color catalog allots 10 pages to audio-visual equipment that includes overhead projector tables, locking consoles, TV mounts, deluxe presentation screens, big screen video projectors, LCD projection panels, lecterns, and hands-free sound systems. K-Log also stocks chairs, floor and wall displays, bookcases, steel and wire shelving, coat rack systems, storage cabinets, and fireproof files.

WEBSITE: The website offers monthly super specials, but watch for expiration dates before reaching for the phone. You'll also find a good selection of best-selling items, from oak office furniture and fireproof storage to modular workstations you configure to suit your unique needs and space. Product descriptions, K-Log's price versus list price, and color images accompany the merchandise listings, but there's no online ordering here as of this writing. For K-Log's full line of products, go straight to the print catalog, which contains many more items.

SPECIAL FACTORS: Satisfaction guaranteed; quantity discounts available; price quotes by phone or letter; authorized returns accepted for exchange, refund, or credit (restocking fee may apply); institutional accounts available.

National Business Furniture

735 N. Water St.
Milwaukee, WI 53202
800-558-1010
FAX: 800-329-9349

FORM OF INFORMATION: free print catalog; online catalog

PAY: check, MO, MC, V, AE, DSC

SELLS: corporate and midsize office furnishings

STORE: several locations with outside sales staff (see text)

ONLINE: www.nationalbusinessfurniture.com

Established in 1975, National Business Furniture (NBF) sells quality corporate and midsize furniture for beautiful offices at affordable prices, including bookcases and shelving, conference room tables, cabinets, leather chairs, traditional chairs with classic button-tufting, display cases, and desks. Savings at National Business Furniture, which calls itself "the nation's largest direct marketer of office furniture," reach as high as 50% on many items. NBF's 290-page print catalog includes products not seen in some other furniture dealers' catalogs, namely, portable partitions to create instant rooms, acoustic panels to screen out distracting noises, colorful lockers to conveniently and quietly store personal belongings, and olefin floor mats and runners to wipe shoes and reduce water tracking on tile. Most top-name manufacturers are represented in the 10,000-item catalog, and complete manufacturers' product-line brochures, as well as fabric swatches and wood samples, are available by calling NBF. Local sales reps in branch locations (Atlanta, Boston, Chicago, Dallas, Los Angeles, Milwaukee, Phoenix, and New York) are available for office consultations. NBF provides a 15-year guarantee on products (except for normal wear and for chairs used on a 24-hour basis), and will adjust, repair, or replace them if there are problems with workmanship or quality.

WEBSITE: At the website you can shop by department (breakroom, reception, drafting, conference, training and so on), or by category or style. There's a product-search capability and lots of useful information for the shopper, including shipping and warranty policies, color images and detailed descriptions, and order tracking. Discounted prices are listed next to list and you can order products directly online.

SPECIAL FACTORS: Price quotes by phone or letter with SASE; quantity discounts available; leasing plans available to qualifying companies.

OfficeFurniture.com

735 N. Water St., #400
P. O. Box 510050
Milwaukee, WI 53203–0017
800–933–0053
FAX: 800–468–1526

FORM OF INFORMATION: free print catalog, online catalog

PAY: check, MO, MC, V, AE, DSC

SELLS: small and home office furniture

STORE: no walk-in location; mail-order only; phone hours Monday to Friday 6:30 am– 7:00 pm, Saturday 8:00 am–2:00 pm CST

ONLINE: www.officefurniture.com

If you're in the market for office furnishings for your small office or home, OfficeFurniture.com's discounts of 40% and higher off manufacturers' list prices are just the enticement you've been waiting for. Most products are available "factory in-stock," which means there's no undue waiting. Sharp color photos in the 80-page print catalog detail important aspects of every piece of value-priced office furniture, including bookcases, organizers, panels, reception seating, tables, chairs, desks, and computer furniture. If your order is likely to exceed $1,000, you're invited to phone for a price quote, since additional discounts of 2% to 8% apply to larger orders.

WEBSITE: The website lets you browse by category or brand. Categories include: Desks/Workcenters, Chairs, Bookcases/Wall Units, Modular Workstations, Filing Cabinets, Storage Cabinets, Tables, and Accessories. The brands offered here include Adesso, Altra, Bestar, Bush, La-Z-Boy, Leda, Martin, Maxon, O'Sullivan, Royal Teak, and more. Items have color images with detailed descriptions plus shipping costs.

SPECIAL FACTORS: Satisfaction guaranteed; quantity discounts available; OfficeFurniture.com's own 9-year guarantee (except for normal wear and tear) applies to everything it sells.

Office Supplies and Machines

General office supplies; faxes, copiers, shredders, and other office machines; telephone headsets; shipping materials

If you're still using a single source for your office needs, check out the vendors listed here, then pull your last few supply invoices. When you compare prices—especially on items your firm uses in bulk—you'll no doubt find that you're paying more than you should. And many of the discounters listed here offer the same perks you've been getting: open accounts, quick shipment, special orders, and custom services. You'll find virtually everything you need in this section to keep your office humming—from paperclips to copiers.

For firms specializing in computers, computer-related hardware such as printers and modems, and computer software, see "Computer Hardware and Software," page 441. For furniture such as desks, workstations, chairs, shelving, and the like, see "Office Furnishings," page 455. "Printing and Stationery," page 479, features companies that can custom-print payroll checks, business cards, invoices, rubber stamps, letterhead, postcards, and other items for you and your business, although many of the firms in this section offer some of these services as well. And if you're looking for promotional items, corporate gifts, or clothing imprinted with your company's logo, see the last section of this chapter, "Uniforms and Promotional Products," on page 487.

Find It Fast

BAGS, BOXES, AND STORAGE MATERIALS
Associated Bag, Plastic Bagmart, U.S. Box

BINDERS AND ORGANIZERS FOR BUSINESS AND PHOTOS
Century Photo, StoreSmart Express, University Products

CASH REGISTERS
Business Technologies

COMMERCIAL ARTS SUPPLIES
Reliable

CUSTOM-SEWN COMPUTER DUST COVERS
Co-Du-Co Computer Dust Covers

GENERAL OFFICE SUPPLIES AND OFFICE MACHINES
Quill, Reliable, Viking Office Products

PRINTER/COMPUTER/COPY MACHINE SUPPLIES
Co-Du-Co Computer Dust Covers, Quill, Viking Office Products

PRINTER INK CARTRIDGES
 Quill, Reliable, Viking Office Products

PROFESSIONAL-QUALITY TELEPHONE HEADSETS
 Headsets.com

RESALE PACKAGING AND RETAIL DISPLAYS
 U.S. Box

SHIPPING SUPPLIES
 Associated Bag, Quill, Reliable, ULINE, Viking Office Products, Yazoo Mills

WRITING IMPLEMENTS
 Fountain Pen Hospital

Associated Bag Company

400 W. Boden St.
Milwaukee, WI 53207
800–926–6100
FAX: 800–926–4610
TDD: 800–926–4611

FORM OF INFORMATION: free print catalog and samples; online catalog

PAY: MO, MC, V, AE, DSC

SELLS: shipping and packaging products

STORE: no walk-in location; mail-order only; phone hours Monday to Friday 8:00 am–8:00 pm EST

ONLINE: www.associatedbag.com

If only the world were as straightforward and direct as this company, which has been in the packaging and shipping business since 1938. Is there anyone else out there besides me who gets excited by the prospect of giant rolls of corrugated paper, machines to shrink-wrap everything, zipper-lock bags in every conceivable size, burlap sacks, bubble-lined envelopes, and color-coded trash-bag liners and ties? I feel as though I could systematize and protect my entire life's possessions if only I had the storage space for all the bags, boxes, and wrap I'd need.

Associated Bag's well-organized 200-page color catalog has poly bags, bag-closing devices, envelopes, retail packaging, industrial covers and liners, static control products, safety and clean-up supplies, tapes and labels, mailers, boxes, and shipping and packaging products. From Junior's lunchtime sandwiches to radioactive waste, Associated has the right size and material bag to contain it. Besides a fantastic array of containers and other products, Associated Bag offers pricing that's competitive, even more so when you order in volume. The staff is trained to deal with just about any packaging problem you or your business can come up with, and free product samples are available. This is a great source for small businesses or large projects, such as moving. Associated Bag can customize just about any product for your specifications, and offers imprinting with low minimums.

WEBSITE: The website allows for electronic viewing of the actual print catalog if you have the software installed to download it. It's a handy way to see what the company carries and to read about company policies without having a print catalog in front of you. But you still need to call, fax, or mail in your order, because there's no online ordering capability as of this writing.

SPECIAL FACTORS: Satisfaction guaranteed; products for special applications can be made to order; quantity discounts available and some minimum quantities apply; returns accepted; same-day shipping on orders placed by 8:00 pm EST.

Business Technologies

3350 Center Grove Dr.
Dubuque, IA 52003–5225
800–451–0399
563–556–7994
FAX: 563–556–2512

FORM OF INFORMATION: free brochure
PAY: company check, MO, MC, V
SELLS: cash registers and cash register supplies
STORE: same address; Monday to Friday 8:30 am–5:00 pm

If you'd like to open a retail shop and start small, you could spend a lot for a cash register. Business Technologies has a simple solution: Don't. This company sells Sharp electronic cash registers and cash register supplies (paper rolls, inking supplies, extra tills, etc.) at discount prices—to the tune of about 30% off list. The 1-page brochure shows the basic models with features listed for each. But a telephone call once you've seen the selection will hook you up to the helpful salespeople and support staff at Business Technologies, who will walk you through the pros and cons of different models, and will stand by you after you've made the purchase with technical support, a 1-year warranty, and free programming.

SPECIAL FACTORS: Price quotes by phone, fax, or letter; minimum order: $25.

Century Photo

P.O. Box 2393
Brea, CA 92822
800–767–0777
FAX: 800–786–7939

FORM OF INFORMATION: free print catalog; online catalog

PAY: check, MO, MC, V, AE, DSC

SELLS: office and photo organizers

STORE: no walk-in location; mail-order only

ONLINE: www.centuryphoto.com and www.centurybusinesssolutions.com

If you collect tabloid-sized newspapers, Century Photo, with 45 years' experience, has the perfect scrapbook with screw bindings to help you protect your collection—up to 25 pages. This company specializes in helping people organize, display, and archive their treasured images. For more typical archival or storage needs—family photos and videos, baseball cards, stamps, periodicals, trading cards, and recipes—Century Photo carries photo and slide storage sheets and albums, binders, report covers, video- and audiocassette portfolios, and filing systems, with savings running between 20% and 33%. Certain products such as Crown linen albums, oversize photo binders, and library albums come with free gold imprinting. The 60-page catalog of office and photo organizers (there's also a 48-page photo catalog) has sections of disk storage and CD storage products, including double-capacity static-guard diskette pages, mini-display disk binders, poly or vinyl CD safety sleeves, and CD zipper travel cases. For sorting, identifying, and handling signs, letters, and schedules, there are heavy-weight vinyl envelopes in 22 sizes, with pricing for silk screen color logo imprinting, when you supply the camera-ready color-separated art. Foil stamping and deluxe personalizing are available for other products as well.

WEBSITE: The website is every bit as meticulous and well-organized as you would expect from a company that specializes in organization. No need to use the print catalog if you have internet access, this is a great site and you can order online.

SPECIAL FACTORS: Satisfaction guaranteed; returns accepted for exchange, refund, or credit.

Co-Du-Co Computer Dust Covers

4802 W. Wisconsin Ave.
Milwaukee, WI 53208–3050
800–735–1584
414–476–1584
FAX: 414–476–9329

FORM OF INFORMATION: online catalog only; no print catalog

PAY: check, MO, MC, V, AE

SELLS: all-fabric, custom-fit dust covers for computers and peripherals

STORE: no walk-in location; mail-order only; phone hours Monday to Friday 9:00 am–9:00 pm CST

ONLINE: www.co-du-co.com

Do you consider your computer a friend? If so, you will be as happy as I was to discover Co-Du-Co Computer Dust Covers, a small company that takes a low-tech approach to our high-tech world in the form of custom-made, solid-color dust covers for your computer and peripherals. Why would you want one of these? Well, for one thing, they're extremely affordable. For another, they're attractive. They're also durable. Unlike cheap plastic or vinyl covers, these will never crack or yellow. They're breathable, too, which means you can cover up your equipment immediately after turning it off without causing damage to either equipment or covers. When they need freshening up, never fear. Because they're made of a nifty cotton/polyester blend, Co-Du-Co computer dust covers are completely washable and will continue to look smart and neat for the life of your equipment. And since they're inexpensive, you can buy one for all of your computers and peripherals—your portable, keyboard, scanner, and printer. I love the colors, which range from understated and tasteful—grey, maroon, beige, black, white, and navy—to bold—sassy orange, red, forest green, mustard, turquoise, royal, and purple. Color swatches are shown on the website.

If this company doesn't list your brand and model, they'll custom-make a cover for you based on the dimensions you provide. The website has a section that shows how to measure, but if you're unsure, you can call the customer service number during business hours for assistance. Want your initials or company logo embroidered on your covers? No problem. Co-Du-Co does this, too. Owner Terry Schaefer says, "I am very proud of my little company, which has been in business for almost 18 years." She should be proud. This company is a great find, and these covers would make a wonderful gift for your favorite computer. Place your order online or by fax.

SPECIAL FACTORS: A good fit is guaranteed or cover is remade or refunded; custom orders and embroidery available; wholesale inquiries welcome.

Fountain Pen Hospital

10 Warren St.
New York, NY 10007
800–253–PENS
212–964–0580
FAX: 212–227–5916

FORM OF INFORMATION: free print catalog; online catalog
PAY: check, MO, MC, V, AE, DSC
SELLS: fountain pens, writing instruments, and repair services
STORE: same address; Monday to Friday 7:45 am–5:30 pm
ONLINE: www.fountainpenhospital.com

There are certain items you don't expect to find at good prices: fine writing implements, for example. But Fountain Pen Hospital, in business since 1946, has "the world's largest selection" of modern and vintage writing instruments at great prices. Price comparisons with several other fine-writing-instrument companies showed that Fountain Pen Hospital offers the best deals by far, with prices 20% to 40% less than everyone else's. The 84-page catalog includes some of the best names in the biz: Montblanc, Aurora, Waterman, Namiki, Parker, and many others. This family-run business specializes in new pens as well as vintage instruments made between the 1880s and 1960s. Recent catalog offerings included Delta's Alfa Romeo collection, bright resin colors with sterling silver accents,(30% off list); a Waterford Gold fountain pen from the Arcadia collection (50% off list); and Montblanc's Meisterstück collection, offering a black with gold trim fountain pen with an 18k gold nib . You'll also find wood and leather pen cases and trunks, matching pens and lighters, Filo-fax organizers, and more. Retail prices are listed alongside Fountain Pen Hospital's price so you can readily see the discounts.

Owners Steve and Terry Wiederlight apply lots of TLC to pen repair (call for mailing procedure) and to maintaining their catalog (a new one is sent out approximately every 3 months).

WEBSITE: Log on for more on the firm's history, latest product arrivals, and plenty of super specials. At the website, you'll find a wonderful variety of fine writing instruments with detailed photos, descriptions and secure online ordering.

SPECIAL FACTORS: Satisfaction guaranteed; price quotes by phone or letter; returns accepted within 7 days for exchange, refund, or credit.

Headsets.com

1 Daniel Burnham Ct., 310 C
San Francisco, CA 94109
800–450–7686
FAX: 415–929–5980

FORM OF INFORMATION: free print catalog; online catalog

PAY: MC, V, AE

SELLS: telephone headsets

STORE: no walk-in location; mail-order only; phone hours Monday to Friday 7:00 am–4:00 pm PST

ONLINE: www.headsets.com

"All of our representatives are busy assisting other customers at this time. Please stay on the line and your call will be answered by the next available representative in the order it was received." *Click.* Muzak. Does hearing this on the other end of the phone drive you absolutely batty? If you have to spend 40 minutes on and off hold with an airline company in the middle of your workday. for example, wouldn't it be great to be able to do something productive, like tidying up your office instead of sitting there like a jerk, staring out of the window? Ah, if only you had a professional-model telephone headset. But who can afford such a luxury? You can!

Headsets.com, America's leading headset discounter, is a company that sells nothing but high-quality headsets and headset accessories at true wholesale prices. When you see the prices at this website, you may wonder how this company is able to do it. The reason is that most headsets are manufactured in the Far East, sold to an importer or a major headset distributor, then purchased by a local dealer who sells them to us, the end user. Headsets.com has eliminated the layers of distribution and thus the added mark-ups—straight from the factory to you means they can charge around 45% to 60% less than a conventional retailer. But good prices are only the beginning.

At Headsets.com you get customer support before and after the sale, a 1-year warranty, and a complete, no-questions-asked, money-back guarantee. The models here include over-the-head, on-the-ear (won't mess up your hairdo), and factory-reconditioned wireless models (brand-new, the latter are prohibitively expensive for most people). Headsets.com also has accessories such as DC adapters to eliminate the need for batteries, extension cords, and training adapters (allows two headsets to connect to a single phone so supervisors can listen in with trainees). All models come with an optional noise-canceling feature that can be added on for an extra cost, and many colors are available. What are some other reasons to buy a telephone headset? Headsets prevent neck and shoulder strain, free up your hands and thus increase productivity, and make hearing easier for people in loud environments.

WEBSITE: After visiting the website, getting a feel for this company's commitment to service and support, and reading about the advantages of telephone headsets, you're going to want to buy one.

SPECIAL FACTORS: 60-day money-back guarantee.

Plastic Bagmart

67 Bond St.
Westbury, NY 11590
800–343–BAGS
516–997–3355
FAX: 516–997–1836

FORM OF INFORMATION: free catalog with SASE

PAY: check, MO, MC, V, AE

SELLS: plastic bags

STORE: same address; Monday to Friday 9:00 am–5:00 pm, Saturday 9:00 am–3:00 pm

The little 8-page catalog from Plastic Bagmart has just the right bags for your business, home, or industry and offers discounts up to 60% below supermarket prices. Here you'll find reclosable zipper bags; flat, heat-sealable poly bags; trash liners; take-out bags for merchants; rolls of poly tubing; FDA-approved bags for food and packaging; cellophane bags; handy bags on a roll; printed ice bags; foldover shirt bags; heavyweight storage bags; doorknob and newspaper bags; garment bags; disposable poly gloves; packing list envelopes; and sealing equipment. There's a bag here for just about every need and in just about every size imaginable. Quantity discounts apply, and you can mix and match cases to earn them.

SPECIAL FACTORS: Satisfaction guaranteed; price quotes by letter with SASE; returns accepted within 10 days; minimum order: 1 case; prices include shipping.

Quill Corporation

P.O. Box 94080
Palestine, IL 60094–4080
800–982–3400
FAX: 800–789–8955

FORM OF INFORMATION: free print catalog (see text); online catalog
PAY: check, MO, MC, V, AE
SELLS: office supplies and equipment
STORE: no walk-in location; mail-order only
ONLINE: www.quillcorp.com

In business since 1956, Quill Corporation is one of those names immediately recognized among business managers, institutional buyers, and individuals purchasing office supplies and equipment for offering the best prices; savings can reach as high as 83% off list. In addition to the mega 600-page master catalog, Quill publishes smaller special-interest catalogs you can request that make shopping easier for your more targeted needs. Catalog subjects include computer supplies, professional services (financial, accounting, legal), health care, business furniture, school supplies, warehouse express (shipping, janitorial, safety equipment), and Quill's CD-ROM catalog.

WEBSITE: I like the website, where you can order your office supplies online, take advantage of specials, and get a good sense of all the products this company sells. With more than 14,000 products to handle, the Quill website is surprisingly easy to navigate.

SPECIAL FACTORS: Satisfaction guaranteed; institutional accounts available; returns accepted; goods shipped only within the U.S.; minimum order: $20.

Reliable Corp.

P.O. Box 1502
Ottawa, IL 61350–9914
800–359–5000
FAX: 800–326–3233

FORM OF INFORMATION: free print catalogs
PAY: check, MO, MC, V, AE, DSC
SELLS: office supplies and equipment
STORE: no walk-in location; mail-order only
ONLINE: www.reliable.com

Reliable sells thousands of office supply products and furniture items at 50% to 80% off suggested retail prices. By phone, fax, and online you can request one or more free catalogs for "Basic Office Supplies," "Computer Supplies," "Furniture," or "Shipping and Warehouse." If you want to receive up-to-the-minute sales announcements, simply provide your email address when you place your catalog request.

Among Reliable's inventory are paper and pens, presentation folios, binders, computer furniture, workstations, cleaning supplies, media storage, leather chairs, cordless phones, fax machines, corporate gifts, lamps, task chairs, breakroom supplies, shipping supplies, imprinted goods, specialty items, and designer laser paper. Your savings increase even more if you can buy in quantity. This firm ships products within an hour of receiving your order, with free delivery standard on all in-stock items. Reliable offers an unconditional guarantee with a 30-day free trial that includes computers and electronics.

WEBSITE: At the website, when perusing the online catalog index, you need to move your little mouse over the main category and then onto the subcategory to link to the page. (I know you can do it.) There are no links from the main categories. The products all have thorough descriptions and clear images to look at, and secure electronic ordering is available.

SPECIAL FACTORS: Satisfaction guaranteed; institutional accounts available; minimum order: $25.

StoreSmart Express

180 Metro Park
Rochester, NY 14623
800–424–1011
585–424–5300
FAX: 800–424–5411
or 585–424–5313

FORM OF INFORMATION: free print catalog; online catalog

PAY: check, MO, V, MC, AE

SELLS: multi-media storage products

STORE: same address; Monday to Thursday 9:00 am–5:00 pm, Friday 9:00 am–4:30 pm

ONLINE: www.storesmart.com or www.visualhorizons.com

StoreSmart Express specializes in over 5,000 multi-media storage products to organize your business cards, CDs, audio and videotapes, office, and home. The 40-page catalog presents a varied selection for storing and protecting just about anything you need to protect. Business is booming at StoreSmart as customers discover that these products are useful in organizing all areas of their business and home. The catalog also features peel and stick and non-adhesive pockets in sizes from 2" x 2" all the way to 26" x 39". The pockets make your proposals easy to identify, information easy to find, filing cabinets more organized, and much more. The pockets act as a permanent protector of the information, yet the information can be removed and replaced easily. The prices are excellent in both small and large quantities. There is no minimum order and samples are available on many items. Call for a quote for large quantities.

WEBSITE: The online version of the catalog lists all available sizes and dimensions in table form, along with price breaks. It's easy to order online, by phone, fax, mail, or mail.

SPECIAL FACTORS: Satisfaction guaranteed; rush service available; Rush service available.

ULINE

2200 S. Lakeside Dr.
Waukegan, IL 60085
800–958–5463
FAX: 800–295–5571

FORM OF INFORMATION: free print catalog; online catalog

PAY: check, MO, MC, V, AE, DSC, DC

SELLS: shipping supplies

STORE: no walk-in location; mail-order only

ONLINE: www.uline.com

Whether you're running a mom-and-pop business out of your home or are in charge of a warehouse, ULINE is the source for every kind of packing need. This family-run, reader-recommended business has warehouses in Illinois, Minnesota, New Jersey, and California; orders are shipped from the location nearest you to ensure the quickest and most cost-effective service. The handsome 280-page catalog features anti-static products, bags and bag sealers, boxes, bubble and cushioning material, tape and tape dispensers, envelopes, foam, labels, mailers, packing list envelopes, strapping, stretch wrap, tags, tubes—everything from aerosol products to vermiculite. And ULINE has over 500 different box types in stock—one of their biggest advantages over other shipping-supply houses. At ULINE, the more you buy, the more you save—there are quantity price breaks on all items. ULINE will even give you a free gift (a baseball cap, a mug, a tote bag, or gourmet coffee, for instance) when your order exceeds $250.

WEBSITE: ULINE's website takes you to a table of contents, organized alphabetically, where you can click on the item of interest, view it, read the description, and then order it online.

SPECIAL FACTORS: Satisfaction guaranteed 100%; returns must be made within 30 days.

University Products, Inc.

P.O. Box 101
Holyoke, MA 01041–0101
800–336–4847
FAX: 800–532–9281

FORM OF INFORMATION: free print catalog; online catalog

PAY: check, MO, MC, V, AE, DSC, DC

SELLS: archival-quality materials for conservation, restoration, and preservation

STORE: no walk-in location; mail-order only

ONLINE: www.universityproducts.com

For over 30 years, University Products, Inc., has been a leader in providing archival-quality materials for conservation, restoration, and preservation, as well as library and school furniture and supplies. The "Archival Quality Materials Catalog" of over 200 pages details standard archival products, such as conservation paper and boards, tapes and adhesives, photo supplies, framing and matting supplies, display materials, and conservation tools and equipment. But you can also discover unexpected or hard-to-find items, such as solid aluminum and bookcase time capsules, unbuffered acid-free tissue paper, archival hat boxes, bridal boxes, artifact/specimen storage cartons and trays with clear-view covers, collectible display cases (for that precious Fender guitar or high school football from your youth), and museum pest kits that are pheromone traps and lures for controlling clothes moths, cigarette beetles, and cockroaches. Disaster supplies, which can serve institutions and home owners, include a sensor-activated Water Alert, newsprint paper for drawing spills away from documents, and Rescube for transporting water-soaked books. Professionals or hobbyists who rely on slides, prints, and negatives in their work can choose from storage boxes, enclosures, envelopes, folders, preservers, marking pens, mounts, a mounting press, inspection gloves, and slide sorter.

In the "feel good" department, it's wonderful to know that University Products sponsors a $5,000 annual award for distinguished achievement in conservation of cultural property, and that its product line, designed specifically to meet the needs of museums, brings that same high quality to individuals.

WEBSITE: New products and monthly specials can be viewed at the website and ordered online, but the full inventory can only be seen in the printed version of the catalog.

U.S. Box Corp.

1296 McCarter Hwy.
Newark, NJ 07104
800–221–0999
973–481–2000
FAX: 973–481–2002

FORM OF INFORMATION: $5 print catalog; online catalog

PAY: check, MO, MC, V, AE

SELLS: gift, jewelry, resale, and fashion packaging

STORE: no walk-in location; mail-order only

ONLINE: www.usbox.com

What is it I love so much about the catalog from U.S. Box Corp.? Perhaps oohing and ahhing over the pages of fanciful packaging and gift boxes is nearly as fun as opening them. U.S. Box Corp. has been selling retail and gift packaging since 1948. This is primarily a business-to-business firm, but it offers products that consumers use routinely: wrapping paper, tape, gift boxes, ribbon, and mailing bags, for example. If you can fulfill the $100 minimum order, you'll enjoy prices as much as 60% lower here than those charged for comparable items in variety and stationery stores. Some but not all items must be ordered in a minimum quantity—say, by the carton or roll. Additional discounts of 5% apply to orders over $500, and up to 25% on totals of $2,500 plus. Samples of the goods may be purchased at unit cost plus $5 shipping; this is recommended, since returns are not accepted.

The U.S. Box Corp. catalog is nearly 100 pages of dazzling tissue paper in plain and prints, ribbons (curling, paper raffia, woven metallic, etc.), bows, cording, giftwrap for every occasion or mood, and accessories such as printed labels and hot-stamped enclosure cards. It will convince you that for every product, there's a box or bag best suited to show it off, and this includes jewelry boxes, food boxes, corrugated liquor bags, clear plastic boxes with dividers, hat boxes, zip-up vinyl pouches, packing materials that are as pretty as the boxes, and much more. This catalog is fun and will wake up any creative person's imagination. Even if you don't have a retail shop, you'll find practical uses for many of these pretty and clever containers. The Jewelry section is great if you sell and display jewelry, because you'll find folding boxes, handle-lock bags, tiny totes, velvet jewelry pouches, display risers, tiny marble pedestals, miniature mahogany boxes, and a lot more. Consolidate your packaging needs or go in with a friend and you'll easily meet the $100 minimum order.

WEBSITE: The website offers a wide selection of packaging supplies with a greater variety than the catalog, plus new products are added daily There is online ordering.

SPECIAL FACTORS: Samples available at unit cost plus $5 shipping; returns not accepted; minimum order: $100.

Viking Office Products

950 W. 190th St.
Torrance, CA 90502
800–711–4242
FAX: 800–762–7329

FORM OF INFORMATION: free print catalog; online catalog

PAY: check, MO, MC, V, AE

SELLS: office supplies, furniture, computer supplies, stationery, printing services, etc.

STORE: no walk-in location; mail-order only

ONLINE: www.vikingop.com

With your first order from Viking Office Products, established in 1960, you'll receive the 609-page full-line catalog of over 12,000 office products, at discounts up to 69%. Offerings in sale catalogs are priced at discounts as high as 79%, savings that add up when you consider how quickly supplies get depleted. Rely on Viking for great deals on printers, ribbons, and cartridges; computer furniture; computer paper and labels; diskette data cartridges; myriad office supplies; and all kinds of business machines. Viking offers quantity pricing on many items, and always prints the list price alongside Viking's discounted one so you can compare and appreciate the savings you'll reap. With competition in the office supplies industry so fierce, this company has learned to excel by offering great prices and exemplary customer service. Delivery is free on orders of $25 and up, and Viking offers *same-day* delivery in major cities around the U.S. when you order by 11:00 am. Where will you get faster service than that? In addition to the general catalog—one you'll want to park on your desk shelf for frequent reference throughout the year—Viking issues these specialty themed catalogs: "Monthly Sale Book," "One-stop Print Shop," "Paper Catalog," "Office Machines," and "Mailing and Warehouse Supplies." Everything at Viking is guaranteed for 1 year, and all products come with a 30-day money-back return. This company wants—and deserves—your business. I've used this company for many years and have never had a complaint. Viking has only grown bigger and better over time.

WEBSITE: The website is designed for both comfort and speed. You can look for items using the product search engine, or browse by category. All products have the list price next to Viking's discounted price. There are other convenient features, too, such as your own customized order list—How many times have you flipped through a catalog trying to find that exact brand of paper you ordered last time?—and an instant supplies search that finds the compatible toner, say, for your printer's brand and model. Hooray for Viking! I really like this site and heartily endorse this company. Online ordering is available at the website.

SPECIAL FACTORS: Satisfaction guaranteed; institutional accounts available; shipping free on orders over $25.

Yazoo Mills, Inc.

P.O. Box 369
New Oxford, PA 17350
800–242–5216
717–624–8993
FAX: 717–624–4420

FORM OF INFORMATION: free print catalog; online catalog

PAY: check, MO, MC, V, AE, DSC

SELLS: shipping and mailing tubes, and custom-made cores

STORE: no walk-in location; mail-order only

ONLINE: www.yazoomills.com

Everything comes from somewhere—the name for Yazoo Mills comes from a town in Mississippi, and those tubes you find inside rolls of fax paper come from Yazoo Mills. Yazoo also makes carpet cores, cable reels, heavy blast casings for mining companies, and shipping tubes for posters and other works on paper. I knew a painter of very large pictures who used to search the dumpsters of Manhattan for gigantic carpeting tubes, perfect for rolling up his unstretched canvases for storage. If only he'd known about this gem of a company. Shipping tubes, which range in length from 12" to 85" and in diameter from 2" to 12" are sold by the case with plastic inserts for plugging the ends—at discounts up to 80% below art-supply shop prices. For custom sizes and colors, or for acid-free stock, call for a price quote; Yazoo routinely does job-specific manufacturing.

WEBSITE: Yazoo has kept up with the times with a nifty website. It's simple to use: Just click on the product (mailing and shipping tubes), click on the size, and place your order online.

SPECIAL FACTORS: No shipping charges within the continental U.S.; minimum order: 1 carton of stock tubes.

Printing and Stationery

Stationery, invitations, letterhead, logo design, check printing, business cards, bills of lading, invoices, postcards and other custom-printing services

Jazz up your company image with some new letterhead and business cards. Increase efficiency and save time and money with preprinted business checks, invoices, and shipping forms that you can feed through your printer. Need a rubber stamp to identify your child's books, some monogrammed stationery, or customized invitations? Some of the firms here can do that, too. At Modern Postcard, Color Card, and Color Printing Central you can get postcards printed for much cheaper than anywhere else I've checked. Don't pay full price for printing services! All of the companies in this section can save you lots of money.

Find It Fast

ADDRESS LABELS
Checks in the Mail, Invitation & Promotion Hotline

BROCHURE AND CATALOG PRINTING SERVICES
Color Printing Central

BUSINESS CARDS
Checks in the Mail, Color Card, Color Printing Central, Invitation & Promotion Hotline

CHECK-PRINTING SERVICES
Checks in the Mail

FOLDING CARDS
Color Card

POSTCARD PRINTING SERVICES
Color Card, Color Printing Central, Modern Postcard

POSTER PRINTING SERVICES
Color Printing Central

PERSONALIZED CARDS AND STATIONERY
Current, Invitation & Promotion Hotline

WEDDING INVITATIONS
Invitation & Promotion Hotline

WRAPPING PAPER
Current

Checks in the Mail, Inc.

P.O. Box 350060
New Braunfels, TX 78135
866–639–2432
FAX: 800–800–2432

FORM OF INFORMATION: free catalog; online catalog

PAY: check, MO, MC, V, AE, DSC

SELLS: check-printing services

STORE: no walk-in location; mail-order only; phone hours Monday to Friday 7:00 am–9:00 pm Saturday and Sunday 8:00 am–6:00 pm CST

ONLINE: www.checksinthemail.com

The designs offered by Checks in the Mail are among the liveliest available from the big check-printing firms. The Anne Geddes line, for example, features those now-famous photos of real babies as potted sunflowers, pea pods, cabbages, and others. There are scores of designs for personal checks, offered in wallet and carbonless duplicate styles, and in 3-to-a-page desk sets. Other options, such as logos, designer typestyles, and message lines, are also available. Business checks are offered in a choice of formats and designs, in continuous-feed and laser-printer styles. There are plenty of accessories here, too, including stamps, labels, covers, and wallets that you can coordinate with your chosen check design. Surely your insurance company will appreciate that your return-address label and monthly check to them match! Prices are close to half what you pay when you order them from your bank. The checks are guaranteed to be printed to your bank's standard, and confidentiality of your bank data is assured.

WEBSITE: The website is lots of fun because you can view all of the designs, and under each check design is a list of suggested accessories (a matching embossed vinyl check cover, for example). Secure online ordering is available.

SPECIAL FACTORS: Satisfaction guaranteed; checks can be ordered on U.S. banks only.

Color Card

1065 Islip Ave.
Central Islip, NY 11722
800–875–1386
FAX: 631–232–1392

FORM OF INFORMATION: free sample package; online catalog

PAY: check, MO, MC, V

SELLS: postcards, folding cards, and business cards

STORE: same address; Monday to Friday 9:00 am–5:00 pm

ONLINE: www.afullcolorcard.com

I am always so delighted to find a good printer, with reasonable rates, who accepts camera-ready work online, because the printers where I live aren't so great and they're definitely on the expensive side. Color Card, in business for over 20 years, offers quality full-color printing at reasonable prices. This company is dedicated to improving their products and services, while keeping their prices low. Color Card has maintained their introductory price of $95 for 500 4" x 6" postcards for over five years now and they have no immediate plans to change it. They have even significantly lowered some of the prices of their services since their introduction.

Color Card has spent over $3 million in the last three years updating their facility. This includes state of the art prepress, including two new scanners. The press room has three new presses including a brand new 4-color Heidelberg speedmaster with dryer (Heidelbergs are synonymous with quality in the print industry). The finishing department has been improved as well with a new 45" computerized cutter and a film laminater, used to apply their lamination, optional on their postcards and standard with their business cards.

If you would like to receive a free sample package of their work, you can fill out a request form at the website and one will be mailed to you.

WEBSITE: At the website you can download an order form which can be faxed or mailed in, or you can call in your order.

SPECIAL FACTORS: Because each order produced is a custom job, no order may be returned for credit under any circumstances; Color Card will reprint any order that contains abnormal imperfections, at their option.

Color Printing Central

<table>
<tr><td>

800–309–3291

877–574–0284

FAX: 954–784–0341

</td><td>

FORM OF INFORMATION: online catalog only; no print catalog

PAY: check, MO, MC, V

SELLS: brochure, postcard, catalog, poster, and business card printing

STORE: no walk-in location; mail-order only

ONLINE: www.colorprintingcentral.com

</td></tr>
</table>

This company is a great source for color printing of brochures, catalogs, posters, postcards, and business cards. I have been in the publishing industry for almost 20 years, and have extensive experience with some of the largest printing companies in the country, as well as countless small local and regional printing companies for smaller jobs. I was very happy to find this company. They are extremely friendly and helpful, the service is timely, the quality is excellent, and they have some of the best prices I have researched. Plus, their prices include real color proofs, not just online proofs— which is often not offered by online printers. Prices for all products are listed on the website. If you find a better price anywhere, email them or give them a call, chances are Color Printing Central can beat it.

They support both Mac and PC platforms and offer templates to download for all of their products in the most popular computer graphics and layout programs. If you need help with a software program not listed at their site, just let them know, most likely they can still work with your files.

SPECIAL FACTORS: No refunds once proof is signed and order is confirmed.

Current

1005 E. Woodman Rd.
Colorado Springs, CO 80920
877–655–4458
FAX: 800–993–3232
TDD: 800–855–2880

FORM OF INFORMATION: free print catalog; online catalog

PAY: check, MO, MC, V, AE, DSC

SELLS: stationery, wrapping paper, cards, and gifts

STORE: outlets in CA, CO, OK, and OR

ONLINE: www.currentcatalog.com

Looking through the Current catalog and website, you'll be struck by the interesting and somewhat out-of-the-ordinary items carried here in addition to the company's great-priced stationery, cards, and other paper goods, for which it is generally known. It's a great source for gifts. But this is still a good place to find gift-wrap items (paper of every conceivable pattern and theme, ribbons and bows, gift boxes and bags), invitations, note cards, greeting cards, stationery, scrapbooking supplies, organizers, and calendars. Here's a sampling of what else you'll find at Current: household items such as gift wrap organizers, refrigerator magnets, tiny vases, bags, garage-sale stickers, windsocks, holiday treat bags, and wooden furniture repair crayons; and gifts for children and others, such as bug barns, hop balls, snowcone makers glass photo paperweights, candle holders, magnetic shopping list pads, glass angels, and more.

WEBSITE: The website features online ordering and the full inventory, fully photographed with detailed descriptions.

SPECIAL FACTORS: Satisfaction guaranteed.

Invitation & Promotion Hotline

68 Hawkins Rd.
Manalapan, NJ 07726
800–800–4355, ext. 921
732–536–9115
FAX: 732–972–4875

FORM OF INFORMATION: free flyer; online catalog

PAY: check, MO, MC, V, AE, DSC

SELLS: printed wedding invitations, calligraphy, stationery, party favors, holiday cards, and promotional items

STORE: by appointment only; phone hours Monday to Friday 9:00 am–5:00 pm EST

ONLINE: www.invitationhotline.com

An invitation to a wedding or Bat Mitzvah tells the guests a lot about you, whether you like it or not. But must you pay a lot to send the right message? When you're budgeting for a big event, Invitation & Promotion Hotline can trim the cost of invitations, reply cards, wedding stationery, birth announcements, favors, programs, and other printed items (e.g., letterhead stationery and business cards) by 25% (save more on volume and multiple orders).

Here's how it works. You can view stationery albums, those large books put out by card and stationery manufacturers that feature page after page of samples. Or, if you have internet access, sit back, put your feet up and browse through over 90 albums of designer invitations at Invitation & Promotion Hotline's website. When you find a style you like, you can order online, but only for some manufacturers. For the manufacturers that you cannot order online from write down the book and style numbers, then call Invitation & Promotion. They'll get it to you for 25% less than if you ordered it locally. Accuracy is guaranteed or Invitation & Promotion will replace it for free. If you need advice or don't have access to the manufacturers' books, feel free to call Invitation & Promotion. They understand everything about the selection process and can help you find the right item for your taste, needs, and budget, compose the wording, custom-design the work, figure out foreign-language orders, and even address envelopes in calligraphy. The 1-page flyer lists some of the manufacturers Invitation & Promotion Hotline discounts, but since they're adding new manufacturers regularly, it's best just to call or visit the website.

SPECIAL FACTORS: Complete satisfaction guaranteed; price quotes by phone or email.

Modern Postcard

1675 Faraday Ave.
Carlsbad, CA 92008
800–959–8365
760–431–7084
FAX: 760–431–1939

FORM OF INFORMATION: online catalog only; no print catalog

PAY: check, MO, MC, V

SELLS: postcard designing, printing and mailing services

STORE: same address; Monday to Friday 9:00 am–5:00 pm

ONLINE: www.modernpostcard.com

Modern Postcard creates full-color postcards from start to finish—typesetting, individual drum scanning, direct-to-plate digital imaging, printing, shipping, bindery, and complete mailing services. This is good for the customer in a number of ways. First, you can create a totally customized postcard by sending them a slide, photograph, scanned image, or transparency, along with the text and any other specifications you may want (type of material used, layout, etc). You can also make customized cards using Modern Postcard's professional-quality stock images and multiple backside layout designs for no additional charge. The site also offers more complicated build-it-yourself programs for professional graphics designers. Another advantage of Modern Postcard's in-house production and mailing is that it saves you money. Since they don't have to work through a mailing house, Modern minimizes shipping, allowing them to offer cheap mailing options (for large orders shipping costs about 21 cents per card or 34 cents for deluxe-sized cards). Note that this does not translate into a longer turnaround. They manage to send off your cards a mere seven days after the order is confirmed (and artwork is supplied). If you're still looking for a catch, don't hold your breath because they also have state-of-the-art printing equipment, and all their cards are printed on ultra-premium brilliant white card stock with a nontoxic aqueous coating. Sounds impressive, doesn't it? Their graphics designers have even created custom-made programs to aid in color calibration.

As could be expected from a company selling high-quality graphics, Modern Postcard's website looks sharp and is easy to use. Each time you load their homepage it has a new postcard picture on the front, an immediate testament to the quality of their work.

SPECIAL FACTORS: Client is 100% responsible for accuracy of layout and compliance with postal regulations; no refunds once order is confirmed; no partial refunds for work not completed.

Uniforms and Promotional Products

Uniforms, workwear, and footwear for the medical, food-service, and other industries; imprintable clothing and miscellaneous goods for promotional purposes and corporate gifts

When I first left home at eighteen to make it on my own, I moved with my sister to Juneau, Alaska. We both got jobs as busboys at a popular seafood restaurant named Annabelle Lee's. I was a skinny little thing and had recently got what I thought was a stylish short hairdo. My busboy's uniform consisted of a pair of black pants, a white shirt, and a red vest. To my shock one day when I was dutifully busing tables, a restaurant patron addressed me as a boy, "Boy, can you bring me another cup of coffee?" I delivered the cup, convinced that once the gentleman who addressed me got a closer look he would clearly see that I was a girl and apologize. He didn't. The next day I went to a jewelry store to get my ears pierced. I picked a lovely pair of stainless steel and turquoise studs for the piercing. When I went into work the next day, I tied a bow in my hair to complete the feminine picture. The same gentleman who had mistaken me for a boy two days before called me over to his table. Ah ha, I thought to myself, he has realized his mistake and is going to apologize. I walked over to the table and the man said, "Boy, why are you wearing earrings and a bow in your hair?" Perhaps if the restaurant could have afforded "busgirl" outfits, I need not have been embarrassed.

The firms listed in this section specialize in uniforms, clothing and other products that can be screen-printed, embroidered, or embossed with your company's name or logo. Some of the clothing is quite specialized—for people in the restaurant, catering, or medical professions. Other clothing is more all-purpose—janitorial jumpsuits, polo-style shirts, and baseball caps, to name a few. If your business requires uniforms other than suit and tie, you're apt to find what you need here at good discounts.

Businesses looking to strengthen employee loyalty, up their name recognition with clients, or reward good customers will be interested in the firms below that offer good deals on items of all kinds—from golf balls, totes, and key rings to pens and clocks—all custom-printed with your company's name, of course.

Find It Fast

CUSTOM LOGO DESIGN SERVICES
Cheap Aprons/Allstates Uniform, Tafford Manufacturing

FOOD INDUSTRY CLOTHING
Cheap Aprons/Allstates Uniform

GENERAL WORK CLOTHING AND CASUAL APPAREL
4imprint, Cheap Aprons/Allstates Uniform

IMPRINTED PROMOTIONAL PRODUCTS
4imprint, Best Impressions Promotional Products Catalog

MEDICAL INDUSTRY CLOTHING
Cotton Scrubs, Tafford Manufacturing

MEDICAL INDUSTRY SHOES
Tafford Manufacturing

MISCELLANEOUS PROMOTIONAL PRODUCTS
4imprint, Best Impressions Promotional Products Catalog

4imprint

101 Commerce St.
Oshkosh, WI 54901
888–298–8190
FAX: 800–355–5043
TDD: 800–982–9152

FORM OF INFORMATION: free print catalog; online catalog

PAY: check, MO, MC, V, AE, DSC

SELLS: imprinted promotional products

STORE: no walk-in location; mail-order only; phone hours Monday to Friday 7:00 am–6:00 pm CST

ONLINE: www.4imprint.com

According to Dick Nelson, president of 4imprint, employees, friends, members, and donors of your company all have one thing in common: the need for appreciation and recognition. 4imprint was founded on this idea. This mail-order company offers businesses like yours hundreds of high-quality imprinted promotional or corporate-identity products at the lowest prices. They back up this latter claim with a "lowest prices" guarantee. The greater the quantity, the lower the per-item price.

Where and how can imprinted items be used? Here are some ideas offered by 4imprint: when opening new accounts, to build trade-show or store traffic, to support community service activities and fund-raisers, to commemorate in-house events (picnics, anniversaries, open houses), to use as employee incentives and rewards, to reward customers for early orders, and on and on. The 60-page catalog features a variety of apparel: polo shirts (all cotton, various weaves and textures, solid colors, tri-colored, long- and short-sleeved, etc.), neckties, oxford-style shirts, rugby shirts, turtlenecks, rain gear, sweatsuits, jackets (denim, parka, Polar-tek, etc.), caps, and more—all imprinted with your company's logo. You'll also find just about everything else you can imagine—from auto accessories, clocks, candy, and glassware to magnets, mugs, toys, and watches. Detailed text explains how to order and how to submit your logo. A 1-color design is included in the price. You can request a free sample of any merchandise to inspect its quality before ordering.

WEBSITE: The website lets you search for products by category and order directly online. As is often the case with online versus print catalogs, there are items to be found on the website that don't appear in the catalog, and vice versa. There are also web-only specials you'll want to check out. What's also nifty about this site is you can submit your logo along with your order.

SPECIAL FACTORS: Goods guaranteed to be delivered exactly as ordered, or order will be rerun, refunded, or credited; quantity discounts available; institutional accounts available.

Best Impressions Promotional Products Catalog

345 N. Lewis Ave.
Oglesby, IL 61348
800–635–2378
FAX: 815–883–8346

FORM OF INFORMATION: free print catalog; online catalog

PAY: check, MO, MC, V, AE, DSC

SELLS: imprinted promotional products

STORE: no walk-in location; mail-order only; phone hours Monday to Friday 7:00 am–6:00 pm CST

ONLINE: www.bestimpressions.com

What are promotional products? They're items like coffee mugs, pens, or mouse pads imprinted with your company's logo, designed to inspire employees, reinforce a positive company image with clients, and spur new sales leads. Or put another way, they're for people who, like most of us, love to get free stuff. The Best Impressions catalog features items for every company's budget: mugs, glasses, sports bottles, balls, balloons, bean-bag buddies, fortune cookies, pocket knives, key chains, calendars, address books, digital desk clocks, holiday ornaments, candy jars, picture frames, calculators, notepads, and of course pens and pencils. Savings can run up to 50%, depending on the item and quantity ordered, and prices include execution of your design in one color in one imprint area (additional colors are extra). Camera-ready artwork is required, or it can be produced by the firm's art department for an additional fee. Each product has a minimum order—48 baseball caps, 24 umbrellas, 500 Post-it notes are typical examples—but many minimums can be lowered (surcharges apply). And selected products are available for accelerated shipment, at no extra charge—see the catalog or website for details.

WEBSITE: The online catalog lets you click on a category—Drinkware, Magnets, Office, Fun Times, Lapel Pins, Giveaways, Tools, Leisure, Carry-alls, Clocks, Writing,

Gift Ideas, Calendars, and Clocks—and see examples of these items with quantity price breaks. They have online ordering available.

SPECIAL FACTORS: Price quotes by phone; quantity discounts available; institutional accounts available; minimum orders vary by item.

Cheap Aprons/Allstates Uniform

Catalog Sales, 599 Canal St.
Lawrence, MA 01840
800–367–2374
FAX: 978–689–2483

FORM OF INFORMATION: free print catalog; online catalog

PAY: check, MO, MC, V, AE

SELLS: monogrammed or screen-printed food-industry uniforms, aprons, chef's apparel, table linens, work clothing, etc.

STORE: same address for showroom; Monday to Friday 9:00 am–5:00 pm, Saturday 9:00 am–1:00 pm

ONLINE: www.cheapaprons.com

If you own a restaurant, are a caterer, run a business, or even have a weekend bowling team that needs a morale booster in the way of team caps, you should know about Cheap Aprons and Allstates Uniform, sister companies supplying workwear and casual apparel that's custom-monogrammed or screen-printed with your logo. Cheap Aprons' 32-page color catalog offers aprons of every kind (wrap, café, bib, full-length bistro, waist, etc.), button-down shirts in plain and patterned, bow ties, polo shirts and T-shirts, tuxedo shirts, chef's apparel, table linens, baseball-style caps, sweatshirts, and more—all at reasonable prices that include a free 1-color screen-printed logo. Cheap Aprons offers quantity discounts on every item, as well as a logo-design service.

In Allstates Uniform's 16-page catalog you'll find other types of workwear—work jackets, coveralls, waterproof rain suits, utility smocks, T-shirts, caps, and tank tops among them. The screen-printing is included in the good prices, and quantity discounts are listed here as well.

WEBSITE: The website is for Cheap Aprons only, and presents their full inventory complete with photographs and descriptions. Here you'll also find a monthly website-only special that's usually an excellent deal. Online ordering is available.

SPECIAL FACTORS: Satisfaction guaranteed; see catalogs for returns policy; custom logo design is available; specify which catalog you want when you call.

Cotton Scrubs & Co.

P.O. Box 1014
Montgomeryville, PA 18936
888–225–7162
FAX: 215–643–4922

FORM OF INFORMATION: free print catalog; online catalog

PAY: check, MO, MC, V, AE, DSC

SELLS: all-cotton scrubs and accessories for medical professionals

STORE: 3 locations in PA; call for addresses and hours

ONLINE: www.cottonscrubs.com

Doctors, nurses, veterinarians, techs—these and other medical professionals spend their time and energy helping us and our loved ones feel better. Cotton Scrubs & Co. is a newish venture of Tafford Manufacturing (see listing this section) dedicated to helping the caregivers feel comfortable as well. Imagine a surgeon dressed in a gaily decorated cartoon alligator print being the first person your child sees when he comes out of anesthesia. The styles, colors, and prints offered here make the whole experience more human. And medical professionals will jump for joy at the all-cotton fabric that breathes and is easy to care for, in cuts that provide a soft, natural fit. Scrubs are also available in linen, corduroy, and hemp. Since these items come directly to the consumer from the manufacturer, you'll save an average of 20%. In addition to the good selection of scrubs (drawstrings and tops, tunics, skorts, scrub dresses, etc.) there are a number of amusing and useful items here: reading glasses, themed and matching earrings, pendants, and pins; comfort shoes and socks; color-coordinated stethoscopes; and more. Sizes run from XS to 4X. I really like the drawstring pants here—in comfortable knit jersey, corduroy, even soft-washed denim. Drawstring pants are great for exercising, as pajamas, or just lounging around the house. You won't find a better selection for less anywhere else.

WEBSITE: This is a nice website with some very cool features. When you shop by print, color, style, or collection, a list of each type comes up and by rolling your mouse over the name of the item, swatches and illustrations of styles will appear to the right of the screen. Click on the item name to see photographs and prices. If you like what you see (I did), you can order it online.

SPECIAL FACTORS: Unworn garments may be returned within 30 days for refund or exchange.

Tafford Manufacturing, Inc.

P.O. Box 1001
Montgomeryville, PA 18936
800–697–3321
FAX: 215–643–4922

FORM OF INFORMATION: free print catalog; online catalog

PAY: check, MO, MC, V, AE, DSC

SELLS: uniforms, shoes, and accessories for the medical professional

STORE: 3 retail locations in PA; call for addresses and hours

ONLINE: www.tafford.com

Compared to the average catalog of uniforms for health-care professionals, Tafford Manufacturing has the best fashion buys for the dollar. The firm manufactures its own uniforms, which means you beat at least one markup, and the size selection is great—from XS to 6X, petite to tall. The 72-page color catalog shows mostly women's clothing, although most of the scrubs and warm-ups are unisex. Say good-bye to the intimidating doctor or nurse dressed in clinical white. You'll find many colors, prints, and styles here, designed to suit every figure type, including maternity styles. The catalog also shows cardigans, jackets, shoes (from traditional "nurse" styles to clogs and Birkenstocks), emblem pins, reference books, and brightly colored basic equipment—stethoscopes, blood pressure kits, scissors, otoscopes, etc. Both the retail and the discount prices of the clothing are given so you see how much you're saving—usually

20% or 30% on the regular retail. The main difference between this and sister company Cotton Scrubs (see listing this section) is that most of Tafford's wearables are a poly/cotton blend, and therefore less expensive. Consult your colleagues before ordering, because if you buy as part of a group, Tafford also offers special services, such as swatches and samples, volume discounts, and custom embroidery and logo silk-screening.

WEBSITE: Some of the medical uniforms pictured online look so good, you may end up ordering a few items for yourself. You can request a print catalog or browse online at this comprehensive and well-organized website that also has online ordering capability. Click on Sale Items for pages and pages of internet bargains.

SPECIAL FACTORS: Satisfaction guaranteed; unworn, undamaged, unwashed returns are accepted within 30 days for exchange, refund, or credit.

Special Needs

Adaptive clothing, tools, gadgets, and home and office aids for children and adults with special physical or medical needs, including products for people with postoperative conditions, limited mobility, the elderly, left-handed, allergy-sensitive, ample-sized, and hearing and visually impaired

If you're fortunate enough to be youngish, of average size, in excellent health, with no disabilities, then you probably take for granted, as many of us often do, all the little activities and pleasures in life that come easily and naturally. The companies in this chapter provide all kinds of products to restore dignity, help out, and make life more fun for people who are extra large, visually impaired, hearing impaired, have limited strength or mobility, or have physical conditions requiring special clothing, furniture, or personal accessories. From seat belt extenders, and Braille playing cards to all-cotton bedding, left-handed baseball mitts, and support hosiery, you'll find a lot here that you and your loved ones will appreciate.

Find It Fast

ALLERGY-SENSITIVE
National Allergy Supply

DIABETICS OR POOR CIRCULATION
Support Plus, SupportHosiery.com

DISABLED CHILDREN'S CLOTHING
Special Clothes

ELDERLY OR LIMITED MOBILITY
Amplestuff, Comfort House

EXTRA-LARGE PEOPLE'S PRODUCTS
Amplestuff

HEARING AID BATTERIES AND REPAIR
ABC Nationwide Battery Club

HEARING IMPAIRED
ABC Nationwide Battery Club, Comfort House

LEFT-HANDED AIDS, GADGETS, TOYS
The Left Hand

POST-BREAST SURGERY PRODUCTS
Bosom Buddy Breast Forms

POSTOPERATIVE OR MEDICAL CONDITIONS
Comfort House, Special Clothes

SUPPORT HOSE
Support Plus, SupportHosiery.com

VISUALLY IMPAIRED
Independent Living Aids, The New Vision Store

ABC Nationwide Battery Club

18700 Main St., Ste. 101B
Huntington Beach, CA
92648–1713
800–432–7114
714–375–3742
FAX: 714–375–9682
TDD: 714–375–3071

FORM OF INFORMATION: free brochure

PAY: check or MO

SELLS: hearing aid batteries, new and reconditioned hearing aids, and repair services

STORE: same address; also Garden Grove, CA; customer service phone hours Monday to Friday 9:00 am–5:00 pm, Saturday 9:00 am–12:00 noon PST

EMAIL: abcbttry@gte.net

Until speaking with the nice owner of ABC Nationwide Battery Club, I had no idea that hearing aid batteries have to be replaced a few times a month, depending on size and usage. If you're a hearing aid wearer, however, you're all too aware of this fact—and keenly familiar with the expense, too. Company founder David Thorpe came up with a simple but effective way to save you hundreds of dollars. ABC sells batteries directly to you at true wholesale prices, about 72% less than you'd pay in a store. Even if you're smarter than the average Joe and already buy your hearing aid batteries cheaply through a group such as AARP or one of the giant discount chains, you'll be pleased to know that ABC Nationwide Battery Club beats everyone's price.

All 5 hearing aid battery sizes are available here in 4-cell packs. At this writing the popular size 13, 312, and 675 batteries are only $2.50 per package, normally $5 in stores! And prices plunge even further when you take advantage of the fantastic deals such as the "baker's dozen special": Buy 12 packages and get one package for free (3-year shelf life guaranteed). But it gets even better. Are you one of those people who never sends in the paperwork to get your rebate? ABC will prepare the paperwork for you and pay the postage to process manufacturers' cash rebates—which means, in every instance, you'll get an additional dollar off every package you buy. Now *that's* amazing!

I don't know of any other company that would do this for its customers. Then again, it's this kind of courtesy and attention to consumers' needs that's made ABC one of the largest single retailers of hearing aid batteries in the U.S. Talk to David Thorpe just once and you'll know you're dealing with a highly ethical man who just wants to help seniors save money. In addition to hearing aid batteries, ABC Nationwide Battery Club sells new and reconditioned hearing aids, offers repair, upgrading, and remaking services, and sells warranty plans for all working hearing aids. Be sure to inquire about these, because ABC's prices are startlingly low here, too. Call or email ABC with your order, specifying your battery size or color (each size is color-coded, so that's all you really need to know), and you'll get new batteries in a couple of days, along with an already stamped envelope in which to send your payment by U.S. check or money order. Now isn't that nice? This is a refreshingly honest and trusting business that can help senior citizens and others save a lot of money.

SPECIAL FACTORS: Satisfaction guaranteed; hearing aids repaired and shipped anywhere in the world.

Amplestuff

P.O. Box 116, Dept. PP
Bearsville, NY 12409–0116
845–679–3316
866–486–1655
FAX: 845–679–1206

FORM OF INFORMATION: free print catalog; online catalog
PAY: check, MO, MC, V, AE, DSC
SELLS: products and books for plus-size and supersize people
STORE: no walk-in location; mail-order only
ONLINE: www.amplestuff.com

One evening, Amplestuff president Bill Fabrey received a call from a 540-pound man across the country in the hospital for an emergency appendectomy. His most serious suffering was caused by humiliation for lack of a hospital gown that fit him. Bill made sure the very next morning there were 4 hospital gowns waiting for the grateful patient when he woke up. There aren't many businesses with this kind of concern and personal rapport with their customers. Amplestuff's motto, since 1988, is "make your world fit you," and the 44-page catalog is devoted to hard-to-find products that big people all over the world will surely appreciate. Items such as airline seat belt extenders; fanny packs ("you shouldn't have to be slender to wear a fanny pack"); large-size socks, aprons, and hospital gowns; silver- and gold-plated bangles in 8", 9" or 10" sizes; extra-large clothes hangers; extra-large bath towels; reach extenders; a portable bidet; 10" car steering wheels (for more leg and stomach room); blood pressure kits; high-limit scales; hygiene products; and more are offered, with photographs and descriptions of each. There are also size-friendly videos and books, including exercise videos, art books, and a resource guide to the best books related to the larger-size population.

Bill Fabrey says half of his business dealings are in communications, since there are very few sources out there knowledgeable about improving the lives of ample-size people. Amplestuff's voicemail is often on, but the staff always returns calls promptly.

WEBSITE: Amplestuff's website lists descriptions of the products they carry in their print catalog. There are links to size acceptance organizations, super-size clothing stores for men and women, and related magazines and sites. Online ordering is available.

SPECIAL FACTORS: U.S. funds only; quantity discounts on some items; satisfaction guaranteed; orders by phone, fax, and mail—no email orders.

Bosom Buddy Breast Forms

2417 Bank Dr., Dept. WCO1
P.O. Box 5731
Boise, ID 83705–0731
800–262–2789
208–343–9696
FAX: 208–343–9266

FORM OF INFORMATION: free brochure; online catalog

PAY: check, MO, MC, V, DSC

SELLS: Bosom Buddy breast prostheses

STORE: no walk-in location; mail-order only; phone hours Monday to Friday 9:00 am–5:00 pm MST

ONLINE: www.bosombuddy.com

This company has been producing and selling the "Bosom Buddy Breast Form" by direct mail since 1976. Founder Melva Smith found a way to turn her own experience with breast cancer into something positive with the invention of an all-fabric external breast prosthesis that's helped thousands of women around the world. The Bosom Buddy costs about 50% less than other breast forms on the market, and is a more comfortable alternative to the hot and heavy silicone versions. It's ideal for active women—golfers, joggers, swimmers, and the like.

The Bosom Buddy is made from luxurious nylon softened with fiberfill, backed with 100% cool cotton next to your skin. The unique design incorporates the use of smooth, tiny glass beads cushioned in fiberfill pillows to give the form weight and balance. The shape and balance can be adjusted, and the breast forms are interchangeable (fit both left and right sides). The forms fit into a regular bra from size AAA to DDD, and come in 2 different shapes and 3 different skin-tone shades. The brochure has all the details, but if you still have questions, call B&B's staff and they'll be glad to help.

Wholesale customers: A starter set of 6 breast forms is required on the first purchase. The minimum order for subsequent orders is 3 breast forms or $100.

WEBSITE: The attractive and easy to use website features the same information as the brochure, complete with pictures, customer testimonials, and Medicare information. At press time, they were in the process of developing secure online ordering. In the meantime, you can print out an order form and fax or mail it back or call their toll-free number.

SPECIAL FACTORS: Satisfaction guaranteed; returns accepted; Medicare-approved.

Comfort House

189-V Frelinghuysen Ave.
Newark, NJ 07114–1595
800–359–7701
973–242–8080
FAX: 973–242–0131

FORM OF INFORMATION: online catalog only; no print catalog

PAY: check, MO, MC, V, AE, DSC

SELLS: tools and gadgets to make life easier

STORE: no walk-in location; online only; phone hours Monday to Friday 8:00 am–4:30 pm EST

ONLINE: www.comforthouse.com

Unfortunately for some of you, Comfort House, the source for products "to make your life easier," has discontinued their print catalog and is now only found online. Fortunately for those of us who have access to the internet, this is a great website—easy to use, comprehensive, logically organized. Comfort House, in business since 1991, sells things such as long-handled light bulb changers that anyone might find useful, as well as pineapple peelers, lamp switch enlargers, zipper pulls, and seat-lift chairs designed specifically for those with limited strength. There are doorknob turners, various gripping devices, exercisers, sleeping and bathing aids, travel accessories, gardening tools, cooking aids, and much more. Whether you're experiencing the inconvenience or discomfort caused by pregnancy; a chronic medical condition, such as back pain or poor circulation; low vision or hearing; limited mobility; incontinence; allergies; arthritis; or any other physical encumbrance, Comfort House has the ingenious gadget or product to help you. Although this is not a discount vendor, Comfort House is included here because it is simply a great collection of products that can help people perform everyday tasks more easily and more safely, as well as cope with changed conditions that happen to all of us eventually. The website shows current specials and closeouts where savings can be significant. In addition to what's shown at the website, Comfort House accepts special orders for any of thousands of products for general personal care, incontinence, mobility assistance, or needs associated with orthopedics, ostomy, laryngectomy, mobility, and urology. They also have a new hotel and hospitality shop which caters to owners of b & b's and small inns.

Wholesale customers: Wholesale terms are available to drug, medical, and surgical-supply stores, schools, institutions, government agencies and to the hospitality industry. Inquire on company letterhead for terms and pricing.

SPECIAL FACTORS: Satisfaction guaranteed; returns in unused condition accepted within 30 days.

HearingPlanet.com

100 Westwood Place Suite 300

Brentwood, TN 37027

800-HEAR-NOW

800–432–7669

615–248–5910 ext. 211

FAX: 615–248–5903

FORM OF INFORMATION: online catalog

PAY: check, MO, MC, V, AE, DSC

SELLS: hearing aids and home products for the hearing impaired

STORE: over 950 clinics nationwide, check website or call for locations and hours

ONLINE: www.hearingplanet.com

★

If you are among the 28 million people in the U.S. who experiences hearing impairment, but have been turned off to hearing aids because of their prohibitive cost, then HearingPlanet may be able to help. This fast-growing company works with a network of professional audiologists nationwide to sell and dispense hearing products at a low cost to consumers, 30% to 45% off typical retail prices. Customers can contact HearingPlanet by phone or via the internet (live chat) to set up an appointment at the office of one of over 900 affiliated local professionals throughout the U.S. These are professional audiologists or hearing-aid retailers who conduct all tests and fittings. HearingPlanet arranges the visit for you, and all payments are made through them with no additional hidden costs owed to the audiologist or hearing aid manufacturer. By conducting their business in this fashion, HearingPlanet is able to sell the best hearing aid products available on the market at the guaranteed lowest prices. If there isn't an affiliated audiologist in your immediate area, HearingPlanet will make arrangements to locate one and get them onboard.

WEBSITE: At the website, you will find the best and latest computer chip technology available for hearing aids. These discount hearing aids come in three different categories: digital, programmable, and conventional. HearingPlanet and their representatives will work within your budget to review all of the options that are available to you.

In addition, the website presents a score of other hearing-related products, including special telephones and communication devices for deaf and hard-of-hearing individuals; telephone ring signalers; special cell phones that are hearing aid compatible; clocks, watches, and wake-up alarm products; notification devices for indoor and outdoor use; hearing aid batteries; wireless listening devices for television viewing; and more. The website also provides useful information on the effects and cause of tinnitus, information on alternative therapies, a live chat hookup with a professional audiologist during the hours listed above, and an FAQ section.

SPECIAL FACTORS: The price quoted for the purchase of hearing aid instruments includes a full evaluation, ear mold impressions, fitting of the device, 45-day follow-up service for necessary adjustments, a 45-day trial period with a 100% guaranteed refund, and 1-year warranty against repair, loss, or damage; financing is available; for wholesale terms, please inquire.

Independent Living Aids

200 Robbins Lane
Jericho, NY 11753
800–537–2118
516–937–1848
FAX: 516–937–3906

FORM OF INFORMATION: free catalog in print, cassette, or disk form; online catalog

PAY: check, MO, V, MC, DSC

SELLS: aids for the visually impaired

STORE: no walk-in location; mail-order only; phone hours Monday to Friday 9:00 am–5:00 pm EST

ONLINE: www.independentliving.com

For more than twenty years, Independent Living Aids has been distributing unique and hard-to-find aids to people who are visually handicapped. The 80-page color catalog features hundreds of items to help individuals with special needs live more comfortably and safely. A sampling of their products includes large-face watches and desk clocks; magnifiers (handheld and clip-ons for eyeglasses); desk lamps; floor lamps, and other lighting to enhance visibility; recorders; calculators; and all kinds of "talking" items—from clocks, telephones, and bathroom scales to thermometers and money identifiers. You'll find canes and walkers, writing guides for checks and envelopes, large-face playing cards and other games in Braille, including Monopoly, Scrabble, and Battleship. There are personal care items, such as mirrors; cooking aids, such as tactile meat thermometers; bath and shower items, such as a bathtub transfer bench; accessories for diabetic care; books about and for the visually impaired, such as large-print cookbooks; and computer software that adapts to any computer. The prices on most items are very reasonable, but Independent Living Aids also runs specials and has a wholesale division, where savings generally run over 20%. The real plus with this company is that they offer hard-to-find items, many of which would be useful for the rest of us and our aging parents, as well. The catalog is available in cassette, disk, or print form.

WEBSITE: The website is really terrific and allows you to view the entire inventory and order online. Well designed websites like this one make print catalogs unnecessary, in my opinion, if you have online access.

SPECIAL FACTORS: Wholesale customers must have a resale number; returns must be made within 30 days.

The Left Hand

17540 Sterling Lake Dr.
Ft. Myers, FL33912
TEL/FAX: 239–985–9553

FORM OF INFORMATION: online catalog only; no print catalog

PAY: check, MO, MC, V, AE

SELLS: left-handed tools, sports gear, and other products for children and adults

STORE: no walk-in location; mail-order only; phone hours Monday to Thursday 1:00 pm– 4:00 pm EST

ONLINE: www.thelefthand.com

If you're right-handed and have ever tried to use scissors with your left, you know it's nearly impossible. Now consider that everything from cars to clothes to kitchens is designed with the right-handed person in mind. When Ross Perot, Bill Clinton, and George Bush were running for the presidency a few years back, the media commented on how very odd it was that all three were lefties. The truth is, there are millions upon millions of left-handed people, but few consumer products designed with their special needs in mind.

The Left Hand intends to correct that. Owners Carolyn and John Williams have put together an eclectic selection of items—some whimsical, others necessary—geared to the needs of left-handed children and adults. You won't find most of these items in stores, and everything carried at The Left Hand has been hand-picked, and family-tested and -approved. The catalog offers baseball items (pitcher, catcher, baseman, and fielder gloves); office supplies, address books, aluminum rulers, computer accessories (keyboards with numeric and arrow pads positioned on the left, ergonomic mouse models, joysticks for lefties); hand tools (tape measure, Swiss army knife, ergonomic pruner); products for kids (notebooks, scissors, coloring books, rulers, handwriting helpers); kitchen and cooking implements (can opener, peeler, corkscrew, measuring cups, knives of all kinds, pastry servers); scissors (manicure, pinking, household, barber, etc.); and more.

WEBSITE: Online you'll find the secure online ordering, full-color photos and product descriptions, as well as helpful links to other websites with merchandise and information of relevance to lefties.

SPECIAL FACTORS: Satisfaction guaranteed; returns accepted within 30 days of receipt for refund, exchange, or credit; may be subject to a 15% restocking fee.

National Allergy Supply, Inc.

1620 Satellite Blvd., Ste. D
Duluth, GA 30097
800–522–1448
770–623–3237
FAX: 800–395–9303

FORM OF INFORMATION: online catalog only; no print catalog

PAY: check, MO, MC, V, AE, DSC

SELLS: nondrug products to avoid airborne allergens

STORE: no walk-in location; mail-order only; phone hours Monday to Friday 8:00 am–7:00 pm, Saturday 9:00 am–5:30 pm EST

ONLINE: www.nationalallergy.com

National Allergy Supply is the nation's largest discount allergy products supplier. A spot check on several items showed this company's prices to be 20% and more below retail. National Allergy Supply is designed for people who suffer from sneezing, runny nose, swollen and itchy eyes, coughing, wheezing, postnasal drip, and many other allergy and asthma symptoms. Ryner Wittgens started this company thirteen years ago as a result of his daughter's being diagnosed with six different airborne allergies. He made it his goal to find the best products out there for people like his daughter, for whom ordinary household environments full of pet dander, dust mite allergen, dust mold, chemical gassing of carpets, and toxins from household cleaners make life difficult, if not dangerous. Even if you're not allergy-prone, there are lots of ways to make your environment cleaner and healthier. You'll find all-cotton bedding, nondown comforters, air cleaners, carpet treatments, vinyl and cotton gloves for people with chemically sensitive skin, household cleaners, skin- and hair-care products, floor dusters, vacuum cleaners specially designed to eliminate 99.97% of allergens, in-home asthma treatments, respiratory masks, breathing and sleeping aids, window fans, and much more.

One gets the sense that the company has selected only the best one or two manufacturers in each category, and explanatory text accompanies each product with descriptions about its benefit to allergy-sensitive people. There are plenty of testimonials from happy customers, and the company guarantees 100% satisfaction on all their products. National Allergy Supply keeps a staff of highly trained reps who are available to answer all of your questions.

WEBSITE: At the website you'll be able to check out all of the products, take advantage of special clearance items, get information about allergies, and order directly online. A search button lets you search for products by manufacturer, description, category, or idea. Each product is described and accompanied by a color photo.

SPECIAL FACTORS: Satisfaction guaranteed; Canadian customers must pay by credit card.

The New Vision Store

919 Walnut St., 1st Fl.
Philadelphia, PA 19107
215-629-2990

FORM OF INFORMATION: free product list; website

PAY: check, MO, MC, V, AE, DSC

SELLS: aids for visually impaired

STORE: same address; phone and store hours Monday to Friday 11:00 am–4:00 pm EST

ONLINE: www.thenewvisionstore.com

Bill Ankenbrant understands the challenges faced by visually impaired persons. Visually impaired himself, he launched his store and mail-order company to "provide products that promote hope and independence for every customer wherever possible." The 11-page typewritten product list, which also comes out in Braille twice a year, presents a variety of necessary but hard-to-find items, some of which are discounted, others discounted 20% if you buy in small quantity, but all at reasonable prices. The New Vision Store offers such products as canes (auto-fold, rigid fiberglass, folding support canes, and others); flame-retardant oven mitts; raised-number timers, clocks, and calculators, as well as large-print, talking, and Braille versions; magnifiers of all kinds; labeling supplies, such as kits, labeling guns, Braille-embossing guns, as well as tapes for clothing, magnetized tapes, and labels of every kind; bill organizers; talking thermometers; a variety of sunglasses; small electronics, such as Walkmans, desk recorders, and desk radios; mailing supplies, including free-matter-for-the-blind labels and two- and four-cassette mailers; a variety of user-friendly watches; desk accessories such as rulers and pens, as well as signature guides and slates of different sizes for note-writing; and Braille paper by the ream. The New Vision Store also offers services such as cane repair (for a $3 labor charge at this writing they'll make your cane like new with elastic, new sections, tips, and reflective tape) and Braille embossing (send in a greeting card and they'll emboss it for you for $3).

WEBSITE: The website lists all of the products offered. If you mention that you are ordering on information found at the website, you will receive an additional 5% off of the order you are placing. Ordering can be done by phone or mail, but not electronically.

SPECIAL FACTORS: If you need a product not found in the catalog, The New Vision Store will find it for you; request in writing for shipping Free Matter for the Blind; see company literature for other shipping fees and policies.

Special Clothes

P.O. Box 333
East Harwich, MA 02645
TEL/FAX: 508–896–7939

FORM OF INFORMATION: $1 print catalog; online catalog

PAY: check, MO, MC, V

SELLS: adaptive clothing for children and adults with disabilities

STORE: no walk-in location; mail-order only

ONLINE: www.special-clothes.com

Special Clothes was founded in 1987 by Judith Sweeney, whose interest in developing adaptive designs was inspired by her experiences as an educator involved with children with special needs. Special Clothes helps children for whom dressing is a daily struggle; plus, this year they have added basic clothing for adults with disabilities to their line. Because the company prices the clothing by size, pricing is not inflated, and there are quantity discounts that enable you to cut costs further. All garments of knit, fleece, or denim are 100% cotton, most garments are latex-free, and functional features such as snap crotches, bib fronts, and gastrostomy-tube access are inconspicuous. The 40-page children's catalog has clothing for toddlers to size-20 teens. (There's a handy sizing chart included that helps you choose the right size for your child.) Among the clothing and accessories offered are all-cotton bodysuits with snap crotches and optional

G-tube access (Special Clothes will conceal the access opening with a stitched-on pocket), available in solid colors and a variety of styles; snap-on bodysuit extenders that add four inches to the torso length; a travel bag to carry catheterization items safely, easily, and discreetly; all-cotton absorbent briefs and nylon protective pull-ons; feeding bibs, jeans and trousers, culottes, heavyweight flannel diapers, pajamas, swimwear, socks, slippers, mittens, jackets, ponchos, orthopedic sneakers, and more. All clothing is available in a variety of colors, closure options, G-tube access, length, etc. Special Clothes' Birthday Club will give your child a greeting card and a 15%-off coupon when you send in your child's name and birth date.

WEBSITE: You can find out all you'll need to know about this wonderful company by logging on to their website. The online versions of both the children's and adult's catalogs are easy to use. Just click on an item of clothing to read about and see a line-drawn image. Once you've made your selections, there's a printable order form that you can fill out and mail or fax in. Online ordering may be available in the future.

SPECIAL FACTORS: See catalog for returns policy; custom orders are available (but not returnable).

Support Plus

P.O. Box 500, Dept. WBM
Medfield, MA 02052
877–808–0024
FAX: 508–359–0139

FORM OF INFORMATION: free print catalog; online catalog

PAY: check, MO, MC, V, AE, DSC

SELLS: women's support hosiery, supportive footwear, footcare items, undergarments, and daily living aids

STORE: no walk-in location; mail-order only; phone hours Monday to Thursday 8:30 am–9:00 pm, Friday 8:30 am–7:00 pm, Saturday 9:00 am–3:00 pm EST

ONLINE: www.supportplus.com

Support Plus has been in business since 1972 offering products geared toward the older woman (although men can use many of these products as well). Here you'll find an extensive selection of medical and support hosiery; aids to daily living (folding reading glasses, shopping bags with wheels, decorated canes, back-support products, reachers, travel chairs and cushions, and walkers); an excellent selection of shoes; health-care products for feet, skin, arthritis, and back pain; safety products for your bathtub and shower; incontinence products; and undergarments. If you are someone who suffers from, but mostly ignores, your own foot problems, you will be amazed by all the gadgets, elastic aids, massage tools, and other items offered in the catalog for people like yourself. Although discounts here aren't deep—sale items may run from 15% to 25% off regular prices—Support Plus nevertheless is a good company to know about because of their solid customer-relations policies and the thoughtful selection of products.

WEBSITE: More products are available online than in the print catalog. Here you'll find online ordering and some terrific sale and clearance items. If you don't see something you want, call.

SPECIAL FACTORS: Unscuffed shoes can be returned for refund or exchange; price quotes by phone for quantities in excess of 12 pairs.

SupportHosiery.com

856 Highway 206	**FORM OF INFORMATION:** free brochure; online catalog
Suite 6B	**PAY:** check, MO, MC, V, AE, DSC
Hillsboro, NJ 08844	**SELLS:** men's and women's therapeutic support hosiery
877–525–7224	
FAX: 908–359–9471	**STORE:** no walk-in location; mail-order only; phone hours Monday to Friday 9:00 am–5:00 pm EST
	ONLINE: www.supporthosiery.com

Did your doctor tell you to buy support hose? Then you know how expensive they can be. SupportHoisery.com sells compression stockings at 35% to 50% below retail and is an authorized dealer for Jobst, Juzo, Medi, Sigvaris, and Venosan. SupportHosiery.com also sells their own manufactured brand, RxFit, where you can reap the most savings; this "house brand" is the same high-quality product sold in retail stores under more famous brand names. You'll appreciate the prices here on support products including sheer support (pantyhose, thigh-highs, knee-highs), men's socks, maternity pantyhose, 20–30 and 30–40 surgical weight (pantyhose and thigh-highs), anti-embolism stockings, and diabetic socks. They'll match any internet competitor's price on any brand, any time. Call them to arrange a competitive price match (no additional discounts apply). And they charge no shipping on your orders over $60. You've suffered enough; now give your pocketbook some relief.

WEBSITE: The website has size charts and offers secure online ordering if you wish, or you can call, mail, or fax in your order. The site also has a valuable FAQ page with lots of articles and information on pregnancy and varicose veins, swollen legs, the benefits of compression hosiery, and more.

SPECIAL FACTORS: 100% satisfaction guaranteed; authorized returns accepted within 30 days of receipt for refund, credit, or exchange; shipping free within U.S.

Sports and Outdoor Recreation

Camping, Hunting, and Survival

Clothing and gear for camping, hiking, rugged outdoor activities, hunting, and survival; military surplus goods

When my sister and I were teenagers, living in California, we used to like to drive to Stinson Beach and Mendocino to camp by the ocean with a group of friends. Our idea of camping was to hang out on the beach until after the sun went down and the lifeguards had gone home, and then we would get our sleeping bags out of the car and pick a spot on the side of the hill above the beach. There were no dunes, just the beach and then a dry grassy hill. We couldn't sleep on the beach or the night patrol would find us, so it was the long grass on the incline for us. By the time the sun came up we had all slid, slowly in our sleep, to the bottom of the hill. When we woke up we'd go into town to get some pecan waffles and fresh coffee at a very quaint little restaurant. As you are probably guessing by now, I am somewhat of a camping expert.

This chapter is for people who enjoy camping, fishing, hiking, wilderness backpacking, and hunting. The companies in this section have everything one needs for outdoor living and survival, from camp stoves and heavy-duty rain tarps to brush-clearing machetes and state-of-the-art bows and arrows. There are some truly wonderful deals on camping equipment and surplus goods, up to 70% off in some cases. There's no need to take the minimalist approach that I once mastered.

Campmor

P.O. Box 700
Saddle River, NJ 07458–0700
800–CAMPMOR
800-226-7667
201–825-8300

FORM OF INFORMATION: free print catalog; online catalog

PAY: check, MO, MC, V, AE, DSC

SELLS: camping gear and supplies

STORE: 810 Rt. 17 N., Paramus, NJ; Monday to Friday 9:30 am–9:30 pm, Saturday 9:30 am–6:00 pm

ONLINE: www.campmor.com

Since 1978, savvy mail-order shoppers have turned to Campmor for savings up to 50% on gear and equipment for outdoor activities and recreation. You'll be thrilled to know that when I did a price comparison with another major camping discounter recently on backpacks, tents, and sleeping bags, Campmor came out way ahead on all three. Most of the offerings in the 232-page newsprint catalog cater to the needs of campers, hikers, and backpackers of all ages, with special sections for "kids" (e.g., children's outerwear and snow and ski accessories). You'll find major manufacturers represented even in the super-discount sections of the catalog and website, with items such as packs (back, fanny, day, dog, internal and external frame), hiking boots and running shoes, fleece clothing, underwear, rainwear, hats and balaclavas, and gloves and mitts. Equipment is plentiful, including compasses, first aid/wilderness medicine kits, lanterns, flashlights, stoves, cook sets, water filters and purifiers, and watches. You'll also find tents, sleeping bags, inflatables, mountain racks, reflective vests, antifog lens cleaner, a portable urinal, and an assortment of survival items (survival cards, waterproof matches, 10-mile signal mirror, 120-hour candles). What's so delightful about this catalog, are the informative line drawings and detailed product specifications.

WEBSITE: The website boasts a catalog of more than 10,000 items and web bargains priced below catalog prices (you must mention the website to get the lower price when you call). Additional savings are available by clicking on Products of the Week and Hot Deals, where name-brand manufacturers offer drastically reduced items. The links to related sites are broad and useful, covering parks and recreation, outdoor organizations and clubs, and outdoor magazines available on the internet. To receive up-to-the-minute sale and new-product information, sign up for Campmor's TrailMail.

SPECIAL FACTORS: Returns accepted for exchange, refund, or credit; institutional purchase orders accepted ($200 minimum order); additional discounts available for nonprofit organizations.

Camptown USA

303 Jansa Dr.
Shoreview, MN 55126
651–340–8358

FORM OF INFORMATION: online catalog only; no print catalog

PAY: check, MO, MC, V, AE, DSC

SELLS: camping gear and supplies

STORE: no walk-in location; mail-order only; phone hours 9:00 am–5:00 pm CST

ONLINE: www.camptownusa.com

Your tent, sleeping bag, and mattress pad can mean the difference between a fun outing and a miserable one. Camptown USA wants to be your single source for camping, hiking and outdoor supplies. They have a large selection of name-brand products to offer you at very low prices. Their expertise, personal attention and friendly service are not easily found in the larger retail chains. Prices here average about 30% below retail and they list the original retail price next to their discounted price on all items. The website is very easy to use with clear pictures and detailed descriptions. Categories include: tents, sleeeping bags, mattresses, stoves, cookware, backpacks, heaters, first aid, picnic items, coolers, binoculars, GPS, radios, and outdoor games. You'll also find links for camping guides and a directory for RV parks and campgrounds by state.

SPECIAL FACTORS: Satisfaction Guaranteed. Authorized returns within 30 days for refund or exchange; an additional 20% restocking fee can be applied if the return is made after 30 days or not in the original packaging;

Military Surplus & Survival

435 W. Alondra Blvd.
Gardena, CA 90248
800–441–8855
FAX: 310–324–6909

FORM OF INFORMATION: free print catalog; online catalog

PAY: check, MO, MC, V, AE, DSC

SELLS: camping and hunting clothing and equipment; survival and disaster preparedness items; military surplus food and equipment

STORE: same address; Monday to Friday, 9:00 am–6 pm, Saturday 9:00 am–5:00 pm, Sunday 11:00 am–5:00 pm

ONLINE: www.majorsurplusnsurvival.com

A male friend of mine recommended this company after he found a 10′ by 20′ length of camouflage netting for under $20 that he wanted to use on his wrap-around windows in the bedroom as curtains. (Did I mention that he was single?) You're going to love this company, based out of a 60,000-square-feet warehouse in California. Savvy shoppers can save up to 90% off regular retail by shopping from Military Surplus & Survival's print or online catalogs. Customers who prefer to shop by print catalog will receive six to eight catalogs a year, 48 to 64 pages long, each emphasizing a different theme—"Disaster Preparedness" or "Outdoor Recreation," for example.

WEBSITE: When you log on, get ready for the wonderful world of disaster preparedness and survival in the face of unforeseen circumstances. Some of the items you'll find at the website include: military wool blankets; knives, airguns (no real guns) and supplies; hammocks and mosquito netting; vintage combat gear; tents and sleeping bags;

earthquake survival kits; water storage items; Mylar blankets; European-issue wool and cotton long underwear and T-shirts; dehydrated food in bulk; camping cookware; first-aid kits; Dickies-brand work wear; Potassium Iodate; and bio-chemical protection suits. My favorite items: the MRE's (military-issue Meals-Ready-to-Eat). Most of these items are storable up to 5 years and are heat-and-eat (no water required). Choose from entrees, full meals, and side dishes. You can also buy full-meal MREs, which includes an entree (chicken-, pork-, veggie-, or macaroni-based), side dish, cookie, crackers, spread, and accessory pack. (When was the last time you served 72 people for under $20?) The prices here are incredible, and not just on the MREs. Be sure to check out the Super Savers section, a monthly selection of unbelievable bargains in very limited quantities that you are unlikely to find at these prices anywhere, items such as a black-out kit, a gas mask and air filter, surgical utensils, handcuffs, and a night vision monocular. Shopping here is extremely practical. Don't even consider buying summer camp gear for your kids until you've first checked out the deals here.

SPECIAL FACTORS: At press time the company had suspended international shipping due to import/export laws; items are returnable within 30 days for refund,

The Sportsman's Guide

411 Farwell Ave., Dept. WBM
So. St. Paul, MN 55075–0239
800–882–2962
FAX: 800–333–6933

FORM OF INFORMATION: free print catalog; online catalog

PAY: check, MO, MC, V, AE, DSC

SELLS: outdoor clothing and footwear, hunting and camping gear, military surplus, etc.

STORE: no walk-in location; mail-order only

ONLINE: www.sportsmansguide.com

For more than 26 years, The Sportsman's Guide, brainchild of Gary Olen, has been selling outdoor gear (and plenty of indoor products) at prices 68% below what others sell it for. New items receive deep discounts from the get-go, closeouts are priced even lower, and special buys do better than closeouts. If you join the Buyer's Club ($29.99 at this writing) for 1 year, you save an additional 10% and receive notice of special Members Only bargains. What could The Sportsman's Guide have for you? How about thermal underwear, flannel-lined denim shirts, Thinsulate swampwalker boots, hand-held CB radios, women's Dr. Marten boots, women's Timberland leather slip-ons, and women's Harley Davidson shoes. Inventory holdings vary with each shipment, so one time you might catch a deal on a tree stand or a reconditioned Harmon Kardon surround-sound receiver and new Sherwood 6-speaker system, and another time, luck into some Ray-Ban X-Rays sport sunglasses. There's a tempting section of government surplus gear and clothing, with specials on such items as BDU pants, West German military-issue parkas , "search and rescue" boots, and French military-issue hip bags. You can't predict what The Sportsman's Guide will offer you next—which is why it's called "The Fun to Read Catalog"—but you can always count on low prices.

WEBSITE: The website is every bit as much fun as the catalog, with more than 2,500 products and Deals of the Day, as well as online ordering capability. Happily, high technology hasn't squelched owner Gary Olen's enthusiastic sales personality, which jumps out at you with every click of the mouse: "Ridiculously low prices! Iron-clad guarantee!" Even if you're not in the market for outdoor or camping gear, this is a fun site to browse for the odd item bargain priced for your yard, home, or your kids.

SPECIAL FACTORS: Satisfaction guaranteed; returns accepted for exchange, credit, or refund; see catalog for restrictions on ordering and shipping of certain goods.

Team and Individual Sports

Clothing, footwear, and equipment for all kinds of indoor and outdoor sports and athletic activities

My mother and father took me and my two sisters skiing in the Sierra Nevadas when we were eleven and twelve years old. My parents rented equipment because it was cheaper than buying. One time, even though I was fairly inexperienced, boldness overcame me and I decided to chuck the snowplow technique and point both skis directly downhill so as to gain speed. One of my skis caught on something and I plummeted forward, made one full revolution, and landed on my back with both skis still firmly connected to my ski boots. Normally (with good ski equipment) the skis release during somersaults. I couldn't get up because of the pain (I had fractured my left tibia) and lay in the snow as my sisters came to my side and took off their skis to assist me. A helpful stranger screamed from the chairlift that they should cross the skis to signal to the ski patrol that someone was injured on the mountain. They misunderstood the instruction and thought that they were supposed to cross my skis while they were still attached to my boots. They discussed the peculiarity of crossing my skis, but as I seemed to be in a great deal of pain, they thought it best to just comply. My sisters came toward me, kneeled down opposite each other by my legs, and each reached for one of my attached skis to initiate the crossed ski signal when an off-duty ski patrolman appeared on the scene. Whew! If only my parents had known about some of the companies in this chapter they could have purchased skis with better release action.

No matter what your sport—skiing, scuba diving, kite flying, golf, soccer, kayaking, swimming, tennis, etc.—you'll find clothing, footwear, and equipment to be in full gear from the companies in this chapter. If organized sports are your thing, there are firms here that specialize in outfitting whole teams. Discounts of 40% and more are routine. And if you don't mind buying last year's ski equipment, for instance, savings can run as high as 60% or more.

For camping, survival equipment, or hunting, see "Camping, Hunting, and Survival," page 513. For firms that offer foul-weather gear, swimwear, and clothing for athletes and nature lovers, see the "Clothing for Women, Men, and Children" section, page 29. For companies that sell larger boating and marine supplies, see "Auto, Marine, and Aviation," page 95. For workout equipment, see the "Fitness and Exercise" section, page 281, of the "Health, Beauty, and Fitness" chapter.

Find It Fast

BOATS AND WATER SPORTS
Bart's Water Sports, The House, Overton's, SOAR Inflatables, Water Warehouse

BOWLING
Beach Bowl Pro Shop

CYCLING
Bike Nashbar, Performance Bicycle

GOLF
GolfDiscount.com, Golf Haus, Virtual Fairway

RACQUET SPORTS
Holabird Sports

SCUBA EQUIPMENT AND APPAREL
Divers Direct, Snorkel City

SKIING AND SNOWBOARDING
Al's Ski Barn, The House

SNORKELING EQUIPMENT
Divers Direct, Snorkel City

SOCCER
Acme Soccer and Widget Works

SWIMMING POOL EQUIPMENT
Water Warehouse

VOLLEYBALL
Spike Nashbar

YO-YOS
BFK—The Yo-Yo Store

Acme Soccer and Widget Works

P.O. Box 811	**FORM OF INFORMATION:** free print catalog
Carrboro, NC 27510–0811	**PAY:** check, MO, MC, V, AE, DSC
800–333–4625	**SELLS:** soccer gear and athletic shoes
FAX: 888–800–2263	**STORE:** no walk-in location; mail-order only; phone hours Monday to Thursday 8:00 am–12:00 midnight EST

Soccer moms: Stop despairing at the coming of spring. Sure, your kid has outgrown her shin guards and needs some new cleats. But Acme Soccer knows this, and that's why the company purchases manufacturers' overstocks of soccer gear and can sell it to you at prices that are 50% to 60% off the regular retail price. The 32-page color catalog has items for kids and adults, including soccer shorts; T-shirts with cool slogans and pictures, as well as plain ones and the designer logos the kids flip for; soccer shoes of every type and style, designed for indoor courts as well as muddy fields; socks; knit hats and visor caps; gloves; shin guards; equipment bags; single-color team shirts; nylon windbreakers and other jackets; and soccer accessories and gifts. This is a good source for discounted athletic shoes if you're lucky enough to find your shoe size and preferred brand. A recent catalog, for example, had men's and women's running shoes from Adidas, Nike, New Balance, and others in very limited styles and sizes marked down to half the original sticker price.

Note to Spanish-speaking customers: Acme welcomes your calls and has Spanish-speaking reps to assist you.

SPECIAL FACTORS: Acme recommends that you call before placing your order, since some of the items are stocked in limited quantities; returns accepted on clean, unused, or defective merchandise (see catalog for details); no C.O.D. orders.

Al's Ski Barn

207–865-0740
877-865-0740

FORM OF INFORMATION: online catalog only; no print catalog
PAY: MO, MC, V, AE
SELLS: ski equipment and snowboards
STORE: no walk-in location; mail-order only
ONLINE: www.untracked.com

Skiing is an expensive sport, but it just got cheaper. Al's Ski Barn is a virtual ski shop that acquires surplus ski equipment or equipment from outfits that are going out of business, and then sells it directly to you off their website—at savings that reach up to 60% and more. All equipment is still warrantied by the manufacturer, but it may be last year's stock. (Next year your brand-new equipment will be last year's model anyway!) When you visit Al's user-friendly, uncomplicated website, you'll see what they currently have in stock. The stock changes periodically when new equipment comes in, so if you don't find what you're looking for right away, check back. Next to each item is the retail price and then Al's Ski Barn price. The savings are *really* significant. Al's carries top-name skis, boots, and bindings from such famous makers as Atomic, Blizzard, Dynastar, Head, K2, Kastle, Lange, Look, Marker, Nordica, Salomon, Tyrolia, and Volkl. Don't forget to check out the Bargain Stall, where the drastically marked-down sale items will blow your boots off. If you want, you can join Al's Ski Barn's emailing list to receive the word when new inventory is added.

SPECIAL FACTORS: Returns within 7 days of receipt; all equipment warrantied by manufacturer.

Bart's Water Sports

P.O. Box 294-WBM
North Webster, IN 46555
800–348–5016
574–834–7666
FAX: 574–834–4246

FORM OF INFORMATION: free print catalog; online catalog

PAY: check, MO, MC, V, AE, DSC

SELLS: water sports, marine/boating, and personal watercraft goods

SHOWROOM: Hwy. 13, North Webster, IN; Monday to Saturday 9:00 am–6:00 pm

ONLINE: www.bartswatersports.com

In 1972, Bart Culver, a recent undergraduate in biology from the University of Indiana with a love for water sports, started selling water skis by mail. Decades later, Bart's Water Sports is still housed in North Webster, Indiana (population 1000), but now boasts a state-of-the-art facility, employs a staff of experts who can answer all your water sports questions, and maintains a loyal worldwide customer base. This company has weathered the uncertain wakes of commerce by selling everything related to water sports at discount prices—up to 40% on many items, with savings even greater on closeouts, specials, and BLEMs (factory-new goods with a minor cosmetic blemish that won't affect performance). Bart's promises the absolute lowest prices on every item stocked, including wakeboards, PWC (personal water craft), accessories, boating and marine equipment, water skis, wet suits, kneeboards, vests, sportswear, snorkel gear, children's pool toys and floats, videos and interactive media, gear bags, deck and pool accessories, and much more.

WEBSITE: The online catalog is friendly, comprehensive, and offers secure electronic ordering. Check it out often if you're looking for great bargains: There's a terrific closeouts section updated frequently, where the discounts run as high as 60%, quantities are limited.

SPECIAL FACTORS: Satisfaction guaranteed; returns accepted within 60 days (including closeout items); minimum international order: $300.

Beach Bowl Pro Shop

1970 E. Osceola Pkwy., #219
Kissimmee, FL 34743
888-545-2695

FORM OF INFORMATION: online catalog only; no print catalog

PAY: check, MO, MC, V, AE, DSC

SELLS: bowling balls, bags, shoes, shirts, and accessories

STORE: no walk-in location; online only; phone hours Monday to Friday 2:00 pm–6:00 pm EST

ONLINE: www.beachbowlproshop.com

I know, I know, the first thing you're going to ask is, "How can I afford to have something as heavy as a bowling ball shipped to me and still save money?" Beach Ball Pro Shop, located in sunny Florida, takes a generous attitude if you live in the continental U.S.: Shipping is free! Add to that discounts up to 50% off suggested retail price, and I don't know why you'd want to shop anywhere else. Beach Bowl Pro Shop is the best source for bowling balls from some of the best makers: AMF, Brunswick, Columbia, Ebonite, Hammer, Storm, and Track among them. This online merchant also sells bags, shoes and shirts for ladies and men, and accessories such as ball spinners (for polishing and sanding your balls). The online catalog is straightforward and easy to use. Owner Oscar Teran, a retired military base bowling center manager, promises to beat all legitimate retail prices. Be sure to check out the specials—factory seconds and closeouts—where savings run even deeper. I like small companies like this one that offer great, personalized service, high-quality merchandise, and real bargains.

SPECIAL FACTORS: Shipping free within the continental U.S.; all merchandise covered by the original manufacturer's warranty; nonwarranty returns subject to a restocking fee (see website for details).

BFK—The Yo-Yo Store

19306 Windrose Dr. **Rowland Heights, CA 91748** **626–912–9696**	**FORM OF INFORMATION:** online catalog; free print catalog **PAY:** check, MO, MC, V, AE, DSC, JCB **SELLS:** yo-yos and related parts and accessories **STORE:** no walk-in location; mail-order only; phone hours Monday to Friday 9:00 am–4:00 pm PST **ONLINE:** www.yoyostore.com

Somehow, yo-yos never seem to go out of style. On the contrary, they're more popular than ever. The Yo-Yo Store, a division of BFK Sports, has the largest selection of yo-yos and accessories at the lowest prices anywhere. The well-developed website is set up to make online shopping easy and fun. Here you'll find 50-plus models by the best known manufacturers, as well as web specials, books, parts, bearings, strings, collector yo-yos, and more. They have a Fun Stuff category which has kites, whoopee cushions, stink bombs, spin tops, squirt pens, and more. And there's no need to embarrass yourself in front of friends as you struggle with your yo-yo. BFK—The Yo-Yo Store sells numerous instructional videos so you can master every kind of slick trick.

SPECIAL FACTORS: Satisfaction guaranteed; new, unused returns (some exceptions) accepted within 15 days for exchange, refund, or credit; minimum $30 on international orders.

Bike Nashbar

6103 State Rte. 446
Canfield, OH 44406
800–627–4227
FAX: 877–778–9456
APO/FPO: 304-683-5635
APO/FPO FAX: 304-683-5636

FORM OF INFORMATION: free print catalog; online catalog
PAY: check, MO, MC, V, DSC
SELLS: bicycling accessories, apparel, and equipment
STORE: same address; call for hours
ONLINE: www.nashbar.com

Bike Nashbar is one of the country's top sources for casual and serious cyclists. They publish an 80-plus-page catalog which includes everything for your cycling needs, from helmets to toe clips and front brakes to rear derailleurs. In business since 1973, Bike Nashbar sells its own line of cycling accessories and clothing. In addition, you will find they carry a full line of parts and accessories from the industry's leading vendors. If you're looking for saddles, shoes, chains, wheels, pedals, handlebars, tools, nutritional items, bags, racks, sunglasses, forks, tires, tubes, pumps, lights, computers, or training equipment, Bike Nashbar has it all. Rain or shine, winter or summer, Bike Nashbar will keep you riding all year long.

WEBSITE: Wow! This online catalog is so extensive that you needn't bother with the print version unless you don't have internet access. You'll find thousands of products at the website organized by manufacturer or category. There's also a search engine that lets you search for merchandise by keyword. Updated daily, the website is much more current and comprehensive than the print catalog. There are also closeouts you'll only find out about by shopping online. Secure electronic ordering is offered here.

SPECIAL FACTORS: Satisfaction guaranteed; guaranteed lowest prices.

Divers Direct

1020 NW 6th St. Suite A
Deerfield Beach, FL 33442
800–DIVE–USA
954–429–0116
FAX: 954–429–8572

FORM OF INFORMATION: free print catalog; online catalog
PAY: check, MO, MC, V, AE, DSC
SELLS: scuba equipment and apparel
STORE: 7 store locations in Florida
ONLINE: www.diversdirect.com

Divers Direct was founded in 1984 and was formerly known as Holiday Diver, because the company founder Wayne Senecal started running scuba-diving trips off Key Largo, FL, from a boat that he docked behind a Holiday Inn. The company began selling online in late 1996 and mailed its first print catalog in fall 1998. They stock over 25,000 different products for scuba divers and snorkelers of all kinds and offer only top quality brands at the most competitive prices with full manufacturers' warranties. You'll find some of the best diving equipment products here, like Aeris dive computers, O'Neil wetsuits, JBL and Riffe spearguns, Pelican dryboxes, Sea & Sea underwater cameras, Sealife cameras, Tusa dive masks, Citizen dive watches, and many more products and manufacturers.

WEBSITE: The website offers closeouts and specials and online ordering, as well as diving-related links and membership to the Direct Rewards, where you earn points on each purchase that can be applied to free gear, exotic travel and other cool stuff.

SPECIAL FACTORS: Satisfaction guaranteed; returns accepted for exchange, refund, or credit.

GolfDiscount.com

888-394-4653
425-957-3626
FAX: 425-373-3153

FORM OF INFORMATION: online catalog only; no print catalog

PAY: cashier's check, MO, MC, V, AE, DSC

SELLS: golf equipment and gear for men, women, seniors, and left-handed people

STORE: no walk-in location; online only; phone hours Monday to Friday 7:00 am–5:00 pm, Saturday and Sunday 10:00 am–4:00 pm PST

ONLINE: www.golfdiscount.com

If you love to surf (the internet, that is) as well as to golf, then GolfDiscount.com is the place for you. GolfDiscount.com brings almost a quarter century of experience in the golf retail business to golf enthusiasts looking to pay about 20% less than they would at retail. There's a page of fan email from satisfied customers (quite a few of whom were left-handed golfers ecstatic to have found southpaw-friendly clubs), which is always heartening to see. This site carries clubs by the top-name manufacturers—including Cobra, Ping, Callaway, Taylor Made, Top Flite, Power Bilt, Cleveland, Titleist, Adams, Odyssey, Wilson, Nicklaus, and many others—as well as putters, golf shoes by FootJoy, Bite, Reebok, Etonic, Dunlop, and Mizuno, golf balls, travel covers, and even accessories such as ball retrievers, spikes/wrenches, rule books, grips, and sunglasses.

Straightforward and easy to use, this site has something some online shops lack: customer service. If you have questions, you can call and speak to a helpful sales rep who will even find the clubs you're looking for if GolfDiscount.com doesn't happen to be showing them at present on their site. You can also chat live online, if that's your thing. And there are separate online sections that cater exclusively to women, seniors, kids and left-handed people. All merchandise comes with the manufacturer's warranty. GolfDiscount.com also provides imprinting. You can have your corporate logo on golf balls, caps, shirts, and other items.

SPECIAL FACTORS: Satisfaction guaranteed; returns accepted within 30 days, but customer pays shipping; no personal checks accepted.

Golf Haus

700 N. Pennsylvania
Lansing, MI 48906
517–482–8842
FAX: 517–482–8843

FORM OF INFORMATION: free price list
PAY: check, MO, MC, V
SELLS: golf clubs, apparel, and accessories
STORE: same address; Monday to Friday 9:00 am–5:30 pm; Saturday 9:00 am–5:00 pm

"If we can't save you money, we don't deserve your business!" The folks at Golf Haus are earnest all right, which I like in a company. They specialize in one thing—saving you money on golf-related gear and equipment—and they have been doing it well for thirty years. The price list Golf Haus sends out is so frequently updated that it almost makes more sense to call. Here you'll find the lowest prices—up to 70% below list—on clubs, bags, putters, balls, and other golf equipment and accessories by major manufacturers including Powerbilt, Cobra, Wilson, Titleist, Taylor Made, Ping, Spalding, Mizuno, and many others. In addition, recent offerings have included such items as Gore-Tex rainsuits, spikes, airline travel bags (holds clubs and bag), and gloves. If you have a golf fanatic in the family, you'll do well to call Golf Haus before making any major purchases.

SPECIAL FACTORS: Free shipping and insurance on orders within the continental United States; minimum order: $75.

Holabird Sports

9220 Pulaski Hwy.
Baltimore, MD 21220
410–687–6400
FAX: 410–687–7311

FORM OF INFORMATION: free price list; online catalog

PAY: check, MO, MC, V, AE, DSC

SELLS: racquet sports equipment, athletic footwear and clothing

STORE: same address; Monday to Friday 9:00 am–5:00 pm, Saturday 9:00 am–3:30 pm

ONLINE: www.holabirdsports.com

Holabird Sports, established in 1981, carries equipment, clothing, and accessories for a good number of sports, but its specialty is racquets—prestrung, unstrung, and custom strung—for tennis, squash, and racquetball. Prices here are great—sometimes as much as 40% off suggested list. The free flyer is basically a no-frills price list that presents, among other things, racquet models by all the major brands, plus "Best Buy" racquet specials in limited quantities. Since you won't find detailed product specifications or photographs here, only product names and great prices, you'd do well to visit their website and review many of their products online. Holabird stocks over 3,000 items, among them a large selection of shoes (in regular and junior sizes) for aerobics, tennis, soccer, racquetball or squash, walking, running, cross training, and basketball, as well as rugged boots for hiking or work, plus men and women's athletic clothing. You'll also find portable stringing machines, ball hoppers, ball machines, and wind screens (many of these large items ship free of charge), and an eclectic assortment of other racquet-sport-related goods: reflective gear, Teva Wet Climber sandals, ladies clogs, joint supports, heart-rate monitors, videos, sports bags (including backpacks and fanny packs), sports gloves, eyeguards, socks, watches, visors, and personal sports radar gadgets. Holabird has a staff of professionals to custom-string rackets, but racquets can be purchased unstrung (deduct $6 from price) for stringing by do-it-yourself kit.

WEBSITE: The website is easy to use and features online ordering. Many products are listed here, and most are pictured. An informed consumer will appreciate this no-non-sense online catalog.

SPECIAL FACTORS: Authorized unused returns accepted within 7 days; small additional shipping charge outside continental U.S. and to APO addresses; call for price quotes.

The House

300 S. Owasso Blvd., Dept. WBM

St. Paul, MN 55117

800–409–7669

651–482–9995

FAX: 651–482–1353

FORM OF INFORMATION: free print catalog; online catalog

PAY: check, MO, MC, V, AE, DSC

SELLS: snowboarding, skateboarding, wakeboarding, and windsurfing equipment and accessories

STORE: same address; Monday to Friday, 9:00 am–6:00 pm, Saturday 9:00 am–1:00 pm

ONLINE: www.the-house.com

The House, established in 1983, is as much a philosophy as it is a business, "dedicated to no rip-off pricing so you can ride more!" Buying directly from manufacturers enables The House to save you from 20% to 50% off the price of sailboards, rigs, sails, snowboards, boots and bindings, clothing, accessories, and more. Whether your venue is snow, street or water, you'll reap the greatest savings by purchasing from The House. The House issues two catalogs—one for sailboarding, the other for snowboarding. Be sure to specify which one you're interested in. Each catalog gives important board specs for products, along with recommendations for choosing the best board based on such factors as rider weight and foot size. The House also sells equipment and clothing for children.

WEBSITE: At the website, you can enter nine different shops: Boot Shop, Binding Shop, Shoe Shop, Clothing Shop, Board Shop, Snow Shop, Wind Shop, Wake Shop, or Skate Shop. Once you get into a shop, click onto the category you want and you'll see full color images of items with pricing, and descriptions which include board specs. There is online ordering.

SPECIAL FACTORS: Satisfaction guaranteed; authorized returns accepted within 30 days.

Overton's

P.O. Box 8228, Dept. 57612
Greenville, NC 27835
800–334–6541
252–355–7600
FAX: 252–355–2923

FORM OF INFORMATION: free print catalog; online catalog

PAY: check, MO, MC, V, AE, DSC, JCB

SELLS: boating accessories and water sports goods

SHOWROOM: locations in Greenville, Charlotte, and Raleigh, NC; call for addresses and hours

ONLINE: www.overtons.com

Overton's is the place to shop if you're looking for discount boating and marine accessories, water sports equipment and gear, kiddie water play accessories, personal safety equipment, and anything else related to weekend boating, recreational poolside lounging, serious surfing, water skiing or tubing, snorkeling and diving, or wind gliding. Here you'll find top manufacturers of hundreds of products including apparel (belts, eyewear, footwear, men's shorts, rain gear, etc.); boating accessories (boat covers, heaters, lights, mooring hardware, navigation equipment, fuel systems, toilets); gifts and gadgets (kids' floating trampolines, boat telephones, remote-control toy boats); personal water craft (PWC) apparel and accessories; SUV/truck accessories; and water sports gear and equipment (diving equipment, kneeboards, pool accessories, wetsuits, flotation vests). If web surfing isn't your thing, you can request one of Overton's two print catalogs ("Water Sports," or "Marine and Boating"). Overton's lowest price guarantee states if you find a published price that's lower than theirs, they'll refund your money plus 10%.

WEBSITE: When Overton's, self-proclaimed "World's Largest Water Sports Dealer," offers its online shoppers a "power search" of the entire database of inventory, power is what the shopper gets. You can browse under Boating, Water Sports, Personal Water Craft, SUV/Truck and Apparel categories, or search by a long or a short product description, by part number, and vendor. The website also has great bargain-basement deals on goods in every category, so check here first.

SPECIAL FACTORS: Satisfaction guaranteed; quantity discounts available; unused returns accepted within 30 days for exchange, refund, or credit.

Performance Bicycle Shop

P.O. Box 2741
Chapel Hill, NC 27514
800–727–2453
FAX: 304–683–2001

FORM OF INFORMATION: free print catalog; online catalog

PAY: check, MO, MC, V, AE, DSC

SELLS: bicycle parts and cycling apparel

STORE: retail outlets in CA, CO, IL, MD, NC, OR, PA, VA, and WA

ONLINE: www.performancebike.com

If it's good enough for the U.S. Cycling Team, it should be good enough for the rest of us. I'm talking about the technical clothing and bicycle parts and accessories sold at Performance Bicycle. Performance Bicycle claims to be the largest retail and mail-order supplier of bicycle parts and accessories in the U.S. The prices here can be excellent, especially if you scan the pages for sales and closeouts. This company, in business since 1981, will give you a price that's lower than anyone else's—a promise they back with a guarantee. The color catalog is appealing and easy on the eyes, with vivid photos and descriptions. However, if you have access to the internet, I strongly advise you to check out the online catalog first.

WEBSITE: Online you can not only view hundreds of products—books/videos, car racks, glasses, helmets, indoor storage hardware, lights, locks, pumps, saddles, wheels, tools/lubes, packs, ultralight camping gear, electronics, nutritional products, and much more—but also check out weekly specials and clearance items that offer unbelievable deals on last-season's goods—some as low as 70% off; hop to other bike-fanatic web links; join a chat; and order online. I liked the Custom Bike section of the website, where you're led step by step through the process of building your own unique bicycle using custom components of your choosing.

SPECIAL FACTORS: Satisfaction guaranteed; returns accepted for refund, credit, or exchange (see print or online catalog for details)

Snorkel City

866–254–0032

FORM OF INFORMATION: online catalog only; no print catalog

PAY: MC, V, DSC

SELLS: snorkeling equipment

STORE: no walk-in location; mail-order only

ONLINE: www.snorkelcity.com

The folks at Snorkel City have over 50 years of combined experience in the sport of snorkeling and scuba diving. As certified instructors and divemasters, Snorkel City has handled thousands of pieces of snorkeling gear and personally used many different brands from around the world. As they explain it, if they offer it to you, it is quality equipment that will last for years and continue to provide the best possible experience for you while you are in the water. They know what makes a good piece of equipment and they sell it for less than you'll find at other locations. Savings on masks, fins, snorkels, wetsuits, snorkel sets, gear bags, dive knives and lights average around 30% for adults and 25% off in the kids section.

Snorkel City also offers masks with pre-ground optical prescription lenses as well as custom-ground prescription lenses.

SPECIAL FACTORS: Returns within 30 days of receipt; 20% restocking fee; some restrictions apply, see website for details.

SOAR Inflatables

20 Healdsburg Ave.
Healdsburg, CA 95448
707–433–5599
800–280–SOAR
FAX: 707–433–4499

FORM OF INFORMATION: free print catalog; online catalog

PAY: check, MO, MC, V

SELLS: inflatable boats and accessories

STORE: same address; Monday to Friday 10:00 am–5:00 pm (no dealers)

ONLINE: www.soar1.com

There are only 3 other companies in the world, according to SOAR Inflatables owner Larry Laba, that make inflatable canoes, and his are less expensive because he manufactures and sells them factory-direct to the consumer. SOAR, by the way, stands for "Somewhere on a River." The boats are 12′ ($1,425), 14′ ($1,595), and 16′ ($1,775)—prices as of this writing. Why spend that much when a regular canoe could cost as little as $500 (or up to $3,000)? Because, says Laba, his boats can be rolled up to fit into a backpack, a car trunk, an RV, and any airline storage unit. You can't do *that* with a rigid canoe. For regular (noncommercial) use, your SOAR Inflatable will last a lifetime. And these canoes handle virtually any condition a rigid canoe can, including Class 3 white water—this from a customer who did it. SOAR Inflatables are fun and reliable, as witness the dozen or more testimonials from happy customers in the flyer that comes with the 8-page color catalog. These customers range from urban apartment-dwellers and families with children to professional river guides, and they all echo the same themes: easy maneuverability, extreme ruggedness, versatility, and convenience.

Rolled up, the canoes weigh between 52 and 68 pounds, and they come with 2 seats, a double-action hand pump, straps to keep your inflatable tightly rolled, and a repair kit. Other items available in the catalog include collapsible paddles (and kayak paddle converters), duffel bags, padded seats with backs, a pump that hooks up to your car battery, and more. The catalog provides details for canoe aficionados, such as abrasion resistance, buoyancy, and drag. SOAR offers quantity discounts to businesses, ranging from 10% to 30% off, depending on the number purchased.

WEBSITE: For more about these remarkable boats, visit the website, where you can read all about them, check out monthly sales, request a catalog, see the photo gallery of happy customers, and read testimonials from SOAR owners. Online ordering is available.

SPECIAL FACTORS: Satisfaction guaranteed, with a 30-day trial; limited 5-year warranty.

Spike Nashbar

601 Packard Ct.
Safety Harbor, FL 34695
800–774–5348
FAX: 800–370–3424

FORM OF INFORMATION: free print catalog; online catalog
PAY: check, MO, MC, V, AE, DSC
SELLS: volleyball gear and apparel
STORE: no walk-in location; mail-order only
ONLINE: www.spikenashbar.com

Spike Nashbar, established in 1990, has competition volleyball gear, clothing, and accessories, and offers outstanding deals on some items if you buy in quantity or select from the Special Buys merchandise available in limited quantities and sizes. The 48-page color catalog has nets and balls for indoor and outdoor play, volleyball pumps, indoor and outdoor clothing and undergarments for men and women, shoes, kneepads, wraps and braces, sunglasses, and volleyball-related books, videos, novelties, and jewelry. Spike Nashbar will custom print and number your team's logo onto clothing.

WEBSITE: And don't miss the website. The online catalog features more than 4,800 in-stock products and closeouts. Click on a manufacturer or a product category to navigate around. This company offers a lowest price guarantee.

SPECIAL FACTORS: Satisfaction guaranteed; quantity discounts available; returns are accepted for exchange, refund, or credit.

Virtual Fairway

72–785 Highway 111
Palm Desert, CA 92260
760–346–5863
FAX: 760–776–7123

FORM OF INFORMATION: online catalog only; no print catalog
PAY: check, MO, MC, V
SELLS: used golf balls
STORE: no walk-in location; mail-order only
ONLINE: www.virtual-fairway.com

Sometimes the simplest, least-complicated things in life are the best. Virtual Fairway is just such a company. Several years ago, Cindy Carpino and her husband started a business so that Cindy could be a working mom at home with their children. Her husband, a golf fanatic, came up with the idea of a company that would sell nothing but used golf balls over the web, and the rest of the story is a happy one for both the Carpinos and their satisfied customers.

Golf balls are expensive. Period. And quality, high-grade, used golf balls at close to 50% less than they cost brand-new is the solution. For low-handicap and scratch golfers, used golf balls are great for practice. For mid- and high-handicap golfers as well as beginners, used golf balls will save money as you perfect your stroke. The inventory changes at Virtual Fairway, but past specials have included Top Flite Strata Distance at $15/dozen. Among the selections were Titleist DT Wound (90 or 100) for $12.00/dozen, Wilson Titanium Spin (90 or 100) at $15/dozen, Titleist Professional (90 or 100) for $25/dozen, all the way down to Pinnacle Gold LS, ($10/dozen),and Top Flite XL ($8/dozen). The selection regularly features a half-dozen leading brands in a spectrum of choices. If the prices don't snag you, the e-letters from happy Virtual Fairway customers from all over the world will. Whether you're golf-obsessed or merely a novice, this is an address you'll want to visit. Virtual Fairway offers discounts for purchasing 3 dozen versus 1 dozen golfballs, but the prices are already deeply discounted. You can order by phone, fax, mail, or right on the site.

SPECIAL FACTORS: Satisfaction "guaranTEED"; special orders welcomed. Free shipping on orders over $50.

Water Warehouse

6950 51st St.
Kenosha, WI 53144
800–574–7665
FAX: 800–323–5932

FORM OF INFORMATION: free print catalog; online catalog

PAY: check, MO, MC, V, AE, DSC

SELLS: swimming pool supplies and equipment

STORE: 5102 Green Bay Rd., Kenosha; Monday to Friday 10:00 am–7:00 pm, Saturday 9:00 am–5:00 pm, Sunday 11:00 am–4:00 pm

ONLINE: www.waterwarehouse.com

"America's Swimming Pool Experts," in business since 1965, carry not only the pool equipment and chemicals you'd expect, but also innovative products such as solar blankets (guaranteed for 6 years), Kreepy Krauly's automatic cleaners and Arneson's Aqua Critter, high-rate sand filter systems, and pool alarms. Water Warehouse offers hundreds of products for your pool or spa at savings of up to 25% to 50% on every order. Whether your pool is in-ground or above-ground, standard or custom size, in a one-season or four-season climate, Water Warehouse has the necessary sanitizing chemicals, algaecides, test kits, water purifiers, and floating chlorinators. If you don't yet have a pool, you're invited to consult by phone with knowledgeable staff about a variety of above-ground pool kits, do-it-yourself in-ground pool kits, and any other pool-related questions, especially those pertaining to custom and install-it-yourself pools (call the customer hotline, 800–574–7946, for free measuring installation packet, how-to video, price sheet, and installation guide). Shop the Water Warehouse for diving boards, aquatic exercise equipment, toys and games, pumps, liners—everything but the water!

WEBSITE: The website is terrific, with online ordering capability, product pictures and descriptions, web-only sale items, a comprehensive FAQ with helpful tips on pool maintenance, and much more. Check it out!

SPECIAL FACTORS: Satisfaction guaranteed; returns accepted within 30 days.

Tools, Hardware, and Shop Machines

Hand and power tools, hardware, and heavy machines and equipment for hobbyists, do-it-yourselfers, mechanics, electricians, plumbers, professional shopworkers, and woodsmen

If power tools are to grownups what toys are to kids, then this chapter will make you happy. The firms here offer the do-it-yourselfer, woodworker, hobbyist, woodsman, professional machine-shop worker, and small-time mechanic a wealth of hand and power tools, hardware and parts, electronics and abrasives, and heavy-duty machinery—much of it at rock-bottom prices. The tools run from hex wrenches and fine wood chisels to complete work benches and professional machinery, and the hardware includes hard-to-find specialty items, as well as nuts and bolts. There are even plumbing and electrical supplies here.

Find It Fast

ABRASIVES AND RELATED TOOLS
Econ-Abrasives, Red Hill

HARDWARE, TOOLS, AND MACHINES
Coastal Tool & Supply, Enco Manufacturing, Harbor Freight Tools, Northern Tool & Equipment, Wholesale Tool, Woodworker's Hardware, Woodworker's Supply

HOBBYIST TOOLS
Hot Tools, Micro-Mark, Wholesale Tool, Woodworker's Supply

ONLINE AUCTION OF TOOLS AND MACHINES
Harbor Freight Tools

RECONDITIONED TOOLS
Tool King

SURPLUS ELECTRONICS COMPONENTS, TOOLS
All Electronics, H&R Company

WOODCUTTER/LOGGER EQUIPMENT AND SUPPLIES
Bailey's, Northern Tool & Equipment

All Electronics Corp.

P.O. Box 567, Dept. WMO
Van Nuys, CA 91408
888–826–5432
818–904–0524
FAX: 818–781–2653

FORM OF INFORMATION: free catalog, $5 outside the U.S.; online catalog

PAY: check, MO, MC, V, AE, DSC

SELLS: surplus electronics and tools

STORE: 905 S. Vermont Ave., Los Angeles, CA; Monday to Friday 9:00 am–5:00 pm, also 14928 Oxnard St., Van Nuys, CA; Monday to Friday 9:00 am–6:30 pm, Saturday 9:00 am–5:00 pm

ONLINE: www.allelectronics.com

If you're an electronics nerd and want to get your hands on such items as a geophone vibration sensor, a 110-watt switching supply, a socket connector, a miniature bullet camera, or a deluxe crimp tool, you've just found a great resource. Inventors, technicians, and hobbyists will find all sorts of treasures here for making robotics, building computers, repairing antique radios, restoring electric trains, creating remote-control toys—in short, any project that requires common and hard-to-find electronic devices. All Electronics has been offering new and "pre-owned" electronics for over 30 years, keeping apace with the ever-changing needs of technology. Be aware that the product inventory is always changing, so if you don't see something in the current catalog, you can always check back later. All Electronics also purchases excess inventories.

WEBSITE: If you're a web shopper, you can view and order the inventory online. Most items have pictures and when you click on "more info," a detailed description and larger image pop up, plus a secure online shopping cart. If you prefer, you can download the print catalog from here.

SPECIAL FACTORS: Satisfaction guaranteed; returns accepted within 30 days of receipt in original condition for full refund or exchange.

Bailey's

44650 Hwy. 101
Laytonville, CA 95454–0550
800–322–4539
707–984–6133
FAX: 707–984–8115

FORM OF INFORMATION: free print catalog, $6 outside U.S.; online catalog

PAY: check, MO, MC, V, AE, DSC

SELLS: "woodsman" supplies

STORE: same address; also 196 Edwards Dr., Monday to Friday 7:00 am–6:00 pm; and Jackson, TN, Monday to Friday 7:00 am–5:00 pm

ONLINE: www.baileys-online.com

Bailey's bills itself as "The World's Largest Mail Order Woodsman Supplies Company—Selling at Discounted Prices." While it may not be the fanciest motto, you won't hear the lumberjacks, arborists, log-home builders, and chainsaw guys loyal to this company complaining. Thumbing through the 116-page color catalog will transport you into a different world, a world where Wild Ass Pants, chain grinders, tree saddles, and competition throwing axes are everyday items. The serious woodsman will find all types of chainsaws and related parts, equipment, and accessories; logging tools and gear; fire-fighting equipment; forest management supplies; and of course a complete selection of outdoor clothing and boots designed for safety and durability for rough-hewn types. The catalog also offers books and videos on everything from tying knots to tree-climbing techniques, as well as themed gift items and real-wood business cards. Bailey's good prices are further discounted if you buy in quantity.

WEBSITE: The website has the same friendly attitude as the print catalog—they even have video snipets online to demonstrate a few of their most popular products. Here, you'll find their full line of products, internet specials, and even helpful tips. "Chain saw chains can seem very confusing if you are not familiar with the different characteristics," begins one Buying Tips section. Thank goodness the nice people at Bailey's will take the time to educate us. If you find something that suits your fancy here, you can order right online.

SPECIAL FACTORS: Satisfaction guaranteed; authorized returns accepted within 90 days of receipt, with some restrictions.

Coastal Tool & Supply

510 New Park Ave.
West Hartford, CT 06110
877–551–8665
860–233–8213
FAX: 860–233–6295

FORM OF INFORMATION: online catalog only; no print catalog

PAY: check, MO, MC, V, AE, DSC

SELLS: hand, power, and air tools

STORE: same address; Monday to Friday 8:00 am–5:00 pm, Saturday 8:00 am–4:00 pm

ONLINE: www.coastaltool.com

Coastal Tool & Supply, "the discount tool people," brings us power tools, air tools, and hand tools at "everyday low, low, discount prices." Among the many products you'll find drills, cordless drills, saws, routers, sanders, polishers, rotary hammers, demolition hammers, grinders, compressors, pneumatics, dust systems, vacuums, biscuit joiners, and planers. All merchandise is brand-new and first-quality, in the original factory packaging with factory warranties, yet priced up to 50% less than you'd pay retail. Because Coastal's customers range from state agencies and professional builders to home woodworkers, the staff people are used to fielding a wide range of requests. Call them if you don't see what you're looking for in the catalog. I've found them to be extremely courteous and helpful. When you enter Coastal's online "shopping plaza," you'll be zipped to a screen where you can browse by manufacturer or by category. The website has some wonderful features, such as a gift center that offers suggestions for that special handyperson in your life; a chat room where you can get your questions answered by the tool doctor; highlights from recent newsletters; specials of the month; a factory-service locator; and much more. This is web shopping at its best. Secure online ordering is available. You can subscribe to receive Coastal's free e-newsletter that will keep you up to date on tool innovations, store specials, and features related to building.

SPECIAL FACTORS: Satisfaction guaranteed; returns (in condition received) are accepted for exchange, refund, or credit.

Econ-Abrasives

P.O. Box 1628, Dept. WBM
Frisco, TX 75034
800–367–4101
972–335–9234
FAX: 972–377–2248

FORM OF INFORMATION: free print catalog; online catalog

PAY: check, MO, MC, V, DSC, AE

SELLS: abrasives and related products

STORE: no walk-in location; mail-order only, phone hours Monday to Friday 7:30 am–5:00 pm CST

ONLINE: www.econabrasives.com

If you only need sandpaper once in a while, you can stick to shopping at your local hardware store. But when volume purchases of sanding belts, sheets, blocks and disc bases, and drums are in order, Econ-Abrasives can save you money on its mail-order line of industrial-grade abrasives for home and professional use. The free 32-page catalog is chock-full of data on product materials, specifications, and uses. If the grit you need doesn't appear in the catalog, Econ can make it for you, since they are the manufacturer. The company also carries specially shaped forms for sanding crevices, recesses, turnings, and the like. You can also order handheld scrapers, router and drill bits, wood chisels, sanding wheels, steel wool, safety gear, and many more sanding-related products. In case you're embarking on a new aspect of woodworking or using a new tool, the catalog provides a glossary of common abrasive terms and suggestions for the best tools for different jobs.

WEBSITE: Econ-Abrasives has their full inventory online with secure online ordering available. Check out the Bargain Shop where you'll find closeout specials on bargain sandpapers.

SPECIAL FACTORS: Price quotes by phone or letter; $25 minimum on orders using credit cards.

Enco Manufacturing Company

**400 Nevada Pacific Hwy.,
Dept. WBM**

Fernley, NV 89408

800–USE–ENCO

FAX: 800–965–5857

FORM OF INFORMATION: free print catalog;
online catalog

PAY: check, MO, MC, V, AE, DSC

SELLS: machinery, hand and power tools,
hardware, safety equipment, etc.

STORE: locations in AZ, CA, FL, GA, IL, MN,
OH, TX, and WA

ONLINE: www.use-enco.com

Enco Manufacturing Company, in business over 56 years, grew from a tiny manufacturer of lathe accessories into one of the largest industrial distributors of name-brand tools in the U.S. And yet, among the thousands of products in the 700-plus page catalog, many are suitable for homeowners, amateur woodworkers, hobbyists, or artists—basically anyone who needs easy-to-handle portable power tools or has a shop where they can set up more heavy-duty items. Savings between 30% and 50% off list price are common, with the best prices available on Enco's own line of products.

The product index, a whopping 15 pages long, kicks off with abrasives, air tools, and arbors; rolls into blades, calipers, and clamps; dives into dust-collector accessories, fasteners, and gauges; and barrels full speed through micrometers, pliers, safety gear, and sheet metal equipment—with many products to be discovered. Enco's centralized Parts Department can ship most parts from stock, and Enco's reference library carries handbooks and multivolume titles on subjects ranging from blueprint reading and rapid automated prototyping to harnessing the power of AutoCAD. With more than a dozen branches, Enco automatically routes your call to the nearest location and undoubtedly has the large or small items you need for industry or home. Enco's slogan is "The right tool at the right price," and one would be hard-pressed to challenge this.

WEBSITE: At the website you will need to download the print catalog to see the inventory. Once you have a catalog, you can order items from a secure electronic online order form.

SPECIAL FACTORS: Quantity discounts and institutional accounts available; C.O.D. orders accepted; minimum order: $25; if you find a lower advertised price on any identical part, Enco will beat the price by 5% (see website for details).

Herbach and Rademan

353 Crider Ave.
Moorestown, NJ 08057
800–848–8001
856–802–0422
FAX: 856–802–0465

FORM OF INFORMATION: free print catalog, $5 for international; online catalog

PAY: check, MO, MC, V, DSC

SELLS: new and surplus electromechanical, robotic, and optical components

STORE: no walk-in location; mail-order only

ONLINE: www.herbach.com

If you've got an imagination, Herbach and Rademan's 116-page catalog will spark it. Established in 1934, Herbach and Rademan sell a fascinating mix of surplus bargains—chiefly electronics, robotics, scientific equipment, optics, and mechanical devices. Past catalogs have featured power supplies, CCTV (closed-circuit TV) cameras, monitors, stepper motors, security equipment, gear head motors, blowers, synchronous motors, robotic kits and components, relays and contactors, compressors, instruments and tools, transformers, magnets, laser devices, switches, infrared devices, timers, motion detectors, heating and cooling devices, and lots more. Even if you're not a mad scientist, electronics nerd, or genius inventor, there's lots of stuff here anyone, electromechanically inclined or not, can use: microscopes, wire strippers, educational kits, phone accessories, digital scales, heavy-duty outlet strips and surge suppressers, model trains and cars, goggles, compasses, cabinet slides, parts bins, tool cases and cabinets, battery chargers, inkjet printers, weather balloons, and reference books on technical topics. Herbach and Rademan also run closeout and "grab bag" sales—and will purchase large quantities of your surplus current, quality electromechanical components, optics, relays, computer peripheral devices, and other similar items. Smaller quantities of special items are also purchased. Call to inquire.

WEBSITE: You can view color photos of most products by clicking on the product category in the table of contents. There is online ordering. Or, you can download and print out an order form and then call or fax in your order.

SPECIAL FACTORS: Satisfaction guaranteed; price quotes by phone, fax, or letter; returns with original packing materials are accepted within 30 days; minimum order: $25, $50 on open account, $100 on orders outside the U.S. and Canada.

Harbor Freight Tools

3491 Mission Oaks Blvd.
P.O. Box 6010
Camarillo, CA 93011
800–444–3353
805–388–2000
FAX: 800–905–5215

FORM OF INFORMATION: free print catalog; online catalog

PAY: check, MO, MC, V, AE, DSC

SELLS: tools, hardware, industrial equipment, machinery

STORE: 98 stores in 26 states, see website for locations and hours

ONLINE: www.harborfreight.com

Harbor Freight Tools can save you up to 70% off list prices on home tools and industrial equipment, machinery and hardware, and unexpected products that are the delight of seasoned catalog shoppers. However, Harbor Freight's reputation has been built on equipment and accessories used in welding, woodworking, automotive work, and outdoor maintenance. The catalog experience is akin to wandering through a hardware shop where you find something you need at every turn. Among the products featured in the color catalog are laser tools, air compressors, ai fastening tools, concrete mixers, lawn and garden tractors, motors, pumps, storehouses, tarpaulins, power and hand tools, propane stoves, generators, and shop and safety equipment.

WEBSITE: The website is really fun. It features, among other things, an online auction that invites shoppers to bid on hand and power tools, gardening equipment, and many other products; a clearance center; and online ordering of selected items in categories that include Automotive, Hand and Power Tools, Hardware, Electrical, Outdoor, Air Tools, Lawn and Garden, Household and Tarp. They have "live" help available Monday through Friday from 9:00 am–4:00 pm PST. If you need another incentive to shop Harbor Freight, remember: Shipping is free on orders over $50 within the continental U.S.

SPECIAL FACTORS: Returns accepted within 30 days for full refund or replacement. No questions asked.

Hot Tools

P.O. Box 615
Marblehead, MA 01945
800–777–6309
781–639–7100
FAX: 781–631–8887

FORM OF INFORMATION: online catalog
PAY: check, MO, MC, V
SELLS: wood-burning tools and accessories
STORE: no walk-in location; mail-order only
ONLINE: www.mmnewman.com

If you're a sail maker, kite smith, bird carver, or woodworking hobbyist, you're caught between a rock and a hard place when it comes to wood-burning tools and hot knives. You can go for the really cheap, handheld junkers that are available in craft shops—inexpensive but not intended for heavy-duty use; or you can spring for the second tier—the sophisticated, professional versions that will set you back several hundred dollars. M.M. Newman, the parent company of Hot Tools, has solved this problem by creating and manufacturing affordable, high-quality wood burners and passing the savings directly to the consumer without a middleman. Unlike the hobby-shop models, the Hot Tool has a generous 64" cord and slim design, is lightweight, has a handle that stays cool, and features a heat shield, slide-on changeable tips, and heating elements under the tip. When you call or fax Hot Tools (or contact them through their website), they'll send you several pages of flyers with photographs and detailed descriptions of their products. The Hot Tool wood burner with standard tip is priced at $34.95 at this writing. You'll also find #8 needle tips, reshapable blank tips, feather tips, multigroove tips, and buttons tips, as well as circle and round tips from $1/16"$ to $3/16"$—all for $5.75 each, except for the two multigroove tips, which are more. The helpful text gives step-by-step instructions on how to carve realistic feathers and do other fine work.

Other offerings include a complete wood-burner kit, a stencil maker, a library marking tool, a lacquer burn-in knife, and a hot tacking tool. You'll also find the Hot Knife, intended for cutting and melting synthetic materials such as sailcloth, spinnaker cloth, indoor/outdoor carpeting, etc. These tools are good values, great quality, and will last a long time.

Wholesale customers: Wholesale prices are offered on purchases of 12 or more items; resale number is required for wholesale.

SPECIAL FACTORS: Hot Tools will gladly replace any defective product; C.O.D. orders accepted.

Micro-Mark

340 Snyder Ave.
Berkeley Heights, NJ
07922–1595

800–225–1066

908–464–2984

FAX: 908–665–9383

FORM OF INFORMATION: free print catalog; online catalog

PAY: check, MO, MC, V, AE, DSC

SELLS: model-building tools and supplies

WAREHOUSE STORE: same address; store hours Wednesday to Friday 1:00 pm–5:00 pm, Saturday 10:00 am–5:00 pm

ONLINE: www.micromark.com

If your hobby or profession is building models, making miniatures, toys, musical instruments, dolls, or other small-scale items, then you must check out Micro-Mark, "the Small Tool Specialists." Both selection and prices are great here. Micro-Mark sells over 2,500 tools and supplies at a discount—up to 40% off retail on adhesives, cleaners, and lubes; clamps, jigs, and specialty tools; electronic items; files and sanders; hand tools; kits; knives and cutters; measuring, marking, and vision products; model ship and railroad items; organizers and display cases; painting, weathering, and decaling tools; power tools and accessories; resin, wood, and metal; scenery; soldering and electrical supplies; and even books and videos.

WEBSITE: If you like the convenience of shopping online, you'll love the website. It's easy to browse the entire inventory or search for items by category. You'll also find special offers posted here.

SPECIAL FACTORS: Returns accepted within 30 days of receipt for refund or credit.

Northern Tool & Equipment Co.

P.O. Box 1499, Dept. 24619
Burnsville, MN 55337
800–533–5545

FORM OF INFORMATION: free print catalog; online catalog

PAY: check, MO, MC, V, AE, DSC

SELLS: tools, equipment, engines, and generators for loggers, construction workers, handypersons, and mechanics

STORE: 40 outlets in FL, GA, IA, MN, NC, SC, TN, TX, VA, and WI

ONLINE: www.northerntool.com

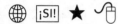

Do-it-yourself items and power tools from Northern Tool & Equipment Co., formerly Northern Hydraulics, are perfect for use by farms, garages, and rental stores, as well as in-home workshops and light industrial operations. The over-300-page master catalog, with discounts up to 50%, features such heavy-duty machinery and equipment as gas engines; generators; painting, welding, and sandblasting equipment; hoists and presses; log splitters; hydraulic pumps; and tillers, mowers, and lawn tractors. Northern also sells air compressors and air tools, lawn and garden equipment (trimmers, cultivators, garden carts, blowers, sprayers), protective gear, and boating accessories. You'll find trailer parts, Go-Karts and parts, tires, casters and wheels, and such up-to-the-minute items as meat smokers, solar panels, stock pot sets, and security lights and alarms—all discounted.

WEBSITE: The online catalog is informative and easy to use, and features secure online ordering. The Red Hot Deals section changes weekly, and here you'll find close-outs or overstocked merchandise in limited quantities—priced to sell.

SPECIAL FACTORS: Authorized returns accepted for exchange, refund, or credit.

Red Hill Corporation

P.O. Box 4234
Gettysburg, PA 17325
717–337–3038
FAX: 717–337–0732

FORM OF INFORMATION: free print catalog; online catalog

PAY: check, MO, MC, V, AE, DSC

SELLS: abrasives and refinishing products

SHOWROOM: Supergrit Abrasives, 1540 Biglerville Rd., Gettysburg, PA; Monday to Friday 8:00 am–5:30 pm

ONLINE: www.supergrit.com

Founded in 1978, Red Hill Corp. specializes in the gritty side of life: abrasives of all kinds. Red Hill is able to pass great savings on to the customer by purchasing huge quantities of first-quality closeouts from manufacturers and distributors, and by scanning the inventory of manufacturers in 14 other countries to find the best deals. You'll reap savings of up to 50% here on flap wheels (great for irregular-shaped surfaces or for removing paint or rust); sanding gel (for removing fine scratches from nonporous surfaces); sanding sticks (for hard-to-reach areas); discs of every size and description; paper rolls; buffing pads and bonnets; grinding discs; cloth shop rolls; sanding sheets; sand screen; scuffing pads; and much more. Whether you've got a heavy-duty, industrial-sized job or fine work in your hobby shop, Red Hill will definitely have the product you're looking for in the 48-page color catalog. In addition, the catalog offers sander parts and accessories, auto-body refinishing products, masking tape, tack cloths, a stick for cleaning sanding belts when the grit gets clogged, a selection of glue guns and glue sticks, and more. When your order exceeds $50, Red Hill lets you choose a free gift.

WEBSITE: Although it doesn't present the company's main inventory of products, the website is definitely worth checking out because it shows special sales on current closeout goods not listed in the print version. You'll find some amazing deals of discontinued or overstocked merchandise at incredible discounts with secure online ordering.

SPECIAL FACTORS: Price quotes by phone or letter on special order sizes; quantity discounts are available; minimum order: $25.

Tool King

11111 W. 6th Ave.
Lakewood, CO 80215
877–975–8665
303–963–4511
FAX: 303–963–4512

FORM OF INFORMATION: online catalog only; no print catalog

PAY: MC, V, AE, DSC

SELLS: manufacturer reconditioned tools

SHOWROOM: 4 stores in CO; call or see website for addresses and hours

ONLINE: www.toolking.com

Tool King, one of America's largest tool distributors since 1978, sells only the finest "like-new" manufacturer reconditioned tools. How does a tool become reconditioned? Because many companies have liberal return policies, customers can return products for any reason. Once a customer opens and/or returns a product, the item can't be sold as new—it must be identified as reconditioned. It is returned to the manufacturer and is completely reinspected and quality-checked to assure it meets all factory specifications. Manufacturer reconditioned tools are not only of the highest quality because they have been checked twice, they cost about 30% less than their new counterparts. Plus, every reconditioned tool is backed by a full manufacturer warranty along with Tool King's satisfaction guarantee. Tool King sells air, automotive, cordless, drill/drivers, gardening, hand, power, and router/rotary tools. The brands they carry include DeWalt, Porter-Cable, Makita, Bosch, Milwaukee, and Toro, just to name a few. Tool King has a lowest price policy which means if you should find a lower price on any tool they sell, they will attempt to beat the final price.

SPECIAL FACTORS: Returns within 30 days of receipt for refund or exchange; free shipping and $6 handling fee for any size order within the continental U.S.

Wholesale Tool Co., Inc.

P.O. Box 68, Dept. WBM
Warren, MI 48089
800–521–3420

FORM OF INFORMATION: free print catalog; online catalog

PAY: check, MO, MC, V, AE, DSC

SELLS: tools, hardware, and machinery

STORE: locations in MI, FL, IN, MA, NC, OK, and TX; see catalog or website for addresses and hours

ONLINE: www.wttool.com

Established in 1960, Wholesale Tool Co., Inc., publishes an 860-page, easy-to-use catalog of industrial tools and supplies of value to the professional contractor, woodworker, and surveyor as well as the weekend handyperson. This is more than a catalog; it's a resource book to keep on your shelf year-round. Here you'll find, at discount prices of about 30% off list, the usual roundup of name-brand tools (saws, drills, lathes, routers, drill presses, grinders, sanders and air tools) and the supplies that go with them (blades, bits, pads, dies, spindles, wheels, back plates). In addition, there are indicator and base sets, micrometers, tachometers, calipers (5 pages), digital readout systems, indexable mills, mill accessories, deburring tools, tool holders, knurls and knurling tools, reamers, countersinks, metric broaches, parts washers, sprayers, vacuums (wet/dry), coolant systems, skimmers, angle plates and tables, thread repair systems, phase converters, motors (single and three phase), torches, and welding equipment—a collection of products not often seen together in a catalog. The do-it-yourselfer or small business owner can count on Wholesale for socket sets, hammers, wrenches, pliers, power tools, abrasives, safety gear, casters and wheels (also in sets), drawer slides, storage bins, tool boxes, cleaning equipment, brooms, screwdrivers, staplers, magnets and demagnetizers, etching tools, tags and stencils, magnifiers, and automotive tools. For materials handling, there are work positioners, portable electric lifts, light-duty scissor lifts, post lift tables, machinery-moving kits (to handle up to 60 tons), pallet trucks, hand trucks, drum-stacking racks, dollies, utility carts, self-dumping hoppers, wheelbarrows, and crossover truck boxes for full-sized trucks.

WEBSITE: This firm has their entire inventory online in a well organized and easy to use site, which also has secure ordering available. Searches can be made by category, item number, or manufacturer. All products are pictured clearly with detailed descriptions.

Woodworker's Hardware

P.O. Box 180
Sauk Rapids, MN 56379
800–383–0130
FAX: 800–207–0180

FORM OF INFORMATION: free print catalog; online catalog

PAY: check, MO, MC, V, DSC

SELLS: cabinet and furniture hardware

STORE: no walk-in location; mail-order only; phone hours September to April: Monday to Friday 8:00 am–8:00 pm, Saturday 8:00 am–12:00 noon; May to August: Monday to Friday 8:00 am–5:00 pm CST

ONLINE: www.wwhardware.com

If today's homes and apartments serve our needs so well, a major reason is the hardware used on or in cabinets, dressers, computer tables, entertainment centers, and storage areas—the very hardware Woodworker's Hardware specializes in. The catalog offers more than 6,000 items including hinges, knobs, slides, pulls, latches, and supports. Woodworker's also carries specialty bins (wastebaskets that slide out of sight) and shelving, wire organizers, lazy Susans, caddies, appliance garages, and items you might not expect but certainly could use, such as keyboard trays, strip lighting, putties, fasteners, glue, and brass rail fittings. If you don't see what you need in the catalog, call for product availability and prices. Prices here are up to 20% below other woodworker's supply discounters.

WEBSITE: The website includes the full line of merchandise, online ordering, product descriptions and images, and online specials. This will no doubt be one site you'll want to bookmark if you're a do-it-yourselfer, particularly since, if you register, you can build your own custom catalog of your favorite hardware items.

SPECIAL FACTORS: Satisfaction guaranteed; price quotes by phone or letter; quantity discounts available; authorized returns (unused, undamaged goods) accepted within 30 days.

Woodworker's Supply, Inc.

1108 North Glenn Rd.
Casper, WY 82601–1698
800–645–9292
FAX: 800–853–9663

FORM OF INFORMATION: $2 print catalog; online catalog

PAY: check, MO, MC, V, DSC

SELLS: woodworking tools and equipment

STORE: locations in WY, NC, and NM; call for addresses and hours

ONLINE: www.woodworker.com

For nearly 30 years, Woodworker's Supply has been "where the experts buy their tools," often at savings up to 30% on comparable goods sold by other supply houses. The 155-page color catalog has a major advantage over some of the heftier tool catalogs of similar products: If you're *not* an expert but rather a novice or hobbyist, the inventory will seem more accessible and suitable for smaller projects. There are shelf pins and shelving supports; audio-video hardware; kitchen and decorative hardware; shellacs and stains; wood fillers and putty; casters and tee-molding; furniture, computer, and table hardware; caning and chair seats; glues and gluing tools; tung oil, varnish, and Danish oil; and woodworking books and plans. Woodworker's Supply has an ample selection of hand tools, power tools, carving, turning, scraping, and wood-burning tools, bench components and clamps, shop and drilling accessories, spray equipment and lacquers, sanding tools and accessories, air nailers, and machinery accessories. Woodtek's line of machinery is offered at the back of the catalog in a dedicated section featuring widebelts, machine stands, a belt/disc machine, large convertible sanders, a heavy-duty 36" radial drill press, dust collectors, overarm router, hollow chisel mortiser, and more. There's also a toll-free technical service number you can call for assistance with your Woodtek machinery. Woodworker's Supply can bring you the "tools of the trade" with the atmosphere and personalized attention of a local shop, and this firm offers a low-price guarantee and a 90-day no-hassle returns policy.

WEBSITE: Woodworker's Supply has their entire inventory online in a well organized and easy to use site, which has secure ordering available. Search by category, brand, or part number. All products are pictured clearly with detailed descriptions.

SPECIAL FACTORS: Satisfaction guaranteed; returns accepted within 90 days for refund or replacement.

Toys, Games, and Party Supplies

Games, Toys, and Fun

Educational and fun toys and games for children and teachers; board and card games for adults; magic tricks for all ages; toy model kits

I love researching the companies to put in this chapter, which is devoted to yanking children (and adults) away from the television set. Children of all ages—and that includes us "grown-ups"—will find great companies here that sell discounted games and toys that encourage thinking, constructive activity, and creative interactions. Games aren't just for kids. Grown-ups will love Cheapass Games and Phoenix Model Company, both of which cater to a more mature (if you can call us that!) consumer. If you're into magic, check out Magic Tricks. Everyone should be able to master a little trick or two. Finally, teachers will find a wonderful company in this chapter, ClassroomDirect.com, that has their specific classroom and curriculum needs in mind. But parents will appreciate this company, too.

Every year around holiday time, a favorite media topic is what to buy for your kids, which toys are dangerous, what's the hot toy, and other tiresome topics. But I'll add my two cents worth to the mix and recommend a great website: Dr. Toy (www.drtoy.com). Sponsored by The Institute for Childhood Resources, a not-for-profit organization, Dr. Toy has reviews of good toys and games for children, categorized by age. This is a good source for parents who don't want to shop at that backward-R place or give in to the latest fad toy. The items Dr. Toy recommends are chosen for their educational and entertainment qualities, as well as their ability to stay outside of or at the very top of the toy chest. You will always get terrific ideas from this site.

Find It Fast

ADULT AND TEEN BOARD AND CARD GAMES
Cheapass Games, TURN OFF the TV

ART AND CRAFT SUPPLIES
ClassroomDirect.com, TURN OFF the TV

BABY AND TODDLER TOYS
ClassroomDirect.com, Constructive Playthings, TURN OFF the TV

BOARD AND CARD GAMES FOR CHILDREN
Cheapass Games, ClassroomDirect.com, Constructive Playthings

COMPUTER GAMES
ClassroomDirect.com

EDUCATIONAL TOYS AND GAMES
ClassroomDirect.com, Constructive Playthings, TURN OFF the TV

MAGIC TRICKS
Magic Tricks

MODEL TOY KITS
Phoenix Model Company

MUSICAL TOYS
Constructive Playthings, TURN OFF the TV

PARENT AND TEACHER AIDS
ClassroomDirect.com, Constructive Playthings, TURN OFF the TV

PHYSICAL EDUCATION AND PLAYGROUND EQUIPMENT AND TOYS
ClassroomDirect.com, Constructive Playthings, TURN OFF the TV

SIX-SIDED DICE, POLYHEDRA DICE, FAKE MONEY
Cheapass Games

STICKERS
ClassroomDirect.com, Stickers 'N' Stuff

Cheapass Games

827 NW 49th St.
Seattle, WA 98107
206–526–1096
FAX: 206-526-1097

FORM OF INFORMATION: print catalog (see text); online catalog

PAY: check, MO, MC, V

SELLS: original dice, card, and board games and accessories

STORE: no walk-in location; mail-order only; phone hours Monday to Friday 9:00 am– 5:00 pm PST

ONLINE: www.cheapass.com

"You and your friends are living pleasant and complete lives in Happyville. You are highly trained and well-paid sous-chefs, who have decided to climb to the top of a tall building, as fast as you can. Devil Bunny Needs a Ham. And he's pretty sure that knocking you off the building will help him get one. Perhaps he is right. Perhaps he is not." This is a description of Devil Bunny Needs a Ham, one of the many games that Cheapass Games has designed and produced. This little gem of a company sells original board, card, and dice games at incredibly inexpensive prices, with other names like Kill Doctor Lucky, Unexploded Cow, Give Me the Brain!, Devil Bunny Hates the Earth, and Lord of the Fries. At this writing, the most expensive black-and-white game was $7.50, with many starting at $2! How is this possible? Because, as founder James Ernest rightly reasons, most of us already own—or can cheaply obtain—the dice, the play money, the pencils, and the pawns needed for any game. What Cheapass does is invent and design their own games, print them out in black ink on colored card stock (the boards for the board games are cut into sections for you to reassemble), and then mail them to you with instructions. They have recently started to make full-color games, as well, under the name of James Ernest Games. These range from $6.95 to $15. As Mr. Ernest says, "You don't need to pay forty bucks for a game that's overproduced and underdesigned." All games are fully described on the website.

Cheapass also sells some of the game pieces as well, such as multicolored dice and solid and transparent polyhedra. At the website, you can also get free games, subscribe to the "Players Club," which allows you to pay one sum and then get games mailed to you as soon as they're released, and check out accessories such as Cheapass buttons and comics. The appeal of this company isn't just that their games are so cheap—this is a group of witty, funny, and original people who have an impressive collective background in gaming and designing.

If you don't have internet access, you can request a print catalog.

SPECIAL FACTORS: Resellers/wholesalers should inquire for terms; overseas customers call or email for shipping fees.

ClassroomDirect.com

P.O. Box 830677

Birmingham, AL 35283–0677

800–599–3040

877–698–1988

FAX: 800–628–6250

FORM OF INFORMATION: free print catalog; online catalog

PAY: MC, V, AE, school purchase orders

SELLS: educational equipment, furniture, supplies, games, learning aids, software, etc.

STORE: no walk-in location; mail-order only; phone hours Monday to Friday 8:00 am– 5:00 pm CST

ONLINE: www.classroomdirect.com

If you are a parent, teacher, child-care worker, camp director, or work with children in any way, get ready for your new favorite company. If you have a kid who loves to play board and card games with you, you are probably always trying to find ones that are unusual, challenging, and educational. You can't find these items at the big chain stores. I'm not kidding when I say that the 385-page color catalog from ClassroomDirect.com is worth its weight in gold. Founded by a former elementary school teacher, ClassroomDirect.com calls itself "your deep discount educational superstore." I've never seen such great stuff at such amazing prices. Three-quarters of the massive print catalog is devoted to every kind of school supply you could imagine: fantastic arts and crafts materials from basic glues, papers, and markers to items such as building blocks; teacher helpers such as stickers, dictionaries, display boards, and stackable organizer bins; audio-visual equipment, including headsets, public address systems, and overhead projectors; educational aids, such as talking globes and flash cards; wonderfully smart board games and card games; motivators, such as prize pencils, certificates, and crowns; room decorations galore; early childhood furniture, mats, physical games, and play stations; books, workbooks, and materials for language arts, math, science, and social studies; kid- and teacher-sized chairs, tables, and computer stations; and storage and cleaning items, to name but a few! The other quarter of the catalog is devoted to every kind of educational software you could dream up, as well as computer accessories.

And I've only scratched the surface! You'll be filled with ideas when you start thumbing through these pages. Take this book along on your next train trip and bring along plenty of stick-em flags. In addition to phenomenal selection and prices, ClassroomDirect.com provides free shipping on orders over $149, has a lowest price guarantee, and an amazing 1-year satisfaction guarantee (see catalog or website for details).

WEBSITE: If you have access to the internet, I have really good news for you: Prices at the ClassroomDirect.com online catalog are even better than those found in the print catalog! The website performs great PR for the company: It's well designed, easy to use, extremely comprehensive, and gives online shoppers lots of perks, like free craft ideas and lesson plans, product reviews, freebies, closeouts, and web-only specials. You can place your order electronically here.

SPECIAL FACTORS: Satisfaction guaranteed; no goods shipped outside the continental U.S.

Constructive Playthings

U.S. Toy Company, Inc.
13201 Arrington Rd.
Grandview, MO 64030–1117
800–448–1412
FAX: 816–761–9295

FORM OF INFORMATION: free print catalog; online catalog

PAY: check, MO, MC, V, DSC

SELLS: toys and educational products

STORE: CA, CO, FL, IL, KS, PA, TX; call or see website for address and hours

ONLINE: www.constplay.com

It doesn't take long for your innocent toddler to get sucked into the materialistic vortex of toy marketing, TV show and movie linkage, and fast-food/toy cobranding. It's nice to know there's a company out there that specializes in wholesome, growth-oriented toys that children will love, despite the fact that they're "educational." Constructive Playthings offers a "lowest price guarantee" on everything they sell, and carries the kinds of items you won't easily find in the mega kids' stores. (If you've ever tried to find wooden building blocks at the mall, you know what I'm talking about.) Since 1953, Constructive Playthings has been in the business of selling classic toys for less, with an emphasis on early educational toys: science and craft projects, musical play mats, real steel tool sets, kid-friendly furniture, giant tumble balls, books, tapes, videos, and outdoor playthings, such as plastic baseball bats, and sand diggers. The products here are built to last and designed to promote creative, safe play. Teachers, day-care workers, or parents of children 8 and under will jump for joy when they see the wonderful catalog from this nice company. *Please note:* If you operate a day-care center or teach in a school, request the 200-page "School Catalog," where the focus is more on group play and institutional settings.

WEBSITE: At the website, you can view the inventory by category or by age group, check out seasonal sale items where bargains abound, and order online.

SPECIAL FACTORS: Satisfaction guaranteed; returns accepted for exchange, refund, or credit; institutional accounts available.

Magic Tricks

2768 Columbia Rd.
Gordonsville, VA 22942
540–832–0488
FAX: 508–267–5822

FORM OF INFORMATION: online catalog only; no print catalog

PAY: check, MO, MC, V, DSC

SELLS: magic tricks for all ages and skill levels

STORE: no walk-in location; mail-order only

ONLINE: www.magictricks.com

Here's a great store that every parent will be glad to know about. Your child is going to amaze his friends with the inexpensive, clever tricks from this wonderfully unique store. Magic Tricks is a real magic shop, in business since 1971, located near the University of Virginia (where generations of coeds have been trying to get their term-paper assignments to disappear). You're going to love shopping online here, where you can click on a product category—Card Tricks, Coin Tricks, Close-up Magic, Club/Stage Magic, Animal Magic, Mentalism, Related Arts, Magic Accessories, Tables and Cases, Magic Books, Videos, Magic Kits, Posters, Memorabilia, and Bargain Basement—and read about and view items grouped by difficulty level. All of the magic tricks sold here come with instructions. Level 1 tricks are appropriate for beginners and require little skill or practice. (Because of small parts, these tricks are not recommended for children under 5.) Level 3 and up are for the serious hobbyist. Some of the more difficult tricks require skills that are not explained in the instructions, such as the ability to palm a card. Instructions for these special skills are available in books and videos that are also carried here.

What you *won't* find at Magic Tricks are pyrotechnics or flash paper, gambling devices (loaded dice, marked decks), real cheapie low-end magic tricks, poorly made effects, or tricks that are too difficult or complicated to perform correctly. Magic Tricks makes up and sells their own magic sets because they found the tricks in commercial magic sets were not a good value. There are lots of other wonderful features of the website you'll want to explore, such as the "special interest" tricks and scripted routines designed for teachers, bartenders, salespeople, and others for whom an injection of magic couldn't hurt their effectiveness. You'll also find links, magic answers, magic trivia, a magic museum, and much more here. This is a great source of gifts for all ages.

SPECIAL FACTORS: Children under 18 should order by mail, since telephone and online orders can only be taken from the actual credit card holder; only items that were defective or damaged at time of arrival may be returned, with preauthorization required.

Phoenix Model Company

P.O. Box 15390
Brooksville, FL 34604
325–754–8522
FAX: 352–754–1882

FORM OF INFORMATION: free print catalog; online catalog

PAY: check, MO, MC, V

SELLS: toy model kits

STORE: no walk-in location; mail-order only; phone hours Monday to Friday 8:00 am– 5:00 pm EST

ONLINE: www.phoenix-model.com

When I was growing up, there were so many cool toy model kits to choose from. My father used to spend hours piecing together, glueing, and then painting countless figures that would adorn our house. I was delighted to discover that the Phoenix Model Company, "Your Discount Hobby Warehouse," still sells great classic models such as dinosaurs, horror-movie characters, and super heroes, as well as the standard-fare ships, military aircraft, and vintage automobiles—at prices that are way below what you would pay at a retail toy and hobby shop. Log on to the fun and friendly website to view over 12,000 toy models and model-building accessories: hobby items including plastic model kits; prebuilt vinyl models; die-cast metal collectibles and toys; wooden model kits; replicas; real flying powered aircraft; paints, airbrush kits, tools, and supplies; and books and videos. Children of all ages can choose from a huge inventory of cool cars, trucks, trains, planes, boats and motorcycles, war figures, James Bond, *Star Wars, Lost In Space, Star Trek, Planet of the Apes, Speed Racer,* The Beatles, Japanese robots, aliens, monsters, motorized banks, scale models of the White House and Capitol Building, armored knights, horses, pirate ships, Godzilla, King Kong, and many more. No matter what kind of model you're looking for, Phoenix either has it in stock in their 18,000-square-foot warehouse or can quickly search out the item for you. The website features full-color illustrations, a "lightning fast" search engine, and monthly specials and Crazy Sale items.

SPECIAL FACTORS: Shipping free on orders over $150 within the continental U.S.; full-credit return policy for damaged or unsatisfactory merchandise returned within 30 days, excluding books and software; wholesale inquiries welcome.

Stickers 'N' Stuff, Inc.

245 West Sycamore Ln. Dept. WBM	**FORM OF INFORMATION:** $2 catalog and samples; online catalog
Louisville, CO 80027–2235	**PAY:** check, MO, MC, V
303–661–0200	**SELLS:** novelty stickers
FAX: 303–665–8779	**STORE:** no walk-in location; mail-order only
	ONLINE: www.stickersnstuff.com

Stickers, stickers, stickers! What child doesn't like to see a sticker next to a good grade on a test? Teachers love to give stickers as much as kids love to get them, and this company makes it easy for every teacher to give stickers, with prices as low as 6 cents for stickers that usually cost 25 cents! The wide variety of stickers here includes prisms (rainbow effect), chrome (foil background), hologram, pearlescent, scratch-and-sniff, velvety fuzzies, and glowing neon. Smiley faces and stars are just the beginning; designs include bunnies, butterflies, clowns, bears, flowers, birthdays, rainbows, horses, angels, ice cream cones, unicorns, snakes, and airplanes. Stickers 'N' Stuff also offers some wonderful collections, with the least expensive being the 410-sticker grab bag. Other collections include an endangered species set, holiday and seasonal stickers, a unicorn grab bag, and economy paper stickers. You'll find heart-shaped adhesive bandages, sticker "earrings," and sticker-collecting books here, too.

WEBSITE: You can view many of these stickers online and order them right at the website. The online catalog is easy to use and has color images of many stickers that will give you letter-decorating and inexpensive-gift ideas.

SPECIAL FACTORS: Satisfaction guaranteed; quantity discounts available; returns accepted for exchange, refund, or credit.

TURN OFF the TV

12 Nepco Way
Plattsburgh, NY 12903
800–949–8688
FAX: 425–558–4781

FORM OF INFORMATION: free print catalog; online catalog

PAY: check, MO, MC, V, AE, DSC

SELLS: family games and activities

STORE: phone hours Monday to Friday 9:00 am–5:00 pm EST

ONLINE: www.turnoffthetv.com

I have a friend who has a kid who lives without a television. What does he do? He plays a lot of board games and card games with his mother, makes art, and lures her into games of darts, basketball, and catch. She doesn't mind playing with her son. "I figure in only a few short years he'll be a teenager and hate my guts," she says. If this sounds like your scenario, you're in luck. TURN OFF the TV, founded in 1994 by the husband and wife team of Tim and Nancy Zier, is a great little company that sells all kinds of interesting games, puzzles, and crafts designed to bring family and friends together through a colorful, free, print catalog and a nice, organized, easy to use website.

At the website you can search in a number of ways—by title, keyword, or manufacturer. There are also helpful lists such as award winners, great gifts under $20, latest and greatest, and TOTV's picks. TOTV sells active games to get you moving; board games of every type and description and for all ages; books full of ideas for daytime fun; cards for all ages; cooperative games where everyone is a winner; crafts; educational games that are entertaining yet full of learning, in areas such as math, science, geography, and music; party/group games; puzzlers; fun strategy games that teach cognitive thinking skills; and travel games especially suited to packing in the car or suitcase. Did you think games were limited to those stacks you see at the backward-R place? The goods here are so unusual and creative you'll be amazed. You will want to bookmark this site and use it frequently to buy presents for those endless birthdays your kid is always getting invited to. Nothing here is expensive, and these are goods you and your children can keep and use over and over again for hours of fun. Now *that's* a bargain. I doubt there's a kid out there who'd rather watch TV than play a game with his mom or dad. Unplug for a day and give it a try.

SPECIAL FACTORS: 30-day money back guarantee.

Parties, Holidays, and Events

Party and catering supplies; party favors and decorations; festive packaging; gift wrapping and holiday decor

For my son's third birthday I spared no expense or energy to create a castle-themed party for him. I collected five refrigerator boxes from a couple of local appliance companies and carved, cut, glued, and painted them into a castle with a drawbridge that filled half of the living room. My sister created a life-size replica of my son as a knight out of clay, wood, fabric, and paint. We blew up enough balloons to hang in big bunches from the ceiling and to cover every surface of floor. Even now, at the age of ten, my son remembers and talks about the castle birthday party and asks if we can have another castle party. The idea of doing it again makes me so sleepy, I ask him, "Won't it be just as much fun to invite all your friends over and get a couple of bales of hay to play in?" "No," he replies, "It won't."

Parents know that one of the biggest annual expenses is The Birthday Party. Somehow, the guest list keeps getting bigger, the party favors more elaborate. If you're throwing a kid's party, you'll find great sources here: Companies that supply piñatas, balloons, penny candy, party favors, and more at tremendous savings, compared with your local mall superstore. Likewise, if you're hosting an event, say, a fund-raiser, retirement party, or a Super Bowl get-together, you'll want to check out the party suppliers here for themed decor, custom-imprinted items, such as napkins and matchbooks, and great catering supplies. And you organized types who have special closets full of gift wrap, matching ribbons, and notecards will love the companies in this section that sell wrapping and packaging supplies. You'll never want to shop for these items in a store again. These are some of my favorite catalogs to have around.

Find It Fast

CHILDREN'S PARTY FAVORS, CANDY, CHEAP TOYS, STOCKING STUFFERS
Oriental Trading, Paradise Products, Party & Paper Worldwide, Stumps-ShindigZ, U.S. Toy

CUSTOM ENGRAVING AND IMPRINTING
M&N International, Oriental Trading, Stumps-ShindigZ

GIFT WRAP AND DECORATIVE PACKAGING SUPPLIES
Party & Paper Worldwide

M&N International, Inc.

P.O. Box 64784, Dept. WBM
St. Paul, MN 55164–0784
800–479–2043
FAX: 800–PARTY–ON

FORM OF INFORMATION: free print catalog,
$6 outside U.S.; online catalog

PAY: check, MO, MC, V, DSC

SELLS: party supplies

STORE: no walk-in location; mail-order only

ONLINE: www.mninternational.com

For inspiration on your next party, prom, dance, or shower at very affordable prices, take a look at M&N's "Bright Idea" book. You'll find anything and everything you might need to make your event memorable, and the variety will send your imagination flying. The color catalog is published in the spring and fall, and each edition features seasonal themes rounded out with year-round party staples. The fall/winter catalog has decorations and supplies for back-to-school, Halloween, Thanksgiving, Hanukkah, Christmas, and New Year's, as well as for sports parties, Oktoberfest, Chinese New Year, Bastille Day, south-of-the-border fiestas, Old West, Hawaiian luaus, Mardi Gras, and much more. Best of all, they guarantee the lowest prices possible on everything, so you can't go wrong by shopping here. Birthdays, anniversaries, weddings, and every other reason to celebrate are covered in this catalog as well, with banners, party hats, festive tablecloths, party favors, and more. In the Caterer's Corner you'll find items that will help make serving easier and more elegant, such as place cards, centerpieces, serving platters, candles, warming racks, chef hats, and special carry-home containers. M&N also offers promotional materials for your company, and will engrave wine glasses, pens, wooden nickels, lollipops, and more with your company insignia.

WEBSITE: The website offers a selection of products in many categories. You can browse around and order the products you seek right online.

SPECIAL FACTORS: Satisfaction is guaranteed; quantity discounts are available; authorized returns are accepted for exchange, refund or credit (15% restocking fee); institutional accounts are available.

Oriental Trading Company, Inc.

P.O. Box 2308
Omaha, NE 68103-2308
800–875–8480
FAX: 800–327–8904

FORM OF INFORMATION: free print catalog; online catalog
PAY: check, MO, MC, V, AE, DSC
SELLS: party goods, novelties, toys, etc.
STORE: no walk-in location; mail-order only
ONLINE: www.oriental.com

In business since 1932, the "World's Biggest Toy Box" sells everything a novelty shop would sell—at prices up to 50% below what you would normally pay in a store. In this toy box you will find everything from porcelain dolls dressed in period costumes to black tissue-paper Halloween cats—with a great deal in between, including jester hats for both adults and children, feather wings, red devil wigs, costumes for dogs, butterfly and ladybug wings, clown shoes, funny eyeglasses, neon wigs, plastic helmets and swords, gorilla costumes for adults, string lights, craft supplies, hand puppets, and much, much more! They also sell many year-round items, such as stickers, party hats and decorations, and party favors. Trust me: You won't be able to put this catalog down without ordering something—even if you don't have kids. Many items are sold singly, but others are sold by the dozen, gross, or pound.

WEBSITE: The website has thousands of items. Here you'll be able to view a good selection of their many fun products and order directly online. You'll be amazed at how much $20 can buy.

SPECIAL FACTORS: Quantity discounts available; authorized returns (except food, candy, and costumes) accepted after contacting customer service within 5 days of receipt of goods. At this time they are not able to ship international orders that are placed online.

Paradise Products, Inc.

P.O. Box 568, Dept. WBM
El Cerrito, CA 94530–0568
800–650–0336
FAX: 510–524–5890

FORM OF INFORMATION: free print catalog; online catalog
PAY: check, MO, MC, V, AE, DSC
SELLS: party paraphernalia
STORE: no walk-in location; mail-order only; phone hours Monday to Friday 7:00 am–5:00 pm PST
WEBSITE: www.partymaster.com

This is one company worthy of its name! As you flip through the pages of this catalog, you'll soon realize this company sells everything you might need to turn your next party or event into a fun-and-savings paradise. With savings of 50% below typical retail prices, you'll be able to pull off a memorable and festive event without emptying your wallet. Paradise Products sells decorations and supplies for over 60 different themes, including the big holidays of Halloween, Thanksgiving, Christmas/Hanukkah, and New Year's, and others, such as Mardi Gras, Fourth of July, St. Patrick's Day, Valentine's Day, and Mother's Day, not to mention disco, county fair, circus, outer space, Caribbean, pop culture, Hollywood, sports and many other fun themes. Glitzy streamers, golden crowns, ice-sculpture molds, and tissue centerpieces will give your event that exciting touch, while matching dining accessories, candles, and aprons will help the event go off with ease and flair. On most items, the prices go down when you buy in quantity.

WEBSITE: The website is pretty basic. You can choose a browse button or search button on the home page. The browse button takes you to a list of party themes which are links. Click on a link and you'll get a chart-like page with products available under the category you've chosen. When you click on a product name, a page with a brief description and photo will appear. Online ordering is available.

SPECIAL FACTORS: Prices include UPS ground shipping; allow up to two weeks for delivery; minimum order for catalog $20; minimum order for website $25; minimum order for international and Canadian orders $100; minimum order for APO/FPO $25, or a $3 service charge applies; $15 added to order for APO/FPO customers; authorized returns within 30 days of sale, subject to restocking and freight both ways.

Party & Paper Worldwide

800–631–3310
847–543–9779
FAX: 847–265–9799

FORM OF INFORMATION: online catalog only; no print catalog

PAY: MO, cashiers checks, MC, V, DSC

SELLS: party supplies

STORE: no walk-in location; website only; phone hours Monday to Friday 8:00 am–6:00 pm, Saturday 10:00 am–6:00 pm EST

ONLINE: www.partypro.com

I like companies like this online party supply store: What you see is what you get. Party & Paper Worldwide buys direct from the manufacturers, which saves you from 15% to 60% off normal retail. Secure online ordering, free shipping on orders over $40 (within the contiguous U.S.), and a customer-service department reachable by phone (toll-free) make this an easy place to like.

The online catalog has thousands of items in dozens of categories and themes, including Anniversary Supplies, First Birthday, Balloons, Candles, Cards and Sta-tionery, Centerpieces, Dinnerware, Gift-wrap Supplies, Graduation Supplies, Party Favors/Decorations, Catering Supplies, Party Themes, Scrapbooking, Seasonal Party Supplies, Signs/Banners/Flags, Stemware, and Wedding Supplies. If you've thrown a party lately, you know how much little things add up, such as the tablecloths and din-nerware. Gorgeous piñatas shaped in many whimsical designs, from mermaids and unicorns to ballet slippers, fish, and basketballs, are only $9 at this writing, and Party & Paper Worldwide also sells the piñata filler (party favors and candy). You'll find incredible deals, too, on greeting cards, gift wrap, tablecloths, and many other items. The selection is too vast to outline here, so pay this online vendor a visit next time you log on to the internet.

SPECIAL FACTORS: Free shipping within the continental U.S. on orders over $40; complete satisfaction guaranteed or your money fully refunded.

Stumps-ShindigZ

One Party Place	**FORM OF INFORMATION:** free print catalogs; online catalogs (see text)
P.O. Box 305	
South Whitley, IN 46787-0305	**PAY:** check, MO, MC, V, AE, DSC
	SELLS: party decorations, supplies, and favors; large theme decorations
800–348–5084	
260–723–5171	**STORE:** no walk-in location; mail-order only
FAX: 260–723–6976	**ONLINE:** www.stumpsparty.com

Stumps-ShindigZ, founded in 1926, introduced the first full-color catalog featuring themed prom kits, such as "Starry, Starry Night" and "A Night in Venice" in 1960. This company may very well be responsible for thousands of first kisses! This mail-order party-supply company sells Mylar balloons, buttons, car decorations, candles, centerpieces, columns, crowns, curtains, favors, flowers, fund-raising candy, garters, lights, float and parade materials, photo albums, sashes and scepters, stickers, streamers, tiaras, and more to make large-scale events—for schools, theaters, weddings, reunions, and holidays—memorable and festive. And, yes, Stumps' prices are wholesale—up to 40% below retail. Besides, ShindigZ, their four seasonal, special-occasion catalog, Stumps also has four other catalogs catering to slightly different needs: "Prom," "Everything Elementary" (for teachers, principals, and PTAs—from fun squeeze bottles and stickers to lapel pins, pencils, and ribbons), "Spirit and Homecoming, and "Celebration and Fantastic." Each of these branches has a corresponding online catalog that you can access from Stumps-ShindigZ's main website. They have a long history of excellent customer service and can help you plan your next event as well as sell you everything you need and things you couldn't even imagine needing.

WEBSITE: Once you're at www.stumpsparty.com, you can click on a link that takes you to one of Stump's sister websites to view and buy all different types of products online, depending on the nature of your event. The choices here are almost mind-bending. At all of these online stores, you'll find great prices on a wide selection of goods, and free event-planning guides with checklists, budget charts, and tips. Send an email from the website for a free consultation with the on-staff party planner, who can offer everything from wedding tips to decorating advice.

SPECIAL FACTORS: Satisfaction guaranteed; quantity discounts and institutional accounts available; authorized returns, except worn clothing and imprinted or customized items, accepted within 15 days for exchange, refund, or credit (15% restocking fee possible); minimum order: $15.

U.S. Toy Co., Inc.

13201 Arrington Rd.
Grandview, MO 64030–2886
800–832–0224
816–761–5900
FAX: 816–761–9295

FORM OF INFORMATION: $3 print catalog; online catalog

PAY: check, MO, MC, V, DSC

SELLS: novelties, party favors, and fund-raising items

STORE: 7 locations in CA, CO, FL, IL, MO, PA, and TX; see catalog for addresses and hours

ONLINE: www.ustoyco.com

If you're a parent, teacher, day-care or camp director looking for inexpensive, imaginative party materials, the prices in this catalog will make you smile. Some of the party toys and decorations are priced as low as a penny apiece! U.S. Toy Co. offers a vast array of carnival/party and seasonal decorations, masks, novelty toys, costumes, festive tableware, stuffed animals, grab-bag prizes, balloons, and many more items developed for their exclusive sale. If you've thrown a birthday party for youngsters lately, you know that the guests' "party bags" end up costing you more than the cake, the decorations, and everything else. You'll absolutely flip for the items carried by this company, little goodies such as troll-doll rings, tiny bubble bottles and wands, and crazy spectacles—all priced by the dozen. (These make great stocking stuffers, too.) Prices at U.S.

Toy are up to 70% lower than retail, and the variety is outstanding, with literally thousands of items to choose from. There are decorating supplies for just about every holiday and occasion. Some of these products are sold by the case or in large quantities, but most items are available singly or in fewer quantities.

WEBSITE: The website lets you browse the inventory, read product descriptions and view images of the merchandise, and order online.

SPECIAL FACTORS: Institutional accounts are available; orders under $25 incur a $5 charge.

Travel

Money-saving travel and vacation companies geared toward luxury, adventure, personal or community enrichment, volunteerism, education, or extreme frugality; smart moving options

This section includes firms that in one way or another could save you money on your next move, airline ticket, cruise, or cross-country or European trip. Travel is a big industry, so there's a lot of information out there, as well as a mind-boggling number of choices. If you have the creativity—and in some cases, flexibility—to nail down your itinerary in a slightly unconventional way, there are lots of ways to save money and benefit personally in other ways.

One newsletter I'd recommend if you travel a lot—or wish you could—is *Consumer Reports Travel Letter* (CRTL), produced by Consumers Union. This is a well-regarded publication for both business and recreational travelers. CRTL conducts in-depth comparisons of accommodations and prices in the U.S. and abroad, and does regular features on airline food, travel scams, travel agents, airline booking systems, and more. Each monthly issue of CRTL runs around 24 pages; a year's subscription costs $39 at this writing, or $59 for two years. Call 800–234–1970, or write to Circulation Department, *Consumer Reports Travel Letter,* P.O. Box 53600, Boulder, CO 80322 for information.

In addition to the company listings in this chapter, here are some basics to get you started with saving money.

CONSOLIDATORS/BUCKET SHOPS

Consolidators, also known as bucket shops, are companies that buy cruise slots, blocks of rooms, and plane seats from airlines, hotels, and charter agents at wholesale prices, and then resell them for less than the hotels, airlines, or often the charter operators themselves could. Although travel agents are the main customers of consolidators, individuals may buy from some of them, too, saving as much as 20% to 30% on APEX fares and much more on full economy tickets.

One good way to find the best airfares is to do a search for travel consolidators using your favorite search engine on the web. Or if you go to www.About.com, you can ask their travel expert to help you find the best ones. Once you have a handful of airline consolidators, contact each of them for a price quote. You'll be glad you took the trouble. Below are some who have good reputations.

Unitravel Flights For Less, one of the oldest consolidators in the business, books mainly international flights, sells directly to individuals, and can save you up to 35% off typical prices. Contact Unitravel at least a month before you want to leave and allow for some flexibility, as tickets might not be available until shortly before the day of departure. The toll-free number is 800–325–2222 for more information.

Economytravel.com claims to have the lowest international airfares on the web. You can save from 10% to 40% by booking your international flight through this firm. Check out the website (www.economytravel.com) where policies are clearly explained. You can get great deals on international airfare, cars, and hotels here.

STA Travel, "the world's largest travel company for students and young people," is another bucket shop that deals with individuals. STA has offices in major California cities, as well as in the District of Columbia, Chicago, Boston and Cambridge, New York City, Philadelphia, and Seattle; call 800–777–0112 for the location nearest you, or log on to the website: www.statravel.com.

HOTEL BROKERS

If you have a credit card, belong to an automobile club, use a discount telephone long-distance service, or are otherwise listed somewhere on the American information grid, you've no doubt been solicited to join a dining and travel club. Depending on how frequently you travel, the annual membership, if there is one, might be worth it for the discounts.

Another way to save on your hotel stays, however, is to book through a hotel broker, who may work like a consolidator or an independent agent, providing reservations and confirmations, often at a discount. Many of these services require prepayment to the service for the room and stay. The services listed below act as agents and allow you to pay the hotel in the customary way.

Quikbook, a long-respected booking service, has been selling discounted rates on upscale hotel rooms since 1988. Choose from over 100 cities including Albuquerque, San Francisco and Vancouver. Rates at its network of more than 1,000 properties run from 20% to 60% off regular prices. Quikbook can be reached at 800–789–9887 or

212–779–7666; at their website (www.quikbook.com); or through the mail, Quik-book, 381 Park Ave. South, New York, NY 10016.

Central Reservation Service, founded in 1987, is a free hotel discount reservation service that offers one of the best selections of New York city hotels. If you book through them, you'll save from 10% to 40%. The very friendly staff speaks both Spanish and English. Call 800–555–7555 or 407–740–6442; the address is Central Reservation Service, 220 Lookout Pl., Ste. 200, Maitland, FL 32751. The website is www.room-connection.com.

HOME EXCHANGES

One of the cheapest ways to save on hotel bills, especially if you're traveling with children, is to stay in someone else's home. *International Home Exchange Service/Intervac* is an organization that compiles three directories a year listing thousands of homes worldwide (most are outside the U.S.). The apartments and houses in this directory are available for exchange and rent, so you don't necessarily have to exchange your own home to take advantage of a good deal. For more information, write to Lori Horne and Paula Jaffe, 30 Corte San Ferrando, Tiburon, CA 94920, or call 800–756–4663. The web address is www.intervac.com.

In a city such as New York, where every single hotel room may be booked for the weekend, it's nice to know that there are thousands of vacant apartments available for less than a hotel would cost—with a number of advantages, namely more space, use of a full kitchen, and no doubt better ambience. These are listed under "Bed and Breakfasts" in the yellow pages of the local phone directory or weekly entertainment newspaper classifieds. Just about every major city has companies that make their business out of connecting owners with overnight guests.

LAST-MINUTE BOOKINGS

There's so much cool (and free) information on the web. I've got to pass along a site I discovered called Webflyer (www.webflyer.com) that compiles all the cyber deals the airlines, hotels, and car rental companies are offering for last-minute travel and then posts them once a week. You get to access this information for *free*. You'll find these in Webflyer's section called Deal Watch. Deal Watch allows you to select the city you want to fly from, stay in, or rent a car in. For example, I selected New York as the departure city. For that following week, one of the airfare options included a round trip to Phoenix, AZ on America West for $208. Departure and return times and dates vary and are restricted for each trip. Some flights are for specific departure and return dates—others can be within a 6-month period. When you find a good deal, you're responsible for calling the airline to make the reservation—and you'd better do it quickly! New deals are added on Mondays and continually added throughout the week with the majority of the deals up by 3:00 pm on Wednesdays, mountain time. A FAQ page answers most questions. This is a *great* way to book spontaneous and extremely affordable trips to see your long-distance friends and loved ones.

CHEAP INTRA-EUROPE TRAVEL

If you're traveling around Europe, the following two options work in basically the same way: You pay one flat fee for a span of time (30 or 60 days, for instance), which entitles you to nearly unlimited travel within that time span. Deals vary depending on your age and itinerary. If you want to hop around Europe by bus, *Eurolines* claims to be the cheapest mode of travel in and around the European countries. Their website address is www.eurolines.com. Then of course there's the most famous mode of all: via romantic European trains where you're apt to fall in love with a mysterious Italian over a glass of wine. Go to the Eurailpass website for more information (www.railconnection.com) or call them toll-free at 888–RAIL–888.

Find It Fast

AUTOMOBILE TRANSPORTING SERVICES
A2B Automobile Moving

DISCOUNT CRUISE PACKAGES
Vacations to Go

DISCOUNT OUTDOOR VACATIONS BY BUS
Green Tortoise

GENERAL TRAVEL AGENT SERVICES
Expedia.com

LEARNING OR COMMUNITY-SERVICE TRAVEL PACKAGES
Elderhostel, Volunteers for Peace

MOVING SERVICE
Help-U-Move

UP-TO-DATE, COMPREHENSIVE COURIER TRAVEL INFORMATION
International Association of Air Travel Couriers

A2B Automobile Moving

2661 W. Whittier Blvd., Ste. G
La Habra, CA 90631
562–690–3949
FAX: 562–691–7650

FORM OF INFORMATION: price quotes

PAY: bank check, MO, MC, V, AE

SELLS: automobile, pickup truck, and van transport services

STORE: no walk-in location; online and telephone only; phone hours Monday to Friday, 8:00 am–5:00 pm PST

ONLINE: www.shipacar.com

Moving? Save time, money, and mileage—and reduce your overall stress—by having A2B Automobile Moving transport your car, van, or truck to your new home. A2B can save you 20% to 40% over moving van rates. They have daily pickups in more than 100 major cities nationwide and can promptly deliver your vehicle to your new location anywhere in the continental U.S. This company, founded in 1995, has specially designed trucks and licensed, insured carriers. Major corporations recommend A2B for relocating employees, as do individuals, whose positive letters pepper the website. Although you can get a free price quote online, the real purpose of the website is to present some very basic information about the company and what it offers. Your best bet is to call A2B or email them with questions you're bound to have.

SPECIAL FACTORS: Vehicle transportation within the continental U.S.; for Canadian destinations, inquire; member of the Better Business Bureau.

Elderhostel

11 Avenue de Lafayette
Boston, MA 02111–1746
877–426–8056
TDD: 877–426–2167

FORM OF INFORMATION: free catalog (see text); website

PAY: MC, V, AE

SELLS: inexpensive learning adventure packages for seniors

OFFICE: same address; Monday to Friday 9:00 am–9:00 pm

ONLINE: www.elderhostel.org

"I can't imagine an Elderhostel-free retirement"—so says one of the many happy clients whose life has been enriched by this wonderful organization. If you're 55 years or older and you want to see the world without spending your children's inheritance, Elderhostel is the way to travel. Imagine studying the literature of Jane Austen in the White Mountains of New Hampshire; traveling to Greece to explore the spectacular art and architecture; or conducting field research in Belize to save the endangered dolphin population. Elderhostel was started in 1975 with 220 participants and a few programs; now it offers 10,000 programs in 90 countries every year, plus 300 service programs that bring volunteer energy to worthy causes around the world. The cost for programs is low, ranging from $500 for a week-long program in the U.S. that includes meals, rooms, instruction, and field trips, to $3,000 for 2½ weeks in Europe that includes airfare. And since Elderhostel is a 501(c)(3) organization, expenses incurred to participants are generally tax-deductible! When you call Elderhostel or visit the website, you'll be asked to choose which of the programs you are interested in: "U.S. & Canada," "International," or "Adventures Afloat."

WEBSITE: The excellent website has a great FAQ section for first-time visitors that answers everything from whether you have to have a roommate ("no": 65% of Elderhostel travelers request and get single rooms) and whether those with special physical needs can be accommodated ("yes": most of the time). You can submit an electronic order form right on the website to have free literature mailed to you.

SPECIAL FACTORS: A deposit is required to process your registration for a program.

Expedia.com

FORM OF INFORMATION: online catalog only; no print catalog

PAY: MC, V, AE, DSC

SELLS: travel agent services

OFFICE: no walk-in location; online only

ONLINE: www.expedia.com

I have a relative who always brags at family events that each of his family members flew round-trip across the country for $99. Never mind that he earns six figures each year. What really irks me is that I want to know his secret. Does he spend his weekends scouring airline deals in the newspaper and online? It used to be a mystery, but maybe I've now solved it. Expedia.com, one of the many monopoly pieces in Bill Gates's Microsoft game, is just about the greatest online travel agent I've found. And it just keeps getting better and better each year. This one-stop travel agent can help you find the very best deals on hotels, rental cars, air travel, cruises, and vacations, and then you can plan and book your trip right at the website. I hate to say it, but Bill Gates has made travel agents obsolete. If you have a live travel agent who will spend hours on your little trip to the Midwest, the one you want to pay less than $100 round-trip for, then you're very lucky. The sad truth is, travel agent fees are so low these days due to internet competition that few of them can afford to give you this kind of time.

Once you log on to Expedia.com and register (for free), you'll be privy to a world of great travel services. For example, Expedia.com stores a list of your itineraries on My Trips page, so you don't have to enter the same information over and over every time you want to visit your folks on the prairie. With Fare Tracker, choose up to 3 air routes you would like them to track, and then Expedia.com will post the latest fare on a regular basis. Ah hah! Now I can compete with that relative of mine! Expedia.com's search engine, which posts airfares, hotels, car rentals, cruises, or vacation packages, is really fast. The best I've used. Other great features at the website: Bargain Fares (Expedia.com negotiates directly with 20 name-brand airlines to offer savings from 10% to 60%); Traveler Tools (including flight status; currency converter; driving directions; restaurants; weather; and more); Mileage Tracker (where you can keep track of those unwieldy frequent flyer miles from umpteen airlines); travel-related news articles; price comparison; a free newsletter with travel deals of the week; and lots more. Expedia.com has won numerous awards over the years for great service, the lowest prices in most cases, and a consumer-oriented attitude. Once you start booking your own trips and saving money as you do, you'll never go back to using a travel agent again.

SPECIAL FACTORS: Customer-service telephone numbers are published on the website.

Green Tortoise

494 Broadway
San Francisco, CA 94133
800–867–8647
415–956–7500
FAX: 415–956–4900

FORM OF INFORMATION: free print catalog; online catalog

PAY: traveler's check, MO, U.S. bank draft

SELLS: adventure bus tours in North and Central America

OFFICE: same address; daily 8:00 am– 8:00 pm

ONLINE: www.greentortoise.com

Ready for an adventure? Green Tortoise is a San Francisco–based company that organizes "adventure" tours to some of the most remote and beautiful places in North and Central America. This isn't the type of bus tour where elderly blue-haired people sit in air-conditioned, perfumy seats and look out the window at the scenery passing by. Green Tortoise travelers ride in one of the "legendary sleeper coaches." They don't sit up all night with their heads against the window; the seats convert to mattresses (with fitted sheets) on raised platforms and bunk beds. In the morning, you've usually arrived somewhere incredible. By day you "swim, cook breakfast, explore caves, climb mountains, raft down-stream, stand under waterfalls, walk through forests, cook dinner, build campfires, visit towns, meet people, or just plain take it easy." Green Tortoise trips aren't for everyone. In fact, the website, which has the same information as the print catalog, has a section on the type of people who *shouldn't* travel on Green Tortoise. These might include people who don't enjoy the outdoors, those who can't tolerate diversity and togetherness with strangers, rabid teetotalers, people with young children, and those unwilling to do some work. (Meals and meal preparation and cleanup are cooperative.) Because of the style of travel, Green Tortoise trips are amazingly inexpensive. Destinations include Alaska, Baja,

Costa Rica, Grand Canyon, Death Valley, Yosemite, the Mayan ruins in Mexico, and many others. There's lots more to learn here, so I suggest you check out the website.

WEBSITE: The website is extremely friendly and informative. There's really no need to order a print catalog if you have internet access. You'll still need to call to make your reservation, though, as all trips have to be confirmed by phone to verify space and availability.

SPECIAL FACTORS: No personal checks accepted; travel with children must be pre-approved through main office.

Help-U-Move, Inc.

85 Commercial Way
East Providence, RI 02914
401–434–4630
FAX: 401–434–5178

FORM OF INFORMATION: online catalog only, no print catalog

PAY: MO, MC, V, AE, DSC, Electronic check

SELLS: you-pack-they-drive moving services

OFFICE: same address, Monday to Friday 9:00 am–6:00 pm

ONLINE: www.helpumove.com

Let's say you're a debt-burdened graduating college student who needs to move his dorm or apartment furniture to a city two states away to begin a new job. Or let's say your elderly mother is moving out of the family home into an assisted-living situation, and she wants you to have the family heirlooms in your home halfway across the country. As common as these situations are, the options until now haven't been satisfactory. One option: Hire a mover, which is prohibitively expensive; another option is to pack up the things yourself and drive the stuff in one of those run-down, dangerous rental trucks. Help-U-Move, which is one of the oldest "you load, we drive" moving companies in the U.S., offers a third alternative that's low cost and hassle-free. Help-U-Move delivers a 28'-long semi-trailer (called a *pup*) to your dorm, apartment, or house and allows you adequate time to load your belongings. They return when you're finished loading and deliver the pup to the new location for you to unload. Once you're finished unloading, you call them and they remove the pup. It's easy. Best of all, you save money by packing the stuff yourself, and you're only charged for the actual footage you use. Even if you hire someone to help you load and unload, you'll still end up paying less here. The pup can hold a large house full of furniture ($28' \times 8' \times 8\frac{1}{2}'$), but you can rent as little as $3'$ of the pup.

Help-U-Move's informative website has answers to most of your questions, a section of testimonials from satisfied customers, and allows you to track your shipment online. At the website, you can obtain a free price quote by email; you can also get a quote over the phone. Help-U-Move wants your business; if you get a cheaper quote from another company, give them a chance to beat it.

SPECIAL FACTORS: Help-U-Move does not perform same-state moves, local moves, or moves under 250 miles; free price quote by email or phone; member Better Business Bureau.

International Association of Air Travel Couriers

P.O. Box 847
Scottsbluff, NE 69363-0847
VOICEMAIL: 308-632-3273
FAX: 308-632-8267

FORM OF INFORMATION: free information packet; website

MEMBERSHIP: $45 for one year; $50 outside U.S. (see text)

PAY: check, MO, MC, V, AE

SELLS: up-to-the-minute courier travel information, discounted air travel

OFFICE: same address; Monday to Friday, 9:00 am–5:00 pm; another location in the UK

ONLINE: www.courier.org

International Association of Air Travel Couriers (IAATC) is the premier clearinghouse for consumers who wish to travel as couriers to foreign destinations. Being a courier is a superdiscount way to travel, but it's not easy to find out about whom to book with and how to do it. After speaking with a company representative, I learned some of the many pitfalls of the courier industry, and it became clear to me why one would want and need to join the IAATC. For one thing, courier companies (of which there are hundreds) come and go, sometimes weekly. You could book with a company and find yourself out of luck come travel day. For another thing, new flights and opportunities spring up hourly, and some of these last-minute deals are unbelievably cheap. You won't be able to get this hard-to-find information from anyone as accurately as from the IAATC, which specializes in customer service. The IAATC "does not sell tickets or profit in any way from your courier flight. Its mission is to provide up-to-date information on all courier travel opportunities available to couriers, while working to support air courier travel as a way to see the world on a shoestring."

Courier flights work like this, in short: Companies need to send packages overseas. If they send them cargo, the packages might spend 2 to 3 days in customs before even getting on the plane. If companies want to send packages on regular flights (getting overseas in a few hours), airline regulations require that they be accompanied by a live body. That's where you enter in. You take the packages as your check-in luggage and hand over the package to the waiting representative when you arrive at the destination airport. You might have to give up some of your carry-on luggage allotment, which is the downside. The upside is that your fare will be up to 85% less than you'd pay otherwise! The U.S. cities from which air-courier flights originate as of this writing were New York, Los Angeles, San Francisco, Miami, Chicago, Newark, and Washington, D.C.

A one-year membership to IAATC is $45 ($50 outside U.S.), which entitles you to telephone support, and a fax-on-demand system, IAATC's online access system for couriers, and a bimonthly subscription to both the *Travel Guide International* (formerly *The Shoestring Traveler*) and the *Air Courier Bulletin*.

SPECIAL FACTORS: Information is for foreign destinations only; no domestic travel service; customers must pay in U.S. funds or British pounds.

Vacations to Go

1502 Augusta Dr., Ste. 415
Houston, TX 77057
800–338–4962
713–974–2121
FAX: 713–978–6003

FORM OF INFORMATION: online catalog only; no print catalog

PAY: major credit cards (see text)

SELLS: cruises

STORE: same address; Monday to Friday 7:00 am–10:00 pm, Saturday and Sunday 9:00 am–6:00 pm CST

ONLINE: www.vacationstogo.com

There's a lot of fierce competition out there between travel agents looking to book your dream vacation. Vacations to Go calls themselves "America's premier discount cruise specialist," and I was impressed with their no-nonsense approach. They claim to offer the lowest prices available (up to 75% off) on cruises 99% of the time, which they accomplish by being one of the largest sellers. This means that they have access to discounts and special fare programs that aren't available to the rest of the nation's travel agents. If the prices go down after you've booked your trip, they'll refund the difference.

Besides their regular low fares you can take advantage of last-minute specials. Luckily, "last minute" to a cruise line means 3 months from departure, so that's plenty of time to plan.

The website has articles on a variety of topics for the cruise traveler, including information for singles traveling alone (some cruise ships offer social host programs), families traveling with kids (Does the cruise ship I'm interested in offer child care, a teen activity center, or planned youth activities?), details on different cruise ports (What can I expect to find in Anchorage, Alaska?), and the pros and cons of booking your airfare on your own or using the cruise line's air/sea program (the latter refunds your money in case of flight cancellation or delay). If you can get up and go in the next couple of weeks, you'll find amazing deals in the Last-Minute Markdowns section.

Vacations to Go has been in business since 1984, and their "cruise counselors" are easy and pleasant to talk to. When you're ready to ask questions or to make a reservation, you need to call, as there's no online ordering at the site.

SPECIAL FACTORS: The type of credit card accepted is determined by the cruise line on which you'll be traveling; quantity discounts available; smoke-free cruises available.

Volunteers for Peace

1034 Tiffany Rd.
Belmont, VT 05730
802–259–2759
FAX: 802–259–2922

FORM OF INFORMATION: free newsletter; website

PAY: MC, V, AE

OFFERS: placement service in short-term international workcamps

ONLINE: www.vfp.org

You're an idealistic person with a strong commitment to social change. You yearn to travel to faraway places but don't have a lot of money. You love people, and you're not afraid of hard work. Does this describe you? If so, you should get hooked up with Volunteers for Peace (VFP), a Vermont nonprofit 501(c)(3) membership organization that's been coordinating international workcamps since 1982. VFP is a member of the Coordinating Committee for International Voluntary Service (CCIVS) at UNESCO and works in cooperation with Service Civil International (SCI), the Alliance of European Voluntary Service Organizations, and the International Youth Action for Peace (YAP). Their services include providing consultation and a placement service for workcamp hosts and volunteers, linking people with programs that foster international education, voluntary service, and friendship worldwide.

The type of work you might be doing in a VFP workcamp is construction and restoration of low-income housing or community buildings; environmental projects such as trail building, park maintenance, and organic farming; social services, such as working with children, the elderly, physically or mentally handicapped, refugees, minority groups, drug/alcohol recovery, AIDS education, and arts projects; and historic preservation and archaeology. Work projects can be of any type, because they arise from the needs of the local host community. Generally, 10 to 20 people from 4 or more countries arrive on a given day in a host community, and are housed in a school, church, private home, or community center. Living arrangements are cooperative, like a family, with volunteers coordinating and sharing the day-to-day activities, such as food preparation, work projects, and recreation. The registration fee (beginning at $200, as of this writing) covers room and board and insurance; you pay airfare. Anyone 18 and up can volunteer. Most workcamps occur June through September and are 2 to 3 weeks in duration. The free newsletter gives a good overview of VFP and includes photos from some of the more recent workcamps.

WEBSITE: The website, which has a wealth of information about VFP, allows you to order the free newsletter and a variety of other books and material online. If you decide to join VFP ($20/year at this writing), you'll receive the *International Work-camp Directory*, which lists and describes the more than 2,000 programs in over 70 countries from which you can choose. If you can find a cheap way to get to the host country, Volunteers for Peace will then provide you with an unbeatable opportunity to serve, to learn, and to discover at a bargain price.

SPECIAL FACTORS: No foreign language proficiency is required.

Wacky, Weird, and Wonderful

Caskets; ostrich products; refrigerator magnets and other magnetic products; spy equipment; decor and collectibles in bad taste; uncommon goods

I spend a lot of time and energy trying to find great companies that will sell directly to consumers without a middleman. The time may not be far off when we'll be able to purchase absolutely everything necessary for human survival by phone, mail, or click of a mouse and have it delivered to our front door. What I'm interested in, of course, is not only the convenience, but also the *economy* of shopping this way.

Every once in a while I find a company so wonderful in its originality that it deserves a special place in this book. Every company here has a great website or catalog that makes you think outside of the box in one way or another. Moreover, some of these vendors will save you up to 60% off the normal retail price.

Find It Fast

OSTRICH MEAT, LEATHER, AND FEATHERS
Ostriches On Line

POP CULTURE DECOR
Archie McPhee

REFRIGERATOR MAGNETS AND OTHER MAGNETIC PRODUCTS
Fridgedoor.com

SURVEILLANCE AND COUNTERSURVEILLANCE EQUIPMENT
Spy Outlet

UNUSUAL HOME DECOR AND GIFTS
Uncommon Goods

WOOD AND METAL CASKETS
Direct Caskets

Archie McPhee & Co.

P.O. Box 30852
Seattle, WA 98103
425–349–3009
FAX: 425–349–5188

FORM OF INFORMATION: free print catalog, $2 for Canada, $5 for International; online catalog

PAY: check, MO, MC, V, DSC

SELLS: pop culture "stuff"

STORE: 2428 Market St., Seattle, WA; Monday to Saturday 9:00 am–7:00 pm, Sunday 10:00 am–6:00 pm

ONLINE: www.mcphee.com

If you've never laughed at an ethnic joke, believe that the decor at Graceland is in bad taste, or think Captain Kirk is a type of cereal, then you need this catalog. Archie McPhee is a real store in Seattle, as well as a mail-order vendor, that sells inexpensive, must-have, useful, or just highly entertaining items skewering or celebrating the very best and worst of our popular culture. I adored the 48-page color print catalog, but as is more often the case than not these days, I recommend that you skip the print version and go straight to the online catalog; it's more comprehensive and up-to-date.

WEBSITE: Now here's a website you'll want to spend some time in. The menu bar at Archie McPhee's online catalog offers such categories as Amusements, Lifestyle, Lounge, Fashion, Tiki Island, and Enlightenment. Here's just a tiny sampling of goods you'll want to buy at Archie McPhee: a metal lunchbox decorated with art from Bolshevik propaganda posters; a "sneaky" spoon that extends to 21 inches for ice cream snatching; your favorite Hindi god finger puppets—Brahma, Ganesh, Garuda, and Kali; a wiggly hula girl in her grass skirt for your car dashboard; nun, rabbi, and red-devil punching puppets; a handbag made of cloth that looks like an armadillo; and last, but not least, angel snot. Believe me, I've barely scratched the surface!

While you're logged on to Archie McPhee, you might as well take the nerd quiz, which automatically calculates your score to see how you stack up next to some of the highest-scoring nerds of all time. I scored only 23 out of a possible 100, not even close to Gandhi or *Mayberry RFD*'s Goober. It's never too late to change, though. You'll have a lot of fun shopping here, which you can do electronically. Don't forget to "join the cult" and receive Archie McPhee's free e-newsletter with notices of member-only specials, freebies, and contests. From now on this will be one of your favorite sources for gifts.

SPECIAL FACTORS: 90-day satisfaction guarantee.

Direct Caskets, Inc.

1215 Second Ave.
New Hyde Park, NY 11040
800–732–2753 (east coast)
800–772–2753 (west coast)

FORM OF INFORMATION: online catalog only; no print catalog

PAY: MC, V, AE, DSC

SELLS: wood and metal caskets

STORE: same address; Monday to Friday 8:30 am–5:00 pm, Saturday 11:00 am–4:00 pm; also locations in Huntington Station, New Hyde Park and Brooklyn, NY, and 3 locations in CA; call for hours and addresses

ONLINE: www.directcasket.com

From researching and writing this book every year, I have a never-ending sense of amazement about the kinds of things one can buy online and have delivered. I've also gained respect and appreciation for the win-win attitude of some vendors who understand that selling goods to consumers at wholesale prices will end up benefiting the seller. Sure, his per-item profit will be lower, but his volume will soar as savvy consumers seek out honest vendors who don't try to rip them off. Direct Casket, Inc., will have your frugal granny grinning from her grave, because this company saves consumers hundreds and in some cases *thousands* of dollars on the single-most expensive component of funeral services: the casket.

What Direct Casket has accomplished is fairly controversial and may revolutionize the industry as more and more of us become aware of our rights. A report by Consumer Affairs Commissioner Jules Polonetsky, which you can read at the website, warns of deceptive trade practices and the growing monopolization of the funeral industry by giant conglomerates. The last thing you'd want to believe when you're in a state of grief is that the funeral director is ripping you off. But look at the prices at

Direct Casket's website—funeral home price versus theirs—and you'll be stunned. The markup is downright abusive.

Direct Casket offers consumers a reasonable alternative: a complete line of lovely wood and metal caskets that can serve most major religious affiliations in the continental U.S.—priced at 50% to 75% less than the mortuary or funeral home charges! All caskets are guaranteed to arrive next-day or second day, at your request. I was riveted by the company's website, which got me thinking about all kinds of issues I hadn't thought of before. You'll find information about what you should know about caskets; how to handle a funeral director's reaction to your not purchasing the casket from them; the law and your rights; plus, frequently asked questions and news articles related to this great company. Besides the incredible savings you'll reap, the most important aspect of Direct Casket, from a consumer's point of view, is their customer support. They'll advise you on how to deal with your funeral director, steer you away from those whom they know to be corrupt, and generally stand behind you 100%. This company empowers consumers to soar through a difficult and painful experience with dignity.

SPECIAL FACTORS: Products guaranteed to be delivered on time and in excellent condition; any product may be returned for a full refund if customer is not fully satisfied; goods delivered within continental U.S. only.

Fridgedoor.com

21 Dixwell Ave.	**FORM OF INFORMATION:** online catalog only; no print catalog
Quincy, MA 02169	
617–770–7913	**PAY:** check, MO, MC, V, AE, DSC
FAX: 617–689–0601	**SELLS:** novelty, refrigerator magnets, custom fridge magnets, and magnetic supplies
	STORE: no walk-in location; mail-order only
	ONLINE: www.fridgedoor.com

Fridgedoor.com was founded in 1997 by Chris Gwynn as a part-time endeavor. By 1998, Fridgedoor.com was so successful it became a full-time operation with a group of friends and family to help fill orders, keep UPS and the local post office happy, and answer customer inquiries. The goal of this company is to be the single largest stop for all things magnetic: novelty magnets, custom magnets, and magnetic supplies.

You'll find this website quite entertaining. The categories here are Novelty, Custom Magnets, and Supplies. Within those categories you can browse by brand or subject. Subject matters for Novelty Magnets include: Animal; Celebrity and Sports; Classic TV Shows; Comic and Superhero; Dress-up; Food, Drinks, Flowers, and Gifts; Humor, Talk and Miscellaneous; Movie and Music; and State and City. Within each of those subjects, you'll find subcategories such as: Cows on Parade, Betty Boop, Gumby and Pokey, Dick and Jane, and Freaks and Pulp Fiction. Some of my favorites in the Humorous Magnets I and II subcategories are: a picture of a 1950s housewife holding a chocolate cake with "Stressed is desserts spelled backwards," a picture of an old women in a bathing suit with "Growing Old is not for Sissies," and, a picture of three old women smiling and wearing witches outfits with "They tell me that you'll loose your mind when you get older. What they don't say is that you won't miss it very much." The magnets here average around $3.50 each.

Fridgedoor.com also offers a complete line of custom promotional magnets for your business which include: business card magnets, retail style magnets, real estate magnets, information magnets, and die-cut magnets.

A really cool thing they carry is magnetic inkjet paper sheets that are designed for inkjet printers so you can turn your computer artwork into creative magnets. Use them just like paper. You can custom-make your own magnets with pictures you create or pictures of you, your children, the dogs, the cats—everybody! What a great gift idea.

In addition to magnets, Fridgedoor.com also carries card sets, mugs, journals, calendars, journals, notepads and photo albums featuring quotations from some of the world's most adept writers, thinkers, and poets.

SPECIAL FACTORS: Returns within 30 days in resalable condition, with original packaging intact, for a full merchandise refund, exchange or credit; package the merchandise in the same or similar box as it shipped, include the invoice number; custom orders are custom and are not returnable.

Ostriches On Line

2218 N. 75th Ave.
Elmwood Park, IL 60707
888-RING-OOL
708-452-7596
FAX: 708-452-7510

FORM OF INFORMATION: free print catalog, online catalog

PAY: check, MO, MC, V, AE, DSC, Wire T/T transfer, C.O.D.

SELLS: ostrich meat, feather products, ostrich leather hides and products, ostrich oil, ostrich farming supplies and references

STORE: same location; visits by appointment

ONLINE: www.ostrichesonline.com

For those of you who haven't tried it, ostrich steak tastes like filet mignon. But the advantage over beef is that it's 99% fat free and has fewer calories, less cholesterol, and less fat than skinless chicken or turkey! And if you're someone who buys only organic meats and vegetables, you'll be happy to know that these ostriches are free-range animals void of steroids or antibiotics.

Hooray for Ostriches On Line, a company that will deliver fresh or frozen ostrich meat to your doorstep for considerably less than you'd pay for mail-order beef. Prices go down when you order in quantity. The food products include ostrich meat (filets, steaks, roast/stir fry/stew/kabob meat, ground meat, burgers/patties, jerky, sausage, whole leg) and ravioli. About half of the 64-page print catalog, which is a spiral-bound, printed version of the website, is devoted to a dizzying range of other interesting products—feather boas and plumes (ostrich, turkey, peacock, pheasant, guinea hen, and swan) in every style and color imaginable; ostrich leather products; ostrich-related toys and collectibles; feather and lambs-wool dusters; gift items, such as hand-painted ostrich egg shells; recipe books; and ostrich-oil cosmetics. If you're an ostrich farmer or want to become one, here's where you'll find reference material, such as videos, software, and books about ostrich farming, ostrich feed, and incubation systems. The price of the print catalog is refundable with your first order.

WEBSITE: I recommend the online catalog, which lets you navigate around with ease to view and read about all the products. The online version is more extensive than the print catalog and has a great deal more information. For example, you'll find a helpful "Ostrich Farming Database and Reference Library" at the site with articles and resources of interest to the new or prospective farmer, such as handling chicks, ostrich diet, and handling ostrich hides. You can also subscribe to the online newsletter for free. By the time you've thoroughly checked out this information-intensive website, you'll feel like an ostrich expert. Secure orders can be placed online.

SPECIAL FACTORS: Shipping is by least-expensive way and is not included in prices listed; quantity discounts apply; wholesale accounts welcome; authorized returns accepted within 10 days of receipt; custom-dyed or hand-painted products and meats are nonreturnable (see catalog for details of returns policy); 25% restocking fee may apply; minimum U.S. order is $15.

Spy Outlet

2468 Niagara Falls Blvd.
Tonawanda, NY 14150
716–695–8660
FAX: 716–695–7380

FORM OF INFORMATION: $5 print catalog; online catalog

PAY: check, MO, MC, V, AE, DSC

SELLS: surveillance and countersurveillance equipment

STORE: 2468 Niagara Falls Blvd., Tonawanda, NY; Monday to Friday 9:30 am–5:00 pm, Saturday 10:00 am–3:00 pm

ONLINE: www.spyoutlet.com

Anyone who's read Dashiell Hammett knows the life of a hard-boiled detective has its unglamorous moments. Lurking behind curvaceous dames you should never trust is a single naked truth that, as one of his salty heroes laments, "one day you could wake up dead." But seriously, in our day and age, you don't have to be a private dick to want to know whether your phone is being tapped, your apartment is being bugged, or your elderly mother is being cared for properly when you're not there to supervise.

WEBSITE: The print catalog costs $5 and isn't as up-to-date as the website, so if you have internet access, go the electronic route. Log on to the aptly named Spy Outlet website and you'll start to get an idea of how far surveillance and anti-surveillance equipment have come since Hammett's day. For example, I was astounded to see a color pinhole camera not much larger than an American quarter. Wow! The categories of products featured here include Video Surveillance, Privacy Devices, Telephone Recorders, Lockpicking, Vehicle Tracking, Voice Changers, Tape Recorders, and Books and Videos. I know what you're wondering: Who shops here? A wide range of customers, including law enforcement, nursing homes, day-care centers, and hobby-ists. Because Spy Outlet is the leading importer of these specialty electronics, buying from the website or print catalog saves you money because there's no middleman.

I enjoyed clicking around the site to see the James Bond–like gadgets—vehicle tracking systems that transmit global-positioning-system location data to you on a regular basis, which you can access right over the internet; home drug-test kits; video cameras disguised as clocks and smoke detectors; sunglasses with rear-view vision; books and videos on everything from creating a new identity for yourself to how to become a private detective; and much more. I recommend this site to any mystery writer looking for some good ideas! You can order right on the website, and customer service people can talk to you and answer your questions if you call during business hours.

SPECIAL FACTORS: Due to the nature of this equipment (may be for one-time use only) items are not returnable; check local, state, and federal video- and audio-taping laws to make sure you are in legal compliance.

Uncommon Goods

303 W. 10th St., 2nd Fl.
New York, NY 10014
888–365–0056

FORM OF INFORMATION: free print catalog; online catalog

PAY: check, MO, MC, V, AE, DSC

SELLS: home and personal accessories, and gifts

STORE: no walk-in location; mail-order only; phone hours Monday to Friday 9:00 am–9:00 pm, Saturday and Sunday 12:00 noon–7:00 pm EST

ONLINE: www.uncommongoods.com

There are some people who are very hard to shop for when it comes to gifts. What do you get someone who already has everything? Something different, of course. Uncommon Goods, where you'll find anything but the ordinary, offers creatively designed, high quality merchandise at affordable prices. They sell original products for the home as well as an assortment of hip and unusual personal accessories and gift items. In addition to providing unique items of outstanding quality, they also endeavor to feature merchandise created in harmony with the environment and without harm to animals or people. Categories here include Accents, Bed and Bath, Dining, Paper, His and Hers, Gifts, Occasions, and Collections. What kind of uncommon things can you get here? Here's a few examples of what you'll find: Buddha Bulb, a light bulb that has an image of Buddha within the orb; record bowls made out of old LPs; Puzzle Ottoman, a soft fuzzy ottoman shaped like a puzzle piece; a pizza cutter featuring Gaston, a loveable dog who's catching the blade in his mouth; a clock with a frame made from a bicycle cog; a duct tape wallet; and, a Dying of Chocolate cookie jar made in the shape of a large woman who seems to have passed out after consuming most of the contents of a box of chocolates.

Note: Some products offered are a little bit pricier than others; but there's still a wide selection of very affordable items.

WEBSITE: Since the website is designed so nicely and is easy to use with online ordering and live help, I recommend you save a tree and do your shopping electronically.

SPECIAL FACTORS: Satisfaction guaranteed; returns accepted within 30 days of purchase date.

Favorite Web-shopping Sites

Useful websites with e-tailer links, bargain finders, vendor reviews and rankings, and information for smart consumers

What I'm calling a *web-shopping site* is any electronic address on the web that makes shopping easier or more convenient for you, or makes you a smarter consumer. As an expert in bargain hunting, I find these websites incredibly useful for people at all internet skill levels who want to find good deals on the web.

INTERNET MALLS

A web-shopping site may be an internet mall—a collection of e-vendors all selling their wares under one electronic "roof." My favorite internet malls—the ones I've included in this chapter—are those that feature mini-reviews and sometimes actual consumer ratings of the member vendors and their services. Some web-shopping sites present themselves as being primarily content- and editorial-driven, with linkage to vendors their secondary function. These sites feature articles, reviews, rankings, and even chat boards for consumers to share information about positive and negative web-shopping experiences. However, without the all-important electronic links to vendors, it's doubtful these internet malls could exist, since the links often pay the bills—the electronic equivalent of "rent."

The internet malls I've included in this chapter are among the places I visit frequently when I'm looking for interesting web vendors. Some have free e-newsletters you can subscribe to telling you about the latest and greatest deals, consumer alerts, new e-commerce trends, new products, and new web vendors. As a researcher of consumer bargains, I've found all of these helpful in different ways. But for an ordinary shopper these are good places to start.

PRICE-COMPARISON SITES

One of the best known price-comparison sites is mySimon. With more than a dozen main product departments to choose from, mySimon is one of the most comprehensive price-search sites around. Google, a popular search engine site, recently launched Froogle, a new service that finds information about products for sale online. In theory it's a great idea, one that could empower consumers and encourage businesses to be more competitive.

However, I've been disappointed on occasion when using generalized shopping robots. The reason is that the database used to compare products and prices is only as broad and deep as the number and quality of the participating merchants. (Be especially wary of shopping-robot sites that charge vendors to participate, which skews the results and brings the unbiased nature of the service into question.) I have often done a price comparison search on a specific product offered by one of the vendors in this book and have had companies come up in the search that are charging more for the item, but not the company that I know has the best deal. Electronic price comparison is useful, but somewhat limited.

COUPON AND SPECIAL-DEAL SITES

Are you a coupon clipper? Then you'll love coupon-and-deal websites. It is a business that lists regularly updated rebate programs, special sales, limited-time offers, customer incentive programs, discount coupons, and free shipping promotions from the best-known online vendors. The two I like best are A Huge Deal (www.ahugedeal.com) and Insane Coupons (www.insanecoupons.com). Both of these sites let you search by store, by category, or by the deal's expiration date. That means, if you are a fan of some of the big mail-order catalogs or famous mall stores, you can check to see if they are running any specials this week. Some of the deals are up to 50% off regular retail.

Find It Fast

CONSUMER ARTICLES
About.com, Consumer World, Esmarts, Yahoo! Shopping

FEATURED BARGAINS
Consumer World, Esmarts, Yahoo! Shopping

LINKS TO ONLINE VENDORS
About.com, BizRate, Consumer World, Esmarts, Yahoo! Shopping

PRICE COMPARISON TOOLS
BizRate, Consumer World

WEBSITE REVIEWS OR RANKINGS
About.com, BizRate, Esmarts

About.com

FEATURES: over 700 individual, highly specialized "environments" presenting consumer articles and resources, vendor links, ask-the-expert chatboards, etc.

ONLINE: www.about.com

About.com calls itself the "leading network of niche vertical sites for users and marketers." *Whah?* Let me translate, because it took me a while to understand About.com. But once I got it, I became a huge fan. About.com makes a great home page, by the way.

The first thing you'll notice when you log on to About.com is a small photo of a person: the kind of person you see everyday at the grocery store. Who are these normal-looking people? Each day a different "guide" is featured. A guide is a real person—not a media creation—a genuine expert on a particular subject who has gone through About.com's rigorous application, screening, training, and trial processes, and has graduated with flying colors. There are more than 700 of these expert guides, with more added each week, in every subject you could imagine from A to Z—action-figure collecting to young adult books. (Well, okay, A to Y.) Each of these guides has a well-developed site within About.com where you can read frequently updated articles on the guide's area of expertise, click on links to related web vendors or other website resources, ask the expert a question, join a chatboard to share your interest with others of like mind, and much more.

To give you a concrete example: Say you wanted to buy wine online. Click on the wine expert at About.com. Read short, well-written articles on a variety of subjects; check out recommended wine books; access the glossary of wine grapes; read about how to buy wine over the internet; and then click on a recommended vendor. *Voilà!* You've just gone from a novice to an educated consumer in a matter of minutes. Want a specific wine recommendation? Ask the expert. She's required to answer you. That's part of her job as an About.com guide.

I really like this site and have used it many times. It's a bit like an ideal small town where every resident is really good at something and happy to share his or her know-how for free.

BizRate

FEATURES: consumer and staff reviews/ratings of web vendors, with links
ONLINE: www.bizrate.com

It's nice to know that someone is looking out for the consumer in the big, anarchical world of web shopping. Luckily, BizRate's practices also help the internet shops themselves, so it's a win-win situation for everyone. If shopping on the internet is intimidating to you, it just got less so. BizRate is dedicated to helping shoppers find quality online merchants by providing a site where you can view the results of consumer and BizRate staff reviews and ratings.

Since the first time BizRate was featured in this book a couple of years ago, it's just gotten better and better (and bigger and bigger). Here you'll find the top companies—those that scored highest in overall customer satisfaction—updated weekly. You can also search by category (apparel, computers, food and drink, pets, and hobbies, to name a few) and see how different internet vendors fared in the ratings. What's good about this site is that it's not just an internet mall, but a living, changing compendium of companies with descriptions of their products and services, as well as links to their home pages.

BizRate makes it simple to find companies offering good prices. Search results are organized by "price," sorting the companies in a given price category in descending order (highest-scoring companies are those that consumers were most satisfied with vis-à-vis their pricing). There's lots more here, including a nice reference section about consumer rights and company responsibilities. This is a site all internet shoppers should get to know.

A caveat for bargain shoppers: At this writing there were thousands of vendor "members" of BizRate. Although membership is free, not every great company on the web chooses to be part of or is accepted by BizRate. Also, some of the stores that do choose to be part of BizRate pay for premium placement in sections of the marketplace. In plain English, this means that when you're looking for a list of women's apparel vendors sorted by price, the top-rated company will be the cheapest *among BizRate's vendor members,* but by no means the cheapest to be found on the world wide web. It's important for bargain shoppers to realize that a web "mall" or shopping site is only as good as the stores it includes. In the case of BizRate, you'll find solid, mostly well-known companies, but ones I'd hardly consider "discount."

Consumer World

FEATURES: consumer articles, product alerts, discount-store price finder, links to hundreds of online vendors

ONLINE: www.consumerworld.org

This is one of the best web-shopping sites. Consumer World has it all—a free weekly e-newsletter that tells you about scams, deals, consumer news, new products, and new web vendors; hundreds of links to unique and interesting internet vendors in all categories, including bargain shops and outlet stores where savings run deep; wonderful articles on consumer-relevant subjects (companies who track down the authors of "anonymous" consumer complaints on chat boards, bargain-of-the-week airfares, auto dealers' dirty tricks, to name a few); a bargain-price finder; a consumer resource section; and much more. It's very easy to find your way around this site—excellent interface! What would I call this site? It's not really a mall. It's more like an interactive magazine. I love that it's so rich in content, yet so useful and practical. I give this site 5 out of 5 stars. It would make a great home page for those of you who love to shop or love to read about things that make you a smarter consumer.

Esmarts

FEATURES: proprietary reviews of internet shopping sites, shopping links, newsletter, message board, etc.

ONLINE: www.esmarts.com

There's something about Esmarts that's friendlier than most web malls. For one thing, Esmarts doesn't even call itself a mall, but rather "the *community* for bargain shoppers." You get a good feeling when you log on to the aptly named Esmarts. Click on one of 14 categories (Flowers, Computers, Groceries, Music, Travel, etc.) and you don't just get a list of vendors with links. You also get thoughtful and well-researched short essays about internet merchants in that category that cover price, service, selection, and other elements contributing to a positive web-shopping experience. The Buying Guides for computers, for example, offered links to computer bots with accompanying reviews of each one; links to information sites, auctions, and sale sites; coupons and freebies; and links to manufacturer sites. Other neat aspects of Esmarts include a newsletter, membership rewards (where you can collect points for free merchandise), coupons, shopping tips, and a shopping board where you and others can sound off on positive and negative shopping experiences.

It's really a consumer guide that's designed to help the wary e-shopper find reputable vendors selling at a bargain. Go to Esmarts and you'll see that web shopping can be fun, enlightening, inexpensive, and—yes—even friendly. I really like this site and recommend it to anyone looking for intelligent life along the information superhighway.

Yahoo! Shopping

FEATURES: vendor links and shopping services and resources
ONLINE: shopping.yahoo.com

Yahoo! Shopping is a section of the famous mega portal Yahoo! For those of you who aren't familiar with Yahoo!, it is a location on the internet that offers a full spectrum of services, such as email, news, travel services, search engines, and much, much more. Many people use Yahoo! as their home page because it provides just about everything any internet user will ever need. But I focus on the Shopping section of Yahoo! here for the simple reason that this company has really done it right. The first thing you'll notice about Yahoo! is its user-friendly interface. If you want to go shopping but don't have a clue where to start, log on to Yahoo! Shopping and first check out the weekly specials and deals. These are often amazing, classy sales or promotions happening at the best-known stores. When you're ready to shop, a search bar lets you search by product category or by key word, if there's a specific product or brand you seek. Other consumer-friendly features, all free: Yahoo! Wallet, where your shipping, billing, and credit card information are stored and can be automatically and quickly accessed whenever you are in a store's online checkout; Buyer Protection Program, a free service that protects you against fraud when you purchase through Yahoo! Shopping; and, Research and Compare where you can compare products in ten different categories. I love Yahoo! Shopping, and so will you.

The Gift Guide

A highly selective list of fun, creative, quirky, useful, and interesting gifts—most under $40—for children, hostesses, best friends, siblings, significant others, parents, and everyone else

The key to gift giving, I've decided, is to understand the recipient and come up with something that will make that person happier, healthier, more relaxed, more excited, more content, and so on. Keeping this in mind, then, know that practical underwear for your hubby would be out. Tie-died boxers, on the other hand (ones you decorated yourself), would be in. But no matter how eccentric the gift, it is definitely the thought that counts.

Below are gift ideas—most of the items $40 or under—that jumped out at me from different companies I've researched. In many cases, it's the company—rather than the gift—that impressed and inspired me for one reason or another and made me want to share my enthusiasm with readers.

THE BEST (AND EASIEST) PRESENT—GIFT CERTIFICATES

Gift certificates, of course, are the best presents you can give, particularly if the receiver is unusually fussy or someone you don't know very well. Gift certificates are *not* no-brainers. I consider them to be among the most thoughtful of all presents. Lots of online vendors offer gift certificates and make it really easy for both buyer and recipient. The gift certificate is assigned a code number that the buyer merely types in at the time of purchase instead of typing in a credit card number. It's an effortless way to make someone really happy. And you know they'll be getting something they really like or need.

Here are some stand-out companies that offer gift certificates:

BLACKSTONE AUDIOBOOKS: for your favorite artist friend who likes to listen to stories while she sculpts. Help her pick out some great literature to inspire her.

FIRE MOUNTAIN GEMS: for your favorite artsy-craftsy teenaged girl. Every page of this jewelry-making catalog has fabulous items that she will want to use to design her own earrings, bracelets, and necklaces.

THE LEFT HAND: for your favorite southpaw. This catalog of tools, games, gifts, and accessories for left-handed people has something for everyone: from your 6-year-old to your grandpa, including hand tools, kitchen items, computer accessories, sports equipment, and whimsical gifts.

MAGIC TRICKS: for your favorite youngsters. The tricks here are fun to read about and are designed for all ages and skill levels. All kids get a big kick out of this gift.

MYMUSIC: for anyone who likes music (beware of those who don't). They'll be able to choose from a great selection including the "essentials" section with CDs by Marvin Gaye, Sara Vaughn, Joni Mitchell, Bob Dylan, Otis Redding, Van Morrison, and more.

NEW GLOBAL MARKETING: for your favorite closet cigar smoker. She will like this hip little company that scans the world for the best deals on cigars, both brand-name and lesser-known boutique lines. Best of all, now she won't have to sneak them.

NORTHWESTERN COFFEE MILL: for your favorite coffee drinker. She hates it when she wakes up in the morning and reaches for the bag of coffee beans only to find it empty. You can purchase a gift certificate for any amount—for either a single occasion or up to one year of installment shipments so she need never run out again. (At least until her shipments are over.)

THAT FISH PLACE/THAT PET PLACE: for your favorite aquarist. Since you don't know whether he'll want real plants, fake coral, or a miniature shipwreck to decorate his aquarium floor and to provide intellectual stimulation for his guppies, give him a gift certificate and let him decide for himself.

WHOLESALE TOOL CO., INC.: for your favorite friend who uses tools for work, play, or just to keep the old homestead in one piece. There's always another tool to make the job go easier.

ZAPPOS: for your sister. There isn't a woman on this earth who won't find something to love at this wonderful store. You just can't have too many pairs of shoes.

COLLEGE-AGE KIDS, TWENTY-SOMETHINGS, ADULT CHILDREN

Antique broom labels collection—for that 20-something niece, who has just gotten her first apartment. These pretty labels feature original American commercial art picturing flowers, birds, cats, sailors, and more, and make adorable decorations for any kitchen. Collection of 30 different broom labels. $12. (Original Paper Collectibles)

"Bare Essentials" box of Mexican ingredients—for your son who loves to cook. This box includes dried chile anchos, dried chile mulatos, dried chile pasillas, canned chile serranos, Mexican oregano, and Herdez brand salsa verde. $28. (The CMC Company)

Charcoal black or red stretch chair cocoons—for your college kid, whose furniture collection consists of metal folding chairs she and her roommate "borrowed" from the film department. Perfect, because these nifty chair covers are designed to transform ordinary folding chairs into hip, marvelous party seating. $35 each. (Masacco New York)

Coffee-of-the-Month club—for your hardworking grad student who is always short of three things: money, coffee, and sleep. She'll get a 1-pound bag of fresh, gourmet coffee, delivered to her apartment every month. Help her earn her law degree and you may be able to hit her up for some free legal advice later on. $85 to $165. (Northwestern Coffee Mills)

Computer code briefcase—for your computer geek son, who's just landed his first job. This solidly constructed, black vinyl briefcase has a slew of text encoded in old-school monitor green. If it was translated it would reveal "The Lovesong of J. Alfred Prufrock" by T.S. Eliot. $29.95. (Archie McPhee)

Flames briefcase—for your daughter, who's just landed her first job. "The Man" may have stolen her soul, but he can't steal her style. This briefcase is the perfect accessory to express her attitude without getting a pay cut or demotion. Comes in matte black vinyl with silver metal fittings. $29.95. (Archie McPhee)

Haute collection of miniature perfumes gift set—for your boss' daughter, who just turned twenty. These beautiful, miniature versions of famous designer perfumes come in a boxed set and are affordable because they are so tiny. The five-piece gift set includes Tresor by Lancome, Safari by Ralph Lauren, Poeme by Lancome, Noa by Cacharel, and Arpege by Lanvin. $33.99. (Fragrance Wholesale)

Spiral-sliced smoked ham—for the young newlyweds on their first Christmas. You know they're strapped for money, and food makes the perfect gift. Now they can invite friends over for a feast. $48.95 (includes shipping). (Amana Meat Shop & Smokehouse)

DADS, UNCLES, FATHERS-IN-LAW, AND GRANDFATHERS

All-fabric computer dust covers—for your dad's first computer system. He's tickled pink now that he's finished his computer course and has a new toy to play with. Make him even prouder by giving him covers—in his favorite color, of course—for his equipment. About $25. (Co-Du-Co Computer Dust Covers)

Brand-new American flag and flagpole—for your patriotic grandpa who loves to tell war stories and has a raggedy old flag he hangs out with pride each Flag Day, Fourth of July, and Veterans Day. These well-made flags come in every size imaginable, with a variety of pole configurations. $ varies. (American Flag and Gift)

Coffee-table art book—for your shy father-in-law. He'll think you spent a lot of money, and will be impressed that you knew who his favorite painter was (his daughter tipped you off, of course). $ varies. (Scholar's Bookshelf)

Left-wing literary magazine subscription—for your dear old dad, recently moved to an assisted-living community, where he believes all the old fogeys on his hallway are boring and conservative. He's got the time to read now, so why not jazz up his days with some new ideas to chat about over bridge. $ varies. (Delta Publishing Group)

Rope sandals—for your hippie parents who've just bought a farm in Vermont. They're retired and want to spend their twilight years off the grid, traveling to Third World countries, and growing their own organic herbs. I can't think of anyone better suited for these nifty sandals, which can go from beach right into the ocean. $19.99. (Dave's Discount Rope Sandals)

Traditional Russian hat—for your sweet old uncle, who loves to tell stories of his adventures around the world when he was a young man. This is the same kind of hat worn by the Russian navy—in an animal-safe version. $25. (Baltic Rim)

Waterford pen from the Marquis collection—for your grandfather, who sits in his room much of the day writing his memoirs. This beautiful ballpoint pen has a handcrafted metal body with a red gunmetal finish. $19.95 (Fountain Pen Hospital)

MOMS, AUNTS, MOTHERS-IN-LAW, AND GRANDMOTHERS

Amplified phone—for your dear old mother, who can't carry on phone conversations very well anymore, but insists that she is *not* hard of hearing. This nifty phone has an amplifier that makes voices loud and crystal clear. She'll say you shouldn't have, but she'll be glad you did. $79.95. (Hearing Planet)

Face Care Kit—for your lovely aunt, who has beautiful skin and wants to keep it that way. She can cleanse with cleansing gel, massage on Earth and Sea Polish, tone with Lavender and Rose Mist, moisturize in the daytime with Sunrise Creme, and moisturize nightly with Royal Jelly Creme. These five precious facial products come in a gold, tinted, clear cosmetic bag. $26 (Kettle Care)

100 pink tulips—for your proper mother-in-law, who finally warmed up to you when you discovered your mutual love for gardening. Spend an afternoon with her planting these amazingly inexpensive lovelies, and she'll appreciate you anew each spring. $35. (Van Engelen)

Swiss Army SwissCard—for your handy mom, who always seems to have a Band-aid, tissue, or flashlight when someone needs it. She will flip for this dandy item, which fits together into the size and shape of a credit card. It has toothpick, nail file, straight pin, mini-ruler, letter opener, scissors, ballpoint pen, tweezers, and a screwdriver tip. $19.95. (Cutlery Shoppe)

Black, all cotton, knitted shawl—for your Italian grandmother. At first she'll be confused because she'll think you got her a shawl like the old Italian women wear in the small villages like the one her mother came from. But then, you'll explain to her that shawls and ponchos are all the rage among young people this year and then she'll be quite pleased. $49. (Bluefly)

FRIENDS, SIBLINGS, AND SWEETHEARTS

Box of bread-dipping herbs and spices—for your favorite pal who embarrasses you at Italian restaurants by asking for a third basket of bread to dip in the olive oil, vinegar, and cheese mixture. Now he can dip in the privacy of his own home with this selection of four jars of herbs and spices to make his own bread-dipping oils. $18.95. (Wildtree Herbs)

Cloud Comfort queen feather bed—for your clinically depressed wife, who seems to be spending a lot of time in bed lately. Make her happy with this extra-plush bed filled with white goose feathers and white goose down and covered with a 195-thread count cotton twill cover. $165 each. (Linen Place)

Cruelty-free faux leather gloves—for your best friend, who is a vegan, subscribes to *The Nation,* and takes her van to every protest within 100 miles. It gets cold being chained to a tree, so get her some vegan (nonanimal product) gloves that she'll feel good about wearing. $12.95. (Pangea Vegan Products)

Diversity T-shirt—for your brother, who gets more active and more in-your-face radical every year he's in that wheelchair. Show him you finally "get it" by buying him a shirt with a message designed to get others to open their minds to the culture of disability. Some of the slogans are designed to shock; others are hilarious. $15. (The Nth Degree)

Faux alligator handbag inspired by J.B. Tods—for your best friend, who has very classy taste but is opposed to the idea of a handbag costing the same as a used car. This cute, classic-looking, animal-friendly bag comes in red, brown, or black. $44. (AnyKnockOff.com)

G.I.-style jungle hammock—for your old college buddy, who dreams of becoming a performance poet and, as a result, lives in a tent or on your couch much of the year. He'll really like this mortgage-free hanging home, which has a nylon/poly-coated roof for rain-free sleep and a heavy-duty cotton canvas body and floor with sturdy zipper closure. The no-see-um mesh mosquito netting keeps those pesky critters away while he sleeps in your backyard. $39.95. (Military Surplus & Survival)

Magnum P.I. Hawaiian Shirt—for your lovable boyfriend, who likes to dress up in "party shirts" when you go out on dates. This traditional Hawaiian shirt, of 100% cotton, is the very flower-and-bird design worn by Tom Selleck in his 1980s TV show, and is such an Americana classic that it is featured in the Smithsonian Museum. He'll be a walking-talking conversation piece at the next party! $49.99. (AspencreekSport.com)

Makita cordless drill set—for your favorite sister. She's turning 50, and she's still not married, so it's time she learns how to do her own handyman work around the house. This 9.6 volt drill comes with two batteries, one charger, a keyless chuck, and a plastic tool case. $69. (Tool King)

Ravishing reptile python-look baguette purse—for your favorite cousin, who thinks she has a better sense of fashion than you do. She'll love this Gucci, Prada, and Fendi inspired durable handbag that comes in eye-popping pink, chocolate brown, or natural. $29. (Freda LA)

Sterling silver white pearl necklace—for your girlfriend, she'll think you spent a bundle of money on her and she'll love you more. This 16" necklace has lustrous pearls joined together with sparkling sterling silver links to form a striking circle. The circle of *love*. $49.99 (ClassicCloseouts.com)

Three-piece Chicago-style pizza set—for your sister, who's a mom of three, works full-time, is PTA president, volunteers as soccer coach, and coleads a Brownie troop every other week. Does she have time to make her kids pizza from scratch? Sure! This dandy kit comes gift-boxed with a 14″ × 11.5″ slant-side, deep-dish pan, a 14″ perforated crisper, a pizza cutter, and recipes. $21. (A Cook's Wares)

KIDS AND TEENS

Comic book subscription—for your niece or nephew who loves superheros. Have a comic book delivered monthly to their doorstep. Make an advance order (2 months in advance) of comics like *Bone, Sonic the Hedgehog, Grendel, Hellboy, Akiko, Cerebus, Batman, Daredevil,* and much, much more. $2.25 to $3.50 monthly. (G-Mart Comics)

Cool Tricks: Mastering the Art of Yo-Yo Play video—for your teenage son. You never thought he'd get into this retro toy, but boy were you wrong! If he could permanently attach his finger to his Pocket Rocket, he'd do it. This 38-minute video demonstrates 80 tricks. $14.99. (BFK—The Yo-Yo Store)

Dragonfly kite—for your brood of young nieces and nephews. Get them outside and away from the television screen with this 100% silk, handpainted, three-dimensional dragonfly kite. 38" x 45". $38. (Pearl River)

The Fascinating World of Bees book—for your young nephew who loves insects and bugs. This 32-page, beautifully illustrated, paperback book will give him basic information about bees in a logical, easy to understand manner. $8.95. (Brushy Mountain Bee Farm)

Jump Start First Grade—for your neighbor's bright 6-year-old. This educational software turns the computer into a fun learning tool. The girl will get a head start on reading and spelling, and you'll be able to enjoy an uninterrupted cup of coffee with your neighbor for a change. $12.99. (Softwareoutlet.com)

Mini-kaleidoscope kit—for your starry-eyed daughter. She can make her own magical scope from this nifty little kit, which includes a 9-inch-long triangular kaleidoscope that comes with patterns for 12 different color wheels. Substitute image wheels or discs for infinite color image possibilities. $11. (Glass Crafters)

Pine needle basket kit—for your daughter who loves to make things. All the materials she'll need are included. The kit guarantees success. In a few hours she'll have a beautiful basket she can be proud of. $24.95. (The Caning Shop)

Quick Chess—for your granddaughter or grandson so they can spend a little more time with grandpa and then beat the pants off of him. This is a great way to introduce kids to the game of chess. For ages 6 and up. $10.99. (TurnOffTheTV.com)

"Unexploded Cow"—for your favorite irreverent teen. It's the summer of 1997, and there are two big problems in Europe that deserve a common solution: mad cows in England and unexploded bombs in France. You and your buddies are out to earn money, make friends, and take home medals. Oh, and blow up a few mad cows along the way. This and the other clever homemade board games from this company rule! $7.50 (Cheapass Games)

THANK-YOU GIFTS

Bag of paperwhite narcissus bulbs—for your trustworthy neighbor who watched your house over the holidays. She'll love these easy-to-grow bulbs that she simply places in a bowl on top of marbles or pebbles and fills with water up to the roots. Five weeks later she'll enjoy a gorgeous, fragrant bouquet blooming in her own living room. Great for the mid-winter doldrums. $9.95/ten. (Dutch Gardens)

Brownie and cookie gift basket—for your dad's home-care worker, who is there every day feeding him and taking care of him when you can't be. You happen to know she has a sweet tooth, so surprise her with these elegant baked goodies as a way of saying, "Thanks for all you do." $ varies. (Bellows House Bakery)

Design-a-Mug—with "Best Coach" for your child to decorate and personalize with special nontoxic crayons. His design bakes on right in your own oven. $9.99. (Constructive Playthings)

Handmade wood-slat lunch basket—for your favorite hostess, who has invited you over for dinner more times than you can count. She loves to unfold a blanket in her meadow and have tea and scones with friends on a hot summer afternoon, so this little basket will come in handy. $22. (West Rindge)

Pretty note cards with envelopes—for your hair stylist at holiday time. Is there anyone who doesn't appreciate nice and useful note cards? It's an inexpensive but thoughtful way to thank her for all of those great hair days. $4. (Current)

Seashell sampler—for that special preschool teacher who has more boundless energy at the end of her day with 14 toddlers than you do when you come to pick up your single child. She'll find 101 uses for this assortment of 200 shells, great for craft projects, good-behavior tokens, and party bags. $25. (Benjane Arts)

A Guide to Buying by Mail, Phone, and Internet

Print Catalogs, Online Catalogs, and Price Quotes

PRINT CATALOGS

The first mail-order catalogs were issued early in the last century. Even so, the mail-order craze didn't really take hold until the middle to late 1970s. In fact, in 1978 when the first edition of this book was published, then called *The Wholesale-by-Mail Catalog,* the editorial staff was in the odd position of having to convince many of the companies to sell directly to consumers so we could put them in our book. Most companies at that time sold merchandise one way: out of their brick-and-mortar stores. Few mailed out print catalogs. Many didn't believe this type of buying would catch on. *Will consumers buy something they can't touch, see, or smell first?* was a question we heard again and again.

Fast forward to the dawn of a new century and millennium. Most of the firms in this book issue print catalogs, and have for years now. These range from glossy tomes laden with color photos to a few photocopied pages listing products and prices. Some are free; others cost a few dollars, a fee that's intended either to weed out frivolous requests or to offset printing and postage costs. To receive a print catalog, you must request it, although if you're a recent customer, some companies will automatically send you the latest catalog.

Sometimes one catalog is all you want. For help in getting off someone's mailing list for good, see "Direct Marketing Association," page 640. With the cost of publishing and postage on the rise, however, many vendors who have become confident about selling directly to consumers are taking the next step, to electronic catalogs.

"REFUNDABLE" CATALOGS. Companies *want* catalog shoppers to place orders from the catalog they requested. Therefore, as an incentive, they offer to deduct the catalog fee from the first order, which should be placed within 6 months of receipt of the catalog, unless a specific time limit is stated. Reimbursement can be done a number of ways. Two common methods are: (1) to deduct the catalog fee from the *grand total* of the order (the order *plus* tax, if applicable, and shipping charges), adding the words "less catalog fee" beside the deducted amount; and (2) to submit a company-issued refund coupon with the order, deducting the coupon amount from the *product total*. If you don't place any orders from the catalog, you won't qualify for a refund of the fee.

ONLINE CATALOGS

An online catalog is located at the company website. For some businesses, you may have to click on a link to get to the shopping area of the website. A common way this is indicated would be Begin Shopping or Enter Store. Once you get to the online catalog, you'll notice that some are quite utilitarian and plain: Here's the product information; here are the prices; here's the order form. Others are extremely elaborate and may include an About Us section that details the history of the company and presents snapshots and bios of the top employees; an FAQ section that answers any and all customer-service queries; and lots of fancy bells and whistles to make you want to return again and again. Frequent-buyer clubs, web-only specials, informative text and articles, a personal shopper, ask-the-expert—these are the types of features one might find at a high-end website. Most online catalogs have "shopping carts" that let you add items as you browse the site, just as you would in a supermarket. When you proceed to "check out," you have the option of removing items from your cart before making the final purchase decision. All online catalogs should have a customer-service number or email address in case you have questions. Customer-service options vary from a live person on the other end of a toll-free phone number, to email, to "live chat," where you type in your questions in real time and get them answered immediately on your screen.

For information about "secure" electronic ordering, see "Ordering Online," page 615.

PRICE QUOTES

Some companies have neither a print nor an online catalog, but sell by "price quote" instead. When stock moves in and out quickly—as it can at outlets and at companies that sell discontinued or deeply discounted products—goods are sold on a price-quote basis, rather than by catalog. Another reason companies sell by price quote is so that they can avoid excessive overhead. Their "store" may consist of nothing more than an office, where a staff person acts as agent between manufacturer and customer. There's no inventory, no showroom, no fancy catalog—just a small staff. Name-brand products sold this way include appliances, electronics, cameras and similar equipment, tableware, furniture, carpeting, perfume, bedding, and wallpaper. (Price quotes are also given when the customer seeks an item not found in the company's catalog.) A price quote, simply put, represents the cost of a specific item from a company at the time of the quote, and can usually be obtained by phone, letter, fax, and email.

ADVANTAGES TO PRICE QUOTES. You may not know much about buying by price quote until you read this book, but once you learn about it, it may become your favorite way to shop for bargains. Why? Because vendors will reward you generously in the form of deep discounts for all the hard work you do for them. To request a price quote, the shopper needs to get beforehand some standard information: the manufacturer's name, the product's model number, and the color or pattern name or code. The quote is usually honored for a limited time or until stock is gone. Find out if the price you receive includes, or is exclusive of, tax, shipping and handling, insurance, and other charges.

FINDING THE INFORMATION. One of the reasons mail-order prices are low is that you, the shopper, do your own product research *before* seeking a price quote. You need to get the name of the company that manufactures the product you're interested in, the *manufacturer's* product code (also called model number or style number or pattern name), and in some cases, the product's size and color. Maybe you saw the item in a catalog, a magazine, an ad, or a friend's home or office. Since those sources won't always provide the detailed, current, and accurate information you need, it's a good idea to check factory cartons or product tags in local stores as well as manufacturers' product brochures, sometimes available in stores and often at the company website.

How to Order

Reasons for shopping by mail, phone, or online vary from person to person—for convenience, out of necessity, for lowest price, or maybe just for the excitement of getting a package at home. What matters is that your shopping experience be satisfactory and that products meet your expectations.

ORDERING BY MAIL

Always order from a company's most recent catalog. If you have an older one but you know the products are fairly consistent, call to confirm that the product is available and what the current price is. If you order from an out-of-date edition, you risk delaying delivery if the firm has to contact you about price differences and payment. Generally speaking, you'd do better to request a new catalog.

Place your order using the form in the catalog, making sure to affix your preprinted address label to the indicated space on the form. If your catalog is a pass-along without an order form, write up the order on your own paper, using a form from another catalog as an example of the kinds of information to include. You'll need to know code numbers, item names, quantity of each item being ordered, price per item, tax if applicable, and shipping charges. Take your time, so you don't forget such important information as your name, delivery address, and phone number; the name and address of the firm you're ordering from; payment information (see "Payment," page 617); and special information, such as an additional address if the item is being shipped as a gift or if the order is being billed to someone other than yourself. Respect any minimum-order requirements. Attach a *copy of the order* to the catalog and file it.

SECOND CHOICES AND SUBSTITUTIONS. Indicating a *second choice* on the order form means that you will accept a different color of the same product if the first color is not available. Indicating that you will accept *substitutions* means that if the product you want is out of stock, you will accept an available product comparable in function, quality, and price to the one you originally wanted. If that kind of substitution is fine with you, say so on the order form or letter. Companies are prohibited by law from making substitutions without the buyer's *written* authorization. If neither a second choice nor a substitution is acceptable to you, write in red *on the order form,* "NO SECOND CHOICES OR SUBSTITUTIONS ACCEPTED."

ORDERING BY PHONE

Giving an order by phone can be easier and faster than mailing in an order. If you opt to order by phone, you'll need to have the same information you would include in a mail-order. Therefore, you should fill out the order form *before* placing your call—including the address label, which has encoded information the operator might ask for, and home and business telephone numbers. However, your phone order will probably be processed more quickly than a mail-order would, and if an item is out of stock, the customer-service rep probably will be able to tell you at the time of your call.

When you're ready to call, have before you the completed order form, your credit card, and note-taking materials. The operator will facilitate the steps of placing the order. You, in turn, should obtain the following information from the person taking your call:

- the operator's name and/or operator number;
- the policy on returns, in case your product carries exceptions to terms listed in the catalog;
- when new stock will arrive if an ordered item is not currently available;
- expected shipping date;
- how the order will be shipped (items together or separate);
- the grand total that will be charged to your credit card;
- your order number.

Before the transaction ends, the customer-service rep may tell you about additional products on special discount. Give a listen in case there's something you've been meaning to pick up when the price was right. If you do add a product to your order, be sure to jot it down, including the price, and ask for the final total. Add the date of the call to your notes, and attach the record to the catalog for safe keeping.

ORDERING ONLINE

I still know some people who won't place an order online for fear of having their credit card information stolen. Oddly, these same people are willing to give their personal information to a total stranger over the phone! If you're a new internet shopper, I suggest arming yourself with information. The FTC "Consumer Protection" website has articles to help you understand online auctions, secure credit card transactions, internet privacy policies, and other subjects for the novice e-shopper. (See "Obtaining Help," page 639.)

Nowadays, chiefly because vendors wanted to nip consumer paranoia in the bud before it got out of hand, the great majority of online catalogs offer "secure ordering." Don't make me explain the technology. Suffice it to say that your credit card number and other personal information are encrypted so as to discourage would-be thieves from obtaining it. As a result, more and more shoppers feel comfortable purchasing merchandise online. Does the technology work? Yes. Is it secure? Yes, as secure as any other type of shopping from home.

If a vendor doesn't offer secure online ordering, the website will say so. Chances are, if the mode of electronic ordering isn't secure for the customer, the company won't even offer the option. Doing so would leave them open to all kinds of legal trouble should your information be stolen. Online vendors who don't offer secure electronic ordering will often have an order form that you can print out, fill out with a pen, and mail or fax in.

Most secure electronic order forms are virtual copies of paper ones. Just type in the information fields with your name, billing and shipping addresses, and type of payment. Be sure to double check such fields as quantity, color, and size, as well as dimensions and other specifications before you click the "buy" or "submit form" button.

Once you have electronically submitted your order, most online vendors will send you an email with your order and tracking numbers, and will sometimes update you by email with notification that your package has been sent. However, it's always a good idea to print out a copy of the order form as well as the order number, just in case there's a glitch in the system. That way you have some type of paper proof of your online transaction. To deal with online vendors in the case of problems, see "Obtaining Help," page 639.

The most common way to order online is by credit card using the secure order form. However, some people still prefer to order by telephone. Most online vendors allow this option, although some make it unappealing to do so by having an answering machine rather than a live person at the other end of the line. Be sure to check for customer service hours, usually posted on the website. Fax and mail are other ordering options, but you first need to check the section of the website that details the company's policies. There you'll be able to determine if the company accepts orders by mail or fax, and you'll find the appropriate address and fax number if they do.

BUYING AT WHOLESALE

A wholesale buyer operates, or represents, a business that intends to resell the purchased items as they are or in another form. If your order or your business qualifies, you can buy at true wholesale from the firms in this book that have a star icon among the symbols. Wholesale orders are subject to any one of the special sales terms below:

LETTERHEAD OR BUSINESS CARD: to show you're acting as a company, not as an individual.

RESALE NUMBER OR BUSINESS CERTIFICATE: to show your activity is part of a business enterprise registered with local authorities and to qualify for exemption from sales tax.

BANK AND CREDIT REFERENCES: to obtain invoice billing or to open an account.

LIMITED OPTIONS OF PAYMENT: to protect the vendor's interest. Payment could be limited to a check or money order or include credit card.

MINIMUM ORDER: to qualify as a wholesale purchase. Minimums can be stated as dollar amounts, number of items, yardage—whatever applies to a particular type of product.

How companies handle wholesale and retail catalog requests varies, from sending out the same catalog with a discount price schedule attached to the wholesaler's catalog, to issuing separate catalogs for retail and wholesale buyers with different products available to wholesalers. Although wholesale catalogs give a pared-down version of product information compared to retail catalogs, they do make sample orders available. Also, they charge less for shipping than retail buyers would pay. At such price breaks, it's not unreasonable to be charged a restocking fee of 10% to 25% if merchandise is accepted for return. The savvy wholesale buyer will stay away from orders labeled "final sale, no returns accepted."

For some firms in this book, wholesale buyers' terms are indicated in the text. If wholesale orders are accepted, make sure you honor the company's terms when you place your order.

PAYMENT

The FTC Mail or Telephone Order Merchandise Trade Regulation Rule may not mean anything to you now, but in the event you are due a refund on an order placed by mail or phone, it will come into play. Did you pay for your order on *credit* using a credit card, or did you *prepay,* using a check or money order or debit card?

PREPAID ORDERS. Orders paid for with checks (personal, certified, bank, teller's, cashier's), money orders (bank, postal), and debit cards are considered *cash* payments under the FTC Rule. Each form of payment has its pluses and minuses.

Personal checks are convenient, inexpensive, and accepted by most firms. The canceled check serves as a receipt for the purchase, and it is automatically returned to you with your bank's monthly statement of checking account activity. The "memo" portion of the check, filled out when you placed the order, keeps a record of the firm's address and telephone number. On the down side, a firm will usually wait for your check to clear before shipping your order, adding a delay of up to 2 weeks to your delivery date. Also, if omitted or underpaid charges must be added to your total, a second check might have to be sent to make up the difference, adding to the delay.

A certified check is a personal check that has been marked "certified" by the bank on which the check is drawn. A "certified" stamp means that the bank has frozen in your account the amount indicated on the check, thereby guaranteeing the availability of the funds to the vendor. This guarantee eliminates payment-related delays. The fee for a certified check ranges from $5 to $9; like a personal check, this check is returned to you in the monthly checking account statement. If a firm requires a certified check, common when fulfilling a first order, it is likely to accept a bank check, a teller's check, or a cashier's check, each of which represents a guarantee of funds.

Both banks and the U.S. Postal Service (USPS) (through post offices and postal carriers in rural areas) sell *money orders.* A bank will charge between $1 and $3, with no cap on the amount. A postal money order costs less, but is limited to a maximum of

$700. Both come with receipts attached, either a copy underneath the money order or a stub that should be filled out with the company's name and address and the money order amount. If the date of the money order is not automatically printed on it, be sure to add the date when you fill in the name of the firm and your name and address.

You won't automatically receive proof of a money order's having been cashed the way you would with a check, but a bank money order can be traced, payment can be stopped, and a refund can be issued. A postal money order can be replaced if it is lost or stolen (as long as you have the receipt), and copies of a cashed money order can be obtained from the USPS within 2 years of its being cashed. A reminder: *Immediately* fill in the blanks on a money order, and separate it from the receipt when you're done. If the money order is stolen or lost, you can't get a replacement if you don't have the filled-in receipt.

CREDIT, CHARGE, AND DEBIT CARDS. Let's start with *debit cards* since they are a hybrid of the more familiar credit card and personal check. When you pay with a debit card, your bank receives an invoice for your purchase and electronically deducts the total of the invoice from your account (checking, savings, money management). That payment is viewed as a cash payment by the FTC, not a credit card payment.

Credit and charge cards are not identical creatures, but when you use one or the other to make a purchase, the procedure is the same. You must provide the vendor with the account number of the card (make sure the firm accepts that card), the expiration date, your phone number, and your signature, if ordering by mail. The advantage to using these cards, besides getting to pay later for a product you enjoy now, is that any unforeseen or overlooked charges, such as shipping costs, can be added to the card, thereby preventing a shipping delay. You're probably wondering what distinguishes the two cards. Simply this: A credit card (MasterCard, Visa, Discover) allows you to carry a balance from month to month and requires only a minimum payment while charging interest on the total unpaid balance; a charge card (American Express) requires you to pay the entire balance on each statement. Because vendors incur charges (from the card-issuing companies) when they accept credit and charge cards, their minimum-order requirement is usually higher than it would be for a prepaid order.

ELECTRONIC MONEY. There are new ways to pay when you order online that have sprung up as a result of security concerns. They also address the fact that people without credit cards felt they were being discriminated against, because vendors would refuse to ship merchandise until personal checks had cleared. Several forms of electronic payment, sometimes called electronic money, are being developed in order to simplify purchasing online. Some methods of electronic payment work in concert with your ATM card, requiring you to fill in a personal ID number, or PIN, when you place your order, to authorize the sale. The money, then, comes directly out of your checking account. Others allow consumers to transfer cash value to a card. These are called "stored-value" cards, and work something like express cards you use when traveling by car to avoid stopping for highway tolls. There are other types as well, some in development even as we go to press. If you want to find out more about this new form of internet money, go to the Federal Trade Commission website (www.ftc.gov), where you can read more about the different forms and the pros and cons to each.

RETURN POLICIES

Policies differ among companies, so you should check on a policy *before* you order (the Special Factors entry in the company listing often addresses this). Catalog firms will generally accept returns within 10 to 30 days of receipt of the order (although I've seen return windows as short as 7 days and as long as a year). Products purchased on a price-quote basis (that is, when a catalog is not offered) are usually not returnable unless defective. Certain items not covered by general return policies include those that have been personalized, logoed, or monogrammed; custom-made; or purchased as surplus or on final sale. Likewise, if you ask a company to special order a product. Returns of undergarments and swimsuits are generally not accepted, but there are exceptions, especially if a package is unopened (see "Returns," page 629).

Finally, before you spring for an expensive item with lots of moving parts, ask the firm to fax you a copy of the manufacturer's warranty. Then take a look at "Evaluating Warranties," page 635, for help in deciding if the warranty holds any value for you.

CANCELING YOUR ORDER

By ordering goods or services by phone, mail, or online, you create a *contract of sale* between yourself and the firm providing them. According to the FTC Rule, you cannot cancel that order or stop payment on a check or money order simply because you've changed your mind about the purchase. (Remember, you contacted the company; it didn't solicit you.) Contract law varies from state to state, but rescinding an order could open you up to legal action by the firm.

What if your concern is that the company is about to fold, taking your money with it and not delivering the goods? Then stopping payment might be a prudent step. But barring such a situation, keep in mind that most mail-order and online firms guarantee satisfaction (they want your repeat business) so goods can be sent back when they arrive. If you *really* don't want to go through with an order you've already placed, speak to representatives of the firm *first*. For whatever reason, they might be able to work with you to everyone's satisfaction.

Shipping, Handling, Insurance, and Sales Tax

A *major* consideration when weighing the advantages and disadvantages of shopping by mail, phone, and online is the combined cost of shipping, handling, insurance, and tax.

SHIPPING COSTS

Shipping costs discussed in this section apply to purchases that are made from U.S. firms *and* are being delivered to addresses in the U.S.

SHIPPING COMPUTATIONS. One reason for confusion among mail-order shoppers when they try to tally their own orders is that shipping charges can be computed a number of ways.

Postpaid   This method is simplest for consumers because the shipping and handling costs are incorporated into the price of the item. The price, therefore, is not subject to an additional shipping charge. (Tax is another matter, covered below.)

Itemized   This method is also simple but not necessarily cost-efficient. The firm indicates the cost of shipping in parentheses at the end of the product description or after the product price or code number. The amount you pay might not match the meter strip on the delivered package, though. Perhaps the amount you were charged included handling and packing, or maybe the company uses the charge as a means of taking in some extra bucks. If you sense too large a difference between actual cost and the amount you paid, you can discuss it with the company and see what happens, if anything.

Numeric   In an effort to get consumers to order several items at one time, rather than one here, one there, some companies charge shipping based on *the number of items you order,* not on their cost, weight, or destination. The charge on the first item is usually the highest, with successive items costing less: "$1.50 for first title, $.75 for each additional book." Sometimes after a specified number of items, charges are eliminated entirely!

Flat order fees   Here's another easy-to-calculate method since one charge is applied to an entire order no matter how many items are included or how much they weigh. Too good to be true? Yes, if your selection is exceptionally heavy or fragile or isn't a standard size. Read the catalog for exceptions that can also apply to orders sent to more than one address.

Free shipping   Is it possible? Could shipping actually be free? Yes, if the cost or quantity of your order meets a standard stated in the catalog. For example, orders "over $100" might not be charged shipping; likewise, for multiple units (say, two dozen) of one color, style, or size. Such an arrangement is common among smaller companies and is usually contingent upon shipping to *one* address. Recent consumer surveys indicate that the number-one reason shoppers often choose one mail-order vendor over another is free shipping. Knowing this, a lot of smart print and online catalog vendors are beginning to offer this benefit. I like it! They're right!

Purchase amount   With this method, the shipping charge based on the *total purchase amount* of an order is determined using a 2-column table found on the catalog order form. Locate the total cost of your purchases in the left column; then look across to the corresponding shipping charge in the right column. For example, if your total purchase amount is between $25.01 and $50, your shipping charge might be $6.95. If your purchase total is $300.01 and over, your charge might be a maximum of $14.95. This method seems unfair if your order consists of a $400 ring, as opposed to a heavy $150 microwave oven. In such cases, a company might apply itemized shipping charges; and most set a maximum limit on the cost of shipping, generally, below $20.

Weight and distance   This is the method that tempts buyers to "forget" to add in shipping because figuring out the charges seems complicated. It involves using a chart of weight and/or distance, doing arithmetic, and rereading catalog product descriptions for notes about trucking. In a "simple" case, you would total the *weight* of your purchases, locate the zone or area you live in on the chart, and then figure out the shipping charge. But some products are "trucked," and you have to know if one of yours fits that category. Usually the catalog codes will tell you with an extra letter at the end. If your catalog doesn't have a rate chart, or if computing the charge is more than you bargained for, you have options. The best is to pay by credit card so the company can simply add the shipping to the total without delaying your order. Next best is to phone the shipping department of the firm. Add the figure they give you to your order. The last way, which could cause a shipping delay, is to send a check for the order and request to be billed for the shipping.

SAVING ON SHIPPING COSTS. If placing a large order appeals to you because of potential savings on shipping, invite like-minded friends and associates to order when you do, especially if a holiday is coming up and shipping to one address is convenient for all. If ordering solo, wait a day after filling in the order form before calling or mailing it in, in case you decide to buy an extra item you were on the fence about.

MODES OF DELIVERY

Regardless of how firms arrive at shipping charges, they tend to ship goods by standard ground courier (UPS would be an example), U.S. Postal Service (USPS), trucks, and overnight delivery services (sometimes called "Air Delivery").

STANDARD GROUND COURIER. For mail-order, many businesses prefer to use firms such as UPS, because overall it costs less than the USPS and automatically insures each package up to $100. One possible disadvantage, from a customer's view, is that delivery is made only to street addresses, not to post office boxes.

U.S. POSTAL SERVICE (USPS) / PARCEL POST (PP). Parcel post (fourth-class mail) delivers to post office boxes, an advantage in favor of the higher charge, compared to UPS's rate. If PP delivery is imperative, do the following two things: (1) Across the top of the *order form,* in large red letters, write, "DELIVER BY PARCEL POST ONLY; COURIER NOT ACCEPTABLE." (2) In a conspicuous place on *your check,* write "GOODS TO BE DELIVERED BY PARCEL POST ONLY." By cashing the check the firm agrees to honor this arrangement and, therefore, should ship by PP.

TRUCK. Here's that term for a tricky form of shipping mentioned earlier, "Truck." It means that an item, because of its size or its location in a *manufacturer's* warehouse (not the mail-order firm's premises), must be shipped by truck, not UPS or USPS/PP. If your order includes some items that can go by mail and some that *must* go by truck, the whole order might ship by truck.

How do you know which products require trucking when you place your order? The catalog will contain the following terms if a product requires shipment by truck: "FOB" (free on board) or "freight," followed by "warehouse" or "manufacturer" or the city from which the goods will be trucked. What, then, does "FOB manufacturer" mean? It means that trucking charges are billed from the *manufacturer's* location, not the mail-order firm's warehouse. A product coming to you from the manufacturer is most likely being drop-shipped to you en route to another, nearby destination. You can ask the mail-order firm if your item is being drop-shipped, and if so, where the manufacturer's warehouse is so you can estimate trucking costs. If quick delivery is important to you, ask the mail-order firm to find out before you order if the manufacturer has the item in stock, and if it does, if it can ship by overnight service.

Trucking presents additional considerations: The charges, collected *upon delivery,* must be paid in cash or by certified check. These charges can mount up if you've ordered something heavy traveling from far away. Deliveries are usually left on the sidewalk in front of your home or business, not inside the door. Sometimes, for additional cash fees, drivers will carry the delivery inside, but not always, especially if you're in a nonelevator building. Additional fees come into play if you require advance notice of delivery or your order is not part of a larger trucking shipment. Sometimes, because of trucking charges, you might do better to buy appliances or heavy-duty equipment from a local retailer that delivers.

AIR DELIVERY. Most mail-order and online vendors will ship your purchase overnight if you request it—for an extra charge. If you're in a hurry but want to save some money, request "second-day" delivery. Some companies in this book—for example, food vendors selling highly perishable goods like caviar, or greenhouses selling fresh-cut flowers—always ship their goods via air delivery. Obviously, they wouldn't be in this book if they didn't make it worth your while from a financial point of view. These firms have high-volume-usage arrangements with the big air-delivery firms enabling them to bring down the normally high cost of overnight delivery and pass those savings along to you, the consumer. If you're really itching for that purchase—say, for a last-minute birthday present—inquire about the cost of air delivery. It might not be as much as you expect.

HANDLING

Sometimes a fee for "handling"—the processing and packing of your order—is charged as a part of the "shipping and handling" cost. Sometimes it's a separate fee of $1 to $5. Whether applied alone or in tandem with shipping, handling (and shipping, for that matter) can be subject to state tax.

INSURANCE

When should you pay for it? If your order is being delivered by the USPS, ask to have it insured, since insurance isn't automatic. Charges are usually quite reasonable at 85 cents for goods valued at $50 and below, and $1.85 for shipments valued from $51 to $100. If the contents of your package are valued at more than $500 but less than $25,000, the shipment must be registered, too. Note also that not all goods are insurable by the USPS (some edibles, for example, or extremely fragile and valuable antiques). If your purchase is uninsurable, ask the mail-order firm to use a service that will insure it.

UPS *automatically* insures packages for up to $100. UPS's charges for each $100 worth of insurance on the same package get added into the shipping charge. If you encounter an order form that says shipments are made by UPS, yet there's an insurance charge printed on the form, don't pay it—insurance is already part of the UPS shipping.

Insurance claims occur most frequently because goods are lost or damaged during shipping. As soon as you notice damage to your shipment, call the customer service department of the firm *you ordered from,* and ask what the procedure is for making a claim. The answer will depend on how your goods were shipped and on the policy of the mail-order company. However, if you have documentation of having received and/or insured the order (a signature in a UPS log, an insurance receipt from the USPS), the company has enough to verify and process your claim, and eventually to reimburse you or issue a replacement order. If the goods don't arrive and you can't prove that they were insured, the firm might send a replacement order anyway. If you paid for your purchase with a credit card, you might qualify for a charge-back, provided you follow the *creditor's* procedure for obtaining one. (See "The Fair Credit Billing Act," page 641, for information on this.) If you're unable to resolve your claim to your satisfaction after persistently using all the options, contact the agencies listed in "Obtaining Help," page 639, and present your case to them.

SALES TAX

For years, one of the joys of shopping by mail was that purchases were exempt from sales tax if they were shipped to an address *outside the state* where the mail-order firm (or its branch offices or its representative) was located. Those unfortunate enough to live in the same state as the mail-order firm or its branches and representatives paid tax on goods as well as on handling, shipping, and packing.

These days, more of us are being numbered among "the unfortunates" as state governments seek to benefit from the success of mail-order shopping (what will happen regarding online shopping is not yet known) by imposing a "use" tax on orders shipped *into* a state! No matter how you feel about paying a sales tax on a mail-order, if the order form says "Add applicable taxes for shipments to WY, WV, and ID addresses only," and you live in one of those states, you must calculate and add in the correct percentage of sales tax. If the form says "Add applicable sales tax for your state," you must do so. If you have questions about purchases that you expect to deduct or take depreciation on, speak to an accountant or a local tax authority.

SHIPMENTS ABROAD

If you want your order shipped outside the continental U.S., *before you order* be sure to find out from the catalog, the website, or a customer-service representative about policies and regulations that could affect your shipment.

SHIPMENTS TO AND FROM CANADA. The North American Free Trade Agreement (NAFTA) has eliminated some but not all tariff problems. Also, some products are not allowed to be shipped out of country. The maple leaf icon in the symbol row indicates which mail-order companies will ship to Canada, but to be sure all items in your order can go there, speak to the vendor's reps.

SHIPMENTS TO APO/FPO ADDRESSES. Let's start with the carriers that *do not* ship to these addresses: UPS and Federal Express. Not surprisingly, the USPS will ship to an APO/FPO address but not on a C.O.D. basis. The USPS, the carrier used by most mail-order companies for this kind of shipping, uses parcel airlift (PAL) to a military dispatch center, which, in turn, ships packages overseas on a space-available basis (SAM, space-available mail). Packages can't exceed 70 pounds and must be no larger than 108 inches in combined length and girth (the same restrictions that apply to regular first-class mail). Firms that ship to APO/FPO addresses—indicated by the flag icon—might charge additional handling fees, so you might want to get a shipping estimate before you place an order.

SHIPMENTS WORLDWIDE. The globe icon indicates that a company ships worldwide. But such shipping isn't a simple matter for the consumer: Import restrictions, duty rates, and conversion rates are important concerns for the mail-order shopper. Experts in these areas should be consulted before you place an order to an address outside the U.S. and Canada (Israel, Japan, Europe, for example). Also, before sending any money, read a company's catalog closely or have the firm, if it sells on a price-quote basis, mail you a shipping quote.

Receiving Your Order

Mail-order shopping is a two-way street with rights and responsibilities falling to both the consumer and the vendor. Here are some guidelines on how to handle your order when it arrives and what to do if it doesn't.

ACCEPTING DELIVERIES

CHECKING THE PACKAGE. First of all, when the order arrives from the trucking service, UPS, or the USPS, inspect the crate, box, or bag for *extensive* damage. If you think the packaging has been through too much—and therefore suspect damage to your order—you don't have to sign for or accept the delivery. (If someone else is accepting the delivery for you, advise that person to make the same inspection.) See "Returns," page 629, for details about returning shipments.

If the box, crate, or bag seems fine, sign for it. While you shouldn't put off opening the delivery, neither should you tear into it with excitement. Open the package with care, paying attention to any instructions on the box, and put aside the packing materials. Retrieve a copy of your order form or an invoice from inside the box or from the plastic envelope attached to the shipping carton. If none is enclosed, get the copy you filed away with the catalog and begin to inspect the contents.

What are you checking for? Damage to goods, an incomplete ("short") order; substitutions you didn't authorize; errors in size, color, style, or model; missing parts; instruction sheets or booklets; warranty forms. If the item was customized (printed, engraved, monogrammed), check wording and spelling slowly and out loud, letter by letter. If you ordered an ensemble, make sure all the pieces were shipped: belts, hats, scarves, vests, ties, ascots. If you ordered a tool or something electronic, use it—after reading instructions carefully—as soon as possible, to make sure it works as it should and does what you were expecting it to do. Check the item for signs of use to make sure you weren't sent a demonstration, reconditioned, or returned item as "new." (If you were, you could return it or negotiate for a lower price.) Don't mail in the warranty card until after you've tried out the item. See "Returns," page 629, on what to do if you decide to return an item.

DAMAGED OR INCOMPLETE DELIVERIES. If goods are damaged, inform the seller right away. Speak calmly and politely as you describe the condition of the order and how you think the problem could be corrected. If the damage seems to have occurred during shipping, the seller will ask you to file a complaint with the delivery service. In that case, ask the seller for the following information: the *seller's* shipping address, the date of shipment, the seller's account number with the delivery service, relevant shipment codes, and any other information you might need. Then, *file the claim with the delivery service,* and send a copy of the complaint to the seller. If you think photos will help your cause, enclose them with the original complaint. Sometimes purchases made with a credit card are entitled to extended warranties, so contact the issuer of your credit card if you used it to purchase the damaged goods.

Should you receive a short shipment, don't get upset. The seller might have included a notice saying that the pieces will be shipped separately. Check also for an option notice, which would be sent if an item were out of stock. (See "The Option Notice," page 628, for information on this.) If a company doesn't back order, it will enclose a refund check with the order or send a refund check under separate cover or, if you paid by credit card, bill it for the adjusted total. What if you don't find a notice about the missing items? Look in the catalog to find out if certain items get shipped from the manufacturer or separately by the vendor. If no such information is apparent, call the firm right way.

Contact the firm immediately if customized products have errors in them—even if a special occasion is months away.

DELAYED SHIPMENTS

What feels like a long time to you may not constitute an actual delay in the legal sense, as outlined in the FTC Mail or Telephone Order Merchandise Trade Regulation Rule. However, if a company does delay shipping your order, you need to know your basic rights and obligations. The FTC Rule, a federal rule, was created to address the problem of late delivery as it concerns shopping by mail, phone, and online. "Mail- or telephone-order merchandise" means the goods the customer orders from the seller by mail or telephone. Telephone-order merchandise can be ordered directly or *indirectly* by telephone, *including fax machines and computers.*

The FTC Rule contains certain principles that the mail-order consumer ought to know, as well as exemptions to its protection and *obligatory* actions on the part of the buyer when there are problems. When state or local laws exist for purposes similar to the functions of the FTC Rule, whichever law affords the *consumer* the most protection is the law that takes precedence.

GENERAL TERMS OF THE FTC RULE. An important term to understand is the word *ship.* The FTC Rule states that a seller must *ship*—not "deliver"—goods within 30 days of receiving an order that is properly completed, unless the firm, in its catalog, advertisement, or promotional material, asked for more time. A "properly completed order" means that the check or money order sent as payment is good and made out in the proper amount; your credit is good if an order is charged; and all necessary information for processing the order is available. The 30 days start counting as soon as the firm receives your payment, but the count stops if the payment is dishonored. For credit card payments, the countdown starts when the seller receives valid account information, *not* when it puts the charges onto the card.

If there are any problems with the order, the 30-day clock doesn't begin until they're fixed. Problems could include any of the following: Your check or money order is dishonored by the bank or made out for less than the total cost of the order; your credit card doesn't receive authorization from the issuer; the order is missing such information as your address or the color you want—anything that stands in the way of completing the order. Once the problem is eliminated—proper payment is received or credit is approved or missing data is supplied—the 30-day countdown begins. Therefore, to prevent delay, you should be attentive to details when you write up your order and, if placing it by phone, be as organized as possible to avoid making errors.

EXCEPTIONS TO THE FTC RULE. To every rule there are exceptions. If a firms asks you to allow more than 30 days for shipment—"allow 6 to 8 weeks for delivery"—then the 30-day limit doesn't apply. In addition, some goods and purchases don't receive protection under the FTC Rule: seeds and growing plants; C.O.D. orders; purchases that require you to say "no" to prevent shipment, such as book and record clubs (also called negative-option plans); and subscriptions to magazines and other "serial deliveries." The FTC Rule applies to catalogs that require payment or compensation, but it does *not* apply to gifts that really are "free."

The firms you order from know all about the FTC Rule. Therefore, if your order is covered under the FTC Rule, the firm knows there's a specified procedure it must follow if it can't ship your order within 30 days. Likewise, to protect your rights under the terms of the FTC Rule, you must know what they are. The next few sections will tell you.

THE OPTION NOTICE. If you submit a properly completed order, and the seller can't ship within 30 days of receiving your order or by the time specified in its catalog, ads, or promotional material, it is obligated to send you an *option notice*. An option notice, to comply with the FTC Rule, tells you that there is a delay in shipping the item you requested. A new shipping date might be mentioned. If it is, and the date is up to 30 days later than the original deadline or another date specified by the firm, you should be given the choice of consenting to the delay (accepting the new delivery date) *or* of canceling the order and receiving a refund. (See below for orders shipped over 30 days after the original date.) The option notice, under the FTC Rule, must state that if you do not respond to the notice, you're giving your implied consent to the delay. (That means if you get an option notice and you don't respond to it, the delay is okay with you.) If you choose to cancel the order—and it's definitely your right to do so under this circumstance—the cancellation must reach the firm *before* it ships the order. That's why acting immediately is important when dealing with mail-order issues.

If the seller gives you a new shipping deadline that's over 30 days after the original date, or it can't give you any revised shipping date at all, the option notice must clearly say so. Read the following statement carefully, since it describes a procedure different from the one in the paragraph above: The notice must say that your order will be *automatically canceled* unless (1) the seller receives, within 30 days of the original shipping date, your consent to the delay, and (2) the firm is able to ship the order within 30 days after the original deadline and has not received cancellation of the order from you as of the time of shipping.

Notices must be sent by first-class mail with a cost-free way to respond to the notice, such as a prepaid business-reply envelope or postcard (the ones that say "Postage will be paid by" or "No postage required if mailed within the United States"). Reply immediately, especially if you want to cancel your order. For protection, photocopy the cancellation order (the card, letter, or form that you send), and send it "return receipt requested" so you'll know the exact date it was received. If the order goes out any time after the date the firm received your cancellation order, and you have proof, you can refuse to accept delivery, sending the order back to the seller at the seller's expense and claiming a prompt refund or credit.

THE RENEWED OPTION NOTICE. Let's say a firm has sent you an option notice stating a revised shipping deadline. If the firm can't meet the revised shipping deadline, it must send you, *before the date of the revised deadline,* a renewed option notice. This second notice, and any that come after it, must state that if you do not consent *in writing* to a new shipping date or to an indefinite delay, the order will be canceled. According to the FTC Rule, the consent to the second delay must reach the seller *before* the first delay period ends, or the order must be canceled.

Even if you agree to an indefinite delay, you have the right to cancel the order at any time before the goods are shipped. Note also that the seller, if it is unable to ship within the delay period, may cancel the order and that it must cancel the order under various circumstances.

THE FTC RULE AND REFUNDS. Under the terms of the FTC Rule, how you paid for your order determines the time frame within which you receive a refund, should you or the firm cancel the order. Regardless of how you paid for the order, however, the FTC Rule provides for a prompt refund. For prepaid orders, the firm must send you a refund check or money order by first-class mail within 7 business days after the order was canceled. If you used a debit card, tell the firm at the time of cancellation because it needs to treat that payment as cash, the way it would for a money order or check. It must reimburse your *account* within 7 working days *or* send a refund check. According to the FTC Rule, payments made by credit card must be refunded (credited to your account as a void of the charges made for the goods) in one billing cycle. Firms can't substitute credit vouchers for their own goods in lieu of making a reimbursement.

Returns

A lasting mail-order relationship depends on satisfied customers, and firms know that sometimes delivering satisfaction means accepting customer returns. To do that, sellers have policies that spell out the procedures and conditions for making a return. The customer's right to return products also depends on the nature of the problem, the conditions under which the return is made, and laws made at local, state, and federal levels

Before you order by mail or online, read the catalog carefully because it tells you the firm's policy on returning items, including how soon after receipt they must be returned, whether you need authorization from the seller, reasons for which returns can be made, and which types of goods are nonreturnable. Generally, special orders, "final sale" items, truly wholesale purchases, intimate apparel, and custom-made items are *not* returnable. However, if the firm made an error or the product was defective, some "nonreturnables" will be accepted for exchange. "Implied Warranties" provide information on laws that apply to product performance and to the rights of consumers beyond those stated in catalogs, so it's wise to read them. See "Implied Warranties," page 634.

OBTAINING AUTHORIZATION

The phrase *authorized returns accepted* appears frequently in the Special Factors portion of the listings. An "authorized return" is a return you have called the company about and for which you have received an authorization number (also called an "RMA"). The company expects you to use that number on all correspondence pertaining to the return and on the outside of the package when you ship it back.

Before sending back goods, you should check for packing inserts that detail the return procedure; if no inserts are found, read the catalog for instructions. Also, the back of the order statement sent with your goods might have a return form printed on it. If it does, use that for your correspondence, filling it in completely and correctly. If it doesn't, write a straightforward, *factual* letter that states (1) the reason you're returning the item, (2) the price and the order number of the item, (3) the date the package was delivered to you, and (4) how you would like the situation resolved. For example, do you want a refund check, an exchange, a repair, a credit to your charge account, or a store credit toward a future purchase? Avoid wordiness, threats, and emotional arguments at this point. Keep a copy of the correspondence—a letter or the company's return form, and notes of your phone conversation with the company, especially the authorization number and the name of the person you spoke to.

RESTOCKING FEES

A restocking fee offsets the company's cost to rehandle a product when returning it to inventory. Fees are stated in catalogs and range from 10% to 15% of the cost of the item (some items, such as frames, may go as high as 25%). Pay attention to catalog notes about fees when buying furniture, electronics, and appliances. If an item is returned because of a defect or shipping error, a restocking fee usually is not charged.

SENDING THE ITEM

Under "Accepting Deliveries," page 625, I advised setting aside packing materials until the contents of the package have been examined. If an item needs to be returned, package it in those same materials, if feasible or if requested by the firm, and make sure any insurance coverage equals the full value of the item (see "Insurance," page 623). Before sealing the package, enclose the return form or your *dated* letter, double checking that you included your name and address, the product's order number, the authorization number and/or name of the person who approved the return, and what you would like done (repair, exchange, refund, or credit). File a copy of the correspondence, any notes, and your invoice with the catalog.

REFUNDS AND CREDITS

By reading the catalog before you order, you'll know *in advance of returning a product* what a company will and will not do when it accepts a return. Knowing this is important when you state in your letter what you would like done. To ask for a refund from a firm that only offers a choice of replacement or repair will delay resolution of the problem. However, many firms *do* have refund policies, so if you want a credit to your charge account, include the necessary information in your letter, and if you want a refund check, specify the mailing address that should be used.

EXCHANGES

If you're exchanging the returned product for an identical item (without the defects), say so in your correspondence. But if you're exchanging the product for a completely different item, provide the same information you would give if you were ordering the item new: the code number from the catalog, the size and color, the price, and other relevant information. It's best to talk to a customer-service representative before exercising this latter option, as a difference in price between the two items could be problematic.

POSTAGE REIMBURSEMENT

Generally, firms do *not* pick up the customer's cost of shipping and insuring a return. A few exceptions, however, will accept "postage collect" returns or hire UPS to pick up the package at no charge to the buyer. Others will reimburse their customers for shipping and insurance. Since *federal* law does not require reimbursement of these costs—even when the seller makes a mistake—companies tend not to reimburse for them.

However, since the buyer benefits from the law that offers the most consumer protection, check your state and local laws in case they provide for reimbursement.

Guarantees and Warranties

People use the terms *guarantee* and *warranty* interchangeably, but they are somewhat different. In Special Factors, the expression *satisfaction guaranteed* represents a firm's pledge to stand behind the products and services it sells. That promise is backed up by each firm's policy on returns (see "Return Policies," "Returns," and "Implied Warranties," pages 619, 629, and 634, respectively). In contrast, a warranty is a written policy covering the performance of a specific product, and, like a guarantee, it is available without charge. An "extended warranty," however, is a *paid service contract* for a particular product.

Since warranties are regulated by state and federal laws, you have certain rights with regard to achieving product satisfaction. Therefore, it pays to know the terms of each policy so you can get the best warranty value for your product and avoid paying for services (such as repairs or replacement) that ought to be paid for by another party (for example, the manufacturer or the seller).

THE WARRANTY ACT

Before I get to the terms of the Magnuson-Moss Warranty—Federal Trade Commission Improvement Act (the Warranty Act), a word about oral promises made by salespeople. An oral "warranty" that assures product performance and customer satisfaction has no value *unless it is also given in writing*. The Warranty Act, enacted in 1975, regulates printed warranties. It requires that all terms and conditions of warranties be expressed in "simple and readily understood language"—in other words, plain speech. For products costing over $15, a copy of the warranty must be available to the buyer *before* purchase. Stores are supposed to post warranties on or near their products or keep them on premises in a binder of warranties, posting a conspicuous notice about its location. Mail-order firms honor the law by making copies of warranties available to potential customers *upon request*. Therefore, if along with a price quote you ask to receive a copy of a warranty, you're entitled to have your request fulfilled.

The party making the warranty (the warrantor) is required by the Warranty Act to describe the policy using the terms *full* and/or *limited*. Sometimes multiple warranties will apply to a single product if it has parts that are covered differently. The warranty covering each of those parts can be designated as full *or* limited.

FULL WARRANTIES. A *full warranty* provides for the repair or replacement of the product at *no cost* to the buyer. This provision includes removing and reinstalling the item, if applicable. A full warranty exists for a certain amount of time, which must be stated, and its provisions must be transferable to another party for the full term of the policy. So, if a relative passes a small appliance on to you during the term of the warranty, you are entitled to the benefits of the warranty, should you need them within the covered time. The duration of *implied* warranties (see "Implied Warranties," page 634) may not be limited by the terms of the full warranty and may last, under some state laws, up to 4 years.

After you inform the seller of a problem, repair should be made within a "reasonable" amount of time. If a reasonable number of attempts have been made to repair the product, and it still doesn't work properly, a "lemon provision" entitles you to replacement of or refund for the product.

For marketing research and product development purposes, many firms enclose registration cards with their products, inviting consumers whose products are covered by a full warranty to register them with the warrantor. Such registration is a voluntary act and should be so stated on the card. Registration is *not necessary* to protect your rights under the warranty.

LIMITED WARRANTIES. A *limited warranty* offers fewer benefits (less coverage) than does a full warranty, and is not subject to the "lemon provision." Under a limited warranty, the buyer can be held responsible for some costly aspects of product repair or replacement: removal, transportation, and reinstallation of the product and labor costs for repairs. In order to validate the policy, the buyer can be required to return the warranty card to the firm. Also, the warrantor *can limit* the terms of the policy to the original purchaser and make a prorated refund or credit for the product.

There is also something called an *implied* warranty (see "Implied Warranties," page 634), the duration of which can be limited by the warrantor, but not shortened. If the implied warranty time is limited, the warranty must state: "Some states do not allow limitations on how long an implied warranty lasts, so the above limitation may not apply to you." However, the warrantor may not put a limit on the extent of the protection you are entitled to under an implied warranty.

An informed buyer has more leverage in attaining product satisfaction than one who has no knowledge of consumer protections and seller obligations under the law. Here are some additional provisions of the Warranty Act:

- If a firm receives your complaint within the warranty period, it must take action to remedy the problem according to the terms of the warranty.
- If a product comes with a written warranty, the warrantor can't exclude the product from protection under implied warranties.

- A warrantor is allowed to exclude or limit consequential damages from coverage under both full and limited policies provided the warranty states: "Some states do not allow the exclusion or limitation of incidental or consequential damages, so the above limitation or exclusion may not apply to you." See "Implied Warranties" and "Consequential Damages" on the following pages for more information.
- All warranties must tell you whom to contact, where to take or mail the product, and how to reach the warrantor (name, address, or toll-free phone number).
- Both full and limited warranties must state: "This warranty gives you specific legal rights, and you may have other rights that vary from state to state."

IMPLIED WARRANTIES

Unlike the Warranty Act, which is a federal law, an implied warranty is a *state* law that offers protection against major hidden product defects. Every state has implied warranties covering every sale *unless* the seller states that the product is being sold "as is," a declaration that means no warranties or guarantees are offered. However, even if a firm sells a product under a no-guarantee policy ("as is"), if that product comes with a written warranty, the implied warranty of the *buyer's* state is valid on that item. Although states vary in some aspects of the terms of the implied warranties, many offer similar kinds of provisions.

WARRANTY OF MERCHANTABILITY. This common implied warranty means that a product must work properly when used in its customary fashion. For example, a toaster should toast at varying degrees of lightness and darkness; a vacuum cleaner should pick up ordinary household debris—or liquids if that's its function. If a warranty of merchantability exists in your state, and you have purchased a product that doesn't do what it's supposed to do, most likely you will be entitled to a refund for that product.

WARRANTY OF FITNESS. This warranty applies to cases in which the seller has identified or recommended a particular purpose or use for a product. So, if the seller indicates that a sleeping bag is appropriate for use in sub-zero temperatures, it should offer warmth in that situation. You should still check the product literature to verify such a claim. If none is available, call the manufacturer. Whether through product ignorance or misguided good intentions or a profit motive, the seller might not be entirely accurate. The manufacturer should have reliable information about product fitness.

CONSEQUENTIAL DAMAGES

Consequential (incidental) damages result when the malfunction of a product causes *other* property to become damaged or destroyed. According to the FTC's example, consequential damage has occurred if the use of faulty antifreeze causes a crack in an engine block. Likewise, an incidental damage has occurred if a properly installed home aquarium begins leaking at its seams and damages the carpet.

Although written warranties usually entitle the buyer to consequential damages, warrantors are permitted to exclude this provision under both full and limited warranties. If such damages are exempted, the warrantor must still state: "Some states do not allow exclusion of limitation of incidental or consequential damages, so the above limitation or exclusion may not apply to you."

There are two important consumer entitlements in the provisions for consequential damages: (1) compensation for the damage or loss of the property, and (2) repair or replacement of the defective product. You can see why, given something as costly to repair or replace as an engine block, a seller might declare an exemption of damages. And if your state *allows* exclusion of limitation of incidental damages, the value of the product and its warranty will be greatly reduced from the buyer's point of view.

EVALUATING WARRANTIES

With so many products at competitive prices and similar features, a buyer must also weigh the value of a warranty *before* making a purchase. As you read the warranty—and you really should *read* it—pay attention to what you know about yourself as a product user (Are you rough on gadgets? Careless about or attentive to maintenance?) and what you know about the type of product in general. For example, what usually goes wrong with a cassette player or a VCR? Do you have reason to be concerned about being able to get such an item repaired or replaced, based on your experiences? You can also review the warranty in terms of the following questions:

- Is it a full or a limited warranty?
- Is the whole product covered or only specific parts?
- From date of purchase, is the warranty period a number of days (30, 45, or 90 days) or months (6 months) or years (1, 2, or 5 years)?
- Whom do you contact for repairs? The manufacturer? The seller? A service center? (And note where each is located.)
- Who is responsible for removing, delivering, and reinstalling the product? (This is especially important for large appliances.)
- Must repairs be made by an "authorized" service center or representative? Where is the closest one located?

- Is a temporary replacement provided while your product is being repaired or serviced?
- Are consequential damages excluded? If so, would malfunction of the product lead to considerable damage and loss?
- How is reimbursement on a pro rata basis calculated (according to time, use, or price)?
- If the product can't be repaired, are you entitled to a refund or a replacement?

To evaluate a warranty, consider (as if you were in a horror film) *all* that could go wrong with a product and how soon after purchase things could go wrong. Then determine how much loss, inconvenience, and expense you could bear concerning this particular product. Your answers will help you decide if the product and its particular warranty are worthwhile for you.

COMPLYING WITH WARRANTY TERMS

By virtue of being human, we all mean to do things we should do, but often we don't actually do them—following instructions and reading contracts, for example. Here are some reminders to help you take advantage of the protections in warranties and fulfill the obligations of any buyer.

- Read the warranty card—or have someone read and explain it to you.
- Read the instructions or operating manual *before* using the product, even if you're sure you know what to do. There could be some delightful feature you don't know about, or less optimistically, an important warning, such as "Do not turn on unit until compartment is filled with water."
- Follow the instructions for using the product.
- Understand the conditions that void a warranty: misuse, mishandling, and neglect of the product; improper installation; repair or service by an unauthorized party; commercial use of a noncommercial model; and use of the product at the wrong voltage. Anyone who uses your property should know how to operate it.
- Keep the warranty and dated proof of purchase together, in a spot reserved for such records.
- If you must send in proof of payment to qualify for a rebate, photocopy the receipt and store it with the warranty.
- Maintain the product as suggested in the manual, and resist the impulse to perform do-it-yourself repairs. Improper maintenance or tampering with the product could void the warranty.

When in doubt, let the manufacturer or service center answer questions about maintenance and use—because if you violate the terms of the warranty, it will become void and the cost of repairs will fall to you.

OBTAINING SERVICE

If your product stops working or malfunctions, don't panic. Try following these suggestions:

- Refer to the operating manual or instructions, specifically the troubleshooting section. Make sure you're not trying to get the product to do something it wasn't intended to do.
- Speak to a friend who may have knowledge about common problems or who can run through your product's setup procedures, to make sure you installed the item correctly.
- Contact the warrantor—unless the seller offers service under the warranty— from information on the warranty card.
- Describe the problem, state when it occurred, and indicate whether you want a repair, replacement, refund, and/or consequential damages. If you visit a service center, bring a copy of the warranty and proof of payment; include the same if you send a letter. Your rights and the form (and extent) of compensation will vary depending on the terms of the warranty and the laws for your area.
- If you drop off a product or the repair service picks it up, get a signed receipt with the date the item should be ready, approximately how much the repairs will cost, and the serial number of the product, if it has one.
- Any product you ship out for repairs should be insured for its full value, and a letter enclosed stating the problem, the date it occurred, and what you would like done.
- If you call or visit the warrantor or the seller, follow up with a letter stating what was said during the conversation. Photocopy the letter, and send it by certified mail to the person or agency you talked to.
- Log the actions taken in the process of your honoring the warranty: Indicate dates of phone calls, visits, and actions as well as expenses for them.
- If, after 3 to 4 weeks, you have not heard from the seller or the manufacturer in response to your letter, write again. Ask for a reply within 4 weeks, enclose a photocopy of the *first* letter, and mail the second correspondence using certified mail. Address the letter to the person you've been dealing with; if you don't have a specific contact, send the letter to the attention of the warranty department or the head of customer relations.

- Deal with one party at a time: the manufacturer *or* the seller, not both. If one does not resolve the issue, then contact the other. Neither can afford to do business with a party that doesn't hold up its end of the relationship.
- Before you accept a product that has been repaired, have it demonstrated. If you recognize quirks that repairs should have eliminated, point them out. Better to have the problem checked there than to take the item home and go through the procedure again.
- When you pay for the repairs, get a guarantee on parts and labor. This will protect you from paying for repairs again if the item malfunctions shortly after you start using it.
- Under the "lemon provision," if the product repeatedly malfunctions after being repaired, and it is covered by a full warranty, you can most likely get a replacement or a refund. In a letter to either the manufacturer or the seller, detail the history of the problems and the repairs, ask for a replacement or a refund, and enclose a copy of the warranty. If the warranty is limited, not full, the terms may still entitle you to a replacement or a refund. Send the same correspondence as for a full warranty to either the seller or the manufacturer.
- Your state's laws covering implied warranties and consequential damages may provide protections not given in the product warranty. Find out what the laws in your state are.
- If a malfunctioning product has caused you physical injury, contact the appropriate attorney.
- For problems that have not been resolved to your satisfaction, despite your good-faith actions and the passage of a reasonable amount of time, your local consumer-protection agency can provide advice.
- Other agencies and organizations exist to help consumers with unresolved product disputes. See "Obtaining Help," page 639.

Complaints

COMPLAINT PROCEDURES

Telling a company that you received a defective product is not complaining; neither is pursuing your rights under a warranty. But what if you have acted in good faith to resolve a problem, only to end up with unsatisfactory results? Then it's time to make a formal complaint, which involves writing a complaint letter.

THE COMPLAINT LETTER. No matter how angry or frustrated you feel over the matter, keep your letter neat, formal, assertive, and respectful. Follow proper letter-writing format to include the date of the letter, your name and address, and reference to your customer account number. Give accurate and complete product and payment information: the order (or product) number or code, descriptive details, and payment data (credit card information, debit account number, etc.). State your specific complaint ("I have not received a reply." "The appliance still does not work." "No refund check has been received."), and provide a *brief* history of the problem. Mention that you're enclosing *copies* of previous letters (both to and from various parties), the warranty, proof of payment, proof of repairs, and other relevant documents. (Later, be sure to enclose them, and return all originals to your file.) State what you think would be a fair resolution to the problem, and indicate that you're offering the firm one last chance to settle the issue before seeking outside help. Explain that if a reply isn't received or a resolution reached within 30 days, you will report the firm to the appropriate agency or agencies (the U.S. Postal Service, Better Business Bureau, Direct Marketing Association, Federal Trade Commission, and/or another group). If after 30 days the matter hasn't been resolved, take the promised action.

OBTAINING HELP

The challenge consumers face when trying to get help is not knowing what kind of help they need and which agency to turn to. One great resource is the *Consumer's Resource Handbook,* published by the Federal Citizen Information Center. Log on to www.pueblo.gsa.gov for more information about this guide, which provides advice, consumer tips, names, addresses, and phone numbers for every organization and agency out there that can help with all your consumer complaints.

Another great place to get information about internet vendors and your rights as a web shopper is the "Consumer Protection" website of the Federal Trade Commission. This official-looking website's unwieldy web address is www.ftc.gov/ftc/consumer.htm. Here's where you'll find the most complete and recent information on a variety of subjects relating to e-commerce: alerts to low-cost PC scams, a guide to online payments, guides to internet auctions (buyers and sellers), shopping safely, unsolicited emails, and so on.

Regardless of which organization helps you, you'll need to provide a copy of your final complaint letter along with copies of the documentation you enclosed. (Keep the originals for your file.) The agencies described below have their own ways of handling consumer mail- and phone-order problems, so be understanding if the help they can provide falls short of your dream solution. Some groups will investigate individual complaints while others will accumulate complaints until they have enough to take action.

CONSUMER ACTION PANELS (CAPS). CAPs offer third-party dispute-resolution programs for specific industries. In addition to investigating consumer complaints, they provide consumers with service information and members with suggestions for improving consumer service. For example, the Major Appliance Consumer Action Program (MACAP) helps with problems involving major appliances. Call 800–621–0477 for information, or write to MACAP at 20 N. Wacker Dr., Ste. 1231, Chicago, IL 60606.

BETTER BUSINESS BUREAUS (BBBS). Business and professional firms fund the self-regulatory agencies known as Better Business Bureaus. They maintain files on firms that are useful for answering consumer inquiries about a firm's selling history; monitor business practices such as advertising and selling; and make service information available to consumers. Since most BBBs have programs for mediation and arbitration, and the power to make awards (binding arbitration), they really can assist in resolving consumer complaints.

If you want to contact a BBB, look for an office closest to the *company* you're concerned about. You can call to request a directory of offices (703–276–0100) or write to the Council of Better Business Bureaus, Inc., 4200 Wilson Blvd., Ste. 800, Arlington VA 22203–1804. Be sure to enclose a SASE with your request. Once you've located the appropriate office, write to request either a "consumer complaint" form or a "consumer inquiry" form. Better yet, visit the Better Business Bureau website at www.bbb.org, where you can get most of the information you need right at the site and can even file a complaint online. There's lots of good information here as well, such as consumer tips, news, and alerts.

DIRECT MARKETING ASSOCIATION (DMA). A trade organization of direct marketers and mail-order companies, the Direct Marketing Association is the largest and oldest organization of its sort, with more than half its membership comprised of non-U.S. firms. The DMA maintains a Mail Order Action Line (MOAL) to assist in resolving nondelivery problems involving *any* direct-marketing firm, not only member firms. You can seek help by *writing* to MOAL. Send a copy of your complaint letter and all the documentation to Mail Order Action Line, DMA, 1111 19th St. NW, Ste. 1100, Washington, DC 20030–3606. After your complaint is received, the DMA will contact the firm and attempt to resolve the problem, making a request that you allow the firm 30 days to act.

If you get too many direct mailings and solicitation calls, the DMA's "Telephone Preference Service" and "Mail Preference Service" can reduce them. Your name will be kept on the DMA's lists for 5 years, lists that most reputable firms consult before sending out a mail campaign. You can reduce *mail* by writing to Mail Preference Service, DMA, P.O. Box 9008, Farmingdale, NY 11735–9008. Give your name and home address (this procedure won't work for business addresses), state that you don't want direct mail, and write "HOME" on your request. You can reduce *solicitation calls* by writing to Telephone Preference Service, DMA, P.O. Box 9014, Farmingdale, NY 11735–9014. Give your name, home address, and *home* telephone number, state that you don't want solicitation calls, and write "HOME" on your request. If you continue to receive calls, speak to the marketer directly, and if a third party seems to be using another firm's list of customers, tell the referring company that you want the practice stopped.

THE FEDERAL TRADE COMMISSION (FTC). This law-enforcement agency protects the public against business practices that are anticompetitive, unfair, and deceptive. It accepts complaint letters, which form the basis of files on firms. If a large number of complaints is received or the problems are of a serious nature, the FTC may decide an investigation is appropriate. They may seek court injunctions and/or the imposition of fines as stiff as $10,000 for each day the violation continues. Your letters about firms that don't follow FTC regulations are important, so do take the trouble to report them.

THE FAIR CREDIT BILLING ACT (FCBA). The FCBA was passed in 1975 as part of the FTC's Consumer Protection Act to give mail-order shoppers who pay with credit cards some recourse in the event of nondelivery problems. The FCBA created a procedure for consumers to settle billing errors such as, but not limited to, charges for goods and/or services that were not accepted or not provided or delivered as agreed. Read the entire procedure carefully, as it includes deadlines and steps that should not be overlooked.

1. To activate FCBA protection, you must *write to* the "billing error" address that appears on your monthly statement. Do not call the customer service telephone number on your bill.
2. In your letter, give your name, address, and account number; the dollar amount of the error; and the reason you think the error occurred.
3. This letter must reach the creditor *within 60 days* after the first bill with the error was mailed to you. Send the letter by certified mail, return receipt requested.
4. The creditor is obligated to acknowledge your correspondence in writing and within 30 days of its receipt, unless the problem is corrected before then.
5. While an amount is being disputed under this procedure, it does not have to be paid. Neither does the related portion of the minimum payment nor the related finance charges have to be paid.
6. If the creditor finds an error, the creditor must send you a letter explaining the correction, credit the disputed amount to your account, and remove related finance charges. If the creditor finds that you owe a portion of the disputed amount, the finding must be explained in writing.

7. If the creditor finds the bill correct, it must send you a letter explaining the reasons and stating the amount you owe. When this is the outcome, you're liable for missed minimum payments and finance charges that accrued pending resolution.

8. If your state laws allow you to pursue the matter against the *seller* rather than the creditor, you can further dispute the amount. Within 10 days of receiving the creditor's justification of the charge, send the *creditor* a letter saying that you still refuse to pay the disputed amount. At this point the creditor can begin collection proceedings against you. Therefore, it might be wise for you to contact a local consumer protection agency for options to handle the problem.

If state law allows withholding of payment from a seller, then under the FCBA you can dispute the *quality* of goods or services. This coverage holds for credit-card purchases over $50 made in your state of residence or within 100 miles of your mailing address. If the credit card used was issued by the seller, the limits do not apply. Before doing anything, contact a local consumer protection agency for advice.

THE U.S. POSTAL SERVICE (USPS). Another organization to turn to for help is the USPS, which has a reputation for resolving around 85% of the complaints it acts on. Under provisions of the U.S. Code, the USPS has the power to go to court, obtain a restraining order, and withhold mail delivery to a company—a debilitating circumstance, surely, for a mail-order firm. To enlist the support of the USPS, you have two options: Send a copy of your final complaint letter and documentation to the Chief Postal Inspector, U.S. Postal Service, Washington, D.C. 20260, or write directly to the postmaster of the post office serving the firm with which you're in dispute.

BANKRUPTCY COURTS. How can a bankruptcy court help? It might be able to offer information on orders and refunds that seem to have gone astray. You should contact a bankruptcy court if letters to a company have gone unanswered for an inordinately long time and attempts to reach it by phone have yielded only disconnect messages. Tell the clerk at the U.S. Bankruptcy Court nearest to the firm the reason for your call. If the company has filed for reorganization under Chapter 11, ask for the case number and any information or forms you need to file a claim. Under Chapter 11, a hierarchy of creditors exists to protect a business against its creditors' claims. Your claim will join the roster after claims by suppliers, utilities, banks, and others. Filing doesn't guarantee that you'll get your money back, but it is an option available to you, so why not use it?

Index

speakers, 135, 137, 266, 312, 414, 415, 417, 425, 435

Special Clothes, Inc., 509

Spike Nashbar, Inc., 536

spiral staircase kits, 329

sporting goods and equipment, 46, 266, 270, 521, 522, 523, 530, 531, 532

Sportsman's Guide, The, 518

Sportswear Clearinghouse, 47

spy equipment, 594

Spy Outlet, The, 594

STA Travel, 574

Starr Organic Produce, 221

State Line Tack, 10

stationery, 273, 476, 483, 484

stemware, 368, 381, 383, 386, 387

Stencil House of N.H., 398

stencils, 398

Stickers 'N' Stuff, Inc., 563

stickers, 558, 563

storaging and organizing, 456, 457, 465, 469, 471, 472

StoreSmart Express, 472

Strand Book Store, 129

stringed instruments, 433, 434, 438, 439, 440, 460, 472, 474

studio furniture
  art, 194, 198, 199
  music, 425, 432

Stumps-ShindigZ, 570

Sultan's Delight, 223

sunglasses, 18, 33, 36, 45, 46, 270, 277, 278, 279

Sunshine Discount Crafts, 154

support hose, 511, 512

SupportHosiery.com, 512

Support Plus, 511

supportive footwear, 511

surveillance equipment, 594

swimming pool equipment, 49, 538

swimwear
  men's, 33, 36, 45, 49
  women's, 33, 36, 35, 45, 49

Szul, 62

t-shirts, 43, 45, 46, 47, 55, 67, 177, 521

table linens, 320, 491

table pads, 350, 359

tablecloths, 46, 320, 491

tableware, 33, 366, 368, 369, 383, 386, 387

Tafford Manufacturing, Inc., 493

Tartan Book Sales, 130

Taylor's Cutaways and Stuff, 186

tea, 212, 221, 223, 226, 230, 290

telephones, 266, 312

telescopes, 135, 138

televisions, 135, 136, 137, 259, 261, 263, 266, 312, 313, 314, 315, 417

TextbookX.com, 131

Thai Silks, 187

That Fish Place/That Pet Place, 11

therapeutic support hosiery, 511, 512

Think Ink, 155

ties, 33, 38, 66, 67

Tiffany lamps, reproduction, 372

tin ad reproductions, 85

Tire Rack, The, 110

tires and wheels, 104, 107, 110

toddler's clothing, 25, 26, 27

Tom Thumb Workshops, 157

Tomahawk Live Trap Co., 12

Tool King, 551

tools, 259, 260, 265, 270, 540, 541, 543, 544, 546, 547, 548, 549, 551, 552, 554

tote bags, 18, 20, 273

towels, 33, 46, 48, 270, 320, 321, 322

toys, 36, 259, 260, 263, 266, 268, 270, 560, 567, 571